D1460492

Feminists, Islam, and Nation

Feminists, Islam, and Nation

GENDER AND THE MAKING OF MODERN EGYPT

• *MARGOT BADRAN* •

PRINCETON UNIVERSITY PRESS

PRINCETON, NEW JERSEY

Published by Princeton University Press, 41 William Street,
Princeton, New Jersey 08540
In the United Kingdom: Princeton University Press,
Chichester, West Sussex

Library of Congress Cataloging-in-Publication Data

Badran, Margot
Feminists, Islam, and nation : gender and the making of
modern Egypt / Margot Badran.
p. cm.
Includes bibliographical references and index.
ISBN 0-691-03706-X
ISBN 0-691-02605-X (pbk.)
1. Feminism–Egypt–History. 2. Women–Egypt–History.
3. Muslim women–Egypt–History. I. Title.
HQ1793.B33 1994
305.42'0962–dc20 94-19055 CIP

This book has been composed in Laser Sabon

Princeton University Press books are printed on acid-free paper and meet the guidelines
for permanence and durability of the Committee on Production Guidelines for
Book Longevity of the Council on Library Resources

Printed in the United States of America

5 7 9 10 8 6 4

TO THE MEMORY OF MY PARENTS

MARGARET WOODS FARRANTO

JOSEPH DOMINIC FARRANTO

• CONTENTS •

PREFACE ix

NOTE ON TRANSLITERATION AND TRANSLATION xiii

ABBREVIATIONS xv

INTRODUCTION 3

PART ONE: RISING FEMINIST CONSCIOUSNESS 29

CHAPTER 1
Two Lives in Changing Worlds 31

CHAPTER 2
Claiming Public Space 47

CHAPTER 3
Thinking Gender 61

CHAPTER 4
Egypt for Which Egyptians? 74

PART TWO: THE FEMINIST MOVEMENT 89

CHAPTER 5
The House of the Woman 91

CHAPTER 6
City Sisters, Country Sisters 111

CHAPTER 7
Recasting the Family 124

CHAPTER 8
Educating the Nation 142

CHAPTER 9
Women Have Always Worked 165

CHAPTER 10
Traffic in Women 192

CHAPTER 11
Suffrage and Citizenship 207

PART THREE: THE WIDENING CIRCLE 221

CHAPTER 12
Arab Feminism 223

NOTES 251

BIBLIOGRAPHY 317

INDEX 339

• PREFACE •

I FIRST HEARD of Huda Shaʿrawi when a fellow American graduate student suggested I study her. Who was Huda Shaʿrawi, I silently wondered. He confessed that he too had never heard of her until he moved into a flat on Huda Shaʿrawi Street in the center of Cairo. After making inquiries he discovered that she had led the first feminist movement in Egypt early in this century. I instantly became interested. This was in the 1960s, when "women's history" had scarcely been imagined. I had no idea how to go about researching this feminist leader except by "asking around," as one would seek out a lost friend. One day I met two women who had been close to Huda Shaʿrawi: her lifelong feminist associate Saiza Nabarawi and her niece Hawwa' Idris, also a committed feminist. They became the first women in a long chain who over the months and years led me to far corners of Cairo, to Alexandria, to Minya, and beyond Egypt. These many women unlocked their memories, shared their personal papers, and opened up their private libraries to me.

Newly armed with names of women writers and titles of books, I marched to the old Dar al-Kutub in Port Saʿid Street where I discovered a cache of women's magazines and newspapers from the 1890s. At al-Azhar, where I was studying Arabic, I borrowed books on women and Islam and debated at great length with my teacher, Shaykh Yahiya Hashim. A few years later I began graduate studies at Oxford University where I continued my historical investigation of Egyptian feminism under the supervision of Albert Hourani, writing a dissertation entitled "Huda Shaʿrawi and the Liberation of the Egyptian Woman." By this time women's studies and women's history were taking shape as disciplines, and I eagerly plunged deeper and deeper into more research, continually thinking and rethinking Egyptian feminism as I moved between Egypt and the West. Earlier fruits of this labor have appeared in two books and numerous articles I published in the 1980s and 1990s.

With the completion of this book the pleasurable moment has come to remember those who helped me along the way and to offer my thanks. I start with Bruce Craig, then a graduate student in Cairo and now Bibliographer for Middle Eastern Studies at the Joseph Regstein Library of the University of Chicago, for introducing me to Huda Shaʿrawi. I am deeply grateful to the women in Egypt who started me on my journey into Egyptian feminism, who accompanied me along the way, and without whom this book, which tells their story, would not have existed. Hawwa' Idris and Saiza Nabarawi opened their personal archives of correspondence, memoranda, and photographs, and their collections of books and journals. Hawwa' Idris loaned me her copy of Huda Shaʿrawi's memoirs. Mary Kahil, one of the last of the old *salonnières*, placed me in contact with numerous women and also turned over private papers to me. Andrée Fahmy shared memories of her father, Morcos Fahmy, and a rare copy of his 1894 book with me. Huda Shaʿrawi's daughter-in-law Munira ʿAsim, her granddaughter Nini Lanfranchi, and her great-granddaughter Bassna Sadek Chastaing shared family memories. A list of pioneering feminists, to whom I am grateful for long hours of conversation about the past, appears in the bibliography. I would like to thank especially Inji Aflatun, Naʿima al-ʿAyyubi, ʿAzizah Haykal, Eva Habib al-Masri, Ihsan al-Qusi, Bahigah Rashid, Aminah al-Saʿid, Duriyah Shafiq, and Hilanah Sidarus.

There are numerous people who have contributed in other ways to the shaping of this book. I am grateful to the late Albert Hourani for his careful supervision of my D.Phil. thesis, generous time given to discussion, his critical readings of my other writings, and for his friendship and support over the years. I thank Carl Brown, who first introduced me to the history of the modern Middle East and who has ever since encouraged my work, for reading the final version of this book. Others who have read the manuscript in whole or in part, or have made contributions through discussion and debate, include Yesim Arat, Marilyn Booth, Antoinette Burton, Virginia Danielson, John Esposito, Leonore Fernandez, Mary Harper, Marieme Helie-Lucas, Deniz Kandiyoti, Ann Lesch, Philippa Levine, Huda Lutfy, Magda al-Nowaihi, Afaf Marsot, Ann Mayer, Valentine Moghadam, Karen Offen, Donald Reid, Leila Rupp, Nükhet Sirman, Lucette Valensi, and Kamala Visweswaran.

Over the years I have received generous institutional and financial support. I would like to thank the American Research Center in Egypt, the Fulbright Commission—with special appreciation to Cairo Director Ann Radwan for her generous help—the Ford Foundation in Cairo, the Social Science Research Council of New York, and the Annenberg Research Institute in Philadelphia. I completed the writing of the book as a Visiting Fellow at the Department of Near Eastern Studies, Princeton University. I would like to thank Carl Brown for first inviting me to Princeton several years ago and for welcoming me back once again. I am grateful to Avram Udovitch, who extended a kind welcome as the department chair and who, together with Mary Craparotta, Judy Gross, and Mary Alice McCormick, extended all the support one could hope for in the final stages of book preparation. I thank Sumaiya Hamdani for her efficient assistance in recovering materials from Firestone Library for me. I am grateful to Firestone Library reference librarians and bibliographers Joyce Bell, Hedi Ben Aicha, Nancy Pressman, and Audrey Wright, and to Azar Ashraf, Special Collections Assistant at the Near East Library, who have been generous with their expertise. I thank Gail Group, Leszek Mazur, and Mark Lewis for computer support. I would like to express special appreciation to my editors at Princeton University Press, Mary Murrell and Lauren Lepow, whose care and skills in the process of making a manuscript into a book have indeed been impressive.

I feel fortunate to have the family and friends who over the years sustained me and offered me hospitality in many places. While it is impossible to acknowledge them all, here I would like to offer thanks to Nelly Hana Boulus, John and Evgenia Farranto, Joan and Ted Cregg, Andrée Famhy, Azara Leong, Deborah Pellow, Leila Ibrahim, Ann Radwan, Frank Woods, Elizabeth and James Wueste, and Pat Waddy. I can never express adequately the profound gratitude I feel toward my late parents, Margaret Woods Farranto and Joseph Dominic Farranto, for the strong encouragement they offered my entire life. Finally, I would like to express my appreciation to Ali Badran, who as a husband and friend of many years has generously supported this project.

• NOTE ON TRANSLITERATION AND TRANSLATION •

I FOLLOW the Library of Congress system of transliteration. Diacritics, except for the hamza and ʿayn, are omitted as a convenience to nonspecialists. The two main exceptions to the system are: (1) common English forms such as Cairo, harem, feddan, etc.; and (2) some personal names and other transliterated words that appear as cited in particular works in Western languages. Sometimes the *g* sound in colloquial Arabic is used in a name rather than the classical *j*.

All translations are mine unless otherwise stated.

• ABBREVIATIONS •

AFU Arab Feminist Union
D "Dhikrayati"—Nabawiyah Musa's memoirs published serially in her *Majallat al-Fatah*
E *L'Egyptienne*
EFU Egyptian Feminist Union
FO Foreign Office
HI Hawwa' Idris
HS Huda Shaʿrawi
HSM Huda Shaʿrawi, unpublished Arabic memoirs (HI copy)
IAW The International Alliance of Women for Suffrage and Equal Citizenship. It is referred to throughout the text variously as the International Alliance of Women and the International Alliance, and sometimes as the Alliance. From 1904 to 1923 this organization was called the International Woman Suffrage Alliance (IWSA).
M *al-Misriyah*
MAQF *Al-Mar'a al-ʿArabiyya wa Qadiyya Filastin: al-Muta'mar al-Nis'ai al-Sharqi*
MNA *Al-Mu'tamar al-Nisa'i al-ʿArabi*
NM Nabawiyah Musa
SN Saiza Nabarawi
WIDF Women's International Democratic Federation
WILPF Women's International League of Peace and Freedom
WWCC Wafdist Women's Central Committee

Feminists, Islam, and Nation

• INTRODUCTION •

The rise of women's feminist consciousness in the nineteenth century heralded the beginnings of what in many ways would be the most potent force in the creation of modern Egypt. I refer to women's coming into an awareness that being born female meant that they would lead their lives very differently from those of similar classes and circumstances who were born male. I refer to women's questioning *why* this was so, under what authority, and *what* they started to do about it. The *why* was the beginning of an analysis of patriarchy—that is, the power men had accorded themselves, irrespective of class, to make rules and to impose their rules on women to keep them subordinate. The *what* was feminism—ideas and actions expressed individually and collectively about personal life, family life, societal life; about being Muslim or Christian, about being a member of the Egyptian nation; in short, about being a woman in its totality and plurality of meanings—about gender and power.

This is a book about Egyptian women and the feminism they created. Egyptian feminist women imagined a dynamic gender culture within a rethought Islam and a reconstructed nation. *Feminists, Islam, and Nation* is the story of women's agency and their insistence upon empowerment—of themselves, their families, and their nation. It is *their* story, constructed out of their own narratives and records, aiming to convey the process and vision of their feminism. It is a story of transcendence—the transcendence of patriarchal and colonial containment—and triumphs, and of unfinished business, of a journey begun.

The history of Egyptian feminism is about middle- and upper-class women assuming agency—the capacity to exercise their will, to determine the shape of their own lives and to partake in the shaping of their culture and society. Three stages may be discerned in women's assumption of agency. In the first stage, occurring in the latter decades of the nineteenth century, some women gave voice to a rising "feminist consciousness" through the poems, stories, and essays they published. The second and third stages, which are those of individual and collective forms of public activism, form the core of this book. In the second stage, during the first two decades of the twentieth century, domestically secluded women made initial forays into society, embarking on invisible everyday "feminist" activism through philanthropy, intellectual programs, and teaching. The third stage began in the early 1920s when women engaged in a highly visible, organized feminism, creating the first explicitly feminist association, al-Ittihad al-Nisa'i al-Misri (the Egyptian Feminist Union or EFU).

The earliest manifestations of upper- and middle-class women's nascent "feminist consciousness" surfaced as a new culture of modernity was being shaped in nineteenth-century Egypt. Women gave expression to this new gender awareness at the moment the old urban harem culture, predicated on female domestic seclusion and other stringent forms of family-based patriarchal control of upper- and middle-class women, was eroding in the midst of pervasive and hard-to-control modernizing change.[1] Upper- and middle-class women observed how men in their families were freer to innovate while they were more restricted. As women expanded their female circles, they discovered different ways that they *as women*—across lines of class, religion, and ethnicity—were controlled. As they imagined new lives, women began to withhold complicity in their own subordination.

While their country experienced increasing Western economic and political intrusions, Egyptian men articulated two major discourses of revitalization and empowerment: Islamic modernism and secular nationalism. Islamic modernism constituted a call to Muslims to reexamine Islam in terms of contemporary realities. It aimed to rescue religion from narrow or erroneous interpretations, opening up Islam as a vital force in women's and men's daily lives plunged into uncertainties by massive economic and technological change. The discourse of secular nationalism, articulated in the wake of colonial occupation, involved collective self-review as part of a project of national reinvigoration to win independence. Feminist women legitimized their own discourse of revitalization and empowerment in the discourses of Islamic modernism and secular nationalism. To this day Egyptian feminism has affirmed its Islamic and nationalist dimensions.

Nineteenth-Century Transformations

The roots of twentieth-century Egyptian feminism are found in the nineteenth century. To know more fully what upper- and middle-class women with a gender awareness were moving away from and striving toward we must look to the shifting cultures of nineteenth-century urban Egypt.

Urban Harem Culture

The site of the first emergence of women's "feminist awareness" and nascent "feminist expression" was the urban harem. At the opening of the nineteenth century, the domestic seclusion of women prevailed in the urban upper and middle classes, and among the rural gentry, while gender segregation was observed, in varying degrees, by all classes. Upper- and middle-class men had the economic means to keep "their" women in domestic seclusion. Men of the urban poor and the peasantry did not; moreover, the labor of "their" women was needed outside the house.[2] Urban women of all classes and women of the rural gentry veiled their faces if and when they went outside. Peasant women did not veil because the custom was incompatible with their work in the fields, although bedouin women who tended flocks covered their faces. Confining women to the home, rendering them invisible, and segregating them from all men except close relatives were hallmarks of urban upper- and middle-class harem culture. The Arabic word *harim* (from which the English-language loan word *harem* derives) applied both to women and to the women's quarters of the house.[3] Neither domestic confinement nor veiling the face was ordained by Islam, although both had been imposed on women in the name of religion.[4] These practices were also enforced because of deeply held sexual and moral beliefs, which were likewise associated with religion. Domestic seclusion and veiling in Egypt were not practiced solely by Muslims but by Jews and Christians as well.

"The woman" was perceived as essentially, or exclusively, a sexual being, unlike "the man," who was only partly understood in terms of his sexuality. Women were held to possess a more powerful sexual drive than men, posing a threat to society because of the chaos or *fitna* they could unleash. It was popularly believed that the mere proximity of a woman to a man would lead to sexual relations. To make matters still more fraught, women's sexual purity was linked to the honor of men and the family, while men's sexual purity was not linked to their own honor nor to that of their women and family.[5] Restricting women to their homes and camouflaging them if they went out were deemed necessary to the preservation of their purity and with it the honor of their men and families. Equally demanding the sexual purity of "their" women, lower-class and peasant men relied on community surveillance of behavior and the imposition of severe penalties on both sexes for violations of the moral code.

Among the wealthy upper classes, elaborate architecture as well as large household establishments catered to the maintenance of strict divisions between the sexes. Eunuchs (castrated male slaves) guarded women and children, accompanied them if and when they went outside, and controlled all entries into the household. The eunuch was answerable to the master alone, whose women and children he protected and whose orders he obeyed. Eunuchs exercised considerable power over women, even to the extent of controlling their access to their own money. The *kalfa* (matron or housekeeper) presided over the female servants, including both free women and slaves. The latter were more numerous in elite houses, although supplies of slaves dwindled after the traffic was outlawed in 1877. Meanwhile, at the other end of the spectrum with less space and limited domestic help, ordinary middle-class families found it harder to maintain strict separation of the sexes at home.[6]

Around the age of puberty, which could be as early as nine, urban middle- and upper-class girls started to veil and were kept more closely guarded. In all classes girls were commonly married—without their free consent, contrary to the requirements of Islam—around the age of thirteen.[7] Wed at an early age, women could continue to be molded by their elders after being "secured" in their station in life. Toward the end of the century, an Egyptian medical doctor argued that early marriage for females was physically unhealthy.[8] About the same time, the patriarch of the Coptic Church set sixteen as the minimum marriage age for Coptic women.[9] Nevertheless, the marriage age for females generally remained low into the early twentieth century.[10]

In the upper classes during the nineteenth century, a Muslim woman was often a co-wife (*durrah*). Under certain conditions, Islam allows a man to have four wives. In the nineteenth century, polygamy was common in wealthy harems, although less frequent among the middle class. By the turn of the century, polygamy was diminishing but had by no means disappeared. Islam also permitted men to take slaves as concubines. It was common practice during much of the nineteenth century among the Turco-Circassian ruling class and the rising Egyptian Muslim elites to obtain such women from the Caucasus. When a concubine gave birth, the child was the legitimate offspring of the father, who usually married the mother. In this way women of humble origins might improve their status. The decline of concubinage was another corollary of the disappearance of slavery in Egypt.[11]

Confinement, invisibility, restricted movements, controlled "choices": these were the tropes of urban harem culture that were threatened with erasure as modernity was scripted onto the Egyptian cultural canvas.[12]

The Rise of Modern Culture

Nineteenth-century Egypt saw the rise of the modern state, expanding capitalism and fuller incorporation into the European-dominated world market system, secularization, technological innovation, and urbanization. These forces, changing the lives of Egyptians across lines of class and gender, assailed urban harem culture.

Early in the century, Egypt won de facto independence from the Ottoman Empire when Muhammad ʿAli, who had been sent by the sultan to end the French occupation (1798–1801), broke with Ottoman control and established himself as ruler. To protect the autonomy of Egypt and his own power, the new ruler embarked on an ambitious program of "modernization," at the center of which was building a strong army. The state also imposed a shift from subsistence agriculture to cultivation of cotton as a cash crop for export. It initiated industrialization schemes, created modern health and education systems, set up the country's first printing press, and made urban improvements. Technocrats, mainly but not exclusively male, were brought from Europe, while Egyptian men were sent abroad for training.[13]

By the 1860s and 1870s, the pace and scope of modern transformation accelerated under the rule of Khedive Ismaʿil. The basis of a modern transportation and communications system was laid out. The railroad that connected Cairo and Alexandria in 1853 was extended and reached Minya in Upper Egypt in 1867.[14] The Suez Canal opened in 1869, providing a new route to the East. By 1875 some nine hundred carriages were in use on the newly paved avenues in the capital. Carriages were not only used for transport but became a form of recreation for women and men alike. Khedive

Isma'il's daughter Cemile even donned a military uniform and drove her own carriage.[15]

Khedive Isma'il promoted the creation of a new residential area in Cairo by making grants of land to wealthy Egyptians and foreigners to build modern villas. In the new area called Isma'iliyah, west of the medieval city, people of diverse religious and ethnic identities lived side by side, unlike the practice in the medieval city where religious and ethnic groups lived in separate quarters. Architectural forms catering to female isolation also began to disappear. Older inward-oriented domestic buildings, with women's quarters on the upper levels and shielding devices such as fretted windows, gave way to structures that were not designed to render women invisible. Not only were females less hidden away but in the new quarter they could view ways of life different from their own. Soon there were "two cities," the old and the new with their different social and cultural practices existing side by side.[16]

The opera house built to celebrate the opening of the Suez Canal in 1869 provided new entertainment for upper-class women. Screened loges reached by a private staircase were installed for women.[17] In *Hadith 'Isa ibn Hisham* satirist Muhammad al-Muwaylihi wrote wryly of respectable ladies watching European theatrical performances of love stories on stage: "But for their refinement, we would have thought that they were women of low virtue."[18]

A pioneer in the 1880s was Princess Nazli Fazil (ca. 1840–1913), niece of the deposed Khedive Isma'il and daughter of Mustafa Fazil, who had lost out to Isma'il when the law of succession changed. Fluent in Turkish, Arabic, French, and English, she broke ground as the first woman to open a salon—one frequented by men, mainly intellectuals and politicians who debated political and social issues, including "the woman question." Mixing unveiled with male guests Nazli violated strict gender conventions, but as a member of the royal family she had special leeway.[19]

In the same decade modern journalism made its appearance in Egypt. Syrian Christian men emigrating to Egypt from Ottoman provinces of the Arab East were prominent in creating the new (general) press, and Syrian Christian women soon founded journals for women.[20] As literacy continued to spread, women and men published more and more books.

With increasing steamer traffic on the Mediterranean and through the Suez Canal Europeans and Americans visited Egypt in growing numbers. The Thomas Cook Company took its first organized group tours up the Nile as travel to the East became possible for the middle class.[21] Visits to harems became standard fare for Western lady travelers.[22] Although a common language was lacking, Egyptian and Western women observed each other, engaging in limited exchange.[23] By the end of the century French became more widespread in elite harems, opening up greater possibilities for communication.[24]

Egyptian women of the elites observed European women in their own milieus when they began to travel to Europe, which was replacing Turkey as a holiday destination, in the company of their husbands, fathers, and brothers. Aboard ship they removed their veils and cloaks, displaying the latest in European dress.[25] In Europe, not only did Egyptian women observe other lives at first hand but they also behaved differently themselves, commingling in public with their husbands.[26]

In Egypt men who were neither husbands nor close relatives began to enter private quarters. These were European doctors, mostly French, but also Italian, English, and German. Royal and upper-class families suspended their rules of strict gender segregation when it came to health.[27] Photographers constituted another group of unrelated males entering the private space of upper-class harems. Here no life-and-death justifications might be given for the breaching of gender barriers. Moreover, producing images of uncovered female faces constituted a double unveiling, and one that could not be fully controlled by the subject or her guardians.[28]

By the end of the century trams were introduced into Cairo and Alexandria; in 1898 separate female compartments enabled women of ordinary means to move about more freely. Modern department stores opened, offering new shopping possibilities and a novel pastime for well-to-do women who had formerly relied on women peddlers to bring goods to their houses. Huda Shaʿrawi related that when she started shopping for herself at Chalon, a new department store in Alexandria, those around her "looked upon me as if I were about to violate the religious law or commit some other crime."[29] Upper-class women also began to take excursions on the pleasure boats that appeared on the Nile. To the south of Cairo, Helwan, boasting sulfur springs, new European-style hotels, and open-air theaters, became a winter resort for affluent Egyptians and foreigners. Huda Shaʿrawi recalled, "In the days when women were still veiled, Helwan offered a more relaxed atmosphere in place of their routine seclusion in Cairo."[30]

Women's Education

Programs of the expanding Egyptian state, and the changes they wrought, directly and indirectly pitted the state against the family over the ordering of female life. In the early decades of the nineteenth century when the state attempted to assume the education of women and prepare them for new societal roles, it incurred initial resistance from families but gradually made headway.[31]

In 1832 women received training under the auspices of the state for the first time when it opened the School for Hakimahs (medical aides or "doctoresses"), attached to the new military hospital at Abu Zabal outside Cairo.[32] This training was inspired by the drive to control venereal disease, rampant among the troops, and by the need to reduce infant mortality in the underpopulated country. At first, when families refused to send their daughters to the school, black slaves were recruited from Ethiopia; however, Egyptian women from modest homes soon began to attend when the school's success was proven and the economic benefits became clear. Establishing the

School for Hakimahs was the limit of the state's early success in offering training and education to women. In 1836 the Council for Public Education explored the possibility of starting state schools for girls but concluded that such a plan was premature.[33] Although Muhammad ʿAli had been unable to start a state school system for girls, he set an example that the elites followed when he hired European women to teach his daughters at home.[34]

What the state was unable to accomplish private initiative could. A Mrs. Lieder from the English Church Missionary Society set up a school in the 1830s, creating a precedent for schools run by religious societies, mainly from Britain, France, and the United States. The first Egyptian-run schools for girls were founded in 1853 under the impetus of the innovating Coptic archbishop who, the following year, became Patriarch Cyril IV. The communal and foreign schools attracted middle-class girls, mostly Christian.

In the second half of the century when the state renewed earlier efforts to promote female education, it encouraged advisers to prepare the public for the idea. ʿAli Pasha Mubarak, a technocrat, and Shaykh Rifaʿi al-Tahtawi, a religious scholar, in their respective books, *Tariq al-Hijaʾ wa-al-Tamrin ʿala Qawaʿid al-Lughah al-ʿArabiyah* (The way to spell and practice in the rules of the Arabic language, 1869) and *al-Murshid al-Amin lil-Banat wa-al-Banin* (The faithful guide for girls and boys, 1875) argued in favor of education for both sexes, marshaling both instrumental and Islamic arguments.[35]

In 1873 Tcheshme Hanim, a wife of Khedive Ismaʿil, became the patron of the first state school for girls, the Siyufiyah School. The following year the Foundation for Awqaf (pious endowments), under the lead of minister of awqaf ʿAli Mubarak, opened the Qirabiyah School. Run by Syrian Christian headmistresses Rose and Cecile Najjar, these schools served daughters of high officials and Circassian slaves in elite households; the latter were raised like their young mistresses and often became wives of officials. Construction had begun on the Banat al-Ashraf (Daughters of the Nobility) School in 1878, but when the khedive was deposed the following year the project was abandoned. Despite the new initiatives, however, upper-class families still preferred to educate their daughters at home under the direction of European governesses who provided instruction mainly in French.[36]

Middle-class women's lives were most changed by expanding opportunities for formal education. In 1889 the government created the Saniyah School, which after the turn of the century instituted a teachers' training program. A section for girls was opened at the ʿAbbas Primary School in Cairo in 1895.[37] To improve on the limited education the colonial state offered females, Egyptian nationalists created their own independently funded girls' schools under the aegis of provincial councils. Among the earliest were a primary school in Fayyum and a teachers' training school in Mansurah. The state set up a second teacher's training school for girls at Bulaq in Cairo and opened the Wardiyan Women Teachers' Training School in Alexandria in 1916. A girls' section was also started at the Hilmiyah School for Boys.[38]

Around the turn of the twentieth century, for the first time a few upper-class girls began to attend schools. They were sent to private foreign schools, especially those operated by French nuns; some went to the American College for Girls, founded in 1909. (Several EFU members were educated in these schools.)[39] The colonial state never provided secondary education for women. Whatever secondary schooling women received during the colonial period was in private institutions.

Reordering Islam

At the beginning of the nineteenth century one of Muhammad ʿAli's first measures as ruler was to bring the center of religious learning at al-Azhar under his control, breaking its economic independence and limiting its jurisdiction. During the century a process of secularization was initiated, bringing education and law under the purview of the state.[40] A secular educational system developed alongside, and soon overtook, the religious educational system. The proliferating Western missionary schools meanwhile formed their own "system."[41] It was the introduction of new secular state schools and private schools that opened up formal education to women. There had been no space for females in the religious educational system of al-Azhar, although a few girls perennially attended *kuttab*s (Quranic elementary schools), mainly in the villages, learning Quranic recitation.

In the realm of law there was a secularization of commercial, civil, and criminal codes leaving only *ahwal shakhsiyah*, or personal status law (also called family law), under the jurisdiction of Islam.[42] Christians had their own separate personal status code. Egyptians were at once members of a religious community (*ummah*) and citizens of a secular nation-state (*watan*), albeit one in which Islam was the official religion. Persons were born into a religion and of necessity were classified accordingly. Officially an individual had to belong to a religion and therefore be governed by its personal status code. For Muslims apostasy has been a crime punishable by death. The practice of religion, and the ways it is interpreted to guide behavior, have been left to competing interests. As the state increasingly regulated the public life of Egyptians, relinquishing to religious authorities the ordering of their family life, women were caught in a difficult position. Islam had been used to shore up family-based patriarchal controls and prerogatives. It fell to feminists and other progressives concerned with issues of gender to untangle what religion actually prescribed from what was alleged to be required by Islam.

While al-Azhar also retained authority in the pronouncement of religious doctrine, here too the state tightened its grip by appointing the mufti, the official who issued *fatwa*s, religious interpretations or rulings in response to particular questions. During Ottoman rule Istanbul appointed the mufti, but early in the nineteenth century this task was assumed by the new Egyptian state. The mufti could influence behavior by making conservative or liberal pronouncements. The state might give him a free hand to deal with ordinary matters of women's and men's personal lives, but the mufti was expected to lend religious legitimacy to matters of special interest to the state. We shall see, for example, that muftis did not pronounce in favor of women's rights to vote and to be elected to parliament until the state, advancing its new revolutionary agenda in the 1950s, signaled it was ready for this. Although the formal domain of the Islamic authorities had contracted, Islam remained a religious and cultural force in daily life that could be politicized to serve different purposes.

While the official purview of establishment Islam was contracting, Shaykh Muhammad ʿAbduh articulated the discourse of Islamic modernism. He advocated a return to the practice of *ijtihad* (independent inquiry), calling upon Muslims to look to the scriptural sources of their religion for fresh inspiration. This gave Muslims, men and women alike, a tool to interpret religion themselves and to apply Islam anew in their lives. In this way some women and men came to see that the domestic cloistering of women and the imposition of the face veil were not religious prescriptions. They also discovered that other practices ordained by Islam, such as obtaining a woman's consent in marriage, were ignored, while men often abused their rights to divorce and polygamy.[43]

In the late nineteenth century and for the first two-thirds of the twentieth century, the reforming, revitalizing doctrine of Islamic modernism accorded space for a feminism within the framework of the religious culture and provided a congenial climate for its evolution. When Egyptian Muslim women who are the subject of this book adopted an explicit feminist identity, they did not see this as threatening to their religious identity. To the contrary, they felt that their feminism enhanced their lives as Muslims. With the rise of a politicized populist conservative Islam in the 1970s, 1980s, and 1990s, the space accorded feminism contracted and a hostile environment was created. True to their feminist heritage, contemporary feminist women insist on retaining their space within Islam. In the current contest over religious interpretations concerning gender Egyptian Muslim women as feminists hold their ground and draw upon their own history.

Engendering the Nation

In the second half of the nineteenth century Egypt experienced growing encroachment by the West in its economic life. The country had become a major source of raw cotton for England following the loss of supplies during the American Civil War, while the opening of the Suez Canal in 1869 created a vital link between imperial Britain and India. In 1882, the British occupied Egypt on the pretext of safeguarding the khedive and foreign economic interests during the ʿUrabi revolution, which was led by Egyptian military officers seeking access to the higher ranks monopolized by the Turco-Circassian ruling elite and the achievement of a broader integration to Egyptians into the civil administration.[44] Huda Shaʿrawi's father, Sultan Pasha, initially a supporter of the ʿUrabists, was implicated in assisting the British intervention. Nabawiyah Musa's father, Musa Muhammad, benefited from the eventual opening up of the higher military ranks to ordinary Egyptians.[45]

British colonial rule interrupted the process of economic and social development begun under the direction of the previously autonomous Egyptian state. The political economy was redirected to serve British needs.[46] British men and women were imported into Egypt as government advisers, technicians, private tutors, teachers, school administrators, nurses, and doctors to buttress the colonial state and economy. Education became primarily geared toward training men to enter the lower and middle ranks of the bureaucracy and to fill key technical needs in such areas as irrigation engineering. The education and training of women that had earlier been encouraged by the modernizing Egyptian state was truncated.[47]

Egyptian nationalism evolved around the idea of a territorial nation or *watan* as a galvanizing counterforce to Western colonial occupation. This was a secular notion of nationalism as distinct from the "nations" within the Ottoman Empire defined by religion and ethnicity. While this idea of secular nationalism was being articulated, Egyptian women, Muslims and Christians alike, were sharpening their thinking about gender and the new idea of nation.

The very language of the British authorities broadcast their denial of an Egyptian nation. The British consul general of Egypt from 1883 to 1907, Evelyn Baring, Lord Cromer, and his fellow colonizers referred to Egyptians as "natives" or the "native race," avoiding the term "Egyptian." Moreover, the word "native" in the imperial vocabulary connoted a subject "race," the colonized other. As "natives," Egyptians were merged into a category that included all the colonized others. Much as women under patriarchy had been unrecognized and subsumed into a larger category, so Egyptians were lost in the anonymity of "native." As women had gone nameless, so did Egyptians. If colonial authorities generally refused to utter the word "Egyptian" because it would affirm a national identity, occasionally they employed it in the service of denigrating comparison, as when Egyptians were compared with Syrians living in Egypt; the latter, in Cromer's words, possessed "strength and *virility* of character" and, unlike women, they had the "power of inductive reasoning."[48] The Syrian in Egypt might be commended in order to diminish the "Egyptian," but, as an "Oriental," the Syrian also belonged to the category of the subordinate others. Cromer intoned: "Want of accuracy, which easily degenerates into untruthfulness, is, in fact, the main characteristic of the Oriental mind. The European (like the male) is a close reasoner."[49] Colonialism rendered Egyptians, men and women alike, nameless and nationless, while together they were gendered female. It was no accident that the recognition of "Egyptianness" and of gender arose simultaneously.

Within a broad collective will to end colonial occupation, differences emerged in the articulation of nationalist ideology and activism across lines of class and gender.[50] The nationalism of male secular progressives, mainly upper-class, included a call for women's advance that envisioned new societal roles for them as part of national empowerment. The nationalism of conservative men, mainly from the modest middle class, extolled women's domestic roles as part of their defense of an Islamic cultural authenticity.[51] When feminist women began to enter public space early in this century as educators and philanthropists, they insisted they were playing vital nationalist roles, as we shall see in chapter 2. Other, more conservative, women claimed their nationalist contributions as mothers and homemakers.

With the start of the First World War, the British placed Egypt under a temporary protectorate, ending all vestigial legal ties with the Ottomans. After the war, when the British were slow to remove the protectorate status and prevented Egyptians from attending the Versailles peace meetings, the entire nation rose up in revolt. From 1919 to 1922 Egyptian feminist women played key roles in the militant national independence struggle alongside male nationalists, and they stood in for them during their absence. Women's nationalist militancy together with their sustained commitment to feminist principles is the subject of chapter 3. When the British were finally forced to issue a unilateral declaration of independence, Egyptians assumed responsibility for their internal affairs—although British advisers, and lesser employees, were still abundant in the government ministries—while the British retained authority in foreign affairs and kept a military presence in Egypt. After the "independence" of 1922 and the promulgation of a new constitution the following year, the nature of the Egyptian national struggle changed and with it the nationalist-feminist nexus, as we shall see. Under colonialism all Egyptians had been concerned about issues of identity, rights, and sovereignty. Under patriarchy women were concerned with issues of their identity and rights and how authority was shaped and exercised. Women's commitment to nationalism was, if anything, heightened by their feminism. During the independence struggle, especially in the final phase of militancy, nationalist men welcomed women's support in the nationalist struggle. It was then that progressive nationalist men's rhetoric of women's liberation was most vocal. After independence the nationalist discourse of liberal men dropped much of its "feminist" dimension while men competed for political power. Moreover, nationalist men deprived women of the formal political rights of citizenship. To combat national forms of patriarchal domination, some women established a feminist organization within which to pursue nationalist goals and feminist goals.

Egyptian women as feminists conducted another kind of nationalist campaign abroad, in the context of the International Woman Suffrage Alliance. The EFU produced a journal in French called *L'Egyptienne*, in part to correct the national image of Egypt abroad. Egyptian feminists tied the campaign against state-licensed prostitution to a nationalist campaign to end the Capitulations, which accorded extraterritorial privileges to foreigners in Egypt. Egyptian feminists in the international feminist forum also called for attention to the violation of national rights of Palestinian Arabs. On many fronts, Egyptian feminists confronted international feminists with issues of imperialism they preferred to ignore.

The Emergence of Women's Feminist Discourse

The first women who manifested new awareness about gender were born in the middle decades of the nineteenth century. They published books of poetry and prose, biographical dictionaries, and articles and essays in the (male) press as early as the 1870s and 1880s, at a time when publishing itself was still new to Egypt.[52] One of the earliest contributions toward rethinking gender involved the recovery of women's past achievements. Two women who emigrated from Lebanon to Egypt, settling in Alexandria, published the first biographical dictionaries of women. Maryam al-Nahhas (1856–1888) published *Maʿrid al-Hasnaʾ fi Tarajim Mashahir al-Nisaʾ* (Dictionary of the exemplary in the lives of famous women) in 1879.[53] Zaynab Fawwaz (1860–1914) published *al-Durr al-Manthur fi Tabaqat al-Khudur* (Pearls strewn in the women's quarters) in 1894.[54] These compendiums provided models for women. Naming women and according them a public identity was radical at the time. Recalling his childhood in that period, writer Salamah Musa wrote: "Once I was struck by my sister because I had called her name in public."[55]

Writer ʿA'ishah al-Taymuriyah (1840–1902) confronted women's domestic seclusion. Instruction at home that gave women the ability to put pen to paper to communicate with others was still not something they could routinely expect as their due. In *Nataʾij al-Ahwal fi al-Aqwal wa-al-Afʿal* (The results of circumstances in words and deeds), published in 1887, she revealed her early yearnings to acquire literacy, rather than instruction in needlework. She went on to master Arabic, Turkish, and Persian, succeeding in becoming a writer and poet through her own determination and with the help of a supportive father. The daughter of Kurdish litterateur Ismaʿil Pasha Taymur and a Circassian concubine, she was raised in the shelter of an elite harem. After marrying at the age of fourteen she put her writing aside. Twelve years later, upon losing her husband and her father, she returned to her pen. In the period following the death of her only daughter Tawhida in 1873 at the age of eighteen, ʿA'ishah al-Taymuriyah published two *diwans* (collections of poetry): one in Arabic called *Hiyat al-Tiraz* and another in Turkish called *Shakufa*. A third in Persian was destroyed by her own hand before it could be published. Contemporary Syrian poet Warda al-Yaziji[56] praised al-Taymuriyah. Future writers Lebanese Mayy Ziyadah and Egyptian Malak Hifni Nasif (Bahithat al-Badiyah) and other women hailed al-Taymuriyah as a founding mother of feminist expression.[57]

In *The Results of Circumstances in Words and Deeds* al-Taymuriyah confessed to unseen sisters in similar circumstances: "I have suffered in this cave of isolation [the harem]. Compassion for all people [women] who have encountered what I have encountered and who have been struck by the same blows has led me to fashion a tale which would distract them from their cares when thoughts crowd in and would entertain them drawing them far from the grief they feel . . . in the exile of solitude which is harder to bear than exile from one's homeland."[58] Sharing a consciousness of gender with other isolated women was a first step in building a sisterhood.[59]

Literacy also gave secluded women a chance to speak to men, to expose their complicity in keeping women behind and to interrogate such actions. Al-Taymuriyah wrote in *al-Adab* in 1889, "Oh, men of our homelands, oh you who control our affairs, why have you left women behind for no reason?"[60] In a short book published in the 1890s called *Mir'at al-Taʿamal fi al-ʿUmur* (The mirror of contemplation of things) al-Taymuriyah decried the "marriage problem" and domestic ills rampant in her class as men tyrannized over women, trying to keep them suppressed while they took their own liberties. She protested that men were too free and women too "incarcerated."

Some women deployed their newfound literacy to expound a narrow view of women's lot and thus to hold back their own sex. When Hanna' Kawrani, a Syrian Christian, attacked women's suffrage, then being debated in England, in the newspaper *Lubnan* (Lebanon), Fawwaz responded, upholding women's struggle for political rights in *Jaridat al-Nil* (The newspaper of the Nile) in 1892.[61] Countering Kawrani's essentialist and religious arguments for restricting women to the home, Zaynab Fawwaz retorted: "We have not seen any of the divinely ordered systems of law, or any law from among the corpus of religious law (in Islam), ruling that woman is to be prohibited from involvement in the occupations of men. Nature has nothing to do with this . . . woman is a human being as man is, with complete mental faculties and acumen, and equivalent parts, capable of performing according to her own abilities."[62] Fawwaz's strong feminist voice resonated in her prolific essays and articles, which were collected and published in *Kitab al-Rasa'il al-Zaynabiyah* (Zaynab's letters) in 1897 and reprinted in 1910.[63]

By the 1890s, the new communion of women, initiated by exchanges of letters and circulation of books, expanded and took new forms. Upper-class Egyptian women pioneered in collective debate on their lives when Eugénie Le Brun—a Frenchwoman turned Muslim, married to Husayn Rushdi from the Turco-Circassian landowning elite (and later prime minister)—opened the first salon for women. Huda Shaʿrawi, who had adopted Le Brun as an elder friend and mentor, was the youngest woman to attend the salon, where veiling and seclusion were among the topics of debate. As a convert studying Islam Le Brun had discovered that the seclusion of women and covering the face were not religious prescriptions but simply social conventions.[64]

When middle-class women founded the women's press, they created a wider forum for their voices and for the discussion of matters that concerned them.[65] Hind Nawfal (ca. 1860–1920), the daughter of biographer Maryam al-Nahhas, inaugurated the women's press in 1892, when she founded *al-Fatah* (The young girl). The editor explained: "Its sole principle is to defend the rights of the deprived and draw attention to the obligations due. . . . We ask the gracious and learned ladies to consider *al-Fatah* their newspaper in the East. It will express their ideas . . . defend their rights, review their literature and knowledge, and take pride in publishing the best of their work."[66] Knowing full well that the woman's voice was considered *ʿawrah* (literally, pudenda; more generally construed as anything having sexual connotations) and therefore something to be "covered" or unheard, the editor issued a disclaimer: "But do not imagine that a woman who writes in a journal is compromised in modesty or violates her purity and good behavior."[67] Women whose words would reach the public (mainly a female public) would not, by the very act of writing, transgress moral codes and commit sins of sexual impurity. Three other journals appeared before the close of the century: Louisa Habbalin's *al-Firdaws* (Paradise, 1896), Alexandra Avierino's *Anis al-Jalis* (Woman's companion, 1898–1908), and Esther Moyal's *al-ʿA'ilah* (The family, 1899–1904). The founders of the first two, like Nawfal, were Syrian Christians and the third a Syrian Jew. The women's press was didactic, focusing mainly on the enhancement of women's family roles and on education as serving these roles.

Though the women's press was not radical in content, its mere existence was. Through writing for publication, women collectively transcended their domestic confinement, beginning to acquire a public "presence," and by claiming their names and voices they took responsibility for themselves and accepted accountability. The women's press afforded larger numbers of women, mainly middle-class women, the chance to speak and be heard. In making their voices heard, writing women challenged the ideology of ʿawrah used to silence women. This early "unveiling" of women's voices was paralleled by a literal unveiling, as some (non-Muslim) women began to uncover their faces. Issues of respectability, voicing, and sexuality were all bound up with women's moves into society.[68]

It was Muslim women like ʿA'ishah al-Taymuriyah and Zaynab Fawwaz who were the most outspokenly radical in their day. Their vehicles of expression were their articles in the "mainstream" (male) press and their books. These were women who were heralded, revered, and claimed as foremothers by the feminist activists of the early twentieth century. Al-Taymuriyah and Fawwaz, born in the middle decades of the nineteenth century, stood at the beginning of the feminist tradition in Egypt.[69]

The Emergence of Men's Feminist Discourse

Women had already begun to manifest their discontent and had taken steps to ameliorate their lives, when a questioning of patriarchal practices and institutions surfaced within the patriarchal establishment itself. Men's starting points were quite different from women's. While women were motivated by reflection upon their own lives and in the first instance sought improved conditions for themselves, men began more abstractly. It was the search to explain their country's backwardness that first led men to articulate feminist formulations. These were highly educated men with legal training and exposure to European thought.

In the early 1890s, a young graduate of the khedivial law school in Cairo, Murqus Fahmi, worked on a treatise setting out his analysis of Egypt's backwardness and proposing reform. He argued that the country was backward because women were backward and that women's condition was a consequence of their oppression by men within the family. Fahmi had begun to draft the first systematic critique of patriarchy in Egypt when he learned of a tragedy and decided to convey the operations of patriarchy through a dramatization of this event. The result was a four-act play, *al-Mar'ah fi al-Sharq* (The woman in the East), which Fahmi published in 1894.[70]

The incident had recently happened not far from Fahmi's childhood home in the Egyptian Delta. A young woman from a landowning family had grown up on a country estate where she had been educated by a French tutor. When her parents decided she should marry and provided a prospective husband, the young woman at first refused but in the end was forced to submit to their designs. After her marriage, when contact was made between the woman and the man she had wanted to marry, her husband had the man murdered. The woman in turn killed her husband and then herself. The young woman's aborted life frames Fahmi's exposition of the dire workings of the patriarchal order and the complicity of both sexes in its perpetuation. The plea for liberation of Egyptians and especially women from the tyranny of custom is made more compelling by the reality and the metaphor of the lost life.

Fahmi narrated the oppression of female domestic "imprisonment" (the term al-Taymuriyah used). Men claimed that they confined women to protect them. They insisted that women, who were weak and lacking in moral fiber, were given to treachery and sexual infidelity. Fahmi, without agreeing with the premise, noted that men confined women not simply to control honor but to control the patrimony. The play pivots around the young woman's struggle for self-expression within the context of home and family. Fahmi focused his lens on the fissures in the crumbling elite patriarchal order of late-nineteenth-century Egypt, articulating the contest between "traditional" patriarchy and emergent feminism through the contest between two brothers, one a reactionary and the other a progressive.

The reactionary brother intones: "Free choice is not permitted to woman. It violates the dictates of her own sex. It goes against her very nature and reason for being. Exercising free will only causes woman to be lowered in the eyes of man. No one could trust such a woman nor be saved from her cunning." A woman's free choice, the freedom of a woman to choose her spouse, as a man can, is opposed to the well-being of society: "If we permit the woman to choose her husband we'd also have to allow her free movement and the opportunity to meet men in order to find someone she likes, the way man moves freely from one house to the other to choose his partner. This would harm society morally and materially," he adds, "because woman by her very nature is fickle." For order to be preserved in family and society, "the woman must remain imprisoned in her house and the freedom of choice kept from her." This is divinely ordained: "God Almighty, himself, has created her to be the ornament of man who may treat her as he will."[71]

This conventional argument for the domestic seclusion of women as a source of stability and honor is turned on its head through the voice of the progressive brother. "Incarceration [of the woman in the house] brings shame upon women and their men the same way that confinement brings shame to the family of those jailed." He pursues the implications of the reactionary argument: "If he [the man] allowed her [the woman] to be free her morals would become corrupt and she'd bring disgrace upon herself and him that could never be eradicated. Man, unfortunately, does not grasp the full meaning of what he says. Doesn't he see that he makes a declaration of mistrust tantamount to saying if the woman is not imprisoned like a thief she would commit evil? Doesn't he see by speaking this way it is as if his wife had already disgraced him since the intention alone to commit an improper act is enough to tarnish his honor?" Only "purity and virtue" issuing from a woman's conscience can confer honor.[72]

Linking the private with the public, Fahmi contends that family despotism is mirrored in state despotism. Lack of family unity is reflected in lack of national unity. Barriers are placed between Egyptians not only by gender but by creed. Giving his characters names common to Muslims and Christians alike, Fahmi spoke to all Egyptians using secular arguments, imagining a secular society governed by secular laws, including personal status laws. His was a radical and lone voice calling for secularization of family law.

All women must be freed from tyrannies in their everyday family lives. They must be given education and allowed other rights their religions have accorded them. Only then will the family be strengthened and, in turn, the nation. Optimistic, Fahmi announced in his introduction: "The day is coming when the rights of woman will be honored. The attention given this and the beginnings by the gentle sex to defend their rights taken by force, by oppression at the hands of men, are sure signs we are close to emerging from darkness into light . . . it is not impossible that we shall move from words to deeds."[73]

In 1894, the year *The Woman in the East* appeared, Qasim Amin, a Muslim judge, published *Les Egyptiens*, defending current gender practice among upper-class Egyptians from attacks the French duc d'Harcourt made in his book *L'Egypte et les Egyptiens* in 1893. Objecting to this patriarchal apologia Princess Nazli Fazil invited Qasim Amin to her salon to hear the views of Islamic reformist Shaykh ʿAbduh and other progressives on the subject of women in Egypt.[74] Five years later, in 1899, Qasim Amin published *Tahrir al-Marʾah* (The liberation of the woman). Striking similarities to Murqus Fahmi's writings suggest that Amin, and Muhammad ʿAbduh, Ahmad Lutfi al-Sayyid, and others who are said to have had a hand in the book, were familiar with *The Woman in the East*.[75] Amin, however, addressed a Muslim audience, employing Islamic modernist arguments to justify his call for gender reform. Amin, like Fahmi, depicted patriarchal oppression. As part of religious reform and national regeneration Qasim Amin called for an end to female seclusion, which he demonstrated had nothing to do with Islam. Abuses of divorce and polygamy must be eliminated. Women must be educated. Unlike Fahmi, who ignored the matter, Amin also called for an end to face veiling, which likewise had nothing to do with Islam. Intense outrage was directed toward the proposal to unveil, broadcasting not merely its practical implications but its larger symbolic significance. Fearful about their customary privileges conservatives and reactionaries were outraged when this respected Muslim man, a member of the judicial establishment, tore away the Islamic cover of the patriarchally imposed practices of veiling and domestic incarceration of women. In 1900 Amin published *al-Mar'ah al-Jadidah* (The new woman), applying secular arguments to his call for female, and hence national, liberation.

Amin's books have since been widely, if incorrectly, acclaimed as the founding feminist texts in Egypt. Unlike the earlier works by women and Fahmi's book, they provoked heated controversy.[76] The outcry against Amin was intense because of his status as a male Muslim and respected judge who not only insisted that his views conformed with Islam, but also used secular arguments.[77] The ideas of Fahmi, a Copt—as of women—could be more easily dismissed.[78]

Conceptual Challenges and the Politics of Presentation

Here, before proceeding to the main body of the book, I would like to address issues relating to definitions of feminism and to what can be called the "politics of presentation" of feminism and, more generally, of issues of gender and culture.

Defining Feminisms and Feminists

Egyptian women first used the term "feminist" to define themselves and their organization al-Ittihad al-Nisa'i al-Misri—which they called in French l'Union Féministe Egyptienne—in 1923. *Nisa'i/yah* is an ambiguous term in Arabic that can signify anything pertaining to women; sometimes it denotes "feminist" and sometimes "feminine." The term *féminisme* was originally coined in France in the 1880s but was not widely used until the early 1890s, after it had come into use as "feminism" in England.[79] "Feminism" first appeared in the United States in the 1910s. Just a decade later nisa'i began to be used to signify "feminist" in Egypt.[80] The Arabic Academy in Cairo recently adopted a word for patriarchy, *abawiyah*, but it has yet to adopt a word for feminism.

The basic definition of feminism used in this study, which derives from the experience of Egyptian women as feminists in the nineteenth and twentieth centuries, includes the awareness of constraints placed upon women because of their gender and attempts to remove these constraints and to evolve a more equitable gender system involving new roles for women and new relations between women and men. It assumes women's independent agency and constitutes a discrete discourse, which appropriates elements of other discourses, especially those of Islamic modernism and nationalism. My use of "feminist" is deliberately fluid and broad in order to be inclusive rather than exclusive, as I believe that to narrow the Egyptian feminist experience is to distort and diminish it. EFU women, who articulated their own feminism in their own society and circumstances, saw their feminism as a specific expression of a generic or "universal" phenomenon. In other words, they did not perceive that the process of redefining gender roles and relations in ways more favorable to women, which they came to identify as "feminism," was the property of the West, or of the East. They did not see their feminism as derivative or as an alien intrusion, as some antagonists have done. In the early twentieth century under colonial occupation and during the period of incomplete independence, critics depicted feminism as a manifestation of Western cultural imperialism, while there are still those to this day who view feminism as a vestige of Western colonialism. The way people view feminism is a function of their histories, agendas, and politics. It is important to contextualize feminism in time, place, class, and groupings defined by ethnicity and creed. However, it is also illuminating to open the analytic lens to view feminism through a wide angle, consciously blurring internal distinctions across various divides such as those of class and ethnicity to see the wider culture of feminism. Definitions of feminism are ratified by concrete experience and change in any given place over time.

I wish to make clear how I use the terms "feminism" and "feminist" and such constructs as "feminist consciousness" and "feminist" activism. When I apply any of these terms to ideas and actions prior to 1923, when one can first date Egyptian women's use of "feminist" and "feminism," I employ them simply as analytical devices. The term "feminist consciousness," of course, was not coined until later in the century in the United States. Thus I identify certain late-nineteenth-century and early-twentieth-century women as "feminists" because of their ideas, agendas, and actions, not because they themselves did. I call such women as ʿA'isha al-Taymuriyah (d. 1902), Zaynab Fawwaz (d. 1914), and Malak Hifni Nasif (Bahithat al-Badiyah, d. 1918) feminists. I also refer to Huda Shaʿrawi and Nabawiyah Musa as feminists before they associated themselves with the term as founders of the Egyptian Feminist Union. Nabawiyah Musa soon conducted her "feminism" mainly outside the framework of the EFU, not bothering about the feminist label. Hence, even after the term circulated in Egypt, I refer to some women as feminists who did not necessarily adopt this explicit identity. The feminists introduced in Part Two, who are at the core of this study, include the EFU leadership and members, and women who were EFU members at one time, or were nominal members but who supported the EFU agenda in general and periodically rallied round certain issues. Feminists also include women engaged in what I call "everyday feminist activism," mainly those pioneering in entering the professions or in building new institutions of civil society.

During the period of feminist history that this book treats, Egypt experienced colonial occupation and an incomplete independence with pronounced vestiges of colonial intrusion. It was also a period when the majority of the countries in Africa and Asia that have experienced colonialism and imperialism were still under imperial rule. Where feminisms existed in Africa, Asia, and the West, they were caught up in the world of the colonizers and the colonized. I use the phrase "national feminisms" to denote feminisms that existed in particular countries. Feminisms in colonized or semi-independent countries such as Egypt, Syria, India, and the like were "nationalist feminisms" and were explicit about this. Feminisms in colonizing countries such as Britain and France were "imperial feminisms," although British and French feminists were not always highly conscious of this. I describe in chapter 2 subtle forms of Egyptian women's "everyday nationalist activism" and in chapter 3 their engagement in militant nationalist feminist activism. The workings of imperial feminism and Egyptian nationalist feminists' engagement with imperial feminism are illuminated in various parts of the book: for example, chapter 10 addresses the intersections of imperialism and prostitution; chapter 12 explores the interconnections of imperialism, gender, and the Palestinian national struggle. It is chapter 12 that deals with the birth of Arab feminism, that is, pan-Arab feminism—both acknowledging and blending the nationalist feminisms of individual Arab countries—that Egyptians played a major role in consolidating.

Feminists, Class, and Culture

Writing the history of women and of feminism in Egypt—and elsewhere, for that matter—makes one conscious of the challenges of dealing with gender and class. In some forms of Marxist analysis women have been subsumed under class and have been seen primarily to express and serve interests of class—the class interests of fathers and husbands. To simplistically conflate women's concerns with the interests of men of their class robs women of agency. Also one has to take into account that women, for reasons of gender, may try to subvert, remake, or transcend class cultures or to achieve class mobility. We shall see in chapter 1 the divergent ways upper-class Huda Shaʿrawi and modestly middle-class Nabawiyah Musa operated within and beyond their classes and how the latter positioned herself to change class. When women increasingly pioneered in the professions in the 1930s, they helped to shape the culture of the expanding middle class.

In the previous section, in discussing broad social, economic, and political transformations in the nineteenth century and, more specifically, women's education, I have begun to illuminate how different class cultures took shape. The upper class and upper middle class socially spoke mainly French, less often English, and acquired European manners. The middle and lower strata of the middle class and the lower class spoke Arabic and retained familiar ("indigenous") modes, but these were by no means "pure" or static. Although it is possible to make these general observations, the reality is more complicated. It is too reductive to label the upper class "Western" and the modest classes "Eastern" or "authentically indigenous" as is frequently done in popular discourse. Huda Shaʿrawi, from the upper class by virtue of the wealth of her father (whose sole language was Arabic; her mother's languages were Circassian and Turkish) spoke French as her everyday language in her Cairene social circles. She spoke Arabic at women's nationalist meetings at her house during the independence struggle and both Arabic and French as a leader of the feminist movement in the 1920s, 1930s, and 1940s. She spoke Turkish with her mother and Arabic when visiting her family home in Upper Egypt. Shaʿrawi recalled in her memoirs, with evident pain, her failed attempts to acquire literacy in Arabic. Upper-class girls "who would not become judges," as Shaʿrawi was told, were deemed not to need Arabic; by contrast, the men of their class, because of their wider societal roles, were allowed to study Arabic and were more exposed to the language in their public life. Middle-class Nabawiyah Musa and Bahithat al-Badiyah habitually spoke, read, and wrote in Arabic but also knew French and English, which they studied in state schools. Both also had encounters with Western women in Egypt, mainly through their intellectual and professional lives.

Feminist and other innovating women, as well as those unexpectedly left without male support, often live at the intersections of classes and unsettle conventional constructions of class. Throughout this book we shall see how the rising feminist culture transcends class, creating a certain cross-class culture, and also how class inflects feminist culture and agendas.

Veiled Battles

Veiling was a contentious issue in early-twentieth-century Egypt, as indeed it is at the latter end of the century. As a cultural practice and as a symbol the veil must be situated in historical context. In my discussion of urban harem culture I noted that veiling in the form of covering the face was imposed on city women cloistered in their houses as well as on the less secluded lower-class women. I have shown how women, as they deepened their gender awareness, began to discover that the practice was erroneously imposed as a religious prescription. In nineteenth- and early-twentieth-century Egypt the Arabic word *hijab*, veil, signified covering the face and was used as a generic term. There were various specific terms for the piece of cloth, such as *burqa* and the Turkish loan word *yashmak*. In the 1970s in Egypt with the "return to the veil," hijab does not refer to hiding the face but simply to covering the head, while the less common cloth covering the face is called a *niqab*. In this study of late-nineteenth- and early-twentieth-century practice I employ the terms "veil" and "veiling" as they were used then.

In the first two decades of the twentieth century feminist women like Huda Shaʿrawi and Bahithat al-Badiyah retained the veil. Both argued that uncovering the face was premature because society was not ready for it, but both expressed a conviction, without remorse, that it was a matter of time before the veil would disappear. In Part One of this book I discuss how these and other feminist women during this period used veiling as a "feminist device," aiding their own and other upper- and middle-class women's entry into society. Nabawiyah Musa, on the other hand, stood out among early Muslim feminists for removing her face cover during this period, around 1909. As a pupil in a school for girls run by the colonial state, she had been required by the education authorities to veil. It may have been in part an act of nationalist defiance when she unveiled not long after leaving the state system to run the primary school for girls Egyptian nationalists opened in Fayyum. Nabawiyah Musa, being unmarried, was freer to unveil than Bahithat al-Badiyah and Huda Shaʿrawi, who both had husbands. Bahithat al-Badiyah died in 1918 without having unveiled. Huda Shaʿrawi unveiled in 1923 at the beginning of the organized feminist movement and the year after her husband's death. Unveiling was never part of the Egyptian feminist movement's formal agenda. In Egypt in the 1920s and 1930s women, encouraged by an independent feminist movement, decided for themselves if and when to unveil, unlike their counterparts in Turkey and Iran, where the state took measures to impose unveiling. Chapter 5 deals with the Egyptian feminists' approach to unveiling. When Shaʿrawi unveiled her face, she kept her head covered, thus observing what today would be called "veiling." Later she alternated between covering and not covering her head. In her "official portrait" as a feminist leader, which still hangs in the premises of the EFU (now called the Huda Shaʿrawi Association), her head is covered, giving her the aspect of a contemporary veiled woman.

For feminists—except perhaps for Nabawiyah Musa—veiling has been first and foremost a gender issue. For nationalist men in Middle Eastern countries it has been primarily a nationalist issue. Anticolonial nationalist movements in Arab countries have taken diverse positions on the veil. In Algeria, which experienced a protracted French colonial rule (1830–1962) that was aggressively culturally assimilationist and where a large French settler community was implanted, retaining the veil became a mode of nationalist defense. Before and after the French tried to instigate unveiling as a cultural form of colonial assault, the veiled woman as the "authentic" Algerian—as Algeria—became a symbol of anticolonial resistance. In Egypt where the circumstances and policy of British colonialism were different—where indigenous culture was less massively and directly assaulted, which is not to underestimate the cultural impacts of British colonialism in Egypt—Egyptians did not muster the veil as a weapon of cultural defense.[81] Among the upper classes flaunting their preference for the French language and things French became a form of anti-British defiance. In Egypt the "new woman," was deployed against the colonizer, and deployed herself against the intruder. Clinging to a "traditional model" of "the woman" clothed in some pure "authentic" dress was not a dominant nationalist strategy in Egypt. Liberal Egyptian nationalist men and nationalist feminist women did not turn the veil into a nationalist flag. Conservative nationalist men, whose voices were not to carry the day, clung to veiling as an icon of the "Islamic" culture—and the kind of theocratic political system they hoped for—that they saw slipping away.

Out of the Prison of Colonialism

A common counterattack on women's assumption of agency as feminists—on behalf of gender and nation—has been to discredit feminists, and feminism, by branding them Western agents of colonialism. The charge of derivative feminism, a reductive and agency-depriving mode of thinking, still lingers. Some narrators of the history of Egyptian feminism imprison it in a frame story of Western colonialism, ironically sustaining a colonialist scripting they abhor by according it overarching explanatory power. A corollary pursuit has been to apply an East-West litmus test to Egyptian feminists. East equals authentic and good; West equals alien and bad. Such a reduction obscures the complexity of cultures—especially in a country like Egypt at the crossroads of three continents—and forecloses the notion of hybridity. What surfaces is an essentialized notion of some "pure" Eastern or Western culture perpetuating the polarization and politics of difference that colonialism constructed. In countries that were not colonized, such as Turkey and states in the Arabian Peninsula, feminism is not attacked for being Western.

Egyptian feminism was not a subtext of colonialism or "Western discourse," but an independent discourse that simultaneously engaged indigenous patriarchy and patriarchal colonial domination.

Positionings

Over three decades as I have moved back and forth, living and working in Egypt and other parts of the Middle East and the West, mainly the United States and England, I have observed the "situatedness" of debates, theories, and arguments. In particular contexts certain sensibilities are sharpened while others are muted; certain questions are raised and accorded priority. I have been struck by how historical feminism and contemporary movements engaging questions of gender have been considered in intellectual and feminist circles—circles comprising Egyptians and foreigners from the East and the West—in Egypt, and how sharply this vision differs from that in the

West. Today in Egypt feminist women and those sympathetic to feminism view their feminist past as "indigenous," as an integral part of Egyptian history. Contemporary feminist concerns engage specific issues, such as women's retaining their place in the work force, the building of new institutions of civil society, and women's ability to sustain free choice about their personal lives in such matters as dress and mobility. Feminists and other liberal and progressive women are concerned about countering threats from conservative populist Islamist forces to push women back to the home and dictate how their lives are to be conducted. Meanwhile, Egyptian feminists and other progressives living in the West sometimes take apologetic positions on conservative or reactionary practices, sacrificing the urgencies of gender issues that women feel in Egypt to a nationalist defense of "Islam." By the end of the 1980s in Egypt, feminists, pro-feminists, and some intellectual women within the Islamic movement began to articulate converging views on a number of gender issues, especially women's right to remain in the work force.

Assessing the Egyptian feminist past is far from simple. There are feminist and Islamist women in contemporary Egypt, for example, who equally claim Nabawiyah Musa as one of their own. Some young Islamist women have noted that Huda Shaʿrawi was pictured wearing hijab, "after she unveiled." There are multiple identities, multiple political projects, multiple ways of constructing culture and evoking historical memory.

My intent in this book is to present the Egyptian feminist movement until the middle of the twentieth century—the collective, organized movement and individual, pioneering activists—as the movement saw itself and as feminist women saw themselves, constructed their agendas, and reconstructed their experiences. I have used women's records and documents: I took extensive oral histories, examined women's memoirs, correspondence, essays, speeches, journalistic articles, poetry, fiction, bylaws of women's organizations, sets of demands, petitions, oaths of allegiance, and slogans; I have looked at the records of the Egyptian Feminist Union and examined its two official organs and its occasional publications. Of necessity this lengthy research was conducted in Egypt and over a period of many years. The first "incarnation" of this book was written mainly in Oxford where it was presented as a doctoral thesis in 1977. Over the years since then I have extended my research in Egypt and thought and rethought the Egyptian feminist past. Since my first writing a populist conservative Islamist movement has emerged, which has gained a considerable following among women and has exerted its own force in society. Into the 1980s I was still discussing contemporary gender issues and the feminist past with feminists who had known and worked with the first generation of feminist activists, Huda Shaʿrawi, Nabawiyah Musa, and others. Meanwhile, I was lecturing, writing, and attending symposia both in Egypt and in the West, mainly the United States. My initial positioning at the start of this project was as a researcher resident in Egypt; over the subsequent years my positioning has moved freely between Egypt and the West.

Organization of the Book

This study of the rise and evolution of feminism from the late nineteenth century to the middle of the twentieth century is arranged in three parts comprising twelve chapters, ordered both chronologically and thematically.

Part One: Rising Feminist Consciousness

This part, dealing with the period from the 1880s to the beginning of the 1920s, focuses on the continuing emergence of women's gender awareness. Huda Shaʿrawi and Nabawiyah Musa—respectively, an upper-class founder and leader of the first organized feminist movement and a middle-class everyday activist pioneering in education and the workplace—whose vision and experiences form a vertical thread through the book are first introduced in this section. Chapter 1 explores their early lives and evolving gender consciousness, observing how they acquiesced or innovated in their early lives. Chapters 2 and 3 investigate how these and other middle- and upper-class women pioneered in invisible everyday feminist activism, creating new female institutions in public space, and entered male-dominated public institutions while concurrently giving expression to fresh ways of thinking about gender. The section culminates with chapter 4, examining women's nationalist militancy, together with their sustained feminist activism, during the movement leading to independence in 1922.

Part Two: The Feminist Movement

This part, forming the core of the book, focuses on the 1920s, 1930s, and 1940s. It deals with the entire period of the first organized feminist movement, the movement that Huda Shaʿrawi led as founder and head of the Egyptian Feminist Union from 1923 to her death in 1947. Women as active members of the EFU, the "political feminists," supported and were supported by the "pragmatic feminists," many of whom, like Nabawiyah Musa, belonged to the EFU but concentrated their energies in the everyday arenas of social service and professional life.

The development of organizational apparatus, which is discussed in chapter 5, and the prioritization of the goals of the EFU-led movement order the internal flow of Part Two, which is thus, to a certain extent, chronologically mapped. Yet this movement is driven also by the trajectory of individual women's societal pioneering, as the "two movements (the political and the pragmatic) within a movement" were highly interactive.

The EFU-led movement, together with pioneering feminist philanthropists, attempted to extend social services to lower-class urban women—a process that had begun before the EFU was formed—from the 1920s through the 1940s, and to villagers from the late 1930s; their efforts are the subject of chapter 6. The EFU campaign to reform the personal status code, an immediate priority in the 1920s, and later to advise on the everyday functioning of the family are dealt with in chapter 7. Promoting education and women's roles in the work force constitute the concerns of chapters 8 and 9; chapter 10 examines the EFU campaign to end state-regulated prostitution. Chapter 11 focuses on the attempts by the EFU, and other feminists, to win political rights for women.

Part Three: The Widening Circle

This part concentrates on the period from the late 1930s through the 1940s when the EFU played a key role in bringing Egyptian and other Arab women together to defend the Palestinian national cause. Coming together for this Arab nationalist cause, women went on to articulate and institutionalize pan-Arab feminism. The two-decades-long experience and the vision of the Egyptian feminist resonated in the agenda of Arab feminism.

• PART ONE •

Rising Feminist Consciousness

• CHAPTER 1 •

Two Lives in Changing Worlds

Two women born in the late nineteenth century shaped the history of feminism in Egypt in the first half of the twentieth century. Huda Shaʿrawi, whose background was upper-class, led an organized feminist movement. Nabawiyah Musa, of modest middle-class origins, expressed her feminism as a pioneering educator of women. The experiences of these two women reveal the play of class and gender in the construction and reconstruction of their lives.

Exploring the rise of feminist consciousness during the early formative years of the lives of Huda Shaʿrawi and Nabawiyah Musa is this chapter's central concern. For Huda Shaʿrawi this period extends from 1879 to 1900, the year she resumed conjugal life after a seven-year separation. For Nabawiyah Musa this period runs from 1886 to 1907 when she capped her formal education. The "formative years," determined by key turning points in the two women's lives, coincidentally end for both at the age of twenty-one.

Our investigation draws upon these women's memoirs, which give insights into the processes whereby women learn what it is to be a "woman," ways they react to the "fixed" constructions of "woman," and how they attempt to redefine the category "woman." The women's autobiographical accounts provide clues about what propelled them and shaped their respective visions as they acquiesced or innovated in their everyday lives. A juxtaposition of these two lives discloses gender commonalities as well as differences linked to class and circumstance in the unfolding of women's growing feminist awareness and activisms. Along with illuminating evolving feminisms, a look at the early lives of Huda Shaʿrawi and Nabawiyah Musa provides a window on upper- and middle-class female life of the period.

This chapter suggests how women become feminists and the complexities of the category "woman." The term "feminist" is neither fixed nor easily definable. It is constructed (or emerges) out of experiences and perceptions, and is expressed both in voicings and in silences. Debates on whether feminism in Egypt and more generally in much of the third world is Western have included in the circumference of interrogation political issues of authenticity, national-cultural "treason," and social ir/relevancy—such matters that stack the cards for the legitimizing or discrediting of "feminism." Examining the unfolding of feminism(s) in the context of Egyptian women's experiences and reflections renders such interrogation redundant.[1] Looking for an essential "cultural purity" underlying such debates over feminism is futile. Cultures are constructed; they are fluid and thus continually in the process of construction. "External elements"—external to class, re- appropriated and woven into the fabric of the "indige- pt historically has appropriated and absorbed "alien ele- ly vital indigenous culture. Attempts to discredit or to on cultural grounds, used by feminists and detractors rojects predicated on divergent ways of understanding, lture and on the willingness or perceived need to perpet- East" and "West."

Huda Shaʿrawi

Huda Shaʿrawi was born Nur al-Huda Sultan in 1879 at Minya in Upper Egypt on her father's vast estate. Muhammad Sultan Pasha, who was known later in life as "the King of Upper Egypt," had risen from modest beginnings as *shaykh al-balad*, or village headman, through the provincial administration. Toward the end of his life, aided by the policy of the Turco-Circassian ruling elite to draw native Egyptians from the provinces into the central government, he became president of the Assembly of Deputies (Shura al-Nuwwab) and, after it was dissolved, a member of the Consultative Council (Majlis al-Shura). It was in that period that he established a household in Cairo. Sultan Pasha played a role in the ʿUrabi revolt, which included the aim of bringing more Egyptians into high military ranks. Later, by helping to secure the allegedly endangered throne of Khedive Tawfiq, he played a hand in assisting the entry of the British into Egypt.[2] His daughter rejected any notion of her father's collaboration with the British; indeed, she suggested that their growing entrenchment in the country hastened his death in 1884.[3]

While her father was an old man at the time of Huda's birth, her mother Iqbal was still in her teens. Born in the Caucasus, Iqbal as a young child fled to Istanbul with her mother following her father's death in skirmishes with the Russians. Life in Istanbul was tenuous for refugees from the fighting in the Caucasus. After an infant daughter was kidnapped, Iqbal's mother sent her daughter to Cairo where she was reared in a harem of the Turco-Circassian elite.[4] A companion to the young daughters of the household, girls like Iqbal from Turkey and the Caucasus were later given as concubines or brides to men of the Turco-Circassian or new Egyptian elites. Thus Iqbal was presented to Sultan Pasha; according to the dispersal of his properties set out in his *waqf* (religious endowment) Iqbal never achieved the status of legal wife. However, Turco-Circassian consorts had their own status and brought prestige to the houses into which they entered.

Huda was five years old when her father died. She grew up in her father's Cairo household presided over by her mother and a *durra* (co-wife), Hasibah. Upon the death of Sultan Pasha his sister's son ʿAli Shaʿrawi had become the legal guardian of Huda and her brother, and the *wakil*, the agent or executor, of their late father's estate. ʿAli Shaʿrawi, who lived in Minya, made periodic visits from Upper Egypt. Huda's upbringing included lessons at home given by tutors she shared with her brother ʿUmar, two years her junior.

When Huda was twelve her mother arranged her betrothal to her cousin and guardian, ʿAli Shaʿrawi, and Huda married him the following year. At fourteen she separated from her husband, returning, under family pressure, when she was twenty-one. During the period of "independence" Huda resumed her lessons and expanded her world.

In the first decade of the twentieth century, Shaʿrawi helped to found a philanthropic society and organize lectures for women. She was active in the national independence movement from 1919 to 1922. In 1923, the year after independence (and the year after her husband's death) when Huda Shaʿrawi was forty-four, she founded al-Ittihad al-Nisaʾi al-Misri (the Egyptian Feminist Union) and led a feminist movement until her death in 1947.

Huda Shaʿrawi had been at the head of the first organized feminist movement for more than two decades when she began to dictate her memories in Arabic—not in her everyday French—to her secretary ʿAbd al-Hamid Fahmi Mursi, but death overtook her before she completed the task. Her story, which tapers off in the mid-1930s, is told in two voices. She recounts the first part of her life before she became a public figure with an introspective, innocent voice; often lyrical, it flows in a stream of consciousness, caressing pains and pleasures. In contrast, her voice in the second part is that of the chronicler, self-conscious and calculating, as she set out to record the public, organized feminist movement. With the eye of a mature feminist Shaʿrawi retells the story of her early years, charting the rise of her gender consciousness. She delineates the acquisition of control over her life when she gained, unexpectedly and by default, a seven-year moratorium from marriage. Shaʿrawi shows how she expanded her life within the parameters allowed by her class and circumstances. A dominant trope in the representation of her early life is awareness of gender despite acquiescence in the patriarchal culture of her class.[5]

Shaʿrawi initiates the portrayal of her life with a grounding in genealogy.[6] Speaking of her forebears, she situates herself in the context of class. She registers her Turco-Circassian connection through her mother; she recites her Egyptian father's public achievements as testimonials to his role in building and expanding the administrative apparatus of modern Egypt. Shaʿrawi reveals how her upper-class Turco-Circassian/Egyptian status with its privileges and its prices structured her life and how she responded to this.

As a child Huda was deeply distressed by the preferential treatment given her brother, even questioning her own identity as a daughter.

> I used to imagine that I was not my mother's daughter—that my real mother was a slave girl who had died, and the truth was being withheld from me.

> Firmly convinced of this, I suffered all the more. I could keep everything suppressed until nightfall but as soon as I laid my head on the pillow, I was overcome by anxieties and frightening thoughts moved me to tears. . . . I dreamed often that huge beasts were pouncing on me, baring their fangs in my face, and that when I sought refuge with my mother I would find that she had taken my brother in her arms and turned her back on me. "I am not your child!" I would scream, "You have lied to me! Tell me the truth! I am not your child! I am not your child!"[7]

In seeking an explanation for the favor shown her brother, raising the question with her mother's co-wife Hasibah, the young Huda discovered the significance of gender. "I once asked *Umm Kabirah* ('Big Mother,' [Hasibah]) why everyone paid more attention to my brother than to me. 'Haven't you understood yet?' she asked gently. When I claimed that as the elder I should receive more attention she replied, 'But you are a girl and he is a boy. One day the support of the family will fall upon him. When you marry you will leave the house and honor your husband's name but he will perpetuate the name of his father and take over his house.'"[8]

Although she was pained by comparisons with her brother, Huda also profited from having a male sibling. She shared his lessons when tutors came to the harem. She studied Quranic Arabic, Turkish (the language her mother spoke), and calligraphy. Like other girls of her social class she studied French, which was then replacing Turkish among the elites in Egypt. The Italian woman who instructed her in French also taught her to play the piano, an accomplishment then becoming fashionable for upper-class girls.

By nine Huda had memorized the Qur'an, an unusual feat for a girl. However, she had not progressed far in the Arabic language and asked for instruction.

> Of all the subjects, Arabic was my favorite. . . . I asked him [her Qur'an teacher] to teach me Arabic. The next day, when he arrived carrying an Arabic grammar under his arm, Said Agha demanded arrogantly, "What is that?" to which he responded, "The book Miss Nur al-Huda has requested in order to learn grammar." The eunuch contemptuously ordered, "Sayyidna Shaykh, take back your book. The young lady has no need of grammar as she will not become a judge!" I became depressed and began to neglect my studies, hating being a girl because it kept me from the education I sought.[9]

Shaʿrawi recounts how an itinerant woman poet who came periodically to stay in the family house did not suffer from the same limitations and constraints as women in the household. "Sayyidah Khadijah impressed me because she used to sit with the men and discuss literary and cultural matters. Meanwhile, I observed how women without learning would tremble with embarrassment and fright if called upon to speak a few words to a man from behind a screen. Observing Sayyidah Khadijah convinced me that, with learning, women could be the equals of men if not surpass them."[10]

Shaʿrawi recalls the shrinking of her world after puberty and the beginning of gender segregation. "From the time we were very small, my brother and I shared the same friends, nearly all boys, most of whom were the children of our neighbors. The boys remained my companions until I grew up—that is, until I was about eleven—when suddenly I was required to restrict myself to the company of girls and women. I felt a stranger in their world—their habits and notions startled me. Being separated from the companions of my childhood was a painful experience. Their ways left a mark on me."[11] Early marriage for upper- and middle-class girls was the pattern into the first decades of the twentieth century, with marriages arranged by family members or guardians. When Huda was twelve, Iqbal heard that someone from the palace wanted to seek her daughter's hand in marriage. Such an offer could not be refused, so Huda's mother and her legal guardian, ʿAli Shaʿrawi, took action. The two decided that Huda would marry her cousin-guardian ʿAli Shaʿrawi, some three decades her senior, who was also the executor of her father's estate. This would assure that the fortune in lands and real estate Huda had inherited from her father, who had owned over four thousand feddans (a feddan is a little over an acre) at the time of his death, would remain in family hands.

Shaʿrawi was kept in ignorance about the matter. Only when it became necessary to extract her formal consent to the marriage, as required by Islamic law to make the marriage contract valid, did she discover what had been planned for her.

> To my utter astonishment, ʿAli Pasha Fahmi announced: "The son of your father's sister wants your hand in marriage and we are here on his behalf." Only then did I understand the reason for the various preparations under way in the house, as well as a number of other mysteries. With my back to the men, I cried without speaking or moving. I stood sobbing by the window for nearly three hours. Occasionally passers-by glanced up sympathetically. Eventually ʿAli Pasha Fahmi and Saʿd al-Din Bey asked, "Whom do you wish to designate as your wakil to sign the marriage contract?" I said nothing, and after a long silence, Said Agha whispered in my ears, "Do you wish to disgrace the name of your father and destroy your poor mother who is weeping in her sickbed and might not survive the shock of your refusal? Upon hearing these words, which pierced my heart, I replied, "Do whatever you want," and rushed immediately to my mother's room.[12]

Shaʿrawi recorded her reaction to betrothal to her already married cousin. "I was deeply troubled by the idea of marrying my cousin whom I had always regarded as a father or older brother deserving my fear and respect (as I had been previously made to understand). I grew more upset when I thought of his wife and three daughters who were all older than me, who used to tease me saying, 'Good-day, stepmother!' When my brother and I were small and our guardian-cousin called on us, I did not find him gentle. He was especially abrupt and curt with me, but treated my brother better. All of this alienated me from him."[13]

Huda's mother, after a certain amount of wrangling, was able to persuade ʿAli Shaʿrawi to agree to have the marriage contract stipulate that the union be monogamous. This meant leaving his first wife. If he took another wife while married to Huda, the marriage with her would automatically end. The *ʿismah*, the writing into a marriage contract of conditions formulated by the wife, was (and is) uncommon, since most men would object as ʿAli Shaʿrawi initially had.[14]

Shaʿrawi reconstructs her wedding festivities as a fleeting moment of splendor, "a night I had fancied would last in all its beauty and majesty forever, a night when my sorrows and agonies vanished." But it "passed away like an enchanting dream." Dismissing the "sorrows and agonies" of her childhood, she wistfully conjured up this period as one truncated like the trees felled in the garden, which were "sacrificed at the call of a single night."[15] "Bitter reality followed. I wept for my trees. I wept for my childhood and for my freedom. I saw in this barren garden a picture of life—the life I would live cut off from everything that had delighted me and consoled me in my melancholy childhood."[16] At thirteen marriage catapulted Huda into an instant adult, yet the child in her remained. "For a long time I did not fully appreciate that my new status as a married woman required a solemn demeanor and obliged me to appear with the poise of a perfect lady, for owing to my youth I was still under the influence of a child's life and subject to its rulings. I would play whenever I had a chance. In the afternoon or evening, when I heard my husband's footsteps on the stairs, I was the first among the women to escape behind a curtain (custom ordained that a woman hide at the approach of a man other than her husband)."[17] Within a year it was discovered that Huda's husband had returned to his former wife when she became pregnant, whereupon Huda separated from him for a period that she managed to stretch into seven years. Huda had remained in her late father's house following her marriage rather than moving to the household of her husband's father as was customary. Thus she continued her life in her paternal house.[18]

During her separation, with her formal married status affording her a measure of autonomy, Huda acquired some control over her day-to-day life. Once again she attempted to obtain tutors in Arabic and once again she failed. She was more successful in continuing her study of French with Mme Richard, a Frenchwoman and widow of a French engineer who had worked on irrigation projects in Upper Egypt under the jurisdiction of Huda's late father.[19] A fondness grew between the two women which was sustained until Mme Richard's death in 1920.[20]

During this period Shaʿrawi expanded her limited circle of friends and acquaintances. Three women stand out as having influenced her life in quite different ways: they were ʿAdilah Nabarawi, ʿAtiyah Saqqaf, and Eugénie Le Brun—Egyptian, Turkish, and French, respectively.

ʿAdilah Nabarawi, who resided with her husband in Paris, returned periodically to Cairo. A strong friendship developed between Huda and ʿAdilah, who were contemporaries. Huda recalls their excursions to the opera house with its separate entry for women leading to screened boxes in the balcony. While ʿAdilah had been a companion for outings, Huda's relationship with ʿAtiyah Saqqaf unfolded within the confines of Huda's late father's house, to which ʿAtiyah, a distant relative of her mother, had come from Arabia (where she had lived during her marriage) for an extended stay following her divorce. ʿAtiyah's renditions of her unhappy marriage and the lost custody of her two sons moved Huda. At the same time, the reclusive ʿAtiyah's attempts to control Huda and to monopolize her attention, especially when friends called, rankled.

Huda's brother ʿUmar had helped her to enlarge the borders of her life. It was during a boating trip on the Nile that he had arranged that Huda met Eugénie Le Brun, a Frenchwoman many years her senior, who was married to Husayn Rushdi, a wealthy landowner and future prime minister. Huda speaks of the instant affection that developed between the two women. Huda's mother, her mother's co-wife, Hasibah, and ʿAtiyah Saqqaf were all reclusive women, and her friend ʿAtiyah Nabarawi spent much of her time in Paris, but through Le Brun the young Huda Shaʿrawi was able to extend her movements. Eugénie Le Brun, "a dear friend and valued mentor," Shaʿrawi writes, "guided my first steps in society and looked out for my reputation."[21] Such chaperoning of a young woman was necessary to maintaining honor and respect, especially, as Huda points out, since she was separated from her husband. In the 1890s Le Brun hosted the first women's salon in Cairo, where a variety of issues, including veiling, were debated. At the time Le Brun was working on her book, *Les répudiées* (The divorcées), wishing to show that it was not Islam but "social customs" which oppressed women. While attending sessions at the religious courts that heard personal status cases—to which only the poor brought their grievances—Le Brun discovered how badly husbands treated their wives.[22] Shaʿrawi recalls that Le Brun, who "nourished my mind and spirit," used to read parts of the manuscript to her.[23]

Eugénie Le Brun became a surrogate mother to Huda and a counterpoise to her real mother. Le Brun, originally an outsider but connected to Egypt through marriage, was freer than Egyptian women, or Egyptian-raised women, yet at the same time as an insider by marriage she was tied to local conventions. It was the blurring of borders that allowed the special relationship between Eugénie Le Brun and Huda Shaʿrawi to evolve. Iqbal, ushering her daughter into an early marriage, had eased her along the "expected path" for a woman of her class and attended to ensuring her daughter's material security. Eugénie Le Brun provided a different stimulus, constituting an important intellectual and feminist force in Shaʿrawi's life. Shaʿrawi discloses the significance of this relationship: "Mme Rushdi died a few months after the death of our national leader, Mustafa Kamil. Qasim Amin, 'The Defender of the Woman,' followed them the same year (1908). Thus, Egypt lost three valiant strugglers in the service of her cause. Both my brother and my husband . . . shared my grief for my departed friend. I had come to rely heavily upon her good counsel but even after her death I felt her spirit light the way before me. When I was about to embark on something, I often paused to ask myself what she would think, and if I sensed her approval I would proceed."[24]

Shaʿrawi resumed her marriage in 1900 at the age of twenty-one when her brother announced his refusal to marry until she did so. In 1903 she gave birth to a daughter, Bathna, and in 1905 to a son, Muhammad. For the next several years Huda Shaʿrawi devoted herself to maternal duties. She is careful to mention that she suckled her children, rather than giving them over to wet nurses as was then common among women of her class. She also notes the special care bestowed on her daughter, who was sickly as an infant, and declares that it was only when her daughter became robust that she resumed her outside interests. Shaʿrawi traveled with her mother and her daughter Bathna to Turkey in 1905, when she was pregnant with her son, and to France for the first time with her husband in 1908. In 1914 Huda suffered two losses: her mother and her brother. She grieved deeply over the death of her brother ʿUmar, a major support in her life. His death was a crucial event and turning point for Huda.

Nabawiyah Musa

Nabawiyah Musa was born in the town of Zagazig in the eastern Delta province of Qalyubiyah in 1886.[25] Her father, Musa Muhammad, was a captain in the army. As she wrote, "Egyptian officers only reached this rank after great effort because the senior levels of army officers were all in the hands of the Turco-Circassians before the ʿUrabi revolt."[26] Nabawiyah saw her father only "in dreams," as he had died on a military mission to Sudan before she was born. She says nothing of her mother's origins or early life and even omits mention of her name. Nabawiyah depicts her mother as a strong woman who as a young widow chose not to remarry but to raise her two children on her own with the income from her late husband's military pension. Nabawiyah's mother moved with her daughter and her son, who was two years older than his sister, from Zagazig to Cairo in order to advance the boy's schooling.

In Cairo Nabawiyah acquired her first rudiments of learning at home, wresting help from her brother. Eventually she entered the Girls' Section of the ʿAbbas Primary School (established in 1895). She was in the third class to graduate, passing the state primary school examination in 1903, and scoring higher in the Arabic exams than future writer ʿAbbas al-ʿAqqad and future prime minister Mahmud al-Nuqrashi, who took the examination the same year. She went on to register herself in the Teachers' Training Program at the Saniyah School. Upon graduating in 1906, she became a teacher in the Girls' Section of the ʿAbbas School. The following year she petitioned the Ministry of Education for permission to sit for the state baccalaureate examination, which during the colonial period was given only to boys (there were no state secondary schools for girls). Preparing for the examination at home, she came out in the top third. Continuing to work as a teacher Nabawiyah attempted unsuccessfully to enroll at the Egyptian University, founded in 1908. In 1909 she was invited to teach in the university's new extracurricular Section for Women, and her lectures were published in *al-Ahram* in 1912.[27] Nabawiyah Musa meanwhile became the first Egyptian woman school principal at the Girls' School in Fayyum, starting her long career in administering schools run by the Ministry of Education and provincial councils and, later, in her own private schools. In 1924 she became inspector of girls' schools. An outspoken critic of education policy and the behavior of state employees, citing what today would be called sexual harassment and misconduct, she was fired from the Ministry of Education in 1926. Afterwards, she devoted herself to running the two private schools for girls she had founded.

As a young teacher Nabawiyah Musa began to publish articles in Cairo newspapers, mainly in *al-Muqattam* and *al-Ahram*. She wrote under the pseudonym Damir Hayy fi Jism Raqiq (A Living Conscience in a Delicate [or fettered] Body) because it was forbidden for employees in the Ministry of Education to publish articles in the press. She later edited a woman's page for the weekly *al-Balagh al-Usbuʿi*. In 1937 she founded her own journal, *Majallat al-Fatah* (The magazine of the young woman). Nabawiyah Musa also published several books. In 1920, during the height of the independence struggle, she published *al-Marʾah wa al-ʿAmal* (The woman and work), a feminist and nationalist manifesto that advocated developing the productive forces of women.[28] Her other books included *al-Ayat al-Bayyinat fi Tarbiyat al-Banat* (The clear verses in the education of girls), *Diwan al-Fatah* (The collected poems of the young woman), and a novel, *Riwayat Nabhutub*.

In 1942 Nabawiyah Musa was arrested and jailed for speaking out against the government's compromising position when British tanks drew up in front of Abdin Palace. With this her career and her journal came to an abrupt end, although she was successfully defended by the pro-feminist lawyer Murqus Fahmi. Her final fight was to obtain her retirement pension from the government. She died in retirement in 1951 at the age of sixty-five, bequeathing her schools to the state.

At the height of her career and still in the thick of the battle Nabawiyah Musa began in 1938 to publish her memoirs serially in her *Magazine of the Young Woman*.[29] Nabawiyah Musa's voice is feisty, full of anger and irony; it is strident and strong. This self-made woman of modest origins opened her life narrative with a piece called "How I Started My Work Life and When My Troubles Began," establishing what would be a trope of trials and triumphs with a focus on her own educational formation and her mission in the education of other women. In representing her life as struggle, she projects a defiant early self, resurrecting a girlhood when, in a piecemeal and steady way, she assumed control and invented her own life. She did not acquiesce in the plans of others (family and society) for her life but navigated her way out of the path prescribed by class and gender.[30]

Nabawiyah Musa obtained a sense of her secondary status as a girl when her mother made efforts to advance her brother's schooling but ignored hers. She tells how she learned to read and write Arabic by memorizing with her brother from books he brought home from secondary school and later from military college. However, when she progressed from the mnemonic to the creative, composing her first verse, her brother denigrated her efforts. An uncle witnessing her brother's slight cajoled her, Nabawiyah Musa writes, asserting that when she completed her education no one would be able to "touch you in writing," and adding, "I'll send you the first part of a grammar book so you will know the rules."[31] She relates: "The next day the book arrived. I read it and started to apply the rules to the stories I read. My thinking at that time was directed toward realizing my uncle's prediction and giving attention toward education."[32] Nabawiyah Musa speaks in her memoirs of the inspiration she drew from the poems of ʿA'ishah al-Taymuriyah. It is not clear, however, exactly when she first gained access to al-Taymuriyah's works.[33]

After memorizing the Qur'an, Nabawiyah proceeded to interpret verses by herself. A relative studying at al-Azhar, the center of Islamic learning, objected to her independent reading of a Qur'an, saying that it was "heretical" and that even he as a student of religion would not proceed without a mentor. She recalls, "I wanted to know the interpretations he had learned at al-Azhar. I swore to him that if I benefited from his learning I would praise him in verse but if I didn't I'd scorn him." When he blundered through a blatant misreading of a Quranic verse, Nabawiyah fulfilled her vow.[34] Clearly she was announcing that she believed in her own ability to read and interpret the holy scriptures and was bold enough to assert her confidence within the patriarchal family.

As Nabawiyah relates, she was no more than fifteen years old when she concluded that she was unlike other women. This revelation occurred during the annual festivities at the departure of the camel caravan carrying the *mahmal*, the cover for the Kaʿbah, the Black Stone, in Mecca. When Nabawiyah's mother had for the third time forced her to join other women in viewing the procession from the apartment of a friend overlooking the route, she balked. She could not fathom how the women could watch the same ceremony year in and year out. When she asked an old woman who had viewed the ceremony at least thirty times, the woman replied that it relieved the monotony of her days. The woman, for her part, was amazed when

Nabawiyah turned her back on the procession, burying her head in a book. On the way home Nabawiyah overheard the old woman laughingly tell a friend: "'That is the strange girl I saw earlier today looking at the *mahmal* with her back rather than her eyes.' At that moment I understood that while I might consider something abnormal in someone else, another might consider something abnormal in me. . . . The exceptional is the abnormal and it was about time for me to know the truth that I was more abnormal than others. What is customary is not abnormal. The abnormal is what goes against custom that everyone observes, right or wrong."[35]

Armed with her state primary school certificate, Nabawiyah challenged maternal authority over continuing her schooling. "I wanted to continue my education at the Saniyah School. I learned from my brother that if I wanted to be admitted into the third year I had to know arithmetic, which was taught in the second year. . . . I asked my mother to get me a private tutor. She consulted her uncle who repeated the famous proverb, 'Teach girls to say words of love but not how to write.' So, my mother refused to get me a tutor. She also neglected to teach me how to say words of love and I am ignorant about this until now."[36] Again with help from her brother—who brought her the needed arithmetic book and from whom she "stole time" to learn the ABC's of English—she prepared herself. She then announced to her mother that she intended to enter the Saniyah School. "She [her mother] got upset and considered it a violation of the rules of decency and modesty and an affront to my good upbringing and religion. She went around telling her relatives about the absurdity. Everyone who heard about my passion to enter the Saniyah School backed my mother's refusal. But I had made up my mind to make my wish come true no matter what."[37] Nabawiyah Musa continues her story.

> I realized it was best to keep quiet for the time being and simply try to enter the Saniyah School without saying anything to my mother. If I succeeded in getting accepted I could then face my mother. So I kept everything under cover and carried out my plan in secret. I stole my mother's signet stamp, went to the Saniyah School, filled out the application form, and stamped it with my mother's signet. My handwriting on the application form was shaky. I was not sufficiently accustomed to writing and did not hold the pen well. The school secretary and teachers were surprised by the daring of the girl who had come to apply on her own. To make them accept me I wrote that I would pay tuition. Most of the girls at the Saniyah School were given free education because people were not eager to educate their daughters. I believed that an application from a girl paying tuition would not be refused.[38]

Passing the entrance examination was a high moment. Nabawiyah Musa relates: "I flew home with joy to tell my mother that I had been admitted to the Saniyah School. She said, 'If that's true it is the end of you and me.' I said, 'I have been admitted and am starting school. If you stick to your refusal I'll enter as a boarder and pay my expenses out of the pension [of her father].'"[39] Her mother capitulated. When her brother arrived home the following weekend, he said he would disown his sister. She gave him a flippant rebuff and the matter ended there. Nabawiyah Musa continues: "On Saturday I went to the Saniyah School. I was shy and afraid because it was strange. Staying at home, I didn't see any men except my brother. That day I saw many male teachers and servants. I was critical of any incorrect movement or word on the part of these teachers. I used to measure my own actions by the millimeter so that I would not deviate from the strict behavior instilled in me under the supervision of my mother and the stern looks of my brother."[40]

By continuing her schooling Nabawiyah Musa seized the opportunity to continue to advance herself and to loosen fetters imposed by family and society. The Ministry of Education of the colonial state shored up various retrogressive practices, stalling new initiatives. The state schools for girls, administered mainly by British headmistresses and staffed largely with British teachers, were highly authoritarian. Girls in the state schools were required to veil after unveiling had already begun, notwithstanding the touting of liberal ideas by colonial authorities.[41] Englishwoman Florence Davson pontificated: "Implicit obedience to those above them is inculcated at all the schools, for no Egyptian girl can have a happy home-life unless she is prepared to give perfect submission to her husband or father." Davson justifies authoritarianism on the basis of what she sees as monolithic and unchanging imperatives of indigenous patriarchy, deflecting attention away from the repressive colonial agenda of keeping "the natives" locked into conservative practices.[42]

After obtaining her certificate from the Saniyah Teachers' Training Program in 1906, Nabawiyah Musa started to teach in the Girls' Section of the ʿAbbas Primary School. She quickly discovered discrimination in pay between the male and female teachers.

> My salary was six pounds. At that time the salary for the graduates from the Higher Teachers' Training School for Men was ten pounds a month. I was unhappy that the government treated us [women] in our pay the way that inheritance operates, that is, giving women half the amount men receive. I don't question that it may be all right concerning inheritance because what one inherits is not through one's own effort. But for the woman to do the same work as the man and receive half his salary is unjust. I was furious. I taught as the young men taught. The government did not have many secondary schools [and none for girls] and all of us [women] teachers were in primary schools. Why did the ministry discriminate, paying them not only one or two pounds more but nearly double what they paid me? I worked with great effort so that I would be equal to the man in jobs and everything else.[43]

When Nabawiyah Musa inquired about the discrimination, she was told that men earned more because they held not only teacher training certificates but also secondary school diplomas. She resolved that she would sit for the state baccalaureate examination, even though there were no state secondary schools for girls in Egypt, "so that the Ministry of Education will not have any excuse for not treating me equal to men."[44]

> I filled out the application to sit for the baccalaureate examination and sent it in on time to the Ministry of Education. The men of the ministry went into an uproar over it. They talked about it everywhere. They thought it preposterous that a young woman who had not attended high school should sit for the examination. Mr. Dunlop [the British education adviser] came to me at the ʿAbbas School with my application in hand. He gave it to me laughing and said, "It seems that you have not read the baccalaureate curriculum; if you had you would not have sent this request." I said, "On the contrary, I have almost completed it." He said, "You are dreaming. Take my advice and withdraw the application and don't submit another one unless you can promise me that you will pass the examination." I said, "Has anyone who submitted an application to sit for the examination promised you to succeed before actually taking it?" He said, "You are my student and I am interested in your welfare." I said, "Everyone is your student, Sir, and surely you are as interested in their welfare as in mine." He said, "You should know that if you fail, my opinion of you will go down." I said, "Thanks be to God, I am a step above the women servants; neither you nor anyone else can consider me a servant. . . . My status at work cannot be lowered." He said, "You are stubborn, but I repeat my advice. Withdraw your application."[45]

Nabawiyah Musa describes her experience in taking the examination. While the male students sat for the examination at the former ministry building in Darb al-Gamamiz, she took hers in a special room set aside at the Saniyah School.

> I used to take the Sabtiyah tram from the ʿAbbas School, which passed the Saniyah School and then went to Darb al-Gamamiz. The male students living in Sabtiyah and nearby neighborhoods rode the same tram. This tram did not have a special compartment for women, and so my brother accompanied me coming and going. We would sit at the back of the tram not to attract the attention of the male students but their talk poured over my head. Some of them vowed to beat the girl student if she failed in the examination. And of course she would fail. She applied to sit for the examination only to show her beauty and charms. They paid no attention to me because I was not the person of their imagination. They thought that I was a frivolous, showy girl. The girl sitting at the back of the tram was modest, and no one would think for a moment that she could even read. When my brother heard what they said he smiled at me but I was careful not to answer his smile with one of my own. I got off the tram one stop before the Saniyah School and entered the school from the back door because I knew that male students had gathered in a crowd outside the front door of the Saniyah School to catch sight of me. I did the same when I left. . . . My examination committee consisted of three persons: one Frenchman and two English-

> women. One of the two Englishwomen, the headmistress of the Saniyah School, greeted me with reprimands and mockery whenever I entered or left the room, saying such things as, "You are conceited. Surely you will fail. Why did you submit your application and cost us money in preparing a separate committee for you?"[46]

Succeeding in her examination, Nabawiyah Musa records her victory:

> When the results of the examination were announced, I was among those who passed. I think I was thirty-fourth out of two hundred who passed. This news was well received by the [Ministry of Education] employees and by my fellow students. That was in 1907. Of course, I didn't have any fellow women students. It was not until 1928 that the next Egyptian woman would sit for the baccalaureate examination. My success was big news. The papers published the story under large headings with bold letters such as "First girl student wins the baccalaureate diploma" and "Egyptian female superiority." Had I conquered France at that time my name would not have reverberated more. . . . It seems that those who corrected my examination were afraid someone might think that Nabawiyah Musa was a man, and decided to add a title to the name that would dispell any doubts, and so they wrote *Sitt* [Lady] Nabawiyah.[47]

Nabawiyah Musa won a pay raise, and as the first woman teacher to receive a salary equal to male teachers set the precedent of equal work for equal pay for the two sexes to which the postindependence Egyptian government adhered.[48] The colonial state made Nabawiyah Musa the exception, only paying one woman equally. British colonial authorities did not permit any other Egyptian women to sit for the secondary school certificate examination as long as they remained in power.

The public and private were closely connected for women teachers like Nabawiyah Musa. Ministry of Education policy did not allow a woman to teach after marriage, which meant that most women taught for only a limited time before leaving the profession. Nabawiyah Musa, however, had no intention to quit her job or to marry. Unlike Huda Shaʿrawi, who reluctantly acquiesced in marriage, Nabawiyah Musa rejected marriage in clear defiance of social convention. Her education and work were integral to this defiance. "It [marriage] repelled me, and perhaps my leaving home at the age of thirteen to go to school was because of my hatred for marriage. If I had not worked I could not have remained unmarried. I did not have adequate resources for my needs."[49]

Nabawiyah Musa relates how several suitors who learned about her through her newspaper articles sent letters to her presenting themselves for marriage. Her brother urged her to accept the first offer that seemed sound to him. She tells how she turned each one down, explaining her reasons. She earned more money than the suitors. She was not interested in a combination of marriage and career—even if that option had been available to her—scorning what would later be called the "double burden." The burden she wanted to avoid, however, was not simply a practical one but included the general weight of male domination that came with marriage. In her memoirs, she rails against marriage. "I hated marriage and considered it dirt and had decided not to soil myself with this dirt. Since childhood, I had believed that marriage was animalistic and degrading to women and I could not bear [the thought of] it."[50] Speaking about her escape from a state that would have entailed her reconfinement to the domestic sphere she declares, "I preferred to live as the master of men, not as their servant."[51] Nabawiyah Musa came to be critically outspoken about marriage in her memoirs, although earlier she had been publicly discreet on the issue.[52]

The lives of the two women, united by gender and divided by class, displayed certain strikingly similar circumstances. Both women grew up without fathers. Both were raised in female-headed households by illiterate mothers. Both had a brother with whose lives they could make comparisons and who helped them in particular ways. Both struggled for their own educational advance. Both wanted to perfect their Arabic, though only Nabawiyah Musa was successful.

Comparisons with brothers made Huda Shaʿrawi and Nabawiyah Musa aware that males were privileged over females. Huda Shaʿrawi's brother was given greater attention. Nabawiyah Musa's brother viewed education as his due, while she had to fight for hers. Both women understood that they, unlike their brothers, were expected to live domestically centered lives. Resentment and frustration fueled these women's attempts to forge new roles. They both experimented, not finding their mothers' lives exemplars for their own. Nabawiyah Musa broke away in her teens by availing herself of new opportunites the state provided: going to school and working as a teacher in the government educational system. Before the age of twenty Huda Shaʿrawi had frequented the first women's salon, but it was only thereafter that she designed a public life for herself, creating social service and intellectual associations, as we shall see in the following chapter.

For Huda Shaʿrawi the privileges of class were also constraints. She reveals how she submitted to the life prescribed for her. She found marriage her only option. Through marriage within her class the upper-class woman secured her social status and consolidated her material well-being. Marrying against her will, it was only by default that Huda gained a temporary respite from marriage and the chance to more freely fashion a life for herself. It was unthinkable for upper-class girls of her day to go to school. Work was even more unimaginable. Neither served the interests of upper-class patriarchy. As a young woman Huda Shaʿrawi was bound by the confines of the class whose privileges kept her beholden.

The situation of middle-class families was quite different. They stood to gain by allowing their daughters to take advantage of the schooling and employment opportunities the state had opened up. The state offered the education that middle-class families could not provide for their daughters at home. The state also made jobs available to women that would confer new status as well as enhance their material well-being and that of their families.[53] Prevailing attitudes about women, however, exerted a counterforce. Determined to advance herself, Nabawiyah Musa well understood the connection between economic need and female dependence; she rejected social conventions that would prevent her from improving her position in both class and gender terms. However, once women like Nabawiyah Musa worked for the state, that state itself exerted its own gendered controls.

We shall see in the succeeding chapters how class, and the ways women could maneuver within the context of class, set Huda Shaʿrawi and Nabawiyah Musa on divergent, but not wholly separate, paths. We shall see as well how gender and nation could unite women across the divisions of class.

• CHAPTER 2 •

Claiming Public Space

THE PERIOD of discreet public activism from the turn of the century to the early 1920s was a critical moment in the history of feminism in Egypt. During this time between the initial stirrings of feminist consciousness in women like Huda Shaʿrawi and Nabawiyah Musa, and indeed many others, and the start of the organized feminist movement, upper- and middle-class women increasingly left confinement in the home to claim new roles in society. They did this while outwardly "respecting" the dictates of harem culture. Most Muslim women continued to veil, but for those with a feminist consciousness the veil became camouflage for "invisible" feminist activism. Women of the minorities, Copts and other Christians, Jews, and local Syrian women, had begun to unveil but did so quietly as they proceeded to fashion new lives for themselves.

Previously, class rather than religion and ethnicity had primarily defined women's social practice and the interactions of the sexes. Around the turn of the century, religious and ethnic affiliations increasingly superseded class as a determinant of women's social behavior in the middle and upper strata. There were cultural, economic, and social reasons for this. Veiling and female seclusion were seen to be Islamic. When in the midst of massive economic and cultural change in Egypt women began to disdain these practices, non-Muslim women were less constrained to uphold the old ways. Moreover, for minority families engaged in commerce and trade with Europeans it became expedient to allow their daughters to break with such "backward" conventions and to project a "modern" aspect. Veiling, which had been a mark of social status, was increasingly becoming a stigma. The Copts were often commercial agents for Europeans and acted as their consular representatives in provincial towns, while Syrians had wide Mediterranean trading networks. Also, more Coptic and Syrian Christian women than Muslims had benefited from school education by then, which gave them their own incentives to innovate.[1]

Muslim women of the middle and upper classes experienced more pressures to perpetuate the institutions of veiling and seclusion because these were deemed Islamic religious requirements. The outrage directed at Qasim Amin's book *The Liberation of the Woman*, which demonstrated that veiling and seclusion were not Islamic prescriptions, caused many (men) to defend these customs. But, as mentioned earlier, underneath this attack on veiling and seclusion lay an attack on a traditional prop of patriarchy in upper- and middle-class mainstream culture.

National consciousness, however, soon overtook considerations of gender, class, and religion. Early in the twentieth century, Egyptian women generated a nationalist discourse that both legitimized and advanced their innovations. In Egypt nationalist women deployed the idea and practice of the "new woman" against the colonizer, rather than clinging to custom as a weapon of cultural defense, as would later happen in Algeria.[2]

Early in this century, middle- and upper-class women in Egypt, whether veiled (as were the majority) or unveiled, reduced their domestic seclusion but generally upheld norms of gender segregation. Most Muslim women continued to cover their faces until the 1920s. Those with a feminist awareness had come to scorn the veil, but wore it to facilitate their forays into public space.[3] They did not wish to call undue attention to themselves and their experiments. Nabawiyah Musa became an exception among Muslims when she unveiled around 1909; she appears to have done this when she was in Fayyum, where veiling was not common. Moreover, she fastidiously covered herself with an *ʿabayah* (an enveloping black cloak) and headscarf, maintaining a modest demeanor in keeping with Quranic prescription and society's prevailing notions of decency. Indeed, she dressed this way to the end of her life, long after most other middle- and upper-class women had abandoned the ʿabayah. Women were still constrained by the force of the conventional patriarchal moral code: they did not want to experience abuse, verbal or physical; they wanted to strengthen their position and to allow society more time to adjust to change. Husbands and male relatives could also obstruct women: it is significant that when Nabawiyah Musa unveiled, she had neither a father nor a husband, and by then had neutralized her brother's attempts to control her life. Women's moves away from confinement and into new roles in society were pragmatic and piecemeal, and were governed by a longer vision. They were fought for in the name of Islamic modernism and Egyptian nationalism, as well as on humanitarian and educational grounds.

Minority women (Christians and Syrians, as well as non-Arab minorities—Greeks, Jews, and Armenians), although freer to innovate, and thus set precedents, could not confer legitimacy; Muslim women were more constrained, but only they could lend cultural legitimacy to new behaviors. Although middle-class Syrian Christians led in discarding the accoutrements and practice of domestic incarceration, paradoxically they also led in creating a cult of domesticity. Middle- and upper-class Muslim women who were slow to remove their veils and break with conventions of gender segregation were at the forefront in articulating a feminist ideology.

Philanthropy and Social Service

When women of the upper and middle classes pioneered in creating modern secular philanthropic associations and social service societies to help needy women and children, they gave themselves a door to the outside world and new social roles, building on religiously based humanitarian traditions.

Islam and Christianity in Egypt share a long history of assisting the poor. Both religions had a system of *awqaf*, or pious bequests, whereby individuals of either sex could place property in a waqf (singular of *awqaf*) for the benefit of others. Bequests could take many forms, such as schools, hospitals, orphanages, hospices, or drinking fountains. The terms of the bequest were documented, and the administration of the waqf was undertaken by a *nazir*, or executor. Muslim women (and Copts in Egypt who were subject to Islamic laws of inheritance) could inherit in their own right and legally dispose of their property on their own. Historically, they used the Islamic system for making endowments. In medieval Cairo, for example, a significant number of women were benefactors of mosque schools, which men alone could attend.[4] Early in the twentieth century Nabawiyah Musa complained about this continuing practice: "Whenever women do give something for education, it is for men's education." She cited the example of Aminah Hanim, the daughter of Salim Pasha al-Silahdar, who had placed lands in a waqf for the Islamic university al-Azhar.[5] She might also have remarked upon Princess Fatma Isma'il's generous bequest of lands and jewels in 1908 to assist the project of the new Egyptian University where her own sex could not matriculate, as Nabawiyah Musa herself had unhappily discovered the year it opened.

Another form of religiously prescribed assistance to the needy was almsgiving, equally enjoined upon Muslims and Christians. On special occasions such as marriages and religious feasts families distributed food, clothing, or money to the poor. On a regular basis large houses traditionally fed, clothed, and sheltered many persons. The less well-off gave to others in keeping with their means. Huda Sha'rawi recalled ritual foods prepared in her childhood home for distribution to the poor on feast days.[6] Her cousin, Hawwa' Idris, remembered the large numbers who were regularly clothed and fed by Sha'rawi, who as an adult continued her family's charitable traditions.[7]

At the end of the nineteenth century, a new approach to helping the poor was taken by Muslims when the Islamic reformer Muhammad 'Abduh, inspired by practices he had observed in Europe, founded al-Jam'iyah al-Khayriyah al-Islamiyah (Islamic Benevolent Society) in 1892, which opened training workshops for boys. In 1901, a group of Muslim men in Cairo created the Jam'iyat Ta'lim al-Banat al-Islamiyah (Islamic Society for the Education of Girls) to foster the education of Muslim girls. Such religiously affiliated societies focused on education, including religious and moral formation, and practical instruction.

Religious and ethnic minorities had evolved ways to cater to the needs of their own communities. From the late nineteenth century, Coptic welfare societies were established such as the Tawfiq Coptic Society, created around 1880, which opened a girls' school in al-Faggalah and a boys' school in Azbakiyah. Most of the Coptic societies were connected with church dioceses.[8] The Syrians in Egypt also created a network of communally based philanthropies, as did resident Greeks, Jews, Armenians, as well as Italians, Maltese, Austrians, and others.[9]

It was women who extricated social service from the exclusive hold of religious (or religiously affiliated) institutions in Egypt when they created the first secular philanthropic societies and other non–religiously connected social service projects. In 1909 Huda Shaʿrawi and other Egyptian women formed the Mabarrat Muhammad ʿAli, creating a dispensary for poor women and children.[10] The immediate impetus was the alarming infant mortality rate reported the year before, but there was also a nationalist impetus. Earlier, British women had created the Lady Cromer Society, which operated a foundling home and dispensary for poor women and children. Several upper-class Egyptian women had joined the society, including Iqbal Hanim, Huda Shaʿrawi's mother, but Shaʿrawi herself consciously refused for nationalist reasons to affiliate herself with colonial philanthropy.[11]

Upper-class women, with royal patrons, formed the membership of the Mabarrat, which rapidly expanded. Among the early members was Mary Kahil, who gave generous financial support. Hidayah Barakat, who joined later, became a consummate organizer. For both these women, the Mabarrat Muhammad ʿAli remained a lifelong concern. The Mabarrat did not go on to open a school for maternal and child health as Shaʿrawi had suggested, but it successfully ran the much-needed dispensary and later expanded its medical services. This association, unlike many others, endured.[12]

Early this century, Aminah Hanim Afandi gave her support to a committee of Egyptian and British women who established a school for the training of midwives at the Citadel in Cairo.[13] The project fell under the jurisdiction of the British director of the School of Medicine, Dr. Keatinge. Women from the committee told Dutch feminist and physician Aletta Jacobs when she visited the school in 1911 that Dr. Keatinge "does not want to allow it to become a flourishing program under capable women's leadership." Jacobs further noted in her travel memoir, "These women assured me that they wouldn't stop trying to get it under their leadership."[14] The women's committee also wanted to raise admissions standards, drawing from graduates of the new primary schools for girls, and to set a minimum age of sixteen. Despite the discouragement from the top, the women's committee met with some success. By 1914, when the school was turned over to the Department of Public Health, 118 women had earned certificates.[15]

In 1911 another kind of crisis propelled Egyptian women into collective action once again. The Italian invasion of Libya spurred middle-class Malak Hifni Nasif (1886–1918), a feminist writer and speaker better known under her pseudonym Bahithat al-Badiyah (Searcher in the Desert) and a former teacher, to establish a relief society. She also created a center to train nurses on her property in the Munirah quarter of Cairo.[16]

Still by no means was it easy or always possible to draw upper- and upper-middle-class Egyptian women into corporate relief work. In 1912 when refugees from the Balkan Wars streamed into Alexandria, Djavidan Hanim, the wife of Khedive ʿAbbas Hilmi II, was unable to elicit the support of upper-class women in the aid operations she organized at Ras al-Tin Palace. Instead, lower-class women were mobilized as paid helpers.[17] The same year, a group of men started the Jamʿiyat al-Hilal al-Ahmar (Red Crescent Society), but it was not until the Second World War that the Women's Committee of the Red Crescent Society formed under the leadership of Nahid Sirri.

Some upper-class women (founders of the Mabarrat Muhammad ʿAli) and some middle-class women, including Ihsan al-Qusi (later to be a founder of the Egyptian Feminist Union), created Jamʿiyat al-Mar'ah al-Jadidah (The New Woman Society) in the aftermath of the first nationalist demonstrations of 1919. The society, located in the Munirah district of Cairo, set up a crafts workshop to give poor girls in this populous neighborhood a means to earn money. The girls were also taught to read and write and were given instruction in hygiene and general guidance.[18] Huda Shaʿrawi, who contributed financially to the society and donated equipment to the workshop, was made honorary president.

The innovations introduced by the modern, secular philanthropic society had important gender and class implications. The site of assistance shifted from facilities run as waqfs to the premises of the philanthropic society, usually located in poor quarters of the city. Members of the philanthropic society were now brought into direct contact with the people they helped, lessening the segregation of rich from poor. Previously, when contact between the two occurred at all, it was customary for the poor to go to the rich for assistance; now the rich went to the poor, whom they could see for the first time in their own harsh environment. By pioneering in creating the modern philanthropic society as a collective effort and an alternative to individual charity, women created new networks and bonds among themselves. Together they honed and expanded the organizational and managerial skills some had already developed as mistresses of large households.[19] Through the women's secular philanthropic associations social assistance was removed from an exclusively religious context. Social assistance came to be understood as not solely a religious obligation but also a civic and national responsibility for Muslims and Christians to shoulder together as Egyptians.[20] Thus Egyptian women created space for themselves in the public arena in which to perform collective roles as citizens rather than as members of separate religious communities.

Some women like Huda Shaʿrawi already possessed a feminist awareness that impelled them both to innovate and to reflect upon the impact of their new enterprise on themselves and on the women they sought to help. For others involvement in philanthropy and social service created a new gender awareness. Women with a feminist awareness were conscious of the emancipatory effect their benevolent work was having upon themselves by enabling them to enter the public arena where they could perform important social roles.[21] They also hoped, naively, that by helping to meet the basic needs of lower-class women they might assist them on the path toward gaining their fuller rights as women. Other philanthropic women saw their work more simply as giving succor. Later we shall see how philanthropy and social service became part of the agenda of organized feminism and how nonfeminist women continued to experiment in the delivery of social services.

Intellectual Associations and Programs

As they took first steps into society to assist others, upper- and middle-class women more deliberately set out to help themselves by starting intellectual societies and programs.[22] Programs of lectures brought together women of the two classes who would not normally meet, as well as women of different ethnic backgrounds: Egyptians, Syrians, and Europeans. Some of the founders and members of these associations were women with a feminist consciousness, while others were perhaps ripe yet still unawakened to feminism. Most women pioneering in collective intellectual projects were eager to expand their knowledge and create new social roles. Some women, however, worried about new trends and deviation from what they believed was Islamic prescription. Yet even if their thinking was conservative, their activism as pioneers in associational life was bold.

One of the early intellectual societies in Cairo was formed, not by women with a feminist consciousness, but by more conservative women. In 1908 a group of women of the upper strata (mainly upper-middle-class) under the leadership of Fatma Rashid created the Jamᶜiyat Tarqiyat al-Marʾah (Society for the Advancement of the Woman). The society held talks and published a journal of the same name. Members celebrated "woman's place" in the home in the language of conservative Islam.[23] The name of the organization may have been an "Islamic response" to *Tahrir al-Marʾah*; Rashid's husband was among the vociferous opponents of Qasim Amin's book. With the avowed goal of reinforcing women's "traditional" domestically centered family roles, these women contributed to the shaping of a cult of domesticity, yet at the same time by their very existence *Tarqiyat al-Marʾah*, the association and the journal, supported new public activities for women. Both, however, were short-lived.[24]

Other Muslim women subscribing to a more liberal interpretation of Islam forged ahead to find new roles in society. Giving and attending "public" lectures—outside the premises of women's associations—was an important step in women's outward-bound itinerary. Huda Shaᶜrawi helped organize lectures by and for women. The first lecture in 1909 compared the lives of Egyptian and European women and included a discussion of veiling. The topic was chosen by Shaᶜrawi, and the talk given by Marguerite Clément, a Frenchwoman, in Egypt on a study mission sponsored by the Carnegie Foundation. Clément, who had first met Huda Shaᶜrawi in the women's loges at the opera suggested giving a talk to women. Shaʿrawi obtained the backing of Princess ʿAyn al-Hayah. A member of the University Council, ʿAlawi Pasha, provided a hall at the new Egyptian University for the lecture.[25] The talk proved a success.

Soon Egyptian women who had benefited from school education began to give lectures to women. They obtained space after hours in the offices of the liberal paper *al-Jaridah*, the organ of the Ummah Party, through the help of the editor-in-chief, Ahmad Lutfi al-Sayyid. Women also lectured in the program run by the Women's Section created at the Egyptian University during its second year; talks were held on Fridays, the weekly day of recess. The women's lectures brought together middle-class women as "teachers" and upper- and middle-class women "students" in the common pursuit of self-development.[26]

The program of lectures at the university's Women's Section, resulting from female demand, provided an opportunity for women to continue their learning informally, which suited the aspirations of most leisured women of some education. The Egyptian University, however, did not allow Egyptian women to matriculate as regular students. The project for an indigenous university had been pushed by progressive nationalist men in Egypt and stalled by colonial authorities fearful of its nationalist implications and unwilling to help finance it. A woman (Princess Fatma Ismaʿil) was the largest single benefactor. The university was both a symbol and an instrument of advancement in a country struggling to end colonial occupation. The same liberal men in Egypt who incorporated women's advancement or liberation into their nationalist discourse, insisting that it was necessary for the liberation of the country itself, had been unwilling to open the university's doors to the first Egyptian woman armed with the state baccalaureate degree. When Nabawiyah Musa defiantly challenged the colonial Ministry of Education in order to sit for the state examination, which she passed in the top quarter, hers was as much a national victory as a triumph for gender. By forbidding her to matriculate at the new Egyptian University, nationalist men exposed the gap between their rhetoric and their practice. Three decades later Nabawiyah Musa told her story.

> I was the first Egyptian girl to obtain the baccalaureate diploma and I wanted to join the university. The university was located in a building at the beginning of Qasr al-ʿAyni Street. When I went to the building the doorman did not allow me to enter. He made me remain in the carriage until he obtained permission from the director of the university to let me in. After he got permission, the university secretary received me in a special room, took my application, and said he would deal with getting my acceptance. Unfortunately, the university secretary was unable to secure my acceptance. The university refused to admit me with the excuse that it had not prepared a special place for women. I was unhappy with the refusal and wrote a long letter to the director of the university blaming Egyptian men for their failures in educating women despite advocating the ad-

vancement of the nation and expounding the cause of its advancement. . . . The university did not care about my letter and did not respond. Shortly afterwards the decision was taken to have lectures for women given by women.[27]

Egyptian nationalist men were also negligent when it came to the selection of a head for the Women's Section. They bypassed their own female compatriot, who held an Egyptian baccalaureate degree, in favor of Frenchwoman Mlle A. Couvreur, a former teacher at the Lycée Racine in Paris, who had been one of the first women in her country to obtain the *agrégation.* Couvreur offered a lecture series on the history of women in Western civilization, which she delivered in French.[28] Nabawiyah Musa presented a series on Egyptian women through the ages. Couvreur's lectures were published in 1910 and Nabawiyah Musa's two years later in 1912.[29] Labibah Hashim, founder and editor of *Fatat al-Sharq* (The young woman of the East, 1906–1939) and a woman of Syrian Christian origin, gave talks on child care that were later published as a manual called *Kitab al-Tarbiyah* (The book on upbringing) in 1911. Rahmah Sarruf, also of Syrian Christian background, spoke on household management.[30]

Malak Hifni Nasif—Bahithat al-Badiyah—was one of the most powerful speakers both at the university and in the offices of *al-Jaridah*. The daughter of litterateur and lawyer Hifni Nasif (trained at al-Azhar and Dar al-ʿUlum) who encouraged her learning, she had been in the first class to graduate from the Girls' Section of the ʿAbbas Primary School in 1901. She then enrolled in teacher training at the Saniyah School, obtaining her diploma in 1905. Bahithat al-Badiyah returned to teach at the ʿAbbas School but had to quit when she married in 1907. The state school system did not allow women to continue teaching after marriage, but neither would her husband—nor indeed would most other husbands. Bahithat al-Badiyah moved to the Fayyum oasis west of Cairo, the home of her husband, bedouin chief ʿAbd al-Sattar al-Bassal, where she discovered he had a wife, as well as a young daughter whom he expected her to teach. Bahithat al-Badiyah observed the sufferings of other women in their marital lives and endured her own. She found solace in her correspondence with the Lebanese poet and writer Mayy Ziyadah, whom she met in the early 1910s, as well as in her public writings.[31] It was after she had gone to the Fayyum oasis that Malak Hifni Nasif took the pen name Bahithat al-Badiyah, writing and speaking out on women and society in contemporary Egypt. She published a collection of her talks and essays originally appearing in the newspaper *al-Jaridah* in a book entitled *Nisa'iyat* (Feminist pieces, 1909), a key text in Egyptian feminist history.[32] Bahithat al-Badiyah was a staunch advocate of women's advancement through education and work. She acknowledged the strides European women had made, but warned against blind imitation. Egyptian women must find their own national mode of expression and Muslims must remain true to their religion. She pointed to unveiled Egyptian peasant women who moved about more freely and had productive roles beyond the house. Predicting that restrictive practices like veiling would not last forever, Bahithat al-Badiyah cautioned middle- and upper-class women to proceed gradually in discarding old ways.

The Women's Section did not survive more than three years, as hostility mounted toward female invasion of "male" space, hostility extending to threats on the life of the university secretary. In 1912 the Women's Section was closed down, and the money saved went to supporting three male students on study missions abroad. A few women managed to enroll in the regular courses, but these exceptions were from the Christian and Jewish minorities or were Europeans.[33]

Early in the second decade of the century middle-class women were speaking at societies and schools not only in the capital but also in provincial towns. More associations and clubs continued to be created in Cairo, providing forums for local women (Egyptians, Syrians, and European residents) and international visitors to speak and exchange ideas. In 1914 women formed two new intellectual societies. Huda Shaʿrawi, Bahithat al-Badiyah, Nabawiyah Musa, and Mayy Ziyadah were active in al-Ittihad al-Nisaʾi al-Tahdhibi (Women's Refinement Union), where Egyptian and European women gathered together for talks and informal exchange. Huda Shaʿrawi and other members of the Women's Refinement Union also founded the Jamʿiyat al-Raqy al-Adabiyah li-al-Sayyidat al-Misriyat (Ladies Literary Improvement Society) for the purpose of resuming women's lectures.[34] Fatimah ʿAsim created Jamʿiyat al-Nahdah al-Nisaʾiyah (Society of the Women's Awakening) in 1916. These associations included middle- and upper-class women as members. The dues were not inexpensive for the time: founding members paid twenty-five Egyptian pounds, associate members six pounds, and corresponding members two pounds a year. The middle-class women who gave talks received free memberships.

Even by 1914 just getting together in "public" space was still by no means easy. Huda Shaʿrawi's recollections about the Ladies Literary Improvement Society indicate the uphill struggle. "I looked for a headquarters for our association, which we did not dare to call a club (*nadi*) because our traditions would not allow it, and in fact it was still not acceptable for women to have a place [in public] to congregate."[35]

Planning new lectures, Shaʿrawi invited Marguerite Clément to return to Egypt to give the inaugural talk.[36] Once again the two collaborated. Since upper-class women still did not speak publicly at that time, it might be argued that Clément became Shaʿrawi's surrogate voice. In the talk entitled "What Can and Must Be the Role of the Egyptian Woman in Social and National Work?" the speaker acknowledged Islam as the source of Muslim women's rights. The freedoms and accomplishments of women in the early days of Islam were contrasted with later backwardness resulting from domestic confinement. Finally, Clément (cum Shaʿrawi) spoke of a process underway when she declared that the path out of seclusion lay in women's participation in social welfare work, which would legitimize their public presence and demonstrate their skills.[37]

One of the members of the Ladies Literary Improvement Society was Lebanese writer Mayy Ziyadah (1886–1941), an important figure in literary and feminist circles in Cairo in the first half of the century.[38] Emigrating with her family from Lebanon around 1908, Ziyadah became a tutor to the daughters of Idris Raghib, the Syrian owner of the paper *al-Mahrusah*. Ziyadah's father became editor of the paper, and it was there in 1911 that she published her first essays. In 1914 Ziyadah began to receive women and men writers and intellectuals in her father's house in Cairo, forming the first gender-mixed salon in the city.[39] A Levantine Christian, Mayy Ziyadah was freer to experiment in this way than Egyptians. Nazli Fazil's earlier salon had not included women other than the hostess herself.

Teaching as Feminist Activism

As women entered public life not only did they create new "female" institutions, but some took up the challenge of penetrating existing "male" institutions. When upper- and middle-class women started social service and intellectual associations and when middle-class women founded their own journals, they constructed arenas where they were not in competition with men and where they had little or no contact with them. Nor were these Egyptian women in professional competition with British or other European women.

When middle-class Egyptian women became teachers or administrators in the state education system, however, they entered a workplace that Egyptian men and British women had monopolized. Behind Egyptian men stood the weight of indigenous patriarchal culture, while British women were shored up by the colonial system, a patriarchal system that controlled them as well.[40] The nature of the indigenous opposition revealed how gender practices such as the separation of the sexes, allegedly Islamic and based on moral principles and religious belief, could be ignored for reasons of expediency by men when it served their economic interests or when men in positions of authority wished to assert their power. What Egyptian women educators had to contend with from the British in the state education system also revealed the intimate workings of colonialism.

Nabawiyah Musa's experience pioneering as a teacher and headmistress (from 1906 to the early 1920s) in the Egyptian public school system illustrates the difficulties women faced at a time when few were adequately educated and the majority of middle- and upper-class women were still secluded and segregated from men. Because of the unavailability of Egyptian women teachers early this century, Egyptian men and foreign women (mainly British) found employment in the state schools for girls. By 1904, however, the

Saniyah School was turning out women teachers. Bahithat al-Badiyah and Nabawiyah Musa, as noted, were among the first. Nabawiyah Musa (unlike Bahithat al-Badiyah), we recall, rejected marriage and domestic reconfinement in favor of working as an educator. We examine Nabawiyah Musa's pioneering activism through her own reconstruction of this experience.

Nabawiyah Musa's victory in passing the state baccalaureate examination positioned her as the only Egyptian woman teacher on a par with male teachers who had graduated from secondary school, making her a threat to Egyptian men and British women ensconced in the colonial public school system. By barring other Egyptian women from taking this examination colonial education authorities stalled a process they feared.

There were two kinds of public schools at the time: schools in Cairo and Alexandria, which were financed and staffed (mainly by British men and women and Egyptian men) directly by the colonial Ministry of Education; and schools in provincial towns, built and financed by provincial councils and run by Egyptian staff. Nationalists supported schools under the auspices of provincial councils as a way to provide Egyptians greater educational opportunities that the colonial state refused to finance. Although these schools enjoyed virtual independence, they ultimately fell under the jurisdiction of the Ministry of Education. Moreover, all Egyptian schools were monitored by the Ministry of Interior as possible sites of nationalist resistance.

Nabawiyah Musa's career as a teacher and administrator in Egyptian public schools was characterized by remarkable professional competence as well as stern resistance to the overweening colonial "superiority" British male and female education officials projected and also to displays of patriarchal authority by Egyptian officials.

After obtaining her baccalaureate in 1907, Nabawiyah Musa lasted two years as a teacher under the authority of a British headmistress in the Girls' Section of the ʿAbbas Primary School in Cairo. In 1909 she seized the opportunity to become the first Egyptian woman headmistress at the primary school for girls in Fayyum. While this gave her freedom from working under a British headmistress she came up against the authority of male provincial officials. She wrote in her memoirs that she was amazed to discover that provincial governors had a power that the minister of the interior himself did not have in the city.[41] The young Nabawiyah Musa would not be daunted, however. After a year her "recalcitrance" impelled her transfer to the Women Teachers' Training School in Mansurah in the middle Delta, where she remained headmistress for four years. Again she resisted infringements on her authority by local officials. After accusing her of anti-British behavior in 1914 at the start of the First World War, she relates, antagonistic provincial officials managed to have the Ministry of Education force her return to Cairo. She was installed as assistant principal at the Bulaq Women Teachers' Training School under the authority of an English principal, Miss Mead. This was not a happy arrangement for either party. In 1916 Nabawiyah Musa was appointed principal of the Wardiyan Women Teachers' Training School in Alexandria, where she remained until 1924 when she was made Inspector of Girls' Education. She accepted this post reluctantly, preferring the greater independence of school administration.

When Egyptian women started to enter the public arena, and especially the work force, people feared the mixing of the sexes and raised the specter of endangered female morality. Women pioneers in education had to be circumspect in their interactions with male colleagues and superiors, and indeed with men in general. Because of the necessary mixing of the sexes at a time when male teachers predominated in the girls' schools, teaching was not then generally considered respectable for Egyptian women, and most families remained hesitant to send their daughters to school. From the beginning of her career as a school administrator Nabawiyah Musa scrupulously adhered to the spirit of the modesty code. This shielded her honor and also helped attract girls to her schools, for families were strict with their daughters.

Nabawiyah Musa's adherence to local norms of dress did not require her to cover her face, as veiling had not been customary in small towns and villages. Photographs and hints in her memoirs suggest that she stopped veiling her face around the time she went to Fayyum. It is telling that she made no direct mention of removing the veil. She simply discarded the face veil, by quiet example paving the way for others.

Nabawiyah Musa made a direct correlation between her modest demeanor and the advance of girls' education in Fayyum. "At that time there were only eighty girls in the school. Most were no older than ten because people, especially the villagers, were not eager to educate their daughters since they believed education would lead to corruption. His Excellency the governor had tried in vain to change this thinking. However, when people saw that my attire was nearly the same as that of the village women they stopped believing that teachers dressed immodestly and began to approve of the school. Not more than three months from the day I started working in the school the number of students exceeded two hundred."[42]

However, while one segment of the patriarchal culture (fathers of girls) approved of Nabawiyah Musa's support of prevailing norms of gender separation, other segments of patriarchal society chose to violate these norms if it suited their purposes. Two examples illustrate this.

Among the most outspoken against the mixing of the sexes, men of religion (shaykhs trained at al-Azhar and at Dar al-ʿUlum) took it upon themselves to be custodians of virtue. Yet when it became possible to replace male teachers with female teachers in the girls' schools in the teaching of Arabic, which the shaykhs monopolized, they opposed this, fighting to maintain their jobs. In 1906 Nabawiyah Musa, who excelled in Arabic, became the first woman appointed by the Ministry of Education to teach Arabic in a state school (the Girls' Section of the ʿAbbas School). She recalls: "The men of Dar al-ʿUlum were stirred up when they heard what for them was the strange news, and deeply offended that a young woman would teach the Arabic language to the fourth-year pupils. They had been the ones to reign supreme in the Arabic language. From this time, the name of Nabawiyah Musa began to appear in a negative rather than a positive light. They [the male teachers] called me the destroyer of men's homes and the one who cut their income and other such epithets, and began to find ways to harm me."[43] She describes how the British woman principal in her school sided with the shaykhs. Was this in order to appease the cadre of male Arabic teachers? Or did Nabawiyah Musa's teaching of Arabic signal a potential threat to British women that an Egyptian woman teacher might take over in "their" fields? Minister of education Saʿd Zaghlul (the future leader of the national independence struggle), however, backed her.

If the shaykhs could ignore the chance to implement gender separation when it threatened their livelihood, for other reasons certain officials in the provincial administration were willing to breach existing barriers between the sexes. As a headmistress Nabawiyah Musa needed to interact with male teachers and superiors, and at the same time she had to uphold principles of gender segregation. To accommodate these conflicting demands she issued instructions regulating male movements on the school premises. She relates how some provincial officials challenged her while she was headmistress in Fayyum, in what was a contest of authority and power.

> I issued strict orders that no man should enter the school except during the working hours from 8:00 A.M. to 3:00 P.M. Outside those hours no man was allowed inside the sanctuary of the school including governorate officials. His Excellency Muhammad Mahmud Pasha who was most correct did not oppose my orders nor interfere with them in any way. Unfortunately, he was transferred from Fayyum and another governor came. This new governor thought it excessive for the headmistress to issue orders about comings and goings and wished to assert his authority. He sent the secretary of the Provincial Council to me at seven o'clock in the evening on official business. I felt it would be damaging if people witnessed an occurrence at the school that might offend them, such as a man going into the office of the headmistress after hours when the teachers and pupils had gone home and she was alone. It would create doubts about the conduct of the headmistress. I found myself obliged to refuse to receive him. The governor was not pleased.[44]

Nabawiyah Musa relates that because of her "insubordination" the governor harassed her, eventually causing her to leave. Later as headmistress of the Women Teachers' Training School in Mansurah she encountered a similar problem. In upholding gender segregation in her schools Nabawiyah Musa exercised authority and control over her environment, claiming an independence that some men found it hard to tolerate. When women break into areas of work where men predominate, they have to contend with male power and control. Nabawiyah Musa upheld gender segregation for moral reasons and expected both sexes to adhere equally to the conventional moral code governing gender relations, which was intrinsically important to her. At the same time she enforced separation as a way to limit the power of men in the workplace, turning a code meant to contain women into one to contain men. "Men," Nabawiyah Musa wrote, "used to think that my strictness [in imposing gender segregation] was in direct opposition to their absolute authority as superiors."[45] They were not wrong.

Nabawiyah Musa also recalls the tightrope she had to walk to avoid antagonizing Egyptian men in the education system, on the one hand, and British men and women, on the other. While moral slurs against her or her school would most inflame the Egyptian public against her, within the colonial education system the greatest weapon her adversaries could and did use was the accusation that she was anti-British. While she could guard against the threat of moral charges, it was more difficult to guard against accusations of disloyalty to the colonial government, all the more so because Nabawiyah Musa was a committed nationalist.

Nabawiyah Musa's success as a school principal was a nationalist victory as much as a gender victory and one that threatened both colonial authorities and segments of the indigenous patriarchy. When she was headmistress at the Women Teachers' Training School in Mansurah, her students came out on top in the state examination for primary school teachers. "People started to talk about this and make comparisons between the Egyptian headmistress and the English headmistress. Before that time people thought Egyptian women were not suitable to be headmistresses. This [success] proved the opposite of what people had thought and they came to prefer an Egyptian over an English headmistress. This opened a door that was closed in the past for Egyptian women to be appointed headmistresses in the schools."[46] As an educator Nabawiyah Musa mounted a parallel "insurrection" against indigenous patriarchy and against patriarchal colonialism.

• CHAPTER 3 •

Thinking Gender

WHILE some women were moving out of confinement in the home into society and creating new public lives, others invaded the larger world mainly through their writing. Some of these women of the pen articulated a new cult of domesticity. Others shaped a feminist ideology.

We have already noted that upper- and middle-class Christian and Muslim women transcended domestic isolation and anonymity in the final decades of the nineteenth century by publishing books, and how middle-class women of Syrian origin, three Christian and one Jewish, founded their own journals in the 1890s. From 1900 to 1914, women started eighteen more periodicals.[1] Syrian Christians retained the numerical edge as founders and editors, but half the new editors were Egyptians, equally divided between Muslims and Christians.

WRITING THE CULT OF DOMESTICITY

The new women's press became the main vehicle for the production of the cult of domesticity. The women's press was a middle-class phenomenon: its founders, editors, contributors, and readers came predominantly from this class, and its language was Arabic, the language of the middle class.[2]

With the women's press, as with women's associational life of the period, there were two orientations: Islamist and secular.[3] While secular women's intellectual associations were progressive, most of the secular women's journals were conservative. With the exception of Labibah Ahmad's Islamist-oriented *al-Nahdah al-Nisa'iyah* (The women's awakening/renaissance), which lasted from 1922 to 1938, the journals with a secular tone were the longest-lived.[4] Forms of feminist expression were evident in some of this period's secular journals, but it was not until after independence that the first explicitly feminist journal was created.

While the women themselves, as publishers or contributors, need not have stepped far outside their houses (most published their journals from their homes), their voices, names, and ideas penetrated the public domain. Most women attached their real names to their words, deliberately discarding anonymity in favor of a public identity. Even the conservative Muslim women who wrote in *The Progress of the Woman* signed their own names.[5]

It is striking that just as the pioneers of the women's press were transcending the confines of domesticity and laying claim to a new occupation, they employed their pens to exalt the very domesticity they were escaping. When

Qasim Amin, in *The Liberation of the Woman* (1899), suggested that there was a life for women in the public sphere, conservative Muslim men such as Talʿat Harb in *Tarbiyat al-Marʾah wa-al-Hijab* (The education/upbringing of the woman and the veil) and Muhammad Farid Wajdi in *al-Marʾah al-Muslimah* (The Egyptian woman), two of the many rebuttals to Amin's book, harped on the centrality of women's family roles, reminding women that their place was in the home.[6] But it was women themselves, in their new magazines, domestic manuals, and advice books, who elaborated and expanded upon this view and made the domestic world more appealing for women.[7]

In her journal *The Progress of the Woman* (1908–1909), Fatma Rashid used the discourse of conservative Islam to stress women's place in the home and the sublimity of their family roles. She echoed the conventional views that her husband, Muhammad Farid Wajdi, had reaffirmed in print. Such a position can be understood in part in the context of a perceived threat to a conventional Islamic identity, a threat felt by both men and women. But while men also used conservative religious discourse to fight what they saw as a threat to their entrenched privileges as men, what other motivations could women have had for adhering to conservatism? They might have fallen under the influence of conservative husbands. Yet it might also be that their own vision of their "Islamic identity" remained locked in a familiar patriarchal mold whose imperatives and symbols they could not easily discard. Unlike feminists they lacked a critical approach to patriarchy.

Why did Syrian Christian or Coptic women from liberal families also extol women's domestic roles? In part, it was safe for women of religious and/or ethnic minorities to promote women's advance by advocating an improvement in their accepted roles. Among minorities women, like men, were constrained; it was not in their general interest to promote "radical" ideas. Indeed, at a moment when they were asserting differences on such sensitive issues as unveiling, they did not want their innovations to appear threatening, thus undermining their acceptability to the majority. Thomas Philipp, who has studied the Syrian community in Egypt during this period, noted that the Syrians "tried to develop a new national identity which would make their acceptance by Egyptian society possible."[8] There were also practical reasons. "Modernizing" women's domestic roles so that their performance would be more proficient fit the larger ethic of thrift and enlightenment, in practical matters such as housekeeping and in matters of health, evolving among the growing commercial and professional middle classes. Many of the new women journalists, especially those of Syrian origin, came from families where men were publishers and journalists, and these men may well have seen a market for journals by women.

Newly educated middle-class women in general, for whom teaching was the most common vocation, found in journalism another use for some of the skills and knowledge acquired at school. They could do so without presenting a threat by restricting their topics to "safe" matters of interest to other women. Among the subjects treated was household economy.[9] As journalists, women could build on an area of expertise acquired through educational training and home experience, a "women's expertise." They could pass on the fruits of their learning to a housebound middle-class female constituency. In an age of increased literacy for women, the arts and skills of family roles and household tasks could be handed down on the printed page and expanded beyond what illiterate mothers of limited experience could impart. This was a historical moment when most educated daughters had illiterate mothers. A generation or so later, more mothers and daughters would be able to partake of a common body of knowledge transmitted in print; indeed domestic manuals would be reprinted many times over.[10]

What was the shape and substance of the cult of domesticity? It idealized the roles of mother and (to a lesser extent) wife, and women's place in the home. In this way, it spoke not only to middle-class women but to upper-class women as well. But the cult of domesticity inspired by these "ideals" and paying homage to them was essentially a practical program for taking charge of, and improving upon, the performance of family and household roles. This practical appeal was quintessentially middle-class. The arrangements and possibilities of upper-class life were quite different. Upper-class women had far more, and usually better-trained, domestic help; they also had more opportunities for escaping a domestically confined world by taking advantage of new forms of recreation and travel.

The cult of domesticity as a practical program aimed to improve women's nurturing skills, household management, and productivity. It took an instrumental approach to family relationships; women's improved performance would enhance family relations. The women's journals dispensed advice on health, hygiene, and child care that was salient at a time of mounting concern over widespread infant mortality. Focusing on preventive care, the women's journals enabled middle-class women to instruct their counterparts on disease prevention; upper-class women, through their charitable dispensaries, were at the same time extending curative assistance to lower-class women.

Education for girls was quickly harnessed to the cult of domesticity; it was put to the service of elevating women's family roles, especially that of mother. The idea that to educate a mother was to educate the nation was infused into the nationalist discourse at a time when Egypt was intent upon revitalization as part of the struggle to free itself of colonial domination. The cult of domesticity thus became a nationalist project, albeit a conservative one.[11]

As more girls attended school, discussion focused on what they should be taught. It was argued that the curriculum in girls' schools should differ from that in the boys' schools so as to prepare female students for their lives as wives, mothers, and keepers of the home. Nabawiyah Musa, however, in her

1920 book, *The Woman and Work*, argued that both sexes should study the same academic curriculum but that girls should receive additional instruction in domestic subjects.

There was a nationalist dimension in the debates on education for girls as future wives and mothers. Many of the early schools for girls were run by Western missionaries. Indeed there were more girls in these schools than in the new state schools for girls. With the availability of state schools, it was argued, girls should attend these in preference to the foreign schools. The curriculum in the state schools, however, was largely based on the British model and many courses were taught in English, by British teachers; still there was Arabic instruction and some attention given to Egyptian and Islamic history. The mothers of tomorrow must be taught in their native Arabic and formed in their own national culture and heritage, and their own ethical and moral systems. This was an argument feminists would later use in promoting teaching as a profession for Egyptian girls.[12]

The cult of domesticity was a discourse that limited women's options. It clearly brought them some benefits when it "modernized" their family and household roles and accorded them higher status. But the context in which the cult of domesticity was shaped is telling. At a time when significant numbers of women were beginning to escape domestic confinement and experiment with new social roles, stressing and revalorizing women's domestic roles was essentially a conservative enterprise. The cult of domesticity was a "modernizing" discourse of containment: it could operate to stem the tide of women out into the public arena, harnessing new skills to old domestic tasks rather than encouraging women to deploy them for new work outside the house. In "modern" terms, it articulated and exalted the old notion that woman's place was in the home. New social, economic, and political roles for women lay beyond this domestic pale.[13]

Before we consider the production of a feminist ideology by other women in Egypt at this same moment, it is important to observe that while the women's press became the major site for the production of the cult of domesticity, this press also presented models of women in public life. Was this a sign of ambiguity or a display of muted (or incipient) feminism? The women's journals continued the project begun in the biographical dictionaries of Maryam al-Nahhas and Zaynab Fawwaz of presenting profiles of meritorious women, sometimes drawing from these earlier sources. These portraits, which became standard fare in the women's journals, subtly subverted the cult of domesticity, even though citations of women's public achievements were tempered by simultaneous homage to their domestic roles.

In the pantheon of "greats" there were Muslim exemplars, paramount among whom were women from the family of the Prophet Muhammad, such as Khadijah, his wife (and the first convert to Islam), a businesswoman for whom Muhammad had worked, and Nafisah, a descendant of the Prophet who was a transmitter of *hadith* (the Prophet's sayings). Islam was thus used to legitimize women's public roles at the same time that it was used to bolster the cult of domesticity. The wide-ranging list of worthies also included Eastern and Western feminists, such as Egypt's Bahithat al-Badiyah, Turkish nationalist and feminist writer Halide Edib, and Lucy Stone, founder of the American Woman Suffrage Association. Women from the West as well as from the East might be taken as models, although essays in the same journals were critical of Western influences. The biographical sketch provided a vehicle for women who might be reluctant to take an overtly feminist stance, such as Syrian Christians, to transmit feminist messages indirectly through this "feminist hagiography," as historian Marilyn Booth has persuasively argued.[14] Through these portraits of women famous for their public achievements, writers in the women's press gently undermined the press's own cult of domesticity. Other women did this more aggressively.

Articulating Feminism

> Woman was not created in order to remain within the household sphere, never to emerge. Woman was not created to become involved in work outside the home only when it is directly necessary for household management, childrearing, cooking, kneading bread, and other occupations of the same sort.[15]

This antithesis of the cult of domesticity, published in a male-run journal by Zaynab Fawwaz in 1892—the same year the women's press was inaugurated—formed part of the early feminist discourse. Fawwaz, and before her ʿA'ishah al-Taymuriyah and Wardah al-Yaziji, had began to repudiate female domestic confinement.[16] Poet ʿA'ishah al-Taymuriyah expressed what she and other nineteenth-century articulators of nascent feminism had undertaken when she wrote in her book of poetry *Hilyat al-Tiraz* (Embroidered ornaments): "I have challenged tradition and my absurd position and have gone beyond what age and place allow."[17]

After the turn of the twentieth century, when upper- and middle-class women were in the final phase of the transition from domestic confinement and invisibility to open and more full lives in a new public culture, Huda Shaʿrawi, Nabawiyah Musa, and Bahithat al-Badiyah eased the process and prepared the way not only by their "invisible" activism, which we have just examined, but also ideologically.

In the early twentieth century, as before, women articulated their feminism in books and in articles (often collected in books) published by the mainstream press that reached an audience of both female and male readers, rather than the more exclusively female audience that the women's journals sought. Egyptian Muslim feminists produced the two major feminist books of the period: Bahithat al-Badiyah's collected speeches and essays, *Feminist Pieces* (1909), and Nabawiyah Musa's treatise, *The Woman and Work* (1920). In 1915, the year after Zaynab Fawwaz's death, her compendium of essays and articles, *al-Rasa'il al-Zaynabiyah* (Zaynab's letters, 1897), was republished. Although of Syrian origin, Fawwaz was also a Muslim, which elucidates her explicit feminist daring, atypical of minority women.

Nabawiyah Musa and Bahithat al-Badiyah reaffirmed and extended Zaynab Fawwaz's insistence that gender roles were socially constructed rather than ordained by nature or divinely prescribed. They argued that not only gender but also sexuality was socially defined. A major theoretical task and strategic imperative for these turn-of-the-century feminists was to establish the idea of gender and sexual similarity.[18] This would pave the way for the final dismantling of female domestic seclusion and would lay the groundwork for the articulation of gender equality and equal treatment. Nabawiyah Musa and Bahithat al-Badiyah rejected the notion of gender difference that enshrined gender inequality to predicate male superiority in favor of a counternotion of gender similarity that affirmed gender equality.[19]

Breaking through old boundaries, these feminists championed roles for women beyond the household. Back in the 1890s Fawwaz had advocated work for women outside the house and had also acknowledged the importance of political rights for women. In the early twentieth century, Bahithat al-Badiyah and Nabawiyah Musa became staunch advocates of education and work for women. When Talʿat Harb repeated the essentialist doctrine that women were inherently different to defend their confinement to the domestic realm, Nabawiyah Musa retorted: "Men have spoken so much of the differences between the man and woman that they would seem to be two separate species."[20] She continued, "As with animals, [the human] female and male are alike, as scientists confirm. . . . [People] forget that it is only when people use their gifts that they develop."[21] She pointed out that peasant women and men, unlike city folk, were thought to be alike because both used and developed their abilities in similar ways. "It is unfair to compare the mind of an urban man with that of his wife. How can one compare the mind of a man of education and experience who has developed himself with that of his wife which has been neglected since infancy? Her mind became rusty through lack of use. . . . Her abilities were suppressed and she was sheltered from life's experiences before her mind could develop naturally."[22]

Essentialists, men and women alike, stressed women's procreative functions as the prime "proof" of the fundamental difference between women and men. Muhammad Farid Wajdi, for example, intoned that "the woman is a noble being created to increase the species, and in this the man cannot compete with her."[23] Nabawiyah Musa asked: "Can the woman procreate alone? Since the man participates with the woman in the creation of human life, would it not be more accurate to say that human beings are noble beings created for the purpose of multiplying the species like all other animals? Are men simply trying to create differences between the sexes?"[24]

Bahithat al-Badiyah, addressing a female lecture audience, absolved Islam and religion in general of complicity in structuring separate roles for the two sexes. "Men say to us categorically, 'You [women] have been created for the house and we have been created to be breadwinners.' Is this a God-given dictate? How are we to know since no holy book has spelled it out. . . . The division of labor is merely a human creation."[25] In another lecture she affirmed that maternal duties did not demand women's imprisonment in the house, nor did they conflict with their roles in society.[26] Dismissing the "nature argument" Nabawiyah Musa asserted, "People can decide for themselves about this [work]; nature has nothing to do with it."[27]

A basic constituent of the notion of gender difference was the insistence upon women's and men's fundamental sexual difference. It was commonly held in Egypt, as in other Muslim and Arab societies, that woman was by nature wholly and exclusively a sexual being—or "omnisexual," as Moroccan scholar Fatima Mernissi puts it—whereas man by nature was only in part a sexual creature. Moreover, women, unlike men, possessed voracious sexual appetites that they were powerless to control, threatening to unleash *fitnah* (social chaos).[28] Feminists refuted this construction of sexuality and rejected practices imposed on urban middle and upper classes in its name, that is, domestic confinement and face veiling. Early Egyptian feminists were well aware that face veiling was a powerful symbolic affirmation of fundamental sexual difference. However, practical considerations and everyday personal politics made Shaʿrawi and Bahithat al-Badiyah take a conservative position regarding the process of unveiling. Bahithat al-Badiyah and Huda Shaʿrawi implicitly acknowledged the sexuality of *both* women and men. They argued that women must keep the veil until men were ready to change—that is, to control their own sexual behavior. Men needed to be resocialized to think of women as more than simply sexual beings. In the harem culture of the past, the only unveiled women were slaves who were sexually available to their masters. Women also needed to know how to conduct themselves when unveiled. Bahithat al-Badiyah wrote, "If we had been raised from childhood to go out unveiled, and if our men were ready for it, I would approve of unveiling for those who want it."[29] Bahithat al-Badiyah and Huda Shaʿrawi adopted a gradualist approach to unveiling both for themselves and for others. Huda Shaʿrawi coaxed a young Egyptian woman, repatriated in her early teens after being raised in Paris, to put on the veil. She promised the rebellious Saiza Nabarawi, the daughter of her late friend ʿAdilah Nabarawi and a future feminist, that they would both unveil later. Bahithat al-Badiyah admitted, "We know that veiling will not last forever." Meanwhile, women should use the veil to protect their forays into the outside world. Thus, instead of hiding the "omnisexual woman," the veil became a feminist tool to assist women in gaining access to public space. When male progressives called for unveiling, Bahithat al-Badiyah let it be known that women would decide for themselves when it was expedient to unveil. She insisted that the man "should not be a tyrant in our liberation as he was a tyrant in our enslavement."[30]

Nabawiyah Musa, who was in the vanguard of Muslim women when she unveiled around 1909, remained modest in dress and behavior, as already noted. By example she helped to desexualize woman's image but never explicitly argued for unveiling. What she did was to shift the focus of the heated and, for her, futile debate on veiling (*hijab*) versus unveiling (*sufur*) to an examination of modesty (*hishmah*) versus immodesty or seductiveness (*tabarruj*). With veils in Egypt becoming increasingly transparent and cloaks becoming more seductive, veiling per se was not necessarily an expression of modesty, as Nabawiyah Musa and Bahithat al-Badiyah both remarked. The idea and practice of hijab had lost its original meaning. Qasim Amin agreed. His portrayal of a turn-of-the-century "veiled" woman proved the point:

> Today I saw a woman walking down Dawawin Street. From the servant preceding her and from her appearance I could tell she was of good family. She was tall, well-built, between twenty and thirty. A leather belt encircled her slender waist, and the folds of her cape clung to the curves of her body. The lower part of the cape around her hips allowed the beautiful embroidery beneath to show through. The top part did not cover her dress at all. The cape was fastened to her head, however, and fell down over her shoulders and upper arms. On her face was a piece of thin muslin, narrower than the face itself, which transparently hid her mouth and chin, just as fine clouds might hide the face of the moon, leaving her eyes, eyebrows, forehead and hair to the crown of her head uncovered. Walking with measured steps, she undulated her body as would a dancer upon the stage and raised and lowered her eyelids languorously, sending beguiling, flirtatious, come-hither glances to passers-by.[31]

Nabawiyah Musa laid out the problem in her introduction to her treatise *The Woman and Work*: "I have dealt with all the subjects relating to Egyptian women, but I have not dealt with what they now call sufur and hijab because I believe these are academic terms, of whose meanings we are quite ignorant. I cannot call the peasant women unveiled because she does not wear the transparent veil that is known to us city women. She goes about her way modestly. . . . I cannot call some of the city women veiled when they go out immodestly covered with ornaments and jewelry, attracting the eyes of the passerby while on their face they wear a veil that conceals nothing but timidity."[32] In her memoirs two decades later, Nabawiyah Musa recalls an encounter on a tram with a woman who, noticing her face uncovered, asked if she were a Christian.[33] Nabawiyah Musa replied, "I see what I should not see of your bosom and your arms from beginning to end, but you can see nothing of me but my face."[34] When a male writer at the Cairo daily *al-Ahram* insisted to Nabawiyah Musa that women must veil, she told him: "Sir, you come from a village. Your mother, your sister, and your cousin leave the house dressed in clothes like mine with a *khimar* covering their head and bosom. What is this veiling you are asking city women to observe?"[35] Not stopping at that she turned conventional wisdom on its head: "Sir, you claim that men are wiser and more rational than women. If women are not seduced by your faces, and some of you are indeed handsome, how could you men who are more rational be seduced by women's faces? You should be veiled, and women should be unveiled."[36]

The veil was clearly more than an emblem of modesty. It was a symbol of the harem culture designed to keep women contained and subordinate, and ultimately for this reason patriarchalists supported veiling. However, as feminists recognized, the practice was on its way out; with time and resocializing of the rising generation, it would disappear—until its resurrection, albeit in a different form, at the end of the twentieth century.

Egyptian women's assumption of new work roles was not hindered solely by conservative indigenous ideology but also by colonialist policy. The colonial authorities allocated a pittance in the state budget to female education, thus preparing just a few women to assume new work roles. Not only did the colonial state save money, it saved jobs for British women as well. Early feminists, especially Nabawiyah Musa, elaborated nationalist feminist arguments when promoting new jobs for women.

The first public articulation of Egyptian women's feminist demands was made in 1911 in a nationalist forum: the meeting of Muslim nationalist men at the Egyptian National Congress in Heliopolis. Bahithat al-Badiyah, prevented by custom from appearing at a male gathering, sent a set of demands that would mobilize the energies of half the nation. In the voice of a nationalist feminist she confronted British colonialists and at the same time addressed the Egyptian patriarchal system. Women must have access to all educational opportunities. They must be able to take up new occupations and enter the professions. Women must also regain their right to participate in congregational worship in mosques, as in the early Islamic ummah. Essential to societal revitalization was family reform, argued Bahithat al-Badiyah, calling for changes in the personal status code, especially provisions relating to marriage and divorce.

At the Coptic nationalist congress that had convened a few months earlier at Asyut in Upper Egypt, no Coptic women had presented feminist demands. This was in keeping with their approach of "innovation without proclamation" as a minority. After national independence, however, Coptic and Muslim women would join forces as Egyptians in organizing a secular feminist movement.

Nationalist Feminism Encounters Imperial Feminism

The same year that Egyptian women placed feminist demands on the agenda at the Egyptian National Congress, they had their first encounter with Western feminists when two leaders of the International Woman Suffrage Alliance (IWSA), Carrie Chapman Catt and Aletta Jacobs, visited Egypt in 1911. The IWSA had been established in Berlin in 1904 by women from suffragist organizations in the United States and northern Europe, who, after decades of struggle, joined forces in the final round of the battle for political rights.[37] Carrie Chapman Catt (1859–1947), former head of the National American Woman Suffrage Association, had redirected her organizing abilities to help spearhead the international suffrage movement as the first IWSA president, serving from 1904 to 1923.[38] Aletta Jacobs (1854–1929), the first woman physician in the Netherlands and president of the Vereeniging voor Vrouwenkiesrecht ([Netherlands] Woman Suffrage Association) from 1903 to 1919, was a member of the IWSA Executive Board.[39]

The IWSA was less than a decade old when it decided to broaden the base of the international suffrage movement by trying to recruit women from beyond the West. With this objective Catt and Jacobs toured Eastern countries in 1911 and 1912.[40] The Western feminists were naive on two counts. First, they surmised they would have to awaken Eastern women to feminism and help them to organize. They were ignorant of the rise of feminist consciousness in Eastern countries and of the many associations women had already formed. A second lack of awareness on the part of Western feminists was more serious. The IWSA Declaration of Principles affirmed that "men and women are born equally free and independent members of the human race," and are "equally entitled to the free exercise of their individual rights and liberty," claiming that the vote was the only way to secure these rights. Western feminists set out to recruit women from colonized countries in Asia and Africa to enter an international suffrage movement that avoided challenging, and indeed contributed to, a colonialism which subverted the egalitarian and democratic ideology enshrined in the IWSA Declaration of Principles.

When Catt and Jacobs arrived in Egypt, upper- and middle-class women were active in philanthropy, giving and attending lectures, pioneering in associational life, and making inroads in journalism and education—in short, they were busy creating a nationalist feminist culture. The visiting feminists had difficulty contacting Egyptian feminists. British woman physician Dr. Elgood whom they met introduced them only to Englishwomen. Elgood, whose husband was with the British military and who knew Nabawiyah Musa through the Ministry of Education where she worked, was well aware that Egyptian feminists were fervent nationalists. Elgood was not about to facilitate links between the Western feminists and Egyptian feminists, no doubt seeing IWSA feminism as subversive to the colonial project, which indeed at certain levels it was while still being an imperial feminism. Despite this lack of assistance Catt and Jacobs managed to meet some Egyptian women, possibly through the women's intellectual societies where Egyptian and Western women commingled. The visitors probably met Bahithat al-Badiyah (who assisted American writer Elizabeth Cooper in her research on Egyptian women)[41] and either Huda Shaʿrawi or Nabawiyah Musa, as Jacobs later remarked that she had met one of the women on the Egyptian delegation to the IAW congress in Rome in 1923.[42]

The immediate interest of the visiting Westerners was to forge international gender solidarity to achieve Western women's own political goal—to obtain electoral rights in their (independent) countries.[43] They wanted to help Egyptian women establish a suffrage association to affiliate with the IWSA. While this would serve their own purpose of widening the international suffragist base, the Western feminists believed this broad solidarity, under Western tutelege, would also serve the needs of women beyond the West, which they claimed were the "universal needs" of women.[44] The visiting suffragists soon realized, however, that it was absurd to discuss votes for women in a country like Egypt where even men lacked political rights, but they shrank from taking up the cause of the liberation of colonized countries, separating national liberation and women's liberation. The Western suffragists did not confront the contradictions colonialism posed for the international feminist movement they were trying to expand. Later, when women from countries still under direct or indirect European imperialist rule entered the international feminist association as "equal" sisters, the force of these contradictions would be felt. I will discuss in chapter 12 how imperial feminism nearly sundered international feminist sisterhood in the late 1930s and 1940s.

The imperial dimension of IWSA feminism and of Western national feminisms created and sustained a tension in the quest for international sisterhood. Catt's report of the Asian tour in her presidential address to the 1913 IWSA conference in Budapest conveys the arrogance of imperial feminism and the tutorial role Western feminists assigned themselves.

> We shall claim little more than that we have blazed a trail which we may point out to other women willing to carry the inspiration and sympathy of our movement to the women of Asia. . . . It is our earnest hope that the other women, comprehending the *unity* [emphasis added] of the women's cause, will be led to carry our greetings to the women of Asia, who just now need the encouragement which Western women, emancipated from the most severe mandates of tradition, can give in practical advice to these women, who for many years must continue to struggle under conditions which obtained in our Western world some generations ago.[45]

Historian Antoinette Burton speaks of the imbrication of imperialism in feminism in her study of late-nineteenth- and early-twentieth-century British feminists' involvement with Indian women. "The conviction that Indian women represented a special feminist burden was one expression of middle-class British 'imperial feminism.' . . . Professions of sympathy and of protectiveness were, together, at the heart of British feminist attitudes toward Indian women and formed the basis of what many British feminists considered to be the international sisterhood of the women's movement. And yet, in the imperial context, theirs was not a relationship of equals, either with Indian women or with other women of the world."[46] Burton points out that British suffrage periodicals "articulated an international feminist vision whose promise of universal sisterhood came into constant conflict with British feminists' determination to lead the world of women to freedom."[47] Harriet Feinberg, in her analysis of Aletta Jacobs's writings on her 1911–1912 trip, detected the same contradiction. Feinberg found two simultaneous voices she labels "encouraging our peers" and "uplifting our native sisters," implying both equality and inequality, and reserving a mentoring role for the Western feminist.[48] A sense of imperial feminism in the French context is revealed by the suffragist Hubertine Auclert (1848–1914). Auclert, it is worth noting, in 1882 had been the first woman to use the term *feministe.*[49] Auclert, who lived in Algeria for about two years as the wife of a French judge, wrote *Les femmes arabes en Algérie*, which was published in Paris in 1900. There she advocated the Frenchification of Algerian women and implied that if Frenchwomen had the vote they would look after the interests of women under French colonial rule. French feminists were part of the IWSA's inner core.[50] In 1939, the international feminist organization took a resolution demanding that women have equal opportunities in all government positions at home and abroad, including colonial service. This was at a time when there were several affiliates from colonized countries.[51]

Catt and Jacobs reported to the 1913 IWSA congress in Budapest that they had found women's emancipation already underway in Egypt.[52] With the visit of Catt and Jacobs in 1911 contact was established between Egyptians and the IWSA. A decade after independence, albeit partial, and the launching of the organized feminist movement in Egypt, the newly formed Egyptian Feminist Union (EFU) became a member of the IWSA. This part of the story belongs to later chapters.

Although Egyptian feminism was a nationalist feminism (of a colonized, not an independent, country) and IWSA's international feminism bore an imperial stamp, still there was potential for mutually beneficial activism. More broadly, there were many other points of contact between Egyptian women and Western women, both inside and outside Egypt. Comparing life-styles, exchanging views, and considering "the other" were common interests from which Western women extracted benefit, as suggested by Billie Melman in her study of British women travelers and residents in Egypt.[53] Egyptian women meanwhile, like men, had been turning toward Europe, attracted by its new technologies and other aspects of its material culture. Egyptians patterned certain institutions, such as the secular philanthropic society and the new private university, on European models. Meanwhile, the West exploited and colonized Egypt economically, politically and culturally. As they experimented with innovation, Egyptian women wanted to preserve religious and national cultural identities—which included a feminist identity—that *they* would redefine. All of this made relations between Egyptian women and Western women complicated and contradictory. Gender brought women together, but only to a point. The nationalist and imperialist projects of these women exerted centrifugal pulls. Relations among Egyptian and western women (inside and outside Egypt) were at once affable and antagonistic.[54] Feminism became part of this tangled web.

In 1918 Egyptian women received a shock when Bahithat al-Badiyah, their most moving feminist orator, suddenly died at the age of thirty-two. Her premature death may have made her feminist mission all the more enduring. It clearly empowered her companions. By a sad irony, the final silencing of Bahithat al-Badiyah's voice gave birth to Huda Shaʿrawi's public voice. At the age of forty, Shaʿrawi took to the podium for the first time to commemorate Bahithat al-Badiyah, promising, in what can only be called a feminist eulogy, to carry on her mission. Shaʿrawi recaptures the moment:

> I felt the dead more steadfast in seeking their rights than the living. The departed want us to take every opportunity we have to carry out the sacred mission they have placed on our shoulders. When I saw men honor the memory of Bahithat al-Badiyah and praise her virtues, I cast away my selfishness in sorrowing over my brother and called upon my sisters to perform their duty to Bahithat al-Badiyah. We conducted a eulogy for her at the Egyptian University. The women requested that I lead it, and thus I took to the rostrum for the first time in my life. How difficult it was to be in her place and not to see her next to me. Later in the difficult days we passed through during the 1919 revolution and afterwards, I used to look to her whenever I felt the need for her unique patriotism and courage. I used to talk to her inside myself. I heard her voice in my conscience.[55]

• CHAPTER 4 •

Egypt for Which Egyptians?

WHEN Egyptian women moved into public space, inventing new roles for themselves or entering "male" professions, they understood their own advancement/liberation as "new women" to be intrinsically connected with the nation's advancement/liberation. "The new woman" occupied a niche in the nationalist rhetoric of progressive men. Egyptian women's feminism and nationalism and Egyptian men's liberal nationalism signaled a united nationalist front during the independence struggle.

When the First World War ended, Egyptians rose up in demonstrations and strikes—the revolution of 1919—demanding an end to the protectorate imposed on the country at the beginning of the war and a termination of British colonial occupation. Women and men, the old and the young, and all social classes sustained a united struggle until independence was achieved. Women worked for the nation in any way they could. Gender rules were suspended.

From the outbreak of the revolution of 1919 to independence Egyptian women were fully involved in nationalist militancy. Feminists and other women engaged in highly visible organized nationalist political agitation and in more masked nationalist political activism in a professional context. Women's experience in the national independence struggle and immediately after "liberation" became the bridge from a gradual pragmatic feminism discreetly expressed in everday life to a highly vocal feminism articulated in an organized movement and a vigorous process of entering and creating modern professions.[1]

DEMONSTRATING NATIONALIST WOMEN

The story of Egyptian women's highly public, highly visible nationalist activism starts in 1919 with the beginning of the nationalist movement's militant phase. But let us first go back to the year 1910 and to Brussels, where al-Hizb al-Watani (the National Party) was holding a congress. An Indian nationalist and feminist woman attending the meeting, Bhikaji Cama, confronted the men: "I see here the representatives of only half the population of Egypt. May I ask where is the other half? Sons of Egypt, where are the daughters of Egypt? Where are your mothers, your wives, and your daughters?"[2] Among the many speakers calling for Egypt's independence one was a disembodied voice, that of Egyptian nationalist Inshirah Shawqi, whose written appeal was read out by a man. She was unable to be present and to speak in her own voice because her country's gender conventions forbade it.[3]

When the First World War drew to a close, Egyptians wanted their independence. On November 13, 1918, three leading nationalist men, Saʿd Zaghlul, ʿAbd al-ʿAziz Fahmi, and ʿAli Shaʿrawi, approached British high commissioner Reginald Wingate declaring their desire for an Egyptian delegation (*wafd*) to go to London to present the nation's demands to the British government. When they were blocked in this, and in their efforts to participate in the peace conference in Paris, the nationalist leaders constituted al-Wafd al-Misri (the Egyptian Delegation) to speak directly for the nation. The Wafd (the name by which it became widely known among both Arabic and English speakers), with Saʿd Zaghlul at its head, broadcast Egypt's demand for national independence. The nationalist movement had turned militant. Attempting to stem the movement the British authorities deported Saʿd Zaghlul and two other leaders to Malta.

The day after the arrests, Egyptians went out in demonstrations and strikes in Cairo and soon after in cities and towns throughout the country. Huda Shaʿrawi described the demonstrations as "sparks flying from the mouth of a boiling volcano ready to erupt. . . . Anyone who saw this sweeping revolution spreading in a way that revealed the depth and force of its fire could tell it was a fire that could not be contained. . . . The revolution manifested itself the same everywhere because there was only one way to act and that was to revolt."[4]

Huda Shaʿrawi recalls how she and her husband worked together in the nationalist struggle. ʿAli Shaʿrawi as vice president of the Wafd stood in for the exiled Zaghlul. Huda Shaʿrawi's husband kept her informed of events so that she and other women could take over if he and other Wafdist men were jailed or exiled. It was a difficult and dangerous time, with ubiquitous British soldiers and police, martial law, curfews, and censorship. Mobilizing the women's network was vital.

On March 14th, Hamidah Khalil, "a woman of the people," became the first woman martyr when she fell to a British bullet in front of the Husayn Mosque in the old city.[5] Two days later upper-class women took to the streets of Cairo denouncing the violence and repression of the British against the Egyptian people and protesting the arrest of the nationalist leaders.[6] The crowd of women, variously estimated from 150 to 300, assembled at the house of Mrs. Ahmad Abu ʿUsbaʿ in Garden City and, leaving their cars and carriages, began their march on foot. Veiled women in procession carried flags with crescents and crosses, brandishing the national unity of Muslims and Copts in the face of colonial "divide and rule." They waved banners with slogans in Arabic and French. "Long live the supporters of justice and freedom!" "Down with oppressors and tyrants!" "Down with occupation!"

The demonstrators delivered written protests to the legations of the United States, France, and Italy announcing, "Egyptian ladies—mothers, sisters, and wives of those who have fallen victim to British designs—present to Your Excellencies this protest against the barbarous acts that the peaceful Egyptian nation underwent for no wrong other than demanding freedom and independence for the country based on the principles advanced by Dr. [Woodrow] Wilson to which all countries, belligerent and nonbelligerent, have subscribed."[7] They proceeded to "Bayt al-Ummah," or "The House of the Nation," as Egyptians called the house of Saʿd Zaghlul. Nearing their destination they were surrounded by British soldiers. Thomas Russell (Russell Pasha), commandant of the Cairo Police, spoke briefly to the women and, on the pretext of going to obtain a permit for the demonstration, left them in the heat of the sun for about three hours. When he returned empty-handed, the women were forced to disperse. They held a second demonstration four days later that met with a similar fate.[8]

The women's militancy posed a challenge to the British commandant of police. In a letter to his son he described his dilemma and solution in doubly patronizing language. "My next problem was a demonstration by the native ladies of Cairo. This rather frightened me as if it came to pass it was bound to collect a big crowd and my orders were to stop it. Stopping a procession means force and any force you use to women puts you in the wrong. Well, they assembled in motor cars, etc., got out and started to walk in a procession. . . . I let them get a little way and then blocked them in with police supported by troops and there the dear things had to remain for an hour and a half in the hot sun with nothing to sit on except the curb stone."[9] In his published memoirs Russell's "dear things" become "ladies" against whom there is a considerable show of force—but no use of force, as this was reserved for the lower class. "At a given signal I closed the cordon and the ladies found their way opposed by a formidable line of Egyptian conscript police, who had been previously warned that they were not to use violence but . . . considerable licence was given them by their officers to practice their ready peasant wit on the smart ladies who confronted them."[10] Thus the colonial police commandant encouraged Egyptian conscript police to engage in coarse taunts against the women demonstrators. Huda Shaʿrawi recalls, "Some of the women started to rebuke the Egyptian soldiers [i.e., police]. A few soldiers became very upset and actually wept."[11]

Women continued to protest. It was only upper-class women who staged single-sex demonstrations. Actors of both sexes from theatrical troupes set out from Opera Square in open carriages chanting patriotic slogans. Ruz (Rose) al-Yusif recalled the fervor of those times when she, Mary Ibrahim, and other actresses made the rounds of Cairo.[12]

Lower-class women rose up more spontaneously in street protests alongside their men. It was these women who were sometimes fired upon and killed, like Hamidah Khalil. Four days after her death, another woman,

Saʿidah Hassan, was killed in popular protests in Bulaq.[13] The funeral procession of still another victim, Shafiqah bint Muhammad Ashmawi, a young widow, turned into a moving show of nationalist solidarity when Egyptians of all classes, women and men alike, followed her flag-wrapped coffin in silent protest. Other "women of the people" who became martyrs included: ʿA'ishah bint ʿUmar, Fahimah Riyad, and Najiyah Saʿid Ismʿail, to name just a few. Many women were wounded and some were killed in the streets or while cheering men on from their windows and balconies. Shaʿrawi and other women collected the names of the dead and wounded and visited their families.[14]

Schoolgirls participated in the independence struggle. Students at the Saniyah School became active, much to the consternation and alarm of their British teachers. Tahiyah Muhammad Isfahani recalled how day students used to keep the boarders informed about events in the city. Hilanah Sidarus, Jamilah ʿAtiyah, ʿAtiyah Abu ʿUsbaʿ, and other pupils distributed circulars at school and delivered them to private houses as well. With the heavy police surveillance it was a dangerous task that the girls undertook. Huda Shaʿrawi believed that the clandestine circulars printed and distributed during the revolution had been effective. Years later, schoolgirls remembered Shaʿrawi's visits to the Saniyah School during that period and how she encouraged their militancy and became their idol.[15]

The 1919 revolution rapidly spread to the provinces where women were also active. Hidayah Barakat traveled to Upper Egypt by train, distributing shopping baskets filled with clandestine pamphlets to teachers at stations along the way.[16] At Asyut in Upper Egypt, Zaynab Talat, with the help of women servants, gave food and assistance to militants engaged in sabotaging the rail line.[17]

When Saʿd Zaghlul and other nationalists were released on April 8, 1919, women and men of all classes went out in a massive demonstration that was a stunning display of national unity but also of class and gender hierarchy. Men marched in front: members of the cabinet, then deputies from the Legislative Assembly, *ʿulama*, judges, lawyers, doctors, government employees, army officers, workers, and male secondary and primary school students. Women followed: upper-class women in cars and finally lower-class women in carts. British troops fired on the demonstrators; four were reported killed.[18]

During 1919 Egyptians continued their militancy. At the end of the year the Milner Mission's arrival in Egypt to investigate the causes of the revolution propelled a fresh round of protests. Two days later, on December 9th, women again took to the streets. After circulating through the city in their carriages, the women proceeded to St. Mark's Coptic Cathedral for a mass meeting. (Mosques and churches were safe national sanctuaries.) There "the women of Egypt" made their first direct protest to the British authorities denouncing the Milner Mission. They also deplored their own ill-treatment during the demonstration.[19] This was the first of many written protests. Most women signed with their husbands' names as "wife of." Huda Sha^crawi and a handful of others signed their own names.[20]

Teaching as Nationalist Activism

While Huda Shaʿrawi and other upper-class women were going out in organized street demonstrations in Cairo, Nabawiyah Musa, as headmistress of the Wardiyan Women Teachers' Training School in Alexandria, refrained from public protest and also restrained the teachers and students in her school. Nabawiyah Musa did not wish to give the colonial Ministry of Education a pretext for closing her school.

During the revolution of 1919, schools in Egypt were sites of nationalist agitation. On the second day of the revolution, male teachers and students from primary and secondary schools and higher institutes went out on strikes and demonstrations. The women students from the Saniyah School, who distributed leaflets, did not go out en masse into the streets. The colonial authorities kept a sharp eye on the schools. In her memoirs Nabawiyah Musa insisted that the threat had been such that "my friend, the English inspector [in the Ministry of Education] was ready to destroy me if my school moved in any way at all." She also believed that an Egyptian superior in the Ministry of Education who was her "enemy" tried to goad her into ordering a strike at her school and thus bringing about her own downfall. She relates: "I called the women and men teachers and told them that schools going on strike did not help the country, in my view. The country is in great need of education. Teachers should be far removed from militancy in the national movement because they are performing great national work that they should not put aside for anything else, however important it might be. Their work is to teach an illiterate nation where ignorance is widespread. We have to sustain our efforts in combating this ignorance. . . . The meeting ended and every teacher went out intent that their students should not strike. All the schools went out on strike except the Wardiyan Teachers' School."[21]

Not only did the entire nation need more schools but women especially were in need of education. Nabawiyah Musa believed that spreading education among women was the highest form of nationalist activism and had the most far-reaching impact.[22] In 1920, during the height of the independence struggle, when Nabawiyah Musa published her nationalist and feminist manifesto *The Woman and Work*, she declared in her introduction that "drawing the attention of women to education and work is the best service we can render this country we are ready to die for. This conviction has inspired me to publish this book in the hope that it will have some effect."[23] Nabawiyah Musa understood the limits of nationalist militancy possible to her and to other women employed in the colonial Ministry of Education.

Middle-class women dependent on the state for employment risked losing their jobs and with this the ability to put their hard-won skills to the use of other women and, thus, their country.[24]

An impulse of quite a different order that also influenced Nabawiyah Musa to dissuade her female teachers and students from going out on demonstrations was her insistence on upholding gender segregation. Genuine commitment to a code and expediency—assuring through maintaining strict gender separation that families would keep sending their daughters to school—seem to have commingled. Nabawiyah Musa explains in her memoirs: "I used to guide my female students in a way appropriate to them as women. I inculcated in them a sense of correctness, decorum, and modesty and therefore did not allow them to go out on demonstrations and mix with male students, as most of them did not know the meaning of manners or decency."[25] Even in the name of nationalism, "taking part in street demonstrations was not fitting to our dignity as oriental women."[26]

In *The Woman and Work* Nabawiyah Musa called for more training for Egyptian women so they could take over jobs from foreign women whose presence constituted "a second occupation."[27] At the beginning of the twentieth century about half of the eight thousand professionals in the labor force in Egypt were European. In Britain marriage rates for women were low in the period before World War I (1911 was the nadir) at a time when the ratio of females to males was greater. "Surplus" women often went off to the far reaches of the empire to serve their own needs as well as imperial purposes.[28] Bringing Egyptian women into the work force was a nationalist imperative and a priority for Nabawiyah Musa, who insisted:

> A nation cannot prosper unless its people are vital and productive. A people cannot be vital so long as half are paralyzed and isolated from the affairs of everyday life. If women do not work, half the nation is unproductive. Egypt has great need for labor. There is no way we can keep Egyptian wealth in our own hands except through the education and training of women. . . . First we neglect the education of women; they remain ill-equipped to work. Then we look down on them, slam the door of work in their face, and welcome foreign women into our homes, entrusting them with our basic needs. . . . Egyptian capital is lost to these foreign women, found perfect, rather than going to our own women, found wanting. Had we spent money on educating Egyptian women, they would have been able to perform these jobs, and we Egyptians would be keeping Egyptian money in Egyptian hands. At a time when we make a great effort to win our political independence, why do we lag behind in fighting for our economic independence while we have the means in our hands?[29]

Nabawiyah Musa was equally concerned about the treatment of the young by foreign educators and the cultural (national and moral) formation they imparted. In subtle and not so subtle ways British teachers and principals deployed their authority to "colonize" students. Nabawiyah Musa tells the story of a visit by British education adviser Douglas Dunlop to her school:

> When we entered the first [classroom] the girl students stood up but they did not raise their hands in salute as was customary in all government schools. The late adviser looked at me and said, "Why didn't the students salute?" I said, "Because they are not in the habit of saluting me." He said, "Why is that?" I said, "Because I want them to retain their dignity. They are not soldiers who must raise their hands in a military salute." He said, "I wonder about you. Haven't you seen the English headmistresses? Why haven't you followed them?" I said, "Sir, I follow them in the right way, not the wrong way. Englishwomen in their own country do not oblige students to give them a military salute, but in Egypt, which is a colonized country, the English headmistresses oblige their girl students to salute them whenever they see them. I am an Egyptian headmistress of an Egyptian school, therefore I must behave like an English headmistress of an English school."[30]

The Wafdist Women's Central Committee

The same year that Nabawiyah Musa published her nationalist feminist treatise in Alexandria, women in Cairo formed a political organization. On January 12, 1920, women gathered once again at St. Mark's Cathedral where they created the Lajnat al-Wafd al-Markaziyah lil-Sayyidat (Wafdist Women's Central Committee, WWCC)—as the name indicates, a group attached to the Wafd.[31] Huda Shaʿrawi was elected president of the WWCC, whose initial members included ʿUlfat Ratib, Regina Habib Khayyat, Mrs. Wissa Wasif, Mrs. Ahmad Abu ʿUsbaʿ, Sharifa Riyad, Ester Fahmi Wissa, Louise Majorelle Wasif Ghali, Ihsan al-Qusi, and Fikriyah Husni. Most had taken part in the demonstrations of 1919. Several were married to Wafdist leaders. The Wafdist women came mainly from large landowning families, but some were from middle-class Cairo families. Upon the creation of the Women's Committee Wafd secretary ʿAbd al-Rahman Fahmi remarked, "The renaissance of the woman in the nationalist movement is occurring in a way that augurs well for the future." He expressed hope that the women's nationalist work would be long-lived and voiced Wafdist men's belief that women would be a positive force in the development of Egypt.[32]

The name of Safiyah Zaghlul, the wife of the Wadf's head, was missing from the list. Although she had close ties with the Women's Committee, Safiyah Zaghlul's primary role in the nationalist struggle was as the wife of its leader. Popular with the people, she also became emblematic of the struggle as "Umm al-Masriyin" (Mother of Egyptians). Born in 1876 into an upper-class family, Safiyah was the daughter of Mustafa Pasha Fahmi, a former prime minister. Educated at home by a German governess, at the "advanced" age of twenty she married the aspiring middle-class lawyer at the National Court of Appeals Saʿd Zaghlul.[33] Marriages across classes were not common.[34] Safiyah's father and her future husband had both frequented the salon of Princess Nazli Fazil in the 1890s where, it has been said, the agreement for the marriage was struck.[35] During the nationalist struggle, when her husband was imprisoned and exiled, Safiyah acted as a link between him and other male Wafd leaders and the people.[36] The night of her husband's arrest, Safiyah Zaghlul told his Wafdist companions who had come to Bayt al-Ummah that it would be open as usual for their meetings.[37] When the men suggested that they remove Zaghlul's papers for safekeeping, Safiyah told them to consider her not a woman but a militant (male) Wafdist.[38]

The WWCC undertook a number of vital tasks during the national independence struggle. When male Wafdist leaders were jailed or exiled, Wafdist women took charge. They maintained contact with Wafdist men, as well as with the British authorities. They handled finances. They kept up morale. They supported workers' strikes, organized boycotts, sold shares in Bank Misr, the new national bank, and collected money and jewelry to finance the cause.[39]

The WWCC played an important role in broadening the base of the Wafd's popular support.[40] Wafdist women worked through female associational networks. Huda Shaʿrawi and other Wafdist women, including Regina Khayyat, Ester Fahmi Wissa, and Fikriyah Husni, were active among members of the New Women Society (al-Jamʿiyat al-Mar'ah al-Jadidah), founded a month after the first women's demonstrations in 1919.[41] The WWCC later surely made contact with women from Jamʿiyat Nahdat al-Sayyidat al-Misriyat (Society of the Renaissance of the Egyptian Woman) and Jamʿiyat Ummuhat al-Mustaqbal (Society of Mothers of the Future), both founded in 1921 by middle-class women. In late 1921 and early 1922 the WWCC solidified links with women's societies in provincial towns. Fikriyah Husni, a WWCC member and schoolteacher from Minya in Upper Egypt, helped wives and daughters of local notables and shopkeepers to establish the Ittihad al-Sayyidat bil-Minya (Women's Union of Minya).[42] Hayat Thabit helped start the Ittihad al-Sayyidat bi-al-Asyut (Women's Union of Asyut), and Khadijah ʿAbd al-Salam headed the new Jamʿiyat al-Ittihad wa-al-Tarqiyah (Society of Union and Progress) in Tanta in the Delta. The latter two societies sent letters of protest to British papers.[43]

Before the WWCC was a year old, a crisis occurred in the Wafdist ranks. A proposal for Egyptian independence, referred to as the Curzon Plan, that Saʿd Zaghlul and other Wafdist men had helped draft in London was brought to Egypt in October 1920 and circulated to various groups for their reactions. The WWCC, however, was not consulted. Wafdist women immediately gathered at Shaʿrawi's summer house in Ramleh outside Alexandria to study a copy that they had managed to obtain. They published their criticisms of the plan in the newpapers.[44] Shaʿrawi wrote to Saʿd Zaghlul in London, deploring the Wafd's failure to consult the Women's Committee:

> We are extremely surprised and dismayed at the way we have been treated. It is contrary to the way you have dealt with us up till now and much different from the treatment we have grown to expect from you. You supported us when we participated with you in the [militant phase] of the nationalist movement. You backed us when we formed our committee and expressed in your telegrams of congratulations and the most noble sentiments and the finest hopes. What causes our dismay to increase even more is that by neglecting us, the Wafd has caused foreigners in Egypt to slander our renaissance by claiming that the women's participation in the Egyptian nationalist movement was not motivated by genuine patriotism, but that the women had simply been used by a group of men in the nationalist movement to mislead the civilized nations into believing in the maturity and advancement of the Egyptian nation and its ability to govern itself. Our renaissance, as you well know, is above that. At this moment when the Egyptian question is about to be resolved, it is patently unjust that the Egyptian Wafd, which stands for the rights of Egypt and struggles for its liberation, should deny half the nation its share in that liberation.[45]

Sha^crawi wanted to know what this implied for the future of Egyptian women. Zaghlul sent an apology, iterating that a society could not advance without the participation of its women.[46]

Meanwhile, strains mounted among the Wafdist male leadership, with personal and political repercussions for Huda Shaʿrawi. Difficulties arose between Saʿd Zaghlul and ʿAli Shaʿrawi while Wafd leaders were in Paris negotiating Egypt's future, causing the two men to part company. ʿAli Shaʿrawi returned to Egypt early in 1921.[47] When Saʿd Zaghlul reached Cairo on April 5th, ʿAli Shaʿrawi absented himself from the group that received the Wafdist leader at the train station and from the reception at Zaghlul's house. Huda Shaʿrawi accompanied the Wafdist women to welcome the returning leader, ably separating her roles as WWCC president and the wife of an estranged Wafd leader. She reconstructs the event:

> When we arrived at Saʿd's house, it was filled with crowds of men and women. Outside the house were two tents, one for men and one for women.[48] I felt somewhat timid being in that throng while my husband, who had diligently served the Wafd, without whose services it would not have gained the trust of the nation, had remained alone at home and thus the nation would not appreciate his worth. While I was in that swelling crowd with such thoughts swirling in my head, I heard the voice of Sayyid Agha [HS's eunuch] calling me to say that Saʿd Pasha was looking for me asking, "Where is the *raisah* (president), where is the raisah?" In the awkward position I was in, I was obliged to conceal myself from the eyes of Saʿd. However, while he moved among the rows of women inquiring, "Where is the raisah so I can thank her?" he chanced to see me as I was going out. I approached him and congratulated him on his safe return. Then I asked Sharifah Riyad and the other women from the Committee to stand in for me next to Saʿd and to give my excuses for leaving, the reasons for which they well understood.[49]

The incident shows Huda Shaʿrawi's adroitness as WWCC president in acting independently of her husband, while displaying the loyalty expected of a wife.

The WWCC was by no means a rubber stamp for the Wafd. When Prime Minister ʿAdli Yakan led a delegation to London to negotiate independence, Wafd head Zaghlul objected and began to struggle against Yakan. The WWCC, however, sent a letter of support to the Yakan delegation. When the negotiations led by Yakan broke down, and the women got word that the Wafd was planning to publicly insult the returning party, the WWCC implored Zaghlul to desist to avoid a display of national disunity.[50]

Meanwhile, differences did not silence the women when Zaghlul was arrested and deported to the Seychelles in late 1921. Huda Shaʿrawi as president of the WWCC sent a letter to the British high commissioner saying: "You cannot stifle the voice of the nation by stifling the voice of the person who speaks for the nation. There are millions who will speak out for the right to liberty and will protest injustice. We shall always protest vehemently the arbitrary and tyrannical measures which you take against us exciting the wrath of the people."[51]

The WWCC entered a period of intense activity. The women told Deputy Prime Minister ʿAbd al-Khaliq Tharwat that they opposed the formation of any new government while Zaghlul was in exile. The WWCC held a mass meeting at Shaʿrawi's house on January 20, 1922. There women signed a petition, to be sent to the British government and circulated to the British press, calling for an end to martial law and the protectorate, and objecting to the formation of a cabinet as long as Zaghlul remained outside the country.[52] The women agreed to a comprehensive economic boycott against the British. They would withdraw their money from British banks, and would refuse to buy British goods and to patronize British doctors, dentists, and pharmacists. The women sealed their resolve with a "religious" oath.

> We swear by God, the merciful and the omnipotent, and all his bountiful messengers and the souls of our holy martyrs and the will of our devout heroes, to boycott the British aggressor, to deny to ourselves and to the people close to us everything that those usurpers have manufactured. By God, their shops are forbidden to us. By God, their factories are forbidden to us. By God, all that is connected to them is forbidden to us. God is our witness, and we steadfastly swear by him. May his curse be upon those who betray their oath. We implore you, God, to bring back to us our honest Saʿd, safely and in good health, for his sake and the sake of his devoted compatriots, and to bring victory to Egypt and defeat to her deceitful enemies.[53]

Adding to the fervor of the evening, girls from the workshop of the New Woman Society sang nationalist songs.

Wafdist women organized committees to sell shares for the national bank, setting examples themselves by buying the first shares.[54] Women's legal ability to control their own money (according to the Islamic *shariʿah*) added leverage to their campaign. While the committees selling bank shares solicited the wealthy, the boycott campaign targeted the general population. The women's boycott committee could reach women as managers of households and steady consumers. Wafdist men praised the women's boycott campaign. Wasif Ghali promised women: "We shall never forget the great service you rendered when you rapidly rose to action to conduct the boycott. It was one of the most powerful and effective of the peaceful weapons in our legitimate struggle."[55] After his return to Egypt Saʿd Zaghlul too applauded the success of the women's boycott.[56]

When ʿAbd al-Khaliq Tharwat and other politicians indicated a willingness to accept British conditions laid out in the Curzon Plan as the basis for Egyptian independence, and there were indications that Tharwat might form a new government, the WWCC called a meeting on February 3rd. They repeated that the conditions set forth in the Curzon Plan did not satisfy the nationalist aspirations of the people and called on Egyptian political leaders to reject it. Again, the women also opposed the formation of any cabinet before the return of Zaghlul and the others in exile, and they demanded the release of all political prisoners and an end to press censorship and martial law. Ihsan al-Qusi's minutes of the meeting found their way to the British, who diligently monitored women's nationalist activities.[57]

In 1922 during the height of the nationalist movement, Huda Shaʿrawi's husband died. Although in mourning, a time when women traditionally remained secluded, she continued to work actively at the head of the WWCC. She told a women's meeting:

> Neither illness, grief, nor fear of censure can prevent me from shouldering my duty with you in the continuing fight for our national rights. I have vowed to you and to myself to struggle until the end of my life to rescue our beloved country from occupation and oppression. I shall always honor the trust you have placed in me. Let it never be said that there was a woman in Egypt who failed, for personal reasons, to perform her duty to the nation. I would rather die than bring shame upon myself and my sisters. I will remain by your side and at your head through good and bad times, with hope in the future while we defend the rights of our beloved country. Repeated hardships . . . will not deter me from fighting for the full independence of my country.[58]

Women's Protests after Independence

On February 28, 1922, the British issued a unilateral declaration of independence. It was conditional upon the so-called Four Reserve Points limiting Egypt's sovereignty; these allowed for a continued presence of British troops, enabled the British to maintain security in their imperial communications, protected foreign interests in Egypt, and enforced the separation of

Sudan from Egypt. These points would be dealt with in the future by a treaty between the two countries. The WWCC and the Wafd both objected.

Huda Shaʿrawi accused the new government headed by ʿAbd al-Khaliq Tharwat of boasting about independence, which "any sane person would consider merely a legitimate right restored to its owner" and, worse still, a right that had been "deformed and dismembered." She looked upon the whole matter as a British ploy to "paralyze our national movement and to calm our frazzled nerves."[59] WWCC member ʿAzizah Fawzi asserted that "the independence Britain gave Egypt was a mere substitution of the word *occupation* for the word *independence*," rebuking those who had violated the national pact.[60]

It is hard to exaggerate the courage women displayed under conditions of martial law on behalf of the imprisoned nationalists. Following the declaration of independence, British troops remained in the country, martial law was still in effect, meetings were banned, and the press and mail were censored. The widespread arrests of Egyptians involved in nationalist activities attested to the real dangers involved. In this environment, the Wafdist women kept up their campaign for the return of male nationalists in detention abroad. In addition to the difficulties posed by the British, Wafdist women faced close surveillance of their activities by the Egyptian government after ʿAbd al-Khaliq Tharwat's installation as prime minister.

Huda Shaʿrawi sent telegrams to the British prime minister and to British papers demanding the release of Saʿd Zaghlul and the others and calling for an end to the tyranny of the British in Egypt.[61] Following a fresh round of arrests of male Wafdist leaders in July 1922, Ester Fahmi Wissa, vice president of the WWCC, wrote a letter in English to British high commissioner Allenby, protesting the "great suppression of liberty and terrorization."[62]

An important link with Wafdists abroad was Louise Majorelle Ghali, a French-born and English-educated woman married to Wasif Ghali, one of the Wafdists arrested in July 1922. She maintained frequent contact with Wafdist leaders detained abroad, sending messages of moral support and receiving word on the prisoners' conditions.[63] On December 2, 1922, she received an unsigned telegram from London: according to word from "the highest quarters" the British government would release Zaghlul when it was satisfied that his presence in Egypt would cause no "untoward effect" in the country.[64] Louise Ghali should focus "his" attention on the fact that assurances were crucial. She maintained contact with Saʿd Zaghlul and others until their release.[65] Zaghlul was freed on March 24, 1923.

Four months later Zaghlul, accompanied by his wife Safiyah, returned to Egypt. Huda Shaʿrawi was on the same boat, returning from a summer in Europe. The WWCC president no longer wore the veil, having removed it a few months earlier in an act of public protest. Saʿd Zaghlul expressed approval, suggesting that his wife do likewise. At their arrival in Alexandria, Wafdist men coming aboard to greet Zaghlul objected when they saw the nationalist leader's wife unveiled. Wasif Ghali insisted that the people would not accept it. Safiyah Zaghlul left the ship veiled. Huda Shaʿrawi disembarked with her face uncovered.[66]

With the return of Zaghlul and the quasi-independence of Egypt Wafdist women were optimistic about their own future. Wafdist men had encouraged their expectations. Zaghlul had noted in his diary that during a 1920 discussion among Wafdist men in London on the condition of Egyptian women, everyone present agreed to work for the integration of women into society once independence was won.[67] In 1922 when Wafdist women were in the thick of nationalist militancy, Wasif Ghali told them, "A social movement cannot achieve its goals unless women have a part in it."[68]

Feminist Nationalism and Nationalist Feminism

On the fourth anniversary of the women's first nationalist demonstration (March 16, 1923), Huda Shaʿrawi called other WWCC women to her house in order to create an independent feminist association. She had just received a letter from the International Woman Suffrage Alliance inviting Egyptian women to attend the IWSA conference in Rome in May. In 1920 Shaʿrawi had organized a delegation from the WWCC to the IAW Geneva conference, but at the last moment the women's husbands had prevented them from leaving. In the call to organize anew Shaʿrawi stressed, " It is in our interest as Egyptian women, as well as in the interest of the Egyptian question, to attend in order to promote the status of the Egyptian woman and demand her rights."[69] The women created al-Ittihad al-Nisaʿi al-Misri, the Egyptian Feminist Union, electing Huda Shaʿrawi president, and agreed to send a delegation to the international feminist conference.

The month after the creation of the EFU, and the year after independence, a new Egyptian constitution was promulgated. The constitution declared all Egyptians equal, with equal civil and political rights and responsibilities. Three weeks later this equality was violated by an electoral law that restricted the exercise of political rights to male Egyptians. It was a moment of disappointment and disillusionment for the women who had fought for their country's liberation. They were now cast as second-class citizens.

The *male* Wafd came to power in 1924, gaining an overwhelming majority in the Chamber of Deputies. Saʿd Zaghlul formed a government. When the new parliament officially opened, Egyptian women not only were missing from the new legislative body but were barred from attending the inaugural ceremonies, except as wives of ministers and other high officials. Foreign women, except wives of ordinary Egyptians, were also admitted.

Nationalist women, who had worked to construct a modern national culture and had struggled tirelessly in the militant national independence campaign, now asked, in effect, "Egypt for which Egyptians?" The late-nineteenth-century slogan "Egypt for the Egyptians" insisted that Egypt belonged to native Egyptians and not to the privileged Turco-Circassians.[70]

This time gender rather than ethnicity became the issue. Nationalist feminist women's oppositional politics, which had previously been aimed against the oppression of British colonialism, were now directed against indigenous patriarchal practices. The WWCC and the EFU jointly picketed the opening of parliament. They prepared placards in Arabic and French with nationalist and feminist demands, which girls from the workshop of the New Woman Society paraded in front of the parliament. The WWCC and the EFU also distributed *Les revendications des dames égyptiennes* (The demands of Egyptian women), a nationalist-cum-feminist map for restructuring the Egyptian state and society, to members of parliament and government officials. Not long afterwards when the king ignored the women's demands in his speech from the throne, Huda Shaʿrawi sent a protest to Saʿd Zaghlul and the cabinet, the Senate, and the Chamber of Deputies.[71]

Although outside the formal system, the WWCC under the leadership of Huda Shaʿrawi continued their involvement in nationalist politics. Shaʿrawi and many other women differed with the male leadership of the Wafd under Saʿd Zaghlul over Sudan, insisting it should not be separated from Egypt, while the male leadership was willing to negotiate with the British. The women registered their protest about Sudan in a new anti-British boycott, which they organized at a mass meeting of women at Shaʿrawi's house on October 30, 1924. Tensions mounted between WWCC president Shaʿrawi and Wafd president Zaghlul. On November 19th, when Lee Stack—the British *sirdar* of the Egyptian Army and governor-general of the Sudan—was killed in Cairo, the British delivered a harsh ultimatum to the Egyptians. The Women's Boycott Committee telegraphed Zaghlul to reject the ultimatum. However, the Egyptian government agreed to the first four points. The WWCC president wired disapproval to Zaghlul and sent an open letter to the prime minister demanding: "Since you have not succeeded while in office to fulfill your promise by positive action, I ask you not to be an obstacle in the path of your country's struggle for salvation. . . . I ask you to step down from governing."[72]

The publication of Huda Shaʿrawi's open letter to Saʿd Zaghlul and of the telegram of the Women's Boycott Committee in the newspaper *al-Akhbar* led to an irreparable rupture between the president of the WWCC and the head of the Wafd. Huda Shaʿrawi resigned as president of the WWCC. Saʿd Zaghlul, facing mounting protests, resigned as prime minister on November 23rd.

Although the final parting of the ways between Huda Shaʿrawi and the Wafd had resulted from disagreement over the British ultimatum, clearly much more was involved. Shaʿrawi and many other Wafdist women were more radical in their nationalism than the male leadership. Women were not ready for compromise with the British. They insisted upon complete national independence and sovereignty. However, the women were prevented from active participation in the nationalist debate within the Wafd. The men of the Wafd wanted the WWCC to function as a rubber stamp. Denied formal political rights, women continued to engage in practical politics, as both men and women had done under colonial occupation when no Egyptian enjoyed formal political rights. When Shaʿrawi and other women felt deprived of the ability to register their views within the context of the Wafd, they withdrew from the arena where their voices were suppressed. They would carry on their nationalism and feminism exclusively in an arena of their own. Huda Shaʿrawi gave up the presidency of the WWCC and, with others, left the nationalist body. They would conduct their nationalism and feminism from then on exclusively within the context of the EFU.

When Shaʿrawi and some of her colleagues left the WWCC, other Wafdist women reconstituted themselves as al-Lajnah al-Saʿdiyah lil-Sayyidat (Committee of Saʿdist Women) under the leadership of Sharifah Riyad, pledging loyalty to Saʿd Zaghlul. Thus, there was also a parting of the ways between women as feminist nationalists and nationalist women prepared to be Zaghlul loyalists.

"From 1924, the Egyptian woman expressed her existence and activity in the heart of public life," Shaʿrawi noted in her memoirs. "The Egyptian woman, from the moment of the first spark of the revolution of 1919, entered public life from the most honorable door, the door of national struggle for freedom and independence."[73]

Shaʿrawi expressed the disappointment she and some of the other women felt over the unfulfilled promises Wafdist men had made during the liberation struggle.

> Exceptional women appear at certain moments in history and are moved by special forces. Men view these women as supernatural beings and their deeds as miracles. Indeed, women are bright stars whose light penetrates dark clouds. They rise in times of trouble when the wills of men are tried. In moments of danger, when women emerge by their side, men utter no protest. Yet women's great acts and endless sacrifices do not change men's views of women. Through their arrogance, men refuse to see the capabilities of women. Faced with contradiction, they prefer to raise women above the ordinary human plane instead of placing them on a level equal to their own. Men have singled out women of outstanding merit and put them on a pedestal to avoid recognizing the capabilities of all women. Women have felt this in their souls. Their dignity and self-esteem have been deeply touched. Women reflected on how they might elevate their status and worth in the eyes of men. They decided that the path lay in participating with men in public affairs. When they saw the way blocked, women rose up to demand their liberation, claiming their social, economic, and political rights. Their leap forward was greeted with ridicule and blame, but that did not weaken their will. Their resolve led to a struggle that would have ended in war, if men had not come to acknowledge the rights of women.[74]

• PART TWO •

The Feminist Movement

• C H A P T E R 5 •

The House of the Woman

WITH THE CREATION of the Egyptian Feminist Union women began a tradition of independent organized feminist struggle.[1] In the shift from hidden feminist activism—first embedded in new social and professional forays into society and then expressed as part of nationalist militancy—to the beginning of a highly visible organized feminist movement, three things occurred: (1) Feminist leaders removed the veil as a political statement signaling at once a final rejection of female containment and invisibility (harem culture) and their appearance on the scene as feminists; (2) Women for the first time in a highly public and unequivocal way used the adjective *nisa'i/yah* to signify feminist instead of the ambiguous "women's";[2] and (3) Women created the structure for their new feminist movement: an association, publications, facilities, and formal affiliation with the international feminist movement. The EFU, born in part as an act of feminist women's separation from the Wafd and its restraining influence, formally committed itself to safeguarding its independence, enshrining in its bylaws (*Qanun Jamᶜiyat al-Ittihad al-Nisa'i al-Misri*) the mandate not to affiliate itself with any political party.

UNVEILING FEMINISM AND FEMINISTS

The EFU made the first public declaration of its feminist program at the International Woman Suffrage Alliance congress in Rome in May 1923. The EFU delegation included Huda Shaᶜrawi, Nabawiyah Musa, and Saiza Nabarawi.[3] Huda Shaᶜrawi explained to the feminist congress that Egyptian women were calling for a restoration of their lost rights. They were reclaiming their own heritage (*turath*). This was a national enterprise, not an imitative one looking to the West. With these assertions Shaᶜrawi sent a signal both to Western feminists and to Egyptian patriarchalists. Establishing historical legitimacy was crucial in a society revering its past and inherited practices, and reclaiming its identity after colonial intrusion. Shaᶜrawi evoked two golden ages: the pharaonic era and early Islam. In ancient Egypt at the height of its glory women had enjoyed equal rights with men, but when the country fell under foreign domination women lost their rights. Later, Islam appeared in Egypt, granting women and men equal rights, but with time these rights had been eroded. By the modern era women in Egypt had been robbed of their legitimate rights.[4] However, the Egyptian feminists qualified this. Declaring that "the only ones to suffer the loss of their rights were a few thousand women living in the main cities of Egypt,"[5] Nabawiyah

Musa explained: "The Egyptian peasant woman still enjoys all her social rights: she goes out with her face uncovered, participates in her husband's purchases and sales, and has a clear idea of agricultural affairs. Man often resorts to her for advice because he is convinced that his wife possesses greater wisdom than he does."[6] In Egyptian feminist discourse the peasant woman symbolized freedom—of the Egyptian nation and of the Egyptian woman.

The early 1920s constituted a turning point both in Egyptian feminism and in international feminism. After independence was achieved in Egypt, nationalist men turned attention away from women's liberation. This was most painfully symbolized in the withholding of the vote from women. It was an opportune moment for Egyptian women to join hands with the international sisterhood.[7] Egyptian women were open to a sisterhood transcending national borders and politically they needed to forge wider gender alliances. With many Western countries finally granting women the vote in the aftermath of the First World War, the IWSA, while sustaining the suffragist cause, now turned its attention to promoting the practice of full and equal citizenship by women. Reflecting its expanded mandate in a change of name, the International Woman Suffrage Alliance in 1923 became the International Alliance of Women for Suffrage and Equal Citizenship (IAW).

With the IAW's emphasis on citizenship and the shift to a multigoal agenda, the formal programs of the EFU and the IAW coincided. Yet there was a fundamental discordance. In its eagerness to lead and shape a global solidarity of women the IAW Western mainstream stressed gender similarity, conveniently ignoring the issue of imperialism.[8] Yet Western feminists well understood that the world was split into colonizers and colonized.[9] Trapped in a sense of their special mission toward women from other parts of the world, Western imperial feminists accorded themselves a tutorial role, arrogating to themselves the privilege of defining feminist goals and methods, and indeed feminism itself. Egyptian feminists, who refused to be targets of remedial feminism, believed they could make international feminist solidarity work for them—furthering their feminist and nationalist agendas—while helping to shape international sisterhood. The complicated path Egyptian and international feminists trod together, and the mounting frustrations Egyptian women felt, are illuminated in upcoming chapters. However, in the early 1920s, when the spirit of international feminism was high, sisterly enthusiasms on both sides muted the deeper divisions and inequalities among women.

Returning to Egypt from the IAW congress, Nabawiyah Musa remained in Alexandria while Huda Shaʿrawi and Saiza Nabarawi took the train to Cairo. At the railway station in Cairo, stepping down from the train, the two women uncovered their faces as a public political act. The large crowd of women greeting them broke into applause. Some cast aside their own veils in imitation. Only the eunuchs guarding the women showed displeasure,

Nabarawi recalled.[10] Veiling was finished as a feminist strategy for piecemeal entry into public space.[11] The veil had become, in Shaʿrawi's words, "the greatest obstacle to women's participation in public life."[12] Covering the face was not only constraining to the individual but emblematic of the whole urban order of female confinement and containment.[13] A contemporary Alexandrian woman remarked: "[The veil] is a sign of utter dependence and also of freedom from responsibility; a handicap to real progress and a symbol of special privilege. In a word the veil represents an entirely different social system. Discarding it, therefore, involves a whole change of psychology. As long as any vestige of the veil remains the system has not changed."[14] Shaʿrawi and Nabarawi carried their unveiling a step further, giving their photographs to the Egyptian papers *al-Lata'if al-Musawwarah* and *Le Journal du Caire.*[15] Two years later, EFU member ʿAzizah Haykal appeared unveiled before the Egyptian king at a state reception in Paris.[16] This would never happen in Egypt, as the face veil, albeit a merely symbolic covering, remained required dress at court until the monarchy ended with the 1952 revolution.

Egyptian feminist leaders not only set an example themselves but, in the pages of their journal *L'Egyptienne*, drew attention to unveiling elsewhere in the region.[17] Turkish women went unveiled to a reception honoring President Mustafa Kamil at Bursa in 1925.[18] Habibah Manshari appeared unveiled in Tunis in 1929 to give a public lecture entitled "For or against the Veil?"[19] Nazirah Zayn al-Din published a treatise called *Sufur wa-al-Hijab* (Unveiling and veiling) in Beirut in 1928. As *L'Egyptienne* told its readers, the young author from Lebanon stressed that words were only one step toward unveiling and that women had to act.[20] In 1928, EFU member Ihsan al-Qusi participated in an oratorical contest at the American University in Beirut, reminding her audience that covering the face was not required by Islam.[21]

On only one occasion did Egyptian feminists publicly demonstrate against the veil. This was during the state visit in 1928 of the king and queen of Afghanistan, when Surayya—who had recently become the first Muslim queen to unveil—was required by Egyptian court protocol to resume the veil.[22] Unveiled Egyptian women stationed themselves at the Qasr al-Nil Bridge; when the Afghan and Egyptian monarchs and consorts passed in an open carriage, they showered them with rose petals.[23]

Covering the face waned in Egypt in the 1920s and 1930s.[24] There were some, however, who continued to argue in favor of the dying practice. Several articles in Labibah Ahmad's conservative journal *The Woman's Awakening* urged retention of the veil. One writer even evoked Western practice to promote veiling, pointing out that both the pope and Mussolini insisted on women's modest attire.[25] Nonetheless by the late 1930s, the veil had largely disappeared. In 1937 the Fatwa Committee of al-Azhar issued a ruling declaring that the Hanafi school of jurisprudence did not oppose unveiling and the Maliki school did not require veiling.[26] In this way the state, through the religious authorities, merely gave its indirect blessings to what women themselves had already achieved and what the peasant majority had always enjoyed.

Unveiling had never been part of the EFU's formal agenda and had been of concern only to urban women. The EFU's formal agenda constituted feminists' challenge to meet the needs both of women and of society in general. The "Demands of the Egyptian Woman," which the EFU and WWCC announced jointly in 1924, remained the single most comprehensive statement of the EFU program. The women drew up thirty-two demands under three headings: political, social, and female (*féminine*). In using the word *féminine* instead of *féministe* and in placing these demands last, women activists displayed a concern not to unduly upset the patriarchy while challenging it.[27]

The six political points were nationalist demands aimed at obtaining full Egyptian sovereignty. They included a call for the complete independence of Egypt and Sudan, a refusal to recognize the British unilateral declaration of independence and the Four Reserve Points without the consent of the entire Egyptian nation, a stipulation for the neutrality of the Suez Canal, and insistence on the termination of the Capitulations (agreements granting extraterritorial privileges and immunities to foreigners).

The nineteen social demands addressed societal and economic issues, mainly in a gender-neutral way. The manifesto demanded the rapid implementation of constitutionally mandated compulsory primary school education. Schools should provide religious and moral instruction, classes in hygiene, public law, and, if possible, music. Age restrictions for students at secondary schools and institutions of higher education should be abolished. There should be an increase in student missions abroad favoring those with the greatest need. Here the use of the pronoun *elles* made it clear that women were most in need. The university should be reconstituted as soon as possible. Foreign books should be translated into Arabic to facilitate university instruction in the national language. There were several demands of a broad policy nature dealing with the national economy. Local industries producing handcrafts should be protected "against the egotism of the capitalist" through new customs regulations and curbs on the influx of foreign luxury items. The Egyptian economy should not be based exclusively upon cotton. Agricultural cooperatives must be created throughout the country. A call for social services included increasing the number of hospitals for contagious diseases, opening sanatoriums for poor children suffering from anemia, and creating public parks for children in popular city quarters. Social reforms proposed included outlawing alcohol and drugs, ending state-licensed prostitution, and reforming prisons.

The EFU and WWCC framed their seven "female demands" with the liberal nationalist axiom that women mirror the advancement of society. They stressed, "If we demand special amelioration of the condition of the woman, it is not in preference for our sex to the detriment of other members of the community but because we are convinced that this is the only way to reform society." The women also reiterated that "the Muslim religion ordains the equality of the two sexes in all domains, especially in education." While education was the cornerstone to women's advancement, they would not rest content with it alone but would demand "our other rights granted in conformity with natural and divine laws." Calling for equality of the sexes in education, they demanded women's access to higher institutes, the creation of secondary schools for girls in the cities and major provincial towns, and replacement of male teachers with female teachers. Women demanded female suffrage, cautiously (and undemocratically) suggesting starting with literacy and property qualifications. They called for reform of the personal status code, especially laws regarding polygamy and divorce, to be accomplished within "the spirit of religion" for "justice and peace to reign in the family." During the course of their movement feminists added other demands to the original list, addressed many issues in an ad hoc manner, and replaced their initial caution in tone and vocabulary with more forceful language.

The EFU-led feminist movement aimed to be all-inclusive. Saiza Nabarawi as editor of the newly founded *L'Egyptienne* (established in 1925) declared: "It is not individually but collectively that we wish to gain our freedom. . . . The emancipation that we envision for ourselves is vast. . . . It is in consideration of the millions of ignorant women that we must plunge forward without ever compromising the movement to attain what we propose."[28] The feminist movement, despite its broad claims, was essentially an urban movement, and moreover a movement of middle- and upper-class women. The feminists approached urban lower-class women through attempting themselves to provide social services and through pressuring the government in this direction. Later feminists pressured the government to provide services to women and men in rural areas while they and other women tried directly to meet the needs of peasants.

The feminist movement was a national, secular movement of Egyptian women, both Muslim and Christian. The movement was secular in that it was not communally based or articulated exclusively within a religious discourse. Egyptian secular feminism situated itself within the parameters of religion, appropriating the discourse of Islamic modernism in a general way to legitimize its overall agenda and most specifically its campaign to reform the religiously based Muslim personal status code. Christian feminists, however, abstained from involvement in the drive to reform the Muslim code and never endeavored to change their own personal status codes. While Egyptian feminists respected religious difference, they refused to allow religion to be a divisive force. Experiences of communal discord under British occupation were still fresh. The EFU explicitly stated in its bylaws that it would not "take part in religious disputes." When in the late 1930s, aiming to broaden its base at home and in the region, the EFU published an Arabic-language journal, it articulated its secular feminism more explicitly in the discourse of Islam.

Founding Mothers

The eleven founding members of the EFU, like Huda Shaʿrawi, were mainly from wealthy landowning families settled in Cairo, but with recent roots in the countryside. They were the last generation of women raised within the conventions of harem culture. The honorary founders also included middle-class women from the new educated elite the schools were turning out, such as Nabawiyah Musa. Middle-class women were fluent in Arabic, their everyday language, while at school they had studied English and French, which they used more occasionally. The founders of the EFU included both Muslims and Christians, married and single women. They were mainly in their thirties and forties: Shaʿrawi was forty-four and Nabawiyah Musa thirty-seven.

At the first meeting of the EFU, Huda Shaʿrawi was elected president, ʿAtiyah Fu'ad treasurer, and Ihsan al-Qusi secretary. The other charter members were Mary Kahil, Wajidah Khulusi, Firdus Shita, Regina Khayyat, Nadiyah Rashid, ʿAzizah Fawzi, Jamilah ʿAtiyah, and Nabawiyah Musa. Among the honorary charter members were Saiza Nabarawi, Labibah Ahmad, Naʿimah Abu ʿUsba, Jalilah al-Bahrawi, Ihsan Haykal, Firdus ʿAfifi, Khadijah ʿAbd al-Salam, and Fikriyah Husni. Having already examined the early lives of Huda Shaʿrawi and Nabawiyah Musa, we now look briefly at some of the other EFU founders and early members.

Mary Kahil, a founding member, was born in 1889 to a father of Syrian Christian ancestry from a large landowning family in Damietta in the Delta and an Austrian mother who, as a young woman, had come to Egypt as an archaeologist. Kahil was educated by Roman Catholic nuns at Notre Dame de la Mère de Dieu School in Cairo and later at Les Dames de Nazareth School in Beirut. Kahil returned to Egypt in 1905 "full of Arab nationalist feelings," as she put it, and concerned about the place of women. Around this time she met Huda Shaʿrawi, whom she found awesome and inspiring. Kahil recalled suggesting to Shaʿrawi the idea of having lectures for women. Kahil was a pioneering member of the Mabarrat Muhammad ʿAli, which remained for her a central lifelong mission, although she participated in and endowed a wide range of social service activities. She was active as both a philanthropist and a feminist with a special interest in social reform.[29]

Regina Khayyat, another founder, was born in Asyut in 1888, the daughter of a large Coptic landowner, Wissa Boctor Wissa, and Angelina Saifi. She spent her childhood in Asyut, where she attended the Pressly Memorial Institute for Girls run by the American Presbyterian Mission. Although located in Upper Egypt, a region legendary for its conservatism, Asyut had been exposed to liberalizing influences. With its large Coptic population the town had been well endowed with schools for girls and boys opened by Christians, both Copts and Western missionaries. Two leading Coptic families, the Khayyats and the Wissas, each founded a school, the former a school for girls and the latter one for boys. Early in the twentieth century, Regina Wissa married Habib Khayyat, a doctor educated at the University of Edinburgh, and soon afterwards moved with her husband to Cairo. By that time she had already witnessed changes. Asyut women had been among the first Egyptians to unveil around the turn of the century. In the capital Khayyat devoted herself to charitable activities, while her husband practiced medicine and later became a senator. In 1926 she founded the Egyptian Young Women's Christian Association.[30]

ʿAzizah Haykal, an early member, was born in 1901 into a wealthy landowning family from al-Mahallah al-Kubra in the Delta province of Buhayrah. Her father, ʿAbd al-Rahman Rida, was a lawyer at the National Courts in Alexandria. In later life he helped found Rabitat al-Islah al-Ijtimaʿi (The Social Reform League), which his daughter, then a grown woman, joined. ʿAzizah attended the school of Notre Dame de Sion in Alexandria. At sixteen she married Muhammad Husayn Haykal, to whom she had been betrothed since the age of nine. Her husband belonged to the progressive al-Jaridah group and was later a prominent member of the Liberal Constitutionalist Party. Haykal is well known as the author of *Zaynab*, a novel whose protagonist is a young peasant woman from the Delta. An early advocate of women's advance, Haykal went on to become an adviser to the Egyptian Feminist Union. ʿAzizah Haykal, like others of her class, frequently traveled to Europe with her husband. In France in 1927, she joined her husband in attending a state reception for King Fu'ad, the first time an Egyptian woman had been present at an official gathering. At the end of her life, looking back on her marriage to one of the early advocates of women's liberation, ʿAzizah Haykal confessed that her liberal husband "evolved after his marriage" when it came to "putting into practice his advanced ideas about women's behavior," and she let her role in this evolution be known.[31]

Bahigah Rashid, another early member, was born in 1900 in Cairo. Her father, Mahmud Sidqi, was an engineer and irrigation inspector who moved his family around the country in the course of his work. Bahigah was of Turkish ancestry on her mother's side; her maternal great-grandfather had come to Egypt with Muhammad ʿAli. She attended American schools in Luxor and Asyut, completing her education at the American College for Girls in Cairo. She took her secondary school diploma in 1919, the year of the revolution, and later she recalled her nationalist fervor as a schoolgirl. It was at this time that she first heard the name Huda Shaʿrawi. In 1919, Bahiga married Hasan Ahmad Rashid, who had been sent to school in England at fourteen and who completed his studies at the University of Durham. She and her husband resided in Cairo, but the two also spent considerable time at the family estate in the Delta where she opened a dispensary for the peasants on the family land and organized lessons in sewing and hygiene for women. Joining the EFU in 1925, she took a special interest in work for married teachers, the rehabilitation of prostitutes, and political rights for women.

Ihsan al-Qusi, the youngest of the charter members, was born in Asyut in 1895 into a family of religious scholars.[32] Her father was Shaykh Ahmad ʿAli al-Qusi, and her mother, Fatma ʿAli al-Laythi, was the daughter of Shaykh ʿAli al-Laythi, poet laureate to Khedive Ismaʿil. Ihsan attended the Pressly Memorial Institute for Girls in Asyut. After finishing primary school, she continued her education with private tutors at home and recalls reading books from her father's library. At the age of fourteen she lost her father, who had encouraged the education of his only child. After she married a few years later she resumed her formal education. Al-Qusi combined a long career in education with a lifelong commitment to feminism. She served for many years as the Arabic secretary of the EFU and was one of its ablest speakers in Arabic.[33]

Saiza Nabarawi, the daughter of Muhammad Murad and Fatma Hanim, was born in 1897 at the Minshawi Palace in the Qurashiyah district of Cairo, where her father was employed. Originally called Zaynab Muhammad Murad, she was raised by a childless cousin of her mother, ʿAdilah Nabarawi, and her husband, Ibrahim Nabarawi, who changed her name to Saiza Nabarawi. Saiza's maternal great-grandfather, ʿAbd Allah Pasha al-Injlizi, was an English convert to Islam who had come to Egypt in the middle of the nineteenth century to help build the new railway. Her stepmother's grandfather Ibrahim Nabarawi had accompanied one of the first missions of medical students to Paris, where he married an Irishwoman who was the daughter of one of his professors. Saiza's stepmother's mother was a Frenchwoman. As a child Saiza was taken to Paris, where her stepparents lived. She attended the Institut Saint Germain-des-Prés and later the Lycée de Versailles. In 1913 her stepmother committed suicide because of troubles with her husband, who was an alcoholic and gambler. The fifteen-year-old Saiza was sent back to Egypt, where she learned that ʿAdilah was not her real mother. This traumatic discovery combined with culture shock to cause her considerable agony. She went to live with her maternal grandfather, Amin Pasha ʿAbd Allah, and his wife, Kami Hanim, although her father exercised authority over her. When her father found her wearing a hat, a garment that was not only insufficiently modest but was also associated with Christians and Westerners, he ordered her to put on the veil. She shut herself in her room for several days, refusing to go out until Huda Shaʿrawi, her late stepmother's close friend, brought her a veil and persuaded her to wear it. Nabarawi was sent as a boarder to Notre Dame de Sion in Alexandria and remained there until 1915. She later wished to enroll in the French law school but her father would not allow it. Her father continued to exercise a restraining influence over her until his death in 1922. Meanwhile, her late stepmother's friend Huda Shaʿrawi provided a more liberal influence in her life. The year after her father's death, Saiza Nabarawi, then twenty-six, became a member of the EFU. Two years later she assumed the editorship of the EFU's new French-language journal, *L'Egyptienne*. She was to remain Shaʿrawi's closest feminist collaborator and a highly articulate exponent of feminism.[34]

Fikriyah Husni, an honorary founding member, was born in the 1890s into a middle-class family in Minya in Upper Egypt, where she received her primary school education. She completed her education at the Saniyah School in Cairo. Her father, a member of the Nationalist Party, introduced her to the world of politics at an early age. As a young student, Husni met the charismatic leader of the National Party, Mustafa Kamil, whom she heard speak at meetings. Husni marched in the 1919 demonstrations and attended the meeting at the Cathedral of St. Mark, becoming an active member of the WWCC. In Minya, where she worked as a primary school teacher, she created a WWCC branch. In the mid-1920s, she returned to Cairo to become principal of the ʿAbbas Primary School for Girls. Husni was active in the EFU's social service projects. In 1926 she was a member of the EFU delegation to the IWSA congress in Paris. At the end of the 1920s she took up a teaching post at the Helwan Women Teachers' Training School.[35]

The EFU expanded considerably in the early years and by 1929 claimed 250 members. There was a monthly meeting for the general membership, whose approval was sought on all important issues, but the routine work was done by the executive board of twenty, which met weekly. The president, Huda Shaʿrawi, along with spearheading the creation of the EFU and being its chief financial patron, took the lead in initiating policy and formulating positions. She was able to mobilize women, but her need to be at the forefront eventually caused some of the other strong-minded members to concentrate their energies within other organizations, while still remaining loyal to the EFU agenda. There were three categories of activists: those who participated in the regular work of the movement; those who rallied round at critical moments or took part in special events; and those who supported the feminist movement by pioneering as "firsts," and through their professions and voluntary associations.

"The House of the Woman"

The EFU convened meetings at Huda Shaʿrawi's house for the first nine years. In 1924, the EFU rented quarters in al-Baghalah in the working-class district of Sayyidah Zaynab where they installed a dispensary for poor mothers and children.[36] Soon a center for instruction in domestic arts and a handicrafts workshop called Dar al-Taʿawun al-Islahi (The House of Cooperative Reform) were installed in the same premises. Meanwhile, in 1925, the EFU Club was started "for the restoration and diffusion of high intellectual and artistic culture." This was a continuation of the still new tradition of women's intellectual associations.[37]

In 1932, the EFU centralized its operations when it opened its large new building complex in Qasr al-ʿAyni Street, which became the official headquarters. When people began calling it the "House of the Woman," the EFU decided to inscribe this name on the building's facade. There was such an outcry, however, that the matter was dropped. Saiza Nabarawi wrote wryly: "To affix the secret name, "Woman," on a building in public view! To announce openly that this creature has a social existence, has an integrity, a personality, and has ceased to be a chrysalis of collective anonymity, oh!"[38] Merely acquiring the building had been a feat. In 1927, the government granted 3,600 square meters to the EFU with a pledge to subsidize the building costs. But when the feminists criticized the repressive measures of Ismaʿil Sidqi, who became prime minister in 1931, the pledge was not honored.[39] EFU members saved the day by raising their own money. Fund-raising techniques included subscriptions, donations, and annual charity galas. Women themselves gave generously in the subscription drive. Aminah Hanim Afandi, Huda Shaʿrawi, and Mary Kahil headed the list of benefactors. Under the Islamic inheritance law in Egypt, which applied to both Muslims and Christians, women inherited in their own right—although a daughter inherited half as much as a son—and they were granted full control over their assets. The ability to generate money through fund-raising events and private donations, along with the perennial financial support of the EFU president, enabled the feminist organization to build its new headquarters and expand its operations—and indeed to sustain its entire movement.[40] The inauguration of the new premises in 1932 confirmed the importance for the feminist movement of political and economic independence. Then young singer and later famous Umm Kalthum—who had performed at the EFU fund-raising galas—sang during the two-day celebrations.[41]

"A house of its own" both symbolized EFU success and made possible an expansion of activities. The new building housed administrative offices, conference rooms, an auditorium, a library, and, later, club facilities for the members and visitors. The dispensary for poor mothers and children was relocated to the building. The crafts workshop for girls was absorbed into the new Ecole Professionelle et Ménagère, which also offered training in domestic science and commercial education.[42] Saiza Nabarawi declared that the new Professional and Domestic School would help create "a conscious [female] working class, which at the moment does not exist, and which Egypt greatly needs in the task of social reconstruction underway."[43]

The auditorium served for public lectures and as a meeting space for young women. The EFU announced that its center "would offer the warmest welcome to foreign feminists passing through Egypt . . . to put into practice the spirit of feminist cooperation."[44] There was ample room to house future projects as well, such as the Dar al-Hadanah, the daycare center for the children of working mothers, which opened in 1946. By bringing women of varied backgrounds together under the same roof EFU members hoped to lessen the distance between women of different classes.[45]

In the late 1930s, the EFU, as part of an effort to extend its activities into the provinces, began projects in Upper Egypt. The feminist organization wanted to establish regional committees to provide information on health and child-care needs of rural Egyptians.[46] In 1937, Huda Shaʿrawi founded dispensaries in Sharq, Samalut, and Zawiyat al-Amwat, villages in her Upper Egyptian ancestral province of Minya, near the provincial capital. The EFU president also founded a school for girls and boys in Zawiyat al-Amwat. In 1944, the EFU set up a branch in the city of Minya, but it was short-lived.

In the mid 1930s, the EFU reached out to the rising generation. New recruits from the upper and the upper middle class formed the Shaqiqat, under the aegis of the EFU in 1933. Most were graduates of the first state high schools for girls: the Shubra Secondary School for Girls and the Girls' College in Zamalek. The president of the Shaqiqat was Hawwa' Idris, a Circassian cousin of Huda Shaʿrawi (the daughter of her maternal uncle Ahmad Idris and his wife Hafsah), born in Turkey in 1919. Orphaned at an early age, Hawwa' and her young sister Hurriyah were brought to Cairo in 1924 to be raised by their elder cousin, Huda Shaʿrawi. Hawwa' Idris attended the American College for six years before transferring to the Girls' College in Zamalek, graduating in 1935.[47] Other members of the Shaqiqat included Aminah al-Saʿid, the Arabic secretary, Surayya ʿAli, the French secretary, Hurriyah Idris, ʿAzimah al-Saʿid, Suhayr al-Qalamawi, Sharifah Lutfi, and Aminah Hamzah.[48] The Shaqiqat mainly engaged in voluntary social service projects in Cairo and did not as a group develop a wider sphere of action. Neither they nor the EFU exploited their full potential. The Shaqiqat lasted as a group until May 1941 when some of them became regular members of the EFU. Although short-lived as an institution, the Shaqiqat left a legacy of individuals who contributed to the cause of women in ways we shall explore in succeeding chapters.[49]

Most progressive men who had argued for women's liberation during the period of colonial occupation had shifted their attention to their own political and professional careers following independence, but a number of sympathetic men were supportive from behind the scenes. Shaʿrawi and other EFU members exploited their contacts among men in high places to acquire information and lobby for their cause. In 1929 the EFU invited a group of professionals, mainly lawyers and educators, to act as advisers to the organization. They included Murad Sid Ahmad, royal counselor and soon to be minister of education; Muhammad Fahmi al-Amrusi, inspector of education; Ahmad Lutfi al-Sayyid, rector of Fu'ad I University; Taha Husayn, university dean and professor of Arabic literature; Mansur Fahmi, assistant dean of the university's Faculty of Letters; Shaykh Mustafa ʿAbd al-Razik, university professor of philosophy; Muhammad Husayn Haykal, writer and politician; Antun Jumayyil, secretary of the Committee of Finances in the Ministry of Finance; Ibrahim Halbawi, lawyer and politician; Zaki ʿAli, a lawyer; and Dr. Shurbagi, gynecologist; Dr. Shahin, director of the Department of Health.[50]

L'Egyptienne

In 1925, two years after its creation, the EFU founded a monthly journal in French called *L'Egyptienne* (The Egyptian woman), the first explicitly feminist journal in Egypt.[51] It was also the first and last feminist journal in French.[52] The names of the EFU journals, along with Balsam ʿAbd al-Malak's *al-Mar'ah al-Misriyah*, signified a shift from titles connoting gender alone (such as *The Young Woman* or *The Gentle Sex*) to those foregrounding gender and nationality.

L'Egyptienne: revue mensuelle politique, féminisme, sociologie-art (The Egyptian woman: Monthly review of politics, feminism, and sociology-art) ran from February 1925 through April 1940. In using French *L'Egyptienne* was targeting an upper-class and upper-middle-class readership in Egypt. The EFU also aimed, for both feminist and nationalist reasons, to reach the international feminist community. The EFU leadership—specifically Huda Shaʿrawi and Saiza Nabarawi, who both regularly contributed to the journal—were unable to write in Arabic; other upper-class women, and many upper-middle-class women educated in foreign schools, were unable to read Arabic. Mass meetings, however, were conducted in Arabic, while Shaʿrawi and other EFU members also spoke publicly in Arabic.

Feminists used *L'Egyptienne* to foster international feminist exchange. In 1935 at the IAW conference in Istanbul *L'Egyptienne*'s editor called the journal "a link in understanding and harmony between our sisters of the East and West."[53] *L'Egyptienne* countered negative images in the West of Egyptian women, and hence of Egypt.[54] Huda Shaʿrawi, in a 1929 public lecture at the American University in Cairo, told her audience: "We found it necessary to put before the eyes of European public opinion a true picture of the Egyptian woman, one other than that presented by writers who have gathered a mass of erroneous information on the Orient. The only way to attack this was to create a women's journal in a European language."[55] In using French EFU feminists could not directly reach a wider base in Egypt and the region. On the other hand, because the EFU employed French, not the language of the majority, their movement was less threatening to adversaries.[56] In 1930, when the EFU celebrated the fifth anniversary of the journal, actor Bahija Hafiz personified *L'Egyptienne* in a *tableau vivant*, declaring: "Although I am a descendant of the pharaohs I am young. That is my strength. For I possess a faith in myself and in the future of my country that can only perform miracles. If I express myself in French it is because I am the messenger of the Egyptian cause on all continents. Wherever I go I spread the truth. My concern for justice elevates me above all parties. That is why I am loved and respected everywhere. Before me all opinions give way because my ideal of regeneration rests in a profoundly social task whose foundations are equity and fraternity."[57]

In using French the EFU also appropriated the new feminist terminology, beginning with the term *feminism* itself. The term feminism had been generated in France in the 1880s; thus elsewhere in Europe and in North America it was also a borrowed term. Wherever it surfaced it acquired a culture-specific constellation of meanings. The term became current in the United States only a decade before it was used in Egypt, so Egyptian and American feminists were formulating their discrete interpretations of feminism nearly simultaneously. Feminism never was or could be monolithic. It never was or could be exclusively Western.

L'Egyptienne was printed by Paul Barbey, the director of the press at the French Institute of Archaeology in Cairo. It sold in Egypt for five piasters an issue, or sixty piasters for a year's subscription, and abroad for an annual subscription of seventy-five piasters. At the time, five piasters for a journal was not inexpensive. The EFU's Arabic journal founded twelve years later sold for one milleme, which was a tenth of a piaster, and the journal Nabawiyah Musa founded the same year cost one piaster. The journal was not supported by circulation. Some revenue accrued from advertising, but most of the financing came from the personal funds of Shaʿrawi.[58]

Saiza Nabarawi served as the editor of *L'Egyptienne* for its entire fifteen years.[59] Huda Shaʿrawi wrote mainly on nationalist questions and Saiza Nabarawi on feminist issues. Jeanne Marques (a Frenchwoman settled in Egypt) served as a salaried editor, dealing with literature and art as well as news from abroad.[60]

As the organ of the EFU-led movement *L'Egyptienne* publicized the work of the organization and articulated its stand on a wide range of issues. The cover of *L'Egyptienne* portrayed a city woman in an ʿabayah, a long all-enveloping wrap, pulling the veil away from her face while a small veiled figure in the background strode toward her, symbolizing a process still underway.[61] A regular opening feature called "Hors-texte" comprised a portrait of a prominent woman, who might be Egyptian or foreign, either Eastern or Western. These portraits—which first appeared before photographs of Egyptian women became usual in the press—gave women public visibility and recognition.[62] Men were also occasionally cited. The inaugural issue of *L'Egyptienne* published the portrait of Aminah Hanim Afandi, wife of the late khedive Tawfiq and mother of the ex-khedive ʿAbbas Hilmi, a woman of legendary generosity known as "The Mother of Benefactors." The pantheon included Egyptian feminists, writers, lawyers, educators, the first woman pilot, and other royal women. Among the foreign women were several members of the International Alliance of Women. The achievements of women were also brought to notice in other sections of the journal, especially "Echos d'Orient" and "Glanes," which circulated news of women from other Arab countries, from other Eastern countries, particularly Turkey and India, and from the West. Not only were living, or recently living, women presented, but those of the more distant past were honored. There were many women of attainments, including the politically powerful, culled from Egyptian and Islamic history to serve as models for the present.[63]

Along with EFU pronouncements and positions on feminist and nationalist issues were contributions of broader cultural interest. This appears to have been part of a strategy to attract a wide readership. Contributors included both women and men, Egyptians, other Arabs, and Europeans (mainly French). Egyptian women included journalist and feminist Fatma Niʿmat Rashid, active in Arabic- and French-language journalism in the 1930s, who wrote for *L'Egyptienne* from 1933 to 1937. She instituted the feature, "Notre Enquête" (Our inquiry), soliciting the views of prominent men on Egyptian women and on feminism. Duriyah Shafiq, a protégé of Huda Shaʿrawi, contributed pieces including an extract from her minor thesis for the Sorbonne entitled "L'art pour l'art en Egypte antique" (Art for art's sake in ancient Egypt).[64] Teacher Duriyah Fahmi and Princess Qadriyah Husayn wrote on ancient Egypt.

Among the non-Egyptian Arab women contributors was the Lebanese poet and writer Mayy Ziyadah; ʿAsmah Zafir, a poet (a great-granddaughter of the Algerian nationalist Amir ʿAbd al-Qadir exiled to Syria); Nelly Zananiri, a novelist of Syrian Christian origin and vice president of L'Association des écrivains de langue française en Egypte (The Association of Writers in the French Language in Egypt, established in 1936);[65] and novelist Amy Kher, also of Lebanese Christian origin.[66] Haghir al-Asqalani reviewed French and English books.

The men who contributed to *L'Egyptienne* included EFU adviser Muhammad Husayn Haykal; Muhammad Aflatun, a member of the Arabic Academy (and father of future feminist Inji Aflatun), who wrote on the Arabic language; and Ahmad Fikri, who wrote on Islamic and French art. ʿUthman Sabri discussed the literature of Arab Spain. Ahmad Shafiq and Ahmad Zaki contributed historical articles. Sociologist ʿAli ʿAbd al-Wahid Wafi wrote on female infanticide in pre-Islamic Arabia and on slavery. University professors of Egyptology Salim Hasan and Sami Jabra wrote on women in ancient Egyptian life and art. Men also published poems. The list included Egypt's "Prince of Poets," Ahmad Shawqi, and those of lesser stature such as Muhammad Zulfiqar, Teo Akad, and Foulad Yeghen. Emil Mosseri, editor of the Jewish journal *L'aurore* (published in Cairo) and Prince Haydar Fazil were occasional contributors.

A common language opened lines of communication between the Egyptian feminists and Frenchwomen; indeed, the pages of *L'Egyptienne* give testimony to the links that existed between them.[67] However, *L'Egyptienne* was not a forum for French feminists, who were busy with their campaigns at home. *L'Egyptienne*'s readers were rarely introduced to such French feminists as activist and lawyer Maria Verone and Avril de Sainte-Croix, president of the Conseil national des femmes françaises (National Council of Frenchwomen) and a campaigner against legalized prostitution in France. The Frenchwomen contributing to the journal were romantics and adventurers: journalists, writers, and poets who often wrote on women and whose feminist interests, if they existed, were probably more focused on the condition of the women they saw abroad than on their sisters at home. These women included Marcelle Tinayre, a well-known novelist and traveler in Egypt and Turkey;[68] Alice La Mazière, a journalist; Alice Guibon Poulleau, who traveled and wrote in Eastern countries; and Myriam Harry, a visitor to Egypt who had earlier met Nazli Fazil in Tunisia and who had interviewed Shaʿrawi and Nabarawi for her book *Les derniers harems*.[69] Marcelle Capy (sister of Jeanne Marques), a journalist, novelist, and author of *L'Amour-Roi*—which advocated pacifism and universal brother- and sisterhood—published short stories and articles on work for women.

Al-Misriyah

In order to communicate more directly with a wider segment of the population and with other Arabs in the national language the EFU created *al-Misriyah* (The Egyptian Woman). In her introductory editorial on February 15, 1937, Shaʿrawi announced that *al-Misriyah* was addressed to

> the leaders of opinion in Egypt and brother Arab states, scientists, men of religious law, journalists, poets, writers, and litterateurs. To reformers and to productive persons in our country, legislators, educators, economists, and various professionals. To the men of politics who are guiding the radar of our affairs and sitting in the seat of government in our country and who are responsible for the well-being of the nation and observation of security and peace. To the youth upon whose ethics and genius we place our hopes. To the Egyptian employee, to the worker, to the peasant on whose activity, sincerity, integrity and proficiency depends the prosperity of Egypt and its advancement. To the woman active in her home, factory, and field. To the good wife in her palace and her hut. To the wise mother under whose guidance the child grows up and matures and at whose feet the devoted child finds paradise. . . . To all the sons and daughters of my country, religion, language, and race I introduce *Al-Majallah al-Misriyah* in its wonderful national dress.[70]

Al-Misriyah employed a different gender iconography. The cover portrayed a peasant woman symbolizing the Egyptian woman and the Arab woman and signaling the intent to widen the class base of the feminist movement. There was no sign of the urban veil. The unveiled woman was the quintessential Egyptian and Arab woman, the culturally authentic woman, and unveiled peasant women were the majority. Nabarawi explained that *al-Misriyah* "aims to elevate the intellectual and moral level of the masses and create lines of solidarity among the different classes of the nation. . . .

Al-Misriyah will be a *minbar* (pulpit) for feminist demands and the tongue of the most noble nationalist hopes.[71] *Al-Misriyah*'s masthead bore the Islamic motto "*Khudhu nisf dinkum ᶜan hadhihi al-humayrah*" (Take half of your religion from ᶜA'ishah). Meaning to signal the compatibility of feminism and Islam, making feminism more accessible to the Muslim majority, it placed Christians on the outside.[72] Despite the symbolism *al-Misriyah* operated mainly as the secular journal of a secular movement; Christians continued to be part of the EFU-led movement, and indeed *al-Misriyah*'s second (and longest-tenured) editor was a Copt.

Al-Misriyah appeared bimonthly (twice as often as *L'Egyptienne*) and was widely accessible at the cost of one milleme, or one-tenth of a piaster, per issue. The new journal expressed and facilitated the opening out of Egyptian feminism within the Arab region. During its three and a half years, *al-Misriyah* had two editors, who worked independently of the editors of *L'Egyptienne*. Fatma Niᶜmat Rashid, who had contributed to *L'Egyptienne*, served as the first editor, stepping down after eight months over differences with the EFU leadership.[73] She was succeeded by a feminist of the new generation, Eva Habib al-Masri, a Copt from Asyut and the first Egyptian woman to graduate from the American University in Cairo (1931).[74] Al-Masri took a master's degree in sociology at Smith College in 1934.[75]

Al-Misriyah, like its French counterpart, dealt with nationalist, feminist, and social/cultural matters. By the time *al-Misriyah* appeared, the EFU's nationalist focus was directed toward Palestine and pan-Arab unity. EFU feminists had shifted from being more purely ideologically suffragist to being more militantly suffragist. With *al-Misriyah* the EFU more comprehensively addressed issues of everyday concern to a broader constituency of middle-class women.

The contributors to *al-Misriyah* were mostly Egyptian women and men whose usual language was Arabic, and who had predominantly an Egyptian-Arab cultural and educational formation. *Al-Misriyah*'s contributors were more numerous and more various than those of *L'Egyptienne*. Among *al-Misriyah*'s women writers were Bint al-Shati', born ᶜA'ishah ᶜAbd al-Rahman, who was a student of Arabic literature at the university when she began contributing to the EFU journal;[76] Jamilah al-ᶜAla'ili, a member of the Apollo school of romantic poets that emerged in the 1930s; Kawkab Hifni Nasif, one of the first women doctors, and a sister of Bahithat al-Badiyah; Naᶜimah al-Ayyubi, the first woman to graduate from Cairo University in law (1933), who was studying at the School of Social Work at the University of Liège in Belgium and reading for a higher degree in law when she wrote for *al-Misriyah*;[77] Sumayya Fahmi, a psychologist who became head of the Maᶜhad al-Tarbiyat lil-Banat (Institute for the Education of Girls); Nafisah al-Ghamrawi, a specialist in physical education and a licensed pilot who later became director of the Maᶜhad al-Tarbiyah al-Riyadiyah lil-Banat (Institute of Physical Education for Girls); Karimah al-Saᶜid, an educator and future deputy minister of education; and Munirah Thabit, lawyer and journalist. Contributions from women such as these were testimony to the considerable gains made by Egyptian women since the days when *L'Egyptienne* had first begun, twelve years earlier.

The men who wrote for *al-Misriyah* came from classes and sectors of society representing a range of views from progressive to traditionalist Islamic. Among the secular liberals were Muhammad Husayn Haykal, Muhammad ʿAli ʿAllubah, and Bahi al-Din Barakat, who were all EFU advisers; Hafiz ʿAfifi, ambassador, politician, and writer; Fikri Abazah, a journalist; ʿAbd al-Razzaq Sanhuri, a leading jurist and distinguished constitutional lawyer; and Majd al-Din Hifni Nasif, brother of Bahithat al-Badiyah, who was a lawyer and a socialist.[78] Contributors among Islamic traditionalists included Shaykh Shafaʿi Labban, a *qadi* (judge) in the shariʿah courts; Muhammad Jad al-Mulla, a member of the Arabic Academy and a teacher of ethics at Dar al-ʿUlum; and Hasan Ibrahim Hasan a professor of Islamic history at Cairo University.

Egypt's men of letters who contributed to *al-Misriyah* included writers Mahmud Taymur, ʿAbbas al-ʿAqqad, and Ibrahim al-Mazini; and established poets such as Ahmad Shawqi, Hafiz Ibrahim, and Khalil Mutran, as well as the younger men of the Apollo group, including Ahmad Zaki Abu Shadi, Muhammad al-Harawi, Ibrahim Najdi, Hasan Kamil al-Sirafi, Mukhtar Wakil, and Sudanese Mustafa al-Tinai. Other contributors were Ahmad Rami, who wrote poetry in colloquial Egyptian Arabic and later composed songs for Umm Kalthum; Kamil al-Tilmisani, a leader in the surrealist movement in art and poetry; and Kamil Kilani, who translated books from European languages into Arabic and founded a press for children's books. The work of men associated with the theater appeared in *al-Misriyah*, such as Tawfiq al-Hakim's play *al-Jins al-Latif* (The gentle sex), performed for the first time at the EFU auditorium, and Muhammad Khurshid's *Masiruhum ilayna* (Their destiny is ours). Zaki Tulaymat, who later established the Institute of Dramatic Arts, and ʿAbd al-Hamid Yunus, a student of Egyptian folklore and later director of the Center for Folklore, also wrote for the journal. Although now known as a seminal Islamist ideologue, Sayyid Qutb (he joined the Society of Muslim Brothers around 1950) during his secular phase as a young writer and critic published poetry in *al-Misriyah*.[79] A list of contributors as varied as these attests to the openness of *al-Misriyah* and the willingness of a wide cross section of society to air their views in a feminist journal.

The gender messages *al-Misriyah* sent were contradictory. This was an inevitable outcome of the policy to accept contributions from such a wide range of people. It might have been the result of a conscious attempt to mix progressive feminist messages with more conservative opinion, thereby attracting a wider readership. Such a symbiosis of views in the pages of a single journal in the late 1930s would not be possible at the end of the century. The contradictions and odd juxtapositions within the EFU-led movement allowed for choices in an age taken up with experimentation but not yet heavily riven by ideological polarization. The EFU and its journals both enabled and expressed the possibilities and contradictions of the feminist experiment. They are also testimony to a complex and vibrant feminist culture.

The two organs of the EFU ceased publication in 1940 at the beginning of the Second World War. *L'Egyptienne* had served the feminist movement for fifteen years and *al-Misriyah* for three and a half years. They were never revived.

The International Connection

The EFU joined the International Woman Suffrage Alliance in 1923, when the organization changed its name to the International Alliance of Women for Suffrage and Equal Citizenship (IAW) and the first year that feminist organizations from outside the West became members. The Women's Indian Association, the Jewish Women's Equal Rights Association from Palestine, and an association from Japan also joined the IAW at this time. IAW members included colonizers and the colonized. The national concerns of women from colonized countries clashed in serious ways with the prevailing international feminism. This clash, as I have noted, was muted by the Western feminist leadership. Eastern feminists at times "ignored" the clash; at other times they contested it, as we shall see in succeeding chapters.

How could the IAW be a sisterhood of equal members when some women were from colonizing countries and others from colonized countries? How could women from colonized countries possibly gain suffrage before gaining national independence? What about Western feminists' racial attitudes and stereotypes? If, as some British suffragists had earlier argued, obtaining the vote would enable women to be better citizens of the empire, would they now use their votes to uphold empire? IAW women from the colonizing countries did not advance a colonial critique. The feminism of members from colonized countries was inextricable from their nationalism; they simultaneously sought national and gender self-determination. IAW feminism also could not respond to those feminisms which emerged in nations without countries, such as certain ethnic groups from the former Russian and Austro-Hungarian monarchies. Because membership in the IAW was country-based, many eastern European national feminist groups, such as the Ukrainians in the new Soviet Union, could not affiliate with the international feminist body. Although African and Asian countries were under Western colonial rule, they were deemed countries, not colonial territories, and therefore were eligible for IAW membership. Both colonial hierarchies and anticolonial contestation were manifest in the IAW arena.

The IAW, which continued to be dominated mainly by western European and American women, chose to ignore the colonial realities in the interest of advancing their idealized universal sisterhood. The IAW Women's Charter affirmed "self-government in the state" but did not affirm the right of self-government of states. The charter demanded gender equality in suffrage but did not confront the issue of political repression of both sexes in countries under colonialism.[80] By ignoring colonial realities it subverted the idea of universal feminism. The IAW in the 1920s, 1930s, and 1940s comprised national feminisms and imperial feminisms under the umbrella of international feminism.

In 1923 Margery Corbett Ashby from Britain succeeded American Carrie Chapman Catt as president of the IAW and remained president until 1946. Her tenure coincided with Shaʿrawi's years in the organization. Although Shaʿrawi and Corbett Ashby worked out a modus vivendi and could be mutually supportive, both felt the underlying tension deriving from their different "positionings." In the eye of the other, Corbett Ashby was an imperialist and Shaʿrawi was a fiery nationalist. Shaʿrawi attended all seven IAW congresses held during her time. Only one of these convened outside Europe, the 1935 congress in Istanbul. The Egyptians had been eager to host a congress, but this never happened. Corbett Ashby termed this impossible for "larger" political reasons. The EFU opposed the continuing British military presence in Egypt and came out against the Anglo-Egyptian treaty of 1936; they took a strong stand against British imperialism and Zionist expansion in Palestine. After the Second World War when the IAW was looking for a venue for its first postwar congress, Corbett Ashby told Catt in a private letter: "Then we thought of accepting the invitation to hold a Congress in Egypt which would have many advantages because it is after all the women of the Near and Middle East who most need the equality work of the Alliance. But recent events in Egypt make it look as if we should be very unwise to plan to go there, especially as the President of our Society, Mme Charaoui, is such a very violent nationalist."[81] Here we see a clear—but not public—declaration of how imperial interests overrode gender interests.

Yet despite fundamental divisions and difficult problems there was also common ground deriving from gender. It was evident from the many fond memories of Saiza Nabarawi half a century later that there had been a sisterly camaraderie among IAW women that was sustained, if sometimes strained, that an international feminist culture had worked at some levels for its members, enabling them to transcend the divisions imposed by national and imperial patriarchal cultures. It was this global sisterhood to which Corbett Ashby paid homage when she returned to Egypt half a century later to celebrate the EFU's fiftieth anniversary.

IAW feminism worked best for Egyptians during the 1920s. But as the 1930s progressed, tensions between the colonized and the colonizers increasingly surfaced. The universalist dimension of IAW feminism was rent as nationalist feminisms asserted themselves in the context of particular events in Europe and the Middle East. As Mineke Bosch observes, "The international suffragists [the IAW] never fully came to accept that not all women are the same and not all women want the same things, or that in fact all such concepts as difference, unity, equality, and sameness are full of complexities which need constant consideration."[82]

From the late 1930s, the EFU moved increasingly toward consolidating a regional feminism—that is, pan-Arab feminism. This development was linked to intensifying Arab nationalisms. The EFU played a major role in the creation of the Arab Feminist Union (AFU), which was officially inaugurated in 1945. While relations remained cordial between the EFU and the IAW, the feminist fulcrum had now shifted from the international to the regional arena.

• CHAPTER 6 •

City Sisters, Country Sisters

DURING its first year the EFU began programs for poor women. Some members conducted social service within the framework of the EFU, while others operated through benevolent societies where they worked alongside women who did not identify with feminism.[1] During the 1920s, 1930s, and 1940s, upper-class women continued to play roles in society through voluntary social service, which remained the major outlet available to upper-class women of ambition and energy who wished to make a mark in public. Middle-class women were freer to experiment. Those inclined to do something less daunting than forging new careers engaged in voluntary social service. While not the founders, administrators, and financiers of the long-lived major secular philanthropies, middle-class women led in professionalizing social service at the end of the 1930s and in the early 1940s, in shaping the new field of social work.

An explicit feminist agenda separated the EFU's approach to social service from that of the philanthropic associations. The feminists contended that alleviating the hardships of poor women was a first step toward creating conditions that would make it more possible for them to gain their full rights as women. However distant such a feminist utopia might be and however limited their means, the EFU possessed a vision.

Feminists and philanthropists directed attention to urban women in the 1920s, but in the 1930s they turned to the needs of both women and men in the villages, where gender segregation was not part of everyday life.

The House of Cooperative Reform

In 1924 the EFU sent a public crier through the streets and lanes of the popular quarter of Sayyidah Zaynab to announce the opening of its new medical dispensary for women and children in al-Baghalah. The feminists located their facility near a major shrine, the tomb of Sayyidah Zaynab, a daughter of the Prophet, where women brought their supplications.[2] The new clinic soon attracted women from the nearby neighborhoods, as well as other quarters of Cairo, and even from the outskirts.

The administration of the EFU dispensary began under the direction of a Japanese woman; the widow of Ahmad Fadli, her own name is missing from the record. A team of male doctors including Sami Kamil, Salim Sabri, ʿAbd al-Halim Waffa, Tawfiq Najjar, and Husayn Jamali examined patients free of charge. Different days were set aside for specialized examinations.[3]

Assisting the doctors were women volunteers such as Hawwa' Idris, then a schoolgirl, who worked at the dispensary during her weekly recess from boarding school. She used to explain the doctors' instructions to patients while handing out medicines.[4] Some volunteers visited homes, instructing women in basic hygiene and health practices. At a 1926 EFU meeting Shaʿrawi appealed for more dispensary volunteers, indicating a shortage of helping hands in what was still a new arena for most women.[5]

In their annual reports the doctors at the EFU clinic exposed the alarming health problems of the poor, especially chronically high maternal and child mortality. There was also a high incidence of venereal disease, particularly syphilis, among the women[6]—data that the EFU used later in their fight against prostitution. Although women flocked to the dispensary in large numbers, there were many who stayed away. Social taboos made women reluctant to see male doctors, especially for gynecological examinations.[7]

Through the operations of the dispensary in al-Baghalah, EFU women observed at close hand the effects of dire poverty on women, especially divorcées and widows without regular means of support. The EFU decided to start a workshop for handicraft training to help needy women earn money. The women themselves rejected the opportunity, probably because they were already far too overstretched in their daily lives. But they offered their daughters instead, saying, "They will learn better than us."[8] The EFU took over rooms adjacent to the dispensary and opened a workshop for girls, calling it the House of Cooperative Reform. Its program served a dual purpose: it taught girls sewing, embroidery, and weaving, and at the same time provided instruction in basic health and hygiene. When they completed their training, the girls were awarded certificates recognizing their achievement.[9] Thus, by its second year, the EFU had set a precedent in operating both a dispensary and a workshop under the same roof. Huda Shaʿrawi hoped the EFU model would be replicated by others in different quarters of Cairo.

To meet the enormous needs of the poor, the EFU was anxious to enlarge its operations. We have just seen in the previous chapter how the feminist organization raised its own money to build new facilities, enabling the feminists to expand their social service program. In 1932 when the new headquarters in Qasr al-ʿAyni Street was completed, the EFU installed its dispensary and workshop, which now became part of the new Professional and Domestic School. In a preview of the program Saiza Nabarawi announced: "It will teach poor girls not only all kinds of handiwork but also cooking, washing, ironing, that is, whatever will help them to become excellent housekeepers. Those wishing to earn their livelihood would be able after three years of apprenticeship to be placed as children's nursemaids, maids, cooks, or workers in clothing workshops. Those accepted among the pupils finishing their elementary studies can take courses in hygiene, child care, moral formation, domestic economy, and civics. Above all our goal is to form women members of the working class conscious of responsibility for their own existence."[10] During the third year girls specialized in a branch of domestic science or studied typing and accounting to prepare for work in a business office. Although Nabarawi rhapsodized about the "female solidarity" that the program would create across the classes, the training school was clearly meant to help women *within* their respective classes. Still, it was something.

The State Follows

Women's private initiative had begun projects that the government had yet to undertake. In 1927, three years after the EFU opened its original dispensary, the government set up a Section for the Protection of Childhood in the Department of Public Health, a department that did not become a ministry until 1936. With the creation of this section, the government assumed some of the tasks the EFU and women's philanthropic societies had undertaken, such as offering instruction in maternal and child health and hygiene, and establishing dispensaries for women and children. The government also expanded training opportunities in midwifery and nursing.

By the end of 1927, the government had opened child-care centers in two popular quarters of Cairo, Bulaq and Darb al-Ahmar, and had set up a mobile unit to serve the poor in Gizah, then on the city's outskirts.[11] Saiza Nabarawi visited the child-care center in Darb al-Ahmar in the old city and, on behalf of the EFU, applauded the government initiatives.[12] While continuing to advocate state intervention the EFU also pressed for the expansion of private efforts, especially in the delivery of maternal and child health care to the provinces.[13] By 1944 there were forty-nine government-run child-care centers in Egypt, but many more were needed.

Feminism and Philanthropy

The two major women's philanthropies, the Mabarrat Muhammad ʿAli and the New Woman Society, expanded their services, respectively, in health care and in crafts training for poor girls. The EFU hailed the work of the women's philanthropic associations, continuing to encourage their activities. Huda Shaʿrawi was enthusiastic about what women could achieve after she and Saiza Nabarawi visited philanthropic societies in New York, Washington, and Detroit in 1925.[14]

Mary Kahil was a feminist best known for her devotion to the Mabarrat and other philanthropies, to which she generously gave of her prodigious energy and considerable wealth. With her powerful personality Kahil rallied others. Ellen Sarruf, of Syrian Christian origin, credited Kahil with drawing her as a young woman to "the social service side of the feminist movement."[15] Kahil seems to have thought of herself as a feminist and a philanthropist in rather separate terms, unlike Sarruf, who felt she was expressing her feminism through social service work. Rather than being consciously driven by her feminism Kahil's philanthropy was rooted in her Christian faith. In addition to supporting secular endeavors she endowed many Catholic charities. Kahil, who dedicated herself to social service, chose not to marry. In 1972, six years before the end of her life, the state honored Kahil for her lifelong dedication to social service.

Hidayah Barakat (1898–1969) also devoted her life to social service. Born Hidayah ʿAfifi, the daughter of the judge Ahmad ʿAfifi, she attended Notre Dame de la Mère de Dieu School in Cairo before marrying Baha al-Din Barakat, a professor in the Faculty of Law at Cairo University. She joined the Mabarrat and became an active member, serving as treasurer. After the revolution of 1952 when the Mabarrat Muhammad ʿAli and the New Woman Society merged, Barakat became president of the new association. In 1969 the state decorated Hidayah Barakat; she died the same day. Her daughter, Layla Barakat Murtagi, a second-generation philanthropist, took over her mother's duties as president of the society.[16]

Regina Khayyat, another EFU founder and nationalist activist in the WWCC, was also prominent in social service. In 1923 she founded an Egyptian branch of the YWCA and served as its head until 1942, when her daughter-in-law Edna Khayyat took over. Coming from a family that had built a school for girls in Asyut, Regina Khayyat was heir to a tradition of public service. She retained her commitment to feminism but directed her everyday energy to philanthropy.[17]

In the 1930s, a younger generation of upper-class women took new initiatives. In 1936, a group of young upper-class women, recent graduates of the Girls' College (Kulliyat al-Banat) in Zamalek found themselves unwilling "just to sit around waiting for husbands like the other girls" but could not even imagine attending university. They acted on an idea inspired by their psychology teacher Zakiyah ʿAziz, who had spoken to them of tuberculosis chronic among the poor. The young women, "who wanted an aim in life," gathered at the home of Layla Doss where they laid the plans for al-Jamʿiyah al-Nisaʾiyah li-Tahsin al-Sihhah (Women's Society for the Improvement of Health) to fight tuberculosis.[18] Other founders included Duriyah and Ida ʿAllubah, Sharifah Mihriz, and Niʿmat Birzi. Eva Habib al-Masri (the new editor of the EFU's *al-Misriyah*), armed with her master's degree in social work from Smith College, soon joined them.[19] "For the sake of respectability," Doss pointed out, the young women had to find an older adult to act as president. They persuaded Ivy Najib Mahmud, an Englishwoman married to an Egyptian and some twenty years their senior, to take on the role.

The society acquired a small premises in the ʿAbdin quarter and was ready for work. Doss recalled the routine of the early days. The young women set out from their headquarters in pairs making the rounds of the quarter to locate tuberculosis victims. It was the first time, according to Doss, that she and her companions, who lived in Cairo's luxurious quarters, had seen the city's crowded and filthy back alleys, let alone entered the hovels of the poor.

Doss and the others saw how the poor lived cramped into one or two vermin-infested rooms. In such conditions of poverty there were no divisions of living space between sexes or ages. Doss related that the close contact with suffering "forged her commitment."

The young women sent reports on the tubercular and their families to the new Section for Chest Diseases under the direction of Dr. Mahmud ʿAbazah in the Ministry of Public Health, which assumed responsibility for medical care. Meanwhile, they distributed food parcels, clothing, blankets, and soap to the victims and their families, and sometimes offered monetary support to families or tried to find work for healthy family members.

As part of the effort to stop the disease's spread the tubercular had to be separated from the healthy members of the household. While the pattern in Europe and North America had been to remove the tuberculosis patients to sanatoriums, here it was decided that the ill should remain at home and the children should be removed to a safe haven. To support this effort required resources, and thus began years of fund-raising. The young women gave lentil soup parties to generate money and also made direct appeals for financial support. Eva Habib al-Masri used the pages of the EFU's *al-Misriyah* to raise public consciousness. In 1939 she wrote: "I don't see why we spend so much money on official functions and are miserly when it comes to the vital needs of this country. What is the use of spending money on compulsory education while our children go to schools hungry and sick? We must combat poverty and improve the economic level of the ordinary person."[20] Years of public advocacy and fund-raising paid off. In 1947 the society opened the gates of Madinat Tahsin al-Sihhah, the City of the Improvement of Health, next to the pyramids of Gizah, where daughters and sons of tubercular parents were given a new home. The children attended a school on the premises that followed the government curriculum. Crafts instruction was also provided.

At a time when they might have followed their elders into what were by then well-established philanthropies, Doss and the other young women instead took the initiative to form their own association where they could define their purpose and take the lead themselves. Some Tahsin al-Sihhah members in addition to Eva Habib al-Masri, such as Layla Doss, joined the EFU. Years later Saiza Nabarawi recalled the excellent relations between the EFU and Tahsin al-Sihhah.[21] The cooperation between the young women's new philanthropy and the EFU was unusual among women's organizations.

Doss was an exemplary social feminist of the new generation. Founding her own society and nourishing it for decades also enabled her to create a life of her own outside conventional marriage. Doss remained for more than half a century at the head of the Tahsin al-Sihhah, which established itself solidly under her direction. She stepped down only in the 1970s. Her time had finally come to enter the university.[22]

Seven years after young women had first worked as volunteers in the EFU dispensary, a group of young upper-class men calling themselves the Pioneers (al-Ruwwad) came together and tried to establish contact with lower-class youth. They set up meeting places, *mahallahs*, in various working-class quarters. Each mahallah had its own character and program, but an emphasis on mutual help and cooperative action was common to them all. Layla Doss recalled that one of the Pioneers, Dr. ʿAbd al-Salam, had helped the women of Tahsin al-Sihhah make contacts in the bazaars where men could move more freely. However, cooperation between the sexes was not the rule; while the young men tried to cut through class barriers, they did not attempt to break down gender divisions.[23]

The Mabarrat Amirah Faryal, active in the 1940s, was unusual in its day for being a gender-mixed social service society. Members believed, according to Suʿad Riyad, that diminishing the distance between the sexes through cooperation in humanitarian activities would lead to wider societal harmony. Representing the Mabarrat Amirah Faryal as a member of the EFU delegation to the Arab Feminist Conference in 1944 Riyad proposed a resolution declaring that cooperation between women and men in creating a sound society was a basic goal of Arab feminism.[24]

Daycare

The 1930s and 1940s were decades both of exacerbated economic hardship for lower-class families and of growing employment opportunities for poor women. Many women found work in the new hospitals and clinics, which were often run by the Red Crescent and the Mabarrat, and in factories. Child care became a growing problem for working mothers. As early as 1924 the EFU and the WWCC had pointed to problems working mothers faced, and called for the creation of supervised children's parks in popular urban quarters. When ʿAli Mahir became prime minister with an agenda of social reform in 1936, the EFU repeated its request, now calling for children's parks in towns throughout the country.[25]

As with other pressing social needs, the EFU did not stop at lobbying, but also addressed the problem by starting its own daycare center in its Qasr al-ʿAyni complex. With two decades' experience in social service Hawwaʾ Idris organized a daycare center called Dar al-Hadanah (The Nursery) in 1946, which she continued to run into the 1980s. Dar al-Hadanah operated a crèche for infants, supervised play for younger children, and provided instruction in reading and writing to older children. Most of the mothers worked at the nearby Qasr al-ʿAyni government hospital. In opening the daycare center, the EFU set another example for the government to follow. However, child care has remained a perennial problem in Egypt, as in many other countries. Even during the socialist period (from 1952 to 1970) when the state mobilized women into the work force on a large scale, it never supplied the necessary support services.[26]

Women to the Rescue in War

By the end of the 1930s voluntary social service had become well established as a respectable activity for women of the upper classes, thanks to their own initiatives. Women had gained considerable experience at providing routine services. Early in the century Djavidan Hanim had been unable to elicit help from upper-class women when refugees poured in during the Balkan Wars, but now such women were quick to enter the arena of emergency relief. At the beginning of the Second World War *al-Misriyah* ran an article titled "Our Duty Today: We the Women of Egypt," exhorting women under the banner of patriotism to volunteer in first aid, and urging the government "to prepare educated women to perform the jobs of men."[27]

Egyptian women organized relief for victims of the 1939 earthquake in Turkey. Nahid Sirri, aunt of Queen Faridah and wife of Prime Minister Husayn Sirri, organized a women's committee that held a raffle to raise money for the victims.[28] The EFU held a subscription drive.[29] The following year women came promptly to the rescue of victims of aerial bombardments in Alexandria. Also in 1940 women responded to the plight of flood victims made homeless in the village of ʿIzbat al-Basri outside Cairo, meeting with young architect Hasan Fathi (later to achieve world renown), who volunteered to help rebuild the lost houses.[30]

Women who participated in these relief operations formed the Women's Committee of the Egyptian Red Crescent Society under the leadership of Nahid Sirri and the patronage of the queen. The Red Crescent Society, which had been created during the First World War and had affiliated to the League of Societies of the Red Cross in 1919, had remained an exclusively male society. Among the early members of the Women's Committee were Sulha Aflatun (mother of future feminist Inji Aflatun), Insaf Sirri (prominent educator), Layla al-Shawarbi, and Gertrude Ghali (a Swiss nurse married to Mirrit Ghali). The Women's Committee organized first aid courses for upper-class women to prepare them to assist the wounded. During the air raids in 1941 the committee set up shelters in Cairo, Alexandria, and Mansurah in the Delta, and visited soldiers in the Red Crescent hospitals and Libyan prisoners of war in Egypt.[31]

Born in response to crises, the Women's Committee continued to perform valiant services during emergencies. Meanwhile the committee involved itself in the routine operations of the Red Crescent, overseeing a large hospital in Ramsis Street, a clinic for tuberculosis patients at Inshas, and numerous dispensaries throughout Cairo. In 1943, a Young Women's Committee attached to the Red Crescent Society was created under the patronage of Princess Faryal.[32] Gertrude Ghali, a member of the Executive Board of the Women's Committee, claimed years later that the women became the most active members of the Red Crescent Society and its real leaders.[33]

Expanding Needs, Expanding Responses

The EFU grew increasingly concerned over the limited capabilities of the existing private social service societies to cope with the needs of the poor. The feminist organization continued to try to stimulate the expansion and coordination of services by private and governmental bodies. The EFU called upon the government to create a higher council for childhood on the lines of a recent French model. Feminists also proposed coordination among private benevolent associations, perhaps following American and British initiatives. Still another idea was to create a supreme council to supervise social service projects of both private and governmental bodies serving both city and countryside.[34]

In 1937 Huda Shaʿrawi invited presidents of the large women's societies in Cairo to become honorary members of the EFU. She also attempted to form a federation of women's societies aiming to more effectively pressure the government. The heads of these associations, however, were not responsive. Saiza Nabarawi, Mary Kahil, and others later attributed this to personal rivalries, as each leader had her own agenda and her own power base. Some of them may also have wished to avoid public association with the explicitly feminist EFU.

From City to Country: The EFU

Meanwhile, feminists turned greater attention to the needs of the rural areas. In 1937 in an article in *al-Misriyah* entitled "The Duty of the Woman in the New Era," Saiza Nabarawi announced the EFU's new focus on rural Egypt. "We believe that the time has come to spread hope throughout the entire country. We shall form regional committees to provide us with knowledge of the vital needs of villagers and in this way achieve contact between the capital and the provinces. . . . Our duty is to raise the living standard of the peasant materially and morally." She stressed that "the EFU deals with numerous problems whose solutions will not just improve the condition of the woman but of the whole society."[35]

Eliciting the interest of city people in the problems of the peasants was an ambitious task. The EFU called upon women, large landowners, and the government to work together to bring services to the people of rural Egypt. The organization advocated that landowners spend time on their country estates and work toward improving peasants' lives. *Al-Misriyah* praised landowner ʿAbd al-ʿAziz Fahmi Pasha who "gave the highest example when he returned to the village from the city to spread education and to raise the standard of life."[36] The EFU also urged doctors and educators to go to the rural areas.[37]

Al-Misriyah tried to arouse a sense of mission in city women toward the peasants. Writer and poet Jamilah al-ʿAla'ili told women it was time to abandon the lecture halls of the city and to carry the feminist message to Egypt's remotest villages where women needed help: "We have been educated but we have not done enough for humanity of which to be proud. Let us address ourselves to the peasant woman who lives under different conditions from ours. How selfish we are. She must take her share of rights like wealthy women."[38] Rashad Rustum exhorted city women to "bring the city to the villages," urging them to help their rural sisters.[39]

ʿA'ishah ʿAbd al-Rahman, proudly identifying herself with the land as Bint al-Shati' (Daughter of the Riverbank) was the only woman of peasant origin to speak out about peasant needs. She also wrote in the press, publishing articles in *al-Misriyah* and *al-Ahram*, and in 1935 published the book *al-Rif al-Misri* (Rural Egypt). While others urged city women to go to the villages, Bint al-Shati'—then a university student in Cairo, at a time when economic conditions were driving peasants to the city—stressed the need for peasant women to remain in the villages to "lighten the darkness."[40] In 1939 the new Ministry of Social Affairs announced that it wanted to enlist the services of Bint al-Shati' in helping peasant women.[41] However, Bint al-Shati' went on to complete her doctorate in Arabic literature and her life took another focus.

In 1937 *al-Misriyah* published a series called "Rakhat al-Fallah" (The prosperity of the peasant), addressing problems of income, land, water, housing, health, and education.[42] The opening article deplored the exploitation of peasants, whose income amounted to three piasters a day and who must be enabled to reap greater profits from the land. A reduction in land rents or an increase in farmers' shares in the crops would increase peasants' income, helping to spread out the wealth concentrated in the hands of the large landlords. It was also suggested that the government sell state lands to the peasants at low cost and initiate land reclamation schemes to provide new arable lands for them.[43] Feminists urged that the government create a cooperative bank for peasants.[44]

L'Egyptienne deplored the lack of clean drinking water in the villages.[45] The government and some of the landowners had begun to install pumps to provide safe water for the peasants, but the staggering needs were far from satisfied. Contaminated water transmitted numerous endemic diseases, such as schistosomiasis, a parasitic disease contracted through contact with stagnant water, usually in irrigation canals, where the parasite incubated in snails. Large numbers of Egyptian peasants were afflicted with this incurable and debilitating disease.[46] The cholera epidemic that broke out in the Delta in 1947 was another result of the water crisis. The EFU continued to press the government to provide villages with clean water.

The EFU also continued to agitate for the extension of health services and educational facilities to rural areas. When fifteen government dispensaries for mothers and children were created in villages in 1927, *L'Egyptienne* immediately appealed for more.[47] A decade later the feminists were still complaining about the lack of facilities in rural areas, asking the government to send mobile health units equipped with doctors, nurses, midwives, and medical supplies to the villages.[48] They insisted that medical services should include basic instruction in hygiene and health, and in new techniques of childbirth and child care. Films might be used to reach the illiterate rural population. In 1944, Nur Marʿai, as an EFU delegate to the Arab Feminist Conference in Cairo, repeated the earlier plea for an extension of health services to rural areas, calling upon the government and private philanthropy alike to respond. She also pressed the government to open vocational training centers in provincial capitals and to create asylums for orphans.[49] The 1923 constitution had called for compulsory primary school education for all Egyptians. By the late 1930s needs had been widely met in the cities but rural areas still lacked facilities. In 1936 the EFU demanded that the government provide education for children in rural areas, emphasizing the need for technical education to help improve agricultural methods. They suggested using the radio (which came to Egypt in 1934) to mount a large-scale educational campaign in the rural areas.[50]

Along with an advocacy campaign the EFU took practical measures. In 1937 it created the Committee for the Improvement of Conditions in the Village, along with several specialized subcommittees. Huda Shaʿrawi tried to enlist the active support of EFU members in projects for villagers. The EFU president took the initiative, laying the groundwork for a model village on her land in Tirsa, not far from Cairo, in the province of Gizah. Members of the EFU lent financial support and participated in planning for the construction of houses for peasants and the installation of a pumping station to provide water for drinking and irrigation.[51] Shaʿrawi also began projects in her ancestral province of Minya in Upper Egypt. In 1937 she opened medical dispensaries in the villages of Sharq, Samalut, and Zawiyat al-Amwat. The dispensary at Sharq was affiliated with an organization called International Public Assistance, created by Egyptians and foreigners before the First World War. Shaʿrawi also set up a school for girls and another for boys in Zawiyat al-Amwat.[52] But most EFU members did not direct their attention in any sustained way to the needs of rural Egypt. Even the EFU youth group, the Shaqiqat, failed to respond.

From City to Country: Philanthropists

Urban women within the framework of philanthropic societies attempted to extend help to rural Egyptians. They opened branches of their associations in the provinces. Women also participated in creating new societies founded explicitly to deal with rural needs.

Tahsin al-Sihhah opened branches in Upper Egypt, beginning with Asyut in 1943 and Minya in 1944.[53] Members of the Cairo headquarters participated in the inaugural ceremonies of new branches that were run by women of the local elite. Among the women who came from Cairo to inaugurate the

Luxor branch of Tahsin al-Sihhah in 1953 were Layla Doss, Munirah al-Bayadi (sister of Muhammad Najib, then president of Egypt), and Jeannette Makar Kamal Bulus Hanna.[54] The Mabarrat Muhammad ʿAli also began to spread throughout the country, opening branches in Minya, Tanta, Sidi Salim (near Tanta), and Zagazig in 1946.[55]

Among the new societies formed exclusively to extend services to the rural areas was the Jamʿiyat al-Sayyidat al-Qibtiyah li-Tarbiyat al-Tufulah (Coptic Ladies' Society for the Education of Children). Anna Dadian Nagib Ghali, an Armenian from Istanbul who had married into the Ghali family, founded this organization to establish free schools for Coptic children throughout Egypt.[56]

A new generation of women also turned their attention to the provinces. A group of young Christian women embarked on an educational mission among peasants in Upper Egypt through the Oeuvre des Ecoles Gratuites des Villages de Haute-Egypte. This society was founded in 1939 by Egyptian Jesuit Henry Habib Ayrut, who had studied the Egyptian peasantry and had recently completed a doctorate in sociology at the University of Lyon. Ayrut enlisted young middle-class women recently graduated from secondary school in voluntary work in Upper Egypt. His supervision undoubtedly made it possible for their families to agree to their traveling out of Cairo on their own. Among the volunteers were Yvette Ayrut, Jeannette Ayrut, Nelly Younan, Nadia Rabbat, Arlette Fumaroli, Mimi Farazli, Marguerite Azzam, and Iris Habib al-Masri. Small groups of women went to Upper Egypt for a few weeks at a time. Accompanied by local townswomen, they visited villages to learn about local needs and at the same time to give basic instruction in health and hygiene, and to distribute *gallabiyahs* (tunics), soap, medicines, and food parcels. The volunteers also gave peasant women literacy lessons. Before leaving an area the volunteers and local townswomen set up permanent centers under the society's auspices. When the women returned to Cairo, they gave talks on the conditions and needs of the peasants.[57]

While the EFU's Shaqiqat did not go to the rural areas themselves, the feminist organization tried to stimulate initiatives among the rising generation. In 1937 Aminah ʿAllubah proposed that students go to villages during the summer vacation to give literacy lessons and basic instruction in health and hygiene under the direction of the Ministry of Education.[58] In 1940 the EFU suggested that the Ministry of Social Affairs institute a compulsory service program requiring women, upon completion of their education, to work in social service in the rural areas for six months.

Fighting Epidemics

Not only were women working for the extension of regular services to the rural areas, but they went to the rescue during major epidemics. In 1944 upon learning that malaria had broken out in Upper Egypt, Cairene women immediately mobilized help. They began relief operations in Cairo, raising money and collecting food, clothing, and medicine to distribute in Upper Egypt. Women organized teams from the Mabarrat and the Women's Committee of the Red Crescent. Nahid Sirri headed the Red Crescent teams, which included Gertrude Ghali, Sulha Aflatun (mother of feminist Inji Aflatun), Sophie Butrus Ghali (mother of the future United Nations secretary-general Butrus Butrus Ghali), Hawwa' Idris, Celine Cattawi, Layla Shawarbi, and Lutfiyah Yusri. The teams working with the Mabarrat included Hidayah ʿAfifi Barakat, Mary Kahil, Aminah Sidqi (daughter of former prime minister Ismaʿil Sidqi), and Firdus Shita. Huda Shaʿrawi participated in the appeals for help but, because of age and poor health, could not accompany the teams to Upper Egypt.[59]

The Mabarrat set up a central relief station in Luxor while the Red Crescent women operated from Esna. Gertrude Ghali described the routine in Luxor. During the day the women, accompanied by nurses, made house-to-house rounds in villages to ascertain conditions. At night they prepared medicines, food parcels, and clothing for distribution. The volunteers operated public kitchens in Luxor and Esna and assisted medical personnel in giving vaccine injections.[60] Teams of women continued to go to Upper Egypt throughout the early months of 1944, and some returned toward the end of the year as well. Not long after the first women's teams had departed, King Faruk visited the relief operations, praising the work of the women volunteers.[61]

Three years later when cholera broke out in the Delta, women again responded. The Women's Committee of the Red Crescent Society and the Mabarrat, in cooperation with the Ministry of Public Health, organized vaccination centers in towns in Lower and Upper Egypt. The women also distributed food, clothing, and money to people in the stricken areas and helped instruct them on prevention.[62]

The cholera epidemic became a heated nationalist issue. The British were widely accused of bringing cholera to Egypt, as British troops had been passing through Egypt from India, where the disease had broken out earlier the same month, and the first cases were reported among Egyptian workers at the British military base at Tall al-Kabir.[63] As president of the EFU, Huda Shaʿrawi protested to the United Nations that the British troops were responsible for the epidemic; she took the occasion to call for an end to the military occupation of her country.

The State Follows Again

In 1939 when the Ministry of Social Affairs was created, it assumed responsibility for services the women's philanthropic associations had been providing and these associations now came under its jurisdiction. They were required to register with the ministry and to submit to its supervision, but they remained largely self-financing. The government stipends that were later given to the women's associations were minimal. The independence the women's philanthropic associations had enjoyed was gone. However, the women had to count it a success when the government finally stepped in to do what they had long urged it to do. Indeed the EFU was vocal in its support of the new ministry. The two systems, the governmental and private philanthropic, now existed side by side.

• CHAPTER 7 •

Recasting the Family

WOMEN'S feminist consciousness first arose in the context of home and family. Women witnessed and experienced ills as daughters, wives, and mothers. ʿA'ishah al-Taymuriyah described marital miseries in the upper-class family in the 1890s, when men sought fortunes through expedient matches. In 1892 the thirteen-year-old Huda Shaʿrawi had been pressured into marriage with her elder cousin to secure the patrimony. Bahithat al-Badiyah's father arranged her marriage in 1909 to a wealthy bedouin chief who, unbeknownst to father or daughter, was already married. She wrote about her own anguish and about the sufferings of other women because of divorce and polygamy. Nabawiyah Musa was so disaffected by what she saw around her that she avoided marriage altogether.[1]

Patriarchal domination remained most entrenched in the family, with modes of control over women varying according to class and circumstances.[2] In the nineteenth and early twentieth centuries patriarchal controls were most pervasive in families of the upper strata. With the erosion of the instrumental hold of males inside the patriarchal family over "their" women as the nineteenth century progressed—a corollary of "modernization" of state and society—the personal status laws, or family laws, became a last bastion of control over women. The patriarchal family would not relinquish this control, nor would the state exact it. Having removed all other areas of law from the jurisdiction of Islam, the state had left Muslim religious authorities in control of Islamic personal status laws.[3] According to the conventional interpretation of Islam, and of Christianity, wives were under the authority of husbands. Women inherited less than men, who were enjoined to support women. In short, women and men had different responsibilities and duties in the family. As members of families, men exerted considerable control over women's rights to participate in the economic, social, and political life of the country. It is important, obviously, to bear in mind that there was no monolithic family—constructions of family varied considerably across the classes; that there have always been exceptions to "rules" within class; and that family-based controls over women were not total, and women have found ways to resist domination.

Certain observations can be made about Islamic ideological constructions of marriage, sexuality, and gender deriving from interpretations of the sharʿiah. For women all expression of sexuality is restricted to monogamous marriage. Men are able, fulfilling certain conditions, to engage in polygamous marriage and are allowed up to four wives at one time.[4] Men may divorce (by *talaq* or repudiation) their wives; women do not have the same right, although there are other ways a woman can remove herself from marriage. Muslim men can marry non-Muslim women "of the book," that is, Jews and Christians. However, Muslim women may not marry non-Muslims, nor may non-Muslim wives inherit from their husbands. Inheritance plays a fundamental part in structuring the patriarchal family. In Sunni Islam women receive half of what men in the same capacity inherit (this is the one area of Muslim law that also applies to Christians). At the same time, husbands are required by law to support their wives. While wives have no material obligations, they do have service obligations. Islam structures the patriarchal family to function so as to secure the protection of the unit and its members. Accordingly, it qualifies the prerogatives it gives to men.

Using Islamic modernist arguments feminists aimed to ameliorate the functioning of the family through curbing men's abuses of their prerogatives, particularly divorce and polygamy, and men's neglect of their duties, especially support of wife and children. Feminists tried to have the Islamic personal status code altered in such a way that it would protect the contemporary family. Given the appropriation of Islam—an Islam narrowly or mistakenly read—by the patriarchal family and the legal regulation of the family by the al-Azhar–based Islamic religious establishment (largely antagonistic to ʿAbduh's doctrine of Islamic modernism), the task the feminists undertook was exceedingly difficult.

The Egyptian feminists' critique of family law was moderate, if not conservative. They did not challenge the notion of the family predicated on the distribution of complementary rights and responsibilities to women and men. Feminists accepted different gender roles in the family but insisted on equality in difference.[5] They adhered to the mainstream view that women's and men's family roles and relations were ordained by religion. Feminist activists focused their attention upon Muslim men's abuse of their lawful rights and responsibilities; men avoided responsibilities to the family, oppressed women within the context of the family, and deprived women and children of security. Feminists also marshaled secular arguments, insisting that a strong and united family was necessary to a vital and cohesive nation, and that women had a fundamental right to their own well-being and security.

The EFU dealt with the family, and with women's and children's security and roles in the family, in two ways. In the 1920s it concentrated on reforming the family's legal structure, calling mainly for controls of male excesses and abuses. This was the only instance when Egyptian secular feminists, represented by the Muslims among them, focused specifically on a Muslim female constituency, as necessitated by the religiously based system of personal status laws. Employing Islamic reformist arguments in a discourse of persuasion, Muslim Egyptian feminists engaged in a campaign to influence their politically empowered male compatriots to enact changes in the Muslim personal status code. Although the feminists continued to press their case after the 1920s, they understood that chances for success were minimal.

In the late 1930s the EFU tried a different approach in dealing with family issues. Now feminists addressed women themselves, as Egyptians rather than as members of religious communities, whom they advised to protect and enhance their lives in the family through improved performance of their family roles. Conducted in the pages of *al-Misriyah*, this crusade spoke most directly to middle-class women.

Campaigning to Reform the Personal Status Code

In its campaign to change the Muslim laws of personal status, *ahwal shakhsiyah*, the EFU's commitment to Islam was clear, and the organization never deviated from insistence upon reform within the framework of Islamic religious law, the shariʿah.[6] The EFU never approved the secular family code Turkey adopted, although it applauded certain gains for women, especially the abolition of polygamy and the granting to both sexes of the right to divorce.[7] The secular Turkish Civil Code (based on a Swiss model), however, preserved patriarchal privilege: for example, unlike the Egyptian code it declared the husband the head of the family; it also forbade married women to use their father's names, whereas in Egypt women after marriage were legally known by maiden names.[8]

The EFU agenda for legal reform included two demands directly addressing women: the establishment of a minimum marriage age and the extension of the mother's legal custody (*hadanah*) over her children. Both were realized, in 1923 and 1929, respectively. Three demands were aimed at curbing patriarchal excesses: the regulation of men's ability to divorce, the restriction of men's practice of polygamy, and the abolition of the institution of *bayt al-taʿah* (literally, the house of obedience), whereby a husband armed with a court order could force a woman to return to the home she had left without his permission. None of these demands was met. What feminists saw as "patriarchal excesses" men regarded as "patriarchal privileges."

Feminists intended their demands to benefit all Egyptian women. But what were the class implications of the feminist program for legal reform? A minimum marriage age for women stood to benefit middle- and upper-class girls, giving them a chance to extend their education before marriage. As for lower-class women and those in rural areas who would not go to school, this law could be burdensome to them and their families. The extension of the mother's custody over her children also had different implications across the classes. It lengthened a mother's time with her children but also extended her responsibilities. If the child support legally due her was not forthcoming, financial hardship could ensue. Indeed, poor women were perennially in the courts pleading for support due them as mothers, whether as wives or as divorced women with legal custody. Polygamy was still practiced mainly in the upper class, but not exclusively in that class. Bayt al-taʿah appears to have been practiced mainly in the modest strata of society. Divorce was endemic in all classes.

When feminists called for legal reforms that required the intervention of judges, they implicitly raised another class-related problem. Families of the upper strata typically did not use courts in matters pertaining to marriage and divorce, or in issues of wife or child support, but rather settled their affairs privately. A requirement to effect a marriage or divorce in front of a judge and to adhere to legally stipulated conditions would transfer controls from the patriarchal family to an external authority. Men from the upper strata, and perhaps many women as well, objected. Customarily, the courts were used most by the lower classes and peasants. Speaking of personal status reforms Enid Hill remarked, "The poor have taken advantage of modern legislation intended for the whole society while their 'betters' have held fast to traditional forms."[9] Complex intersections of gender, class, and patriarchy concerning family law and its enforcement indicate how fraught was the feminist project to reform the law and protect women.

In seeking a legal minimum marriage age for girls, in June 1923 the EFU directly petitioned the government, as there was still no parliament at the time. Feminists celebrated the favorable outcome as their first victory. In 1924 when the new parliament was inaugurated, the EFU and the WWCC made controlling divorce and polygamy public issues for the first time. In 1927 when the government created a committee to prepare revisions in the personal status code, the EFU again presented these two demands along with others; the work of this committee did not result in new legislation.[10] Two years later the demands were submitted to a second committee, but very little of what the feminists sought was incorporated into the 1929 law.[11] They continued, albeit fruitlessly, to press their case: notably in 1936, when the government established a committee to undertake a completed codification of personal status laws, and after ʿAli Mahir formed a cabinet announcing special interest in social reforms; and in 1939, with the creation of the Ministry of Social Affairs.[12] Let us now examine the demands individually.

A Minimum Marriage Age

The establishment of a minimum marriage age for girls was one of the first two demands the new EFU presented to the Egyptian government (the other was for secondary schools for girls). In the nineteenth and early twentieth centuries, women across the classes in Egypt were married, as a rule, around the age of puberty.[13] Huda Shaʿrawi, who had been married at the age of thirteen, called early marriage "the first obstacle to the development of the young woman."[14] She had most immediately in mind the young urban women whose education could be truncated by early marriage, although by the second half of the 1930s the feminists were concerned about the extension of education to girls in rural areas. The EFU asked in 1923 that the minimum marriage age for girls be set at sixteen. A decree law that same year fixed the age at sixteen for females and eighteen for males.[15]

The new marriage age law turned out to be a relatively easy starting victory for the feminists. But, as Saiza Nabarawi later pointed out, it was a decree law issued before the new postindependence parliament had been instituted. She believed parliament would never have passed such a law.[16] The gain proved to be more illusory than it first appeared and demonstrated the limitations of legal reform. Laws had to be implemented if reform was to be meaningful. When feminists discovered the law was not being applied, they objected.[17] The state itself was negligent in permitting the registrar issuing marriage licenses (the *ma'dhun*) to accept the verbal testimony of two witnesses to determine age in lieu of a birth certificate. The feminists insisted that birth certificates, which had been required by law since 1912, be demanded as proof of age. If it were impossible to produce a birth certificate, the prospective bride's age should be determined after examination by two government doctors;[18] but when this became a requirement, feminists complained that doctors often falsified women's ages.[19] A 1931 law stipulated that no claims against a marriage could be entertained unless marriages were registered.[20] Nevertheless, it continued to be difficult to enforce the marriage age law. *Al-Misriyah* in 1938 published an angry article entitled "The Marriage of Girls under Age Is White Slave Trade," protesting forced marriages of young girls to old men. The EFU suggested that prospective brides be required to produce certificates with photographs and that the government make it a criminal offense for the ma'dhun to authorize marriages of minors.[21] Not only did the law continue to be ignored but twice in 1937 there were proposals in the Chamber of Deputies to abolish the minimum marriage age law altogether.[22] The law was neither dropped nor effectively applied.

Seeking to Restrict Polygamy

The EFU campaigned for the restriction of polygamy (*taʿaddud al-zawjat*), demanding that a man be permitted to take a second wife only if his first wife were sterile or had an incurable illness.[23] Polygamy had been a common practice in the old upper-class harems. While women may once have found it tolerable, feminists argued, this was no longer the case; polygamy was insulting to contemporary women and psychologically damaging. Feminists also attacked polygamy as a threat to the family. Saiza Nabarawi insisted, "It endangers the family more than anything else."[24] Huda Shaʿrawi told *al-Ahram* that polygamy "constitutes an attack on the dignity of the wife and mother and is an obstacle to [creating] a harmonious home generating the moral force able to form and guide the good citizen."[25]

Feminists had firsthand experience with polygamy. When Huda Shaʿrawi's husband returned to his former wife, she separated from him, returning only when he agreed to a monogamous marriage. Second wife

Bahithat al-Badiyah narrated the ills polygamy caused women and children. She observed in Fayyum: "In this wilderness where I live, I do not exaggerate if I say that there is not one married woman around me who is the only wife of her husband. . . . I often ask a woman this question: 'Do you really love your husband as much as you did before he had a second wife?' The answer was always no. In fact, many said they preferred to see their husbands carried away on shoulders [i.e., dead] rather than see them marry an additional wife." Bahithat al-Badiyah insisted: "Divorce is less of a trial than polygamy. The first is misery plus freedom, while the latter is misery plus restriction . . . the husband of two or more wives ought really to be appointed Minister of the Colonies."[26]

Feminists countered the Quranic permission for a man to take four wives, conditional upon equal treatment, with a Quranic verse saying, "You are never able in spite of your efforts to be equitable toward your wives," insisting that it was impossible for a man, as a good Muslim, to practice polygamy.[27] They argued that the Islamic restriction of a man to four wives had to be understood in the context of pre-Islamic Arabia, where men had had vast numbers of wives and such a limit was a more realistic step toward ending polygamy than immediate total abolition. Polygamy, moreover, had been condoned in Arabia at the beginning of Islam because the large numbers of men killed in wars had resulted in a surplus of women. In contemporary Egypt the ratio of women to men was nearly equal. Further, given overpopulation and restricted resources, it was better to limit the birth rate than to encourage population increase by condoning polygamy.[28]

Appealing to national pride Saiza Nabarawi declared in a 1931 article that while Egypt considered itself a progressive nation and the leader of the Islamic world, "in advanced Muslim communities polygamy was considered contrary to the precepts of Islam."[29] Turkey had abolished polygamy in 1926. In Afghanistan after 1928 a government employee who took a second wife would lose his job.[30] Iran restricted polygamy in 1932. Keeping up the pressure *L'Egyptienne*'s editor in 1935 wrote: "This resistance to modern currents in a nation priding itself on being at the head of all progressive movements amazes me."[31]

The only male voice advocating an end to polygamy altogether was Murqus Fahmi's in his 1894 *al-Mar'ah fi al-Sharq*. However, a number of other liberal men favored restricting the practice. Islamic reformer Shaykh Muhammad ʿAbduh, who had witnessed his own mother's suffering as a result of polygamy, had suggested that a man not be allowed to take additional wives without proving his financial capacity before a court and pledging that he would accord his wives equal attention.[32] In 1917 jurist Ahmad Safwat asserted that only Quranic provisions making specific interdictions must be followed in a literal sense; other provisions were open to interpretation: as a person's right to own a slave had been prohibited in Egypt, so could limits be put on divorce and polygamy. This view elicited intense opposition in religious circles.[33] Ten years later minister of justice Zaki Abu al-Saʿud and the shaykh al-Azhar, following ʿAbduh's lead, incorporated recommendations for restricting divorce and polygamy into the 1927 draft proposal for a revised personal status code.[34] The cabinet approved the proposal but the king vetoed it.[35]

Eight years later the shaykh al-Azhar was writing in favor of polygamy in *Majallati*. After unsuccessfully attempting to interview the religious leader, Saiza Nabarawi reminded *L'Egyptienne*'s readers of the shaykh's former stand: when asked about the 1927 draft code, he had told the feminist journal, "I approve of the new draft of the Muslim personal status code and am proud to be among those who designed it." Nabarawi contrasted the shaykh al-Azhar's new position with the progressive thinking of the late Shaykh Muhammad ʿAbduh.[36]

In 1939, feminist Munirah Thabit succeeded in obtaining an interview with the next shaykh al-Azhar, who advanced a socioeconomic argument in favor of polygamy. Accusing feminists of favoring the city over the countryside the shaykh insisted that the man on the land counts his productive labor in the number of his wives and children. For urban women he proposed the individual solution of the ʿismah, whereby women could stipulate in their marriage contract that a husband must not take additional wives. Of course the prospective husband had to agree to the stipulation. In her campaign for the legal restriction of polygamy Thabit suggested that stiff penalties be imposed on men for violations. She disparaged women who would accept a polygamous union. Perhaps her previous experience as the second wife of ʿAbd al-Qadir Hamzah had influenced her stand.[37]

The feminists' campaign against polygamy was a struggle against a dying custom. Polygamy was already growing less common in the upper and middle classes. Among the lower class and peasantry, contrary to the shaykh al-Azhar's assertions, poverty had always limited the practice.[38] But the campaign was more than a fight against a declining social practice; it was an attack against patriarchal supremacy expressed in legalized asymmetrical sexual relations with psychological, social, and economic implications for women. Feminists did not accept the argument that polygamy worked in women's favor by ensuring women support instead of abandonment through divorce. Indeed, they tied their advocacy of women's right to work to their security.

Seeking to Regulate Divorce

Feminists approached the question of a wife's security by demanding regulation of divorce (*talaq*), which is strictly a male prerogative. If polygamy was less common and confined largely to certain strata of society, divorce was widespread across classes and regions. Under the Islamic shariʿah a man could repudiate his wife simply by pronouncing a formula in her presence or absence, with no witnesses, and at any time or place. Feminists observed the lives of countless women and families disrupted by divorce.[39] Huda

Shaʿrawi has spoken about the impact of divorce on the upper-class woman, Bahithat al-Badiyah observed its ravages on middle-class women, and Eugénie Le Brun Rushdi in *Les répudiées* (The divorcées, 1908) recorded the evils of divorce for poor women.[40] Under the personal status code in Egypt men were required to pay a wife alimony for one year and to support children in her custody, but often this money was not forthcoming. Divorce was a potential threat to all women, although its effects varied according to class and circumstances.[41]

The EFU requested that men be permitted by law to divorce a wife for serious reasons only, and only in the presence of a qadi, who would first oblige the two parties to submit to arbitration conducted by representatives from each side. The demand was not met; the 1929 revised code simply declared that divorce pronounced by a man who was intoxicated or under duress was invalid.

Although in Islamic law a wife cannot repudiate her husband, she can apply to a judge to end her marriage. A judicial divorce (*tatliq*) may then be effected. For example, at a wife's request a judge can call for arbitration conducted by persons acting on behalf of each party. If attempts at reconciliation fail, grounds for divorce are then examined. The 1927 draft law discussed what constituted grounds, *darar* (literally, harm or injury), specifically citing such extreme situations as the disappearance of a husband for four years or his affliction with an incurable disease. The proposal further stated that harm could also be inflicted on a woman by words and deeds, to be interpreted in terms of circumstances and milieu or social class, by a qadi who would determine the merits of individual cases. When a marriage is terminated, the judge must assign blame to either husband or wife. Unlike the man, if the wife is to blame she must pay an indemnity. The feminists objected: "The care men take to favor themselves reappears concerning divorce. It is stipulated that any divorce, demanded by a man, however much to blame, will never be followed by compensation on his part whereas if the wife is declared culpable she is compelled to pay compensation. As is evident, the responsibilities are never equal for the two sexes. It is always the one who is called weak who must support the heaviest load."[42] Nonetheless, these provisions for judicial divorce were incorporated in the 1929 law. Man's ability to divorce was still not controlled; a major source of insecurity to women as wives and mothers remained.

Denouncing Bayt al-Taʿah

Feminists wanted bayt al-taʿah purged altogether from the personal status code, strongly denouncing an institution that enabled a husband to obtain a judge's order to forcibly return a wife who had left home without his permission. Such a woman is legally defined as *nashizah* (disobedient/rebellious) and as such is not eligible to obtain a judicial divorce. Nabarawi wrote in 1927: "Isn't bayt al-taʿah a marital home in its most barbaric form? . . . A wife is a companion to her husband, not his slave. . . . A wife should not be forced to remain with a tyrannical husband . . . it is contrary to our modern idea of human freedom. . . . It is [equally] contrary to ideas of humanity according to the Koran."[43] Speaking at the American University in Beirut in 1928 Ihsan al-Qusi insisted:

> *Bait al-taʿa* is more dangerous [for women] than prisons for criminals. Prisoners are guarded by men invested with authority by the law. They are not driven by hate or animosity to take revenge or to transgress the bounds of legally bestowed authority. The husband is clearly an involved guard. No one controls him. To whom can the poor woman condemned to obey him have recourse? He can claim that his incarcerated wife has disobeyed him, so he can insult her and hit her and the courts will not consider this behavior to be outside his legal rights. All these injustices are committed even though the state has a public legislation order that punishes anyone who hurts someone else. All citizens enjoy the protection of this legislation, that is, all except this poor woman. Worst of all, these injustices are committed in the name of a religion that says: "Do not keep them [wives] by force for vengeance. Retain them with kindness or leave them with respect" [Qur'an 4:231, 198].[44]

The feminists pointed out that bayt al-taʿah undermined the foundations of family life. The EFU insisted that a woman's right to ask for a judicial divorce, which was written into the 1929 code, contradicted the notion of forced conjugal life.[45] Indeed in its section on judicial divorce the 1929 personal status code stated: "Misunderstanding between spouses is a source of great evils whose effects touch not only the spouses but their offspring and all persons with whom they are linked by blood or association."[46]

But bayt al-taʿah was not abolished by the 1929 code. Egyptian writer Ihsan Assal, born in the same decade when feminists were campaigning against bayt al-taʿah, created the character Nabilah in the short story "Bayt al-taʿah." By her own wits Nabilah escaped the marital incarceration the law still made possible, but we can only guess at the fate of many real-life women. Bayt al-taʿah was ended only in 1967.

Extending Maternal Child Custody

Unlike divorce and polygamy, privileges and symbols of male power, child custody (*hadanah*) did not generate patriarchal hostility. Three major schools of Islamic jurisprudence had established the principle that custody was to be shared consecutively by parents, the mother taking the children in their early years and the father later; the fourth (the Maliki school) stipulated that a daughter remain with her mother until marriage. Infants and younger children, it was believed, needed maternal love, affection, and compassion, but the maturing child required paternal guidance, discipline, and reason. In Egypt, where the Shafiʿi school predominated, mothers retained custody of daughters until the age of nine and sons until the age of seven.

The EFU favored extension of maternal custody, suggesting that girls remain with their mothers until marriage and boys until puberty, in accordance with the Maliki rule.[47] Feminists chipped away at the conventional gender schema, favoring an expansion of the mother's role and increased influence of the mother over her children, whom she would shape into ideal citizens.

The EFU won a partial victory in 1929 when the new law extended custody for mothers to eleven years for girls and nine years for boys. This did not restrict men's prerogatives so much as postpone their paternal responsibilities. In practice, men of all classes frequently neglected to pay the legally required child support to the mothers of their children, revealing that custody was a responsibility they often preferred not to shoulder.

Shrinking ʿIddah

One matter, which was related to custody, that the feminists had not raised was addressed in the 1929 law, stimulating their response. This concerned the duration of ʿiddah, the period immediately following a wife's separation from her husband by divorce or death when a woman is entitled to support from her former husband (or his family) and any child born is considered the legal offspring of her former or late husband. According to the Hanafi rule the minimum duration of the ʿiddah was three menstrual cycles and the maximum was the remaining period of a woman's pregnancy. The Muslim personal status code in Egypt had set the maximum period of ʿiddah at three years. The 1929 revised code changed this to one year, ending what feminists saw as the one advantage to women of a personal status code based on premodernist interpretation. The EFU protested the reduction of ʿiddah, provoking startled reactions: a three-year gestation period could hardly be asserted in the face of modern medical knowledge. When the Cairo daily *al-Ahram* asked the EFU president to explain, she replied that a protection women had enjoyed for centuries should not be eroded unless at the same time divorce and polygamy, which continued to threaten women's security, were controlled.[48]

Considering Inheritance

Inheritance was another issue omitted from the EFU program for reform, but it was not long before this matter was also raised. While separate codes governed matters of personal status for Muslims and Copts, the one exception, as I have just already noted, was inheritance, which was regulated by a uniform law for all citizens regardless of their religious affiliation. Inheritance law in Egypt was grounded in Islamic jurisprudence—that is, the jurisprudence of Sunni Islam, whereby females receive half of what males in the same capacity inherit.[49] It should be noted, however, that the Copts, who generally do not favor the system of unequal inheritance, often take practical steps to equalize the distribution of their wealth. Coptic journalist, Fabian socialist, and feminist supporter Salamah Musa had suggested in 1923 that the EFU demand equal inheritance for women and men, but the EFU demurred.

A few years later when debates arose over the impending legal reforms, the feminists were pressed once again about inheritance. In 1928 when questioned on the matter by *al-Ahram*, Huda Shaʿrawi replied that the EFU had not formulated a position on inheritance.[50] Hinting at a lack of feminist consensus on the matter, Shaʿrawi was careful to give what she called a personal opinion, saying she did not oppose the Islamic system of inheritance because the unequal gender distribution of wealth was counterbalanced by the uneven distribution of family obligations, which required the husband to pay a *mahr* (dower) and to support his wife.[51] Three years later in a speech at the University Women's Club in Cairo Saiza Nabarawi declared that gender inequality in inheritance was an anachronism. The Sunni Islamic inheritance system had been predicated on the idea that women in the family were supported by men. While this suited early Islamic society, and was indeed enlightened in its day, socioeconomic conditions were quite different in modern Egypt. Now that women were earning incomes and financially contributing to the family, the inheritance system should be reviewed. It was clear what Nabarawi wanted, but she hesitated to say outright that women's and men's inheritance should be equalized.[52] The previous year when journalist Mahmud ʿAzmi had suggested equalizing inheritance, Rashid Rida, a conservative disciple of Muhammad ʿAbduh, publicly attacked ʿAzmi.[53] Rida also berated a woman law school student who advocated equal inheritance, saying that her denial of Islamic teachings on the subject would make her an apostate and consequently "no Muslim should marry her; she should inherit from no Muslim and no Muslim should inherit from her."[54]

In 1931 Aminah Hanim Afandi, "The Mother of Benefactors"—widow of the late khedive Tawfiq and mother of the late ex-khedive ʿAbbas Hilmi—died leaving a will stipulating that her two daughters and two sons all inherit equally. The EFU publicized this in *L'Egyptienne*, but that was as far as the feminist organization went.[55] The EFU refused to challenge Sunni Islam.[56]

The feminists' drive to improve women's condition in the family, and the family itself, through legal reform proved disappointing. For the duration of the EFU-led movement the only major changes in the personal status code occurred in 1929. The EFU president declared that the revised code "came to us . . . deprived of the spirit of reform that should have animated it and failed to respond to the social goal we envision."[57]

The feminists' fight to effect changes in the personal status code was a fight by female Islamic modernists focusing on issues of gender. The feminists demanded that the Muslim personal status code reflect and express contemporary social practice and take into account the sensibilities of women as well as men. Slavery, allowed by the Islamic shariʿah, had been outlawed in Egypt in the late nineteenth century after it had come to be perceived as a humanly degrading practice. Feminists and other women in the early twentieth century had come to find polygamy and arbitrary divorce degrading to women.

The goal of the feminists' legal reform campaign was to enhance and empower Muslim women's family position and roles and thereby to enhance and revitalize the Muslim family itself. The feminists' stance was not a challenge to Islam but a challenge to patriarchal power as anchored in the family. Since the late nineteenth century modern transformations had diminished the power of a patriarchal society, but the upper- and middle-class patriarchal family remained largely intact legally and ideologically. The 1929 personal status code preserved the legal structure of the old patriarchal culture. Setting a minimum marriage age for both sexes, extending maternal custody, and providing limited clarifications relating to the woman's ability to request judicial divorce did not significantly curb patriarchal power and privilege.[58]

Fifty years would pass before significant changes favoring women would appear in the personal status code. This change came in the form of a presidential decree issued by Anwar Sadat, with pressure from his wife Jehan Sadat. Six years later when it was rescinded, a wide spectrum of women rose up in a militant campaign demanding the law's reinstatement. An attenuated version of the law was enacted only on the eve of Egyptian women's departure for the United Nations Forum in Nairobi, marking the end of the UN Decade of Women. The state understood that it would not do for Egyptian women to take their grievances to this international meeting.

Recasting Women's Family Roles

In the late 1930s, the feminists shifted fronts in their battle for family reform. Women could not change laws but they could change the performance of their family roles. Enhanced and expanded roles in the family might serve not only to increase women's stature, bringing them the security they were unable to achieve through legal reform, but also to safeguard women's new roles in the paid work force. Through its new Arabic journal *al-Misriyah* the EFU advised a growing constitutency of middle-class women.

One route to increased authority and leverage for women lay through an expansion of their maternal roles. Feminists built on the principle of expanded maternal authority that the 1929 custody revision ratified. The mother's authority over her children extended into their adolescence, a period of growth that was only beginning to be understood as a distinct stage of life. Until then not only had fathers been considered the key figures in the lives of older children, especially sons, but in middle-class families the mother's role had frequently been usurped by her mother-in-law, who often shared the same household. The mother's assumption of a predominant role in raising her children would lessen her domination by her mother-in-law, a linchpin of family patriarchy.

By the late 1930s middle-class women had broken into new professions, entering the workplace in significant numbers and often competing with men for jobs. The influx, which made many men uneasy, was exacerbated by the persisting economic recession. As working women came under increasing attack as wives and mothers who neglected their home and "natural" roles, feminists stepped up the discourse on the importance of women's family roles. This was by then a familiar strategy of feminists in promoting new opportunities for women in society; it was especially expedient in the 1930s with the rise of Islamist conservatism. Through a focus on women's traditional roles their fragile gains in the workplace might be protected and the way paved for future advances.[59] Advice on making the family function more smoothly and the household operate more efficiently could also help women employed outside the house shoulder their new double burden.

Al-Misriyah provided a forum for broad debate and included male voices. The resulting juxtaposition of views, occasionally odd, was also strategic: it allowed for conservative positions to be aired and in the same venue subtly subverted. Further, including conservative views alongside liberal treatments of family roles might help attract a wider constituency at a time when the EFU was aiming for broader outreach.

Mirroring the feminists' approach to the family's legal structure, discussion on women's activities within the family highlighted conventional roles and responsibilities, displaying no overt quarrel with the "traditional" distribution of authority that privileged men.

In the 1930s, cries went up about the "marriage crisis" (*azmat al-zawaj*). The lamenting voices were mainly male. Muhammad Farid Junaydi published a book entitled *Azmat al-Zawaj fi Misr* (The marriage crisis in Egypt), identifying the crisis as a problem of the urban middle and upper classes. *Al-Misriyah* provided space for airing the problem and proposing solutions. Habib al-Masri claimed, "The gravest illness in Egyptian society is in the home."[60] Journalist Fikri Abazah complained that family members went off in different directions and never so much as sat down together at "the same dinner table." The cacophony of conjugal discord reverberated in "The War of Nerves," by *al-Misriyah*'s editor Eva Habib al-Masri.[61] The problem did not stem exclusively from frayed gender relations; it had an economic base as well. Middle-class men were finding it difficult to afford to marry in times of economic depression.

What did women think? Expanding experience, and with it expanding consciousness, made some younger women more acutely aware of the perils of married life. Yet few followed Nabawiyah Musa and some of the feminist philanthropists in trying out alternative solutions. Suhayr, the protagonist in Muhammad Khurshid's play *Masiruhum Ilayna* (Their destiny is ours), performed at the National Theater, illustrated the dilemma. Suhayr, a twenty-five-year-old Paris-trained doctor who has recently opened a clinic in Cairo, talks about men and marriage with her fifty-year-old mother, Aminah.

SUHAYR: I'd rather remain single than marry a violent, tyrannical man. You women sought a man because you needed one, but I work. I don't need a man to support me.

AMINAH: Are you saying that the girls of today are using education as a shield to protect themselves from men?

SUHAYR: Aren't they right?

AMINAH: We sought our security with men, not protection from them.

SUHAYR: Men knew that and exploited the situation and dominated you as they pleased.

The male-scripted play ended, however, with Suhayr seeking marriage—like most women.[62]

While it remained unclear whether Suhayr would combine work with marriage, the feminists keynoted women's dual roles in the inaugural issue of *al-Misriyah*. A pioneer in law and government service, the EFU's Na'imah al-Ayyubi declared that the woman "must know her duties to family and society."[63] In "The Reforming Woman as a Guide and Educator" early EFU member Bahigah Rashid wrote: "We had hoped that opening the doors of higher education to girls would be the beginning of a new era in which the woman became fulfilled and [at the same time] would lead to the creation of new family life in Egypt." She insisted that the educated woman's influence should not stop with the family but must also be felt in the nation and society.[64]

The space given to the woman's role as wife in *al-Misriyah* constituted a new departure in the discussion on family roles. The earlier cult of domesticity had privileged the maternal role. It had been argued that education would improve women for their roles as mothers; now education and special training were coming to be seen as a must for women's roles as both wife and mother. The article "Between Two Educated Girls," signed "An Honest Listener," noted that "all affairs of life are conducted by specialists except marriage and motherhood." It suggested specialized training as an answer.[65] In a literary competition in 1936 on the theme "The Renaissance of the Egyptian Woman," Duriyah Fahmi reported that some essayists had suggested awarding wives "a diploma in *zawjiyah* (housewifery) confirming [their] preparation for housewifery and giving [them] financial remuneration."[66]

New importance was given to a wife's literacy and general knowledge. An article entitled "The Wife Who Doesn't Read" asked, "If a wife doesn't read, doesn't understand him [her husband], and can't talk with him, what will he do?" The author asserted that "the most important thing in marriage is intellectual friendship. Many homes have been broken because of lack of intellectual and cultural harmony."[67] Another piece, "The Causes of Family Disputes: The Opinion of an Expert Lawyer Based on Numerous Cases from Different Classes," identified the ignorance of the wife and mother as "the most dangerous thing."[68]

The problem of compatibility between spouses, exacerbated by uneven education and different daily lives, afflicted both middle and upper classes. Muhammad Husayn Haykal, the husband of EFU member ʿAzizah Haykal, recorded in his diary: "There are almost universal complaints in the educated sections of the country concerning young men's evasion of marriage or their desire to marry foreigners. . . . The main problem today is that the young women do not progress as they [the young men] do and the gulf between the two groups grows wider."[69]

In an article in *al-Thaqafah* playwright Tawfiq al-Hakim discussed how the two sexes' unequal "progress" damaged their relationships. He claimed that many distinguished male writers—including Muhammad Husayn Haykal, Taha Husayn (married to a Frenchwoman), and Ahmad Amin (married to an Englishwoman)—had been most inspired in their work by European women.[70] Feminists contended that men were responsible for the "failings" of Egyptian women. In 1920 Nabawiyah Musa had pointed out that women were kept from education and opportunities to develop and then they were blamed for the consequences.

In 1937, when it was announced that former prime minister Tawfiq Nasim would marry an Austrian woman, feminists voiced their objections to Egyptian men's marrying foreign women. Feminists wished to tie their male compatriots to the problem of continued constraints on Egyptian women's advancement. If men encouraged women's development, the problem of marital incompatibility among Egyptians would be solved.[71]

While the discourse of advice was generally directed to women, there were a few articles in *al-Misriyah* that broached the subject of the man's responsibilities as a husband. Niʿmat Hamid Muhammad, in a piece forthrightly titled "If You Want a Good Wife, Find a Good Husband," pointed out that a husband's actions had a direct bearing on his wife's behavior.[72] Another article, "The Causes of Family Disputes," emphasized that "each spouse has his or her duties and rights."[73] These themes, however, were not elaborated.

What was "safer" in this still conservative patriarchal culture was admonishing women on how to treat their husbands in order to keep them. A few articles appeared in *al-Misriyah* coaching women to cater to their husbands as a way to win out in "their kingdom." In 1937, poet Jamilah al-ʿAlaʾili counseled the modern bride to be attentive to her husband's moods and sensibilities.[74] In "The Secrets of Happiness in the Home," Rifqah ʿAtiyah Yusuf cautioned wives not to argue with their husbands but to create for them "a climate of happiness and beauty." The wife must know her husband's likes and dislikes. She must avoid jealousy, excessive demands, and monotony in everyday life so the husband will not be bored. She must not spend too much time in visits, to the neglect of home and children, or compete with other women in displays of jewelry and clothes. If the wife heeds this advice, Yusuf tells her reader, "you can dominate your kingdom and the hearts and feelings of man."[75] This advice from an unmarried woman to wives, or potential wives, was not unlike that a male contributor, Muhammad ʿIffat, presented to *al-Misriyah* under the title "Ten Commandments of an Arab Woman to Her Daughter." The "commandments" included the following: "Refrain from appearing happy when he [your husband] is sad and sad when he is happy . . . the more you revere him and make him feel important, the more he will revere you and be generous to you . . . the more you agree with him, the more he will agree with you . . . know that you will not attain what you want unless you prefer his satisfaction to yours and his inclinations to your own." ʿIffat resurrected these precepts from ancient Arabia. It is worth noting, however, that this was a mother's advice to a daughter about to marry a king; perhaps the mother would not have offered the same counsel if her daughter had been marrying a commoner.[76] Yet there is a striking parallel in *Bihishti Zewar* (Heavenly ornaments) by Mawlana Ashraf Ali Thanawi, published in Lahore in 1923, in which this Indian Muslim man offers detailed advice to his female coreligionists on how to please their husbands and in-laws. The book became a popular gift for new brides.[77]

Al-Misriyah offered similar counsel. The wife was told how to keep herself attractive with suitable clothes and makeup, and, through a proper diet and exercise, how to keep fit. There were tips on cookery and menus, on how to decorate a house, and on how to organize servants, as even ordinary middle-class households would have some paid domestic help. If a woman fulfilled her role as wife in these ways, relations between spouses would remain smooth and family life would be harmonious. This conservative counsel hardly sounds like part of a feminist program; it might be construed as a "feminist" ploy, encouraging women to seek security through pleasing men in the absence of alternative means, but most feminists would not support such a strategy.

The feminists confronted the economic dimension of the marriage crisis. In the 1930s the depression brought unemployment and low salaries coupled with a high cost of living, and many middle-class families were hard-pressed. Young men were finding it difficult to acquire the money needed to pay the mahr (dower). There were also complaints that men were seeking to marry women with rich and powerful fathers.[78] *Al-Misriyah* approached the problem in different ways. For one, it attempted to change values. The 1938 union of *L'Egyptienne* editor-in-chief Saiza Nabarawi to the artist Mustafa

Najib was presented as a model marriage built on "a spiritual and intellectual foundation."[79] Marriages made with an eye toward material advance or elevation in status were scorned.[80]

On a more practical front, feminists campaigned to lower the mahr. When Hurriyah Idris, a member of the EFU's Shaqiqat, married in 1935, her aunt and guardian Huda Shaʿrawi agreed on behalf of her niece to a mahr of twenty-five piasters in order to set an example. Journalist Ahmad al-Sawi praised the gesture in *al-Ahram*.[81] The same year when Duriyah Shafiq married Ahmad al-Sawi himself, she also agreed to a mahr of twenty-five piasters.[82]

When the feminists learned that registration fees for marriages would be raised as a consequence of the elevation of the ma'dhun's position, they objected to a proposal they had previously favored in the hope that it might lead to stricter enforcement of the minimum marriage age.[83] In 1938, a bill was introduced in the parliament proposing a bachelor tax.[84] In 1939 *al-Misriyah* reported that the new Ministry of Social Affairs was considering a tax on bachelors from the age of twenty-five and proposing job priority for married men, along with higher salaries and child allowances.[85] In 1940 the feminists urged the government to enact a family allowance program similar to one Turkey had adopted.[86]

There had always been a chorus of male and female voices praising the role of the mother. Was the decibel level turned up in the 1930s as women were making strides in higher education and in the workplace? It seems so. And were women now castigated more sharply for not playing their maternal roles properly or abandoning them altogether? Probably. It was at this same time that *al-Misriyah* published a plethora of articles seeking to help women perform their maternal roles in enlightened, efficient, and imaginative ways.

In "Mothers' Talk" ("Hadith al-Ummahat"), a series in *al-Misriyah*, Magda Hasib dispensed practical advice on child care on a range of topics such as breast-feeding, bathing infants, general hygiene, diet, and exercise.[87] Such advice had been offered since early in the century in the Arabic women's press and in manuals. But now, in the late 1930s, there was a new focus on adolescence as a distinct stage in the maturation process in which women had roles to play. This challenged the conventional wisdom that as children became older they required the attention of "rational" fathers over "emotional" mothers.[88] Two EFU members had studied social work (including subjects like psychology and sociology) abroad: Eva Habib al-Masri in the United States and Na'imah al-Ayyubi in Belgium. They and other new experts urged women to apply child psychology to aid them in their child rearing. Articles addressed the psychological and educational needs of growing children and adolescents, with emphasis placed on the importance of reading.[89] *Al-Misriyah* introduced readers to Kamil Kilani's new press for children's books, which was making Arabic classics accessible to children, as well as translations of Turkish and Persian classics, and of French and English children's books.[90]

Attention was paid not only to nurturing children's minds; on more than one occasion it was suggested that mothers impart knowledge to children about their bodies and sexuality. In "Sex Education" ("al-Tarbiyah al-Jinsiyah"), Sumayya Fahmi, a teacher at the Institute for the Education of Girls, counseled mothers to give children accurate information about sex and reproduction.[91]

As *al-Misriyah* rarely advised men on how to be good husbands, so men were seldom advised on how to be good fathers. ʿIffat Thabit, in "Modern Psychology and Parents," addressed both parents and urged a more active paternal role in child raising. She also warned mothers and fathers against being overprotective of the child so they would not inhibit experimentation and independent thinking.[92] Changes in early socialization of children might help reduce the hold of negative aspects of the past.

The discourse of advice on family roles might have helped instill added confidence and pride in women's work inside the home, but the continued prevalence of divorce indicated that enhanced performance could not guarantee women security as wives.

• CHAPTER 8 •

Educating the Nation

EDUCATION FOR WOMEN at all levels and in all fields was a pivotal goal of the Egyptian feminist movement. No state secondary schools for girls had existed during colonial rule. The first demand was for state secondary schools for girls with the same curriculum as that followed in the schools for boys.

In promoting education for women feminists continued the process begun in the nineteenth century by the Egyptian state, a process truncated after colonial occupation. If male Egyptians suffered from a lack of state-provided education, female Egyptians had been far more disadvantaged by colonial education policies. Because of a lack of adequate state schools for girls those Egyptian women who had received schooling had generally been educated in foreign institutions (French, British, American, Italian, and so forth) that imparted a Western enculturation.

During colonial occupation Bahithat al-Badiyah and Nabawiyah Musa had made educational demands that were simultaneously feminist and nationalist demands. When the EFU called for women's education in the 1920s and 1930s, the demands remained feminist and nationalist, presented this time to the new independent Egyptian state instead of to colonial authorities. In addition to secondary schools for girls, Egyptian feminists pushed for women's access to the university and to higher institutes.

In the 1920s the EFU pressured the state to provide secondary schooling for girls and at the same time tried to win over society to the importance of female education. At the end of the 1920s and throughout the 1930s feminists focused attention on opening the doors of the university and higher institutes to women.

The specter of formal education for women raised fears about respectability and concern about women's family roles, especially their roles as mothers. Further, public education for girls was not simply an issue of gender but also one of class: upper-class girls were kept out of the ordinary state schools by their families and rarely attended university until after the 1952 revolution. In campaigning for education for women, Egyptian feminists implicitly raised and confronted a host of intersecting issues.

SECONDARY SCHOOL FOR GIRLS: EQUAL AND SEPARATE

In the spring of 1923 the EFU held its first mass meeting, and there women agreed to petition the state to provide secondary schools for girls with the same curriculum as that offered in the boys' schools. The EFU presented the demand to the prime minister, together with a resolution the IAW had taken at Rome supporting Egyptian feminists' education demand.[1] Soon afterwards the minister of education, ʿAli Mahir, informed the EFU president of plans for a secondary school for girls.[2] When the Shubra Secondary School for Girls opened in 1925, thirty-seven years after the first state secondary school for boys, the EFU claimed it as their second victory, the first having been the minimum marriage age for girls. Four years later, Egyptian women obtained state secondary school diplomas for the first time since 1907, when Nabawiyah Musa had won her degree.[3]

The Shubra School was placed under the able direction of Insaf Sirri, who remained a lifelong educator.[4] Huda Shaʿrawi and Saiza Nabarawi immediately visited the school to register their public support and to encourage the pioneering pupils.[5] Girls from professional, middle-class families were among the first students. These included Aminah al-Saʿid, whose father had left his medical practice in Asyut and moved to Cairo to enable his daughters to pursue their studies beyond primary school, and Naʿimah al-Ayyubi, the daughter of historian Ilyas al-Ayyubi, a Muslim convert of Syrian Christian origin.[6] Wishing to sustain their support of girls' education and seeing the new school as a recruiting ground for future feminists, Shaʿrawi and Nabarawi made repeated calls, speaking to pupils about the women's movement. Aminah al-Saʿid vividly recalled decades later how she had been inspired by Shaʿrawi, who invited her and another pupil called Suʿad to give speeches in Arabic at EFU functions. Several years later Aminah al-Saʿid helped to form the EFU youth group Shaqiqat, serving as the Arabic secretary. As a regular member she continued to deliver EFU addresses in Arabic.[7] Naʿimah al-Ayyubi also became an active member of the EFU.

The EFU kept up pressure for additional secondary schools for girls.[8] The Hilmiyah and Saniyah Schools were upgraded to secondary schools, and a new secondary school for girls was opened at Helwan, south of Cairo.[9] Secondary schools for girls were also established in the provinces: at Asyut in Upper Egypt in 1932, and in the Delta at Tanta in 1933 and Mansurah in 1937. These schools served middle-class girls.

The state also created two elite schools for girls in an effort to attract daughters of upper-class families who still favored the foreign schools for their offspring. The two institutions offered contrasting options. The College Qasr al-Dubara opened in 1927 in a mansion in Garden City. When Saiza Nabarawi paid a visit she discovered that the state had preserved "aristocratic harem ways" in the school. Girls were kept strictly segregated to the extent that "the masculine element, including the servants, was rigorously banished."[10] She told *L'Egyptienne*'s readers: "To appease male opinion concerning the education of women a large part of the curriculum is reserved for housekeeping, domestic economy, and culinary arts. In this way, men who wish to see their future companions preserve the charms of the Chrysalis of former times applaud the government's effort to reconcile past ways with the present."[11]

The Kulliyat al-Banat (Girls' College), which opened around the same time in Zamalek, another fashionable district, was of a different order. Here the standard secondary school curriculum was followed. The Girls' College was a progressive school offering new subjects such as psychology and instilling a social consciousness in its pupils. Huda Shaʿrawi signaled her approval by sending her two young nieces Hawwa' and Hurriyah Idris to the school.[12] In 1929, the ratio was sixteen teachers to eighty pupils. As already noted several early graduates such as Hawwa' Idris and Layla Doss embarked on voluntary social service and became active in the feminist movement.

While the EFU pressed the government to open schools for girls, feminist educator Nabawiyah Musa took a different initiative, mobilizing a group of wealthy women from Alexandria to form the Society for the Advancement of the Young Woman (Jamʿiyat Tarqiyat al-Fatah), for the purpose of creating a primary school for girls.[13] Nabawiyah Musa expected that members would raise funds and persuade the wealthy to send their daughters to the school, while she, the professional educator, would run the school. However, women of the society argued with her over control of the budget. Nabawiyah Musa won out only to encounter difficulties with officials from the Ministry of Education who she claims tried to undermine her efforts. When she lost the first premises she had rented for the new school—a loss that she attributed to interference by her adversaries—she approached Huda Shaʿrawi, who provided the necessary financial assistance.[14] Nabawiyah Musa finally triumphed, and the Tarqiyat al-Fatah School opened in the then elite Muharram Bey quarter of Alexandria. Nabawiyah Musa's school, which charged an annual tuition of six pounds, soon attracted more pupils than the nearby government school.[15]

A few years later Nabawiyah Musa opened a secondary school for girls called the Banat al-Ashraf School in the ʿAbbasiyah quarter of Cairo.[16] Again, she ran into obstructions instigated by hostile Ministry of Education officials. This time under threat that her building would be torn down, she obtained help from minister of public works Husayn Sirri.[17] Her two private schools, which acquired a reputation for academic excellence as well as for stern discipline, educated generations of women in Alexandria and Cairo.[18]

The availability of new state schools for girls did not necessarily mean that families, even from the more receptive middle class, were ready to send their daughter to these institutions. Education for girls, especially at the higher levels of school, had yet to gain wide acceptance. Not infrequently, girls were withdrawn from school in their early teens by families who had finalized marriage arrangements for them.[19]

In the 1920s and 1930s, feminists embarked once again upon the task some of them had taken up earlier in the century—and nineteenth-century reformers before them—of educating the nation about female education. In their campaign, they evoked the "golden ages" of Islam and Egypt.

Feminists grounded their advocacy of female education in the Qur'an and in Muslim history. In a 1925 public lecture at the American University in Beirut Ihsan al-Qusi stressed that the Qur'an approved of education for women; she turned to early Islamic history for examples of women known for knowledge and piety, to refute the common belief that learning leads to women's ruin. Her list included ʿA'ishah, the young wife of the Prophet Muhammad, a renowned transmitter of hadith (sayings of the Prophet), Zaynab, a granddaughter of the Prophet versed in theology, and Sakinah, a poet in ʿAbbasid Baghdad.[20] In 1933 Saiza Nabarawi also reminded her coreligionists that the Qur'an recommended learning for all Muslims.[21]

Feminists took arguments for women's education from Egypt's pharaonic past. They reiterated what progressive male nationalists had declared earlier: that when Egyptian civilization was at its height, women were advanced. Egypt had fallen under foreign occupation because the country had declined, and the country had declined because women had become backward. Through education women and the nation would be revitalized. The nationalist narrative evoked ancient Egyptian glory, as evidenced by the splendors of Tutankhamen's tomb, uncovered the same year Egypt achieved independence. Feminists heralded women's education as the key to restoring national greatness. In public speeches and articles in *L'Egyptienne*, feminists spoke of women's learned forebears, such as Nefrure, daughter of Queen Hatsheput, who had been educated at Dayr al-Bahri by Sennemut, the architect of her temple; and Sakat, Thant, and Maris, the daughters of twelfth-dynasty governor Khunum Khtub, of the Eastern Desert, who had also studied at temple schools. It was said that nobles used to compete in educating their girls, who studied medicine, astrology, religion, and literature with priests at the temple schools.[22]

Feminists were sensitive to the role of state education in instilling a sense of nation and in the shaping of the citizenry. The EFU demanded that national heritage form an essential part of the school curriculum. The feminist organization called for the creation of a museum of national and social history and a commission for the preservation of national monuments.[23] In 1930 the EFU suggested to minister of education Murad Sid Ahmad that civics be taught in the upper grades of girls' primary schools "to prepare them to become good citizens and to make women conscious of their rights and responsibilities."[24] The minister promised to issue a directive that civics and religion focus "on the rights and responsibilities of the woman *as mother* [emphasis added] and citizen."[25]

Nabawiyah Musa was adamant that Egyptian schools adopt a national curriculum and made sure that this happened in her two private schools. As a student and teacher in state schools under colonial rule she was acutely aware of the culturally and politically subversive aspect of nonindigenous education; the state school system in Egypt had been modeled on the British system and still bore its imprint. She was also sensitive to the alien messages—including ideas about morality—transmitted by foreign teachers.

In 1920 she wrote: "If we entrust the education of our daughters to foreign women, our daughters will imitate foreign ways, whether good or bad, whereas our own teachers can inculcate in our students an understanding of our own culture and morality. They will be able to discriminate and to reject what is not suitable for us. Moral values [that are alien] would pass from the educated girls to those in the process of being educated." She also said, "Our children would acquire a sense of nationalism from their Egyptian teachers that they do not get from foreign teachers."[26] In her own private schools, Nabawiyah Musa assiduously tried to instill in her pupils a firm sense of national identity and pride.[27]

The feminists advocated physical education in the schools, as well as in everyday life. They linked physical fitness with the energy, courage, and independence of character necessary for the contemporary woman. Saiza Nabarawi wrote in *L'Egyptienne*: "Is it wise and logical that the girl who is called upon to become the intellectual equal of the young man should find herself in a condition of great physical inferiority to him?" [28] Nabarawi took care to locate the feminist appeal for physical exercise and sports for women within the framework of Islam: "The Muslim religion, far from placing the body and soul in conflict, places them in harmony; to take care of the one is to take care of the other."[29]

Interest in physical well-being for women was not entirely new. At the beginning of the century Bahithat al-Badiyah had advocated walking as recreation for women. She had insisted: "Veiling should not prevent us from breathing fresh air. . . . It must not . . . cause our health to deteriorate. When we finish our [house]work and feel restless, why shouldn't we go to the outskirts of the city and take the fresh air that God created for everyone rather than putting it in boxes for men only?"[30] In 1920 Nabawiyah Musa had encouraged mothers to arrange sports for their daughters "so that they will be raised with strong minds and bodies."[31]

The EFU called for physical education courses as part of the standard curriculum in the girls' schools, and by the end of the 1920s the government schools began to offer such courses. The Ministry of Education appointed Munirah Sabri as inspector of physical education in the girls' schools. In 1928 under her direction the first annual girls' gymnastics exhibition was held at the Gazirah Sporting Grounds. The second year two thousand primary school girls took part.[32] In a public lecture series organized by the Ministry of Education in 1930, Sabri gave a talk entitled "On Physical Culture."[33] Later the ministry instituted a Girl Guides program as another way of promoting physical fitness for women.

When the government created sports clubs for girls in the second half of the 1930s, the feminists encouraged women to take advantage of them and demanded still more facilities. Keeping up the pressure Na'imah al-Ayyubi, in 1937 in *al-Misriyah*, insisted that more attention to sports in the girls' schools was still needed.[34] In the early 1940s, the Institute of Physical Education for Girls was created and Nafisah Ghamrawi was appointed director.

Women excelled as students. A 1930 report on schools indicated better performance among female students and teachers than among their male counterparts. A girl came out first among the 14,409 primary school candidates. Out of the 958 girls who sat for the examination, 509 succeeded (52.9 percent) while only 43.3 percent of the boys passed. Out of 556 candidates for the *kafa'ah*, the first stage of the bacclaureate, 320 girls passed (57.7 percent), as opposed to 47.5 percent of the boys.[35] In 1939, 28.2 percent of the girls and 29 percent of the boys who sat for the secondary school examination passed. In 1940, 85.1 percent of the girls and 67.7 percent of the boys passed the primary school exam. In the secondary school examinations the same year, 43.6 percent of the girls and 41.3 percent of the boys passed.[36] In Arabic language four of the top five primary schools were girls' schools. Among secondary schools the top three were girls' schools: the Amirah Fawziyah in Cairo, and the secondary schools in Asyut and Tanta.[37]

The success of girls in standard curriculum schools was heartening. But after women had achieved considerable equality in education, new questions emerged. Did women have different or additional needs that were not being met in a curriculum originally designed for men?[38] Toward the end of the 1930s, education was being blamed for the alleged failure of women in their roles as wives and mothers. Among the critics were feminists such as the EFU's Bahigah Rashid, who had expected women's education to be more beneficial to family life. Naʿimah al-Ayyubi wrote in 1937 "We demanded that the Ministry of Education provide equal education for girls and boys so that girls would be qualified for higher education, and [now] the result is ignorance on the part of our girls about the woman's duty toward her family, children, and society." She called for courses in health, child care, home economics, and social work to be added to the standard syllabus in the girls, schools.[39] Social work was then being introduced into Egypt, and al-Ayyubi, who had recently taken a degree in the subject in Belgium, was in the forefront of the new profession.

Declaring before the Chamber of Deputies that the education of girls and of boys should not be identical, the minister of education announced the plan to create schools of feminine culture for primary school graduates.[40] The following year the Ministry of Education opened such schools, which offered a curriculum centered on motherhood and home economics. To help in the effort the government enlisted the talents of pioneers in women's education, including Insaf Sirri, then principal of Amirah Fayzah School; Tawhidah ʿAbd al-Rahman, Matilda Awad, and Munirah Sabri, inspectors in the Ministry of Education; Nur Muhammad, a teacher at the Helwan Secondary School for Girls; and Mrs. Muhammad Ahmad Habib, a specialist in music.[41]

Back in 1920 Nabawiyah Musa had advocated the idea of "equal plus more" regarding women's education. She was one of the first, along with Bahithat al-Badiyah, to argue that without equal educational qualifications women would not be positioned for equal work opportunities. At the same time, women also had to contend with domestic responsibilities that they should be equipped to carry out as efficiently as possible. Among those advocating "schools of feminine culture" or "home economics" in the late 1930s it is likely that many, including government officials, were at the same time advocating a more exclusive domestic destiny for women than Nabawiyah Musa, Bahigah Rashid, and Naᶜimah al-Ayyubi had intended. The trend in the second half of the 1930s toward a renewed emphasis on women's maternal roles emerged at a time when more women than ever before were being educated and increasing numbers were entering the work force. It was also a moment when populist right-wing movements were on the rise in Egypt, as they were in parts of Europe.

Opening University Gates: Equal Together

The private Egyptian University, created during colonial occupation, was reconstituted as a state institution and renamed Fu'ad I University in 1925. The charter proclaimed the university open to all Egyptians but the doors were shut to women. Not surprisingly public opinion did not support women's university education, but many liberal members of the university, including British staff, also opposed women's entry.[42] Yet that same year the government displayed willingness to support university education for Egyptian women abroad, sending a group to England on scholarship, far from conservative eyes at home. Kawkab Hifni Nasif (sister of Bahithat al-Badiyah), Hilanah Sidarus, Tawhidah ᶜAbd al-Rahman, Anisah Naji, Habibah Iwis, and Fathiyah Hamid all entered the medical school at the University of London.

Feminists pushed for women's right to enter the university in Egypt. University rector Ahmad Lutfi al-Sayyid and a few others in the central administration, including dean Taha Husayn, supported the women. The rector took a practical course of action, quietly allowing a small group of women to matriculate in 1929, the first year the Shubra Secondary School had graduated women.[43] Four entered the Faculty of Arts: Suhayr al-Qalamawi in Arabic literature, Fatma Salim in classics, and Zahirah ᶜAbd al-ᶜAziz and Fatma Fahmi in philosophy. Naᶜimah al-Ayyubi entered the Faculty of Law. Al-Qalamawi had originally wanted to study science, but the British dean of the Faculty of Science turned her down. Despite some initial wariness and opposition the experiment continued; the following year women did gain admittance to the Faculty of Science. These university pioneers did well, and the EFU publicized their progress. When Naᶜimah al-Ayyubi finished first in her class in 1931, *L'Egyptienne* proudly announced this distinction.[44]

It was symbolically significant that a member of the first cohort of women at the university entered the Department of Arabic Literature, and that the first two doctorates earned by women were in Arabic literature. It had not been easy for women in Egypt to gain literacy in Arabic. It had not been exclusively among the French-speaking upper class that women had been provided with foreign tutors and had later been sent to foreign private schools. Although Arabic was the everyday language of the middle class it was predominantly the men of that class who were given schooling in the language. Middle-class families continued to send their daughters to foreign schools even after state education for women became available. In 1937 Baha al-Din Barakat, the former minister of education, noted this persisting trend. Like the feminists he was critical of this practice because it produced women who were alienated from their own society.[45] Wadidah Wassif, daughter of an educator and deputy minister for secondary schools in the 1940s, was an exception to the rule, and indeed she became proficient in Arabic.[46] As noted earlier, the teaching of Arabic in schools had been the preserve of men of religion trained at al-Azhar, where Arabic was a cornerstone of the curriculum. It was considered a sacred language—according to Islam the Qur'an was dictated to Muhammad in Arabic by the Archangel Gabriel—and the shaykhs were outraged for both cultural and economic reasons when a woman, Nabawiyah Musa, began to teach Arabic in school. For all these reasons the women's achievement in Arabic was signal.

The university, unlike the schools, was coeducational. The virtue of daughters continued to be a major concern to families and an important reason for their reluctance to send their girls to the university. A woman's reputation could be tarnished by mere proximity to men, and with it the honor of her family and her chances for marriage. Accordingly, measures were taken at the university to keep the sexes separated. Women sat at the front in the lecture halls and were provided with their own common room. Nobel Prize–winning writer Najib Mahfuz, a student at the time, described the scene: "The girl students in 1930 were very few in number, no more than ten of them altogether. They all had the stamp of the harem about them; they dressed modestly, wore no earrings or bangles and sat together in the front row of the lecture hall, as though they were all in the women's section of a tramcar."[47] When her parents reluctantly allowed her to go to university in the 1940s, Wadidah Wassif recalls in her memoirs: "I was properly briefed on how to conduct myself with the boys with whom I would be in contact at close range for the first time. . . . I must at all times observe a distant and reserved attitude. . . . Honor and respectability above all. In all circumstances keep my dignity. No private conversations. No familiarities. . . . I obeyed to the letter. I moved in their midst barricaded by thick ramparts of propriety."[48]

In 1933 when the women at Fu'ad I University and at London University graduated, the EFU celebrated at its new Qasr al-ʿAyni headquarters. Taha

Husayn—whose deanship had been a casualty of the political repression directed against the university by Isma'il Sidqi's reactionary government—gave the principal address and presented the new women graduates of the Faculty of Arts to a large and distinguished audience. Lawyer Muhammad 'Ali 'Allubah introduced the Faculty of Law graduate, placing on her shoulders her new lawyer's robe presented by Huda Sha'rawi.[49] Dr. Sami Kamil, from the EFU dispensary, presented the women doctors who had recently graduated from the University of London.[50] The highly publicized success of the first graduates coincided with the reactionary government's attack on coeducation. Feminist women and liberal men publicly banded together in celebration and defiance.

The battle for university education had to be fought virtually discipline by discipline. In 1925, four years before the first group of women formally entered the university, 'Afifah Iskandar had been allowed to sit in on courses in Egyptology but was not permitted to work toward a degree. The feminists drew attention to her plight, but to no avail. In Egypt, the prestigious discipline of Egyptology remained a male purview. It was, moreover, a field dominated by Westerners until much later in the century: not until 1939 did an Egyptian become head of the university's Institute of Archaeology.[51] The Western archaeological missions in Egypt were also male enclaves. When Princess Khadijah Fu'ad 'Izzat, a niece of the famous *salonnière* Princess Nazli Fazil, pioneered in archaeological fieldwork from 1920 to 1935 with a French team excavating Islamic sites in Morocco, *L'Egyptienne* cited her achievements as a model for other women.[52] In 1939 when Hélène Vacaresco brought a group of women archaeologists from L'Ecole du Louvre to Egypt, *L'Egyptienne* used the occasion to promote archaeology for women.[53]

The Faculty of Medicine graduated its first women in 1936, but Fadilah 'Arif, Nafisah Samahah, and Sarwat al-Tunisi were not permitted to work as interns at the university hospital.[54] Not until World War II, when many of the British staff had left, could women do their residency at the university hospital. But women did excel in the classroom: Fatma Hafiz 'Abdin was first in her 1937 class at the Faculty of Medicine, as *al-Misriyah* took care to announce.[55]

In the 1930s there was another breakthrough when women from the provinces began to attend the university.[56] The first two who came from the Delta entered the Faculty of Arts, both specializing in Arabic literature. 'A'ishah 'Abd al-Rahman, later known as Bint al-Shati', was from a peasant family in Damietta. Her al-Azhar–trained father disdained his daughter's educational aspirations. However, with encouragement from her mother and her own strong will, she found her way to the university in the mid-1930s. 'A'ishah 'Abd al-Rahman went on to write on rural women, as already noted. Later her interest in gender would be expressed in a series of books on the Prophet's wives and daughters applauding the public roles of urban Muslim women.[57]

Rawhiyah al-Qalini, born in Kafr al-Shaykh near Dassuq, displayed a gift for reciting poetry at an early age. Her father nurtured his daughter's talent by sending her first to primary school in Tanta and later to the Amirah Fayzah School in Alexandria for her secondary school education. He also encouraged her to enter the university in 1939. Al-Qalini went on to publish a book on Arab women poets, *Angham Halimah: Shaʿirat ʿArabiyat* (Romantic verses: Arab women poets), as well as a number of other works. In the 1940s she joined the Daughter of the Nile Union (al-Ittihad Bint al-Nil) and came to be called the "Poet of the Feminist Movement."[58]

The Faculties of Commerce, Agriculture, and Engineering were created in 1935. Women were admitted to the Faculty of Commerce in the first year,[59] and they entered the Faculties of Agriculture and Engineering in 1945. The number of women at the university grew over the years. In 1930 women represented only .03 percent of students in higher education and the female ratio remained low throughout the 1940s, but women's enrollment did steadily increase, reaching 7 percent in 1950.[60] At a public lecture at the American University in Cairo in 1935, Huda Shaʿrawi announced that there were currently 88 women studying in the Faculty of Arts, 40 in medicine, 27 in science, 10 in law, and 8 in commerce.[61] By 1940, the total number of women at the university had reached 450.[62]

In the mid-1930s women began to undertake graduate study. The first two took advanced degrees in the Department of Arabic Literature. Suhayr Qalamawi had attended the IAW conference in Istanbul in 1935 as a member of the EFU's Shaqiqat. The same year she published a book called *Ahadith Jiddati* (My grandmother's tales) in the form of debates on women's changing lives between her and her grandmother.[63] After working in journalism briefly and running a weekly radio program she returned to the university to resume her studies with Taha Husayn. In 1937 she became the first Egyptian woman to be awarded the master of arts degree, and in 1941 she was the first to win a doctorate. ʿA'ishah ʿAbd al-Rahman studied with another distinguished professor, Amin al-Khuli, and took her master's degree in 1941, her doctorate in 1950.

In 1942 when Faruk I University was established in Alexandria and a second university opened in Heliopolis in Cairo—the Ibrahim Pasha University, later renamed ʿAyn Shams University—both accepted women as a matter of course. By that time, university-level coeducation was firmly established, but in 1956 an option for separate instruction at this level was provided for women. The Women Teachers' Training College in Heliopolis was reorganized and incorporated into ʿAyn Shams University as the Kulliyat al-Banat (The Girls' College), a facility several kilometers away from the main buildings. In 1962 the millennium-old Islamic center of learning, al-Azhar University, opened its doors to women, creating a College for Girls. This occurred a decade after the revolution of 1952, when the new socialist agenda mobilizing Egyptians of all classes and both sexes was being aggressively pushed. The opening up of this Islamic university to women may have made it easier for women from more conservative families to get a university education. The College for Girls later moved to Maʿdi in the suburbs of Cairo and then to Madinat Nasr where it has remained.[64]

Women not only received an education in the liberal arts and sciences and in law and medicine at the university; they obtained political lessons as well, becoming active in the nationalist political protests at the university in the 1930s and 1940s. Aminah al-Saʿid, a student in the Faculty of Arts from 1931 to 1935, recalled participating with other university women in the political demonstrations and in the three-month student strike that followed Taha Husayn's dismissal as dean of the Faculty of Arts during the repressive Sidqi regime.[65]

Inji Aflatun and Latifah al-Zayyat, who were students in the Faculty of Arts in the 1940s, were both part of left-wing movements on the campus.[66] Aflatun, a landowner's daughter and a graduate of the Lycée Française, where she had been introduced to Marxism, was one of the first upper-class women to attend the university. In 1945 she helped create Rabitat Fatayat al-Jamʿiat wa-al-Maʿahid (The League of University and Institutes' Young Women), which al-Zayyat soon joined. Aflatun recognized intersections of class and gender oppression, seeing both as part of imperialist exploitation. She also insisted that women's liberation was compatible with Islam. She elucidated her views in *Thamanun Milyun Imraʾah Maʿana* (Eighty million women with us, 1948) and in *Nahnu al-Nisaʾ al-Misriyat* (We Egyptian women, 1949). Aflatun combined her radical politics with feminist activism. She met Saiza Nabarawi in 1950 through the Harakat Ansar al-Salam (Movement of the Friends of Peace) and joined the Lajnat al-Shabbat, the Youth Committee Saiza Nabarawi created within the EFU.[67]

Al-Zayyat, unlike Aflatun, tended to focus exclusively on nation and class. However, an awareness of gender surfaced in her 1960 novel *al-Bab al-Maftuh* (The open door), the story of a young woman who finds liberation from middle-class patriarchal restrictions through involvement in nationalist politics at the university.[68] She recently explained: "My heroine had to fight on so many fronts: against tradition, against her father, against British occupation [the military occupation in the Canal Zone that continued until 1956], middle-class values—which was very important for me and were to my mind rotten values of fear, withdrawal, caution, a kind of rejection of life, being always afraid and aware of danger." She claimed her hero's vision as her own but pointed out that their experiences differed, for her protagonist was ten years younger than she. Recently reflecting on the past al-Zayyat confessed: "I have come to realize that the status of women has been of great importance to me despite the fact that I was not mistreated as a woman. Being a political activist as a student I was treated with great respect."[69]

While some Egyptian women blazed trails at the national university, others pioneered in higher education in foreign institutions inside and outside Egypt. Earlier I mentioned the women who went to England in 1925 on the first state-sponsored student mission for training as medical doctors. The same year Munirah Thabit enrolled in the French School of Law in Cairo. Women had first entered the school a few years earlier, but they had all been foreigners. Thabit—the daughter of ministry of the interior employee Hasan Thabit and his wife Anisah, a woman of Turkish origin who had received her education in Alexandria at Saint Vincent de Paul School—took her law degree in 1928 after sitting for her examination in Paris. The year she began law school, Thabit became editor of *al-Amal* (Hope), a pro-feminist Wafdist paper. Thabit, who had been co-opted by the Wafd, was antagonistic to EFU president Huda Shaʿrawi, as indeed was the Wafd itself, but by the later 1930s Thabit had joined forces with EFU feminists.[70]

In 1925 Ihsan al-Qusi, an EFU founder, became the first Arab and the first Muslim woman to study at the American University of Beirut. Accompanying her husband who was a student there, al-Qusi took advantage of the situation to further her own studies. Initially she was only allowed to sit in on classes as an auditor because she lacked a secondary school diploma. She later won acceptance as a regular student, however, and majored in psychology and education. The EFU applauded al-Qusi's "courage" in furthering her education at the age of thirty-four "when one would consider her studies over."[71] While at the university, al-Qusi gave several public lectures on gender issues, arguing against such practices as veiling and bayt al-taʿah. When she became the first woman to graduate from the American University in Beirut, Lebanese women's associations feted her.[72] Announcing the successful completion of her studies *L'Egyptienne* wrote, "We hope her example will serve as a lesson to our young women and persuade them of the necessity for higher education."[73]

After graduating from the American College for Girls Eva Habib al-Masri became the first woman to enter the American University in Cairo. In her memoirs she has recounted going with her father to meet the president of the university, who explained that coeducation was still experimental, and that as a foreign institution the American University would have to tread cautiously. However, nothing in the university statutes prohibited the entry of women, and after some discussion the president agreed to permit Eva Habib al-Masri to matriculate.[74] As the only woman, al-Masri sat next to the male students in class but was provided with space on a veranda as her "common room for one." She became editor of the student paper and in 1932 graduated first in her class, with feminist leader Huda Shaʿrawi in attendance. Al-Masri went on to join the EFU.[75]

Duriyah Shafiq had started her education in Tanta in the Delta at the same convent school her mother had attended; she continued at a similar school in Alexandria. She was one of six children of an engineer father and a mother from an impoverished upper-middle-class family, who had died when she was eleven. Duriyah was sixteen when she passed her secondary school examination. Placing second in the country, she wished to pursue university education in France, but this was beyond her family's means. She wrote to Huda Shaʿrawi of her ambitions, and the feminist leader gave her financial support. Duriyah Shafiq began her studies at the Sorbonne in 1930.[76] As a student in Paris she wrote occasional pieces for *L'Egyptienne*.[77] Shafiq took her *licence* and *doctorat d'état* at the Sorbonne; her major thesis was "L'Art pour l'art dans l'Egypte antique" (Art for art's sake in ancient Egypt), and her minor thesis was "La femme et le droit religieux de l'Egypte contemporaine" (The woman and religious law in contemporary Egypt). When she returned to Egypt Huda Shaʿrawi gave her a warm welcome. However, feeling shunned by other EFU members, she went her separate way. In 1947 when the EFU president died, Shafiq, seeing herself as Shaʿrawi's spiritual daughter, felt mandated to carry on her feminist mission.[78]

A striking number of the pioneers in higher education were feminists. Of those I have profiled all called themselves feminists, except for ʿA'ishah ʿAbd al-Rahman and Latifah al-Zayyat, both of whom nonetheless demonstrated an awareness of gender issues. The first generation of EFU feminist activists, predominantly upper-class women, had been educated in harems or in private schools. Many second-generation feminist activists were university educated, one even holding a doctorate. I will return to these younger, middle-class feminists in the next chapter to show how they combined gender activism with careers.

While women were able to enter the university, they were unable to enter the higher institutes, except for one created for them and whose foundation they had laid. This was the Higher Institute of Social Work for Women, established in 1947. Ten years earlier the Association for Social Studies had opened the first school for social work under the direction of Bertha Kamal Fahmi, a graduate of Simmons College in Boston.[79] *L'Egyptienne* and *al-Misriyah* both announced the school's opening, telling readers how to obtain information about the program. The EFU promoted social work as an expression of nationalism.[80] When the government decided to open an institute of social work, it solicited the help of two EFU members, lawyer Naʿimah al-Ayyubi and educator Ihsan al-Qusi. The Ministry of Education sent the two women on a tour of social work institutes in six European countries in 1946 before establishing the new social work institute in Egypt. Al-Ayyubi had taken a degree at the School of Social Work at Liège in Belgium and on her return to Egypt went to work at the new Ministry of Social Affairs, while Ihsan al-Qusi became the first dean of the Higher Institute of Social Work for Women. During al-Qusi's five-year tenure some 150 women were graduated.[81]

The private school of social work and the state Higher Institute of Social Work for Women signaled the professionalization of a field pioneered by women, mostly from the upper classes, at the beginning of the century through their philanthropic associations. By the 1940s social service had become a profession for middle-class women. Upper-class women continued their voluntary social service, which, as noted in chapter 6, after the creation of the Ministry of Social Affairs in 1939 fell under its jurisdiction.

Claiming Other Arenas: Music, Art, and Sport

Women experimented in gaining new knowledge and acquiring training beyond the realm of schools and the university. Some tried to gain entry into higher institutes, while others pursued more individualistic routes through private study and self-development.

In 1930 the EFU cooperated with the Ministry of Education in creating a series of public lectures for women, which Ihsan al-Qusi inaugurated with a lecture entitled "The Woman in the Past and Future" at the Egyptian Geographical Society. The program was an echo of the lectures women earlier in the century had organized for themselves. Now the government was lending support and men were included among the speakers. A distinguished list of women and men spoke on pharaonic and Islamic history, literature, psychology, health, and contemporary intellectual life, providing those women for whom higher education was neither a choice nor a possibility with an opportunity to expand their knowledge.[82]

Gaining entry into specialized higher institutes proved impossible for women during this period, leaving women only private options in their pursuit of the arts. The Conservatory of Oriental Music, which opened in 1925 with substantial government support, remained closed to women. The new conservatory had grown out of Nadi al-Musiqa al-Sharqiyah (Oriental Music Club), a small group of music lovers who first met in modest quarters in Muhammad ʿAli Street in 1913 to perform and teach oriental music. Oriental music, which remained part of popular culture after it had faded among Westernizing elites, had begun to attract the renewed attention of a few middle- and upper-class enthusiasts.[83]

Music had played an important part in the domestic life of the past. In upper-class harems, music had been performed by household slaves and concubines imported mainly from the Caucasus, or by hired performers.[84] On such festive occasions as weddings, women musicians, singers, and dancers were brought into the harems to entertain guests.[85] Around the middle of the nineteenth century Western entertainers began to appear in the royal harems.[86] When the Khedivial Opera House opened in 1869, the European troupes that performed there further developed the taste for Western music. We noted earlier that loges were fitted out with screens, making it possible for women to attend performances.[87]

In the nineteenth century, when upper-class women were educated at home by European tutors, learning the piano became de rigueur. Huda Shaʿrawi as a girl in the 1880s was taught piano by an Italian woman.[88] Playing the piano continued to be fashionable into the twentieth century. Wadidah Wassif has recalled sessions in Alexandria in the 1930s with her Italian maestro who had taught piano to generations of young women.[89] Some recipients of private tuition became accomplished pianists: Sophie ʿAbd al-Masih, for example, had won two gold medals by the age of nineteen.

L'Egyptienne published her portrait on a frontispiece in 1927, celebrating her acclamation by academies of music in Liège and Paris.[90] By the 1930s, Egyptian women began to be sent for study to the Royal Academy of Music in London.[91]

Piano was considered ladylike for upper- and middle-class women, whereas playing oriental instruments and singing were associated with slave girls in the old harems and professional performers of the lower class. In the early twentieth century, the women who kept oriental music alive were of modest background, often from the provinces. While families may have had some reservations, they also recognized the advantages and allowed their daughters to exploit their musical talents. Singers like Umm Kalthum and Munirah al-Mahdiyah both came from poor families in the Delta.[92] Umm Kalthum, who became Egypt's legendary singer of the twentieth century, was born in the village of Tammai al-Zuhayrah. Her father was a Qur'an reciter who had taught his daughter to sing religious songs and perform at local religious festivals. Because of her unusual talent her father agreed to take her to Cairo, where she trained privately with Shaykh Abu al-ʿIla Muhammad. Before long she was sought after to sing in the houses of the wealthy. We have already remarked that she performed at the EFU's charity fetes.[93]

While rural and lower-class women could obtain training in singing with private instructors, an upper-class woman like Bahigah Hafiz was unable to acquire the instruction she sought in composing Arab music. The Conservatory of Oriental Music—which had been established in 1927, with a grant of ten thousand pounds, by the king—rejected her request to study musical composition. She was told there was no money in the budget for the study she requested. Although the conservatory did not admit women generally, the rejection probably stemmed equally from the fact that the work she submitted did not follow the classical rules for Arab music but added Western rhythms. Hafiz was trying to break free from staid musical traditions, as from the cultural traditions that constrained her life. *L'Egyptienne* drew attention to Bahigah Hafiz and three other women composers: the late Mathilde ʿAbd al-Masih, her pianist daughter Sophie ʿAbd al-Masih, and ʿAziza Musa.[94] Saiza Nabarawi visited the conservatory, pleading for the admission of women. When the effort proved fruitless, she suggested the creation of a women's section.[95] Her suggestion fell on deaf ears.

Not long afterwards, the Congress for Oriental Music convened in Cairo.[96] Interested in conservation, the congress suggested that oriental music be taught in Egyptian government schools, but this suggestion did not bear results in institutions serving either women or men. Two years later, for example, when the Higher Institute of Women Music Teachers was established, it taught only Western music.

Women were equally unwelcome at the Ecole des Beaux Arts. In the old elite harems women had been taught drawing and painting as an appropriate pastime. Some became proficient, such as ʿAtiyah Saqqaf who produced a remarkable portrait of Huda Shaʿrawi in the 1890s. In the 1920s and 1930s in Cairo and Alexandria there were a number of upper-class women painters who had studied abroad; others had trained privately in Egypt like Inji Aflatun who worked with Egyptian-born Swiss artist Margo Villon. The work of women artists was displayed in galleries in Cairo and Alexandria and publicized by *L'Egyptienne.* In 1928 Studio Hidayat mounted a retrospective of the paintings of Mrs. Ghali and Suzy Green. In 1928 and 1929 the Society of the Friends of Art exhibited the paintings of Palestinian residents Amy Nimr, Sabihah Rushdi, and Suzanne Adli. Sculptures by Samihah Husayn were exhibited at the Salon féminin des beaux-arts sponsored by the Cairo Women's Club in 1938. The Industrial Fairs in Cairo featured the work of women artists such as Marguerite Nakhlaḥ, who won a silver medal in 1931 and a gold medal in 1932.[97]

The EFU campaigned for the admission of women into the School of Fine Arts when Murad Sid Ahmad was Minister of Education. The sympathetic minister informed the EFU in 1930 that the school's regulations did not prohibit female students. He let it be known that if a group of women applied he would facilitate their entry, but he was removed from office before this plan could be carried out. The EFU pressed their demand again in 1936 and in 1938, when EFU adviser Muhammad Husayn Haykal was minister of education. Asked to explain why the School of Fine Arts would not admit women, the minister answered: "One cannot ignore the prejudice that causes certain reactionaries to condemn the study and reproduction of the nude in schools and exhibitions. How could they be told that young women were present in the same class?"[98] The "liberal" minister hesitated to take a stand in favor of women that might cause him political harm, blaming this on "reactionaries" and their gender sensibilities. Nabarawi scorned the education minister's expedient submission to atavism. "The demand that the minister hesitates to accept because it seems to him to be contrary to our past traditions," she wrote, "is in conformity with the present and with the development necessary if we truly wish one day to see our women artists compare well with their sisters from the West."[99] She also informed the minister that in Turkey women and men studied fine arts together. Confirming the point *L'Egyptienne* published a photograph of Turkish women in a sculpture class at the School of Fine Arts in Istanbul.[100] Taking the tack she had tried with the Conservatory of Oriental Music, Nabarawi suggested, equally unsuccessfully, the establishment of a separate section for women at the School of Fine Arts, so as "not to frighten the conservatives."

Pressing their case for women's study of music and art, the feminists resorted to the familiar trope of benefits to the family. "Just as music sweetens habits, so do design, painting, and all the decorative arts open to the woman and her family, new horizons of beauty, well-being, and harmony. To nurture artistic taste in the young woman is not only to develop her own talent, which may be ignored, but by sharpening her eye permits her to beautify her home, enriching it with new sensibilities, instilling in all [in the home] a love of the fine arts without which there can be no real civilization for a people."[101]

The feminists supported men as well as women artists, conscious of art as a form of national expression. Sculptor Muhammad Mukhtar was widely known for his statue *The Awakening of Egypt*, a colossal statement in granite of the dual awakening of women and of Egypt. Upon his death in 1934 Huda Shaʿrawi formed a group called "The Friends of Mukhtar" to sponsor annual competitions for young women and men artists and perpetuate the memory of the sculptor and his work. Mukhtar's *Awakening*—a woman pulling a veil away from her face with her left hand and her right hand resting on the head of the Sphinx—stands to this day on the avenue leading to Cairo University.[102]

The new sport of aviation was introduced in Egypt in the 1920s, and soon the first woman pilot made her debut. Obtaining her flying license, Lutfiyah Nadi took her place among the university graduates at the EFU ceremony in 1933. The following year she came in first in an international competition, flying from Alexandria to Cairo.[103] Two years later British woman pilot Beryl Markham landed in Cairo en route from Nairobi to London and on to America in her record-breaking flight, but it appears that the two women pilots did not meet.[104] Later Nafisah Ghamrawi and a few other Egyptian women obtained pilot's licenses.[105] Writing in *al-Misriyah* in 1939 Muhammad Tahir called for more women to take up the sport.[106]

Women pilots sparked the imagination of writers, who found the symbolism irresistible. Feminist writer and poet Mayy Ziyadah celebrated the woman pilot in "Hymne de l'aviatrice égyptienne."[107] Playwright Tawfiq al-Hakim made a woman pilot the hero of *al-Jins al-Latif* (The gentle sex).[108] Al-Hakim's pilot is Magdiyah, "the glorious one," and her husband Mustafa is terrified of flying. Magdiyah and two women friends, a lawyer and a journalist, try to persuade Mustafa to accompany his wife on a flight to Iraq.

KARIMAH [the lawyer]: Long live justice.

MUSTAFA: What is justice?

KARIMAH: Justice is following your wife everywhere just like the old times when a wife followed her husband. If you don't agree she can use *bayt al-taʿah* [house of obedience] to force you.

MUSTAFA: Bayt al-taʿah?

KARIMAH: Yes, since the woman now works, her husband should go where her work takes her.

MUSTAFA: So that's the case. Bayt al-taʿah will be in the airplane.

MAGDIYAH: Or even on Mars.

MUSTAFA: Perhaps. I can believe anything now.

It proved easier for women to conquer the sky than the sea. Women's first attempts at swimming at the seaside in Alexandria were socially perilous. In the early 1930s, Egyptian women began to swim at Alexandria resort beaches formerly the exclusive domain of European residents. With the economic depression some Egyptians who might have traveled to Europe in more prosperous times now remained at home. The demise of veiling and other social changes over the past decade had made it possible for women to enjoy outdoor recreation, as Saiza Nabarawi wrote in the summer of 1932. She remarked with favor on women university students who strolled on the beaches with their brothers, cousins, and friends, and on wives with husbands and children. She wrote in *L'Egyptienne*: "Movement, open air, and exercise have become indispensable to full development: to putting bodies in equilibrium with minds and morals. . . . The young generations raised in the excitement of the vitality of their century are no longer able to adapt to the sedentary life of old or to content themselves with the staid amusements of their fathers. Progress brought by scientific discoveries and the speed of [modern] transportation communicate to them a passion for life different from that of their elders."[109]

Nabarawi's celebration of nature's joys was occasioned by harsh criticism of women at the beaches during the past two summers. Conservatives had expressed censure and the reactionary government of Ismaʿil Sidqi had tried to make political capital of the issue. Minister of education Muhammad Hilmi ʿIsa insisted that the mixing of the sexes at the beach endangered public morality, and that all mixing of the sexes—even at the university—must be stopped. Feminists retorted that if the government was serious about protecting morality, it should close the government-licensed houses of prostitution and should shut down the gambling casinos instead of opening a new one in Suez.[110] The issue of gender mixing faded after the repressive regime left power in 1933.

With the rise of populist Islamist groups later in the decade, however, the issue returned. In 1937 parliament deputy Muhammad Jamil ʿAbd Allah called for a law requiring women's bathing suits to conform to standards of public morality and ending the mixing of the sexes on beaches.[111] Such a law was not passed. In June of the same year it was announced that the minister of the interior had been allocated twenty-five hundred Egyptian pounds to open a Morals Office in Alexandria. This did not happen. Women continued to use the beaches. In the 1980s women's behavior and attire at the beach once again became controversial with the spread of Islamist conservatism.

In the mid-1930s, as feminists defended swimming for women, two women staked a claim on the university tennis courts. Zaynab Hasan—an assistant in the chemistry department, who was the first woman on the staff—and student Aminah al-Saʿid raised eyebrows for taking up the sport and for their costumes, both of which shocked conservative sensibilities.[112]

The Mixing of the Sexes and Education

The mixing of the sexes was a volatile issue in the 1930s and 1940s. The principal site of contention over the mixing of the sexes remained the university. In defending recent gains made by women's entry into the university, the EFU observed in 1931 that a new Egyptian society was in the making. By the 1930s unveiling was widespread among both middle- and upper-class women and gender-mixed social life was growing more common among the upper strata. A few upper-class women had begun to drive automobiles. Middle- and upper-class girls were attending school in greater numbers, while middle-class women were associating with men in university classrooms and in the professions. In affirmation of these societal trends, feminists insisted that national cohesion and vitality required interaction among all Egyptians. To feminists, gender divisions were nationally subversive.[113] Yet unease about the mixing of the sexes persisted. Issues of morality and honor loomed large, and with them underlying unease about erosions of patriarchal power. Families feared a loss of control over their women. Within the state educational system, as in society, there were contradictions: gender segregation was preserved in primary and secondary schools—which indeed were becoming even more segregated as women replaced male administrators and teachers in the girls' schools—and in the higher institutes, while integration of the sexes prevailed at the university.

Although the university remained coeducational, this had not been achieved without trials. The first problems came at the beginning of the 1930s, not long after women had begun to enter the university. Then, as we have seen, a new repressive government tried to exploit the mixing of the sexes to its political advantage. A second threat at the decade's end came from populist quarters and had religious overtones. Neither of these "movements" got very far. On the campus there was no sympathy for segregation, and in society a liberal spirit prevailed. In the 1970s and 1980s, with the rise of populist Islamism, an interest in distancing the sexes through renewed veiling would surface first in the university.

The first crisis occurred after women had been at the university only a year, with the 1930 installation of a government headed by conservative politician Isma'il Sidqi. Progressive minister of education Murad Sid Ahmad was replaced by the reactionary Muhammad Hilmi 'Isa, whom the feminists branded "The Minister of Traditions." This was a time of general repression in Egypt: the constitution of 1923 was abrogated, parliament was suspended, and censorship was imposed. Antigovernment protest began at the university and persisted until the constitution was restored in 1935. During this period, not surprisingly, the university came under attack. A government circular forbade students to express political views under threat of expulsion.[114] Dean of arts Taha Husayn was removed in 1932, and not long afterwards Ahmad Lutfi al-Sayyid resigned as rector. Among the charges against Taha Husayn it was asserted that he encouraged the mixing of the sexes at the university.[115]

Women across the social and political spectrum protested against the Sidqi regime. Their most recent major achievement, entry into the university, was brought under attack by the education minister in a move to inflict damage on feminists and on university officials and students, and at the same time to pander to reactionary tendencies that served to distract the public from the central political issues. Education minister Hilmi ʿIsa, raising the specter of endangered morality, announced that the mixing of the sexes would be forbidden in places of learning. This meant closing university education to women. ʿIsa declared:

> We have taken the decision at the Ministry of Education to forbid the mixing of boys and girls. Certain papers have complained of the dangerous proximity of boys and girls on the beaches of Alexandria during the bathing season. These papers have shown how morality and modesty are violated by this proximity, and authorities have directed attention to the need to protect the youth against these obscenities. Our first task is to put an end to these wrongs and to oppose this mixing [of the sexes] that certain persons wish to introduce into our schools. We will not ignore the dangers of this mixing and shall continue to take note of their pernicious effects. We are always better informed than the public about this matter.[116]

At this very time the government zealously promoted the new program of physical education in the schools and the new Girl Guide movement. Saiza Nabarawi pointed to the government's contradictory approaches to gender and to what we would now call sexism.

> The same young women whom you [the government] desire to see guarded in the house you give as an ideal the hard and active camp life [of the Girl Guides]. Indeed I favor the development of physical culture, which brings to our youth health, vitality, and activity necessary for the expansion of the personality. I do not understand how a body accustomed to free exercise in the open air would be able to accommodate itself to the sedentary life of the house, since the person who is freely developed with a taste for independence and initiative would not be able to endure the constraints and subordination one wishes to impose on her in [the name of] accomplishing her duties of wife and mother. Have we by chance become racists?[117]

Writing in French Nabarawi applies the term "racist" to gender. In Arabic, which she spoke but did not read, *jins* means both sex and race; *jinsiyah*, a related word, means nationality. Her use of "racist" in French, which appears to be a "translation" of the Arabic word for sex and race, clearly signifies "sexism." In an interesting parallel, in late-twentieth-century American usage the term "male chauvinism [*excessive nationalism*]" preceded the coinage "sexism."

When the EFU asked the minister of education about higher education for women, he suggested a teacher training course in a special section that could be created for women at the Higher Institute of Teacher Training; alternatively, families of sufficient means could send their daughters to Europe. The minister proposed these options "because it is repugnant for us to see young women students enter into contact with the male students. And supposing that the interests of knowledge could be served by this mixing, we would never permit it because our work is to protect morality above all. When knowledge and morality are in conflict, we shall never allow morality to be sacrificed."[118]

Feminists demanded that the state act responsibly toward all its citizens and that it recognize women's changed roles in society. The editor of *L'Egyptienne* confronted the minister of education:

> He [the Minister of Education] forgets, no doubt, that the times of seclusion are over and that we live in a postwar era, and that the main task of a minister of public education is to prepare the young, who are entrusted to him, to meet the challenges of the times. Who can deny that in the period of evolution that we have gone through the woman was called upon to play an important role in the intellectual and moral elevation of society? The history of the past twelve years when, by successive stages, the woman was freed from the shackles of the past is testimony to the ceaseless development of her personality. If some people are blinded by outmoded prejudices, obstinately failing to recognize the active part she always takes in all aspects of our national renaissance, it is not the business of the minister of public education to ignore this progress. . . . What a pity for Egypt that in the name of morality (little respected at that) all rights of the individual to knowledge and liberty are suppressed and stifled. The first result of mixed education should have dispelled the fears of the conservatives. It was for naught. . . . Hilmy Issa Pacha tries in his interview [with *al-Ahram*] to revive oriental atavism in addressing the specter of immorality threatening this Muslim country and her ancient traditions, which are not safeguarded by the government. And why this holy crusade? Our world has evolved too much, whether you like it or not, for there to be any question of the harem in the future. . . . It is inevitable that the woman will be side by side with you men. It is not by making her frivolous, ignorant, and self-centered that you prepare her to victoriously take up the battle of life.[119]

The government did not let up and neither did the feminists. Two years later the EFU was still fighting back, accusing the Sidqi government of acting like a colonizer in its own country. The government policy, said feminists,

> admirably serves the imperialist designs of Great Britain. This [colonial] power was always opposed to the development of education in Egypt. Is not ignorance the only way to enslave people and to keep them in a condition in which they are not able to free themselves? . . . It is the same egotistical and personal end that the Sedky cabinet follows today with this deplorable policy. Thus to solidify the dictatorial regime that is imposed on the country it is necessary to stifle

> all seeds of liberty. What greater danger is there than the education of the masses who will [then] become conscious of their rights? Far from understanding that they are only responsible to the wishes of the people, who have the task of freeing themselves from foreign tutelage, our ministers confine all their activity to maneuvers to preserve their power for the longest time. . . . Above all it is secondary and higher education for women that is most vigorously combated in the official circles.[120]

In 1933, the Sidqi government fell, and with it "The Minister of Traditions" and his policies. Feminists and other progressives could breathe a sigh of relief: university doors would remain open to women.

During the 1930s women gained entry to various faculties at the university and their numbers increased. The issue of gender mixing, while dormant, was not dead. Toward the end of the 1930s there was a movement of mounting social conservatism among the lower middle class, where the lingering effects of the economic depression were most felt. The Muslim Brothers were gaining strength among this segment of the population, and women were beginning to be drawn to the conservative Islamic movement. After belonging to the EFU for a year, Zaynab al-Ghazali left in 1936 to form the Muslim Women's Society. In this atmosphere the issue of gender mixing at the university resurfaced. Now religion was used to attack coeducation, and the antagonistic forces were populist rather than governmental.

The EFU could not let religion be deployed to impose gender segregation at the university but did not want to be drawn into a confrontation with religious authorities. A March 1937 article in *al-Misriyah*, "A Quiet Talk: Boys and Girls in the Halls of Learning," informed readers: "Some have asked if we are going to reply to Shaykh al-Azhar concerning his statement that boys and girls should be separated in schools and at the university, and about the approval of a new uniform for the modern Egyptian girl. We do not reply because we think this is being stirred up by a group of people seeking division."[121] However, the following month when the situation seemed to be worsening, *al-Misriyah* published a telegram that the EFU president had sent to Shaykh al-Azhar Mustafa al-Maraghi asking him to "stop the discord that exists between the two sexes in the name of innocent religion and [put an end to] the ill effects of this on the unity and advancement of the nation."[122] Al-Maraghi answered that al-Azhar University was working "to advance unity and strengthen religion and religious ethics in the people."[123]

Al-Misriyah meanwhile published the views of distinguished male liberals. Taha Husayn knew of nothing at the university that would necessitate the separation of women and men. The reputations of the students of both sexes were completely satisfactory in the eyes of the university administration, professors, and families. He told the EFU journal: "Those who call for the separation of men and women do not practice this themselves. Nor do they consider its results. Modern Egyptian life necessitates that the communication between men and women be strengthened. There is no way to prevent this. If you separate women and men in the university and other educational institutions, you will not guarantee their separation outside these institutions. They will meet in cinemas, public lecture halls, and thousands of other places."[124] Playwright and wit Tawfiq al-Hakim, always ready to provoke, advocated the mixing of the sexes throughout the entire state educational system from primary school through university. There might be "some danger" for the girl in a mixed secondary school, but if she passed through this experience unscathed, she would be well equipped for the university.[125]

Again the crisis passed. After the 1952 revolution, the higher institutes also became coeducational, and, as already noted, al-Azhar admitted women. When university education became free and women were mobilized in the country's service under the banner of Arab socialism, large numbers of women went to the university. By then, lower-class and upper-class women and men joined those of the middle class in the halls of higher learning.

• CHAPTER 9 •

Women Have Always Worked

IN THE EARLY 1930s the issue of paid work for women assumed a central place in the feminist campaign. By then, the EFU's struggle for educational advances had borne first fruit. Egyptian women from the middle class had begun to graduate from state secondary schools and the university, and they were poised to move into new jobs. Indeed some had already taken such employment. Lower-class townswomen and peasant women who had "always worked" found fresh opportunities for salaried employment in the textile factories created in the late 1920s by Bank Misr, the new national bank.

For a number of reasons work for middle-class women constituted a far more threatening challenge to middle-class patriarchal culture than did education. Through paid employment women could transcend the confines of domesticity. They could also reduce their dependency upon husbands and male relatives for material support. When a frequent male contributor to *al-Mar'ah al-Misriyah* made this point in an article in 1920, the editor felt constrained to distance the journal from this position by declaring its policy to publish all points of view.[1] If work for middle-class women threatened the control of the patriarchal family over women, it also challenged men's monopoly in the workplace.

The policies of the modernizing state in the nineteenth century resulted in new economic and social formations with profound implications for altering gender arrangements. On the one hand, state policies displaced the labor of lower-class urban women and of peasant women; on the other hand, the state tried to draw women from the lower and middle strata into new productive roles, mainly in the modern sectors of health and education. With colonial occupation certain gains for women as workers and potential workers were lost. The colonial state minimized the training of Egyptian women and thus their possibilities for employment, while at the same time it introduced British women into the labor force in the fields of education and health, precisely those fields in which Egyptian women had begun to make headway.[2]

Feminists like Bahithat al-Badiyah and Nabawiyah Musa were among the few Egyptian women who managed to have access to state schooling under colonial occupation, attending the girls' section of a boys' primary school and a teacher training program. They were among the fewer still accepted in the state school system as teachers. Both women were intimately aware of the adverse economic implications of British colonialism for Egyptian women and for the nation as a whole; they also had firsthand exposure to indigenous patriarchal resistance to women's entering the work force. The experiences of Bahithat al-Badiyah and Nabawiyah Musa informed their feminism and nationalism, leading them to privilege demands for education and work for women as part of a strategy for national mobilization.

Male nationalists of the educated elite viewed women's roles in two ways. Progressives, who tended to come mainly from the upper strata, advocated new societal roles for women as necessary to national liberation. Conservatives, typically from the more modest strata, insisted that women's "true roles"—that is, their "culturally authentic roles" as Muslims and as Egyptians—were those of wife, mother, and homemaker, and that challenges to these roles were acts of colonialist subversion.[3] Conservative patriarchal forces unwittingly "colluded" with the colonialist adversary in keeping Egyptian women out of the work force. This gave British women freer rein to impose what Nabawiyah Musa called the "second colonization."

Following formal independence in 1922, the open advocacy of public roles for women by nationalist men faded as they forged ahead with their political and professional careers. Some liberal men helped women, but only behind the scenes. They found it easy to help a few women but were more wary about opening the "floodgates" to all women. Egyptian feminist women themselves articulated the case for paid work for women: they defended it and legitimized it; as pioneers in the workplace they were the frontline activists.

Advocating Work for Women

Early in the twentieth century, Bahithat al-Badiyah and Nabawiyah Musa brought the debate on work for women into focus, addressing both men and women who upheld the cult of domesticity. They stressed that the vast majority of women in Egypt had always worked. Middle- and upper-class opponents of work for women objected to work for middle-class women; the notion of work for upper-class women could not even be entertained. They did not take issue with the work that lower-class and peasant women already performed.

The economic transformations of the nineteenth century led to a regendering of work in Egypt. With competition from new consumer goods imported from the West and the introduction of intensive cultivation of cotton as a cash crop for export, urban lower-class households and small farms diminished as sites of family-based production. Men sought labor elsewhere or, in the countryside, were impressed into corvée labor. Many lower-class urban women were left isolated in the house, while peasant women were increasingly stranded in rural compounds, which some women abandoned altogether.[4] To early-twentieth-century patriarchal conservatives recently regendered roles were "traditional" and therefore culturally authentic. In 1909 Bahithat al-Badiyah asserted:

> Men say when we become educated we shall push them out of work and abandon the role for which God has created us. But isn't it rather men who have pushed women out of work? Before, women used to spin and to weave cloth for clothes for themselves and their children, but men invented machines for spinning and weaving and put women out of work. In the past, women sewed clothes for themselves and their households, but men invented the sewing machine. The iron for these machines is mined by men and the machines themselves are made by men. Then men took up the profession of tailoring and began to make clothes for our men and children. Before, women winnowed the wheat and ground flour on grinding stones for the bread they used to make with their own hands, sifting flour and kneading dough. Then men established bakeries employing men. . . . I simply want to show that men are the ones who began to push us out of work and that if we were to edge them out today we would only be doing [to them] what they have already done to us.[5]

A decade later during the independence struggle, Nabawiyah Musa urgently called for the mobilization, or remobilization, of women's productive energies as imperative to national liberation. By around 1900 about half of the eight thousand professionals in Egypt's work force were Europeans. The paid work force must be Egyptianized; to this end the doors to the workplace must be flung wide open to women. Nabawiyah Musa drove the point home in her introduction to *The Woman and Work*: "The best way to serve this country we are ready to die for is to direct women's attention to education and work." She declared: "This conviction has motivated me to bring out this book in the hope that it will have some impact."[6] In a chapter titled "Egypt's Need for Women Doctors, Women Teachers, Seamstresses, and Women in Other Professions," she argued:

> A nation cannot prosper unless its people are vital and productive. A people cannot be vital so long as half are paralyzed and isolated from the affairs of everyday life. If women do not work, half the nation's resources are neglected. Egypt has great need for labor. There is no way we can keep Egyptian wealth in our own hands except through the education and training of women. . . . First we neglect the education of women, they remain ill-equipped to work. Then we look down on them, slam the door of work in their face, and welcome foreign women into our homes, entrusting them with our basic needs. Egyptian capital is lost to these foreign women, found perfect, rather than [going] to our own women, found wanting. Had we spent money on educating Egyptian women, they would have been able to perform these jobs, and we Egyptians would be keeping Egyptian money in Egyptian hands. At a time when we make a great effort to win our political independence, why do we lag behind in fighting for our economic independence while we have the means in our hands?[7]

If women's work was integral to national liberation, it was equally fundamental to their own liberation. Bahithat al-Badiyah and Nabawiyah Musa argued that work was a woman's basic right, that she should have the option to work even when economic necessity does not compel it. Bahithat al-Badiyah insisted that "if any of us [women] wishes to work in such professions [as lawyers, judges, or railway engineers], our personal freedom should not be infringed." Echoing the words of Zaynab Fawwaz at the end of the nineteenth century, Bahithat al-Badiyah declared that "if women enter the learned professions, it does not upset the system. The division of labor is merely a human creation."[8] Countering the conventional claim that women's nature prevented them from undertaking work, Nabawiyah Musa flatly stated, "People can decide on [work]; nature had nothing to do with it."[9]

As nations should not be dependent, neither should women: so argued feminists during colonial occupation. The customary system of complementary roles and responsibilities, within which a father and husband economically provided for his dependents, often broke down. As we have noted, men often abused their exclusive privilege to enact divorce, and lack of maintance (*nafaqah*) was the major cause of women's crowding the courts. Nabawiyah Musa was virtually alone in drawing attention to the plight of single mothers, whether widows or divorcées. She argued that these women should be enabled to earn a livelihood rather than being limited to the traditional alternatives: dependency on male relatives or in-laws, charity, remarriage, or menial work. Nabawiyah Musa spoke from the vantage point of a daughter raised single-handedly by a widowed mother.[10]

While men feared loss of control over women in the family and competition with them in the workplace, their arguments against work for women were often expressed as claims that women would neglect their family roles, especially their maternal roles, and that work would bring women into the public sphere and into contact with men, endangering female morality and honor—all of which, they insisted, violated Islam and indigenous cultural norms and constituted an invidious Westernization. Here were echoes of the same fears and excuses expressed concerning formal education for women.

In their campaign feminists addressed these fears and allegations in full awareness of the deeper anxieties they signaled about the erosion of patriarchal power and privilege. When promoting work for women, feminists reaffirmed the centrality of their family roles, especially the maternal role. It became standard to reiterate, as Bahithat al-Badiyah had done in a talk to women at the Club of the Ummah Party in Cairo, that by advocating work she was "not urging women to neglect their home and children."[11] Nabawiyah Musa was equally careful in *The Woman and Work* to issue the same reassurances.

Feminists stressed that Islam was not responsible for keeping women out of work. Nabawiyah Musa wrote: "It is out of ignorance that people say that Islam does not allow women to work. In the cities we see women from lower- and middle-class families working, as well as women from peasant families. Do we call them unbelievers? Our religion does not permit this." Moreover, "these [Muslim] families are the backbone of Egypt and the source of the country's wealth, and [our] advancement depends on them. . . . If women of these families were idle like those of the upper-class families, the whole nation would be lost."[12]

Early in the twentieth century feminists addressed the issue of female sexual purity, which conservatives claimed would be endangered if women worked outside their homes. When feminists did not call for unveiling and insisted on scrupulously modest demeanor for women, their intent, in part, was to deflect attention from the issue of sexuality while women took first steps into new public roles. Coming at the issue of women's work in quite a different way, Nabawiyah Musa argued that the issue was not work itself but the kind of work and the social conditions surrounding it. Many poor women, especially mothers with young children, were forced to do whatever they could to generate income, frequently resorting to working as street vendors or household servants. The social conditions of these jobs exposed them to sexual exploitation. Other forms of work would make women less sexually vulnerable. Some women were so desperate that they found their only recourse in commercial sexual exploitation: prostitution. Nabawiyah Musa also argued that middle-class women's entry into the new professions as men's equals would reduce the potential for their sexual exploitation. She gave the example of women working as doctors on the same level as male doctors rather than working in the subordinate position of nurse, where they might be vulnerable to sexual harassment.[13]

Thus even before the start of the organized feminist movement feminists paid considerable attention to the issue of work for women. In the movement's second decade, women were still advancing similar arguments in defense of women's work, showing how little ground had been gained on the economic front in nationalist and feminist terms. In 1930 Saiza Nabarawi echoed the argument Nabawiyah Musa had made in 1920 that only through economic independence can a nation guarantee its freedom. Nabarawi stressed two themes. First, the nation must wrest control from the financially dominant Europeans over such natural resources as petroleum, phosphate, and manganese. This should be part of a move toward broader diversification and away from overreliance on cotton as the major export crop—which, she argued, brought with it the threat that one day Egypt would no longer be able to feed itself. Indeed, this has now happened. Second, Egypt must mobilize all its human resources, including women.[14]

Feminists continued to marshal religion in defense of work for women. In 1935 when Prince ʿUmar Tusun voiced his opposition, Huda Shaʿrawi answered: "Your Royal Highness, in your view half the nation is composed of creatures without abilities and rights! However, Muslim law preaches the equality of the two sexes and has not assigned the domain of work to one more than the other. . . . It is as if Your Highness has forgotten that our religion had accorded the woman free and entire right to dispose of her goods. She is able to buy, sell, secure a mortgage, to bequeath, and to testify. . . . The Great Lawgiver has high regard for the woman but man in his egotism does not wish to take this into account. He wishes unjustifiably to limit her [field of] action."[15]

Following their strategy in promoting female education, feminists singled out distinguished women in early Islamic history to legitimize public roles for women. Khadijah, the Prophet's first wife and the first convert to Islam, was an entrepreneur who engaged in Meccan commerce and caravan trade before and during her marriage, and indeed had been Muhammad's employer, ʿA'ishah, a later wife, dispensed hadith (teachings of the Prophet). Sayyidah Sukaynah, a distinguished poet, gave talks on literature and poetry; Sayyidah Nafisah, an authority on hadith, was consulted by the leading ulama' of the day, including Imam al-Shafiʿi. In ʿAbbasid Baghdad Zaynab bint Muhammad ibn ʿUthman lectured on *ʿilm al-kalam* (theology) and hadith. In medieval Egypt a woman, Shajarat al-Durr, governed the country.[16]

In promoting work for women, feminists had to deal with opponents' persistent deployment of threatened female morality and the dangers of gender mixing as patriarchal political weapons. Feminists favored ending gender segregation but manipulated the issue to their advantage. Sometimes they took the expedient of advocating gender segregation to promote jobs for women in parallel sectors, mainly in education and health. At other times they opposed the separation of the sexes in the workplace, arguing that women who entered a male-dominated profession could better serve the needs of female clients.

The economic depression of the 1930s occasioned conflicting responses from feminist women and conservative men. Feminists pointed out that during hard times women and children are the first to suffer. They deplored the need of poor divorced or widowed women to remarry over and over just to avoid starvation. "Each of these marriages becomes for them another [form of] subjugation. When they can't find a husband their fate is even worse, for they often have to take to the streets to beg."[17] Or they might have to resort to prostitution.[18] Male conservatives argued that economic depression had caused male unemployment and women should not take jobs that would otherwise go to men. Shoring up their position they harped on women's place in the home.

The reality was that under pressure to keep themselves and their children alive many lower-class women were entering the work force. Given that reality, Saiza Nabarawi found, public attitudes were changing: "The idea that work outside the house is a disgrace for the woman is a prejudice that is more and more disappearing, [causing] the old patriarchal spirit to disappear little by little."[19]

Meanwhile many middle-class women, putting their new education to use, were also taking up jobs and redefining their lives. Nabarawi wrote that "our young women of today do not wish to have to rely first on their father and then on their husband for their livelihood. Conscious of their individuality they want to win respect and to take their share of responsibility. Unlike their elders, they do not consider work a social disgrace but rather a means of liberation."[20]

In the face of conservative movements worldwide international feminist solidarity intensified around the issue of women's work, despite divergent views on how best to protect it. The IAW had declared in Berlin in 1929 that "the economic position of women seems to be just now the most important and difficult problem of the women's movement." Six years later at the Istanbul congress the IAW insisted, "The right to work is now [the] most endangered of all."[21] *L'Egyptienne* told its readers that "above all the problem of work mobilizes the grouping of feminist forces [internationally]."[22] Feminists might rally together at international meetings, bringing wider attention to the problem and offering mutual support, but the EFU, like other IAW affiliates, had to conduct its own campaign at home and had its own particular problems to face. American and European women were trying to hold the line for women in the workplace, especially married women, whereas Egyptian women were still trying to penetrate the work force in greater numbers.[23] Egyptians had to deal with the adverse effects of economic imperialism imposed by some of the very countries from which many sister feminists came. The IAW did not examine the ills imposed by imperialism on women, their families, and their nations.

What about support for Egyptian women's work from male progressives at home? Such support was generally covert and limited. In the 1930s when the EFU's Fatma Niʿmat Rashid asked leading male liberals their views on work for women, they revealed their allegiance to the patriarchal culture. University dean and professor Taha Husayn asserted, "The best work for the woman is [in] the house, but if need constrained or leisure permitted her to work outside the house," he was sure she would do well. This was the same person who promoted his woman student Suhayr Qalamawi as a pioneering university professor.[24] Lawyer Muhammad ʿAli ʿAllubah believed the woman's "natural place" was in the home. It was acceptable for peasant women to work in the fields, but work outside the home for city women could lead to a breakdown of paternal authority and of female morality. This was the same person who gave Naʿimah al-Ayyubi her first job as a lawyer.[25] Writer and journalist Muhammad Husayn Haykal declared that a woman should only resort to work if she did not have a family.[26]

In 1931 students at the Faculty of Law at Fu'ad I University debated the question: "Would women working in male professions cause a relaxing of moral discipline?" The hidden question was: "Should women be kept out of 'male' professions?" Naʿimah al-Ayyubi, then in her third year at the Faculty of Law, was on the team which argued that morality would not be endangered by women in the work force. Her team lost.[27]

Going Forward in Work

EFU leaders promoted work for women, using influence to help place women in jobs and lobbying for new opportunities and for appropriate administrative and legal frameworks to protect women in their new work. Other feminists—those already engaged in professional life, such as Nabawiyah Musa and some of the first-generation university graduates—promoted the cause of work through pioneering in new positions themselves and preparing others to follow in their footsteps.

In Factories and Shops

Egyptian women began to work in the textile factories created as state monopolies in the early nineteenth century, where they performed some of the tasks they had formerly done at home. Women worked alongside men but were relegated to carding and spinning while men did the more skilled work of weaving. Also men operated the new steam-driven machinery, leaving to women the less skilled and lower-paid work.[28] This has been a widespread pattern discernible as industrialization has occurred in various countries and more sophisticated technologies have been introduced.[29] By midcentury, state industries had suffered a decline and factory work for women waned. However, women did not disappear altogether from the factory; in the late nineteenth and early twentieth century, some could be found in textile and tobacco factories, as well as in sugar refineries.[30]

In the late 1920s and the 1930s women found fresh opportunities for employment in new textile factories created by Bank Misr such as the Misr Spinning and Weaving Company factory, which opened at al-Mahallah al-Kubra in the Delta in 1927. Women also took up work at the silk factory in Damietta, another Bank Misr enterprise. When Nabarawi visited the factory in 1930, the director, ʿAbd al-Fattah al-Luzi, raved about the "superiority" (by which he meant the docility) of the girl workers over young men, especially in tasks requiring fine detail and patience. It was a classic case of exploitation: obtaining women to do tedious work for lower wages.[31]

An exceptional woman was Halimah ʿAbd al-Malik from Tanta in the center of the Egyptian Delta, who became a cotton broker. The daughter of a mother and father both active in the grain trade, around the age of twenty ʿAbd al-Malik began to buy cotton from local peasants, which she processed in her own small factory and then sold. She soon opened a second factory and also built a warehouse. Her success earned her the title "Queen of Cotton." The EFU hailed Halimah ʿAbd al-Malik as "an emblem of glory for Egypt and the whole East."[32]

Feminists took advantage of the Agricultural and Industrial Expositions in Cairo to promote women's economic production.[33] Following the Indian example, the EFU urged women as consumers to buy only Egyptian-made fabrics in order to help local industry and to create more jobs for women.

Local industry of a different sort was promoted when Huda Shaʿrawi, as a personal initiative rather than an EFU project, created a ceramics factory in 1925 in Rud al-Farag, a popular quarter of Cairo. She claimed a nationalist motivation in setting up this factory to reproduce Islamic pottery and faience. She might have accomplished a feminist goal at the same time if her factory had provided work for women instead of hiring only men.[34]

The EFU's crafts workshop in the House of Cooperative Reform in Sayyidah Zaynab apprenticed girls in weaving, carpet making, sewing, and embroidery. Some of the products could be finished at home, enabling girls (and future mothers) to combine domestic tasks and income-generating work. The EFU marketed their products at a permanent on-site display. The House of Cooperative Reform was instituted at a time when apprenticeship in "industrial arts" was provided mainly for boys.[35] An exception was the New Woman Society's crafts workshop outfitted by Huda Shaʿrawi, which had opened in 1919. The EFU workshop was expanded and incorporated into the new Professional and Domestic School in 1932.

Egyptian women had been slower to find employment in commercial establishments. Women peddlers (*dallalah*s) from the minorities, mainly Christians and Jews of Syrian origin, had formerly sold dry goods from house to house when middle- and upper-class women lived in domestic seclusion. In the late nineteenth century with the introduction of department stores and modern boutiques women of the minorities made an easy transition to new employment as shopsellers.[36] It was not until the 1930s that Egyptian women in any numbers began to work in retail trade.

The EFU took up the issue of working conditions and employment security for women. Debates raged over protective legislation for women workers versus what was called "labor equality" in Western industrial countries, and reverberated in the IAW in the 1930s. Some Western feminists were antiprotectionist, arguing that special legislation barred women from certain jobs and that maternity regulations would deter employers from hiring women.[37] Egyptian feminists favored protective legislation, believing it would curb exploitation of women and children and protect married women. In Egypt, as in the West, women's right to work was threatened after marriage. Egyptian feminists also feared that women would be replaced by machines, and not just machines themselves but men hired to operate them.

When laws regulating work in industry and commerce were drafted, under guidelines laid out by the League of Nations' International Labor Office, the EFU remarked that "female labor is finally considered as something other than corvée exacted at the mercy of a master or employer."[38] The EFU, which participated in discussions of the draft law, favored a fluid workday to accommodate women's child-care responsibilities, arguing against a rigidly fixed nine-hour workday.[39]

In 1933 when the parliament passed a labor law regulating employment of women in industry and commercial establishments, *L'Egyptienne* printed the text in full.[40] The law constituted a state gendering of work roles in modern industry and commerce. The largest single article (Article 10 with twenty subcategories) enumerated types of work forbidden to women. This included labor considered physically taxing or dangerous, such as working in mines or foundries, manufacturing explosives, coating mirrors with mercury, and handling lead. Work regarded as polluting was also prohibited, such as producing alcoholic beverages, slaughtering animals, and manufacturing materials out of blood, bone, or fecal matter. (Peasant women routinely slaughtered small animals, chiefly fowl, at home and also made fuel out of animal dung, which they dried on their rooftops.) Women were forbidden to operate or to supervise the operation of machinery, yet they were allowed to clean and repair it, except while it was "in motion." Arguments of danger kept women from operating machinery, relegating them to the less technologically advanced sector of production and allowing men free monopoly.[41] Women were generally prohibited from working at night. Exceptions included jobs in river transportation and in seasonal processing of perishable agricultural products, and during national or religious feasts. The night work permitted to women also included jobs in "hotels, restaurants, pensions, cafes, cafeterias, theaters, cinemas, music halls, and other establishments of the same nature."[42] Women were also officially allowed to work in state-licensed brothels, but this was not mentioned in the labor law.

There were various provisions related to the conditions of work. Women must not work more than nine hours a day. They must not work longer than five hours without a break and were to have one hour of rest during the day. Maternity regulations required women to take one month off prior to childbirth and fifteen days afterwards, the latter at half pay, and forbade employers to fire women during maternity leave. These regulations were intended to control exploitation and to offer a modicum of job security for women in a labor law that did not otherwise limit employers' abilities to terminate workers' jobs. At the same time, it might make potential employers reluctant to hire women, especially if they thought the law would be applied. The maternity provisions constituted an affirmation by the state that married women had the right to work in industry and commercial establishments. The right of married women to work was far from a given; in fact the state prohibited work for married teachers. However, the Egyptian law regulated work hours and forbade night work in the factory and trades where men dominated and excepted domains where women predominated, a pattern Joan Scott observed in the West.[43] Or, it might be further added, in areas that provided public entertainment to men, and to a certain extent women. The Egyptian state, like states elsewhere, was ambivalent regarding women's work.

In an article entitled "The Rights of Our Women Workers" *L'Egyptienne* summed up the EFU's views of the new labor law regulating women's work: "Because of the world economic crisis wage labor is becoming more and more a vital necessity for women of the working classes in all countries—[and therefore] we consider the notice [of the law regulating women's work] published by our Ministry of the Interior as the first charter for our women workers and a just outcome of years of efforts and feminist struggles. This is the first step on the road of recognizing the rights of our women workers, which places our country in a wider context, that is, within the context of the international plan of work."[44] The year after the new law was passed, the EFU encouraged workers and artisans to form their own associations to protect their interests.[45]

In 1935 a group of women workers complained to the Labor Office in the Ministry of the Interior about exploitive working conditions, charging that women employed in certain dressmaking establishments, bakeries, and groceries were made to work unlawful hours for low pay and were subjected to insulting treatment. They cited such cases as this: "In the two Tseppas Shops, young women worked from 7 A.M. to 10 P.M. without any rest at midday. Their pay was between 150 and 200 piasters or at the most 300 per month. They were continually moving and worked all day long. Also they had to endure the indecent advances of the shops' customers because otherwise the customers would complain to the owner that the salesgirls spoke badly and the boorish owner would fire the young women."[46] Another complaint concerned women workers in the dressmaking establishment of the Vassilas sisters. These women were paid by the piece, making only several piasters a day. They were subjected to insults from morning to night and were on the point of losing their health.[47]

The women workers contacted the EFU president at the same time. The EFU immediately pressured the government to implement the women's labor law. Huda Shaʿrawi pressed for controls in the workplace. A few months later EFU member and newly qualified lawyer Naʿimah al-Ayyubi was appointed the first inspector of women's work in the Labor Office.[48] The following year Saiza Nabarawi wrote a plea for higher salaries and better working conditions, especially improved hygienic standards, for women workers in an essay in a government-sponsored competition.[49]

Educating the Nation

After independence, as soon as the first secondary school for girls was founded, feminists demanded that the government employ Egyptian women in the state school system, both to fill new positions and to replace men already teaching in the girls' schools. They advanced the essentializing argument that women's "maternal sensibility" enabled them to understand the girls' psychology better than men could. But the feminists also pointed out that women might draw upon their own experience growing up female to guide girls in adolescence, adding "something extra" to the state curriculum originally designed for boys.[50] Feminists were equally adamant that the state replace British women and other foreigners in the state schools with Egyptian women. In 1925 soon after the EFU presented its demand, minister of education ʿAli Mahir informed Huda Shaʿrawi that the government had immediate plans to send four women to England to train as secondary school teachers.[51] The following year fifty women were sent. The early students included Karimah al-Saʿid, Nazla Hakim, Munirah Sadiq, Zaynab Kamal, ʿAsmah Fahmi, and Nazirah Niqula.[52] In 1930 forty women were studying on government grants in England.[53]

The EFU went a step further, proposing that women replace men as teachers in the boys' primary schools. Again they marshaled "maternal" arguments, this time insisting that women were better fit than men to teach the young of both sexes. When education minister Murad Sid Ahmad concurred that women should replace men but claimed a dearth of qualified women teachers, Saiza Nabarawi reminded him that 320 girls had passed the *kafa'ah* (the examination at the end of the first half of secondary school) in 1930.[54] The same year King Fu'ad awarded decorations to several women teachers for outstanding performance.[55] Three years later the EFU campaigned for teaching jobs for the first women graduates from Fu'ad I University, not one of whom had been offered a job in the secondary schools.[56] That year the government opened the Institute of Education to train women university graduates for secondary school teaching,

By 1934 there were fifteen teachers' training schools preparing women to teach in primary schools, as compared to two in 1920, and the number of women in training had increased from almost 500 to nearly 1,500. The state gave women free tuition and meals and sometimes granted them stipends; men received free tuition only. These benefits, and in some instances higher pay for women teachers, were offered as inducements by a state committed to building up a cadre of Egyptian women teachers. Studying women's changing roles in Egypt in 1929 Ruth Woodsmall reported that "women have been given more official recognition in education than in any other field."[57]

Taking over the teaching of Arabic in the girls' schools remained problematic for women. As I have noted, Nabawiyah Musa faced opposition from shaykhs in the early twentieth century when she began to teach Arabic. The battle continued long after independence as the shaykhs persisted in the struggle to hold their own against the encroachments of women, and also of Copts. In 1938 when the Ministry of Education instituted a special program to train women to teach the Arabic language and Islamic culture, *al-Misriyah* hailed it as "a new breakthrough."[58]

Feminists demanded that Egyptian women take over the administration of girls' schools.[59] Back in 1909 Nabawiyah Musa had pioneered as the first Egyptian woman school administrator, first in schools run by provincial councils and later in government schools, capping her career in the state system as principal of the Wardiyan Women Teachers' Training School in Alexandria. Early on, for nationalist and feminist reasons, Nabawiyah Musa had pressed for Egyptian women to be appointed as principals. In 1924, two years after independence, she was still calling for such appointments. Although she was by this time chief inspector of female education in the Ministry of Education, she still found it difficult to make her voice heard. Many years later she said of these frustrated efforts, "The woman inspector can only offer opinions with which senior male officials in the Ministry of Education are likely to disagree, and so her views become cries in the wilderness."[60] Nabawiyah Musa also suggested that the Ministry of Education be divided into two equal sections: one for girls' education and one for boys', but this plan never materialized. In 1926 Nabawiyah Musa was dismissed from her inspector's job, and with this the career of the pioneering woman educator in the state system came to an end. Her relations with her Egyptian and British male superiors in the Ministry of Education had always been fraught with difficulties. She credits the colonial education adviser Dunlop, who was intensely disliked as an archcolonialist autocrat, with keeping her "enemies" at bay in what might be called a policy of gendered divide-and-rule. After his departure and the advent of independence she was without this "protection." It had not been easy for her to forge a career in education. Having to contend with colonialist and indigenous patriarchalist obstructions, she developed an intimidating and authoritarian air unusual in a woman of her day.[61] An exemplary educator and an able administrator, she was often confrontational in the course of duty. It appears that her criticism of certain high officials in the Ministry of Education for conduct that today would be called sexual harassment finally led to her expulsion.[62] From 1926 until 1942 she headed her own two private schools, continuing to set an example of excellence remembered to this day.

Ihsan al-Qusi also pioneered in educational administration. In 1930, through the intervention of Huda Shaʿrawi, she secured an appointment as vice-principal of the Saniyah School, which was still run by a British headmistress. Al-Qusi found it impossible to work with this woman and left after a year to become principal of Muharram Bey Primary School for Girls in Alexandria, remaining for three years. She returned to Cairo as principal of the Helwan Secondary School for Girls and then of the Amirah Fawziyah School in Bulaq. She later became inspector of primary schools for girls in the Ministry of Education, and then inspector of history, civics, and ethics in secondary schools for girls, before leaving the state school system in the later 1940s for the new field of social work.[63]

Another pioneering school administrator was Karimah al-Saʿid, the older sister of Aminah al-Saʿid, whose father had sent her to England to complete her secondary school education. She returned to England in 1926 to attend university as part of the women's education mission sent by the Egyptian government. After teaching at the Amirah Fawziyah School from 1932 to 1936, Karimah al-Saʿid became vice-principal of the Girls' College in Gizah for two years. She became the Ministry of Education's inspector of history in primary and secondary schools for girls from 1938 to 1941. She went on to be principal of the Amirah Fawziyah School, the Saniyah School, and the Kulliyat al-Banat in Zamalek. After the 1952 revolution Karimah al-Saʿid became the first woman to hold the position of deputy minister of education.[64]

In 1930, upon returning from university study abroad, Zaynab Hasan was appointed an assistant in the chemistry department.[65] Four years later, when the first women graduated from the Egyptian university, three women became graduate assistants at the Faculty of Arts. One of them was Suhayr al-Qalamawi, who had just received her M.A. In 1941, armed with her fresh Ph.D. and support from her mentor Taha Husayn, she became the first woman assistant professor, teaching in the Department of Arabic Literature.[66] ʿA'ishah ʿAbd al-Rahman, the second woman to earn her Ph.D., also went on to become an assistant professor in Arabic literature, taking up the position at Ibrahim Pasha University in 1951. She too had been helped by a mentor, Amin al-Khuli, whom she had meanwhile married.[67] The first two university faculty positions for women were in Arabic language and literature at a time when Arabic teaching in schools remained a contested domain for females. Fatma Salim, who obtained her classics Ph.D. in London, went on to teach in the Greek and Latin department at Faruk University in Alexandria, and eventually became department head.

I have noted that discrimination against married women in the work force was a pressing feminist issue in Egypt in the 1930s, as well as abroad. Although school principals could work after marriage, the Egyptian government prohibited some women from continuing to teach in state schools after marriage and hindered others. Women doing teacher training on government scholarships lost their stipends if they married. In Syria, by contrast, women could teach after they married, and if a wife and husband were both teachers, the government attempted to post them to the same place.[68] The Ministry of Education in Egypt kept changing its policies regarding teachers. When Ahmad Najib al-Hilali was minister of education from the end of 1934 to the beginning of 1936 and again at the end of 1937, he lifted the flat ban against married women's teaching. Feminists applauded this but criticized the power given to school authorities to dismiss a teacher if they deemed her family life interfered with her professional duties.[69] The feminists were quick to object to the weapon this gave school principals and others in authority over women teachers. By 1940 the Ministry of Education had disparate policies and regulations for different categories of teachers, reflecting a class bias. Teachers in elementary schools—these were terminal schools, mainly in rural areas, that did not prepare pupils for secondary school—had to quit their jobs after marriage. Primary school teachers could work after marriage with special ministerial approval. Secondary school teachers could teach after marriage but after childbirth were required to take a two-and-a-half-month unpaid leave.

When a group of teachers complained to Huda Shaʿrawi, she took the occasion of the annual EFU commemoration for Qasim Amin to say that "so-called reformers" should focus on "protection of motherhood instead of [condoning] regulations that restrict marriage for women teachers."[70] The ministry policy subverted the state's own efforts to encourage marriage. Nabarawi criticized the Ministry of Education for policies that violated the spirit of Islam, which upholds motherhood, and that created "a very inhumane social inequality," causing the humblest teachers to bear the heaviest burden.[71]

Healing the Nation

Women in Egypt had customarily practiced various forms of healing. Although women healers had become rare in the cities by the twentieth century, they were still found in rural areas.[72] Midwifery, on the other hand, remained a perennial "female profession." The *hakimah* as a female medical professional with training similar to a male physician's had all but disappeared by the beginning of the twentieth century with the phasing out of the School for Hakimahs under British colonial rule. Although the title "hakimah" came to be loosely applied to women working as aides and nurses, the prestige associated with the old state-trained hakimahs had waned.[73] Not only had women been eliminated from the medical profession as hakimahs, but Europeans and Syrians were now encouraged to practice medicine and soon outnumbered Egyptians as doctors. By 1912, only 168 of the 418 doctors in Cairo and only 18 of the 144 in Alexandria were Egyptian.[74]

Early in the twentieth century Bahithat al-Badiyah and Nabawiyah Musa insisted that the profession of doctor be opened to Egyptian women on feminist and nationalist grounds. The EFU sustained this demand. The first Egyptian women doctors, who had been the initial female state scholarship holders to study medicine abroad, began their careers in the early 1930s. Kawkab Hifni Nasif took up residency at the Kitchener Memorial Hospital, a private hospital for women and children, and later became the hospital's first Egyptian director. Hilanah Sidarus, who also completed her residency at the Kitchener Hospital, went on to sustain a lifelong career in private practice, which I will discuss more fully below. Tawhidah ʿAbd al-Rahman became an inspector of health in the government schools for girls and chief inspector in the 1940s. In the 1930s and 1940s women doctors mainly went into public health, laboratory work, and school inspection. They claimed that these areas were more compatible with their family responsibilities.[75]

While some male doctors felt threatened by women's entering medicine, there was little popular objection. To the contrary, women were welcomed and indeed looked up to as doctors. Women doctors performed needed service for women, children, and the poor. When they tended other women there were no problems of modesty to worry patients or their relatives. Yet although women were respected as doctors, the appearance of a woman in this "male profession" might still give rise to a certain confusion. Ibrahim ʿAbd al-Qadir al-Mazini captured the new dilemma in his 1943 novel *Midu wa-Shurukuh* (Midu and his accomplices):

> Sarah asked, "It's laughable for me to be a doctor [*tabib*, noun in the masculine]. . . . Isn't that so?"
>
> She was looking at Midu, so he was forced to say something.
>
> He replied, "No, no, no . . . To the contrary, I mean I think this is excellent . . . that you . . . Why not . . ."
>
> Sarah said, "Yes, why not. Doctor [*Duktur*] Sarah . . . isn't that fine?"
>
> Shakir said, "Sarah the woman doctor [*tabibah*]."
>
> Sarah objected, "Please . . . Dr. [*Duktur*] Sarah . . . No feminine. I don't understand why you should be so stubborn."
>
> Shakir said, "I think it's a question of linguistic usage and good taste, my girl. It's not my rule or Midu's. Isn't that so, Mr. Midu?"
>
> Midu asked, "What? . . . What were you saying?"
>
> He [Shafiq] answered, "I ask would you prefer to see Sarah a man? I mean is she as she is better or is she as; oh, I got mixed up . . . Allow me to begin afresh. Do you prefer . . . No . . . this won't work . . . The stars are not promising."[76]

This fictional encounter illustrates conundrums raised for the two sexes by the regendering of roles: issues of identity and language. In Arabic, as in many other languages, personal nouns and titles have both feminine and masculine forms. As we shall see in chapter 12, the Arab Feminist Conference of 1944 passed a resolution demanding that the feminine ending be dropped from words in the Arabic language.

When al-Mazini's novel appeared, Hilanah Sidarus, who would work as a doctor for more than half a century, was in her first decade of medical practice. Born in 1904, in Tanta, she was the daughter of Marie Nikula Haddad (of Syrian Christian origin), who had gone to school and was fluent in Arabic and French, and Sidarus Girgus (from a Coptic family), who was headmaster of a boys' school. After attending the Coptic Primary School in Tanta, she went on to Cairo in 1914 to finish her primary school education at the Saniyah School, where she also completed the teachers' training course in 1920. She recalled memorizing the poetry of the nineteenth-century feminist writer ʿA'ishah al-Taymuriyah and writing to Nabawiyah Musa, an earlier Saniyah graduate, who was then a school principal in Alexandria, whom she idolized. Sidarus began working as a doctor at the new child-care centers the government had recently set up in the popular Cairo quarters of Bulaq, Darb al-Ahmar, Bab al-Sharʿiyah, and Masr al-Qadimah. In the mid-1930s she told ʿAli Ibrahim, the medical school's dean, that she wished to train as a surgeon. His reply—"Do you wish to become a surgeon while ʿAli Ibrahim is a surgeon?"—put an instant end to her hopes.[77]

In 1935 Sidarus entered private practice as a general practitioner and obstetrician working out of her private clinic in Bab al-Luq in the center of Cairo.[78] She made routine deliveries at women's homes, but complicated cases were sent to the hospital. It remained common practice for women of all classes to give birth at home into the 1950s. In the course of her work Sidarus rendered services to women beyond the strictly medical. Sometimes young women or new brides were brought to her by families to ascertain their virginity. She always pronounced the women virgins because "the penalties were too severe." If a woman was found not to be a virgin, she might be killed; at the very least her future marriage would be ruined and her entire family disgraced. Unlike some male doctors she knew, however, she did not perform operations to repair a broken hymen. Obsession with virginity transcended class lines.[79]

Of all the categories of work in medicine, the most difficult to open up for women was nursing. In the early decades of the twentieth century, the nurses who worked in Egypt were mainly British women; jobs for orderlies, *tamargis*, were filled by Egyptian males. The tamargi was popularly thought of as a nurse; thus nursing was gendered male for Egyptians. Another problem, and a more difficult one, was that nurses worked in close contact with doctors, most of whom were men, and with male patients, a proximity widely considered unacceptable for "respectable women."[80] Many doctors refused to hire women as nurses, and the tamargis, fearing for their jobs, found ways to object as well.[81]

Egyptian feminists promoted nursing as a career for women.[82] The EFU presented a demand to the ʿAli Mahir government in 1936 to "increase the number of nursing schools for women, since the woman displays in this area more sympathy and conscientiousness than the man."[83] Two years later, *al-Misriyah* lamented the continued predominance of male nurses in both government and private hospitals.[84] Gertrude Butrus Ghali, an active member of the Women's Committee of the Red Crescent Society and a nurse herself, encouraged nursing as a profession for women in Egypt. In the late 1940s she took a leading role in planning for an advanced school of nursing at the Sadnawi Hospital, a project that was shelved after the revolution of 1952.[85]

Practicing Law

While women had worked in education and health in the recent past in what could be understood as extensions of their nurturing roles within the family, law was seen as a more alien sphere for women. The rise of the new profession of lawyer (*muhami*) was integral to Egypt's process of secularization. The adoption in the nineteenth century of secular commercial and civil law, based on French models, necessitated a cadre of new, secular lawyers. In the late nineteenth and early twentieth centuries law became the most prestigious profession for men.[86] Lawyers had been at the center of the nationalist movement during the British occupation, and using their training and the prestige of their professional status they launched political careers in the first half of the twentieth century.[87]

Nabawiyah Musa had attempted to qualify as a lawyer early in the twentieth century. As her plans were thwarted by the colonial Ministry of Education we can only speculate on how she might have used such professional training and status to advantage in her nationalist and feminist struggles. While Nabawiyah Musa had not succeeded in becoming a lawyer, there were a few foreign women practicing law at the Mixed Courts in Egypt early this century. Among them was Mme Bernard Michel, the first woman lawyer at the Mixed Courts, and Eva Garzouzi, who was from a prominent Syrian family.[88]

Egyptian women began to enter law in the 1930s and 1940s when opportunities for men were declining in a field that had now become overcrowded.[89] *L'Egyptienne* lauded Naʿimah al-Ayyubi, the first woman to graduate—and with honorable mention—from Fu'ad I University in law. She was hailed in the June issue as "the first Egyptian woman lawyer in the National Courts," but this proved premature, for when al-Ayyubi applied for admission to practice at the National Courts, her application was ignored.[90] Outraged, the feminists went on the offensive, protesting the bar's inaction: "We are told that there is a difference of opinion among the members of the Committee. Some are in favor of admission; others oppose it. The eternal struggle between liberalism and reactionary forces, between justice and despotism. We are pained to think that the bar, which should be the most liberal public body, the most attached to the idea of equity, refuses to accept in its midst a young woman whose abilities and talent would only honor this body."[91] The legal profession was charged to defend justice, insisted the feminists, not to capitulate to old-fashioned ideas that undermined justice. Appealing to national pride, feminists noted that women were accepted as lawyers in Europe. In 1925 the French bar had celebrated the twenty-fifth anniversary of the admission of women. Among Eastern countries, India, Lebanon, Syria, and Turkey had all admitted women to the bar.[92] "Is Egypt now to lose the privileged place it enjoys among the Islamic nations that have taken the country as a model? It seems that our government systematically fights all idea of progress."[93] It was particularly galling for Egyptian feminists to see foreign women practicing law in Egypt at the Mixed Courts when their own sisters were excluded from the National Courts.

Egyptian feminists evoked Islamic history: as women had been proficient in jurisprudence in early Islam, why should women's entering the legal profession be amazing today? "Why accept the woman doctor and be indignant about the woman lawyer?" When a cleric was reported to have declared that women must not practice law because their voices should not be heard in public, the feminists pointed to the contradiction involved in accepting the testimony of women in court.[94]

While adversaries used "nature arguments" to keep women out of the legal profession, speaking for feminists Saiza Nabarawi evoked women's "natural qualities" to opposite effect. The woman lawyer would be "naturally more compassionate and understanding toward a woman client who is the victim of the injustice of men than one of their fellow men." However, when she went on to say that the woman lawyer "would make the most persuasive defense because she understands best the case and state of soul of the unfortunate," Nabarawi implied that women's sensitivities and sensibilities were honed by the experience of subordination.[95]

Inspired by ideas of social service and social reform some of the early women lawyers wished to use law to help those disadvantaged by gender or class, while men often used the law to further political careers. Naʿimah al-Ayyubi confessed to Muhammad ʿAli ʿAllubah that she had been inspired to study law "not as a [mere] occupation, nor for ambitious ends, but as a mission to serve the weak and oppressed."[96]

Before the end of 1933 al-Ayyubi was admitted to the bar. She worked in the office of Muhammad ʿAli ʿAllubah, involved mainly in civil cases for the wealthy, but she did not find this satisfying. When she decided to leave private practice to pursue studies in the new field of social work, she was widely criticized for abandoning this prestigious profession. Al-Ayyubi later recalled that Huda Shaʿrawi's had been the only voice of approval. The feminist leader asserted that while al-Ayyubi had served the rich as a lawyer, through social work she would be able to serve the poor.[97]

Meanwhile, other women lawyers appeared on the scene. Mufidah ʿAbd al-Rahman and ʿAtiyah Husayn al-Shafiʿi took their first criminal case together at Minya al-Qamh in the Delta and successfully defended three men accused of the illegal possession of drugs.[98] Like al-Ayyubi, these two also developed an interest in societal reform. Mufidah ʿAbd al-Rahman later became a member of the committee created by the Ministry of Social Affairs to study the reform of personal status laws.[99] In 1939 ʿAtiyah Husayn al-Shafiʿi became the first woman to apply to practice as a lawyer before the shariʿah courts, where personal status cases were heard. When al-Shafiʿi's application was rejected, the feminists protested, but to no avail.

A group of women lawyers came together to protect their interests, forming the Ittihad al-Muhamiyat al-Misriyat (Egyptian Women Lawyers' Union) in 1943, but the association did not last more than a few months.[100] After the 1952 revolution, women lawyers created another professional association. While the law eventually became a widely accepted profession for Egyptian women, they have yet to become judges as have women in some of the other Muslim Arab countries, such as Algeria and Sudan.

Women of the Pen

In becoming lawyers women had tried to penetrate an already established profession. By contrast they were in the front lines in the creation of modern journalism in the late nineteenth century.[101] Women created their own journals, operating as editors and contributors. Unlike most men in the field, who expected to earn an income there, women entered journalism mainly to debate and to claim a public voice. This remained women's primary motivation throughout the 1920s, 1930s, and 1940s. Saiza Nabarawi made the distinction between journalism as a mission, which it was for most women, and journalism as a trade, which it was for most men. Journalism was not highly esteemed, surely not an elite profession like law. Women journalists were generally of comfortable middle-class background, while male journalists spanned a wider class spectrum. As founders and editors of journals some women such as Shaʿrawi, the founder of the two EFU journals, provided certain opportunities for men to publish their works and air their views.

In the 1920s, 1930s, and 1940s there were many developments in women's journalism. The most striking was that several of the new women journalists for the first time publicly identified themselves as feminists. Indeed, journalism became a major vehicle for articulating the feminist cause. Now Muslim Egyptian women, as opposed to Syrian Christians, predominated as founders and editors of the approximately thirty new women's journals, and contributed more widely to the mainstream male press. Feminists who wielded the journalist's pen included Saiza Nabarawi, Munirah Thabit, Eva Habib al-Masri, Aminah al-Saʿid, Fatma Niʿmat Rashid, and Duriyah Shafiq. All had been members of the EFU at one time. The latter two went on to found their own feminist organizations.[102]

Other women who were liberal but not avowed feminists likewise ran journals. Two had founded their journals early in the century: Malikah Saʿd ran *al-Jins al-Latif* (The gentle sex) from 1908 to 1925, and Labibah Hashim was editor of *Fatat al-Sharq* (The young girl of the East) from 1906 to 1939.[103] In 1920 Balsam ʿAbd al-Malik began *al-Marʾah al-Misriyah*, which continued for three years. Women active in conservative women's associations also operated as journalists. Labibah Ahmad founded *al-Nahdah al-Nisaʾiyah* (The feminist renaissance), which ran from 1922 to 1924 and was the organ of Jamʾiyat Nahdat al-Sayyidat al-Misriyat (The Society of the Renaissance of Egyptian Women), an organization with a conservative Islamic orientation. She herself was editor until 1931. Tafidah ʿAlam, the founder-editor of *Ummuhat al-Mustaqbal* (Mothers of the future, 1930–1937), established the Jamʿiyat al-Shabbat al-Misriyat (Young Women's Society).[104]

New trends during this period adumbrated the eventual wider entry of women into mainstream journalism. Women became editors of journals with political backing directed to broad readerships. As noted earlier, Munirah Thabit had Wafdist backing in 1925 when she started *al-Amal*, which lasted only five years.[105] Fatma al-Yusif, of Lebanese origin, had been known as the actress Ruz (Rose) al-Yusif before turning to journalism. She founded *Ruz al-Yusuf* as a journal of the arts, receiving support from various political sources. Later she converted it into a general interest newspaper that achieved wide success and continues to this day.[106] In the 1920s and 1930s women first appeared as editors of women's pages in papers owned by men: Fatma Niʿmat Rashid in *La Patrie*, Nabawiyah Musa in *al-Balagh al-Usbuʿi*, and Mayy Ziyadah in *al-Siyasah al-Usbuʿiyah*.

Feminists helped shape journalism as they advanced the cause of women. While Saiza Nabarawi's primary identity was as a feminist, she had a distinct sense of herself as a journalist and was well aware of how the two roles were mutually reinforcing.[107] When the editor of *L'Egyptienne* was not invited to the opening of parliament in 1925, as were foreign women journalists, she protested her exclusion to the minister of the interior. Similarly, as I have mentioned, Egyptian women had been refused entry the previous year to the inauguration of the first postindependence parliament; the only exceptions were spouses of high officials. However, as Nabarawi herself suggests, national politics (EFU differences with the Wafd) probably loomed as large as gender in precipitating her exclusion from parliament's opening in 1925. Fellow journalists accorded *L'Egyptienne*'s editor better treatment, inviting Nabarawi to attend the monthly press banquets begun in 1928 to promote good relations between Egyptian and foreign journalists in Cairo. When her turn came to preside over the meeting, she reviewed the role the press had played in the evolution of feminism in Egypt.[108] Five months later when writer Mayy Ziyadah addressed the meeting, she paid tribute to the accomplishments of women writers in Egypt.[109]

Fatma Niʿmat Rashid and Eva Habib al-Masri were two other EFU feminists who took up the journalist's pen to advance the cause of women. Rashid was a contributor to *L'Egyptienne* and in 1937 became the first editor of the EFU's new Arabic journal, *al-Misriyah*. However, several months later she parted ways with the EFU and went on to create the bimonthly *al-Mahrajan* (The festival). When al-Masri took over editorship of *al-Misriyah*, she brought her sociological training to bear in evolving as a feminist journalist. Fatma Rashid, still active in the EFU and eager to protect and further the interests of women journalists, had founded the Association of Women Journalists (Hay'at al-Sihafiyat) in 1936.

While successfully running her two schools Nabawiyah Musa had also continued her journalism. In 1937 she founded *Majallat al-Fatah* (The young woman magazine), an unlikely title for a "weekly political and general magazine." Perhaps in using the name *al-Fatah*, which also denotes an unmarried or virginal woman, she wished to flaunt her independent status while also signifying perennial youth and vigor. Nabawiyah Musa used her journal as a vehicle for social reform, especially educational reform. *Majallat al-Fatah* became a preeminent platform for expressing her feminism. It was through her memoirs published in her magazine that she articulated her feminism most forcefully. In recounting her own experience she most straightforwardly and boldly criticized the conventional gender system and revealed how she had attempted to reshape it. Her memoirs are a stunning critique of patriarchal practices in Egypt.[110] Nabawiyah Musa's journal, and indeed her whole career, came to an abrupt end when she was imprisoned for criticizing the government as conciliatory when British tanks menaced Abdin Palace in 1942.

Second-generation feminist activist Duriyah Shafiq also used journalism to advance the cause of women. While a university student in France she contributed occasionally to *L'Egyptienne*. She became editor of *La femme nouvelle*, a glossy magazine founded with royal backing in 1945 that she declared would serve as "a wonderful bridge between East and West."[111] The same year she also founded the Arabic-language journal *Majallat Bint al-Nil* (Daughter of the Nile magazine) to reach out to a broad middle-class Egyptian readership. Through this journal Duriyah Shafiq built up a constituency that became the base of the feminist movement she would lead through the feminist organization of the same name, Ittihad Bint al-Nil (The Daughter of the Nile Union), which she created in 1948. She also founded a more mainstream political journal called *Bint al-Nil al-Siyasiyah* (The political daughter of the Nile), as well as *Katkut* (The chick), a magazine for children.[112]

Aminah al-Saʿid was the first woman to build a professional career as a paid journalist in the mainstream press. She began her work in journalism in the 1940s. In 1945 she became editor of *al-Marʾah al-ʿArabiyah* (The Arab woman), the new short-lived organ of the recently founded al-Ittihad al-Nisaʾi al-ʿArabi (Arab Feminist Union). Al-Saʿid took her first paid job in journalism at Dar al-Hilal as a reporter for *al-Musawwar* (The illustrated) in the late 1940s. While a fledgling journalist she also tried her hand at other literary forms. After her trip to India as an EFU delegate to the meetings of the All-India Women's Conference in 1946, she wrote a travel narrative, *Mushahidat fi al-Hind* (Impressions of India). She also published two novels, *al-Jamihah* (The shrew) and *Akhir al-Tariq* (The end of the road), and a series of children's stories called *Rawdat al-Tifl* (The child's garden).

In 1954, two years after the revolution, al-Saʿid became the founder-editor of *Hawwa*ʾ (Eve, published at Dar al-Hilal), a weekly aimed at a broad female audience in Egypt and other Arab countries. This outreach helped serve the new revolutionary regime's interests in forming strong ties in the Arab world and in advancing mass mobilization of citizens of both genders. Aspiring journalists from Arab countries, including North Africa where French predominated, were sent to Aminah al-Saʿid for training.[113] In 1956 al-Saʿid became a member of the Board of the Press Syndicate, and two years later vice president. She also went on to become a member of the High Board of Executives in Dar al-Hilal. The first feminist activist to become a full-time professional journalist with a mainstream publishing house, Aminah al-Saʿid was also the only feminist from the pre-1952 period whom the state allowed to continue openly to support the cause of women. She did so as a journalist and remained faithful to her feminist ideals. She publicly advocated reform of the personal status code, still a contentious issue; it is possible that the state tolerated this for its own purposes. Feminist activist journalists Saiza Nabarawi and Duriyah Shafiq, however, were silenced by the regime.[114]

Women in the State

The state bureaucracy was a major and respected source of employment for male Egyptians in this historically highly centralized society. In the 1920s the feminists had begun to campaign for jobs for women in government, accelerating their efforts in the 1930s.[115] While the feminists sustained their advocacy, women began to take up jobs in the modern state bureaucracy. The education and health sectors, seen as extensions of women's nurturing domains in the family, were the first to employ women, offering positions in inspection. In the 1920s, the Ministry of Education led when it appointed Nabawiyah Musa as inspector of girls' schools. Although Nabawiyah Musa interpreted this as a tactic to remove her from the more independent position of school principal, rather than as an affirmative move to bring women into inspection, still it set a precedent. In the 1920s the Department of Public Health, which became a ministry in 1936, also engaged women as inspectors, especially in the areas of maternal and child-care services.

In 1933 Huda Shaʿrawi demanded that women graduates be employed by the government, especially in the Ministries of Education and Public Health. She also recommended that municipalities employ women.[116] During the course of the decade more jobs opened up to women. After the introduction of labor laws for women in 1933, the Labor Office in the Ministry of the Interior, with feminist pressure, created the new position of inspector of women workers in factories and commercial establishments and, as mentioned earlier, hired Naʿimah al-Ayyubi for the job. In the mid-1930s with the growth of the Egyptian film industry and increased importation of foreign films, the Ministry of the Interior created the position of censor and hired Zaynab Kamil to fill the post. The appointment of a woman as film censor aroused objections in parliament. Deputy ʿAbd al-Wahhab Muhammad Salim protested that women were too emotional to work as censors.[117] As state film censor a woman would have the authority to pronounce on issues of public morality; in "traditional" patriarchal culture it was men who decided these matters—and who permitted a double standard to operate.

Soon after its creation in 1939 the Ministry of Social Affairs began to employ women freshly trained in the new field of social work and also drew upon the experience of philanthropist women, including such feminists as Huda Shaʿrawi, Mary Kahil, and Hidayah Barakat.[118] Naʿimah al-Ayyubi, having left law practice to train in social work, became the first woman to work in the new ministry, initially as a volunteer. Among al-Ayyubi's early accomplishments was to supervise the creation of student hostels, including the first women's hostel. Later she organized free public kitchens and free public baths in the poor quarters of Cairo.[119] The Ministry of Social Affairs became known as "the women's ministry," an extension of women's voluntary social service work for the community, itself an extension of women's nurturing roles in the family. The first and only woman to reach the level of minister was Hikmat Abu Zayd, appointed head of the Ministry of Social Affairs in 1964.[120]

At the end of the 1930s, the Ministry of Justice employed women to work in the *majalis hasbiyah*, councils for safeguarding the legal rights of orphans. This could be seen as yet another example of the extension of women's nurturing roles into the state bureaucratic arena.

The EFU also called for women to fill official positions in the international arena after Egypt joined the League of Nations in 1936. When Egypt attended its first session in 1937, the EFU president took the occasion to insist that her government "follow the example of the civilized countries" by delegating women to work at the League. *L'Egyptienne* reproduced a letter to the EFU president from the IAW liaison to the League of Nations, Emilie Gourd, in Geneva, saying that she hoped Egypt would follow the example of the other Muslim country, Turkey, in sending women to the League.[121]

By the late 1940s, women had made significant inroads into government service in the middle echelons. The first women government employees had solid credentials. They had at least a secondary school education and often held university degrees. As a group, their level of education was higher than that of men in government work. However, few women reached the upper rungs of the administrative ladder. As one of the top ten graduates from the Faculty of Law in 1951, ʿA'ishah Ratib qualified for a position in the Council of State. However, as the only woman in the group, she was excluded because of her gender. The EFU protested and hired a lawyer, as she did herself, but to no avail. ʿA'ishah Ratib then joined the Faculty of Law at Fu'ad I University.[122]

The entry of women into high level government posts did not occur until a decade after the 1952 revolution.[123] I have already mentioned the nomination of Hikmah Abu Zayd as minister of social affairs in 1962, an appointment made by President Jamal ʿAbd al-Nasir in the context of his new socialist program, which aimed to give both sexes and all classes access to education and employment. This set a precedent. Afterwards, it became commonplace for a woman to be appointed minister of social affairs. Nine years later ʿA'ishah Ratib was also invited to fill the position. At the Ministry of Education, Karimah al-Saʿid became the deputy minister of education in the 1960s;[124] other government ministries continued to be headed by males. The government was able to draw upon a pool of well-qualified women who could be displayed as high-level tokens while the majority of women were sequestered in the lower echelons. In Egypt, unlike most Western countries, women government employees never suffered salary discrimination. However, it was not until the large exodus of male labor to the Gulf states in the 1970s and 1980s, and the rise of a new aggressive private sector with the return of capitalism, that women in any numbers came to occupy senior posts in the government. These were not the plum jobs they had been during the socialist period, as public sector jobs were now among the least well remunerated.

An Old Profession

Women have perennially worked as entertainers in cities and towns throughout Egypt. Whereas women who entered government service and the new professions were mainly well-educated and middle-class, those who worked as entertainers were predominantly women of modest origins. Although working as a teacher or hakimah was not initially deemed proper, these professions soon became respectable for women, while as a doctor or lawyer a woman gained immediate prestige. Careers in entertainment did not bring women respect or prestige in conventional terms, except for the most accomplished who achieved wide acclaim.

In nineteenth-century Egypt female singers, dancers, and musicians who performed in the houses of the wealthy were commonly slaves from the Caucasus—until the outlawing of the slave trade in 1877 cut off new supplies—as well as lower-class Egyptian women. The majority of the Egyptian performers worked in coffeehouses and in the entertainment halls that sprang up in the nineteenth and twentieth centuries. Until the early twentieth century women singers (*ʿawalim*) in Cairo had their own guild.

In the 1830s and 1840s, Italian and French theatrical companies performed in Egypt, bringing European actresses before Cairo audiences. Trends toward Western entertainment became more pronounced in the 1860s and 1870s during the reign of Khedive Ismaʿil. The opera house opened in 1869, providing a stage for touring European performers and a very few Egyptians. In the 1890s when Helwan was developed as a resort for the wealthy, adaptations of European plays as well as Salamah Hijazi and his troupe could be seen in the new music gardens. Indigenous traditions of entertainment continued alongside new forms.[125]

The twentieth century saw new departures in entertainment. Women from Egypt and Syria began to perform on the stage in Cairo and Alexandria as musical theater became popular.[126] One of the earliest was the singer Munirah al-Mahdiyah. Arriving in Cairo from the Delta around the turn of the century, she first sang in the cafés in ʿImad al-Din Street before turning to the stage, where she became one of the first Egyptian women to appear unveiled. She joined the troupe of Salamah Hijazi around 1915 and before long opened her own theater. Leading political men, including Saʿd Zaghlul, frequented her theater, where nationalist songs were sung in defiance of the British.[127]

In the 1920s and 1930s careers for women as singers and actresses evolved at a time when Najib al-Rihani and Yusuf Wahbi and others opened theatrical companies. Mary Ibrahim, a Copt, became the first Egyptian woman to perform as an actress. However, many of the leading actresses and singers in Cairo and Alexandria were from Syria and Lebanon. Fatma al-Yusif was a Muslim orphan from Lebanon, whom a Christian theatrical family brought to Alexandria and raised. She eventually became an actress under the name Ruz al-Yusif and, as has been mentioned, by the mid-1920s had left the theater for journalism.[128] Syrian singers included Mary Jubran (known as Mary Jamilah), Nadirah, Laure Daccache, Mary Samat, Dawlat Abyad (better known as an actress), and Badʿiyah Masabni. Masabni worked as a singer and actress with Najib al-Rihani's troupe in the early 1920s. She later became the first woman to open her own music hall and even started a weekly matinee for women.[129] Wendy Buonaventura, a writer on "Eastern" dance, finds that "oriental" themes in dance that became popular in the West in the late nineteenth and early twentieth centuries were reexported back to Egypt. Buonaventura claims that the Western "fantasy of Oriental dance filtered through and was taken up and unconsciously parodied by Arab dancers in their desire to emulate Western behaviour and modes of fashion." She notes that Masabni innovated when she played with gossamer veils—not at the time part of the customary repertoire—emulating Western "oriental" dancers of the day.[130] Meanwhile, Bahiga Hafiz's attempted to incorporate Western themes into Eastern musical forms.

ʿAsmahan (1912–1944) was an acclaimed singer and actress who also came from Syria. Born Amal al-Atrash into a Druze family, she emigrated to Egypt with her mother to escape danger during the Druze rebellion against the French in 1925. At the end of the 1920s she began to sing in public, helped by her brother, Farid al-Atrash, himself a famous singer and composer. Much admired, she had a tumultuous life and career.[131]

Successes notwithstanding, careers in entertainment were not considered suitable for "respectable" women of the middle and upper strata of society. Women entertainers performed in front of men and, earlier in the century, were criticized for being hasty in unveiling. In the 1920s and 1930s the feminists tried to change negative attitudes and to promote careers in entertainment for women of any background who wished to be performers. The EFU supported women who pioneered on the stage and in films. *L'Egyptienne*, for example, lauded the performances of the Algerian actress Laila Bin Sidara, who performed at the Opera comique in Paris in the 1920s, while carefully noting that she was the granddaughter of a respected religious leader.[132]

In 1925, Studio Misr was created as one of the Bank Misr's enterprises, and with it film production began in Egypt, creating a new industry that was to reach out to the wider Arab world. The first film was produced by a woman, ʿAzizah Amir. Another woman producer of the period, Aminah Muhammad, directed *Muʿjizat al-Mawsim* (Miracle of the season). Early stars of the nascent Egyptian cinema included ʿAsmahan and the Egyptian dancers Tahiyah Carioca and Samiyah Gamal. While film artists were typically of ordinary middle-class origins, upper-class Bahigah Hafiz, whose futile attempts to become affiliated with the Conservatory of Oriental Music were noted in the previous chapter, was more successful in taking up acting. She played the leading role in the first film production of Muhammad Husayn Haykal's 1914 novel *Zaynab*. Hafiz also founded the Fanar Film Company. She produced *al-Dahaya* (The victims), *al-Ittiham* (The accusation), and *Layla bint al-Sahara* (Layla, the daughter of the desert) for which she also wrote the script and played the leading role.[133] Bahigah Hafiz told Saiza Nabarawi in an interview: "Many have criticized me for having chosen this profession, calling it a great scandal! But have they ever considered the difficulties of all kinds thrown in the way of a woman alone, who is without resources but wishes to remain independent? What pushed me toward the cinema therefore was not mere whim nor a simple wish to appear before the public but my need to create a condition that would guarantee my freedom. . . . Besides, I took this decision only after I had despaired of receiving any encouragement or support from my compatriots."[134] As an upper-class woman in the film industry, Bahigah Hafiz remained the exception that proved the rule.[135]

However, for the exceptional, careers in entertainment defied convention. Umm Kalthum, the legendary "singer of the century" of Egypt, and indeed of the whole Arab world, illustrated this. In her early days in the provinces Umm Kalthum's father, who accompanied her in her singing performances, had made her dress as a boy. She first traveled from her home in the Delta to Cairo in the 1920s. She sang at the *kermesses* of the EFU in the late 1920s and early 1930s, and by the 1930s her career was well underway. Umm Kalthum began to achieve wide acclaim in the 1940s. After the 1952 revolution she rose to unprecedented heights, encapsulating and expressing the feelings and aspirations of the Arab masses. When she died in 1975 the national radio broadcast recitations from the Qur'an, an honor customarily accorded a head of state.[136] Lebanese poet Etel Adnan wrote, "The human river is going to flow behind her coffin. The people are coming from everywhere."

Traffic in Women

THE EFU's battle against state-regulated prostitution raised a host of contentious issues. Feminists brought into the open the double standard, an aspect of patriarchal culture in Egypt that most men felt uncomfortable confronting. The diatribes of conservative men against unveiling, their shrill claims that uncovering the face would lead to women's immorality, were still fresh when feminists began to spotlight the state-condoned sexual latitude men allowed themselves.

Under British colonial occupation, the state recognized and regulated prostitution, extending earlier incipient measures of control. Following independence feminists criticized the Egyptian state for condoning prostitution through continued official regulation. Calling prostitution an indignity to all women, feminists demanded that the independent Egyptian state respect and safeguard the well-being of all its citizens, not humiliate "half" of them. Islam, moreover, was the state religion; by tolerating prostitution the state violated Islam.

In combating prostitution feminists brought to public scrutiny a form of class and gender exploitation. It was poor women who took up prostitution to support themselves and their families, whether needy parents and siblings or their own children. Nabawiyah Musa and Huda Shaʿrawi had long been sensitive to the vulnerability of poor women to sexual exploitation. In advocating training and education for women in *The Woman and Work* Nabawiyah Musa argued that such preparation would give those in need access to decent jobs to secure a livelihood for themselves and those dependent upon them. While pioneering in philanthropy Shaʿrawi had advocated training in income-generating skills for poor women.

Prostitution in Egypt was not simply indigenous; it was multiethnic with imperial and racist dimensions. In the nineteenth and early twentieth centuries, there was a considerable flow of women from Europe destined for prostitution in Eastern countries. Egypt was a major terminus. This influx of European women—some coerced, others willing—was part of a rush for profits in a new El Dorado. The international traffic in women came to be called "la traite des blanches" in French and "white slavery" in English. The origin of the term "white slave" is attributed to French writer Victor Hugo, who wrote to British antiregulationist Josephine Butler in 1870 that "the slavery of black women is abolished in America, but the slavery of white women continues in Europe."[1] The name "white slave" for a prostitute began to circulate in England, loaded with the outrage that slavery evoked while shifting the terms of reference from race and the enslavement of the total human being to gender and the purchase of a woman's sexuality. At the end of the century, when it was discovered that Englishwomen had been forcibly taken across the Channel to houses of prostitution in Belgium, "white slave" came to be applied to women presumed to have been abducted over national borders.[2] The term expressed British outrage against the sexual exploitation of their women by foreigners, but this was still "white slavery" within a European context. When Western women were removed, with or without their consent, to colonized Eastern countries, the term took on a racist connotation. The anti–white slavery forces did not speak of the export of women from Eastern countries. The term "white slave" was applied exclusively to Western women who went abroad to work in the sex trade, implying—inaccurately—that they were all coerced.[3]

The same Western women who were seen as pitiful victims by European anti–white slavery crusaders were despicable pariahs in the eyes of Western imperial rulers. The British commissioner of police in Bombay declared in 1913: "As regards the English prostitute, it has for years been an unwritten law to draw a distinction between her and her foreign European sister. The latter is accepted as an ugly but necessary fact; the former if found, is 'induced' to leave India. This unwritten law is known far and wide and . . . had arisen . . . [for] preserving as far as possible the moral character of the governing race."[4] A clear echo of this attitude is sounded in a conversation in Cairo around the same time, between Egyptian and English teachers, about prostitutes. Nabawiyah Musa recorded this in her memoirs to illustrate how the English in Egypt always "glorified" their country in order to assert colonial superiority: "An Egyptian woman asked the Englishwoman sitting next to her the word for 'prostitute.' The Englishwoman quickly replied that such a creature did not exist in England and thus there was no word," whereupon the Egyptian feminist pointed to the English and other European prostitutes in Egypt, saying that the only difference between them and Egyptian prostitutes was that the latter were subject to regulation while European prostitutes were "free to go about without any restrictions or controls."[5] She was referring to the special legal and financial immunities foreigners enjoyed in Egypt known as the Capitulations. These extraterritorial arrangements, which originated in the sixteenth-century Ottoman Empire as a device to encourage and protect Western commerce, were subsequently instituted in other parts of the empire.[6] In nineteenth-century Egypt, the immunities and privileges of Westerners were further extended.

In the early 1920s when the Egyptian feminists took up their battle against prostitution, they encountered a thriving foreign sex traffic beyond the reaches of Egyptian law, existing alongside indigenous prostitution. While there was some overlap between the two "systems" in terms of both practitioners and clients, the European business was by far the more lucrative and "powerful," and predominated in Cairo and in the maritime cities of Alexandria and Port Said.

"Modernizing" Prostitution

Prostitution in Egypt took new forms in the nineteenth and early twentieth centuries, shaped by the rise of the modern state, the expansion of capitalism, and the country's incorporation into the European-dominated world market system, as well as by urbanization and colonization.

Early in the nineteenth century, in the context of efforts to impose law and order and to effect sanitary measures, the new ruler, Muhammad ʿAli, banished street dancers who practiced prostitution from Cairo to Upper Egypt. This only led prostitutes to regroup in provincial towns, where many successfully continued their operations, while driving mercenary sex in the capital underground. In the 1860s and 1870s, an intensified urban expansion and aggressive modernization brought an increased influx of Europeans, and the state lifted the ban on prostitution in Cairo, imposing a tax on prostitutes. The state also instituted regulatory measures, requiring prostitutes to obtain health certificates and undergo routine medical examinations.[7]

State economic policies which drew Egypt more fully into the European-dominated world market system created conditions that produced new categories of poor women whose desperation made many vulnerable to prostitution. When cheap goods from Europe displaced household-based craft production, lower-class urban women were impoverished. In the rural areas, the state-imposed shift from subsistence farming to producing cotton for export threatened the welfare of the peasant family. Further, the state exacted corvée labor from peasant men, leaving many women in dire straits. New economic hardship caused many poor women to gravitate to the city in search of a livelihood.[8] Still another new category of vulnerable women was created as a result of the state's outlawing of the slave trade in 1877: the newly freed women,. originally from the Caucasus, Sudan, and Ethiopia. Some, but by no means all, freed women found employment through their former owners or with the help of state manumission bureaus.[9]

With expanding urbanization and continued harsh conditions in the rural areas there was a perennial flow of women from the countryside to Cairo and Alexandria. Peasant women increasingly found employment in urban households, which could no longer rely upon fresh supplies of slaves for domestic labor. At the same time, with the boom in the major cities benefiting the middle and upper strata, and prosperity extending to some of the provincial towns, there was expanding work for lower-class women in entertainment, often an avenue into prostitution.

Alongside Egyptians working as prostitutes, there developed a brisk European trade. Along with European technocrats, advisers, and merchants, the state-led modernization in the nineteenth century brought increasing numbers of prostitutes. The expansion of Mediterranean steamship service and the opening of the Suez Canal in 1869 drew a steady flow of women destined to work as prostitutes to Egypt.[10] The foreign prostitutes came mainly from Italy, France, Greece, Russia, and Romania. Jewish women and girls from poor villages and ghettos of Russia and eastern Europe constituted some 70 to 80 percent of the foreign prostitutes in Alexandria in 1903, according to police reports. Throughout Egypt, however, Greeks were the most numerous of the European prostitutes.[11] Like other Europeans, prostitutes, and the "traders" and pimps who exploited them, enjoyed extraterritorial privileges and protections under the Capitulations. European prostitution lay outside the jurisdiction of the local police and legal systems. Muhammad Haykal wrote in *L'Egyptienne*, "Under the Capitulations regime that protects the Europeans in this country undesirable elements have emigrated to colonized countries to make their fortune without any scruples."[12]

The clientele of the sex trade, like the prostitutes themselves, were both Egyptian and European. With the outlawing of the slave trade and the dwindling of new supplies of slave-concubines, prostitution assumed a new role in indigenous elite society.[13] At the same time, markets for prostitutes were created by the expanding resident European population centered mainly in Cairo, Alexandria, and Port Said, by growing numbers of Western travelers to Egypt (including those in transit through the Suez Canal), and by British military forces in Egypt.[14] European prostitutes served men of the Egyptian elites and the wealthier Europeans, while the clientele of Egyptian prostitutes were mainly Egyptians, poorer Europeans, and British soldiers.

Regulating Prostitution, Exploiting Women, Rescuing Women

There was a direct connection between state regulation of prostitution and imperialism. Regulation originated in various European countries out of concern for keeping the military physically fit.[15] State regulation, which had begun in England with the Contagious Diseases Acts of the 1860s, gave rise to a vigorous abolitionist campaign led by Josephine Butler and her Ladies National Association.[16] By 1886, with the repeal of the Contagious Diseases Acts, state regulation was ended in England; however, regulation was imposed in Egypt and throughout the British Empire as part of the imperial obsession with law and order, and to protect the health of British troops.[17]

A movement to combat prostitution organized in Britain by the National Vigilance Association, created in 1885, quickly spread abroad. Vigilance activists attempted to halt the coercion of women and girls into prostitution, setting up watches at railway stations and ports to offer advice to female travelers and steer them to safe lodgings. It was British vigilance activists who initiated the international crusade against white slavery.[18] Secretary of the English National Vigilance Association William Coote organized the first International Congress for the Suppression of the White Slave Traffic in 1899 and helped set up committees in Egypt and other countries.[19] The opponents of white slavery, in trying to dry up the supply of prostitutes through prevention and rescue measures directed at the women themselves, and in pursuing traffickers, worked with state law enforcement authorities. The anti–white slavery activists represented by the vigilance groups, working within the existing colonial framework, were far more congenial to colonial authorities than the abolitionists who demanded legal deregulation, thus threatening to contain the authority of colonial and neocolonial state systems. In Egypt, because the Capitulations restricted the powers of the British law enforcement authorities, those authorities welcomed cooperation with private anti–white slavery organizations. Thus groups opposing the exploitation of women helped shore up the colonial state, and later the neocolonial state.

Building on earlier edicts, British colonial authorities in Egypt issued a decree in 1905 setting out regulations. Prostitution was to be conducted from registered houses restricted to certain localities. Prostitutes, who must not be minors, had to obtain from the police permits bearing their photographs. The women were required to submit to weekly medical examinations; if found infected with venereal disease they were obliged to cease working and undergo treatment at their own expense. Enforcement was another matter. Commandant of the Cairo Police Thomas Russell, whose police career in Egypt from 1902 to 1946 included service in the colonial state and the postindependence state when the British still controlled the police, spoke in his memoirs about the persistence of enforcement difficulties and how police officials had to work with private foreign groups and consular officials.[20]

The earliest efforts to combat prostitution in Egypt were part of the international campaign against white slavery. It was in 1904 with help from William Coote that Baron Jacques de Menasce, a leader of the Jewish community of Alexandria, founded the Alexandria Committee for the Suppression of the Traffic in Women. Analogous committees were also set up in Cairo and Port Said. The colonial authorities granted annual subsidies to these committees, which were composed of members of the minority communities and resident foreigners, but excluded Egyptians.[21]

With its large numbers of Jewish prostitutes Alexandria attracted the attention of German Jewish social reformer and feminist Bertha Pappenheim. In her travels through eastern Europe and the Middle East investigating the traffic in women, she stopped in Alexandria. A pioneer in confronting the problems of Jewish women drawn into the white slave trade, Pappenheim had founded the feminist Judischer Frauenbund (The Jewish Women's Union), continuing earlier work for the rescue and rehabilitation of Jewish prostitutes within the context of a larger feminist campaign.[22]

Pappenheim published the journal of her trip in a book called *Sisyphus Arbeit* (The work of Sisyphus, 1924) to draw attention to the international traffic in women.[23] She tells how she began her investigations in Alexandria with a visit to the German consul, who denied the existence of German prostitutes and sent her to the Austrian consul. The latter explained that the prostitutes, whom he referred to as "merchandise," were of "mixed origins," and that the traders were Italians and Greeks. The Austrian consul admitted that there were many Arab women and children working as prostitutes, but said there was no need to bother with them. Pappenheim met anti–white slavery activist Baron Jacques de Menasce and "Herr C.," a member of the Cattawi family prominent in the Jewish community, finding both men overweening. She recorded that de Menasce was "delighted with the achievements" of his committee and claimed that over the past year with police help the committee had rescued seventeen hundred girls from pimps, and traders. Pappenheim suspected that "the traders" had more accurate statistics.[24]

While visiting houses of prostitution, Pappenheim was told by an accompanying security official responsible for dealing with minors that in 1910 there had been seventy-one cases recorded of females engaged in illegal prostitution: the majority were girls between fourteen and sixteen; however, there were also girls of six, eight, and ten, and one case of a four-year-old girl. The official informed Pappenheim that a ship carrying minors had been prevented from landing in Alexandria, only to unload sixty-four Jewish girls in Port Said. Again, Pappenheim doubted the figures quoted: she mentally increased them tenfold. Pappenheim toured the prostitutes' quarter in Alexandria with a British police officer, speaking with the women in German, English, French, and Italian. Her escort translated the remark of a "tall Arab girl" who caught Pappenheim's attention; she said, as Pappenheim recorded it, "She [Pappenheim] and her whole family will be happy and blessed because she is the first such woman who has spoken with us." Pappenheim cited as examples an Arab, a Polish Jew, and an Italian "worthy of our care and willing to accept it," adding, "But who will take care of them? I could be very useful here." She also recorded the lack of attention they received and the poor hygienic conditions.[25]

A group of European women had recently founded a rescue society called L'Amie de la Jeune Fille, which Pappenheim visited. Listening to a Swiss woman who met ships and sought young women in trouble to help repatriate them, Pappenheim acutely felt the enormity of the problem of sexually exploited women. Around the time of Pappenheim's visit to Egypt, refugees from the Balkan Wars were pouring into Alexandria. One can only speculate on how many of these refugees ended up in prostitution.

The state could not directly stop women, whether Egyptian or foreign, from being impressed into prostitution and severely exploited; indeed, antiregulationists argued that state regulation aided and abetted prostitution by driving it underground. Two testimonies taken in the 1920s provide details of the sexual exploitation of women. An Egyptian woman called Afqar who "appeared to be a minor" and was without a permit explained after her arrest how she had been coerced into prostitution in Cairo.[26] Andrée Guillet, a Frenchwoman, sentenced before the French Consular Court, described her abduction from Marseilles and her forced prostitution in Alexandria and Cairo.[27] Evidence from women like these who were arrested and jailed underscored the point that state regulation did not so much protect women as make them, rather than men, pay the price. Private societies, meanwhile, were limited both in their abilities and in their mandate to fight only foreign prostitution.

Fighting Prostitution and Capitulations

In the 1920s, Egyptian women as feminists and nationalists entered the fight against prostitution, taking it in a new direction. Egyptian feminists were quick to take up the battle against state-regulated prostitution. When the EFU attended its first IAW congress in Rome in 1923, prostitution was an important item on the agenda. The IAW combined the two approaches discussed above: antiregulationist and preventionist. The congress took a resolution demanding an end to state-regulated prostitution and a suppression of the international traffic in women and children. The IAW held that prostitution was not only degrading to the prostitutes but an indignity to all women, and made more offensive still by state sanction. Moreover, as Saiza Nabarawi would argue, by granting prostitution a "legal character" the state "seems to justify and encourage it."[28] The IAW defined prostitution as a moral issue: the committee dealing with it was called the Committee on an Equal Moral Standard. The 1923 congress passed a resolution insisting that the same moral standard—that is, the standard demanded of women—be applied to both sexes, and that both sexes should be equally subject to the law.[29] The EFU had voted in agreement with the IAW positions on prostitution, thus lending support to the international campaign. Reciprocal support was the avowed ideal of IAW feminism: when affiliates agreed on a collective position, the national feminist associations in turn should expect support from the international organization. Reciprocity was not always forthcoming, as Egyptian feminists discovered.

In Egypt, Huda Shaʿrawi, as president of the new EFU, wrote to Shaykh al-Azhar Muhammad Abu al-Fadl to enlist support from Islamic authorities on religious and moral grounds in their campaign against prostitution: "The EFU would also like to request Your Eminence to draw the attention of the government to the houses of prostitution that have spread throughout the country posing a danger to morals and virtues. Recognizing prostitution and licensing it is a great shame for a government of an Islamic country whose constitution states that the official religion is Islam."[30] The EFU gained the praise of the shaykh al-Azhar for its campaign against prostitution and alcohol, winning for the new feminist organization the favorable disposition of the religious authorities. The shaykh al-Azhar told the EFU, "We appreciate the value of this honorable society and its hard work to spread virtue and combat vice."[31] The religious establishment, however, did not push the issue politically. The feminists' antiprostitution campaign did not give rise to a broader social purity campaign in Egypt calling for the imposition of a single standard—the sexual standard society and religion demanded of women. No male forces comparable to those that emerged in many Western countries, including Britain, came forth to press men to keep to the moral standard they demanded in women.

The following year, both the EFU and the WWCC placed "fighting prostitution" on their joint list of demands. But it was the EFU women alone, not their Wafd-linked sisters, who mounted an active campaign against legalized prostitution. The feminists tied activism against prostitution with a drive to end the Capitulations in what would be an intense feminist and nationalist campaign. Egyptian feminists abhorred the Capitulations, not only for "protecting" foreign prostitution but also as an odious infringement upon Egyptian sovereignty sustaining inequalities between citizens and Westerners in Egypt. In their campaign against prostitution, Egyptian feminists struggled against inequalities of gender, ethnicity, and class.[32] The Capitulations privileging Europeans had been abolished in 1922 in the former Ottoman Arab provinces that became Syria, Lebanon, Palestine, Trans-Jordan, and Iraq, and were ended in Turkey when it became a republic in 1923, but they remained in Egypt as an oppressive anachronism. Because prostitution in Egypt was an international business protected by the Capitulations, Egyptian feminists struggled at home and abroad simultaneously to end state-regulated prostitution and the Capitulations. EFU members waged a relentless battle in the international arena until the Capitulations were ended in 1937; only then did they shift their full attention to the domestic struggle.

The EFU first revealed its strategy in the fight against prostitution in Egypt at a 1924 conference organized by the International League for the Suppression of Traffic in Women and Children in Graz, Austria. Huda Shaʿrawi, attending as president of the EFU, told the gathering:

> At the outset, I suggest that if the conference is serious about its objectives, it must motivate governments throughout the world to permanently close down houses of prostitution. . . . The acquiescence of any country in permitting the continuation of these establishments . . . in any country, including Egypt, is in my opinion an insult to human dignity and a trespass on virtue and public sentiment. Condoning these establishments is an encouragement to vice and gives a free hand to those who practice the traffic in women and children. . . . Most unfortunately, in Egypt the Capitulations stand as a barrier to enacting a law that can be applied to non-Egyptians operating houses of prostitution. Therefore, I ask the conference to press governments that have Capitulations treaties to allow the Egyptian government to close the houses of prostitution operated by the nationals of these countries.[33]

The EFU moved cautiously against the Capitulations, simply asking countries protected by these treaties to permit the Egyptian government to close houses of prostitution involving their nationals. Shaʿrawi pointed out that she was the only Easterner attending the Graz meeting. As has been mentioned, Egyptians had been barred from the Committees for the Suppression of Traffic in Women and Children in their own country; they would continue to be excluded until 1943 when many Europeans left because of the Second World War. The International League, as Shaʿrawi underscored, was in reality a "Western league." This was the first and last time the EFU used this forum.

Egyptian feminists instead conducted their campaign against prostitution internationally through the IAW. No other IAW affiliate, however, came from a country where foreign prostitution flourished inside its borders under the protection of extraterritorial laws. Many IAW members were from countries whose nationals enjoyed immunities in Egypt because of Capitulations treaties with Egypt. Egyptian feminists tried to educate IAW women about the Capitulations and their implications for prostitution in Egypt. Saiza Nabarawi told the 1926 IAW congress in Paris that because of the Capitulations "all measures taken by our government are condemned to failure from the start." The EFU proposed that the IAW take a resolution demanding that countries having Capitulations treaties with Egypt give the Egyptian government authority over prostitution houses run by their nationals in Egypt. Nabarawi stressed that if state-licensed prostitution houses remained "subject to many authorities in the same country, it would delay their disappearance indefinitely."[34] The IAW did not pass such a resolution.

At a working session of the IAW's Peace Committee convening in Amsterdam in 1927, Huda Shaʿrawi presented a resolution asking participants to press their governments to end the Capitulations on the grounds that the inequalities they sustained between Europeans and Egyptians and their infringement upon the sovereignty of Egypt constituted a danger to world peace.[35] This resolution was not adopted, but the IAW executive committee did endorse a resolution taken by a recent International Congress against the Traffic in Women and Children. This was a request that the League of Nations and governments themselves, individually or in concert if more than one were involved, take every measure to close houses of prostitution. In forwarding the resolution to Prime Minister ʿAbd al-Khaliq Tharwat, Huda Shaʿrawi insisted that not only the EFU but the great majority of Egyptians wanted the houses of prostitution closed out of concern for the moral and physical health of the people.[36]

With Huda Shaʿrawi, Saiza Nabarawi, and Mary Kahil in the lead the EFU prepared itself for a continuation of the battle at the 1929 IAW conference in Berlin. The campaign brought together Egyptian feminists and British commandant of the Cairo Police Thomas Russell, who provided the women with data from police files to use in their campaign. Under pressure to combat the international drug traffic linked to prostitution, Russell was cooperative. But unlike the feminists, whose help was useful to him for his law-and-order purposes, Russell took a strictly technocratic approach. He kept aloof from the politics of the Capitulations, although he decried the impediments they put in his way.

The EFU went to Berlin with its largest delegation to date and this time met with some success. The IAW passed a resolution declaring that since, under the Capitulations, Egyptian authorities had no jurisdiction over foreign houses or the drug traffic, IAW affiliates should press their governments to "facilitate sanitary and moral action by the Egyptian authorities."[37] This was the IAW's first direct mention ever of the Capitulations. The resolution passed, but it was no easy victory. Mary Kahil had made persuasive pleas in German while Shaʿrawi busily lobbied in French. The Egyptians had a staunch supporter in the head of the French delegation, Marcelle Kraemer-Bach, a lawyer and secretary-general of the Union française pour le suffrage des femmes, who strongly opposed the Capitulations. The British abstained from voting.[38]

In the 1920s and 1930s there were international debates over the use of women police in the campaign against prostitution. In Britain women had initially become police workers at the beginning of the First World War when there was a great shortage of male civilians. The state was eager to enlist women's aid in combating the spread of prostitution brought on by the mobilization of troops. The new British policewomen never enjoyed the rank and full powers that male police had, and after the war most were let go. With this turn of events the international arena, and more specifically the international campaign against the traffic in women, beckoned as new terrain for British policewomen. Commandant Mary Allen, a veteran suffragette and pioneering policewoman, attended the IAW conference in Paris in 1926. Out of this conference came a call for the creation of women police "with the full status and powers of their male colleagues," women police who would deal with cases involving women, youth, and children and would do preventive work among the young. The IAW took pains to make clear, however, "that as this Congress unanimously condemns the regulation of prostitution, the use of women police as 'police des moeurs,' when it is the official instrument of regulation, should be absolutely opposed." The line separating prevention and rescue from regulation was thin. For this and other reasons the issue of women police was contentious.

Commander Mary Allen later showed up in Egypt with police inspector Helene Tagart promoting the idea of women in the Egyptian police force. Neither British Police Commissioner Russell nor the Egyptian feminists favored this. The former insisted that the pay and conditions of men in the police should be improved before the police force was opened to women. Feminists, indicating their schedule of priorities, claimed that society was not ready for women police. However, they argued that women were especially well equipped to fight social ills and when the time was ripe would be effective in prevention, in inspecting houses of prostitution, and in working with women and children who were victims of sexual exploitation.[39]

Shortly after the departure of Police Commander Allen, the London office of the League for the Suppression of Traffic in Women and Children dispatched Miss Higson to Egypt to "enlighten" the Egyptian public about the problem of prostitution.[40] Egyptian feminists who had strenuously tried to enlighten Europeans about the connection between prostitution and the Capitulations were furious. Nabarawi informed the hapless emissary that the Egyptian public—including religious leaders, public health officials, feminists, and many other women—had all taken stands against prostitution and especially against state regulation. Higson circulated a petition demanding an end to state-licensed prostitution and calling for new clauses in the Egyptian penal code to enable Egyptian courts to try cases relating to the traffic in women and children. This elicited a dual feminist response. Huda Shaʿrawi signed the petition on behalf of the EFU while Saiza Nabarawi criticized the lack of explicit reference to the Capitulations, repeating that the start of any real solution required their abolition: "No doubt, after this is resolved by the Western powers," the Egyptian government, "would take energetic measures toward prohibition." Nabarawi hoped that Miss Higson would "show the same energy in international forums, in persuading foreign governments to collaborate with ours toward realizing the noble cause we have in common, that she displayed in Egypt."[41]

The agenda and activism of the London office differed from those of the local branches of the League for the Suppression of Traffic in Women and Children. By the 1920s the Cairo and Alexandria branches of the League were engaged mainly in running homes for unwed mothers. The members of these committees continued to be exclusively Europeans. During the Second World War when many Europeans left the country, Egyptians were invited to join the Cairo branch. The name was then changed to the Egypt Society for the Protection of the Woman and Child.[42]

Egyptian feminists approached prostitution inside Egypt in part as a public health issue. They had an ally in the deputy director of the Department of Public Health, Dr. Shahin, who headed an official commission in the early 1930s making a comprehensive investigation into prostitution and venereal disease. Huda Shaʿrawi supplied the commission with epidemiological data gathered by doctors at the EFU dispensary.[43] The commission distributed a questionnaire to private individuals and groups soliciting recommendations for curbing prostitution and the spread of disease.[44] The EFU followed the progress of the commission, which was also charged with preparing a draft law on the suppression of legalized prostitution.[45]

The Egyptian feminists continued their international activism at the 1933 IAW meeting in Marseilles, a city that served as a major point of departure for women destined to work as prostitutes in North Africa and the Middle East. French feminist and lawyer Maria Verone, president of the Ligue française pour le droit des femmes, organized a mass meeting on prostitution. The press attended, applauding the feminists' boldness in publicly discussing such a subject in Marseilles, a notorious center of prostitution.[46] The IAW urged affiliates to press their governments to ratify international conventions against the traffic in women and children, and to urge their application in colonies and protectorates. The meeting called for the establishment of an office in the East that would utilize the assistance of women and private associations to centralize and coordinate international efforts to combat the traffic in women. Delegates from Eastern countries expressed concerns that this might lead to infringements of national sovereignty.[47] The IAW also advocated the creation of local female police cadres in countries where they did not yet exist. By now Turkey had already appointed its first woman police commissioner.[48] On the issue of the Capitulations silence prevailed.[49] The Egyptians now showed impatience with the European feminists: by refusing to confront the question of the Capitulations the Europeans, they insisted, denied them genuine support. Saiza Nabarawi told a press conference that "the same states which rose up against the practice of slavery in the countries of the East [continue to] tolerate it there in a more infamous and inhumane form." She asked, "How can civilized nations reconcile the rights of the individual to freedom with the prevailing legalized servitude of women?"[50]

At the next IAW conference in Istanbul in 1935, international feminists finally attacked head on the issue of the Capitulations. The decision to convene outside Europe for the first time, more specifically at the meeting point of Asia and Europe, and to adopt East-West unity as the conference's central theme was an acknowledgment by the IAW that their international feminism had been very much a Western international feminism. It was also an indication that Eastern affiliates of the IAW were growing in number and voice. Within the frame of East-West unity, the conference themes were peace, equality, and democracy, all endangered with the rise of fascism in the 1930s.

Along with repeating that the Capitulations protected foreign prostitution in their country, Egyptian feminists argued that the persisting inequalities between citizens and foreigners sustained by the Capitulations endangered peace. Nation-based inequality found resonance for IAW feminists in the question of a wife's nationality, which had emerged as a charged issue in the 1930s. Typically, when a woman married a foreigner, she lost her original citizenship and was assigned her husband's nationality. When the IAW took a stand against this practice, insisting that the woman have the right to choose, Egyptian feminists agreed but explained that the existence of the Capitulations would make it difficult to win support for this position in their country. It was around the issue of a wife's nationality, not the issue of prostitution, that, after years of Egyptian persistence and IAW resistance, the international feminist body finally took a resolution against the Capitulations.

> Considering that the Congress is desirous of seeing the principle of equality applied between the woman and man in the question of nationality; that unfortunately in Egypt because of the Capitulations this principle is not able to be

> applied, thus creating new inequalities and sources of discord in the heart of the Egyptian family, which is subjected to two different legal systems. . . . Considering that the Alliance has the duty to come to the aid of all its affiliated societies, the Congress expresses the wish that this law [the Capitulations], which is contrary to the principles of equality adopted by Modern States, must disappear (all the more so because Egypt is the only country in the world where it continues) and that its suppression will permit Egyptian women to claim complete equality of the sexes with regard to nationality.[51]

It is striking that the IAW tied the nationality question, an important middle-class issue, to its resolution against the Capitulations, rather than prostitution, which affected lower-class women. While the linkage Egyptian feminists had made between their campaign against prostitution and the Capitulations was not formally recognized in the IAW resolution, the Egyptians had finally won IAW condemnation of the Capitulations, an important step in their continuing struggle against legalized prostitution, and a nationalist victory. It was supremely symbolic that the IAW condemned the Capitulations at the very site where the institution had been created four centuries earlier.

At home, after winning the condemnation of the Capitulations by international feminists, the EFU continued to speak out against the nefarious link between the Capitulations and prostitution. In September 1935, when a government commission aired a draft law for the abolition of legalized prostitution and proposed a program for the rehabilitation of prostitutes, the EFU stressed that no law would be effective as long as the Capitulations existed.[52]

Capitulations End, Prostitution Continues

The Capitulations reappeared on the agenda of the Montreux conference in 1937. The EFU made a final public stand in a communiqué from Huda Shaʿrawi to the Egyptian delegation expressing the hope that men at Montreux would come out against the Capitulations as women had done two years earlier in Istanbul.[53] IAW president Margery Corbett Ashby sent a message from the international feminists supporting the abolition of the Capitulations, arguing that this would enable Egyptian women to successfully combat prostitution.[54] The Capitulations were finally ended at Montreux in 1937.

With the Egyptian government now freer to deal comprehensively and aggressively with the problem, Egyptian feminists hoped that their goal to abolish legalized prostitution would soon be achieved. The failure to end the legalized traffic in women could no longer be attributed to outside constraints.

The EFU's journals were available to antiprostitution activists. A judge in the National Court at Damanhu, Shaykh Shafiʿi al-Labban, experienced in cases relating to prostitution and drugs, used *al-Misriyah* as a forum to call for social reform based on a moral renewal grounded in a correct understanding of religion and a return to Islamic legislation.[55] Shaykh Jad al-Mawla, a member of the Academy of Arabic Language and a teacher at Dar al-Ulum known for his writings on morality and ethics, also issued an appeal for reform in the pages of *al-Misriyah*.[56]

Before the Capitulations had ended, feminists had publicized closings of Egyptian houses of prostitution, hoping they would serve as examples. In 1933, the EFU reported that houses had been shut down in Damanhur and were about to be closed in Mansura and Asyut.[57] By 1935 the feminist organization had reported closings in ten towns in Egypt.[58] Continuing its monitoring after the Capitulations ended, the EFU announced in 1940 that the governor of Qalyubiyah was about to close houses in Banha.[59]

While working to shut down houses of prostitution, feminists were equally concerned with the fate of former prostitutes. Feminists advocated training programs for ex-prostitutes in income-generating activities. Arranged marriages were also considered a possible solution.[60] A proposal was introduced in parliament in 1938 calling for a tax on unmarried men. Linking the problem of prostitution with men's failure to marry, feminists supported this bill, which suggested applying the revenue toward rehabilitation programs for prostitutes.[61]

When the Ministry of Social Affairs was created in 1939 licensed houses of prostitution fell under its jursidiction. Saiza Nabarawi called on new deputy minister ʿAbd al-Mu'min Riyad to support the EFU's stand against state-regulated prostitution. The deputy minister temporized, insisting that the matter required further consideration and would have to be approached gradually. The following year, *al-Misriyah* reported that the Ministry of Social Affairs was under attack for desultoriness in combating prostitution.[62]

Feminists were now fast losing both patience and hope. They were angered by the contradictions between pious statements about female morality and a lack of political and official will in combating prostitution. In 1940 the EFU president took the occasion of the annual fete honoring Qasim Amin—who had been severely attacked at the turn of the century for undermining the moral order by advocating unveiling—to strike out: "If those hypocritical reformers were really concerned about morals [or women] they would have directed their attention toward the official houses of prostitution where there are Egyptian women, Muslims and others. If they are sincerely interested in defending morals in the name of religion, let them look at the bars and gambling casinos that are centers of corruption. Why can't people support us in our demands to close these places?"[63]

With the rise of the pan-Arab feminist movement in the 1940s, Egyptian feminists began to fight prostitution regionally. At the Arab Feminist Conference in Cairo in 1944, Bahigah Rashid, representing the EFU and the

Society for the Protection of the Woman and Child, placed the call for the abolition of legalized prostitution on the conference agenda. Urging Arab governments to take action, she spoke of the exploitation of Egyptian and other Arab girls during the Second World War when thousands of foreign troops poured into the region.[64] The women's congress demanded the immediate abolition of legalized prostitution in all Arab countries, the closing of gambling casinos, and an end to licensing women to work in bars. It also called upon governments to create alternative forms of work for poor women.[65] Feminist organizations in the Arab countries would work to promote these objectives.[66]

In 1949, state-licensed prostitution houses were shut down by military order in Egypt. A year after the 1952 revolution state-regulated prostitution was finally outlawed.[67]

• CHAPTER 11 •

Suffrage and Citizenship

EGYPTIAN WOMEN had anticipated that when independence came they would enjoy the full rights of citizenship. The new constitution of 1923 confirmed their assumption. Article 3 pronounced the equality of all Egyptians, declaring, "*They equally enjoy civil and political rights* [emphasis added] and are equally subjected to duties and public obligations without regard to race, language, or religion." Articles 74 and 82 granted universal suffrage (*al-iqtiraᶜ al-ᶜamm*). Three weeks after the promulgation of the constitution, an electoral law was passed, restricting the right to vote and to be elected to men. On the basis of gender, this lesser law swept away rights granted by the constitution, depriving "half the nation" of their political rights in contradiction to the supreme law of the land. The electoral law became an instrument enabling the patriarchy to preserve gender inequality and male hegemony in the new political culture. In the new "democratic" order men arrogated exclusively to themselves the highest authority: the power to rule and shape law. By denying women political rights Egyptian men structured women's subordination in the new polity, mirroring the subordination of women in the family that conservative personal status laws sustained.

Egyptians, women and men alike, had struggled to discard the status of dependent colonial subject for that of independent national citizen. Indeed, women had been central actors in that struggle. At the exhilarating moment of national liberation (partial as it was) women, like men, were poised to shape the new state and society. With independence, Egyptian women did not expect to continue to be dependent subjects, this time in an indigenous gendered hierarchical polity. When the new state acknowledged the equality of all Egyptians in principle but subverted it in practice, disenfranchising female Egyptians, feminists understood clearly that they would have to fight to enjoy their political rights and indeed other rights. The organized feminist movement was born in this certainty.

The new EFU-led feminist movement placed gender equality at the center of the practice of citizenship. Feminists faced the contradictions posed by the continuation of the old patriarchal order clothed in the new garments of democracy. They applied to women the right to self-determination that they and male Egyptian nationalists had applied to the nation during the fight for independence from colonial rule. The nationalist ranks split after independence. Now nationalist women as feminists opposed not only the vestiges of colonialism but the persistence of indigenous patriarchal domination.

At the start of their movement, Egyptian feminists committed themselves to obtaining full political rights for all women in the discourses of secular nationalism and democracy, which accorded an equal place in the new polity for all Egyptians irrespective of gender and religion. Employing the discourse of Islamic modernism, Egyptian Muslim feminists declared also that Islam accorded all Muslims the right to participate in deciding the affairs of the ummah, the community or the "nation" of believers.

Also at the beginning of their movement Egyptian feminists joined forces with international feminists. The American and European founders of the International Woman Suffrage Alliance, on the other hand, had come together in the final stage of long, hard-fought national suffragist campaigns. From the start, the Egyptian drive for suffrage was part of a multigoal movement for full citizenship rights rather than the single-issue campaign it was for IWSA founders. The 1923 congress, as already noted, was a turning point for the IWSA, as many Western countries emerging from the First World War had finally granted political rights to their female citizens. It will be remembered that the International Woman Suffrage Alliance changed its name at that moment to the International Alliance of Women for Suffrage and Equal Citizenship (IAW). This reflected the expanded agenda, combining suffrage activism with a campaign to help women exercise their full rights of citizenship, and to shape the meaning of citizenship itself.[1] But how could the IAW hope to be effective in constructing a new practice of citizenship as long as it failed to confront colonialism and imperialism and their implications for international feminism, as indeed for "national" feminisms?

Demanding Political Rights, Acting Politically

Egyptian women had been found fit to struggle in partnership with the Wafd—as members of the Wafdist Women's Central Committee and as independent supporters—in the intense fight for national sovereignty, but then they had been deemed unfit to share in the practice of national sovereignty. In 1924 in the first (all-male) elections since independence, the Wafd gained the overwhelming majority in the Chamber of Deputies, and the Wafdist leader Saʿd Zaghlul formed a government. Not only had Egyptian women been excluded from voting and being elected, they were also barred from the opening ceremonies of the new parliament, except as wives of ministers and high officials, while foreign women were admitted. The exclusion of women in their own right from the new Egyptian polity could not have been more publicly and powerfully symbolized.

Women responded with their own elections. They held an alternative ballot to "elect" male members of parliament. The women swept the Liberal Constitutionalist Party to power with 77 votes.[2] They gave the Wafd a mere 12 votes, the National Party (conservative on gender issues) 18, and independents 60. *L'Egyptienne* announced the winners in a supplement to its first issue. The EFU also broadcast the results of a questionnaire, revealing that women saw the Liberal Constitutionalist Party as the male political party most likely to further women's demands while they insisted that the EFU was best equipped to handle women's issues.[3] Holding the mock elections was a way for women—clearly mostly EFU sympathizers—to register their discontent with the democracy manqué and with the Wafd.

The Wafd soon made a bid to recover its female constituency by funding a paper for women in 1925 called *al-Amal* (Hope). It was edited by Munirah Thabit, the daughter of a Wafdist government employee, who around this time married a prominent Wafd leader, ʿAbd al-Qadir Hamzah. Through *al-Amal* and the pen of Thabit the Wafd declared itself in favor of female suffrage. While the Wafd used Thabit as a mouthpiece, she could also use *al-Amal* to promote the suffrage cause, to which she was genuinely committed. The antagonism between the Wafd and the EFU feminist leadership, grounded in divergences in nationalist and gender politics, was played out in the antagonism between EFU leaders and Thabit.[4] To this strain was added the outrage of EFU women on feminist grounds when Munirah Thabit became the second wife of ʿAbd al-Qadir Hamzah at the very moment the EFU was fighting to restrict polygamy. The Wafd, more interested in its own political fortunes, did not wage a serious campaign for women's political rights. By the second half of the 1930s, Thabit and EFU women closed ranks in the fight for female suffrage.[5]

At the opening of the new Egyptian parliament in 1924 the EFU and the WWCC jointly presented—at the gates—the demand for the vote for women.[6] The following year, signaling a piecemeal approach to gaining political rights, the EFU suggested that the vote might initially be restricted to women of property or education. Feminists called it an injustice that educated and propertied women could not vote while illiterate men enjoyed this right.[7] However, acting expediently, the feminists revealed a willingness to discriminate among women according to class. In proposing the possibility of an educational qualification for female voters the feminists were also willing to accept a higher standard for women, implicitly agreeing with their opponents that the majority of women were not ready for the vote. When the feminists pointed out that the majority of the male electorate were illiterate, they did not suggest that these men should not vote, thus conceding that literacy and education were not prerequisites for political rights. Yet while the feminists agreed to a more exacting standard for women, they also tried to help women meet that standard. In 1925, discussing the EFU's social service work, Saiza Nabarawi explained, "For the moment the activity of the EFU is directed above all to making the masses aware of the rights of the woman to prepare [them] little by little for the idea of suffrage."[8]

At the 1929 IAW congress in Berlin, Egyptian feminists complained that suffrage had slipped to second place in the international arena, and demanded that political rights be given more attention. More was involved than the issue of suffrage itself. Egyptians were sensitive to the rift that had widened since 1923 between women from "enfranchised countries" and "disenfranchised countries." The enfranchised countries were Western, although not all Western countries were enfranchised. Nabarawi urged women from disenfranchised countries to unite in their struggle.[9] This appears, in part, to have been a move by Egyptians to consolidate forces with Frenchwomen, also deprived of the vote, who were sympathetic to the EFU's efforts to end the Captitulations. Four years later, after the 1933 IAW meeting in Marseilles, Egyptians accompanied French feminists on a tour through the Midi organized by Maria Verone and La ligue française pour le droit des femmes. Egyptian feminists campaigned for political rights for their French sisters at suffrage meetings organized en route.[10] Before their departure Shaʿrawi told an audience in Marseilles, "Frenchmen, you who have always throughout history been the first to free oppressed peoples, now free your own women and support those who are the last to enjoy their lawful rights."[11] Her subtext could not but evoke the tenacity of continued French colonial rule in North Africa, the mandated Arab countries, and other parts of Africa and Asia.

While Egyptian feminists pioneered as suffragist activists abroad, at home in the early 1930s they had another kind of battle on their hands. The reactionary Sidqi government had come to power, suppressing the constitution and suspending parliament, and the feminists joined their male compatriots in the fight to recover their rights. As they had during the struggle for independence, feminists and other women threw themselves into political militancy on behalf of the nation. This time, the adversary was not the colonial overlord but reactionary forces within. When the Sidqi regime announced that elections would be held while the constitution and parliament were still suspended, there was widespread popular outrage. Women once again joined forces with men in the largest political uprisings since 1919. Although undaunted, women were not unaware of the dangers. As Saiza Nabarawi wrote in *L'Egyptienne*, "He [Sidqi] made it known in the press that henceforth women would be treated like men, without consideration of rank or sex."[12] This autocrat poised for reprisals was the same Ismaʿil Sidqi who sought to protect women from the dangers of gender mixing at the university by keeping women away from the halls of learning. Thus Sidqi manipulated gender and sexuality in the service of political power.

Egyptian women formed a broad coalition as they had during the independence struggle and as women tend to do in severe national crises. Feminists, Wafdist women, and supporters of the Liberal Constitutionalist Party went out together in public demonstrations. On May 5, 1931, women gathered at "The House of the Nation" (the home of the late Wafdist leader Saʿd Zaghlul) to visit Safiyah Zaghlul, "The Mother of Egyptians." They then set out in their motorcars in a demonstration through the streets of Cairo to protest the political oppression and to urge their male compatriots to abstain from voting. One of the cars was seized and its occupants taken to the police station in Darb al-Ahmar, a popular quarter of the city. Other women demonstrators immediately descended upon the police station shouting antigovernment slogans, refusing to leave until their companions were released, whereupon they too were arrested.[13] Saiza Nabarawi, who had participated in the demonstration, wrote: "For the first time in our history women were imprisoned for a political question. This inaugurates a glorious page in Egyptian feminism that henceforth will only [further] develop—recognition of the equality of duties inevitably implies equality of rights. . . . Everyone, rich and poor, came together in the various provinces of Egypt to energetically defend the constitution of 1923. They [the women] have also proven that they are citizens conscious of their responsibilities and worthy of defending the liberties of their country, and that they are capable of arousing the oppressed."[14]

When the Wafd and the Liberal Constitutional Party were prevented from holding a national congress in May 1931, they issued resolutions pledging allegiance to the 1923 constitution, calling for a boycott of elections, and declaring that any treaty entered into by a parliament so elected would not be binding. Members of the EFU and other women's associations signed the document, along with former ministers and members of parliament, and representatives of political parties, municipalities and provincial councils, the army, the legal and other professional groups, and workers' syndicates.[15] Women also drew up their own manifesto, which they sent to the national congress organizers, declaring, "We denounce and will not unite with anyone who . . . participates in the elections, whether a husband, relative, or ally, for we will consider anyone who does this to be in revolt against the will of the nation, and we will not allow a father, husband, brother, son, or domestic to commit such an assault."[16]

Women kept up their public militancy, making the rounds of Cairo and urging shopkeepers, government employees, and workers not to vote. During a women's demonstration when police injured a number of children in the crowds surrounding the demonstrators, Shaʿrawi, on behalf of the EFU, expressed sympathy to the mothers of the wounded children.[17] Women and men students went out on a three-month strike at the university. Nationalist fervor also spread throughout the girls' schools, many of which closed down when pupils went out on strike.[18] Women suffered various forms of intimidation. Thirty women from Old Cairo brought a formal complaint before the procurator general stating that "agents" had attacked them at night in their houses to force their husbands and sons to participate in the elections.[19]

When election day came, women went out on another demonstration. Nabawiyah Musa was with a group who went to the district of Cairo called al-Wa'ili; there, from a nearby balcony, they rained down abuse on the local election committee office.[20] Many were arrested and later released with a fine. Women demonstrators at Tanta in the Delta were meanwhile arrested and imprisoned. As had happened in the independence struggle, a number of lower-class women paid "with their blood for the defense of the sacred rights of the people." More than one hundred women signed a message to the families of the women killed by the police on election day.[21] The EFU issued a written condemnation of the maltreatment, arrests, and imprisonment of children.[22] Saiza Nabarawi wrote, "Never has Egypt, even under the domination of the Mamluks [a foreign military slave caste] known such tyranny: suppression of individual freedom, the reign of fraud and violence, arbitrary justice, corruption of public morality, in brief a total contempt for the most sacred rights of the Egyptian people and their national dignity."[23] She drew a parallel with women's earlier militancy: "In 1919 they [women] were one of the most influential factors in the nationalist movement. Today their campaign in favor of the boycott of elections was actively threatened by the authorities, who were angered at the participation of women in political life."[24] The Sidqi regime's attacks on the presence of women at the university, the withdrawal of government-pledged building funds for the EFU, and sensationalizing of gender mixing at the beaches were all moves by the government to strike back at women.

By the end of September 1933, the oppressive Sidqi government had been ousted. Although it had left a legacy of problems, there was immediate relief and hopes for new directions. In trying to suppress women, as part of a wider suppression of liberalism, the reactionary government had given them a chance to demonstrate once again their political skills, to hone them still further, and to reassert with added vigor and enhanced claims their democratic right to vote.

Suffrage at Center Stage

"After a fifteen-year struggle it is time for the Egyptian woman to have the right to vote and to become a member of parliament."[25] This declaration in the Egyptian press in 1934 announced the EFU's intention to bring the suffrage cause to center stage. With the return of liberal forces, the time was ripe for women to push the democratization process further by demanding their political rights. Not only had women once again displayed political will, acumen, and bravery—this time to defend the Egyptian constitution and democratic life, but by now they could also point to their impressive gains in education and in the workplace.

In 1935 IAW leaders came to Egypt to offer their Egyptian sisters support in their suffrage campaign. British president Margery Corbett Ashby and vice presidents Germaine Malaterre-Sellier from France and Rosa Manus from the Netherlands were highly visible during what the press called "The Week of the Woman."[26] Prominent Wafdist and Liberal Constitutionalist politicians joined women at a ceremonial banquet at the Semiramis Hotel. Now, reciprocally, a French voice spoke out for Egyptian women's suffrage. Malaterre-Sellier, the only one of the three visitors who herself was deprived of the vote, suggested to the Egyptian men present that it would be in their interest to have the support and collaboration of women in formal political life.[27]

The issue of women's suffrage was restored to prominence in the international arena two months later at the IAW congress in Istanbul. On a planning trip to Turkey several months before the congress IAW president Margery Corbett Ashby remarked to president of the Turkish Republic Mustafa Kamal, "Ataturk," that Turkish women did not have the vote.[28] However, in December 1934, Turkey became the first Middle Eastern and the first Muslim country to grant women the right to vote and to be elected. These rights were not the result of an independent feminist struggle but had been granted from on high by the state. The Turkish Women's Federation—which had been created in 1924, the year after the state had refused to authorize the new Women's Political Party—lasted as long as it served the state's purposes and did not challenge its authority.[29] The federation dissolved after hosting the IAW congress, which had taken a pacifist stand in keeping with the position of the Western allies, a position at variance with that of the Turkish state. The women's organization saved face by claiming that its purpose had been fulfilled when the vote was won.[30]

With Turkey now the first Muslim country to grant women full political rights, Egyptian feminists seized the opportunity of the IAW congress in Istanbul to vigorously push for their own suffrage. The EFU sent its largest-ever delegation to the IAW congress in Istanbul, which for the first time included new junior members, the Shaqiqat. Ester Fahmi Wissa delivered an impassioned speech at the conference. Saiza Nabarawi put the Egyptian cause before the press.[31] Traveling with other delegates to Ankara at the end of the conference, Huda Shaʿrawi met the Turkish president Mustafa Kamal. She recalls the moment in her memoirs: "It was an unparalleled scene, an Eastern Muslim woman representing the IAW as vice president standing up to speak to the president of Turkey in his own Turkish language, expressing the admiration and gratitude of Egypt's women toward the liberation movement he had led in his country. I said that it was highly exemplary for Muslim countries that their big sister had encouraged all the countries of the East to strive for liberation and advocate the rights of women. I told him, 'If the Turks have called you Ataturk [father of the Turks], I say that is not enough; for us you are Atasharq [father of the East].' "[32]

The Egyptian feminists had monitored Turkish women's advances. In education and work, women's "firsts" in Turkey and Egypt closely paralleled each other. The first woman lawyer pleaded a court case in Turkey in 1929, in Egypt in 1934. The first Turkish woman medical doctor graduated from the University of Istanbul in 1929; in Egypt the first group of women entered the Faculty of Medicine of Fu'ad I University in 1932. However, in political rights, the Egyptian women would not make commensurate advances. Egyptian women would not be able to match the claim of president of the Turkish Women's Federation Latife Bakir that "in the same generation one has seen the Turkish woman move from behind harem grilles to the parliamentary platform."[33]

Back in Egypt, the feminists launched an active suffrage campaign. The EFU president submitted an IAW resolution calling for women's political rights to Prime Minister Tawfiq Nasim. The EFU reiterated that women, having the same duties and obligations as men, must share the same electoral rights.[34] In the language of social justice and progress, the feminists pressured successive governments. When ʿAli Mahir became prime minister in 1936, they cautiously demanded, as a start, that women be allowed to vote and to be elected to municipal boards and provincial councils; they repeated their demand when Mustafa Nahhas of the Wafd took over. Neither Liberal Constitutionalists nor Wafdists acted.[35]

When, as prime minister, ʿAli Mahir announced a government-sponsored essay competition, Saiza Nabarawi took the opportunity to present yet again the case for women's suffrage in an essay entitled "The Feminist Evolution and the Benefits That Accrue to the Public Well-Being." In an atmosphere of rapidly changing governments, she argued that the participation of women in the formal political process would be a stabilizing force in Egypt's volatile political life. She pristinely claimed that women would be above "the melee" of party politics: "The entry of the woman into politics would not put her at the mercy of the struggles and ambitions of the parties." Women would focus greater attention on social issues and "would bring the laws in rapport with the culture" to the benefit of family, society, and state.[36] She proposed the expedient of giving the vote initially to women who held diplomas, who were founders and directors of social service societies, or who were property owners.[37] Nabarawi's essay won first prize, but it was to be twenty years before her arguments would bear fruit.

The growing frustration Huda Shaʿrawi and other feminists experienced at being excluded from the legitimate political process was intensified by the 1936 Anglo-Egyptian treaty, which included a provision for mutual defense and the stationing of British troops in the Canal Zone. Huda Shaʿrawi fiercely denounced the treaty and deplored the fact that women had not been consulted. The EFU called upon women to demand a national referendum of Egyptian women and men before the treaty's ratification. The feminist organization distributed stirring leaflets in Arabic and French to their female compatriots:

> Arise ye women! Arise ye dead! If the dead were able to leave their tombs and if their voices could be heard by the living, it is you women of Egypt, mothers of the martyrs of yesterday and tomorrow, who would be entrusted with the sacred mission to maintain the ideal that you have served for a long time and for which our heroes have died. Rise up everyone and show that you have the right as citizens, as wives, and, above all, as mothers to be consulted on the future of your country, which is also the future of your children. Yes, you have the right and what is more the duty, before the ratification of a treaty, to call for a referendum addressed to all the citizens of Egypt (men and women) permitting them to judge and express freely their views and wishes.[38]

In open letters to Prime Minister Mustafa Nahhas and to members of parliament, Huda Shaʿrawi demanded that the matter be placed before the

Egyptian people.[39] She told *al-Musawwar*: "The treaty is unlawful because the women have not given their approval. . . . This treaty is not a protection but a permanent occupation. Our members of parliament have an enormous task and responsibility before them. In their conscience they must know that they have in their care the future life and glory of Egypt."[40] Palestine and Trans-Jordan were still under British mandatory rule. Shaʿrawi was concerned that as "allies [with Britain] it will be necessary for us to stand up against revolutionary Palestine if Britain asks us to do so."[41] The question of the 1936 treaty further intensified the feminists' desire for the vote.[42]

The chorus of women's voices continued to rise on behalf of their political rights. Now consolidating forces with the EFU, Munirah Thabit insisted in *al-Misriyah* in March 1937 that women must have the vote and must participate with men in governing. Egyptian women had gained equality in education. It was high time that they gained equality in political rights. "A man with only a *kuttab* (Koranic school) education is treated better by Egyptian society than a woman with a diploma."[43] She complained to *al-Ahram* that women had taxation without representation.[44] Schoolteacher ʿAliyah Fahmi insisted that women were needed in parliament to deal with national issues pertaining to mothers and children. She also suggested that at least three seats in parliament be reserved for women.[45]

Liberal Constitutionalist Hafiz ʿAfifi wrote in the opening issue of *al-Misriyah* in February 1937: "In politics as a general principle the woman should enjoy the same rights the man enjoys. It is an abnormality that we in Egypt have still not agreed on the right of women to election even though we have a democratic political system." He seconded the idea of starting by granting educated women the vote saying, "Even the most excessive conservatives would not oppose this. It would be a modest claim to begin with and easy to obtain."[46]

When the journal *al-Misri* asked members of parliament whether they supported political rights for women, six out of the seven questioned replied in the negative.[47] The enfranchisement of women in Turkey, as well as Muslim women in some states in India and in the Soviet provinces of Turkmenistan and Uzbekistan, did not provide the model to Egypt that feminists had hoped it would. In 1938 when Liberal Constitutionalist Muhammad Mahmud became prime minister, he vowed that in his time the vote would not be granted to women. Huda Shaʿrawi tartly responded that if Egyptian women had political rights, they would confront the social ills that kept the country backward.[48]

A Wafdist member of parliament, ʿAbd al-Hamid ʿAbd al-Haqq, proposed in the Chamber of Deputies that the electoral law be amended to grant female suffrage with a literacy qualification. Feminists welcomed the proposal but were skeptical, as it had come from a Wafdist while his party was out of power; they saw it as merely a move to embarrass the Liberal Constitutionalists. Huda Shaʿrawi remarked acerbically that until then "women had not received anything from the Wafd" except an invitation to celebrate the 1936 Anglo-Egyptian treaty. "If he [ʿAbd al-Hamid ʿAbd al-Haqq] is truly convinced of the woman's worthiness to have political rights, can he affirm that there are many members of his party who support that, as well? Can he declare that they are prepared to give the woman her political rights when the Wafd returns to power? If that is the case, let the Wafdist deputies back him in this request; we are certain if this happens that other deputies will also join in with their support."[49] As feminists had suspected, nothing came of the proposal.

On behalf of *L'Egyptienne*, Fatma Niʿmat Rashid solicited the views of prominent male liberals on political rights for women. Muhammad Husayn Haykal and Hafiz ʿAfifi favored equal political rights for women. Ahmad Lutfi al-Sayyid was concerned that people be able to vote wisely; gender was irrelevant.[50] Majd al-Din Saʿfan asserted in *al-Misriyah*: "Real democracy gives every member equal rights and equal duties." He said that it was only fascist states that curtailed women's public functions.[51] Liberals might voice support for women's suffrage but for most it stopped there.

The last IAW congress during Huda Shaʿrawi's lifetime where the Egyptian delegation took up the issue of women's political rights was convened in Copenhagen in 1939. Munirah Thabit, a first-time member of the EFU delegation, connected women's vote with peace, arguing that in order to "reestablish peace and order" governments must enfranchise women.[52] But peace was slipping from sight, and the signs of impending war deflected attention at home and abroad from the suffrage cause. At Copenhagen the EFU was consumed by the Palestine question and the increased Jewish immigration connected with the spreading fascism in Europe, as we shall see in chapter 12.

After the Second World War, Egyptian feminists revived the suffrage issue. At the Arab Feminist Congress in Cairo in December 1944 Huda Shaʿrawi and other Egyptian feminists made a strong case for political rights, this time not just for their compatriots but for all Arab women. As president of the EFU and head of the Arab Feminist Conference Shaʿrawi declared in her keynote address, "The Arab woman also demands with her loudest voice the regaining of political rights, rights that have been granted to her by the shariʿah."[53] Shaʿrawi, we notice, legitimized her call for women's political rights in the discourse of Islam rather than the language of secular democracy. Appealing as well to Arab pride, she noted that "civilized nations" had granted full political rights to women. At the opening ceremonies minister of education Muhammad Husayn Haykal, representing the Egyptian government, pointed to the social and cultural mission of women in the Arab world, indicating that political affairs belonged to men.[54] Privately, where it would do little to help the cause, Haykal confessed his approval of women's suffrage.

During the Arab Feminist Conference it was the Egyptian participants, including men, who addressed women's political rights. Lawyer Mufidah

ʿAbd al-Rahman, decrying patriarchal politics, noted that laws made by men reflected men's interests. To change this societal imbalance it was essential that women participate in the lawmaking process. Former member of parliament and lawyer Zuhayr Sabri argued that since women had the same right to own and dispose of property as men they should have the same right to make laws. No country can call itself democratic, he said, that excludes women from the political process. Dean of the Faculty of Medicine at Fu'ad University Sulayman ʿAzmi criticized men who deprived women of equal opportunities to participate in political life, branding them as selfish people living under the influence of the past.[55]

The first of the fifty-one resolutions produced by the congress called for political rights for women: both the right to vote and the right to be elected. "[The Arab Feminist Congress] demands that all Arab governments work for gradual equalization between men and women in political rights, especially the right of the woman to vote and to be elected. Until governments have the chance to bring about complete equality in all legislative and parliamentary bodies, they are called upon from now to move toward equality in regional councils and appointments to the senate."[56]

In the second half of the 1940s, the movement for women's political rights broadened, and with it the feminist movement itself. Women formerly associated with the EFU now formed their own feminist organizations. These included Fatma Niʿmat Rashid's al-Hizb al-Nisaʾi al-Watani, the National Feminist Party (the first women's organization to identify itself as a political party), and Duriyah Shafiq's Ittihad Bint al-Nil (Daughter of the Nile Union), created in 1944 and 1948 respectively. With the National Feminist Party and the Daughter of the Nile Union, middle-class women were brought into the organized feminist movement on a larger scale. The Daughter of the Nile Union was successful in establishing branches throughout Egypt. Both of these associations combined their suffrage advocacy with a broad social program including literacy for women; they also continued the struggle to achieve reform of personal status laws.

Thus by the second half of the 1940s there were three women's organizations with the shared goal of political rights for women. However, while women could form a broad coalition in nationalist struggles against colonialism and against internal suppression of democracy, they were unable to achieve the same unity in a struggle for their own political rights. Women were unable to transcend differences of class and associational allegiances. Their leaders found it difficult to unite. Shaʿrawi had tried to form a federation of women's societies in the late 1930s to more effectively promote their causes through collective action, but she failed. In 1949 the National Feminist Party and the Daughter of the Nile Union formed an alliance, but it broke up within the first year.

When Huda Shaʿrawi died in 1947, the vote for women was still nine years away. The EFU continued to press for political rights for women. After the revolution of 1952 when the head of the new revolutionary government, General Muhammad Najib, visited the EFU, Bahigah Rashid placed the issue before him.[57]

Egyptian women's final thrust for their political rights bridged the end of the constitutional monarchy and the beginning of the new revolutionary regime. Now focusing mainly on suffrage, the feminist movement evoked a hostile reaction, mainly from popular religious quarters, of the sort that the EFU had not attracted earlier. The problem was not simply that women's intensified drive for political rights was threatening but that a segment of the patriarchal culture, anchoring its ideology and politics in a conservative reading of Islam, had been gaining momentum in the 1930s and 1940s. The era when liberalism held sway with its benign tolerance of feminist activism was coming to a close. Feminist activism in its most symbolically threatening form, a suffrage movement, and patriarchy at its most conservative were on a collision course. However, it was soon cut short by the new revolutionary government, which preempted all independent action.

Duriyah Shafiq headed a militant campaign for political rights, leading women in a sit-in at the parliament in 1951.[58] This provoked an impassioned communication to the king from the president of the Union of Muslim Associations calling for an end to women's organizations that demanded female political rights. The Union of Muslim Associations branded the feminist movement an imperialist plot to undermine Egyptian society.

Following the revolution of 1952, when a proposal for a new electoral law was under consideration, Shafiq published *The White Paper on the Rights of the Egyptian Woman* (*al-Kitab al-Abyad lil-Huquq al-Mar'ah al-Misriyah*), a compendium of arguments by men for and against female suffrage. Constitutional lawyer Sayyid Sabri argued in the language of Islamic modernism that laws must change as social conditions change; since women now formed part of public opinion, they must participate in the formal political process. The Constitutional Affairs Committee of the Senate opposed political rights for women. Shaykh Hasanayn Makhluf, the mufti of Egypt—the highest religious authority empowered to issue official interpretations of Islam—pronounced that Islam opposed political rights for women, while the former mufti, Shaykh Allam Nassar, claimed the opposite. The Fatwa Committee of al-Azhar issued a statement condemning electoral rights for women. The following day Islamic organizations held a conference. They issued a lengthy statement pressing the government to keep the door to fitnah closed, warning of the "chaos" that would ensue from granting women political rights—a liberalization that, they argued, was contrary to Islam, to the constitution, and to the public interest. Two years later Duriyah Shafiq went out on a hunger strike at the Press Syndicate. Only when she received assurances from the highest authorities that political rights for women would receive serious attention did she end the strike.

In 1956, thirty-three years after the EFU first demanded suffrage for women—and ten years after Frenchwomen, whose cause Egyptian feminists supported, obtained the vote—the revolutionary regime granted women the right to vote and to be elected. It was necessary to the new state's republican ideology and the Arab socialism to be articulated in the 1962 charter that all Egyptian citizens possess formal political rights. But at the very moment when Egyptian women had finally acquired full citizenship, Egyptian women, like their male compatriots, lost their right to continue to freely express their views. There would be no free elections and no independent political life. In 1956 the EFU was required to self-destruct as a feminist organization. All other independent organizations with political purposes met the same fate. The EFU reconstituted itself as the Huda Shaʿrawi Association, dedicated exclusively to social service under the government's control.

• PART THREE •

The Widening Circle

• CHAPTER 12 •

Arab Feminism

THE Egyptian feminist movement reached out to other Arabs in the late 1930s and the 1940s. The discourse of Arabism and Islam became more prominent in the articulation of the widening agenda. The EFU played a key role in the institutionalization of pan-Arab feminism, or Arab feminism, as distinct from feminisms in individual Arab nations. The story of Arab feminism is a story of intersections between feminisms and nationalisms—both those identified with individual Arab countries and those transcending territorial boundaries. It is also a story about disjunctures between national feminisms of colonized Eastern countries and Western-dominated international feminism. The institutionalization of Arab feminism emerged from a coalescence in solidarity around a nationalist cause, the Palestine cause. Arab feminism was also, in part, born out of the limitations of international feminism.

In 1936 Egypt's partial independence was enhanced with the signing of the Anglo-Egyptian treaty, although Britain still retained a reduced military presence in Egypt and influence in foreign affairs. In 1937 the Capitulations were abolished and Egypt entered the League of Nations. The lands of the Arab East, on the other hand, had come under Western colonial administration with the final breakup of the Ottoman Empire after the First World War. Syria and Lebanon were placed under French mandate, and Palestine and Trans-Jordan under British mandate, while Iraq came under indirect British control. Nationalist movements in the Arab East were struggling for independence from European colonial rule—except in Palestine, where Arab nationalists confronted both British colonialism and Zionism in a struggle for the survival of the country itself. In the 1920s, 1930s, and early 1940s only in independent Egypt was there space for a highly visible, organized feminist movement. This is not to say that there was no feminist activism or efforts at collective feminist organizing in the Arab East during the mandate period, for there was; but there was no space for militant nationalist feminist movements.

The EFU was poised to play a preeminent role in consolidating pan-Arab feminism. By the time women in the Arab East called upon the EFU to take up the defense of Palestine, the organization had accumulated a decade and a half of experience heading the feminist movement in Egypt and participating in the international feminist movement. The EFU rallied women across a wide ideological and political spectrum in what was another historical moment of joining forces in nationalist militancy, this time pan-nationalist militancy, leading to the consolidation of pan-Arab feminism.

Palestinian Arab Women in National Defense

The pan-Arab feminist movement had roots in the Palestinian national struggle. In this intersection of feminist and nationalist activism were echoes of the earlier emergence of an organized feminist movement in Egypt out of women's nationalist militancy in the independence struggle. The differences, however, were salient.

During the 1920s, 1930s, and 1940s the Palestinian Arabs fought a twin battle against the imposition of British rule and the Zionist project. No other Arab country, before or after, had such a battle to fight for national liberation and national survival. Palestinian women were part of the protracted, widespread, and violent struggle for national sovereignty. Women of all classes threw themselves into the battle. Upper-class urban women organized demonstrations, called congresses, petitioned the mandatory authorities, and created their own organizational structures and networks. They coordinated with the male nationalist leaders but carried on their nationalist agitation separately. Peasant women engaged in armed revolt along with their men, and the women also provided support services to militants. There were a few middle-class women who combined activity in the women's associations with forms of militant resistance.

Palestinian women began their public nationalist militancy in 1920 when they went out on a demonstration and organized their first nationalist association, the Palestine Women's Union. Nine years later as part of the intensification of the Palestinian national movement women organized on a large scale. Following outbreaks of violence that resulted in the death and imprisonment of Palestinian Arabs and widespread destruction, over two hundred women from various organizations convened the first Arab Women's Congress in Jerusalem in 1929. They confronted the British high commissioner with their nationalist demands and went out on a demonstration in the streets of Jerusalem.[1] The women also created their own nationalist organizational framework: a central Arab Women's Executive Committee with Arab Women's Unions to be set up in cities and towns throughout the country. The regulations of the Arab Women's Union in Jerusalem indicated a dual nationalist and feminist agenda. "The objects of the Society shall be to work for the development of the social and economic affairs of the Arab women in Palestine . . . to use every possible and lawful means to elevate the standing of women . . . to assist national institutions, and support any national body in any enterprise which may be beneficial to the country."[2] Whatever the vision, the reality demanded full attention to militant national resistance. In the early 1930s, the Palestinian Arab Women's Unions were engaged in widening the militant base of the increasingly radicalized nationalist movement throughout the country.[3]

Palestinian women also reached out to the international feminist community. Early in 1935 members of the Palestinian Arab Women's Unions of Jerusalem, Jaffa, Nablus, and Haifa met in Haifa where they agreed to join the International Alliance of Women and to send a delegation to the Istanbul congress in April.[4] Sadhij Nassar of the Arab Women's Union of Haifa was elected to represent the Palestinian Arab Women's Union at the Istanbul congress. The Syrian Arab Women's Union, which also joined the IAW that year, sent a delegation as well.

With the start of the Arab revolt in 1936 women intensified their militancy.[5] Some peasant women participated in countrywide strikes and armed revolt, while others provided support to insurgents and guarded family homes and lands. The Arab Women's Unions and other women's groups threw themselves into action. Sadhij Nassar, a journalist as well as a militant nationalist and feminist, was eventually jailed for her militancy, which included "inflammatory" articles.[6] In June 1936 during the strikes and in the midst of widespread repression the Arab Women's Committee (which had recently replaced the Arab Women's Executive Committee) contacted Huda EFU president Shaʿrawi for help.[7]

Egyptian Women to the Rescue: The League of Nations and International Peace Organizations

The EFU responded to the call from the Arab Women's Committee of Palestine by holding an emergency meeting (June 9th): it took a resolution condemning the Balfour Declaration; sent appeals to "the women of the world" and the League of Nations to support the Palestinian women's demand to end Jewish immigration (the committee also sent telegrams to the British foreign secretary and the speaker of the House of Commons demanding an end to their country's repressive policy that violated the rights of the Arab people); and laid plans to launch a financial drive to aid the Arabs of Palestine.[8]

Egyptian feminists also placed the Palestine case before the international peace community. Under the leadership of Fatma Niʿmat Rashid, Egyptian women had recently created branches of two international women's peace organizations. The Egyptian Section of the International League of Mothers and Educators for Peace (ILMEP) created in 1935 included EFU members Aminah al-Saʿid, Suhayr al-Qalamawi, and Jeanne Marques. The ILMEP promoted maternal pacifism, believing the way to peace lay in inculcating pacifism in children. Each national section organized around its own needs. The Egyptian Section worked for peace through national independence. Casting colonial occupation and remnants of colonial occupation as enslavement, the ILMEP's Egyptian Section recognized that "dependent peoples" had the right to realize their independence by any means. Peace could come only with freedom.[9]

The second organization was the Egyptian Section of the Women's International League of Peace and Freedom (WILPF). The WILPF had been founded in 1915 by Western feminists—mainly IAW members and social activists calling for investigation, arbitration, and lobbying for peaceful solutions to disputes among nations.[10] Again Egyptian women declared a firm commitment to peace as well as their country's sovereign right to defend itself, departing from the Western, majority WILPF position. With British troops still in Egypt and the country's defense tied to Britain, Egyptian women's peace activism was nationalist activism.[11] Striving for peace in Palestine, the Egyptian Section of the WILPF became active in organizing talks and public meetings, and engaged in peace work with Jews in Egypt.[12]

In June 1936 the EFU attended two meetings supporting peace and the work of the League of Nations. The first was held in Alexandria on June 4th, less than a week before the feminist group received the appeal from the Palestinian women, and the second in Cairo on June 26th. EFU representatives pointed to the situation in Palestine and the continued British military presence in Egypt as threats to peace. The EFU supported the League of Nations but scorned the organization's efforts to keep peace, given current events in Palestine and the Italian invasion of Ethiopia the previous year.[13] Nabarawi deplored the menace of the imperialist powers whose "belligerent policies" oppressed "peaceful countries of the East under the guise of protecting them." The League of Nations should not protect only the rights of the independent states and colonial powers but the rights of all nations. Nabarawi protested the British military occupation of Egypt as part of this "sad reality."[14] Fatma Niʿmat Rashid decried the world's division into two camps—the imperialist powers and the weak nations—declaring that the Middle Eastern nations were seeking to recover their independence and their dignity. It was the policies of imperialist powers in the region that endangered peace.[15]

At the Universal Peace Congress in Brussels later that year, Huda Shaʿrawi, in the name of the women of Egypt and her "sister nations," asserted that peoples of the East were ready to work for peace under the auspices of the League of Nations, on certain conditions. The League must help to elevate the weaker nations by permitting them to become active members of "human society," and it must guarantee countries under mandate the ability to regulate immigration. The mandatory powers must put the interest and security of populations placed under their trust above all "egotistical considerations"; those powers must also be held responsible for injustices committed in the territories entrusted to them.[16] Treaties were not immutable: treaties imposed without the free consent of both parties should be examined by the League of Nations as the supreme world tribunal. Rather than directing attention simply to arms reduction, a key item on the congress agenda, Shaʿrawi insisted that the causes of wars must be examined including questions of immigration,[17] referring to Palestine.

The EFU and Arab Women: A Regional Approach to the Defense of Palestine

While crises mounted, Arab women not only took the Palestine question to the international peace and feminist communities; they also created their own forums and structures through which to operate. With mass arrests of Arab nationalists following the British recommendation for the partition of Palestine, Anisah al-Khadra, president of the Women's Committee of ᶜAkka, telegraphed Huda Shaᶜrawi. Evoking Muslim solidarity to "rescue the Holy Land," she implored the EFU president to put pressure on Egypt's "ally Britain."[18] In the name of Islam and Arabism, Huda Shaᶜrawi pressed Prime Minister Mustafa Nahhas to support Palestine. At the same time, again evoking Arab Muslim solidarity, the EFU president sent a protest of the British government's actions "on behalf of Egyptian and Palestinian women" to British ambassador to Egypt Miles Lampson.[19] These communications adumbrated the pressure Egyptian feminists would continue to place on their own government and upon the British.[20]

Nationalist women leaders remained active inside Palestine. In February 1938 a delegation of Palestinian Arab women from Jerusalem handed a protest signed by two hundred women to the British high commissioner. The document cited Britain's pro-Zionist policy, the violation of the principles of justice and human rights, and the repressive measures taken against the Arab population, men, women, and children. They charged that "police and military alarm women and children in a most repulsive and cruel manner during their search of houses (in cities and especially in the villages). . . . Ladies are stopped in the streets to be searched in police posts, thus offending their womanly sanctity and alarming accompanying children, [which] is a contempt for the traditions and religions of this country and inconsistent with chivalry and honour."[21] British mandatory authorities had reported to London the month before, in answer to an inquiry, that "searches of women cannot be avoided in the present circumstances" but were being conducted reasonably.[22]

As the Arab revolt intensified, some Palestinians, harassed by the mandatory authorities, escaped into Syria where they set up Committees for the Defense of Palestine. Syrian Bahirah al-ᶜAzmah had organized the Women's Committee for the Defense of Palestine; her husband Nabi al-ᶜAzmah was head of the Central Committee for the Defense of Palestine in Damascus. Bahirah al-ᶜAzmah and Huda Shaᶜrawi communicated about holding a women's congress in Bludan.[23] (The men's committees, with support from Egyptian and other Arab groups, were planning a Pan-Arab Congress for the Defense of Palestine in Bludan, to convene in September 1937.)[24] The British intercepted a letter from Shaᶜrawi to al-Azmah suggesting that representatives be invited from women's associations throughout the East, especially from Iran and India. British authorities moved to stop nationalist cooperation between Indian and Arab women and also put an end to the possibility of a women's conference in Syria.[25] As a result leaders from women's associations in Palestine, Syria, Lebanon, and Iraq met in Beirut on July 7th, 1938, where they drafted a letter to Huda Shaʿrawi. In it they delegated her to represent Arab women in presenting the case of the Palestinian Arabs before the Mandate Commission of the League of Nations, the International Alliance of Women, and any other appropriate forum. They also demanded recognition of the Palestinian Arabs' right to independence in their own country, an end to the project of a Jewish national home in Palestine, and a halt to Jewish immigration into the country; they called for a bilateral treaty between Palestine and Britain on the model of the Anglo-Iraqi treaty to replace the British mandate. President of the Lebanese Arab Women's Union in Beirut Ibtihaj al-Kaddurah signed the letter, together with Bahirah al-ʿAzmah for the Women's Committee for the Defense of Palestine in Syria, Shahindah Duzdar and Zulaykhah al-Shihabi for the Arab Women's Committee of Jerusalem, and Naziq Jawdat for the women's societies of Iraq.[26]

This delegation of authority to the president of the EFU constituted a turning point. In September 1938, speaking for the women's associations in Eastern countries, Shaʿrawi cabled the British ambassador protesting the British endorsement of partition at the League of Nations and the violent repression in Palestine. She declared that women were losing confidence in British intentions to uphold the legitimate rights of the Arabs in Palestine.[27]

The EFU president meanwhile moved ahead to switch the women's conference on Palestine to Cairo. Monitoring the women, British authorities in Cairo reported to London that Shaʿrawi was "in close touch with European and Eastern feminist organizations both national and international."[28] Concurrently plans were underway for the Inter-Parliamentary Congress of Arab and Islamic Countries for the Defense of Palestine, which received the backing of the palace, al-Azhar, and prominent politicians, except for the Wafd. The British opposed the conference but could not prevent it.[29] Framing the women's meeting as a peace initiative, the EFU president announced that the Eastern Women's Conference for the Defense of Palestine would convene at the EFU headquarters in Cairo in October. The announcement read: "To fulfill the promise that we, the women of the East, have made to each other and to our Western sisters at various international congresses to cooperate in spreading harmony among peoples in our countries and to struggle by all legitimate means to prevent war, and in order to assist the League of Nations, to strengthen international peace, and to resolve conflicts between countries by peaceful means, we will convene the Eastern Women's Conference to examine the painful conditions that have afflicted Palestine for many years."[30]

This time the women succeeded in holding their conference.[31] The assembly elected Huda Shaʿrawi president and nominated seven vice presidents:

Wahidah Husayn al-Khalidi and Zulaykhah al-Shihabi from Palestine, ʿAdilah Bayham Mukhtar al-Jaza'iri from Syria, Evelyn Jibran Bustrus from Lebanon, Sabihah al-Hashimi from Iraq, and Nafisah Muhammad ʿAli ʿAllubah and Aminah Fu'ad Sultan from Egypt. The sixty-seven delegates from six countries represented a wide spectrum from secular liberals to conservative Islamists. The Egyptian delegation of twenty comprised EFU members as well as women from different organizations and with diverse ideologies, including Muslim Women's Society president Zaynab al-Ghazali. The Palestinian delegation was the largest, with twenty-six members, including several members of the Arab Women's Committee in Jerusalem.[32] The women were able to maintain the broad unity that they had achieved in 1929 when they formed the Arab Women's Executive Committee. The Palestinian women's collective transcended the factional divisions of the men's national movement.[33] The other delegations included twenty women from Syria, three from Lebanon, four from Iraq, and one from Iran. Conference delegates were members of nationalist/feminist and voluntary social associations. Most of the women came from elite families. Some were middle-class teachers and writers.

Feminist and Islamist women together underscored the need for women's political participation and for solidarity between women and men in upholding the cause of Palestine. Shaʿrawi declared that "the unity of the sexes in defending this just case will show the world that the calamity of Palestine has not only stirred the men of the East, but has equally alarmed the women . . . [who] have hastened to participate with their men in the rescue of Palestine."[34] Islamist leader Zaynab al-Ghazali gave the major credit to women: "In past times, as today, the woman has called for peace and lifted the banner of right to defend the land and its dignity. It is not strange that today she calls for help for her Palestinian sister and sacrifices everything dear shouting in the face of men: 'Rise up from your sleep and be awakened from your foolishness and gather all your power and consolidate your forces.' It is the women in this conference who have awakened everyone to come to the rescue." She continued, calling for the solidarity of the sexes: "In these difficult times, it is inevitable that men and women should cooperate and that their voices should be united. Enough of the disputes that have occurred between the man and the woman, with each scorning the rights of the other."[35] The women delegates unanimously decided to invite men to attend. For the first time, male Arab political leaders and university students could witness the debates of women.[36]

Women were conscious of the importance of their political roles in the national struggle. Faykah Muddaris from Aleppo insisted, "In order to achieve the [nationalist] task we should not rely merely upon kings, presidents, and other [male] leaders but also upon women."[37] In assuming political roles women evoked their past. Iraqi teacher Mary Wazir claimed, "Arab women are repeating history and resuming a duty that women so gloriously undertook in the early days of the Arab conquests."[38]

The women's conference condemned British policy and actions and denounced Zionist activities and aspirations in Palestine. Huda Shaʿrawi blamed the British for treachery to the Arabs and for "attempting to make the Zionists masters over an entire people despite their wishes." She declared: "We want to live in peace and brotherhood with Jewish citizens, and we therefore ask them to cooperate with us to turn the Zionists from the dreams they insist upon turning into reality. We ask them, as well as British women and men, to listen to the appeal of the Arab peoples and to join us in demanding respect for the nation's right to self-determination. We ask them to demand an immediate end to immigration to Palestine and to recognize that the Arab inhabitants of Palestine have a right to their freedom and to their very existence."[39] Palestinian Wahidah al-Khalidi said, "Instead of training the Arabs to run their own affairs, Britain created in Palestine a government of foreigners and Zionist Jews."[40]

Delegates communicated firsthand accounts of events in Palestine, which were otherwise shrouded by heavy censorship. Sadhij Nassar recounted details of the Arab Revolt in which she had been a militant participant.[41] Bahirah al-ʿAzmah, head of the Women's Committee for the Defense of Palestine, spoke of "destruction, torture, and brutality," blaming the British and proposing a boycott of their goods.[42] Secretary of the Arab Women's Committee Matiel Mogannam outlined the continuing acquisition of land by Jews.[43] The Palestinian women repeated calls for an end to Jewish immigration into their country. Akilah Shukri Dib, president of the Society for the Training of Orthodox Girls in Jerusalem, stressed, "We do not wish to deny the Jews a place to live, but we do not want them to take our land from our hands and to build their existence upon our ruins."[44]

The conference declared it the duty of every Arab woman and man to come to the rescue of the Arabs of Palestine, who were struggling for their existence; it denounced Britain's Palestine policy, "based on violence and maltreatment," as an act of hostility toward the Arabs and Islam; and it endorsed the demands of Palestinian Arabs: the abolition of the mandate in Palestine, a nullification of the Balfour Declaration, an end to Jewish immigration to Palestine, prevention of land transfers from Arabs to Jews and foreigners, opposition to partition, amnesty for prisoners, and the return of exiles.[45]

The women's conference attracted considerable attention in the region. Messages poured into Cairo. ʿArif ʿAbd al-Razzaq from the office of the Arab Revolt wrote, "I place hope in you and in the women's association, the source of the women's renaissance in the East, to regain the freedom of the East and to bring it back its glory."[46] Islamic authorities applauded women's activism. Mufti of Palestine Hajj Amin al-Husayni praised the wide impact of the conference in the Arab and Islamic worlds.[47] In Cairo al-Azhar rector Mustafa al-Maraghi, a strong advocate of Islamic unity, sent encouragement to the women's congress.[48]

The British had earlier been pleasantly surprised by the men's Inter-Parliamentary Congress, pronouncing it "less venomous and anglophobe" than expected and its resolutions "very moderate."[49] The British Foreign Office judged the women's conference "more violent than its male counterpart."[50] British ambassador Miles Lampson pointed out in a dispatch to London that "the power of the women in the East, as in France, is far greater than their legal disabilities indicate."[51] The Foreign Office in London advised the British ambassador that because the conference made direct attacks on British policy there should be no acknowledgment of receipt of the conference resolutions from "these vituperative ladies."[52]

After the conference adjourned, in addition to the Women's Committee for the Defense of Palestine in Syria others were organized in Egypt, Palestine, Lebanon, and Iraq. Huda Shaʿrawi headed the permanent central committee in Cairo. The central committee disseminated information and became the main office for fund-raising. A subcommittee was created to collect contributions. Members included Egyptians Mary Kahil, Hidayah Barakat, and Hawwaʾ Idris, Palestinian Katy Antonius, and Lebanese Najlah Kafuri. By December 1938 the women had raised nearly two thousand Egyptian pounds through private subscriptions and charity benefits for Palestine relief.[53] The British high commissioner in Palestine and the acting British consul both expressed concern about the destination of these funds.

The women's central committee in Cairo became an important channel for communications. Messages were sent to Cairo from Palestine with news of detentions and deaths and pleas for help. In December 1938, the Arab Society of Damascus asked Huda Shaʿrawi to intervene on behalf of Subhi al-Khadra, still detained by the British.[54] In February 1939, the Arab Women's Union of Haifa sent word to Cairo about the deaths of women and children in their town; they asked that Huda Shaʿrawi enlist the aid of IAW president Margery Corbett Ashby to call for British women's protests on their behalf.[55] In April, the Arab Women's Executive Committee in Jerusalem contacted the Cairo office about the condition of Arab prisoners in Palestine.[56] In March, ulama from Jerusalem sent a telegram to Huda Shaʿrawi reporting the prohibition of prayers in al-ʿAqsa Mosque and pleading, "We ask you to do whatever you can to make our voice heard and to tell our story to the Islamic world." The EFU president forwarded this to the shaykh al-Azhar. Again, three months later, Jerusalem ulama requested that she publish their protest against the British high commissioner in Palestine for denouncing the mufti of Jerusalem in the Egyptian press.[57]

The women who came together to address the Palestine question discussed the Arab unity that, indeed, the conference symbolized and expressed. Palestinian Nabihah Nasir, an educator and founder of Birzeit College, a secondary school in Ramallah (now Birzeit University), outlined a program that began with Arab economic and cultural unity as a step to political unity. She suggested that Arab countries under mandate create a body to assist them in achieving their independence. Sadhij Nassar, an early proponent of Arab unity, underscored the strategic necessity. She stressed to her Arab sisters at the conference that Zionism was not a threat to the Arabs of Palestine alone but also to those of the neighboring countries. "There is no safety for the Arabs except in unity," she told the women. She also emphasized the need for unity "with the Eastern nations and the Islamic peoples."[58]

Limits of International Feminism

When the EFU went to the IAW conference in Copenhagen in July 1939 it found attendance low. Because of unrest and uncertainty at home, neither the Palestinian Arab Women's Union nor the Syrian Women's Union was able to send a delegation. Luli Abu al-Huda, a Jordanian student at Oxford, attended as a "fraternal delegate." The All-India Women's Conference (now the Indian affiliate of the IAW) and the Jewish Women's Equal Rights Association from Palestine—the latter composed of Western women—were the only other affiliates from Eastern countries. The forced closures of affiliates in Germany, Italy, Austria, and Czechoslovakia and the threat of war kept away many members, and for the first time there was no American presence. With fascism entrenched in parts of Europe and hopes of peace receding, issues of individual and national (ethnic and religious) rights and freedoms, social justice, and democracy dominated the feminists' attention. It was in this context that Egyptian feminists introduced the case of the violated rights and threatened national existence of Palestine.

The old order of international feminism was disintegrating. What was feminism? What was "politics"? What was the relationship between feminism and nationalism? These perennially underlying questions in the world of international feminism came to the surface. Discussion of the proposed declaration of principles gave rise to heated debate, starkly revealing a lack of consensus on what constituted feminism. As Nabarawi reported, the majority felt that feminism must reaffirm its commitment to democracy while others saw this as a move toward "politics." Finally, the congress agreed on a declaration: "If women believe the State to be an organization to secure peace, freedom, justice, and well-being for all, they must hold this conviction with passionate sincerity. Women must keep alive the belief in democracy. There can be no freedom for women when freedom is no longer a recognized right of every individual. The woman's battle is that of all mankind."[59]

In the declaration, the IAW committed itself to democratic citizenship, social justice, and peace. However, Article 1 of the bylaws, entitled "Neutrality," stated, "The International Alliance of Women for Suffrage and Equal Citizenship by mutual consent of its Auxiliaries stands pledged to observe absolute neutrality on all questions that are strictly national."[60] There were issues relating to peace and social justice that transcended national borders which the IAW preferred to eschew as "national" and therefore not "neutral" matters, while there were other issues with national dimensions that the organization addressed.

Underlying the Western ascendancy in the IAW was an unstated political orientation, a set of assumptions that the Western core of the IAW leadership did not see as "political." Saiza Nabarawi characterized the atmosphere at the Copenhagen congress:

> The congress, far from representing global views of women, was too often the echo of the political or racial preoccupations of the so-called democratic states and Zionist groups. Under the cover of defense of democratic principles severe criticisms were leveled against the totalitarian states, and the question of Jewish emigration was among those that most preoccupied the congress. One can say that feminist and pacifist problems were relegated to second place. When one waited to hear women protest energetically against injustices and condemn war, their voices were raised only to condemn certain regimes in accordance with the political interests of their governments. . . . We deplored most strongly the regrettable spirit of intolerance which manifested itself at several points in the congress at Copenhagen that we Egyptians had come to . . . with the sincere desire to interest our European sisters in the problem of peace and humanity which concerns us [all] so that our union would be more solid and our collaboration more loyal and fruitful.[61]

IAW international feminism was grounded in feminisms within nation-states. Membership in the IAW was institutional; a single association from a country was to represent all its women. When it admitted the Palestine Jewish Women's Equal Rights Association in 1923, however, the IAW recognized an affiliate that represented only Jewish women in Palestine rather than all women. In 1935 when the IAW admitted the Palestinian Arab Women's Union, it recognized two "entities" from the same country. In the 1920s and 1930s the IAW implicitly recognized "two states" in Palestine. IAW bylaws and policies were inconsistently applied. Because they did not have an independent state, Ukrainians and other national groups in the Soviet Union could not be represented. The limitations of state-based feminisms were not interrogated while exceptions were arbitrarily allowed.

At Copenhagen the EFU pointed out that the democratic principles IAW feminists upheld were not consistently applied. Earlier in 1939 two feminists had been arrested and jailed. When Frantiska Plaminkova, a staunch feminist and nationalist, was among the Jews arrested in Prague after the German march on Czechoslovakia, the IAW had called upon presidents of affiliates to appeal to the German authorities for her release. However, when Palestinian Arab Sadhij Nassar was jailed by the British mandatory authorities in Palestine, the IAW had remained silent. The EFU wanted to know why. President Corbett Ashby explained that in the case of Plaminkova IAW members had acted in a personal capacity on behalf of a fellow IAW board member. Appealing the case of Nassar—who had represented the Palestinian Arab Women's Union at the previous IAW congress—it was argued, would have involved intervention by the IAW in the political affairs of governments, which IAW bylaws did not permit. This led the Egyptians to conclude that there were "two weights and two measures when it came to the East and the West—totalitarian states and democratic states."[62]

Divergences and tensions surfaced in Copenhagen even before the congress opened.[63] At a preconference meeting of the IAW board, Huda Shaʿrawi raised the issue of injustices toward the Arabs of Palestine. According to Saiza Nabarawi, after Jewish members had proposed that the IAW speak out against states which persecuted and expelled Jews, Shaʿrawi asked that a message be sent to the affiliated Palestine Arab Women's Union concerning the situation in their country. A subcommittee was asked to draft a message. The Jewish delegates objected to the first draft, and by the third draft the message had lost its value. Nabarawi said, "In the face of this pronounced hostility on the part of the Zionist block, Madame Charaoui Pacha [Shaʿrawi] felt it necessary to retire and tender her resignation to the board." Shaʿrawi was asked to withdraw her resignation, which she finally did.[64] Rosa Manus, a Jewish member of the Dutch delegation, wrote about the incident to Carrie Chapman Catt. According to Manus Shaʿrawi "came to present a resolution to the Board which she wanted the Board to accept and put to the Congress in which it was asked that we should take a vote that from now on Palestine would not let in any more Jews. She said that the Arab population was too badly treated by them, that it was the country of the Arabs and that we ought to protest against more Jews going to Palestine. You can imagine that the Board Members did not want to go in for any discussion about it as it was not within the scope of the work of the Alliance but meant mere politics."[65]

Carrying out its mandate from the Arab women the EFU placed two resolutions before the Copenhagen congress. One urged that "mandatory and protectorate states" prevent further acts of violence against unarmed people by the military and police. This resolution was rejected on the grounds that it constituted an intervention in the politics of national governments.[66] The other resolution opposed "immigration imposed on a country without the free consent of its population." Although it was cast as a peace issue arguing that imposed immigration produces conflict,[67] it too failed to pass.

Trying to incorporate the concerns of both the EFU and the Jewish delegation from Palestine, the IAW board proposed a resolution declaring that the problem of emigration required rapid solution, that the IAW condemned countries which expelled people for reasons of race or opinions, and that the problem could not be solved by "forced immigration" of refugees imposed on other populations without their consent. The resolution demanded that an international conference study the entire matter to come to a solution "in a spirit of equity and humanity"; it urged IAW affiliates to stir up public opinion in favor of such a conference and to press their governments to support it.[68] Neither delegation accepted this. The Egyptians objected because the IAW resolution did not equally condemn totalitarian and democratic countries for injustices committed: the Egyptian feminists, of course, had in mind Britain and its treatment of Palestinian Arabs. The board drafted a second resolution. It began as the EFU resolution had, placing the problem in the context of peace, but identified emigration as the problem rather than immigration and objected to "forced immigration." In place of condemning governments that expelled people it spoke of "the defaulting of all governments in regard to this immense human problem."[69]

There was a long and heated debate. The EFU argued in favor of adopting the resolution. The Jewish Women's Equal Rights Association from Palestine objected to it. Dr. Brachayahu, a member of the Jewish Women's Equal Rights Association delegation, reported in *Davar Hapoelet* (the association bulletin) that the delegation saw this and the other two resolutions dealing with immigration as an implicit "attack on the right of Jews to immigrate to their country [i.e., Palestine]."[70] Nabarawi noted in *L'Egyptienne* that the Palestine Jewish delegation wanted the reference to "forced immigration" struck on the grounds that the Balfour Declaration recognized Palestine as the legitimate homeland of the Jews. During the debate Jordanian Luli Abu al-Huda appealed to the congress to vote for the resolution as a show of sympathy to the women of her region. When the EFU delegation requested that the resolution be put to the vote, the request was rejected. "Such dictatorship and partiality on the part of the assembly," wrote Nabarawi, "provoked indignation on the part of the members of the [Egyptian] delegation, who left the hall as a sign of protest. We remarked that after having solemnly saluted the feast of liberty the morning of July 14th one was subjected the very same day to the most shameful injustice and intolerance."[71]

After the congress Saiza Nabarawi reported in *L'Egyptienne*:

> What did we demand? A little sympathy for the unfortunate who suffer in the East from the wrongs of imperialist politics. This testiment of sympathy . . . accords moreover with the declaration of human rights so passionately defended by the Alliance and so warmly voted at one of its sessions. It [the IAW] should have given the Eastern world proof that women are sincere and disinterested when they speak of justice and liberty, that they know how to disavow their governments when they do not apply these principles. To the contrary, by their [the IAW's] refusal to interest themselves in Eastern problems they have proven that their magnificent program addresses itself only to certain peoples of the West, alone deigned to enjoy liberty. Thus they render difficult a loyal and fruitful collaboration between the Eastern and Western worlds. There are flagrant contradictions between theory and practice which we pointed out many times in the course of the congress sessions that rendered the task of the Egyptian delegation particularly difficult.[72]

After the congress Corbett Ashby, trying to preserve international sisterhood, wrote a conciliatory letter to Huda Shaʿrawi saying that the EFU president and the other Egyptian delegates had "raised concern and sympathy" for Arab women in Palestine. The Egyptian delegation had opened the eyes of women from northern countries who were ignorant about Palestine, and northern women would like to know more and to give assistance.[73] Shaʿrawi ultimately opted to remain in the IAW, contending that her departure from the organization "would harm us and benefit our enemies."[74]

Revealing the Eurocentricism of the IAW, Corbett Ashby wrote many years later that women were perhaps "mezmerized [*sic*] by the vastness and immediacy of the Jewish problem whereas the Palestine problem was far off and concerned relatively few people." She added that "the absence of Arab delegations was most unfortunate because though Hoda was a good representative the impact was not the same. Obsessed by war forebodings the delegations needed to talk listen learn in informal contacts."[75] The absence of the Arab delegations was directly related to mandatory constraints and the impending European war. It is telling that the IAW official history *Journey Towards Freedom* (1955) is silent about the contentious matters raised in Copenhagen.[76]

Arab Women: Common Ground, Different Histories

The women who gathered in Cairo in 1938 for the conference on Palestine shared a common Arab Islamic culture. Arabic was their mother tongue and Islam their predominant religion, although many were Christian. As a cultural force Islam also influenced the Christian and Jewish minorities. The women came from countries that had all at one time been under Ottoman rule. The Arab countries east of Egypt (often referred to as the Arab East) were now experiencing European colonial rule, whereas Egypt, which had fallen under colonial occupation in 1882, had enjoyed nominal independence in 1922. While there were commonalities, there were also significant local differences. In the 1920s, 1930s, and 1940s, the everyday lives of middle- and upper-class women in Cairo and Alexandria generally stood apart as freer than the lives of their counterparts in Beirut, Damascus, Jerusalem, and Baghdad.

Women from the Arab East were aware of these differences and relaxed their behavior when they came to Cairo for the conference. Palestinian Sadhij Nassar remarked that although the women had arrived in Cairo unveiled, most of them still covered their faces at home.[77] Najlah Kafuri from Lebanon noted that the women had traveled to the conference without the customary *mahram*, a male chaperone who was usually a close relative.[78] Unveiling, traveling alone, and forging new networks had both symbolic and practical importance.

While veiling was still the general practice in the cities and towns of the Arab East, in recent years there had been modifications in styles of dress. A few women had stopped veiling altogether, while many veiled or unveiled according to the situation.[79] Syrian Sara Shahbandar recalled that she and several other women first removed their veils in nationalist demonstrations in Damascus in 1922.[80] Palestinian ʿAnbarah Salam al-Khalidi gave a public lecture unveiled in Beirut in 1927, a first by a woman from the region and not without adverse comment.[81] Tarab ʿAbd al-Hadi related that many Jerusalem women, Muslims and Christians alike, unveiled during the nationalist demonstration of 1929 and never covered their faces again.[82] In the small towns veiling and domestic confinement remained strict, as Palestinian poet Fadwa Tuqan from Nablus reveals in her memoirs.[83] American researcher Ruth Woodsmall, who traveled in the region in 1929, observed that women often unveiled and exhibited more independence when not in their own countries. She remarked that Syrian women teachers in Baghdad behaved differently from their counterparts at home. Woodsmall also noted that it was only in Egypt and Turkey that the press published photographs of women.[84]

The issue of veiling could still draw the kind of fire from conservatives in the Arab East that it had in Egypt at the turn of the century. In 1928 Lebanese Nazirah Zayn al-Din published a treatise called *Unveiling and Veiling: Lectures and Views on the Liberation of the Woman and Social Renewal in the Arab World.* She used Islamic modernist arguments to condemn covering the face, which she branded as a deviation from religious prescription and an impediment to progress. The ferocity of the attacks directed at her—which she answered with a stern rebuttal—indicated the contentiousness of the issue.[85]

Educational opportunities for women had long been available in the Arab East. As noted earlier, many women who emigrated to Egypt from Greater Syria had been educated at schools in their home countries. In Greater Syria, as in Egypt, the first schools for girls had been created early in the nineteenth century. While the early girls' schools had been run by Christian missionaries, schools for girls were later operated by women from the region as well as by private associations, including Muslim philanthropic societies. With education women went on to create intellectual societies and philanthropic associations. The earliest seems to have been the Bakurat Suriyah, a women's literary society in Beirut that Mariam Nimr Makarius created in 1880.[86] Other societies included the Christian Public Charity Society for Ladies, created in Haifa in 1911, and the Jamʿiyat Nur al-Fiyah, the Muslim Women's Association, and the Women's Renaissance Society in Beirut, all active by the 1920s. By the late 1920s women had moved away from sectarian societies to found the first secular feminist and nationalist associations bringing Muslims and Christians together. The Lebanese Arab Women's Union, the Syrian Arab Women's Union, and the previously mentioned Palestine Arab Women's Union were all created in 1929. An expanding network of women's associations would stand ready to serve the cause of gender and nation by the time the Arab Feminist Conference convened in Cairo after the Second World War.

Consolidating Arab Feminism

The consolidation of pan-Arab feminism occurred as countries of the Arab East were poised for independence at the end of World War II. The Eastern Women's Conference for the Defense of Palestine in 1938 had provided the arena where women could unite on behalf of nation and gender. Before the delegates left Cairo, Shaʿrawi had suggested that feminist unions be created in the individual countries as a prelude to establishing a general Arab feminist union.[87]

At the IAW congress in Copenhagen in 1939, Egyptian feminists had seen more fully the real limits of international feminism. The "solidarity of sisters" and shared ideals that had lured Egyptians to the IAW in 1923 appeared to be chimeras by 1939. Earlier differences had been tolerated, perhaps partly in the hope that with time they could be resolved. Egyptian feminists' experiences with the IAW concerning prostitution, the Capitulations and the international organization's inability to act in a decisive and timely manner had shown the Egyptians how enmeshed IAW feminism was in the agenda of Western imperialism. At Copenhagen Egyptian feminists had seen how the IAW read issues of endangered peace and violations of justice one way in the context of Palestine and another way in the context of Europe. This double standard made Huda Shaʿrawi feel that "it had become necessary to create an Eastern feminist union as a structure within which to consolidate our forces and help us to have an impact upon the women of the world."[88] Indeed as early as 1930 Saiza Nabarawi had asserted that the path toward liberation of Eastern women was different from that of Western women, suggesting that Eastern women should unite.[89] Meanwhile a move toward Arab unity had been growing among women and men in Egypt and other Arab countries.[90]

Egyptian feminists took the lead in calling Arab women together to create a pan-Arab feminist union, an organization that would consolidate their collective vision and strengthen feminist movements inside individual Arab countries, while enhancing their participation in the international feminist movement. In the summer of 1944, Huda Shaʿrawi and two second-generation EFU members, Hawwa' Idris and Aminah al-Saʿid, visited women's societies in Lebanon, Syria, Palestine, and Trans-Jordan, exploring the idea of a confederation of Arab feminist unions. The Egyptian women also met various government leaders who encouraged the idea of a pan-Arab women's conference.[91] The Egyptians and leaders of women's societies in countries of the region subsequently met in Suq al-Gharb in Lebanon to work out plans for such a conference.[92] Back in Egypt, Huda Shaʿrawi as president of the EFU issued the call for the Arab Feminist Conference. The call went out to women from countries of the Arab East, emerging from colonial rule, and to the Maghreb, still under colonial domination. North African women were unable to respond to the call. No call went out to women in the Arabian Peninsula.

The Arab Feminist Congress convened in Cairo in December 1944 with highly visible state support. Queen Faridah was patron of the conference. Minister of education Muhammad Husayn Haykal addressed the opening on behalf of the Egyptian government, which had donated one thousand pounds to the conference. The conference was twice the size of the 1938 meeting, with national delegations composed of representatives from various women's associations in their countries. Along with EFU members from Cairo and a new branch in Minya, the Egyptian delegation to the conference included representatives from the Mabarrat Muhammad ʿAli, the New Woman Society, the Red Crescent Society, the Mabarrat Amirah Faryal, the Cairo Women's Club, the Coptic Philanthropic Society, the Muslim Women's Society, and the Egyptian Anti-Smoking Society, as well as a few women and a few men attending as individuals.[93] The Egyptian delegation constituted the kind of confederation of women's associations Shaʿrawi had tried unsuccessfully to form on a permanent basis. The Palestinian delegation of twenty-five was headed by Zulaykhah al-Shihabi, the Lebanese delegation (twenty-seven) by Rose Shahfa, the Syrian delegation (eight) by ʿAdilah Bayham ʿAbd al-Qadir, Trans-Jordan's (two) by Luli Abu al-Huda, and Iraq's (four) by Nadhimah al-ʿAskari. About one-fifth of the women had attended the previous conference. As before, most of the delegates were from large landowning and rich merchant families whose fathers and husbands had diverse political affiliations. But in 1944 there were more middle-class professional women, mainly teachers and journalists. Also this time nearly half the participants were single women.

The conference theme of Arab unity—among Arab nations, among Arab women, and between Arab women and men—was cast in nationalist and feminist terms. Pan-Arab feminists took up the challenge of constructing citizenship in modern Arab states as independent countries in a postcolonial world. This necessitated restructuring gender roles and relations. Arab feminists strove to further realize the gender dimension of liberal nationalist ideology, which predicated the nation's liberation on that of the woman, at the moment of transition to a new era—an era when nationalist discourse was no longer an oppositional discourse contesting colonial domination, and when Arab women and men would have to decide on how both genders would be incorporated into their new polities. This was the same challenge Egyptians had faced earlier, and it had led Egyptian women to organize a feminist movement to push for the rights of female citizens and to participate in shaping the new state and society. However, unlike Egyptian women, who had formally consolidated as feminists in a newly independent country, women from the Arab East were formulating their collective approach and consolidating their forces on the eve of their nations' independence—with the exception of Palestinian women, who were locked in a struggle for national survival.

The situation for Arab women in 1944 differed from what it had been for Egyptian women two decades earlier. Egyptian women, as feminists-cum-nationalists, had been left to fight their own independent battle as Egyptian male nationalists and "progressives" had thrown themselves into creating and controlling the new polity. Now male Arab nationalists recognized women's societal potential and wished to access it for their purposes. Arab women, nationalists and feminists, were important to the "wider" project of Arab unity. When the EFU women toured the Arab East in the summer of 1944, government leaders received them and encouraged them in planning the Arab Feminist Conference. At home Egyptian political leaders who wished to gain preeminence for Egypt in the project of Arab unity supported EFU efforts to organize and host a pan-Arab women's conference. While Arab men supported the conference, and in so doing acknowledged the societal roles of Arab women, the men also wished to shape those roles as they saw fit.

The conference's keynote addresses revealed the divergence of agendas between the feminists and the patriarchal state. Egyptian feminist leader Huda Shaʿrawi, as conference president, shared the podium with education minister Muhammad Husayn Haykal, the representative of the Egyptian state.

Shaʿrawi mapped out the task ahead, sounding unmistakable echoes of the speech she had given at the IAW conference twenty-one years earlier announcing the start of the Egyptian feminist movement. Women were seeking to recuperate lost rights—rights that religion had accorded to women and men alike, and that women had enjoyed in the early days of Islam. These ungendered rights were essential to the national self-determination and democracy that Arabs sought. All Muslims, irrespective of gender, had rights, indeed duties, to participate in the social, economic, and political life of the Islamic ummah, community. Full citizenship for Arab women in contemporary societies demanded the exercise of all their rights. "The Arab woman who is equal to the man in duties and obligations," Shaʿrawi insisted, "will not accept in the twentieth century distinctions between the sexes that advanced countries have discarded. The Arab woman does not agree to be chained in slavery and to pay for the consequences of men's mistakes concerning her country's rights and the future of her children. In her loudest voice, the woman demands to regain her political rights, which have been granted to her by the shariʿah."[94]

Haykal gendered societal roles and essentialized "woman." He spoke of women's "special" social and cultural roles. Woman's "special affinities" in the intellectual, spiritual, and artistic domains must be exploited. After noting these societal roles, the minister spoke of the woman as the primary producer of the new generation, thus recentering woman in the home and reconfirming the exaltation of her maternal role. "Without doubt," said Haykal, "the conference will deal with the greatest social problem, which is the raising of the new generation in a way that corresponds to the development of a new world in the aftermath of the present war." The representative of the state enunciated women's supportive role, signposting the patriarchal road ahead: "We are at the crossroads like other nations, and the [male] intellectuals, [male] politicians, and great men in the world are now foreseeing the world of tomorrow. The efforts of the Arab feminist conference will have their impact on the Arab countries, and the [male] politicians and representatives of Arab countries will be keen to determine the most appropriate ways to direct their countries in the future."[95]

While Shaʿrawi stressed the feminist challenges ahead, Haykal touted the "great activities" of Egyptian women in the past twenty years in social, artistic, cultural, and philanthropic arenas. There was no acknowledgment, not even a hint, of unrealized goals in the domain of personal status laws or women's suffrage. The agenda of the state, as conveyed by its spokesman, was to narrow women's arena and to harness their "special gifts" for the good of the male-run state and society. It was an antifeminist program meant to ensure the continuation of patriarchal culture, albeit in modified form to suit the new times. Nonetheless the feminist delegates maintained control of the conference—it was their agenda, not that of the state, that was articulated in the working sessions. The rights of the nation and the rights of women were the leitmotifs.

The frame of lost legitimate rights included the vanishing sovereignty of Palestine. Palestinian women took the lead in articulating their country's cause, manifesting a shift away from the earlier primary focus on British colonial policy toward a concentration on the Zionist threat. The increasing Jewish immigration and continuing Jewish acquisition of land were the main concerns. The conference demanded an end to Jewish immigration and called upon Arab countries, groups, and individuals to give financial support to Palestine. Funds should be provided to buy back land acquired by Jews and to publicize the plight of the Arabs of Palestine. Palestinian women acted primarily as nationalists trying to save their country, believing that feminism for them was out of the question. Wadiʿah Khartabil asserted, "While Arab women begin to struggle to enter political life, Palestinian women continue to struggle for life itself."[96]

In 1938 when Arab women came together to deal with the nationalist issue of Palestine, they unintentionally set the groundwork for pan-Arab feminism. In 1944 Arab women convened to shape and institutionalize pan-Arab feminism and within this context to keep alive their commitment to the Palestine cause. Arab women continued to cast the Palestine question as a peace issue. To Eleanor Roosevelt's plea that the Arab women's conference work for peace, Shaʿrawi responded, "I answer her from this podium that working to bring justice to the Arabs of Palestine is one of the strongest pillars of peace in the Arab East."[97] As conference president, Shaʿrawi also sent a telegram to President Roosevelt: "The Arab Feminist Conference convening in Cairo and representing the women of Egypt, Iraq, Syria, Lebanon, Palestine, and Trans-Jordan protests all American propaganda in favor of Zionism and any assistance to it to realize its illegitimate hopes in Palestine, which is indisputably the legitimate country of the Arabs. It is strange that America, which is now fighting all over the world in defense of democracy, is violating the sacredness of these noble principles in respect to Palestine, which is Arab. Arab women will not spare any sacrifice in defense of their noble cause."[98] She also sent communications to British prime minister Winston Churchill and to the British high commissioner in Jerusalem.

The conference agreed upon a comprehensive feminist program, with the rights of women as citizens within a unitary Arab framework to be implemented in their respective countries. In the new construction of citizenship all nationals are equal—irrespective of gender—and must enjoy *the practice* of equal rights. However, the construct of the citizen should not be articulated on a male model, under which the female citizen is subsumed. The realities and needs of women and men as citizens must be acknowledged and addressed.

At the top of the list of fifty-one resolutions was a demand for women's right to vote and to be elected, cautiously calling for a gradual equalizing of political rights for women and men. Arab governments should also appoint qualified women to official posts. It was the Egyptians at the conference who spoke out on the issue of women's political rights. Lawyer Mufidah ʿAbd al-Rahman promised that women would not rest until they won their right to vote and to be elected to parliament. Member of parliament Zuhayr Sabri, who had recently submitted a bill to give women equal political rights, made a strong appeal for a new political culture. He said, "Democracy is the government of, for, and by the people. If the woman is deprived of her right to participate with the man in work and in governing, it means that our democracy is a government of half the people by half the people. This is no democracy. As long as we deprive the woman of her right, we are not a democracy and we must find another name for our system of government."[99]

Along with political rights for women it was reforming personal status laws that most challenged patriarchalists. Arab women demanded reform of their various countries' personal status laws through an enlightened interpretation of the Islamic sharʿiah.[100] Egyptian lawyer Naʿimah al-Ayyubi laid out the framework. A minimum marriage age for girls should be fixed at sixteen. Women must have greater security as wives and mothers. Authorization from a judge should be required for a man to practice polygamy. Divorce must be practiced in conformity with Islamic requirements and must not be used as a weapon against women. Women separated from a husband by divorce or death should obtain custody of children of both sexes until adolescence; at that point a judge would determine which parent was better equipped to look after the child. Al-Ayyubi also demanded that women, like men, be allowed to retain their nationality upon marriage to a foreigner. The conference ratified all but the last suggestion.

Education was at the core of women's nationalism and feminism. In Egypt and throughout the Arab East Western missionary schools had been established in the nineteenth and early twentieth centuries. Later under colonial rule new state education systems were patterned on British and French models, and thus state schools became arenas for inculcating Western culture.[101] Qamar Qazun from Syria stressed the need for an educational system rooted in Arab culture.[102] She called for a standardized system of education among the Arab countries from kindergarten through university, which would enable students and teachers to move easily among the countries. Lebanese educator Zahiyah Dughan identified three educational systems prevailing in Arab countries: a reactionary indigenous system, a new nationalist program, and a Western system. She agreed with Qazun, saying, "We demand that education in every country must now have one character and this must be an Arab nationalist character."[103] Insisting that education be grounded in Arab culture Dughan raised complex questions: What is Arab culture? Who defines Arab culture? Arab women had been restrained and controlled in the name of a conservative patriarchal construction of indigenous culture. Dughan insisted that women must participate in defining and transmitting Arab culture. She was sensitive to the need for a different version of the past: one that legitimized women's present desires and their vision for the future. Women must retrieve their own histories; they must preserve them, interpret them, and pass them on. Echoing earlier efforts to produce women's biographical dictionaries Dughan suggested compiling an Arab women's encyclopedia. The Lebanese educator proposed that Arab colleges and universities teach the intellectual and literary heritage of Arab women and that chairs in Arab women's literature be created. She also called for a pan-Arab women's journal. Women expressed concern about the genderedness of the Arabic language, and the conference adopted a demand that feminine endings be omitted from words. This was submitted to the Academy of Arabic Language in Cairo and other learned societies in the various Arab countries. The proposal seems to have appeared outlandish at the time, but the problem of gender and linguistic structures was one that began to trouble feminists in Western countries in the 1970s.

Women's right to work was a serious conference issue. Iraqi ʿAfifah Ra'uf declared that "the economic freedom of the woman is the basis of her other freedoms." Iraqi Rose Khadduri demanded that the work needs and rights of the poor majority be met.[104] The conference asked governments to explore ways to provide work for needy women, calling for an expansion of technical education to improve agricultural and industrial production as a means of opening up new work. Concerned that women and children be protected in the work force, the conference called for labor legislation regulating their employment. It also demanded that work be open to women according to their qualifications and that their pay be equal to men's. Women should teach children of both sexes and be employed as administrators in the girls' schools. Egyptian Mufidah ʿAbd al-Rahman pointed out that there were qualified women available to fill positions in government.

The Arab feminists agreed on a broad social service program centered on the maternal and child health needs of the poor in both urban and rural areas. Mothers must have access to basic information on pre- and postnatal care, instruction in child care, and general information on nutrition and hygiene. Falak Diyab from Syria proposed creating agencies in Arab countries for the protection of mothers and children, accessing the expertise of women's social service associations as well as drawing upon that of employees—who were mainly men—in the Ministries of Health, Social Affairs, and Education. The conference pointed out that it was important for the state to deal with the needs of orphans and neglected children. Lebanese doctor Jamal Karam Harfush proposed that state and municipal authorities provide recreational clubs and public gardens for poor children.[105]

Feminists approached the problems of prostitution in the context of imperialism, morality, and social reform. The Egyptian Society for the Protection of the Mother and Child stressed that prostitution had increased with the heavy concentration of foreign troops in the region during the Second World War, and linked prostitution with imperialism. Feminists demanded the abolition of state-licensed prostitution and called upon states to institute programs for the rehabilitation of prostitutes. ʿAfifah Ra'uf reiterated the argument that expanded employment opportunities for women would alleviate the problem of prostitution.[106]

The agenda set out by the Arab Feminist Conference strongly resembled the program the EFU had been seeking to implement for the past two decades. To realize its goals for institutional and behavioral change, the Arab Feminist Conference established the Arab Feminist Union, a confederation composed of feminist unions from the several Arab countries. The AFU headquarters would be Cairo, and the Egyptian Feminist Union was given the central coordinating and administrative role. The officers of the AFU were elected from the EFU: Huda Shaʿrawi was nominated president, Hafizah al-Alfi treasurer, and Aminah al-Saʿid secretary. Al-Saʿid was also appointed editor of the AFU's journal *al-Mar'ah al-ʿArabiyah* (The Arab woman). Each of the other national feminist unions was represented by a vice president and a secretary: Zulaykhah al-Shihabi and Sadhij Nassar from the Palestinian Feminist Union; ʿAdilah Bayham ʿAbd al-Qadir and Fayzah al-Mu'ayyad al-ʿAzim from Syria; Rose Shahfa and Jamal Karam Harfush from Lebanon; Emily Bisharat and Luli Abu al-Huda from Trans-Jordan; and Nadhimah al-ʿAskari and Sirriyah al-Khujah from Iraq. Shaʿrawi as AFU president was entrusted with responsibility for the preparation of a draft constitution to be approved by the national feminist unions within six months. In October 1945, the ratified constitution of the General Arab Feminist Union (AFU), was officially published.

In Egypt, the conference passed very much as an ordinary event. The press treated it as a manifestation of changing times and social conditions in which women were given credit for playing a decisive role. *Al-Balagh* praised the women for "sharing the burden of the social renaissance."[107]

British officialdom was relieved by the absence of the strong anti-British tone that had predominated in the 1938 conference. The British foreign secretary was given to believe "that the ladies came out gratifyingly and very properly pro-British." The British ambassador in Cairo was closer to the mark, reporting to London that "even Madame Shaarawi the Egyptian feminist leader who has so long been bitterly anti-British had seen the wisdom of changing her tune and now appeared to be converted to pro-British sentiments," but adding, "I hazard the guess that even if true Madame Shaarawi's conversion is likely to be only skin deep."[108] The British foreign secretary also said: "I understand that some of the speakers at the conference did not confine themselves to the subject of Arab feminism but made outspoken comments on political questions which were contentious in the Middle East." This echoed the mind-set of Western feminists at the IAW conference at Copenhagen when Egyptian feminists' insistent focus on issues concerning social justice in Palestine was deemed "mere politics."[109]

While an imperialist mind-set polarized the world of women's international feminism, inside Arab countries (as in other countries of the world) there were tensions between women and men. It was not enough—and indeed not the point—for Arab men to support Arab women's efforts to construct an enhanced and more unified Arab world as "separate sisters." The women wanted to create a new civil society and political culture in which the two genders would be equally active.

The year after women created the Arab Feminist Union, the League of Arab States came into being (May 1945). At the outset the Arab League functioned essentially as a political alliance of independent Arab states to protect their interests vis-à-vis the outside world and to regulate relations among themselves. The Arab League maintained a conventional approach to internal social systems.[110] The Arab League, like the AFU, comprised six member countries. Palestine was a member of the Arab Feminist Union but not of the Arab League because the country lacked independent sovereign status. Saudi Arabia belonged to the Arab League but was not represented in the Arab Feminist Union.

In anticipation of the forthcoming foundation of the Arab League, the Arab Feminist Conference had passed a resolution of support. Three months later when the pact of the League of Arab States was signed, Huda Shaʿrawi, as AFU president, feted representatives of the Arab League at a reception attended by women and men active in their respective countries. Shaʿrawi applauded the creation of the Arab League but decried the absence of women in the delegations from the Arab countries that had participated in its formation and the lack of women in the permanent delegations. She told the men:

> You have widened the gap between yourselves and your women by deciding to build your new glory alone. We women wish you success in everything that will bring benefit to the Arab world and peace and prosperity to the world at large. We women must continue our struggle in the service of Arabism and humanity. Since both men and women are working toward one goal, it is inevitable that we shall meet one day, brought together in harmony by the necessity of circum-

> stances and events to work toward common goals. You will come to believe that it is imperative for the sexes to cooperate, and we shall enter a new era dominated by a genuinely cooperative spirit. Such an era will truly express the essence of the Arab League. The League whose pact you signed yesterday is but half a league, a league of half the Arab people. Our hope is that a league will be formed that comprises both sexes and all Arabic-speaking countries.[111]

The AFU president deplored the fact that the Arab nations lagged behind others, pointing out that women were being included in several delegations to the forthcoming San Francisco conference to create the United Nations.

Syrian prime minister Faris al-Khuri, attempting to placate the women, repeated a string of platitudes blatantly patriarchal in the mid-twentieth-century world that Arab feminists had helped to raise to new levels of gender awareness. Resorting to a conventional epithet al-Khuri called the woman the "ornament of man." He continued: "Happy is the man who finds a mother or a wife or a daughter to surround him with love, tenderness, sympathy, and attention."[112] The prime minister spoke of the men at the vanguard of the army, saying that no army can gain victory without the support of the rear guard. Women were the rear guard. It was a question of a division of labor; men had "given" roles and women had "given" roles. Egyptian prime minister Mahmud al-Nuqrashi stopped the flow, interjecting that the key word was "given." There was laughter and applause. Finance minister of Egypt Habib al-Masri added that he believed the Syrian prime minister had entered into battle with Huda Shaʿrawi wishing for the first time to be defeated. The prime minister diplomatically agreed.[113]

Arab Feminists and the IAW

In the aftermath of the Second World War international feminism was reordered. The IAW, which had managed to keep alive during the war, albeit minimally, resumed its congresses in 1946, two years after the Arab feminists had reconvened in Cairo. The war had scattered IAW board members, and some had not survived it, among them two Jewish board members exterminated by the Nazis. The organization recruited new members, including Tatiana Feodorova from the Soviet Women's Anti-Fascist Committee in Moscow. She initially agreed to be a board member but almost immediately stepped down to join the new Women's International Democratic Federation (WIDF). The creation of the WIDF in 1945 signaled a major split in the international feminist movement along the East-West axis of the Cold War. Women within the WIDF would weld gender struggle with class struggle in the context of a strong anti-imperialist campaign. IAW feminists, on the other hand, continued in the tradition of Western liberalism. The IAW still failed to confront imperialism and its negative implications for the democracy and feminist ideals the organization espoused.

The IAW held its first postwar congress in Interlaken in August 1946. It was a time for reconsolidating and moving ahead. The congress reaffirmed the IAW commitment to democracy and endorsed the new United Nations Charter. Huda Shaʿrawi headed the EFU delegation, which included Saiza Nabarawi, ʿAsmat Asim, and Munirah Harb. The Lebanese Arab Feminist Union sent the only other Arab delegation. The EFU announced the "greatest victory" since the last international meeting: the formation of the Arab Feminist Union, "a solid united block of women from all the countries of the Arab East," dedicated to working together for the "common ideal of justice, liberty, equality, and peace."[114] The Lebanese Arab Feminist Union explained: "Our aim in taking this step was to unify our efforts in the social and political arenas and to work hand in hand with the Arab League in safeguarding the political rights and interests of the Arab world in general. This important aspect of our work will not, however, make us less zealous in carrying on our efforts for gaining equal rights and [full] citizenship, and for propagating more international feeling and sympathy among womankind and mankind."[115] There were still hundreds of thousands of Arab women and men living under Western colonial domination, deprived of rights of national self-determination and the benefits of the democracy that the IAW upheld.

As delegates to the IAW from their national affiliates Egyptian and Lebanese feminists affirmed allegiance to the new Arab Feminist Union while also reaffirming their commitment to the IAW. At the time of the Arab Feminist Conference, Huda Shaʿrawi and IAW president Margery Corbet Ashby had exchanged telegrams pledging mutual support between the AFU and the IAW. In her closing speech to the Arab Feminist Conference Shaʿrawi had announced the IAW president's wish to serve as a link between Eastern and Western women. Kamala Devi Chattopadhyay from the All-India Women's Conference, communicated Eastern women's solidarity, telling Arab women: "Remember during your deliberations the struggle of India and her participation for the sake of the entire East."[116] IAW feminism now faced more forceful challenges from within by "Eastern feminisms."

In 1946 the most pressing concern for Egyptian and Lebanese women as Arabs was the fate of Palestine. The most contentious issues concerned Jewish immigration, on which IAW statements and resolutions were vague and contradictory. The congress unambiguously recognized the plight of European Jews. Under the rubric "Jewish Refugees in Concentration Camps," the congress expressed "its horror" at the murder of six million Jews by the Hitler regime and drew attention to the "hundreds of thousands" of Jewish refugees still detained, calling upon the UN to secure their immediate liberation.

Interlaken represented the end of an old era and the beginning of a new one in international feminism. There were now two competing international feminist camps: the IAW and the WIDF, old liberals and new radicals, dividing along lines of what would soon be called the Cold War. Within the IAW, though the basic orientation did not shift, there was a changing of the guard as the organization lost the founders and early leaders who had sustained the movement for nearly half a century. In 1946 Margery Corbett Ashby stepped down after twenty-three years as president of the IAW. Interlaken was to be Shaʿrawi's last IAW congress after a quarter of a century of affiliation with the international feminist organization. Shaʿrawi found the IAW unsatisfactory as an arena in which to deal with issues of justice and self-determination concerning Palestine. The following year her final public act as EFU president was a call to the ambassador of Greece asking his country to vote against the partition of Palestine. Two days later she died. Shaʿrawi ended her public militancy, as she had begun it, in a struggle for national liberation.

The EFU had helped widen the feminist circle. The agenda of pan-Arab feminism reflected and extended that of the twenty-year-old Egyptian feminist movement. Through the AFU feminists from other Arab countries hoped to strengthen feminist movements in their individual countries and to accelerate the gains, as well as to help consolidate Arab unity. At the same time they believed that the AFU as a collective would help further their cause in the international feminist arena. The history of the subsequent pan-Arab feminist movement, Arab national feminist movements, and the connections of both with international feminism has yet to be told. I would like to add a postscript on the Egyptian Feminist Union and the International Alliance of Women, and offer some observations about the Arab Feminist Union and Arab feminist movements.

Following the death of Huda Shaʿrawi Shaʿrawi's daughter, Bathna, became president, but as vice president Saiza Nabarawi provided the motive power. Shaʿrawi and Nabarawi had remained true to the feminist and nationalist cause, but the rank and file had grown increasingly exclusionary and complacent over the years. By the end of the 1940s, the EFU had lost its earlier feminist vigor. Nabarawi tried to revitalize the organization. In 1950 she formed the Lajnat al-Shabbat (Youth Committee), attracting a new breed of committed young women epitomized by Inji Aflatun, active in the student and workers movements—she was a founder of the League of University and Institutes Young Women—since the mid-1940s. Members of the Youth Committee sought out women workers in poor quarters of Cairo to politicize them as nationalists and feminists. Nabarawi simultaneously lent her energies to the Movement of the Friends of Peace, an anti-imperialist group opposing the continued presence of British troops on Egyptian soil. In 1952, when violence broke out in the Canal Zone, Nabarawi, Aflatun, and other women activists across the political spectrum—from Islamist Zaynab al-Ghazali to leftist Inji Aflatun—organized the Lajnat al-Nisa'iyah lil-Muqawamah al-Shaʿbiyah (Women's Committee for Popular Resistance) and went out in public demonstrations.

Within the IAW Nabarawi assumed Shaʿrawi's place on the executive board. At the IAW congress in Amsterdam in 1949 Nabarawi was elected a vice president. Nabarawi led the EFU delegation to the IAW congress in Naples in 1952 where there was a confrontation between her and Duriyah Shafiq, who had come as head of the Daughter of the Nile Union. This was Shafiq's attempt on behalf of that organization to usurp the place of the EFU; Shafiq had not attempted such a move during Shaʿrawi's lifetime. The EFU—in 1956 reconstituted as the Huda Shaʿrawi Association—continued as the Egyptian affiliate of the IAW. While the EFU remained in the IAW, Nabarawi would not. At the Naples congress Nabarawi defended African peoples against colonialism in her speech to the assembly while the representative from French Equatorial Africa took "a colonialist position."[117] Nabarawi could no longer operate within the IAW.

Equally this veteran feminist found it increasingly difficult to work with EFU members who for their part were eager for her to quit. The following year (1953), exactly thirty years after helping to found the EFU, Saiza Nabarawi left the feminist organization. She was virtually forced out by members who saw her as too far to the left; some labeled her a Communist. There were surely outside pressures imposed upon EFU women as well as internal differences that brought about her departure. Upon leaving the EFU Nabarawi was de facto out of the IAW, which saved her the bother of quitting. The same year she joined the WIDF as an individual member. From then until her death in 1985 Nabarawi did not cease to agitate against imperialism and racism, and for peace, the Palestine cause, and the needs of the poor as part of her feminist agenda.

The EFU itself in its original form only survived another three years. In the aftermath of the revolution of 1952 as Jamal ʿAbd al-Nasir consolidated power, the state forced the EFU to cease as a feminist organization in 1956. It changed its name to the Huda Shaʿrawi Association and devoted itself to social welfare activities. Indeed, the state stamped out all independent feminist activism. By 1959, Duriyah Shafiq was under house arrest for speaking out against Nasir, and Inji Aflatun was in prison for being a Communist. Saiza Nabarawi, then in her sixties, a strong anti-imperialist voice promoting nonalignment, was active outside Egypt within the framework of the WIDF. Three members of the EFU's Shaqiqat of the 1930s, Aminah al-Saʿid, Suhayr al-Qalamawi, and Hawwaʾ Idris, remained on the scene. Al-Saʿid helped serve the state's drive to mobilize women, but she also managed to keep alive certain feminist issues problematic for the state, mainly in the area of personal status reform. The state needed to appear progressive concerning personal status laws, but it did not suit the purposes of the patriarchal socialist state to tamper with this contentious code. Al-Saʿid was the only feminist who was able to retain a public voice as a feminist. Al-Qalamawi, after stepping down as chair of the Department of Arabic Literature at Cairo University, headed the state publishing association. She was not vocal on gender issues. Idris continued to operate the EFU-established Dar al-

Hadana, responding to the expanding needs of working women for child care that the socialist state failed to meet.

A decade after the consolidation of Arab feminism, independent feminist activism in Egypt ceased under state repression following the revolution of 1952. Independent feminist movements were also truncated in countries of the Arab East in the aftermath of independence, while in the case of Palestine the country itself disappeared with the creation of Israel in 1948.

The Arab Feminist Union was born at the end of an era in Egyptian feminism. The EFU and other Arab national feminist organizations heralded the AFU's comprehensive feminist agenda. There was optimism that a unified Arab feminist movement would hasten feminist achievements in countries of the Arab East in the new era of national independence. The reality would be different. In Egypt and many other Arab countries under highly controlling centralized state regimes there was no space for independent feminist movements—or indeed for independent movements of any kind. Neutralized as an independent body the AFU became quasi-official as a ready-made pan-Arab structure for states to appropriate for their own purposes. The AFU comprised national feminist unions that in turn comprised various women's organizations within given countries. With the consolidation of state systems women's associations were required to be registered with the state, often under Ministries of Social Affairs, which gave them annual stipends and monitored them. In order to attend meetings of the AFU abroad, delegates had to obtain exit and entry visas. In this way states controlled the circulation of women; states also required formal permission from a woman's father, husband, or nearest male "guardian" before issuing her a visa. Both Aminah al-Saʿid, who traveled on state business, and her sister Karimah al-Saʿid, who traveled abroad as deputy minister of education, recalled being required to obtain their husbands' permission to go abroad on official business.[118] States also decided which organization in the country would represent women; groups selected came to be the women's branches of states' political organizations.

At its inception al-Ittihad al-Nisaʾi al-ʿArabi al-ʿAmm called itself in English the General Arab Feminist Union. Later the official name in English became the General Arab Women's Union. What had been born out of independent feminist activism in the mid-1940s had come by the 1950s and 1960s to be harnessed by states to serve their purposes.

Still there was a regional structure in place. Women were accustomed to dealing with governments and states on various levels, as allies and adversaries, in advancing gender causes and, through these, national causes. As patriarchal forces have regrouped—whether as "state patriarchy," "societal patriarchy," or "family patriarchy"—so have feminist forces regrouped in Egypt, as elsewhere in the Arab world. Both at home and within this wider struggle the EFU's legacy has been enduring.

• N O T E S •

Introduction

1. See Deniz Kandiyoti, "Islam and Patriarchy," in *Women in Middle Eastern History*, ed. Nikki Keddie and Beth Baron (New Haven: Yale University Press, 1992), pp. 23–57, esp. p. 35.

2. On lower-class and peasant women in nineteenth-century Egypt see Judith Tucker, *Women in Nineteenth-Century Egypt* (Cambridge: Cambridge University Press, 1985).

3. The word *harim* comes from an Arabic root that denotes a sense of the inviolate, sacred, withheld, or forbidden. See *A Dictionary of Modern Written Arabic*, s.v. "harim." See also *The Encyclopedia of Islam*, s.v. "harim." On the institution of the harem in Turkey see Leslie Pierce, *The Imperial Harim: Women and Sovereignty in the Ottoman Empire* (New York: Oxford University Press, 1993); N. M. Penzer, *The Harem* (London: G Harrop, 1936); and Fanny Davis, *The Ottoman Lady, A Social History: 1718 to 1918* (Westport, Conn.: Greenwood Press, 1986). On life in a late nineteenth-century upper-class Egyptian harem see HS, *Harem Years: The Memoirs of an Egyptian Feminist*, trans., ed., and introd. Margot Badran (London: Virago Press, 1986; New York: The Feminist Press, 1987).

4. The Qur'an (33:53) simply admonishes women to cover their hair and body except for the hands and feet. It was only the wives of the Prophet Muhammad who were enjoined to cover their faces and to observe seclusion. English resident in Egypt Lucy Duff Gordon observed in the 1860s that Christians were more fastidious than Muslims in veiling; see her *Letters from Egypt, 1863–65* (London: Macmillan, 1865). The veiling and domestic seclusion of women were prevalent in the Byzantine lands that Islam conquered, including Egypt. See Germaine Tillion, *Le harem et les cousines* (Paris: Editions du Seuil, 1966).

5. On this ideology, which pervades Muslim societies in general, see Fatima Mernissi, *Beyond the Veil: Male-Female Dynamics in a Modern Muslim Society*, rev. ed. (Bloomington: Indiana University Press, 1987), pp. 27–64, and Fatna A. Sabah, *Women in the Muslim Unconscious*, trans. Mary Jo Lakeland (New York: Pergamon Press, 1984).

6. Edward W. Lane, *The Manners and Customs of the Modern Egyptians* (London: J. M. Dent & Co., [1908] 1871), discusses middle- and upper-class housing and harem practices.

7. See ibid., 1:198–99: Lane noticed early in the nineteenth century that many girls married at twelve or thirteen while some "remarkably precocious girls are married at the age of ten." See also William Nassau Senior, *Conversations and Journals in Egypt and Malta* (London: S. Low, Marston, Searle & Rivington, 1882), 2:169–70, for observations of married women alleged to be nine and eleven years old. Eugénie Le Brun, who lived in Cairo as the wife of an upper-class Egyptian in the late nineteenth and early twentieth centuries, said that this pattern held for her day, although the median age may have risen slightly; see her *Harem et les musulmanes*, 2d ed. (Paris: Librairie Félix Juven, 1902), published under the pseudonym Niyya Salima. HS married at the age of thirteen in 1892.

8. According to German doctor Carl B. Klunzinger, in *Upper Egypt: Its People and Its Products* (London: Blackie and Son, 1878), an Egyptian doctor had asserted in a medical treatise that the optimal marriage age for females was sixteen, for males between eighteen and twenty (p. 195).

9. See E. L. Butcher, *Things Seen in Egypt* (Paris: Librairie Vuibert, 1913), pp. 48–49, who adds that the patriarch issued an encyclical in 1895 saying that young people intending to marry should become acquainted before marriage and that there should be mutual consent to the marriage (p. 51).

10. Elizabeth Cooper, *The Women of Egypt* (London: F. A. Stokes, 1914), reported that middle-class women were betrothed between ten and fifteen years of age and that thirteen to fifteen years was the average marriage age; the upper class tended to wait longer. She noted that the recent betrothal of the khedive's daughter at eighteen had set an example among the elites (pp. 201–2).

11. See Gabriel Baer, "Slavery and Its Abolition," in *Studies in the Social History of Modern Egypt* (Chicago: University of Chicago Press, 1969), pp. 161–90, and E. R. Toledano, "Slave Dealers, Women, Pregnancy, and Abortion: The Story of a Circassian Slave-Girl in Mid-Nineteenth-Century Cairo," *Slavery and Abolition* 2 (May 1981): 53–69.

12. There are accounts of elite harem culture in Egypt by women who experienced this as family members and by women who gained access to harems in various capacities. These accounts provided by women of different positions and circumstances reveal changes over time. Such sources include: Emine Foat Tugay, *Three Centuries: Family Chronicles of Turkey and Egypt* (London: Oxford University Press, 1963); Sophia Lane Poole, *The Englishwoman in Egypt: Letters from Cairo Written during a Residence There in 1842, 3, 4* (London: C. Knight & Co., 1844), and *Letters during 1845–6*, Second Series, 3 vols. (London: 1844–46); Ellen Chennells, *Recollections of an Egyptian Princess by Her English Governess*, 2 vols. (Edinburgh and London: W. Blackwood and Sons, 1893); Niyya Salima (Eugénie Le Brun), *Harem et les musulmanes*; Out El Kouloub's novels, *Harem* (Paris: Gallimard, 1937) and *Ramza* (Paris: Gallimard, 1958), also translated from French into English and introduced by Nayra Atiya, Out El Kouloub, *Ramza* (Syracuse: Syracuse University Press, 1994); and Djavidan Hanum, *Harem Life* (New York: Dial Press, 1931). HS's memoirs are discussed in chapter 1.

13. On Egypt under Muhammad ʿAli see Afaf Lutfy al-Sayyid Marsot, *Egypt in the Reign of Muhammad Ali* (Cambridge: Cambridge University Press, 1984).

14. HS's father, Sultan Pasha, was given a private railway car called Tayr Khayr to use on his inspection tours in Upper Egypt the year the line was put in from Cairo.

15. Tugay, *Three Centuries*, describes Cemile on p. 5. For descriptions of women promenading in carriages in Cairo see Chennells, *Recollections of an Egyptian Princess*, 2:279; Chennells noted that carriage blinds had begun to be raised. See also Edward W. Lane, *Cairo Fifty Years Ago*, ed. S. Lane-Poole (London: J. Murray, 1896), p. 142, who observed that on their outings on the Shubra Road women were starting to wear the white gauze yashmak fashionable in Constantinople.

16. On the development of Cairo during the nineteenth century see Janet Abu Lughod, *Cairo: 1001 Years of the City Victorious* (Princeton: Princeton University Press, 1971); Marcel Clerget, *Le Caire: étude de geographie urbaine et d'histoire economique* (Cairo: Imprimerie E. & R. Schindler, 1934); and André Raymond, *Le Caire* (Paris: Fayard, 1993). For a look at the new Ismaʿiliyah by the Egyptian satirist Muhammad al-Muwaylihi see Roger Allen, *A Period of Time* (Reading, England:

Garnet Press, 1992), pp. 145–46, a translation and study of the third edition of Muwaylihi's *Hadith ʿIsa ibn Hisham* (Cairo: Matbaʿat al-Saʿadat, 1923), pp. 368–69. The work was first published serially in the journal *Misbah al-Sharq* beginning in 1898. The first edition of the book was published in Cairo in 1907. A sense of the culture, and internalized values, relating to living in the "old" and "new" cities, as inherited and played out by men and women in the early decades of the twentieth century may be gleaned from Najib Mahfuz's *Cairo Trilogy*: I. *Palace Walk (Bayn al-Qasrayn)*, trans. William Maynard Hutchins and Olive E. Kenny (New York: Doubleday, 1990); II. *Palace of Desire (Qasr al-Shawq)*, trans. William Maynard Hutchins, Lorne M. Kenny, and Olive E. Kenny (New York: Doubleday, 1991); and III. *Sugar Street (al-Sukkariyah)*, trans. William Maynard Hutchins and Angèle Botros Samaan (New York: Doubleday, 1992). The Nobel Prize–winning author, born in 1911 in the medieval city, moved as a young man with his family to the then fashionable bourgeois quarter ʿAbbasiyah.

17. HS mentions going to the opera house in the 1890s with her friend ʿAdilah Nabarawi (*Harem Years*, p. 63). While women in Egypt could not appear socially with men, in Holland women could not appear at a place like the opera without the company of a man; Dutch feminist and physician Aletta Jacobs (b. 1854) achieved a first when she went to the Amsterdam Theater unaccompanied by a man at the end of the nineteenth century.

18. The quotation comes from Allen, *A Period of Time*, pp. 368–69. On the subject of women as theater-goers in nineteenth-century Egypt see Allen's "Drama and Audience: The Case of Arabic Theatre," *Theater Three*, no. 6 (Spring 1989): 7–20, and Ronald Storrs, *Orientations* (London: I. Nicholson & Watson, 1945), p. 27.

19. On Nazli's salon see Roger Allen, "Writings of Members of the Nazli Circle," *Journal of the American Research Center in Egypt* 8 (1969–1970): 79–84, and Mary Flounders Arnett, "Qasim Amin and the Beginnings of the Feminist Movement in Egypt" (Ph.D. diss., Dropsie College, Philadelphia, 1965); Arnett mentions that Nazli contributed some articles to the press, both under her name and anonymously (p. 73).

20. For extensive studies on the subject see Ijlal Hanim Mahmud Khalifah, "al-Sihafah al-Nisa'iyah fi Misr min 1919 ila 1939" (M.A. thesis, Cairo University, 1966), and Beth Ann Baron, "The Rise of a New Literary Culture: The Women's Press of Egypt, 1892–1919" (Ph.D. diss., University of California, Los Angeles, 1988).

21. See Edmund Swinglehurst, *Cook's Tours, the Story of Popular Travel* (New York: Blandford Press, 1982), and James Buzard, *The Beaten Track: European Tourism, Literature and the Ways to "Culture": 1800–1918* (Oxford: Clarendon Press, 1993), especially sections called "Imperial Tourists" and "Forced Connections" in chap. 5.

22. See Billie Melman, *Women's Orients: English Women and the Middle East, 1718–1918, Sexuality, Religion and Work* (Ann Arbor: University of Michigan Press, 1992), on travel and women's literary production.

23. There is very little written by women in Egypt about their interactions with Western women who came to their country during the nineteenth century; two examples are: HS, *Harem Years*, and Tugay, *Three Centuries*. In contrast to the scant records left by women in Egypt there is a voluminous literature by Western women on their stays in Egypt in the nineteenth century, which included visits to harems. A

few examples are Poole, *The Englishwoman in Egypt*; Duff Gordon, *Letters from Egypt* and *Last Letters from Egypt to Which Are Added Letters from the Cape* (London: Macmillan, 1875); Harriet Martineau, *Eastern Life: Present and Past* (London: Moxon, 1848); and Florence Nightingale, *Letters from Egypt* (London, 1854). For extracts of European women's impressions of harem visits to Egypt (and other Middle Eastern countries) and an analysis of this literature see Judy Mabro, *Veiled Half-Truths: Western Travellers' Perceptions of Middle Eastern Women* (London and New York: I. B. Tauris, 1991); see also Melman, *Women's Orients*, and idem, "Desexualizing the Orient: The Harem in English Travel Writing by Women, 1763–1914," *Mediterranean Historical Review* 4 (1984): 301–39. See also Mervat Hatem, "Through Each Other's Eyes: Egyptian, Levantine-Egyptian, and European Women's Images of Themselves and of Each Other (1862–1920)," *Women's Studies International Forum* 12, no. 2 (1989): 183–98.

24. Irene Fenoglio-Abd El Aal, who has studied the spread of French among the elites in Egypt from the mid-nineteenth century, speaks of the rise of French in upper-class harems; see her *Défense et illustration de l'Egyptienne: aux débuts d'une expression féminine* (Cairo: Centre d'Etudes et de Documentation Economique, Juridique et Social [CEDEJ], 1988), p. 44.

25. See Butcher, *Things Seen in Egypt*, pp. 63–64, and Cooper, *The Women of Egypt*, pp. 130–31.

26. HS records briefly her experience and impressions of trips to Europe around 1909 and in 1914 in *Harem Years*, pp. 84–85 and 101–6.

27. William Holt Yates, *The Modern History and Condition of Egypt: Its Climate, Diseases, and Capabilities* (London: Smith, Elder, 1843), 1:68 and 2:220.

28. I was able to view collections belonging to HI, SN, Bahigah Rashid, and ʿAtiyah Saqqaf, as well as to Prince Hasan Hasan, who has an extensive collection of photographs of women of the royal family. Some photographs of nineteenth- and early-twentieth-century women in Egypt were published in *Harem Years*. For more published photographs see Sarah Graham-Brown, *Images of Women* (New York: Columbia University Press, 1992).

29. HS, *Harem Years*, p. 68.

30. Ibid., p. 52.

31. The most comprehensive source on women's education in Egypt is Zaynab Muhammad Farid, "Tatawwur Taʿlim al-Banat fi Misr min al-Ihtilal al-Baritani, 1882 hatta al-An" (Ph.D. diss., Kulliyat al-Banat, ʿAyn Shams University, Cairo, May 1966). A standard work on general education in Egypt is Ahmad ʿIzzat ʿAbd al-Karim, *Tarikh al-Taʿlim fi Misr* (Cairo: Dar al-Kutub al-Misriyah, 1945). See also *L'éducation de la jeune fille musulmane en Egypt* (Cairo, 1928) by Sophie Babazogli, a schoolteacher of Syrian origin.

32. On the hakimahs see Laverne Kuhnke, "The 'Doctoress' on a Donkey: Women Health Officers in Nineteenth Century Egypt," *Clio Medica* 9, no. 3 (1974): 193–205, and idem, "Women Health Officers," in *Lives at Risk: Public Health in Nineteenth Century Egypt* (Berkeley and Los Angeles: University of California Press, 1990), chap. 7, pp. 122–33; and Amira Sonbol, *The Creation of a Medical Profession* (Syracuse, N.Y.: Syracuse University Press, 1991).

33. For a general account of education in nineteenth-century Egypt see J. Heyworth-Dunne, *An Introduction to the History of Education in Modern Egypt* (London: Luzac & Co., 1939), and ʿAbd al-Karim, *Tarikh al-Taʿlim fi Misr*. For the most comprehensive treatment of female education in Egypt from the late nineteenth century see Farid, "Tatawwur Taʿlim al-Banat fi Misr min al-Ihtilal al-Baritani."

34. See Marsot, *Egypt in the Reign of Muhammad Ali*, p. 94.

35. Al-Tahtawi cited examples of educated women from the family of the Prophet Muhammad, as well as hadith. He also said it was wrong to withhold education from females on the grounds that they were weak and vulnerable and that literacy would lead to moral downfall. On the contrary, he argued that as a result of female education the level of society would be raised and marriages would be more harmonious.

36. The tutor of Khedive Isma'il's youngest daughter, Zaynab, has left an informative account; see Chennells, *Recollections of an Egyptian Princess*.

37. This included state-sponsored study at schools abroad. Cooper was told that the results of the early missions were very positive (*The Women of Egypt*, pp. 166–67).

38. Cooper said that in one of the women teachers' training schools she visited in 1913 there had been 138 applications for 13 vacancies (ibid., p. 165).

39. See Christine Sproul, "The American College for Girls, Cairo, Egypt: Its History and Influence on Egyptian Women: A Study of Selected Graduates" (Ph.D. diss., University of Utah, 1982), p. 63; her source was *American Missionary College for Girls, 1910–1911* (Cairo: Boehne and Anderer, 1911).

40. See Daniel Crecelius, "The Course of Secularization in Modern Egypt," in *Religion and Political Modernization*, ed. Donald Eugene Smith (New Haven: Yale University Press, 1994), pp. 67–94.

41. Cooper remarked on the abundance of private foreign schools for girls: "One cannot pass along the streets of Cairo without being amazed at the number of schools of all kinds, French, English, Italian, that are established for girls" (*The Women of Egypt*, p. 169). She claims that about 30 percent of the Egyptians in the missionary schools were Muslim (p. 165).

42. See J.N.D. Anderson, "Law Reform in Egypt," in *Political and Social Change in Modern Egypt: 1850–1950*, ed. P. M. Holt (London: Oxford University Press, 1968), pp. 209–30, and Noel J. Coulson and Doreen Hinchcliffe, "Women and Law Reform in Contemporary Egypt," in *Women in the Muslim World*, ed. Lois Beck and Nikki Keddie (Cambridge: Harvard University Press, 1978), pp. 37–51.

43. On Muhammad 'Abduh and Islamic modernism see Albert Hourani, *Arabic Thought in the Liberal Age* (Cambridge: Cambridge University Press, 1983), and Charles C. Adams, *Islam and Modernism in Egypt* (New York: Russell and Russell, 1933). Muhammad 'Imarah has published 'Abduh's collected works in *al-'Amal al-Kamilah li-Muhammad 'Abduh* (Cairo, 1972; Beirut: al-Mu'assasah al-Arabiyah lil-Dirasat wa-al-Nashr, 1974), which includes essays on issues concerning women.

44. On British colonial occupation and resistance to it see Robert Tignor, *Modernization and British Colonial Rule in Egypt, 1882–1914* (Princeton: Princeton University Press, 1966), and Jacques Berque, *Egypt: Imperialism and Revolution*, trans. Jean Stewart (London: Faber and Faber, 1972). Timothy Mitchell, *Colonising Egypt* (Cambridge: Cambridge University Press, 1989), analyzes the complex discursive dimensions of the colonizing project.

45. On the 'Urabi revolution see Juan Ricardo Cole, *Colonialism and Revolution in the Middle East: Social and Cultural Origins of Egypt's 'Urabi Movement* (Princeton: Princeton University Press, 1993), and Alexander Schölch, *Egypt for the Egyptians!* (London: Ithaca Press for the Middle East Center, St. Antony's College, Oxford, 1981).

46. See E.R.J. Owen, *Cotton and the Egyptian Economy, 1820–1914* (Oxford: Oxford University Press, 1969), and Charles Issawi, *Egypt: An Economic and Social Analysis* (Oxford: Oxford University Press, 1947).

47. Again, see Farid, "Tatawwur Taʿlim al-Banat fi Misr min al-Ihtilal al-Baritani," and ʿAbd al-Karim, *Tarikh al-Taʿlim fi Misr*. See also Amir Boktor, *School and Society in the Valley of the Nile* (Cairo: Elias' Modern Press, 1936), and Abu al-Futouh Ahmad Radwan, *Old and New Forces in Egyptian Society* (New York: Bureau of Publication, Teachers College, Columbia University, 1951).

48. Quotation taken from Afaf Lutfi al-Sayyid Marsot, *Egypt and Cromer: A Study in Anglo-Egyptian Relations* (London: John Murray, 1968), p. 143 (emphasis added).

49. The earl of Cromer, *Modern Egypt* (New York: Macmillan, 1908); quotation from 2:146.

50. For analyses of male nationalist thought and experience see Berque, *Egypt*; and J. M. Ahmed, *The Intellectual Origins of Egyptian Nationalism* (London: Oxford University Press, 1960); and Israel Gershoni and James P. Jankowski, *Egypt, Islam, and the Arabs: The Search for Egyptian Nationhood, 1900–1930* (New York: Oxford University Press, 1986). I address the gendered nature of nationalism in "Dual Liberation: Feminism and Nationalism in Egypt, 1870s–1925," *Feminist Issues* 8, no. 1 (Spring 1988): 15–34.

51. Juan Ricardo Cole, "Feminism, Class, and Islam in Turn-of-the-Century Egypt," *International Journal of Middle East Studies* 13 (1981): 397–407, and Thomas Philipp, "Feminism and Nationalist Politics in Egypt," in Beck and Keddie, *Women in the Muslim World*, pp. 285–308, have written on class, ethnicity, gender, and religion in the culture and politics of men's nationalism; however, the lines are more blurred than these studies suggest.

52. See Margot Badran and Miriam Cooke, eds., *Opening the Gates: A Century of Arab Feminist Writing* (London: Virago; Bloomington: Indiana University Press, 1990); Byron D. Cannon, "Nineteenth-Century Writing on Women and Society: The Interim Role of the Masonic Press in Cairo—*Al-Lata'if*, 1885–1895," *International Journal of Middle East Studies* 17, no. 4 (1985): 463–84; and Nadia Farag, "*Al-Muqtataf*, 1876–1900: A Study of the Influence of Victorian Thought on Modern Arabic Thought" (D.Phil. thesis, Oxford University, 1969).

53. Volume 1 was published by Matbaʿat Jaridat Misr in Alexandria. Begun in 1873, it was dedicated to Tcheshme Hanim, a wife of Khedive Ismaʿil who founded the Siyufiyah School the same year. Al-Nahhas died before she could complete her project. Zaynab Fawwaz wrote about her in *al-Durr al-Manthur fi Tabaqat Rabbat al-Khudur* (Cairo: Matbaʿat al-Kubra al-Amiriyah, 1312 H.), pp. 515–16, relating that al-Nahhas attended English schools in Syria where she studied Arabic, English, history, geography, and music.

54. For a short biographical note see "Zainab Fawwaz," in Badran and Cooke, *Opening the Gates*, p. 220. Marilyn Booth, who is studying women's biographies in late nineteenth and early-twentieth-century Egypt, analyzed Fawwaz's work in "Biography and Feminist Rhetoric in Early Twentieth Century Egypt: Mayy Ziyada's Studies of Three Women's Lives," *Journal of Women's History* 3, no. 2 (1991): 38–64.

55. Salama Musa, *The Education of Salama Musa*, trans. from the Arabic L. O. Schuman (Leiden: E. J. Brill, 1961), p. 7.

56. Warda al-Yaziji (1838–1924) published a *diwan* called *Hadiqat Rose* (The rose garden) in 1867. She moved to Egypt in 1899.

57. For biographies of al-Taymuriyah see Mayy Ziyadah, *ʿA'ishah Taymur: Shaʿirat al-Taliʿah* (ʿA'ishah Taymur: A vanguard poet) (Cairo: Matbaʿat al-Muq-

tataf, 1926), and Antoine Assaf, "Aichat Asmat Taimur," *E*, Aug.–Sept. 1926, pp. 198–202; for an analysis of Ziyadah's biography see Booth, "Biography and Feminist Rhetoric." A biographical note on al-Taymuriyah appears in Badran and Cooke, *Opening the Gates*, p. 125.

58. Translation by Marilyn Booth in Badran and Cooke, *Opening the Gates*, p. 128.

59. The need for homebound woman to connect with the outer world is conveyed in the autobiography of Palestinian poet Fadwa Tuqan, born in 1917 in Nablus: "I went on feeling completely alone, knowing that there was no one who felt my misery except myself. It was my being that was being stretched taut, torn apart; the heart that was constricted and crushed was my heart; the ordeal that was reaching a crisis was my ordeal. There was no other being to share all this with me, no other person. . . . My existence inside the harem wing of the house made me shrink and recoil, so that I was bottled up inside myself. . . . The poetry I published in the papers was the one social activity I could use as a bridge to link me with others, as I crouched within those ancient walls." *A Mountainous Journey: An Autobiography*, trans. Olive Kenny (London: The Women's Press, 1990), pp. 111–12.

60. Translation by Marilyn Booth in Badran and Cooke, *Opening the Gates*: "Family Reform Comes Only through the Education of Girls," pp. 129 and 132.

61. Kawrani attended the Chicago Fair in 1892, remaining in the United States until 1895 writing articles and giving talks. See Baron, "The Rise of a New Literary Culture," p. 270.

62. Translation by Marilyn Booth in Badran and Cooke, *Opening the Gates*: "Fair and Equal Treatment," pp. 223–24.

63. The book was republished in 1910. Booth speaks of Fawwaz in "Imprinting Lives: Biography, Subjectivity, and Feminism in the Egyptian Women's Press, 1892–1935" (unpublished paper).

64. In her memoirs HS speaks about Le Brun and her salon; see *Harem Years*, pp. 76–82. See also SN, "Vers la réalisation d'un souhait," *E*, Mar. 1926, pp. 38–39. Hungarian Mary Torok, born in Philadelphia, married Khedive ʿAbbas Hilmi (r. 1892–1914). Known thereafter as Djavidan Hanim, she too converted to Islam and discovered the restrictions placed on women that had nothing to do with religion. See her *Harem Life*, p. 162.

65. I first came across the impressive collection of women's journals in 1968 in Dar al-Kutub when the National Library was still housed in Port Saʿid Street. For a listing of the holdings see Mahmud Ismaʿil ʿAbd Allah, *Fihris al-Dawriyat al-ʿArabiyah allati Taqtiniha al-Dar* (Cairo, 1963). On the first seventeen years of the women's press in Arabic see Baron, "The Rise of a New Literary Culture."

66. Translation by Beth Baron, in Badran and Cooke, *Opening the Gates*: "The Dawn of the Arabic Women's Press," p. 218.

67. Ibid.

68. Arnett, in "Qasim Amin and the Beginnings of the Feminist Movement in Egypt," p. 78, quotes *al-Muqtataf*, June 1928, p. 687, as saying that Princess Nazli Fazil was the "first Near Eastern woman to cast aside her veil." This seems to refer to her uncovering her face in the presence of the men who attended her salon, not to her going about unveiled outside. On early unveiling see Beth Baron, "Unveiling in Early Twentieth Century Egypt: Practical and Symbolic Considerations," *Middle Eastern Studies* 24, no. 3 (1989): 370–86.

69. Booth in "Biography and Feminist Rhetoric," relates how second-generation

feminist Mayy Ziyadah celebrated al-Taymuriyah's feminism. The EFU's *L'Egyptienne* extolled al-Taymuriyah and other founding mothers of Egyptian feminism, signaling a sense of continuity and paying homage to their Egyptian feminist *turath* or heritage.

70. It was published by Matbaʿat al-Ta'lif in Cairo. *Al-Ahram* announced the appearance of this "original" book and summarized its thesis.

71. Murqus Fahmi, *al-Mar'ah fi al-Sharq* (Cairo, 1894), act 1, pp. 24–25.

72. Ibid., act 3, pp. 14–15.

73. Ibid., pp. 7 and 8.

74. On Nazli Fazil and her salon see Arnett, "Qasim Amin and the Beginnings of the Feminist Movement in Egypt," pp. 70–86. Husayn Rushdi—the husband of Eugénie Le Brun, who conducted the first women's salon—frequented Princess Nazli's salon. Saʿd Zaghlul, a middle-class lawyer, who became minister of education and later head of the Wafd-led nationalist movement, also attended the salon; there his marriage to Safiyah Mustafa Fahmi, of Turco-Circassian background, was said to have been decided.

75. At the time Amin was taking credit along with blame for his *new* ideas, Talʿat Harb (a lawyer, social conservative, and later leading founder of the first national bank in Egypt) attacked Amin as a plagiarist of ideas—moreover, ideas originating with a Christian (Murqus) and beyond the pale of Islam; he also attacked Murqus himself. In *Fasl al-Khitab fi al-Mar'ah wa-al-Hijab* (The last word on the woman and veiling) (Cairo, 1901) Harb wrote, "Some call Qasim Amin the Luther of the East, but the person who deserves the title is Murqus Fahmi, who published a book in the form of a play in 1894—at the time Qasim Amin was of our opinion defending the morals of the Muslim woman and her veil and defending Muslim civilization—in which he stated everything that [later] appeared in *The Liberation of the Woman* and *The New Woman*."

76. See Arnett, "Qasim Amin and the Beginnings of the Feminist Movement in Egypt," p. 105.

77. Leila Ahmed, *Women and Gender in Islam* (New Haven: Yale University Press, 1992), chap. 8, pp. 144–68, argues that in labeling Egypt and Egyptian women backward and in calling for unveiling, Amin colluded with colonialists.

78. *al-Mar'ah fi al-Sharq* received only two reviews, both unfavorable; one in *al-Lamadur*, edited by a Muslim, and the other in a paper edited by a Copt. Fahmi says in the memoirs he started but never completed that "they treated me like a young harebrain out to undermine the Muslim and Christian religions." Fahmi's daughter, Andrée Morcos Fahmy, kindly gave me access to the memoirs. When *Tahrir al-Mar'ah* appeared, it received at least thirty angry attacks including that of Muhammad Farid Wajdi (a conservative follower of ʿAbduh and co-editor with ʿAbbas al-ʿAqqad of *al Dustur*), "A Look at Woman's Emancipation," *al-Mu'ayyad*, Sept. 20 and Oct. 1, 1899. This essay was expanded into the book *al-Mar'ah al-Muslimah* (The Muslim woman) (Cairo, 1912), which speaks of a separate women's sphere and of the differences between men and women. Another attack came from and Talʿat Harb, in *Tarbiyat al-Mar'ah wa-al-Hijab* (Cairo, 1899; 2d ed., 1905). *Al-Mar'ah al-Jadidah* was also widely attacked; see, for example, Harb, *Fasl al-Khitab*. In *Women and Gender in Islam* Ahmed implicates Amin in the colonialist project to undermine Egyptian culture and society.

79. See Karen Offen, "Defining Feminism: A Comparative Historical Approach,"

Signs 14, no. 1 (1988): 119–57, and idem, "On the French Origin of the Words *Feminism* and *Feminist*," *Feminist Issues* 8, no. 1 (1988): 45–51.

80. See Nancy Cott, *The Grounding of Modern Feminism* (New Haven: Yale University Press, 1987), p. 13.

81. On the cultural project and effects of British colonialism in Egypt see Mitchell, *Colonising Egypt.*

Chapter One
Two Lives in Changing Worlds

1. Theoretical issues raised are informed by my reading of Joan W. Scott, "Experience," in *Feminists Theorize the Political*, ed. Judith Butler and Joan W. Scott (New York and London: Routledge, 1992), pp. 22–40.

2. On the life of Sultan Pasha, including his rise through the provincial administration, his political life in Cairo, his role in the ʿUrabi revolt, and his connection with the British occupation of Egypt, see HS, *Harem Years*, pp. 27–32; ʿAbd al-ʿAziz Rifaʿi, *Sultan Pasha amama al-Tarikh* (Cairo, n.d.); Ahmad Taymur, *Tarajim Aʿyan al-Qarn al-Thalith ʿAshr wa-Awwal al-Rabiʿ ʿAshr* (Cairo: Multazim Tabʿi wa-al Nashr Abd al-Hamid Ahmad Hanafi, [1940]); Qallini Fahmi, *Souvenirs du Khedive Ismail au Khedive Abbas II* (Cairo: Editions de la Patrie, [193?]), pp. 23–25, 89–91; idem, *Mudhakkirat* (Cairo: al-Shinnawi, 1943); Zaki Muhammad Mujahid, *al-ʿAlam al-Sharqiyah fi al-Miʾah al-Rabiʿah ʿAsharah al-Hijriyah al-ʿUrabiyah* (Cairo, 1946), pp. 590–91; Schölch, *Egypt for the Egyptians!*; Robert Hunter, *Egypt under the Khedives, 1805–1879: From Household Government to Modern Bureaucracy* (Pittsburgh: University of Pittsburgh Press, 1984); idem, "The Making of a Notable Politician: Muhammad Sultan Pasha (1825–1884)," *International Journal of Middle East Studies*, no. 15 (1983): 537–44; and Cole, *Colonialism and Revolution.*

3. See HS, *Harem Years*, Appendix, "Sultan Pasha and the Urabi Revolution (1881–2)," pp. 148–52, for her comments on the memoirs of ʿUrabi and for testimony from Qallini Fahmi, her father's secretary.

4. HS, *Harem Years*, pp. 25–26.

5. In 1967 HS's cousin HI loaned me a handwritten copy of the memoirs HS dictated in Arabic to her secretary, ʿAbd al-Hamid Fahmi Mursi, which I translated, edited, and introduced, and published under the title, *Harem Years*. The book was also published in Dutch as *Haremjaren: De memoires van de Egyptische feministe* (Baarn: Anthos, 1987). The manuscript copy contained HS's narrative of her life up to her involvement in the national independence struggle from 1919 to 1922. Her account of the period of the nationalist movement, told in a chronicler's voice, is fragmented. HS gave an account of her father's life and role in the ʿUrabi revolt and subsequent British occupation with the intention of clearing his name; in this she sought the help of her father's secretary Qallini Fahmi. The title given to the English translation, *Harem Years*, was intended to signify the period when HS lived within the conventions of harem culture, before she defied its dictates by unveiling at the moment when she began to lead the feminist movement; the subtitle, *The Memoirs of an Egyptian Feminist*, as well as privileging the identity that HS claimed and for which she has earned a place in her nation's history, was intended to subvert stereotypes that the term "harem" conjures up in the West. Another copy of the memoirs that was in Mursi's possession contains HS's recollections into the middle 1930s as

well as materials written by others. Mursi took his copy of the memoirs to Dar al-Hilal, where the writings were ordered, edited, and published with an introduction by Aminah al-Saᶜid as *Mudhakkirat Ra'idat al-ᶜArabiyah al-Hadithah Huda Shaᶜrawi* (Memoirs of the modern Arab feminist leader Huda Shaᶜrawi) (Cairo: Dar al-Hilal, 1981).

6. HS, *Harem Years*, pp. 23–32.
7. Ibid., 34–35.
8. Ibid., p. 36.
9. Ibid., pp. 39–40.
10. Ibid., p. 42.
11. Ibid., p. 52.
12. Ibid., p. 54.
13. Ibid., p. 55.
14. Ibid., p. 52.
15. Ibid., p. 58.
16. Ibid.
17. Ibid., pp. 58–59
18. Ibid., p. 60.
19. Ibid., pp. 63–64.
20. HS's letters from Helwan and Alexandria to Mme Richard in Cairo between 1892 and 1919 attest to the affectionate ties and HS's concern for Richard's welfare. Letters from the Private Papers of HI.
21. HS, *Harem Years*, p. 78.
22. After Le Brun's countryman the duc d'Harcourt published his book *L'Egypte et les Egyptiens* (Paris: Plon, 1893) blaming Islam for social practices oppressive to women, Le Brun, like Qasim Amin, published a defense of the life of Egyptian women of the upper classes called *Harem et les musulmanes*. *Les répudiées* was published in Paris in 1908.
23. HS, *Harem Years*, p. 78.
24. Ibid., p. 82.
25. Most of the following biographical information comes from NM's "Dhikrayati" (My memoirs), hereafter referred to as *D*, published serially in her *Majallat al-Fatah*, from May 5, 1938, to August 2, 1942. Other sources include Khayr al-Din al-Zirkili, ed., *al-Aᶜlam Qamus Tarajim li-Ashhar al-Rijal wa-al-Nisa' min al-ᶜArab wa Mustaᶜrabin wa Mustashriqin*, a biographical dictionary pubished in Cairo between 1954 and 1959, 2d ed., s.v. "Nabawiyah Musa"; *Nisa' Fawq al-Qima* (Cairo, n.d.), pp. 18–24; Safinaz Kazim, "al-Ra'idah Nabawiyah Musa wa-Inᶜash Dhakirat al-Ummah" (The pioneer Nabawiyah Musa and the revival of the nation's memory), *Majallat al-Hilal*, Jan. 1984.
26. *D*, "My Childhood," 2d ser., no. 1.
27. "Al-Muhadarat al-Nisa'iyah fi Jamᶜiat al-Misriyah" (Women's lectures in the Egyptian University) was published on April 16, 1912, and reprinted in *al-Ahram, Shuhud al-ᶜAsr 1876–1986* (Cairo, 1986).
28. For a comparison between this work and *D* see my "Expressing Feminism and Nationalism in Autobiography: The Memoirs of an Egyptian Educator," in *De/Colonizing the Subject: The Politics of Gender in Women's Autobiography*, ed. Sidonie Smith and Julia Watson (Minneapolis: University of Minnesota Press, 1992), pp. 270–96.
29. The memoirs, appearing in monthly installments, included 91 in the first se-

ries and 61 in the second series, a total of 152 episodes, many repetitive. NM loosely adhered to chronology, making an attempt in the second series to start at the beginning of her life, but she soon abandoned attempts at historical sequence.

30. See my "Expressing Feminism and Nationalism," pp. 278–83.

31. *D*, "My Childhood," 2d ser., no. 1.

32. Ibid.

33. Partha Chatterjee, in *The Nation and Its Fragments: Colonial and Postcolonial Histories* (Princeton: Princeton University Press, 1993), p. 140, discusses nineteenth- and early-twentieth-century Indian women autobiographers. Noting the phenomenon of women grasping the chance to learn through opportunities provided their brothers, he writes, "But the sense of acquiring a skill [reading] that was really meant for somebody else stayed with these early generations of educated women." One wonders to what extent this may have been true of NM.

34. *D*, "My Childhood," 2d ser., no. 1.

35. Ibid., "Some Illogical Customs to Which People Cling," 2d ser., no. 86.

36. Ibid., "How I Entered the Saniyah School," 2d ser., no. 3.

37. Ibid.

38. Ibid.

39. Ibid.

40. Ibid.

41. Musa, *The Education of Salama Musa*, p. 27, says that girls were made to wear the veil beginning at the age of about ten to twelve years. He also notes that the *shaykhs* who taught Arabic would be fired if they abandoned their traditional turban and kaftan. He describes the generally "prison-like" atmosphere of the state school he attended.

42. From an article by Florence Davson in the *Egyptian Daily Post*, written around 1912, quoted by Cooper, *The Women of Egypt*, p. 177.

43. *D*, "Sitting for the Baccalaureate Examination," 2d ser., no. 16.

44. Ibid.

45. Ibid.

46. Ibid.

47. Ibid.

48. Historian Anne-Marie Köppeli, pointing to Western experience, notes that schoolteachers' organizations advanced the first demands for "equal pay for equal work." See her "Feminist Scenes," in *A History of Women in the West: Emerging from Revolution to World War*, ed. Geneviève Fraisse and Michelle Perrot (Cambridge: Harvard University Press, Belknap Press, 1993), p. 497.

49. *D*, "The Result of My Success in the Baccalaureate Examination and My View of Marriage," 2d ser., no. 18.

50. See ibid., where she says, "Since my childhood I believed that marriage was dirt (*qadharah*) that I could not bear. Some might say that it wasn't my choice not to marry but that I could not find a husband. That is not true. Many men used to hunt for women because of their money. I was interested in saving money and still am." See also "My Opinion of Marriage," 1st ser., no. 22.

51. Ibid., "My Opinion of Marriage," 1st ser., no. 22.

52. In her 1920 treatise on women and work and thereafter, until the late 1930s, NM took a positive position on marriage in promoting education and work for women. On her personal and ideological views of marriage see my "Expressing Feminism and Nationalism," pp. 281–82. In the early twentieth century there was a

celibacy "movement" in Britain "until the animal nature of men was transformed," termed by Lucy Re-Bartlett the "silent strike," which also included married women. See Sheila Jeffreys, "'Free from All Uninvited Touch of Man': Women's Campaigns around Sexuality, 1880–1914," *Women's Studies International Forum* 5, no. 6 (1982): 641–44. There was never a celibacy movement in Egypt, nor could such a movement have been tolerated. However, besides NM, some other women important in the feminist movement quietly refrained from entering into marriage.

53. Boktor wrote in *School and Society in the Valley of the Nile*: "Women from the poorest homes were attracted to the teaching profession. . . . Only in the last ten years [mid-1920s to mid-1930s] have more Egyptian girls come into the profession" (p. 184); "Work for a girl of a middle class family or even of a lower social status, is an act of indecency" (p. 75). However, while teaching may have been broadly considered with disdain, when a woman like NM succeeded, she acquired a standing in society she would not have had as an ordinary middle-class housewife. Bahithat al-Badiyah, from the professional upper middle class, did not lose status when she became a teacher.

Chapter Two
Claiming Public Space

1. Cooper, *The Women of Egypt*, p. 433, reported in 1914 that the literacy rate of Muslim women was 2 per 1,000 and for Copts 16 per 1,000; the rates for men were 78 and 188 per 1,000, respectively.

2. Circumstances in Algeria were, however, far different. Frantz Fanon was the first to elaborate upon the use of the veil and other elements of tradition as a mode of defense Algerians employed against the colonizer; see his *A Dying Colonialism* (New York: Monthly Review Press, 1965). For a recent analysis see Marnia Lazreg, "Gender and Politics in Algeria: Unraveling the Religious Paradigm," *Signs* 15, no. 4 (1990): 755–80.

3. See Cooper, *The Women of Egypt*, pp. 183–86 and 129, and Baron, "Unveiling in Early Twentieth Century Egypt."

4. Jonathan P. Berkey, "Women and Islamic Education," in Keddie and Baron, *Women in Middle Eastern History*, pp. 143–57, says that no fewer than five schools were established by women in the Mamluk period (p. 144). Ahmad ʿAbd al-Raziq, *La femme au temps des mamlouks en Egypte* (Cairo: Institut français d'archéologie oriental du Caire, 1973), pp. 19–27, lists women from powerful Cairene families from the thirteenth to the fifteenth century making various kinds of endowments. On different kinds of bequests by individual women see Lenore Fernandez, *The Evolution of a Sufi Institution in Mamluke Egypt: The Khanqa* (Berlin: Claus Schwarz, 1988), and her M.A. thesis, "The Madrasa of Umm al-Sultan Shaʿban" (American University, Cairo, 1976). On women as managers of property, including endowments, see Carl F. Petry, "Class Solidarity versus Gender Gain: Women as Custodians of Property in Later Medieval Egypt," in Keddie and Baron, *Women in Middle Eastern History*, pp. 122–42.

5. NM, "Egypt's Need for Women Doctors, Teachers, Dressmakers, and Other Professions," in *al-Marʾah wa-al-ʿAmal* (hereafter cited as *The Woman and Work*) (Alexandria: al-Matbaʿah al-Qawmi, 1920).

6. HS, *Harem Years*, pp. 46–48.

7. Interview with HI, Feb. 3, 1972, Cairo.

8. Other societies included Jamʿiyat al-Tawfiq al-Qibtiyah, Jamʿiyat al-Iman, Jamʿiyat al-Mahabbah, and Jamʿiyat Thamarat al-Tawfiq. Among the Copts, women's benevolent associations had been attached to local churches since the middle of the nineteenth century. Interview with Munirah ʿAbd al-Malak Saʿd, a teacher active in Coptic philanthropies, Sept. 17, 1975, Cairo.

9. See for example Thomas Philipp, *The Syrians in Egypt, 1725–1975* (Stuttgart: Franz Steiner Verlag Wiesbaden GMBH, 1985), and Gudrun Kramer, *The Jews in Modern Egypt, 1914–1952* (London: I. B. Tauris, 1989).

10. On its foundation and subsequent work see *Oeuvre Mohamed Aly el Kebir* (Cairo, 1950), an official publication, and Afaf Lutfy al-Sayyid Marsot, "The Revolutionary Gentlewomen in Egypt," in Beck and Keddie, *Women in the Muslim World*, pp. 261–76.

11. See HS, *Harem Years*, pp. 94–98.

12. Cooper, visiting Egypt in the early 1910s, noted a recent shift from women's religiously based charity to organized philanthropy. See *The Women of Egypt*, p. 330.

13. Naguib Mahfouz, *The History of Medical Education in Egypt* (Cairo: Government Press; London, 1935), pp. 84–85.

14. From Jacobs, "De Staatsopleiding van verpleegsters in Egypte" (State training of nurses in Egypt), *Nosokomos*, no. 12 (Apr. 10, 1912): 247–50, quoted by Harriet Feinberg in "A Pioneering Dutch Feminist Views Egypt: Aletta Jacobs' Travel Letters," *Feminist Issues* 10, no. 2 (1990): 65–78; quotation on p. 71. See also Aletta Jacobs, *Reisbrieven unit Afrika en Azie* (Travel letters from Asia and Africa) (Almelo: W. Hilarius Wzn., 1913), pp. 265–69. Interested in the spread of medical care Jacobs used to give free medical examinations in a poor quarter of Amsterdam.

15. Mahfouz, *The History of Medical Education in Egypt*, pp. 84–85.

16. See Majd al-Din Hifni Nasif, ed., *Athar Bahithat al-Badiyah Malak Hifni Nasif: 1886–1918* (Literary works of Bahithat al-Badiyah Malak Hifni Nasif) (Cairo: Wizarat al-Thaqafah wa-al-Irshad al-Qawmi, 1962).

17. Djavidan Hanim, *Harem Life*, pp. 194–206.

18. *Nidaʾ Jamʿiyat al-Marʾah al-Jadidah* (Cairo, n.d.).

19. Marsot makes this point in "The Revolutionary Gentlewomen."

20. It is useful to compare the Egyptian women with their European sisters: Marion Kaplan, in "From the Chevra to Feminism: Jewish Women's Social Work in Imperial Germany" (Paper presented to the Colloquium on Women in Religion and Society at the Annenberg Institute, May 1991), argued that through their involvement in religious charitable and social service organizations middle-class Jewish women evolved new roles for themselves in the public arena in late-nineteenth- and early-twentieth-century Germany. She further claims, "For many women, it was the religious social welfare context from which their feminist perceptions and movement grew." She notes that "Jewish women's voluntarism was part of a more general secularization: the transformation of religious values into social welfare." See also idem, *Making of the Jewish Middle Class: Women, Family, and Identity in Imperial Germany* (New York: Oxford University Press, 1991), chap. 7, pp. 192–227. This is similar to the turn-of-the-century Egyptian experience. But while these Jewish women's organizations were sectarian, the Egyptian examples were nonsectarian; the former allowed their German members, as Jews, to retain and strengthen communal bonds, while the latter enabled Egyptians to transcend communal barriers.

21. This was expressed in a talk delivered by Marguerite Clément in Cairo in 1914 incorporating HS's reflections. Interview with HI, Cairo.

22. Baron, "The Rise of a New Literary Culture," pp. 72–79, discusses early women's associations. In "Stepping Out," in *A History of Women in the West: Emerging Feminism from Revolution to World War*, ed. Geneviève Fraisse and Michelle Perrot (Cambridge: Harvard University Press, Belknap Press, 1993), speaking of nineteenth-century Frenchwomen, Michelle Perrot writes, "Philanthropy provided . . . substantial experience that altered women's perceptions of the world, their sense of themselves, and to a certain extent, their public role" (p. 451).

23. See Fatma Rashid, "al-Mar'ah wa-Huququha fi al-Islam," *Tarqiyat al-Mar'ah* 1, no. 10 (1908): 147.

24. This kind of conservative Islamic reformism, grounded in an essentializing construct of gender, would be articulated again by Labibah Ahmad and her journal, *al-Nahdah al-Nisa'iyah* (The feminine renaissance, 1922–1938), and would become more rigorously Islamist with Zaynab al-Ghazali's Jamʿiyat al-Mar'ah al-Muslimah (Society of the Muslim Woman, est. 1935), known as the Muslim Sisters from 1948.

25. HS, *Harem Years*, p. 93

26. See *D*, "The University Old and New," 1st ser., no. 78.

27. Ibid. After NM was turned down by the university, she managed to gain admittance as an external student in the College of Law, then under the jurisdiction of the Ministry of Justice. But when she was ready to sit for the examination, the Ministry of Education, which had authority over her as an employee, obstructed her efforts.

28. A. Couvreur, *Conférences faites aux dames Egyptiennes* (Paris: Peyriller, 1910).

29. See NM, "Women's Lectures in the Egyptian University."

30. Sarruf had attended the World Women's Conference in Europe in 1899 and reported on its program for social, economic, and political rights for women in *al-Muqtataf*, Sept. 1899; see "Mu'tamar Nisa'i al-ʿAmm" (The all women's conference), pp. 675–77.

31. After Bahithat al-Badiyah's death, Mayy Ziyadah wrote on her life and work in a nine-part series in *al-Muqtataf* (from Mar. 1919 to Mar. 1920), later published as a book. See Booth, "Biography and Feminist Rhetoric." A commemorative collection called *Dhikra Bahithat al-Badiyah* was published in Cairo in 1920.

32. The ambiguity of *nisa'iyah*, which can be translated into English either as "feminist" or as "women's" has been discussed. Because of its feminist content, I translate *al-Nisa'iyat* as "Feminist Pieces."

33. See Donald Reid, *Cairo University and the Making of Modern Egypt* (Cambridge: Cambridge University Press, 1990), pp. 53–65. On a comparative note, Swiss universities in the same period allowed foreign women to matriculate but not Swiss women. This information comes from Amy Hackett, who has studied the feminist movement in Germany.

34. Cooper, *The Women of Egypt*, p. 239, speaks of the proliferation of women's societies before 1914.

35. "Kalimat al-Sayyidah al-Jalilah Huda Hanim Shaʿrawi," *M*, Feb. 15, 1937, p. 13.

36. See HS, *Harem Years*, pp. 98–100.

37. "Quel peut et doit être le rôle de la femme égyptienne dans l'activité sociale et nationale?" in Association Intellectuelle des Dames Egyptiennes, *Conférences*

données au Caire chez Madame Ali Pacha Charaoui et à l'Université égyptienne par Mlle Clément (Cairo, 1914), pp. 1–16.

38. The major biography of Ziyadah is Salma H. al-Kuzbari, *Mayy Ziyadah: Ma'sat al-Nubu'* (Beirut: Mu'assasat Nawfal, 1978). On Ziyadah's feminism see Marilyn Booth, "Mayy Ziyada and the Feminist Perspective in Egypt, 1908–1931" (B.A. thesis, Harvard University, 1978), and "Biography and Feminist Rhetoric."

39. Alexandra Avierino had opened a literary salon in Alexandria early in the century, but it was not of the order of Ziyadah's.

40. See Nupur Chaudhuri and Margaret Strobel, eds. *Western Women and Imperialism* (Bloomington: Indiana University Press, 1992).

41. *D*, "My Adherence to the Purity of the Reputation of Education and How It Destroyed My Future," 1st ser., no. 2. "When we left the train at the station in Fayyum I was overtaken by the reception I witnessed for the governor. The roads were blocked. People were prevented from walking in the streets and the way was cleared for the governor, something I had not seen the equal of in Cairo. When we arrived at the governorate building, the governor was received with a military greeting, something I had never known before. I was frightened by it."

42. Ibid.

43. Ibid., "Replacing Men with Women in Public Employment and Its Bad Impact on My Weak Self," 2d ser., no. 7.

44. Ibid.

45. Ibid.

46. Ibid., "Moral Reform of the Mansura School: My Fears after Being Given Full Authority," 2d ser., no 34.

Chapter Three
Thinking Gender

1. For listings of the women's journals see Mahmud Isma'il 'Abd Allah, *Fihris al-Dawriyat al-'Arabiyah allati Taqtiniha al-Dar* (Listing of the periodicals in the National Library) (Cairo, 1936), 2:701–3; Baron, "The Rise of a New Literary Culture," Appendix 1, "Arabic Women's Journals: Egypt, 1892–1919," pp. 340–43; and Fenoglio-Abd El Aal, *Défense et illustration*, pp. 18–19.

2. Alexandra Avierino's *Le lotus* (1901–1902) in French was the short-lived exception that proved the rule. Her Arabic-language journal *Anis al-Jalis* (Woman's companion) ran from 1899 to 1904.

3. Journals with a secular voice included Labibah Hashim's *Fatat al-Sharq* (The woman of the East, 1906–1939), Malakah Sa'd's *al-Jins al-Latif* (The fair sex, 1908–1925), and Balsam 'Abd al-Malak's *al-Mar'ah al-Misriyah* (The Egyptian woman, 1920–1939). The editor of the first was a Syrian Christian; the latter two women were Egyptian Copts. Magazines with a conservative Islamic tone, all founded and edited by Egyptians, included Jamilah Hafiz's *al-Rihanah* (Basil, 1907–1908), Fatma Rashid's *Tarqiyat al-Mar'ah* (The progress of the woman, 1908–1909), Sarah al-Mihiyah's *Fatat al-Nil* (The young woman of the Nile, 1913–1915), and Labibah Ahmad's *al-Nahdah al-Nisa'iyah* (The women's awakening/renaissance, 1922–1938).

4. I have noted the conservative Islamic and feminist forms of expression in journalism in Egypt from the early 1920s through the 1940s in the preface to Fenoglio-Abd El Aal, *Défense et illustration*, pp. 6–12.

5. Exceptions to this trend included feminists. Malak Hifni Nasif assumed the pseudonym Bahithat al-Badiyah. NM wrote articles in the mainstream press under the pseudonym Damir Hayy fi Jism Raqiq (Living Conscience in a Delicate [also connoting "fettered"] Body) because the Ministry of Education forbade teachers and other employees to publish in the press. Her articles under this name appeared in *al-Muʿayyad* and *al-Ahram*. However, she published her book *The Woman and Work* in her own name while employed by the colonial Ministry of Education.

6. Wajdi's *al-Mar'ah al-Muslimah* was translated into Persian in 1958 by Mufid Husayn Malja'i Khalkhali and published in Tabriz by Kitabfurushi-yi Bani Hashimi (1337 H.)

7. Among the advice books written by teachers was Zaynab Mursi's *al-Ayat al-Bayyinat fi Tarbiyat al-Banat* (The clear verses on the education of girls) (Cairo: Matbaʿat Kararah, 1912).

8. Philipp, *The Syrians in Egypt*, p. xii.

9. Cooper, *The Women of Egypt*, p. 187, observed that "all the schools, the missionary and training schools, make a speciality of household economy."

10. Cooper in the early 1910s observed "many papers, novels and books of every kind printed in Arabic . . . when education for the woman had become such a fetish in Egypt, these popular educators are found in every home." She remarked that if mothers could not read, and "few of the women of the older day can read," then the daughters and granddaughters read to them (*The Women of Egypt*, p. 241). Cooper also shows another side: "Teachers tell me that one of the real battles that has to be fought and conquered is the intense conceit of the girl student. It cannot be wondered at when one considers that she takes the varied information she learns within the schoolroom, her knowledge of the sciences, of the world, and books to a home where perhaps she is the only member of the family who can read the evening paper" (p. 167). Schoolteacher Zaynab Mursi in her advice book, *al-Ayat al-Bayyinat firbiyat al-Banat*, counsels newly educated girls to respect their elders.

11. There was an imperial counterpart: women, feminists and others, inside imperialist countries argued that wives and mothers were pillars of empire and as such served imperial interests. Antoinette Burton, for example, writes, "British feminists of the period [late nineteenth and early twentieth centuries] manipulated acceptable cultural notions of woman-as-savior partly in order to guarantee a role for themselves in the imperial enterprise." See her "The Feminist Quest for Identity: British Imperial Suffragism and 'Global Sisterhood,' 1900–1915," *Journal of Women's History* 3, no. 2 (1991): 46–81; the quotation is taken from p. 69. Also see Helen Callaway, *Gender, Culture and Empire* (Houndmills, Basingstoke, Hampshire: Macmillan Press in association with St. Antony's College, Oxford, 1987), esp. "Her Husband's Silent Partner," pp. 42–46, concerning British colonial wives in Nigeria.

12. See Baron, "The Rise of a New Literary Culture," pp. 186–87.

13. Discussions of women's family roles in the early-twentieth-century women's press, according to Baron, "sought to reform the family, and at the same time, enhance the authority of wife and mother in the home." She does not see this as antifeminist—"To the contrary, generating domestic literature and feeding a domestic ideal was part of a strategy to empower women within the accepted perimeters of the home without seriously challenging the boundaries of that home"—but she acknowledges that "middle-class women were empowered and had their power limited in a single stroke." The subject of paid work outside the home was largely avoided,

she contends, because it was "threatening to their [i.e., that of the women writers in the female press] ideal of domesticity" (ibid., p. 200).

14. See Booth, "Biography and Feminist Rhetoric."

15. Article in *Jaridat al-Nil* (1892), translated as "Fair and Equal Treatment," by Marilyn Booth in Badran and Cooke, *Opening the Gates*, pp. 223–24.

16. Al-Yaziji, who was publishing poetry in Lebanon in the 1860s, immigrated to Egypt in 1899.

17. ʿA'ishah al-Taymuriyah, *Hilyat al-Tiraz* (Cairo: al-Matbaʿat al-Amirah al-Sharafiyah, 1909), p. xxx. The book was first published in 1885.

18. Women in early-twentieth-century England also challenged the prevailing notion of the woman as a purely sexual being. See, for example, Christabel Pankhurst, *Plain Facts about a Great Evil (The Great Scourge and How to End It)* (London: The Women's Social and Political Union, 1913); Cicely Hamilton, *Marriage as a Trade* (London: Chapman Hall, 1909; Virago, 1981); and Jeffreys, " 'Free from All Uninvited Touch of Man.' " I am not suggesting that Egyptian feminists were aware of this debate in England but rather that similar issues were being addressed elsewhere around the same time. While some English feminists attacked the idea of the "omnisexual" woman, they accepted the notion (common in Western societies) that men had the stronger sex drive and that this must be restrained. Popular notions of sexuality in Egypt and other Arab and Islamic societies contended exactly the opposite, that it was women who possessed enormous sexual drives.

19. On this and the discussion to follow see my chapter "From Consciousness to Activism: Feminist Politics in Early Twentieth Century Egypt," in *Problems of the Middle East in Historical Perspective*, ed. John Spagnolo (London: Ithaca Press, 1992), pp. 27–48.

20. NM, "The Difference between the Man and the Woman and Their Capacities for Work," in *The Woman and Work*, pp. 21–36, translated by A. Badran and M. Badran in Badran and Cooke, *Opening the Gates*, pp. 257–69.

21. Ibid.

22. Ibid. Yet, while stressing the similarity of the sexes, she also claimed that women were more compassionate than men—an essentializing strand in her social constructionist argument, for she did not imply that this trait was produced by particular experience, such as maternal experience. Departing from conventional logic, she concluded, in an interesting argument, that because women were more compassionate they were more rational than men.

23. Ibid.

24. Ibid.

25. Bahithat al-Badiyah, "Muhadarah fi Nadi Hizb al-Ummah" (A lecture in the club of the Umma Party), in *al-Nisa'iyat* (Cairo: Matbaʿat al-Jaridah Press, 1909), pp. 95–100, translated by A. Badran and M. Badran, in Badran and Cooke, *Opening the Gates*, pp. 227–39.

26. Bahithat al-Badiyah, "al-Mar'ah wa-al-Mujtamaʿ" (The woman and society), in Nasif, *Athar*, pp. 130–35.

27. NM, "The Difference between the Man and the Woman and Their Capacities for Work" in *The Woman and Work*, pp. 21–36.

28. See Mernissi, *Beyond the Veil*.

29. Bahithat al-Badiyah, "al-Mar'ah wa-al-Hijab," in Nasif, *Athar*, pp. 275–79.

30. Bahithat al-Badiyah, "Ili al-Anisah Mayy," in Nasif, *Athar*, p. 320.

31. See Qasim Amin, *al-Kalimat* (Aphorisms), translated by Arnett, in "Qasim Amin and the Beginnings of the Feminist Movement in Egypt," p. 21.

32. NM, *The Woman and Work*, pp. 3–5.

33. American Ruth Woodsmall was told that in Cairo in 1929 when the first Muslim woman drove a car she wore a hat so she would be taken for a Christian. See *Moslem Women Enter a New World* (New York: Round Table Press, 1936), p. 81.

34. *D*, "My Unveiling," 2d ser., no. 15.

35. Ibid.

36. Ibid.

37. The IWSA had in part also grown out of the International Council of Women, created in 1888 as the first international women's organization. On the evolution of international women's organizations including the IAW see Leila J. Rupp, "Conflict in the International Women's Movement, 1888–1950" (Paper presented at the Berkshire Conference of Women Historians, Rutgers University, 1990), and Rebecca L. Sherrick, "Towards Universal Sisterhood," *Women's Studies International Forum* 5–6 (1982): 655–62.

38. On Catt see Jacqueline Van Voris, *Carrie Chapman Catt: A Public Life* (New York: Feminist Press, 1987); Robert Booth Fowler, *Carrie Catt, Feminist Politician* (Boston: Northeastern University Press, 1986); and Mary Gray Peck, *Carrie Chapman Catt: A Biography* (New York: H. W. Wilson Company, 1944). On Catt's brand of feminism and suffragism in the American and international contexts see Mineke Bosch and Annemarie Kloosterman, eds., *Politics and Friendship: Letters from the International Woman Suffrage Alliance, 1902–1942* (Columbus: Ohio State University Press, 1990), chap. 1, pp. 1–6, and chap. 4.

39. On Jacobs see her memoirs, *Herinneringen van Aletta Jacobs* (Amsterdam: Socialistische Utigeuerij Nijmegen, 1924), p. 286, and for a biographical profile see Bosch and Kloosterman, *Politics and Friendship*, pp. 9–12.

40. Jacobs recalls her visit in her memoirs, see her *Herinneringen van Aletta Jacobs*, p. 286. See also Feinberg, "A Pioneering Dutch Feminist Views Egypt." For Catt's impressions during her visit see "Diaries of Carrie Chapman Catt," held by the Library of Congress, Washington, D.C., entries for Nov. and Dec. 1911.

41. Indeed, Cooper dedicated her book, *The Women of Egypt*, to Bahithat al-Badiyah.

42. Feinberg, "A Pioneering Dutch Feminist Views Egypt," pp. 69 and 76n.11. The third woman on the delegation, SN, was a young schoolgirl at the time.

43. For an analysis of IWSA international feminism, British feminisms, and Anglo-American feminist perceptions of "oriental" feminists and women, see Burton, "The Feminist Quest for Identity." See Bosch and Kloosterman, *Politics and Friendship*, chap. 7, "Crisis within the IWSA," pp. 219–24, on the failure to acknowledge differences *within* the IWSA "camp." Bosch speaks specifically about the failure to acknowledge the Jewish identity of those among them who were Jews.

44. See Burton, "The Feminist Quest for Identity," on the imperial nature of this thinking and the self-assigned feminist task of taking on a white woman's burden.

45. Catt's speech quoted in Arnold Whittick, *Woman into Citizen* (Santa Barbara, Calif.: ABC-Clio, 1979), p. 55.

46. Burton, "The Feminist Quest for Identity."

47. Ibid.

48. Feinberg, "A Pioneering Dutch Feminist Views Egypt." If Catt and Jacobs ("too eager" to enlist Egyptian women in a suffragist campaign) were "too blind" to

the colonialism, so was Elizabeth Cooper, visiting Egypt not long afterwards; she did not see that Egyptian women could not engage in a suffrage campaign until they first won the sovereignty of their country toward which their feminist nationalism and nationalist feminism was directed. Cooper condescendingly wrote, "A noted suffragette leader visited Cairo and tried to interest its women in 'Votes for Women,' but her arguments fell on deaf ears, as the Egyptian woman can hardly as yet conceive of a state of affairs where ladies would *care to take an active part in the work of the outside world* [emphasis added], coming in contact with men in a public manner." It is amazing that Cooper could write this after having moved around Cairo under the guidance of Bahithat al-Badiyah, who introduced her to women's societal activities. Cooper, however, pointed to the reality of a gender-segregated (middle- and upper-class) public (*The Women of Egypt*, p. 239).

49. It had been used only once before in print, by Alexandre Dumas *fils* in 1872. See Offen, "On the French Origin of the Words *Feminism* and *Feminist*."

50. On Auclert and later French women's approaches to Algerian women see Marnia Lazreg, "Feminism and Difference: The Perils of Writing as a Woman on Women in Algeria," in *Conflicts in Feminism*, ed. Marianne Hirsch and Evelyn Fox Keller (New York and London: Routledge, 1990).

51. See Whittick, *Woman into Citizen*, p. 141.

52. *Report of the Sixth Congress of the International Woman Suffrage Alliance Held in Budapest from 11 to 15 May 1913*, p. 3, and Whittick, *Woman into Citizen*, pp. 55–59. See also a letter from Catt to the *American Women's Journal* published in June 1912. In this letter Catt says that Egyptian women were even refusing to get married. Since NM was making a point of refusing to marry around this time, it might well be that Catt did meet her and also that she was overgeneralizing from NM's experience. Burton, "The Feminist Quest for Identity," pp. 62–63, mentions Catt's letter.

53. See Melman, *Women's Orients*. The reactions of both sides were, however, mixed. Djavidan Hanim in *Harem Life* said that the Eastern woman "felt herself superior to any western woman" (p. 98). This confirms Harriet Martineau's suspicion that the Eastern woman felt pity for the apparently unprotected condition of the Western woman. See Harriet Martineau, *Eastern Life: Present and Past*, new ed. (London: E. Moxon, 1875). Both drew from their Egyptian experiences.

54. Hatem, "Through Each Other's Eyes," stresses the antagonism.

55. HS, "Dhikra Bahithat al-Badiyah," *M*, Nov. 1, 1937, p. 20.

Chapter Four
Egypt for Which Egyptians?

1. I have addressed Egyptian women's feminism and nationalism in "Dual Liberation" and in "Expressing Feminism and Nationalism." There is a growing literature on the intersections between feminism and nationalism. Deniz Kandiyoti, *Women, Islam and the State* (London: Macmillan; Philadelphia: Temple University Press, 1991), looks at such intersections in some Muslim countries of the Middle East and South Asia; specifically on Egypt see my "Competing Agenda: Feminists, Islam, and the State in Nineteenth and Twentieth Century Egypt" in the same volume, pp. 201–36. Kumari Jayawardena surveys the connection of anti-imperialist and anticolonialist national movements with feminism in *Feminism and Nationalism in the Third World* (London: Zed, 1986). On feminism and nationalism in European contexts see

Richard Evans, *The Feminists: Women's Emancipation Movements in Europe, America and Australasia 1840–1920* (London: Croom Helm, 1977), especially the chapter "Moderates and Radicals," pp. 144–88, which examines connections between nationalist and feminist movements in small countries under foreign domination such as Norway (under the Swedish Crown) and Finland (under imperial Russia) and countries of the Austro-Hungarian Empire. On Ukrainian feminism and nationalism see Martha Bohachevsky-Chomiak, *Feminists despite Themselves: Women in Ukrainian Community Life, 1884–1939* (Edmonton: Canadian Institute of Ukrainian Studies, University of Alberta, 1988). A recent article exploring the Czech experience is Katherine David, "Czech Feminists and Nationalism in the Late Habsburg Monarchy: 'The First in Austria,'" *Journal of Women's History* 3, no. 2 (1991): 26–45.

2. Manmohan Kaur, *Women in India's Freedom Struggle* (New Delhi: Sterling Publishers, 1985) p. 102.

3. Letter from Inshirah Shawqi to the congress of the National Party, in 1910, Private Papers of SN. See also "Watha'iq Mahadir al-Hizb al-Watani al-Misri ʿAmm 1910," *al-Taliʿah*, no. 4 (Apr. 1969): 149–61. Inshirah Shawqi was the aunt of the feminist Fatma Niʿmat Rashid who served briefly in 1937 as editor of the EFU's *M*.

4. HSM, p. 140. The page numbers refer to the typescript made from the original copy of HS's memoirs borrowed from HI.

5. See Ibrahim ʿAbduh and Duriyah Shafiq, *al-Mar'ah al-Misriyah min al-Faraʿinah ila al-Yawm* (The Egyptian woman from pharaonic times to today) (Cairo: Matbaʿat Misr, 1955), pp. 119–20.

6. Ibid., p. 139. For HS on the 1919 revolution, see HSM, pp. 139–42. See also HI, "Ana wa-al-Sharq" (Unpublished MS, Cairo, 1975), pt. 2, pp. 334–42, 354–56. For the most detailed account of the women's demonstration, see ʿAbd al-Rahman al-Rafiʿi, *Thawrat Sanat 1919* (Cairo, 1946), 1:137–40. For interviews conducted half a century later with women who participated in the events of 1919, see Naʿilah ʿAllubah, Muhammad Rifʿat, et al., "Thawrat 1919 Rafʿat al-Hijab wa-al-Yashmak ʿan Wajh al-Mar'ah al-Misriyah," *al-Musawwar*, Mar. 7, 1969. See also Ahmad Shafiq, *Hawliyat Misr al-Siyasiyah* (Cairo: Matbaʿat Shafiq Basha, 1926), 1: 260–61. For British accounts, see Thomas Russell, *Egyptian Service* (London: Murray, 1949), pp. 46–47; and letters from Thomas Russell to his father (est. date, Apr. 1, 1919) and from Dorothea Russell to her father (Apr. 3, 1919), in Russell Papers, Middle East Centre, St. Antony's College, Oxford. See Cheetham to Curzon, 22 Mar. 1919, FO 371 54267/3715, no. 125, for an account of the events of Mar. 8–22, 1919. See also Valentine Chirol, *The Egyptian Problem* (London: Macmillan and Co., 1920), pp. 167–68; Marius Deeb, "The 1919 Popular Uprising: A Genesis of Nationalism," *Canadian Review of Studies in Nationalism* 1, no. 1 (1973): 105–19.

7. al-Rafiʿi, *Thawrah*, 1:137–40.

8. HS, *Harem Years*, pp. 112–14.

9. Letter from Thomas Russell to his father (est. date, Apr. 1, 1919), Russell Papers, Middle East Centre, Saint Antony's College, Oxford.

10. Russell, *Egyptian Service*, p. 208.

11. HSM, p. 141.

12. Fatma al-Yusif, *Dhikrayat Ruz al-Yusif* (Cairo: Mu'assasat Ruz al-Yusif, 1953), p. 54; see also chap. 10.

13. Shafiq, *al-Mar'ah al-Misriyah*, p. 125.

14. List of names in HI Private Papers.

15. ʿAllubah et al., "Thawrat 1919," and interview with Hilanah Sidarus, Dec. 5, 1975, Cairo, and Sept. 10, 1990, Cairo.

16. See Marsot, "The Revolutionary Gentlewomen," p. 271.

17. Interview with her daughter Aminah Saʿid, Mar. 29, 1972, Cairo.

18. HSM, p. 143, and Shafiq, *Hawliyat*, 1:314–16.

19. Milner Papers, Box 164, vol. 12 (c), no. 12, communication 12/12/19 from women of Egypt, St. Mark's Cathedral, and no. 56, communication 8/1/20 from Ladies Committee of Egyptian Delegation, St. Mark's Cathedral.

20. Shafiq, *al-Mar'ah al-Misriyah*, p. 127.

21. *D*, "Maneuvers," 2d ser., no. 70. In the end the situation at her school was out of her hands. With the continued widespread agitation the Ministry of Education eventually temporarily closed the Wardiyan School.

22. Ibid., "The Job of Deputy Headmistress," 2d ser., no. 61.

23. Ibid., pp. 3–5.

24. See my "Expressing Feminism and Nationalism."

25. *D*, "Demonstrations and the Morals of Girl Students," 1st ser., no. 68.

26. Ibid., "The Establishment of the Progress of the Girls' School," 2d ser., no. 75.

27. See my "From Consciousness to Activism."

28. Jeffreys, "'Free from All Uninvited Touch of Man.'"

29. "Egypt's Need for Women Doctors, Teachers, Dressmakers, and Other Professions," in *The Woman and Work*, pp. 65–77.

30. *D*, "Mr. Dunlop and How Strict He Was," 1st ser., no. 46.

31. The Wafd was ten months old at the time.

32. Muhammad Anis, *Dirasat fi Watha'iq Thawrat Sanat 1919* (Cairo, 1963), pt. 1, p. 180, letter from ʿAbd al-Rahman Fahmi to Saʿd Zaghlul, Jan. 14, 1920.

33. On Safiyah's life see Fina Gued Vidal, *Safia Zaghlul* (Cairo, n.d.).

34. Eight years after Safiyah Mustafa Fahmi and Saʿd Zaghlul married, when upper-class Safiyah ʿAbd al-Khaliq al-Sadat wed journalist Shaykh ʿAli Yusuf, who was of modest origins, the bride's father was able to have this scandalous marriage annulled. Originally, the bride's father had consented to the marriage, but after four years of postponement the couple married in secret. Although the scandal arose in part because a bride had married "on her own," the class disparity was a principal cause of it. This incident formed the basis for Out El Kouloub's novel *Ramza* (Paris: Gallimard, 1958). An extract, "The Elopement and the Impossible Joy," translated by Nayra Atiya, is published in Badran and Cooke, *Opening the Gates*, pp. 246–56.

35. Arnett, "Qasim Amin and the Beginnings of the Feminist Movement in Egypt," p. 78.

36. Vidal, *Safia Zaghlul*, p. 34.

37. See Appeal of Safia Zaghlul, 4 Feb. 1922, Cairo, "Mme. Saad Zaghlul Pasha," Consular and Embassy Archives, File 14086, FO 141, Box 511.

38. Vidal, *Safia Zaghlul*, p. 34. The men included ʿAli Shaʿrawi, Ahmad Lutfi al-Sayyid, and ʿAbd al-ʿAziz Fahmi.

39. Interview with HI, Jan. 15, 1968.

40. Jayawardena, *Feminism and Nationalism in the Third World*, p. 9, notes women's roles in helping to mobilize the masses in national resistance movements in certain Asian countries, such as India and Indonesia.

41. Letters from Aminah Thabit to HS between Sept. 1920 and Aug. 1921 in HI Private Papers.

42. Letter from Fikriyah Husni to HS, Apr. 26, 1922. The Women's Union of Minya drew up a *Qanun* (bylaws) and sent it to HS (HI Private Papers).

43. From the Society of Union and Progress of Egyptian Women, Tanta, to the prime minister, *Daily Herald*, *The Times*, *Morning Post*, *Nation*, *Westminster Gazette*, *Daily Chronicle*, *Daily News*, London, received Feb. 10, 1922; and from Hayat Sabet, Asyut, Feb. 21, 1922, to the prime minister, *Manchester Guardian*, *Daily Chronicle*, *Westminster Gazette*, *The Times*, *Daily Herald*, London, "Political Views and Activities of Egyptian Women," Consular and Embassy Archives, File 14083, FO 141, Box 511.

44. HS, *Harem Years*, p. 122. On reactions from various sectors of the population, see Berque, *Egypt*, p. 320. He states that "only the Watani Party [The National Party] dissented, pointing out the all too real risk of a swindle" (p. 320).

45. Letter from HS to Saʿd Zaghlul, Cairo Dec. 12, 1920, in HI, "Ana wa-al-Sharq," pt. 2, pp. 348–49. See also HSM, p. 152.

46. Letter from Saʿd Zaghlul to HS, London, Oct. 27, 1920, in the Private Papers of HI.

47. For details, see HSM, pp. 154–55.

48. Receptions were strictly segregated; however, Zaghlul, as the honored person and national leader, was able to greet the women in their tent (or to allow himself to be greeted by them).

49. HS, *Harem Years*, pp. 123–24. HS reported that the following day Saʿd Zaghlul went to the Shaʿrawi house to see ʿAli Shaʿrawi: "I was glad the following day when he returned and shook hands with Shaʿrawi Pasha" (p. 124).

50. This was another occasion on which HS adroitly managed her two roles as WWCC president and wife of ʿAli Shaʿrawi; see HS, *Harem Years*, pp. 124–25.

51. HS to Allenby, high commissioner, Dec. 25, 1921 (handwriting of Mme Wasif Ghali), "Political Views and Activities of Egyptian Women," Consular and Embassy Archives File 14083, FO 141, Box 511.

52. HS for the Dames d'Egypte, Cairo, Jan. 21, 1922, to Lloyd George, Langdon Davies, Mrs. Barnes, *The Times*, *Morning Post*, *Manchester Guardian*, *Westminster Gazette*, *Daily Herald*, *Daily Mail*, *Daily Chronicle*, *Daily Telegraph*, *Nation*, *Near East*, *New Statesman*, London, "Political Views and Activities of Egyptian Women," Consular and Embassy Archives File 14083, FO 141, Box 511. *Majmuʿat al-Khutab allati Ulqiyat fi Ijtimaʿ al-Sayyidat al-Misriyat bi Dar al-Marhum Husayn Basha Abu ʿUsbaʿ Yawm al-Jumʿah 5 Mayu 1922 wa Yawm al-Jumʿah 27 Disimbir 1922*, p. 5, contains a copy of the petition.

53. Oath published in *Majmuʿat al-Khutab*, p. 10. See HS, "Kalimat al-Ra'isah," in *Majmuʿat al-Khutab*, pp. 6–10, for an account of the Jan. 20, 1922, meeting. See also Shafiq, *Hawliyat*, 2:598. Interview with SN, Feb. 15, 1972, Cairo, who was present at the meeting.

54. List (in the handwriting of HS) of shares sold by special committees, in the Private Papers of HI, includes the following: HS 250, Sharifah Riyad 50, Mrs. Abu ʿUsbaʿ 25, Mrs. Zaghlul 10, Mrs. Sinnut Hanna 6, Mrs. Rafiq Fathi 10, Mrs. ʿAfif Barakat 6, Mrs. Ratib 25, Mrs. Bahi al-Din Barakat 6, and ʿA'ishah Fahmi Hanim 1. "Aryahiyat Sayyidat Karimah," *al-Muqattam*, Feb. 2, 1922, mentions the committee headed by Mrs. Zubaydah Khulusi, announcing that she was selling shares, and mentioning that she herself had donated £E180 to buy forty-five shares of Bank Misr stock. See also HI, "Ana wa-al-Sharq," pp. 381–83; and Eric Davis, *Challenging Colonialism* (Princeton: Princeton University Press, 1983).

55. Letter from Wasif Ghali, on behalf of the Egyptian Wafd, to HS, in *Majmuʿat al-Khutab*, pp. 27–28.

56. See *al-Muqattam*, Oct. 9, 1923. Also, Muhammad Ibrahim al-Jaziri, *Saʿd Zaglul: Dhikrayat Tarqiyat Tarifah* (Cairo, n.d.), pp. 102–6, speaks of the important role of the women's boycott.

57. "Decision of the Women's Central Committee of the Delegation," Cairo, Feb. 7, 1922 (meeting held on Feb. 3, 1922), document signed by Ihsan Ahmad [al-Qusi] (this was crudely translated from Arabic and found its way to the British authorities), "Political Views and Activities of Egyptian Women," Consular and Embassy Archives, File 14083, FO 141, Box 511. Immediately following this document in the same file was a document called "Another Version of the Decision of the Women's Central Committee of the Delegation," signed by Ihsan Ahmad, which in substance matched the previous one.

58. HS, *Harem Years*, pp. 126–27.

59. HS, "Kalimat al-Ra'isah," in *Majmuʿat al-Khutab*, pp. 6–10.

60. "Kalimat al-Anisah ʿAzizah Fawzi," in *Majmuʿat al-Khutab*, pp. 11–17.

61. See telegrams from HS to British prime ministers and press, 1922 and 1923, in "Political Views and Activities of Egyptian Women," Consular and Embassy Archives, File 14083, FO 141, Box 511.

62. Letter from Ester Fahmi Wissa to Allenby, July 30, 1922, from Ramleh, for members of the committee and vice president, in "Political Views and Activities of Egyptian Women," Consular and Embassy Archives, File 14083, FO 141, Box 511.

63. Telegrams in the Private Papers of Louise Majorelle Ghali in the Ghali family archives.

64. Unsigned telegram from London to Louise Ghali, Dec. 2, 1922, in her Private Papers.

65. Telegrams in the Private Papers of Louise Majorelle Ghali. The fragmentary nature of the telegrams makes it impossible to reconstruct the flow of information and reveals, at the same time, how difficult the task of communicating was.

66. Interview with SN, Cairo, Feb. 15, 1972.

67. Saʿd Zaghlul, "Mudhakirrat," National Archives, the Citadel, Cairo, notebook 39 (June 9, 1920–June 7, 1921), entry for Nov. 24, 1920, p. 2380. This reference was provided by ʿAbd al-Khaliq Lashin.

68. Letter from Wasif Ghali on behalf of the Egyptian Wafd to HS in *Majmuʿat al-Khutab*, pp. 27–28.

69. HS, *Mudhakkirat Ra'idat alʿArabiyah al-Haditha*, from the text of the letter reproduced on p. 249.

70. "Egypt for the Egyptians" (*Misr lil-Misriyin*) was a slogan from the time of the revolution of 1881–1882 (also known as the ʿUrabi revolt), calling for an end to Turco-Circassian hegemony in the military and greater participation of Egyptians in running the country. Salim al-Naqqash (d. 1884), of Syrian Christian origin and founder (with Adib Ishaq) of *Misr* (1877), and *al-Tijarah* (1878), is said to have coined the phrase in the 1870s. He also published a six-volume book in 1884 under the title *Misr lil-Misriyin*.

71. See *al-Akhbar*, Nov. 16, 1924, and HI, "Ana wa-al-Sharq," pt. 2, pp. 362–63.

72. *Al-Akhbar*, Nov. 24, 1924.

73. HS, *Mudhakkirat Ra'idat alʿArabiyah al-Haditha*, p. 322.

74. HS, *Harem Years*, p. 131.

Chapter Five
The House of the Women

1. See my "Independent Women: More Than a Century of Feminism in Egypt," in *Arab Women: Old Boundaries, New Frontiers*, ed. Judith Tucker (Bloomington: Indiana University Press, 1993), pp. 129–48.

2. For a discussion of the term and of the problematics of feminism in Egypt during this period see Fenoglio-Abd El Aal, *Défense et illustration.*

3. HS was a widow and the other two were single women whose fathers were dead; thus now, unlike the situation in 1920, there were no spouses or fathers to prevent women from going abroad for a feminist conference.

4. Text of HS speech at the Rome congress in the Private Papers of SN. The speech was published in *Le Journal du Caire*, June 4, 1923.

5. Nabawia Moosa, "Egypt," in *The Report of the Ninth Congress of the International Woman Suffrage Alliance, Held in Rome, 12–19 May 1923*, p. 171.

6. Ibid.

7. A comparative note: Bohachevsky-Chomiak, in *Feminists despite Themselves*, p. 263, speaks of this optimistic moment for women from eastern Europe, when Ukrainian women also affiliated with the IAW during the brief moment when their country became an independent republic before becoming part of the new Soviet Union.

8. Privileging homogeneity would also prove problematic within the Western mainstream. On the inability of IAW feminists to acknowledge difference and what this meant for European Jewish feminists see Bosch and Kloosterman, *Politics and Friendship*.

9. On European feminists' reluctance to confront imperialism when espousing rights for all women see Margaret Strobel, *European Women and the Second British Empire* (Bloomington: Indiana University Press, 1991); with respect to India see Barbara Ramusack, "Catalysts or Helper? British Feminists, Indian Women's Rights, and Indian Independence," in *The Extended Family: Women and Political Participation in India and Pakistan*, ed. Gail Minault (Columbia, Mo.: South Asia Books, 1981), pp. 110–24; and Antoinette Burton, *Burdens of History: British Feminists, Indian Women, and Imperial Culture, 1865–1915* (Chapel Hill: University of North Carolina Press, 1994).

10. This event was described to me by SN. See HS, "Kayfa Ussisat al-Ittihad al-Nisa'i," *al-Hilal*, May 1949, pp. 85–87. The eunuchs' displeasure surely must not have derived simply from women's deviating from the "proper" behavior that the eunuchs were charged to assure but also from the fact that this "revolt" against harem culture foreshadowed an end to their jobs. See also Myriam Harry, *Les derniers harems* (Paris: E. Flammarion, 1933), based on personal interviews with HS and SN in Cairo; and Woodsmall, *Moslem Women Enter a New World*, pp. 53–55 for her account of this unveiling (she met HS and SN in 1929) and its symbolic significance, as well as observations of unveiling by other upper- and middle-class women in Cairo and several provincial towns.

11. On veiling as a feminist strategy see my "From Consciousness to Activism." On the general demise of veiling in Egypt see Baron, "Unveiling in Early Twentieth Century Egypt."

12. "Discours prononcé par Madame Charaoui Pacha," *E*, Dec. 1925, p. 338.

13. As Fenoglio-Abd El Aal puts it, "Sans nier que le voile ait été essentiellement

citadin, il est nécessaire de le considerer comme symbole, et de savoir qu'il a été pris comme tel par les premières féministes: symbole de l'enfermement et symbole non équivoque; la lutte contre le voile n'était, en ce sens, ni inutile, ni illégitime" (*Défense et illustration*, pp. 116–17).

14. See Woodsmall, *Moslem Women Enter a New World*, p. 64.

15. *Al-Lata'if al-Musawwarah*, June 4, 1923, and *Le Journal du Caire*, June 4, 1923. Photographs of HS's unveiled face had already appeared in the Italian press; see *Giornale d'Italia*, May 27, 1923. The news of the unveiling spread in the Muslim world; for example, *The Egyptian Gazette*, June 16, 1923, cited an article in the Jidda paper *al-Qiblah* reporting, "The idea of unveiling Muslim women is gaining ground in Egypt. Huda Shaarawi and Saiza Nabarawi have both appeared without veils in Lataif and these women are both distinguished ladies."

16. *E*, Nov. 1927.

17. For a comparative account of unveiling in the Middle East and South Asia at the end of the 1920s see Woodsmall, *Moslem Women Enter a New World*, pp. 39–70.

18. "Une réception en l'honneur de Moustapha Pacha Kemal," *E*, Nov. 1925, p. 315.

19. *E*, Mar., 1929, p. 44.

20. *E*, May 1928, p. 48. For biographical data and translated excerpts from this book and her second book, *al-Fatah wa-al-Shuyukh*, see "Unveiling and Veiling: On the Liberation of the Woman and Social Renewal in the Islamic World," in Badran and Cooke, *Opening the Gates*, pp. 270–78; and Nazirah Zein Ed-Din, "Removing the Veil and Veiling," in *Women and Islam*, ed. Azizah Al-Hibri (New York: Pergamon Press, 1982), pp. 221–26. Woodsmall, who visited Beirut the year after the book was published, noted that it had been translated into several languages (*Moslem Women Enter a New World*, pp. 403–4).

21. Al-Qusi won second prize. See "Conférence d'Ehsan Amed El Koussi prononcée à l'Université Américaine," *E*, May 1928, pp. 18–25, and Woodsmall, *Moslem Women Enter a New World*, p. 404.

22. According to SN, ʿA'idah Qattawi, Jewish lady-in-waiting to Queen Nazli, was asked to present the Afghan queen with a *yashmak* to cover her face.

23. Interview with SN, Aug. 31, 1972, Cairo, and "La visite des souverains afghans en Egypte," *E*, Jan. 1928, pp. 4–5. See also F. Taillardat, "La fin du voyage du Roi Amanullah," *L'Asie Française*, Feb. 1928; Harry, *Les derniers harems*, p. 51; and Woodsmall, *Moslem Women Enter a New World*, p. 45.

24. Myriam Harry, in "La femme orientale et son destin: l'Egyptienne," *Journal de la femme*, July 21, 1934, speaks of changes in veiling since her last visit to Egypt in 1934, noting that the yashmak had completely disappeared in Cairo and in Alexandria.

25. See *al-Nahdah al-Nisa'iyah*, no. 81 (1929): 275, "Should One Veil or Not Veil?" See Fenoglio-Abd El Aal, *Défense et illustration*, p. 61.

26. This was announced in *al-Balagh*, Sept. 15, 1937.

27. The EFU/WWCC demands were published as *Les revendications des dames égyptiennes* (Cairo, 1925) and also published in the opening issue of *L'Egyptienne*, Feb. 1925.

28. SN, "Revendications et émancipation!" *E*, May 1925, pp. 145–46.

29. Interview with Mary Kahil, Mar. 3, 1972, Cairo.

30. Interview with Edna Khayyat (daughter-in-law of Regina Khayyat), Mar. 9,

1972, Cairo. For a biographical sketch see "Rujinah Khayyat," *al-Mar'ah al-Misriyah* 4, no. 7 (1923): 369–70.

31. Interview with ʿAzizah Haykal, Feb. 12, 1972, Cairo. For a short reference to ʿAzizah Haykal and an analysis of the life and work of her husband see Charles D. Smith, *Islam and the Search for Social Order in Modern Egypt: A Biography of Muhammad Husayn Haykal* (Albany: State University of New York Press, 1983), pp. 52–53 and passim.

32. Interview with Ihsan al-Qusi, Feb. 22, 1972, Cairo.

33. See "Conférence d'Ehsan Ahmed El Koussi," *E*, May 1928, pp. 18–25.

34. Interview with SN, Sept. 1967, Cairo.

35. Information from letters from Fikriyah Husni in Minya to HS in Cairo in 1921 and 1922, in the Private Papers of SN and HI; and ʿAllubah et al., "Thawrat 1919."

36. The address was 45 Yahya ibn Zayd Street.

37. "Rapport de la Présidente," *E*, Mar. 1926, p. 176.

38. SN as told to Harry, "La femme orientale et son destin." Confirmed in interview with SN, Mar. 13, 1972, Cairo.

39. Interview with SN, Mar. 13, 1972, Cairo.

40. For an account of contributions see *L'Union féministe égyptienne: rapport 1928–1933* (Cairo, 1933).

41. See "Discours de Madame Charaoui Pacha à la cérémonie d'inauguration de l'école de l'U.F.E.," *E*, Apr.–May 1932, pp. 11–14, and "In Memoriam," *E*, June 1931, pp. 2–4. See SN, "La Maison de la Femme," *E*, Apr.–May 1932, pp. 2–10, for an account of the inauguration. Prince Muhammad ʿAli (the son of Aminah Hanim Afandi) presided, and numerous male politicians, lawyers, journalists, and educators attended, including ʿAdli Yahan, Mustafa Nahhas, Wasif Ghali, Ibrahim Nuqrashi, ʿAli Shamsi, Ahmad Lutfi al-Sayyid, and Yusuf Qattawi. The festivities for the public were held on April 28th and 29th in the Feminist Union auditorium.

42. See SN, "L'école professionelle et ménagère de l'Union féministe égyptienne," *E*, Feb. 1932, pp. 5–10.

43. "La kermesse annuelle de l'Union féminist égyptienne," *E*, Feb. 1929, pp. 20–21.

44. Ibid.

45. SN, "L'école professionelle et ménagère de l'Union féministe égyptienne," *E*, Feb. 1932, pp. 5–10.

46. See SN, "Wajab al-Mar'ah fi al-ʿAsr al-Hadith," *M*, Mar. 1, 1937, pp. 13–16, and "Laysa al-ittihad jamʿiyah bal huwwa fikrah qawmiyah ʿammah," in "al-Ittihad al-Nisa'i," *M*, Mar. 15, 1937, pp. 25–26.

47. Interview with HI, Jan. 12, 1968, Cairo.

48. List of Shaqiqat from Private Papers of HI.

49. Interview with HI, Feb. 8, 1972, Cairo, and HI, "Ana wa-al-Sharq," pt. 1, p. 34, for information on the activities of the Shaqiqat.

50. List of advisers from the Private Papers of SN. HS said that the EFU was inspired to invite male advisers following the example of European feminist associations. Dr. Shahin was not on this list but was mentioned as an adviser by SN, "Au Governement Egyptien et l'enseignement des jeunes filles," *E*, Sept. 1930, p. 2. The EFU invited men to act as advisers before the 1929 IAW congress in Berlin. See "Conférence prononcée par Mme Hoda Charaoui au Memorial Ewart Hall de l'Université égyptienne [*sic*], le 12 nov. 1929," *E*, Nov. 1929, p. 27. Further, the

previous year the EFU had received a government grant of land upon which to build a large multipurpose facility for its rapidly expanding program, and the organization therefore sought the technical expertise of male specialists; see SN, "L'activité de l'UFE," *E*, May 1928, pp. 10–12. In an interview on Feb. 22, 1972, in Cairo Ihsan al-Qusi said that she had proposed the idea to HS in Cairo during a vacation from her studies at the American University in Beirut. The EFU made the attachment of male advisers formal; this was not the normal practice of European feminist societies, according to Margery Corbett Ashby (Interview, Nov. 9, 1972, London).

51. See Fenoglio-Abd El Aal, *Défense et illustration*, p. 92

52. *Le lotus*, founded by Alexandra Avierino, lasted only from 1901 to 1902. *La femme nouvelle*, financed by Princess Swikiar and edited by Duriyah Shafiq in 1945, was a glossy magazine. La Direction, "Déclaration," *E*, Feb. 1925, p. 5. According to Irene Fenoglio-Abd El Aal, "L'activité culturelle francophone au Caire durant l'entre-deux-guerres," in *D'un Orient l'autre: les métamorphoses des perceptions et connaissances* (Cairo: CEDEJ, 1989), the period of greatest intensity of francophone cultural production in Egypt was from the 1920s through the 1940s. Among sixty-five foreign-language journals published in Cairo forty-four were in French. For an analysis of the use of French by *L'Egyptienne* see Fenoglio-Abd El Aal, *Défense et illustration*, p. 117. In the 1980s a group of Egyptian progressive and feminist women brought out *Les cahiers de Chabramant*, an occasional literary journal.

53. SN, "Discours de Mlle Ceza Nabaroui en The [*sic*] offert à la presse à l'Hôtel Pera Palace le 15 April," *E*, May 1935, p. 37.

54. On Western images of Egyptian and other Middle Eastern women see Graham-Brown, *Images of Women*, pp. 70–91; Melman, *Women's Orients* and "Desexualizing the Orient"; and Mabro, *Veiled Half-Truths*.

55. "Conférence prononcée par Mme Hoda Charaoui au Memorial Ewart Hall de l'Université égyptienne le 12 nov. 1929," *E*, Nov. 1929, p. 8.

56. See Fenoglio-Abd El Aal, *Défense et illustration*, p. 118, who assesses two Arabic journals: the liberal *al-Mar'ah al-Misriyah* (1920–1923), edited by a Copt, and *al-Nahdah al-Nisa'iyah* (1922–1938), with its conservative Islamic tone. She argues that both were constrained by the need to work within a dominant ethic expressed in the linguistic conventions of Arabic, which inhibited the articulation of feminism.

57. "Hors-texte," *E*, Jan. 1930, p. 1.

58. Interview with SN, Aug. 31, 1971.

59. After the journal started, SN, who had been living with her grandfather, moved into HS's household, facilitating the closer collaboration of the two.

60. Jeanne Marques was born in Guadeloupe in the Antilles where her father was an officer in the French navy. She studied in the Faculty of Letters at the University of Toulouse. In 1912, for reasons of health, she moved to Egypt where she devoted herself to writing poetry, essays, and articles for journals in Egypt and France. She remained with *L'Egyptienne* for the duration of its existence. She died in Cairo in 1966.

61. The cover sketch was drawn by Valentine de Saint-Point, editor of *Le phoenix*, a journal published in France dedicated to the renaissance of Eastern peoples.

62. According to a personal communication from Marilyn Booth it was standard to place the biographical sketches on the first page in the women's journals; the early sketches were not usually accompanied by portraits. It appears that *L'Egyptienne*

was a leader in regularly publishing pictures with biographical sketches. In 1936 Woodsmall wrote, "Until fairly recently Egypt and Turkey were the only Moslem countries in which women's photographs were featured freely in the press." See *Moslem Women Enter a New World*, p. 78.

63. According to an interview with SN on Aug. 31, 1971, information that appeared in "Glanes" was culled from the publications of feminist organizations abroad, contacts made mainly through the IAW, and from a Paris-based clipping service called L'Argus.

64. Doria Ragai Chafik, "L'art pour l'art dans l'Egypte," *E*, Apr. 1940, p. 5.

65. She was the author of *Vierges d'Orient* (Virgins of the Orient, 1923).

66. She was born in Alexandria in 1896; her father was a Lebanese Christian, and her mother the daughter of Scottish parents who had settled in the Delta in the middle of the nineteenth century. She was educated at Roman Catholic schools in Alexandria and Cairo. First meeting HS in the 1920s, Kher supported the feminist movement from the sidelines. When HS invited her to speak, she obliged, but her first interest was the social-literary scene in Cairo. She began holding literary gatherings in the 1920s. Kher's books include: *Les sycomores: fresque copte romance* (original date unclear), republished in Cairo by Atlas in 1972 under the cover title *Visages d'Egypte*; *Salma et son village* (Paris: Editions de la Madeleine, 1933); *Le voyage de Nevine* (1935), republished in Cairo by Mondiale in 1972 under the cover title *Visages du Liban, visages de Syrie*; and *Mes soeurs* ("L'enfance de Béatrice," "Epouse de seize ans," and "Shérife") (Cairo: R. Schindler, 1942). She also published books of poetry, including *La trainée de sable* (n.d.) and *Méandres* (n.d.). Interview with Amy Kher, Oct. 19, 1975, Cairo.

67. On the affinity Egyptians of the upper class felt toward the French, and toward the Latin Mediterranean, see SN, "Les véritables bases de la culture égyptienne," *E*, Apr. 1929, pp. 12–18, and SN, "Le congrès de la presse latine," *E*, Jan. 1932, pp. 2–4.

68. The Egyptian feminist leaders met Tinayre in Cairo in 1929 when she spoke at a lecture series on Mediterranean culture organized by the Exposition française. See Haidar Fazil, "Les deux belles conférences de Mme Marcelle Tinayre," *E*, Mar. 1929, p. 9, and SN, "Les véritables bases de la culture égyptienne," *E*, Apr. 1929, p. 15.

69. Myriam Harry's husband was the sculptor Henri Perrault-Harry. He took his wife's name when they married, which Egyptian feminists noted with satisfaction.

70. HS, "Tajdimat al-Misriyah," *M*, Feb. 15, 1937, p. 2.

71. From a speech delivered by SN at the EFU on Jan. 22, 1937. See SN, "A l'Union féministe égyptienne," *E*, Jan. 1937, p. 6, and idem, "Wajib al-Mar'ah fi al-ʿAhd al-Jadid," *M*, Mar. 1, 1937, pp. 13–16. "Al-Akhbar," *M*, May 15, 1937, p. 39, reported that the Lebanese papers *Sawt al-Ahrar*, *al-ʿAsifah*, and *al-Nahar* praised *M* for keeping pace with the spirit of the times, and for being a vehicle of feminism and the voice of the Egyptian woman in the new, independent era.

72. ʿA'ishah, the wife of the Prophet, was called Umm al-Mu'minin (the Mother of the Believers). This saying indicates that the faithful had much to learn about their religion from ʿA'ishah.

73. Rashid was celebrated in "Hors-texte," *E*, June 1936.

74. Al-Masri met HS at her graduation ceremony in 1931 and shortly afterwards joined the EFU. Al-Masri was featured in *E*'s "Hors-texte" in Oct. 1937, the month she took up the editorship of *M*. Al-Masri has recalled her life in *Memoirs of an*

Egyptian American or the Life Story of the First Co-Ed at the American University in Cairo (Jasper, Ark., n.d.).

75. Interview with Eva Habib al-Misri, Dec. 2, 1974, London.

76. In an interview on July 8, 1968, in Cairo Bint al-Shati' said she admired HS and the feminist movement but was not herself an active feminist. In the late 1930s and 1940s she wrote on the condition of the peasants, women and men.

77. Naᶜimah al-Ayyubi had been held up in *E* as a role model. "Echos d'Orient," June 1931, announced that she had finished first in her class that year; in July–Aug. 1931 and in June 1933 she was featured in "Hors-texte."

78. Majd al-Din Hifni Nasif, a younger brother of Bahithat al-Badiyah, who had known HS since he was young, was a supporter of the feminist movement. As a law student in Paris in the spring of 1925, he spoke at La Ligue français pour le droit des femmes on "La femme en Islam," after which Maria Verone, president of the organization, first contacted HS. On behalf of the group Verone sent a letter congratulating HS on the "marvelous work" accomplished for "the liberation of your country and the emancipation of the Egyptian woman." see "Echos d'Orient," *E*, June 1925, p. 163.

79. Sayyid Qutb, who was assassinated in 1966 and has been an inspiration to present-day Islamists, published poems in *M* on Apr. 1, May 15, and Dec. 15, 1938, and on Jan. 1 and 15, 1939, and an article on beauty and femininity on July 15, 1938. On Qutb (1906–1966) and issues of gender see Yvonne Haddad, "The Case of the Feminist Movement," chap. 5 in *Contemporary Islam and the Challenge of History* (Albany: State University of New York Press, 1982), pp. 54–70; idem, "Islam, Women and Revolution in Twentieth Century Arab Thought," *The Muslim World* 124, nos. 3–4 (1984): 137–60; and William Shepherd, "The Myth of Progress and Gender Relations in the Thought of Sayyid Qutb" (Unpublished paper).

80. *Report of the Ninth Congress of the International Woman Suffrage Alliance Held in Rome from 12 to 19 May 1923*, "Woman's Charter," p. 234.

81. Letter from Margery Corbett Ashby to Carrie Chapman Catt, n.d. (est. date late Apr.–early May 1945), in the Carrie Chapman Catt Private Papers, Box 2, New York Public Library.

82. Bosch and Kloosterman, *Politics and Friendship*, p. 224.

Chapter Six
City Sisters, Country Sisters

1. Intersections between feminism and voluntary social service have been explored in such works as Marion Kaplan's study of Jewish women's experience in late-nineteenth and early-twentieth-century Germany, *The Making of the Jewish Middle Class*, chap. 7, "Her Sister's Keeper: Women's Organizations from the *Chevra* to Feminism," pp. 192–227; and idem, *The Jewish Feminist Movement in Germany: The Campaigns of the Jüdischer Frauenbund, 1904–1938* (Westport, Conn.: Greenwood Press, 1979). In contrast, in *Egypt's Other Wars: Epidemics and the Politics of Public Health* (Syracuse: Syracuse University Press, 1990), p. 54, Nancy Gallagher insists that the women's philanthropy must be considered separately from feminism because "the feminists concentrated on eliminating the subordinate status of women in society, while the volunteers focused on the provisioning of public health and welfare services to the needy."

2. Woodsmall, who visited the mosque of Sayyidah Zaynab in 1929, remarked

on the crowds of women with many babies gathered around the tomb of the saint from whom women sought a cure for infertility. Ruth Frances Woodsmall Papers, Box 3A, from Diary, May 12, 1929.

3. Woodsmall visited the dispensary on the "eye day" (ibid., May 27, 1929, Box 3A).

4. Interview with HI, Feb. 3, 1972, Cairo, and her memoirs, "Ana wa-al-Sharq."

5. HS, in "A la veille du Congrès de Paris," *E*, May 1926, pp. 101–4, praised the work of the director and of Fikriyah al-Sulh, whose service was cut short by her premature death in 1926 at the age of twenty-three, but deplored the slackening off of women volunteers. HI, in an interview on Feb. 3, 1972, in Cairo, recalled the lack of sustained commitment by volunteers.

6. See "Rapports des médecins du dispensaire de l'Union féministe égyptienne," *E*, Apr. 1926, and *L'Union féministe égyptienne: rapport, 1928–1933* (Cairo, 1933), pp. 4–5.

7. See Nawal al-Saᶜdawi, *al-Marʾah wa-al-Jins* (Beirut, 1972), on effects of taboos on women's health.

8. SN, "L'Ecole Professionnelle et Ménagère de l'Union féministe égyptienne," *E*, Feb. 1932, p. 8.

9. Interview with HI, Sept. 18, 1975, Cairo.

10. SN, "L'Ecole Professionnelle et Ménagère de l'Union féministe égyptienne," *E*, Feb. 1932, p. 8.

11. See "Rapport de 1927 sur la Section de la Protection de l'Enfance," *E*, Nov. 1928, pp. 13–19, and SN, "Le bien-être et la protection de l'enfance," *E*, Jan. 1928, pp. 6–8.

12. SN, "Une visite au dispensaire de Darb el Ahmar," *E*, Oct. 1928.

13. See SN, "Le bien-être et la protection de l'enfance," *E*, Jan. 1928, pp. 6–8.

14. See SN, "Les clubs féminins en Amérique," *E*, Dec. 1925, pp. 242–349. Winifred S. Blackman in *The Fellahin of Upper Egypt* (London: G. G. Harrap, 1927) mentioned the need for organized private charity in Egypt (pp. 42–43).

15. Interview with Ellen Sarruf, Mar. 31, 1974, Cairo. She was the daughter of Yaᶜqub Sarruf, who brought his family from Beirut to Cairo when she was very young. She attended the American College in Cairo.

16. Interview with her daughter, Layla Barakat Murtagi, Apr. 9, 1974, Cairo. Many of the biographical details in the sketch of Hidayah Barakat were drawn from Marsot, "The Revolutionary Gentlewomen," pp. 271–76. With Hidayah Barakat and her daughters as sources, Marsot gives a slightly different version of the foundation of the Mabarrat from that in HS's memoirs. *Jamᶜiyat al-Marʾah al-Jadidah: The Welfare Modern Woman Society* (Cairo, ca. 1974) gives information on the two societies and their amalgamation. See also Hidayah Barakat, *Nubdhah ᶜan al-ᶜAmal al-Siyasi wa-al-Ijtimaᶜi al- Nisaʾi fi Misr* (Cairo, n.d.).

17. Interview with Edna Khayyat (the daughter-in-law of Regina Khayyat), Mar. 9, 1972, Cairo.

18. Interview with Layla Doss, Feb. 13, 1968, and Oct. 5, 1975, Cairo. For a brief history of the society, see *al-Jamᶜiyah al-Nisaʾiyah li-Tahsin al-Sihhah: Qissat Khamsah wa-ᶜIshrin Sanah: 1936–1961* (The Women's Society for the Improvement of Health: The story of twenty years, 1936–1961) (Cairo, 1961).

19. Al-Masri became a member of the Mabarrat Muhammad ᶜAli, of two Coptic societies that operated orphanages (the Coptic Women's Benevolent Association,

where she taught Arabic, and the al-Salam Benevolent Society), and of Hay'at Tahdid al-Nasl, the Association for Birth Control. Interview with Eva Habib al-Masri Dec. 2, 1974, London. See also her *Memoirs of an Egyptian American.*

20. See Eva Habib al-Masri, "Dars min Jamᶜiyah Nisa'iyah," *M*, Dec. 15, 1939, p. 4.

21. Interview with SN, Mar. 15, 1972, Cairo. See also al-Masri, "Dars min Jamᶜiyah Nisa'iyah."

22. Interview with Layla Doss, May 19, 1990.

23. See Fathallah al-Marsafi, "Al-ᶜUmmal al-Ahdath and the Need for Social Reform," *M*, July 15, 1939, pp. 18–21, and "Ahmad Hasanayn Basha Yatahaddathu ila al-Shabab al-Jil" (Ahmad Muhammad Hassanayn speaks to the youth), *M*, Jan. 1, 1940, pp. 4–6. The Pioneers began with eighteen members; nine years later there were forty-eight, and eventually their numbers reached a few hundred. Interview with Ra'uf Kahil (a founder of al-Ruwwad), Feb. 10, 1973, St. Antony's College, Oxford.

24. *MNA*, pp. 142–46.

25. See HS, "Le Cabinet Ali Maher Pacha et son vaste programme de réformes sociales," *E*, Mar.–Apr. 1936, pp. 6–7, and SN, "Pour l'enfance malheureuse ou en danger moral!" *E*, Dec. 1937.

26. See Mona Hammam, "Women and Industrial Work in Egypt: The Chubra El-Kheima Case," *Arab Studies Quarterly* 2 (1980): 50–69.

27. Eva Habib al-Masri, "Our Duty Today: We the Women of Egypt," *M*, Sept. 15, 1939, pp. 2–3.

28. See "En faveur des sinistrés d'Anatolie," *E*, Jan. 1940, p. 33.

29. Earthquake in Turkey: List of Money Gifts, dated Jan. 27, 1940, HI Private Papers.

30. Personal communication from Hassan Fathy. See his *Architecture for the Poor* (Chicago: University of Chicago Press, 1973), pp. 12–14.

31. Report of Nahid Sirri to the Arab Feminist Conference in 1944, *MNA*, pp. 139–42.

32. Ibid.

33. Interview with Gertrude Butrus Ghali, Sept. 12, 1975, Cairo.

34. See "al-Ittihad al-Nisa'i al-Misri," *M*, Mar. 15, 1937, pp. 25–26; SN, "Pour l'enfance malheureuse ou en danger moral!" *E*, Dec. 1937, pp. 6–8; Eva Habib al-Masri, "al-Ihsan al-Munazzamah fi Misr," *M*, Mar. 1, 1939; "Tanzim al-Ihsan fi Misr," *M*, July 15, 1939, p. 31. Appeals to women to volunteer in social service continued as well; see Jamilah al-ᶜAla'ili, "Wajibuna nahw al-Mar'ah al-Faqirah," *M*, July 1, 1937, pp. 12–14, and idem, "Yajibu an Yakun al-Mada Awsaᶜ min Hadha fi Sabil al-Khidmah al-Ijtimaᶜiyah," *M*, Oct. 15, 1937, pp. 12–13. In 1938 Mirrit Ghali spoke of the inadequacy of private and government-run projects to deal effectively with the needs of the poor; see *The Policy of Tomorrow*, trans. Ismaᶜil al-Faruqi (Washington, D.C.: American Council of Learned Societies, 1953).

35. SN, "Wajib al-Mar'ah fi al-ᶜAhd al-Jadid," *M*, Mar. 1, 1937, p. 13. See also "al-Ittihad al-Nisa'i al-Misri," *M*, Mar. 15, 1937, p. 25.

36. Eva Habib al-Masri, "Min al-Rif ila al-Madinah," *M*, Nov. 15, 1939, pp. 6–7.

37. "Speech of Amina ᶜAlluba," *M*, Feb. 15, 1939, pp. 17–20.

38. Jamilah al-ᶜAla'ili, "Wajibuna nahw al-Mar'ah al-Faqirah," *M*, July 1, 1937,

pp. 12–14. See also idem, "Yajibu an Yakun al-Mada Awsaʿ min Hadha fi Sabil al-Khidmah al-Ijtimaʿiyah," *M*, Oct. 15, 1937, pp. 12–13, in which she appeals for financial contributions for aid to villages.

39. Rashad Rustum, "al-Fallahah," *M*, Nov. 15, 1937, pp. 10–12.

40. Abnat al-Shati' [Bint al-Shati'], "al-Mar'ah al-Muthaqqafah fi al-Rif," *M*, Mar. 1, 1937, pp. 19–20.

41. "Les femmes dans les carrières liberales et les fonctions publiques," *E*, Sept.–Oct. 1939, p. 64.

42. From May 15, 1937, through Dec. 1, 1937.

43. "Rakhat al-Fallah," *M*, Dec. 1, 1937, p. 7.

44. On the housing needs of peasants see Fathy, *Architecture for the Poor*.

45. SN, "La politique paysanne du gouvernement," *E*, Feb. 1938, pp. 3–4.

46. Schistosomiasis afflicted men in far greater numbers than women. In Upper Egypt, to which one strain of the disease was confined, women did not work in the fields, and in the Delta there were fewer women in the fields than men.

47. See "Rapport de 1927 sur la Section de la Protection de l'Enfance," *E*, Feb. 1928, pp. 13–19, and SN, "Le bien-être et la protection de l'enfance," *E*, Jan. 1928, pp. 6–8.

48. HS, "Le Cabinet Ali Maher Pacha et son vaste programme de réformes sociales," *E*, Mar.–Apr. 1936, pp. 6–7, and SN, "La politique paysanne du gouvernement," *E*, Feb. 1938, pp. 3–4.

49. *MNA*, pp. 168–71.

50. HS, "Le Cabinet Ali Maher Pacha et son vaste programme de réformes sociales," *E*, Mar.–Apr. 1936.

51. Interview with HI, Feb. 20, 1972, Cairo, and interview with Bahigah Rashid, Oct. 5, 1975, Cairo.

52. "Une fondation humanitaire," *E*, Nov. 1937, pp. 32–33, and "Harakat al-Isʿaf bi-al-Minya," *M*, Jan. 1, 1938, pp. 26–27.

53. *Jamʿiyat al-Nisa'iyah li-Tahsin al-Sihhah*.

54. Interview with Jeannette Makar Kamal Bulus Hanna, Sept. 26, 1975, Cairo.

55. See *Oeuvre Mohamed Aly el Kebir*.

56. Interview with Anna Nagib Ghali, Sept. 10, 1975, Cairo. Interview with Munirah ʿAbd al-Malak Saʿd, Sept. 17, 1975, Cairo, former teacher in one of the society's schools, subsequently secretary of the society.

57. Interview with Jeannette Ayrut de Bono, Nov. 10, 1975, Cairo. Jeannette Ayrout de Bono, "L'oeuvre des écoles gratuites des villages de Haute Egypte," unpub. memorandum. Interview with Marguerite Azzam, Nov. 18, 1975, Cairo. For a critique of Ayrut's book *Moeurs et coutumes des fellahas* (Paris: Payot, 1938), which was translated and republished several times, see Timothy Mitchell, "The Invention and Reinvention of the Egyptian Peasant," *International Journal of Middle East Studies* 22, no. 2 (1990): 129–50.

58. "Fi Dar al-Mar'ah: Kalimat al-Anisah Aminah ʿAllubah," *M*, Feb. 1, 1937, pp. 18–20.

59. Information on women's voluntary efforts during the epidemic comes from an interview with Mary Kahil, Mar. 3, 1972, Cairo; interview with Gertrude Ghali, Sept. 12, 1975, and subsequent talks, as well as the diary she kept in Upper Egypt in Jan. and Feb. 1944; interview with HI, Feb. 15, 1972, Cairo, and HI, "Ana wa-al-Sharq," pt. 1, p. 229. Gallagher has written on the women's participation in relief work in *Egypt's Other Wars*; see pp. 40–45.

60. Gertrude Ghali captured the horror of the epidemic in her diary. Journalist ʿAsmah Halim recorded her observations in *Sittat Ayyam fi Saʿid* (Cairo: The New Dawn Publisher, 1944).

61. See "Après la visite de S.M. le Roi: les secours aux sinistrés de Haute-Egypte augmentent," *La Bourse Egyptienne*, Feb. 14, 1944, which contains an appeal from HS. See Gallagher, *Egypt's Other Wars*, chap. 3, for the politics of Faruk's visit.

62. See Gallagher, *Egypt's Other Wars*, pp. 135–36. Egyptian writer Andrée Chedid has written a moving novel about the epidemic called *Le sixième jour*. A film, *al-Yawm al-Sadis*, based on the novel was made in Egypt. The novel was translated into English by Isobel Strachey as *The Sixth Day* (London: The Serpent's Tail, 1987).

63. See Gallagher, *Egypt's Other Wars*, chap. 8.

Chapter Seven
Recasting the Family

1. See ʿA'ishah al-Taymuriyah, *Mir'at al-Taʿammul fi al-ʿUmur* (Cairo, ca. 1890s); HS, *Harem Years*; Bahithat al-Badiyah, *al-Nisa'iyat*; and *D*.

2. Azizah Y. al-Hibri, "Marriage Laws in Muslim Countries: A Comparative Study of Certain Egyptian, Syrian, Moroccan, and Tunisian Marriage Laws," *International Review of Comparative Public Policy* 4 (1992): 227–44, reveals the enduring overlay of patriarchal cultures in these legal codes.

3. Christians and Jews in Egypt were subject to their own personal status codes and had their own separate denominational (*millah*) courts. The denominational courts (a total of fourteen), along with the Muslim shariʿah courts, were abolished in 1955 (Law 462), after which the cases of all Egyptians were heard in the National Courts. The personal status codes themselves, however, remained religiously based. See Farhat Ziadeh, *Lawyers, the Rule of Law and Liberalism in Modern Egypt* (Stanford: Hoover Institution on War, Revolution and Peace, 1968), pp. 104 and 115.

4. Slavery existed in Egypt in the nineteenth century. According to the Islamic shariʿah men could engage in extramarital sexual relations with slave women, who could be required to provide sexual services. However, the slave trade was outlawed in Egypt in 1877, and slavery dwindled thereafter as a social practice.

5. On equality in difference see Sumayya Fahmi, "Ma Maʿna al-Musawah," *M*, June 1, 1938, pp. 6–7, 17. On gender complementarity see SN, "L'évolution féministe et les profits que peut en retirer le bien public," *E*, Mar. 1936, pp. 11–18. On equality and difference in French feminism see Karen Offen, "Ernest Legouvé and the Doctrine of 'Equality in Difference' for Women," *Journal of Modern History* 58 (June 1986): 452–84. See also Anne-Marie Kappeli, "Feminist Scenes," in Fraisse and Perrot, *A History of Women in the West*, pp. 483–84.

6. See SN, "Examen du nouveau projet du statut personnel musulman," *E*, Apr. 1927, p. 2.

7. For a strong statement of the EFU position see Fatma Niʿmat Rashid, "Muqaranah bayna al-Mar'ah al-Misriyah wa-al-Mar'ah al-Turkiyah," *M*, May 1, 1937, pp. 10, 31.

8. Yesim Arat in *The Patriarchal Paradox: Women Politicians in Turkey* (Rutherford, N.J.: Fairleigh Dickinson University Press, 1989), p. 45, speaks of the futile attempt in the early 1980s to make changes in these two areas.

9. Enid Hill, *Mahkama! Studies in the Egyptian Legal System, Courts and Crimes, Law and Society* (London: Ithaca Press, 1979), p. 92. Also on the use of the

courts by lower-class Cairene women in the early twentieth century see Le Brun, *Les répudiées*; and later in the century see Malak Zaalouk, "The Social Structure of Divorce Adjudication in Egypt" (M.A. thesis, The American University in Cairo, 1975). On peasant women's use of the courts in the nineteenth century see Tucker, *Women in Nineteenth Century Egypt*, chap. 3.

10. See SN, "Examen du nouveau projet du statut personnel musulman," *E*, Apr. 1927, pp. 2–3.

11. "La nouvelle loi sur le statut personnel musulman," *E*, Mar. 1929, pp. 22–37.

12. HS, "Le Cabinet Ali Maher Pacha et son vaste programme de réformes sociales," *E*, Mar.–Apr. 1936, pp. 6 and 12–14. In 1936, Prime Minister ʿAli Mahir sponsored a literary competition: ten themes were suggested, including women's liberation. SN's essay, "L'évolution féministe et les profits que peut en retirer le bien public," which won first prize, addressed personal status reform; one of the judges was the shaykh al-Azhar, Mustafa al-Maraghi. See SN, "L'évolution féministe," *E*, Mar.–Apr. 1936, pp. 11–18. See also Duriyah Fahmi, "al-Nifas al-Adabi," *M*, Apr. 1, 1937, pp. 12–14.

13. Frank Stewart discovered from recent research in Sinai that bedouin women tend to marry later than other women in Egypt because of their later menarche, which occurs around the age of sixteen owing to poor diets; presumably this was true in earlier times as well. See Frank H. Stewart, "The Woman, Her Guardian, and Her Husband in the Law of the Sinai Bedouin," *Arabica* 38 (1991): 102–29; see p. 110. The average age of menarche in the villages and towns was around eleven to thirteen.

14. HS, "A la veille du Congrès de Paris," *E*, May 1926, p. 100.

15. Law No. 56 of 1923. See J.N.D. Anderson, *Islamic Law in the Modern World* (New York: New York University Press, 1959), p. 48. See also Ziadeh, *Lawyers, the Rule of Law and Liberalism*, p. 123.

16. Interview with SN, Nov. 20, 1975, Cairo. Anderson, *Islamic Law in the Modern World*, p. 44, claimed that the Ottoman Law of Family Rights of 1917, which contained an "empassioned description of evils" of premature marriage, set an important precedent in the region. However, a bill for a minimum marriage age introduced in the Egyptian legislative assembly in 1914 failed to pass. Also see J.N.D. Anderson, "Recent Developments in Sharʿia Law III," *The Muslim World* 41, no. 3 (1951): 113–21, and Anna Y. Thompson, "The Woman Question in Egypt," *Moslem World* 4, no. 3 (1914): 266–72, esp. p. 266. A. C. McBarnet, "The New Penal Code: Offenses against Morality and the Marriage Tie and Children," *L'Egypte contemporaine* 10, no. 46 (1919): 382–86, notes the insertion into the Egyptian penal code of a provision that consummation of marriage with a woman under twelve constituted rape, although the marriage itself was legal; this is cited as an example of procedural reform.

17. Winifred S. Blackman, a British social anthropologist doing fieldwork among the peasants in Upper Egypt from 1922 to 1926, observed that the law was often ignored in the villages (*The Fellahin of Upper Egypt*, pp. 43–33). However, unlike Blackman and Egyptian feminists, Ziadeh claimed that child marriages had been "virtually eliminated" as a result of the law (*Lawyers, the Rule of Law and Liberalism*, p. 123).

18. See "Une victoire féministe," *E*, Dec. 1928, p. 37, and SN, "Une loi n'a de valeur que par son application," *E*, Jan. 1931, pp. 5–8.

19. A Social Thinker, "Marriage of Girls under Age," *M*, Oct. 15, 1939, pp. 28–29.

20. Law 78, art. 99, May 12, 1931.

21. "Zawaj al-Qasirat, Ittijar bi-al-Raqiq al-Abyad," *M*, Aug. 1, 1938, pp. 21–22.

22. The deputies, ʿUthman Sawi Bey and ʿAbduh Mahmud al-Burtuqali, each made separate proposals to that effect; see "Barlamaniyat," *M*, Feb. 15, 1937, p. 29.

23. See SN, "Examen du nouveau projet du statut personnel musulman," *E*, Apr. 1927, p. 2.

24. Ibid., p. 7.

25. Reprinted in French in *E*; see "Une interview de Madame Hoda Charaoui," Apr. 1927, pp. 11–14.

26. Translation by Boktor (slightly modified), *School and Society in the Valley of the Nile*, p. 70. Earlier American women had compared the tyranny of husband over wife with that of England over the American colonies.

27. Qurʾan 4:3 and 3:129, respectively.

28. See SN, "La situation juridique de la femme égyptienne," *E*, Feb. 1931, p. 6, and idem, "La polygamie trouve encore des défenseurs en Egypte!" *E*, Nov. 1935, p. 10.

29. SN, "La situation juridique de la femme égyptienne," *E*, Feb. 1931, p. 6.

30. "Echos d'Orient," *E*, Sept. 1928, p. 33.

31. SN, "La polygamie trouve encore des défenseurs en Egypte!" *E*, Nov. 1935, p. 10.

32. Anderson, *Islamic Law in the Modern World*, p. 49, mentions ʿAbduh's efforts. ʿAbduh's biographer and disciple Shaykh Mustafa ʿAbd al-Raziq, in "L'influence de la femme dans la vie du Cheikh Mohamed Abdue," *E*, Aug. 1928, pp. 2–7, claimed that ʿAbduh's efforts to curb polygamy derived in part from his mother's sufferings. ʿAbduh's writings on polygamy included "Fatwa fi Taʿaddud al-Zawjat" (Religious ruling on polygamy), and "Hukum Taʿaddud al-Zawjat" (The rule of polygamy), in *al-ʿAmal al-Kamilah li-Muhammad ʿAbduh*, pp. 111–18 and 127–35, respectively.

33. See Ahmad Safwat, *Qaʾidat Islah Qanun al-Ahwal al-Shakhsiyah* (Cases of reform of the law of personal status) (Alexandria, 1917); and Ziadeh, *Lawyers, the Rule of Law and Liberalism*, pp. 119–21.

34. See "Hors-texte," *E*, Oct. 1931, p. 2.

35. See Anderson, *Islamic Law in the Modern World*, p. 49. For feminist criticism of the new code of personal status see "Une interview de Madame Hoda Charaoui," *E*, Apr. 1927, pp. 11–13.

36. SN, "La polygamie trouve encore des défenseurs en Egypte!" *E*, Nov. 1935, pp. 9–14.

37. See "Rayy al-Ustadh al-Akbar: Radd Muqtarahat al-Sayyidah al-Fadilah Munirah Thabit," *M*, Jan. 1, 1940, pp. 7–9. In "Taʿaddud al-Zawjat wa-Rayy Fadilat al-Anisah Munirah Thabit," *M*, Mar. 1, 1940, pp. 5–7, Thabit claimed that a woman acquiescing in a polygamous union must be ignorant, coerced, or mad.

38. Tucker's sampling of nineteenth-century court records for Mansurah in the Delta indicates that polygamy was not common among the peasantry; see *Women in Nineteenth Century Egypt*, p. 53.

39. SN, "Examen du nouveau projet du statut personnel musulman," *E*, Apr. 1927, p. 8.

40. See HS, *Harem Years*, pp. 70–75, and Bahithat al-Badiyah, "Bad Deeds of Men: Injustice," from *al-Nisaʾiyat*, in Badran and Cooke, *Opening the Gates*, pp.

135–36. Egyptian-born Lebanese Christian Amy Kher described the effects of divorce on middle-class women in *Mes soeurs*; see also "Sherife," pp. 80–100. In an interview in Cairo on Oct. 19, 1975, Kher provided additional insights. From her sampling of nineteenth-century court records in Mansurah in the Delta Tucker relates that divorce was widespread among the peasants; see *Women in Nineteenth Century Egypt*, p. 53, and for a wider discussion chap. 1. Anderson, writing in 1959, spoke of the high incidence of divorce in Egypt as well as in other Muslim countries (*Islamic Law in the Modern World*, pp. 52–53). For recent information on problems of divorce among poor women in Cairo, see Hill, "Divorce Egyptian Style and Related Matters," in *Mahkama!*, pp. 72–101, and Zaalouk, "The Social Structure of Divorce Adjudication in Egypt."

41. SN, "Examen du nouveau projet du statut personnel musulman," *E*, Apr. 1927, p. 8.

42. Ibid.

43. SN, "A une néophyte," *E*, June 1927, p. 21.

44. See, for example, "Conférence d'Ehsan Ahmed El Koussi, prononcée à l'Université américaine," *E*, May 1928, p. 23.

45. For a statement of these arguments see SN, "Examen du nouveau projet du statut personnel musulman," *E*, Apr. 1927, p. 8.

46. "La nouvelle loi sur le statut personnel musulman," *E*, Mar. 1929, p. 22.

47. SN, "Examen du nouveau projet du statut personnel musulman," *E*, Apr. 1927, p. 3.

48. "Une interview de Madame Hoda Charaoui," *E*, Apr. 1929, pp. 13–14, which published extracts of the *al-Ahram* interview.

49. The two major divisions of Islam are Sunni and Shiʿi. Sunni Islam predominates in Egypt. Shiʿi Islam predominates in Iran; there is a sizable Shiʿi community in Iraq, and there are some Shiʿi in countries of the Arabian Peninsula. In Shiʿi Islamic jurisprudence women and men inherit equally.

50. *Al-Ahram*, Dec. 28, 1928.

51. See HS, "La quote-part de la femme dans l'héritage," *E*, Jan. 1929, p. 2. This article had appeared previously in *al-Ahram*, Dec. 28, 1928.

52. "La situation juridique de la femme égyptienne: Conférence de Mademoiselle Ceza Nabarouy," *E*, Feb. 1931. This lecture was given on Feb. 23, 1931, at the University Women's Club in Cairo; for her remarks on inheritance, see pp. 10–12.

53. Ziadeh, *Lawyers, the Rule of Law and Liberalism*, p. 126; see Rida, *al-Manar* 30, no. 9 (1930): 698–709.

54. Quotation and details about Rida's encounter from Peter R. Knauss, *The Persistence of Patriarchy: Class, Gender, and Ideology in Twentieth Century Algeria* (New York: Praeger, 1987), p. 55, citing Ali Merad, *Le réformisme Musulman en Algérie de 1925 à 1940* (The Hague: Mouton, 1967), p. 318.

55. See "In Memoriam," *E*, June 1931, pp. 2–5. Aminah Hanim Afandi had been a supporter and benefactor of the EFU and was much revered by HS.

56. As in all areas of personal status, inheritance had important class implications. The wealthy resorted to a number of tactics to assure that their property passed on as they wished; still special arrangements had to be made to "equalize" or increase inheritance for females. Among peasants women typically did not take possession of their rights to land as heirs but left it to their male siblings to cultivate in return for part of the harvest and lifelong protection (see Tucker, *Women in Nineteenth Century Egypt*, pp. 44–45 and 49–50); however, sometimes women did wish to take possession of inherited land or to take over a usufruct, as indicated by court cases

Tucker examined. On the tendency of women to leave their land to their male siblings elsewhere see Martha Mundy, "Women's Inheritance of Land in Highland Yemen," *Arabian Studies* 5 (1979): 161–87; and Vanessa Maher, "Divorce and Property in the Middle Atlas of Morocco," *Man: Journal of the Royal Anthropological Institute*, n.s., 9 (1974): 103–22.

57. HS, "Quatrième anniversaire de *L'Egyptienne*," *E*, Feb. 1929, p. 4.

58. J.N.D. Anderson, in "The Role of Personal Status in Social Development in Islamic Countries," *Comparative Studies in Society and History* 13, no. 1 (1971): 16–31, asserts that the improved status of women and a feminist demand influenced the legal reforms. The Egyptian feminists did not agree, nor did the the revised personal status code of 1929 law prove his point.

59. Earlier in the century when women were making first steps into new jobs, NM and Bahithat al-Badiyah, while promoting work for women, were careful to exalt their maternal roles. See the former's *The Woman and Work* and the latter's *Nisa'iyat*. See also Badran, "From Consciousness to Activism," pp. 28–29. Looking at the discourse in the middle-class women's Arabic-language press from the 1890s to 1919 Baron argues that "generating domestic literature and feeding a domestic ideal was part of a [their] strategy to empower women within the accepted parameters of the home *without seriously challenging the boundaries of that home* [emphasis added]" ("The Rise of a New Literary Culture," p. 200).

60. Habib Hanin al-Masri, "Interviews with Prominent Men," *M*, May 15, 1939, pp. 6–10.

61. Fikri Abazah, "The Voice of Youth," *M*, Feb. 15, 1937, pp. 27–29, and Eva Habib al-Masri, "The War of Nerves," *M*, Oct. 1, 1939, pp. 2–3.

62. Muhammad Khurshid, "Masiruhum Ilayna," *M*, June 15, 1938, pp. 30–33, and July 1, 1938, pp. 34–36.

63. Na'imah al-Ayyubi, "A Voice from Europe to *al-Misriyah*," *M*, Feb. 15, 1937, pp. 33–36.

64. Bahigah Rashid, "The Reforming Woman as a Guide and Educator," *M*, Feb. 15, 1937, pp. 21–22.

65. An Honest Listener, "Between Two Educated Girls: A Good Aid for Solving the Marriage Crisis," *M*, Oct. 15, 1939, pp. 28–29.

66. Duriyah Fahmi, "The Literary Competition of 1936: A Résumé of the Opinions That Were Written on the Theme of the Development of the Renaissance of the Egyptian Woman," *M*, Apr. 1, 1937, pp. 12–14. Back in 1911 Labibah Hashim in *Kitab fi al-Tarbiyah* (A book on upbringing) (Cairo: Matbaʿat al-Maʿarif, 1911), p. 91, had also suggested that wives have a salary.

67. "The Wife Who Doesn't Read," *M*, Aug. 1, 1939, pp. 33–34.

68. *M*, Apr. 1, 1940, pp. 22–24. The same writer repeated the message in "Misery of Families," *M*, June 1, 1940, pp. 32–33, in which he says, "Lack of education on the part of the woman is the main source of misery in the family."

69. Translated extracts of the diary appear in Charles D. Smith, "Muhammad Husayn Haykal: An Intellectual and Political Biography" (Ph.D. diss., University of Michigan, 1968), pp. 98–99.

70. Tawfiq al-Hakim, "Ta'thir al-Mar'ah ʿala Kuttabina al-Mu-ʿasirin" (The impact of the woman on our contemporary [male] writers), *al-Thaqafah*, Apr. 11, 1939, pp. 6–8. On the feminist reaction see "Tawfiq al-Hakim, ʿAdu al-Mar'ah al-Misriyah Faqat" (Tawfiq al-Hakim only the enemy of the woman), *M*, May 1, 1939, pp. 7–8.

71. "Along the Road by a Passer-by: The Proposed Marriage of Nasim Pasha to

an Austrian Girl," *M*, Oct. 15, 1937, pp. 32–34. For further discussion of the problem of Egyptian men's marrying foreign women see "Risalat Muqadammah min al-Sayyidah Munirah Thabit ila Wizarat al-Shu'un al-Ijtimaᶜiyah" (Introductory letter from Mrs. Munirah Thabit to the Ministry of Social Affairs), *M*, Oct. 15, 1939, pp. 6–11; Munirah Thabit, unlike other feminists, expressed the view that only Egyptian men in high official positions and in the Foreign Office should be required to marry Egyptian women.

72. Niᶜmat Hamid Muhammad, "Idha Arjutum Zawjat Salihah fa-Awjidu al-Zawj al-Salih," *M*, Nov. 15, 1939, pp. 21–23.

73. *M*, Apr. 1, 1940.

74. Jamilah al-ᶜAla'ili, "al-ᶜArusah" (The bride), *M*, June 15, 1937, pp. 21–22. For similar advice, see Rifqah ᶜAtiyah Yusuf, "Asrar al-Saᶜadah al-Manziliyah" (Secrets of domestic happiness), *M*, June 1, 1939, pp. 25–26, and "Athar al-Tanwiᶜ fi Hayat al-Bayt" (The impact of organization on household life), *M*, Dec. 15, 1939, pp. 10–12.

75. Rifqah ᶜAtiyah Yusuf, "Asrar al-Saᶜadah al-Manziliyah," *M*, June 1, 1939, pp. 25–26.

76. Muhammad ᶜIffat, "The Ten Commandments of an Arab Woman to Her Daughter," *M*, Sept. 1, 1939, p. 17. This was said to have been the advice the daughter of ᶜAwf ibn Mahlam al-Shayban was given by her mother when al-Harith ibn ᶜAmr, the king of Kinda in Arabia, wanted to marry the daughter.

77. Ayesha Jalal mentions this in "The Convenience of Subservience and the State of Pakistan," in Kandiyoti, *Women, Islam and the State*, noting that the book is a contemporary best-seller in Pakistan. See also Barbara Daly Metcalf, *Perfecting Woman. Maulana Ashraf Ali Thanawi's Bihishti Zewar: Partial Translation with Commentary* (Berkeley and Los Angeles: University of California Press, 1990).

78. "The Marriage Crisis and Its Social Impact on the Future of the Country," *M*, Feb. 1, 1940.

79. "Happy Marriage," *M*, July 15, 1937, p. 4.

80. "ᶜIlaj Azmat al-Zawaj," *M*, Sept. 1, 1939, p. 23.

81. The article appeared on Aug. 13, 1935. See HS, *Mudhakkirat*, p. 407.

82. Interview with Duriyah Shafiq, Apr. 10, 1974, Cairo. See "Une sensationelle innovation qui prend le caractère d'une réforme sociale," *E*, Aug.–Sept. 1935, pp. 32–33.

83. "Barlamaniyat," *M*, July 15, 1937, p. 36.

84. Linking prostitution to men's failure to marry, the Ministry of Health proposed that revenues from the bachelor tax go toward the rehabilitation of prostitutes. "Barlamaniyat," *M*, June 5, 1938, p. 40.

85. "The Complaint of Honorable Families and the Cure of the Marriage Crisis," *M*, Dec. 15, 1939, p. 16.

86. "Akhbar," *M*, May 1, 1940, p. 30.

87. Magda Hasib, "Hadith al-Ummahat," *M*, Feb. 15, 1939, p. 37; Apr. 1, 1939, pp. 28–29; Apr. 15, 1939, p. 35; Oct. 1, 1939, pp. 25–27; Feb. 15, 1940, pp. 24, 28. Similar articles by others included Isis Habib al-Misri, "ᶜIndama Yarfudu al-Tifl an Yakul," *M*, Nov. 15, 1937, p. 30; Muhammad Wasfi, "Irda' al-Tifl," *M*, July 15, 1938, pp. 21–23.

88. Na'imah al-Ayyubi, "An Opinion on the Education of the Girl in Egypt," *M*, May 1, 1937, pp. 18–21.

89. In 1920 NM had written on the importance of reading in the moral and

intellectual formation of girls and boys; she emphasized the merits of reading for girls at a time when literacy for females was seen as tantamount to their moral collapse. See "The Effects of Books and Novels on Morals," in *The Woman and Work*. A translation of this essay appears in Badran and Cooke, *Opening the Gates*, pp. 259–62.

90. Kamil Kilani, "Madha Yutali'u al-Atfal?" *M*, July 15, 1938, pp. 15–16. Kilani was an employee in the ministry of awqaf who held a literary salon in Hasan al-Akbar near ʿAbidin. Interview with Mahmud Amin al-ʿAlam (Kilani's son-in-law), June 1974, Oxford.

91. Sumayya Fahmi, "al-Tarbiyah al-Jinsiyah," *M*, Mar. 15, 1938, pp. 13–15, and Apr. 15, 1938, pp. 15–16. The random way children in Egypt picked up knowledge about sexuality is vividly portrayed in novels by Egyptian writers Mahmud Diyab, Edwar al-Kharrat, and ʿAbd al-Hakim Qasim, who surely drew on their own encounters and observations growing up in the 1930s. Magda al-Nowaihi has examined this in "Gender as Seen through Children's Eyes in Modern Arabic Literature" (Paper presented at the Colloquium on Women in Religion and Society at the Annenberg Institute, May 1991).

92. ʿIffat Thabit, "Modern Psychology and Parents," *M*, Aug. 1, 1939, pp. 27–30.

Chapter Eight
Educating the Nation

1. SN, "L'évolution du féminisme en Egypte," *E*, Mar. 1925, p. 45.

2. SN, "Dans les domaines de notre action," *E*, May 1925, pp. 108–9.

3. France had begun a state system of secondary schooling for girls in 1880, but the opportunity that boys had for secondary schooling leading to the baccalaureate was granted to girls only in 1925, the same year this occurred in Egypt. See Karen Offen, "The Second Sex and the Baccalaureate in Republican France, 1880–1924," *French Historical Studies* 13, no. 2 (1983): 252–86; see p. 252.

4. Insaf Sirri was married to Mansur Fahmi, professor of philosophy at Fu'ad I University. His doctoral thesis at the Sorbonne, published under the title *La condition de la femme dans la tradition et l'islamisme* (Paris, 1913), provoked heated controversy in Egypt; see Donald Reid, "The 'Sleeping Philosopher' of Nagib Mahfuz's *Mirrors*," *The Muslim World* 74, no. 1 (1984): 1–11. Ruth Woodsmall recorded in her Diary on May 2, 1929, an evening spent with Sirri and her husband comparing "Eastern" and "Western" social practices. At the Arab Feminist Conference in Cairo in 1944 Sirri reviewed Egyptian middle- and upper-class women's move from domestic isolation to active participation in society. See Insaf Sirri, speech, *MNA*, pp. 115–19.

5. See SN, "L'enseignement secondaire féminin en Egypte," *E*, Nov. 1927, pp. 5–10.

6. Al-Saʿid, daughter of Ahmad al-Saʿid and Zaynab Talʿat who had been an activist in Asyut during the 1919 revolution, was one of six siblings (she had four sisters and a brother) and had first attended the Hilmiyah School. Interview with Aminah al-Saʿid and Karimah al-Saʿid, Jan. 21, 1968. Al-Ayyubi had begun school in Alexandria before moving to Cairo, where she also attended the Hilmiyah School. Interview with Naʿimah al-Ayyubi, Feb. 8, 1975, Cairo.

7. Interview with Aminah al-Saʿid, Mar. 29, 1972.

8. SN, "Deux interviews avec S.E. le Ministre de l'Instruction Publique," *E*, July 1930, p. 3.

9. For a teacher's recollections of the Hilmiyah School see ʿAsmah Fahmi, *Dhikrayat ʿan Madrasat al-Hilmiyah al-Thanawiyah lil-Banat* (Memoirs of the Hilmiyah Secondary School for Girls) (Cairo, 1955).

10. SN, "L'enseignement secondaire féminin en Egypte," *E*, Nov. 1927, p. 9.

11. Ibid.

12. HS's daughter, Bathna (b. 1903), had been educated by private tutors at home.

13. See NM, "Private Education," in *The Woman and Work*, pp. 49–65.

14. *D*, "The Establishment of Tarqiyat al-Fatah School," 2d ser., no. 75, and "The Help of Huda Shaʿrawi," 1st ser., no. 14.

15. Ibid., "How My School Was Supported by the Visit of His Majesty, the Late King," 1st ser., no. 13.

16. It will be noted that NM called her school after the aborted Madrasat Banat al-Ashraf, whose construction, begun in 1878, was halted the following year with the deposing of Khedive Ismaʿil.

17. He was married to Nahid Sirri, later founding head of the Women's Committee of the Red Crescent. On the incident see *D*, "The Egyptian Is a Stranger in His Own Country," 1st ser., no. 12.

18. See ibid., "How the Flashy Girls (*mutabarijat*) Disliked My Schools," 1st ser., no. 89, in which she speaks of her strict dress code and the reactions of parents and students.

19. Andrée Chedid draws upon memories of the period to sketch a poignant account of the sudden withdrawal of a young upper-class girl from school in order to marry; see her novel *From Sleep Unbound*, trans. from the French by Sharon Spencer (Athens, Ohio: Swallow Press, 1983), pp. 32 and 45–46.

20. See "Nos féministes à l'étranger," *E*, Apr. 1925, pp. 82–84. Books published around that time on women in Islamic history included Muhammad Jamil Bayham, *al-Marʾah fi Hadarat al-ʿArab* (Beirut: Dar al-Nashr lil-Jamʿiyin, 1926), and Qadriyah Husayn, *Shahirat al-Nisaʿ fi al-ʿAlam al-Islami* (Cairo: al-Maktabat al-Misriyah, 1924). Zaynab Fawwaz had included Muslim women distinguished for their learning in *al-Durr al-Manthur fi al-Tabaqat Rabbat al-Khudur*, published in 1894.

21. See SN, "A la dérive," *E*, July–Aug. 1933, pp. 2–9.

22. Yusuf Niyazi, "al-Marʾah al-Misriyah fi al-ʿAhd al-Farʿuni," *M*, Apr. 15, 1937, pp. 15–16. See also, for example, Henri Henne, "Les conditions de la femme dans l'Egypte antique," *E*, 0ct.–Nov. 1926, pp. 19–26; Fikriyah ʿAbd al-Majid, "al-Marʾah ʿinda Qudamaʾ al-Misriyin," *M*, Nov. 15, 1937, p. 35; and Iris Habib al-Masri, "al-Marʾah ʿinda Qudamaʾ al-Misriyin," *M*, Mar. 15, 1937, pp. 9–12. Jules Tixerant, "La femme à l'époque de Tout-ankh-amon," *E*, Dec. 1925, pp. 350–57, notes impressions of Greek travelers to Egypt.

23. SN, "A l'Union féministe égyptienne," *E*, Dec. 1932, pp. 2–3. On her first visit to France in 1908 HS had been struck by the French reverence for their historical monuments and how monuments and museums further fuel a nationalist spirit. See HS, *Harem Years*, p. 84.

24. SN, "Deux interviews avec S.E. le Ministre de l'Instruction Publique," *E*, July 1930, p. 4. See also *The Egyptian Gazette*, Aug. 18, 1930, "The Egyptian Woman: A Feminist Minister of Education, Demands of the Feminist Union."

25. "Le Gouvernement Egyptien et l'enseignement des jeunes filles," *E*, Sept. 1930, p. 6.

26. NM, "Egypt's Need for Women Doctors, Teachers, Dressmakers, and Other Professions," in *The Woman and Work*.

27. Many years later a former student remembered her most for this. See "Mudhakkirat Mudarissah," *al-Jumhuriyah*, Nov. 16, 1970, no. 16 in the series Mudhakkirat Mansiyah edited by Hafiz Mahmud.

28. SN, "Le développement de la culture physique en Egypte," *E*, May 1929, p. 3.

29. Ibid.

30. Bahithat al-Badiyah, "A Lecture in the Club of the Umma Party," in *al-Nisa'iyat*.

31. NM, "How the Egyptian Girl Should Be Educated," in *The Woman and Work*, pp. 37–48.

32. See Woodsmall, *Moslem Women Enter a New World*, pp. 178–79.

33. "Echos d'Orient," *E*, Dec. 1930, p. 36.

34. Na'imah al-Ayyubi, "An Opinion on the Education of the Girl in Egypt," *M*, Apr. 15, 1937, p. 9.

35. Statistics quoted in SN, "Le Gouvernement Egyptian et l'enseignement des jeunes filles," *E*, Sept. 30, p. 3.

36. "Excellence of Girls in the Results of the Primary and Secondary School Examinations," *M*, Aug. 1, 1940, pp. 8–9.

37. W. F., "To Those Who Ask for Limits in Educating the Girl," *M*, Aug. 1, 1940, pp. 10–11.

38. There seems to have been a growing debate in the 1930s on the issue of different educational needs of women based on the differences between the sexes. Sayyid Qutb (still in his secularist phase) in "Thaqafat al-Mar'ah al-Misriyah," *Majallat al-Shu'un al-Ijtimaʿiyah* 1, no. 4 (1940): 34–38, argued that women's inherent differences and the maternal and domestic roles they must play necessitate a different education for them. Later in his book *Social Justice in Islam*, trans. from the Arabic by John B. Hardie (Washington, D.C.: American Council of Learned Societies, 1953), he posits a social construction of women's emotionality.

39. Naʿimah al-Ayyubi, "An Opinion on the Education of the Girl in Egypt," *M*, May 1, 1937, pp. 18–21.

40. "Discussion in the Chamber of Deputies on Educating Girls," *M*, May l, 1937, pp. 38–39.

41. Ahmad Musa, "On Schools of Feminine Culture," *M*, Oct. 1, 1937, p. 32.

42. Reid, *Cairo University*, p. 105.

43. See Ahmad Lutfi al-Sayyid, *al-Muntakhabat* (Cairo, 1938), pp. 27–28.

44. "Echos d'Orient," *E*, June 1931, p. 30.

45. Baha al-Din Barakat, "Systems of Educating Girls," *M*, Apr. 1, 1937, pp. 4–5.

46. Wadidah Wassif became a translator from Arabic into English. In her memoirs she has vividly recalled her days at a state school and the experiences of girls studying Arabic with Shaykh Rifaʿat.

47. Najib Mahfuz, *Mirrors*, trans. Roger Allen (Minneapolis: Biblioteca Islamica, 1977), pp. 106–8.

48. Wadidah Wassif, unpublished memoirs, Alexandria. For a biographical profile of Wassif see Badran and Cooke, *Opening the Gates*, p. 92.

49. Na'imah al-Ayyubi, in *Dhikra Faqidat al-ʿUrubah Huda Hanim Shaʿrawi* (Cairo, 1947).

50. See SN, "A l'Union féministe égyptienne," *E*, Dec. 1933, pp. 7–9.

51. This was Sami Gabra, a contributor to *E*. See Donald Reid, "Indigenous Egyptology: The Decolonization of a Profession?" *Journal of the American Oriental Society* 105, no. 2 (1985): 233–46.

52 SN, "L'activité d'une grande dame égyptienne," *E*, May 1938, pp. 12–22. Interview with Princess Khadijah Fu'ad ʿIzzat, Feb. 15, 1972, Cairo.

53. "Travaux des femmes archéologues en Egypte," *E*, Feb. 1939, p. 38. Vacaresco, originally from Romania, was the president of a French geographical society called La Femme et l'Univers. "Prix Hélène Vacaresco," *E*, June 1939, p. 34, announced an upcoming competition the society was sponsoring for women writing in French on women in "faraway lands" or in the French provinces.

54. "Echos d'Orient," *E*, Mar.–Apr., 1936, p. 36.

55. "Al-Akhbar," *M*, June 15, 1937, p. 30.

56. In 1939 feminist Naʿimah al-Ayyubi was instrumental in the opening of the first hostel for women, which facilitated university study for women from outside Cairo.

57. Interview with Bint al-Shati' (ʿA'ishah ʿAbd al-Rahman), July 8, 1968, Cairo. She published two autobiographical works: *Sirr al-Shati'* (Cairo: Ruz al-Yusuf, 1952), in the form of stories from the countryside where she grew up; and *ʿAla Jisr: Usturat al-Zaman* (On a bridge: A myth of the time), Cairo: Dar al-Hilal, 1967), a more conventional account that speaks of her husband and marriage. See also C. Kooij, "Bint al-Shat': A Suitable Case for Biography?" (Paper published by the Institute for Modern Near Eastern Studies, University of Amsterdam, 1982).

58. Interview with Rawhiyah al-Qalini, Apr. 11, 1974, Cairo. She worked for a period as headmistress of a girls' school at Mosul in Iraq. She was a member of the Poetry Committee and the Society of Litterateurs in Cairo. Among her other books is a volume on Sufi poetry.

59. Munirah Thabit mentioned in her memoirs that the Ministry of Education wanted to create a higher commercial school for girls but the Alexandria Chamber of Commerce opposed this. Women who worked in the private commercial firms tended to come from the minorities. See *Thawrah fi al-Burj al-ʿAji: Mudhakkirat fi ʿIshrin ʿAm* (Cairo: Dar al-Maʿarif bi-al-Tibaʿah wa-al-Nashr, 1945).

60. In 1925, illiteracy among women was 96 percent (men's 78 percent); in 1930, 95 percent (men's 76 percent); in 1940, 92 percent (men's 73 percent); in 1945, 90 percent (men's 68 percent); and in 1950, 87 percent (men's 63 percent). Reid, *Cairo University*, 113.

61. "Echos d'Orient," *E*, Dec. 1935, p. 33.

62. "To Those Who Ask for Limits in Educating the Girl," *M*, Aug. 1940, pp. 10–11.

63. *Ahadith Jiddati* (Cairo: Dar al-Qawmiyya, 1935; 2d ed. 1959).

64. See A. Chris Eccel, *Egypt, Islam, and Social Change: Al-Azhar in Conflict and Accommodation* (Berlin: Klaus Schwarz, 1984), pp. 377–98.

65. Interview with Aminah al-Saʿid, Mar. 29, 1972, Cairo.

66. On women in the left-wing movements see Giuseppe Contu, "Le donne comuniste e il movimento democratico femminile in Egitto fino al 1965," *Oriente Moderno*, May–June 1975, pp. 237–47; and Selma Botman, "Women's Participation in Radical Egyptian Politics, 1939–1952," *Khamsin*, no. 6 (1987): 12–25. On

the general student movement see Ahmed Abdalla, *The Student Movement and National Politics in Egypt* (London: al-Saqi Books, 1985); and Joel Beinin and Zachary Lockman, *Workers on the Nile: Nationalism, Communism, Islam, and the Egyptian Working Class, 1882–1954* (Princeton: Princeton University Press, 1987), pp. 340–42.

67. Interviews with Inji Aflatun, Sept. 17, 1975, and Mar., 1988, Cairo, when Aflatun told me about her intention to publish her memoirs. She died in 1989 before completing her task. Saʿid al-Khayy edited and introduced *Mudhakkirat Inji Aflatun* (The memoirs of Inji Aflatun) (Kuwait: Dar Suʿad al-Sabah, 1993). I learned of this after submitting my manuscript to the press but would like to draw attention here to its publication.

68. The novel was republished in 1989 with a new introduction by the literary critic Faryal Ghazul. She calls her recent collection of short stories, *Shaykhukhah* (Old age) (Cairo: Dar al-Mustaqbal al-ʿArabi, 1986), "a celebration of self-reconciliation . . . which no man could have written." Her latest book is *Hamlat Taftish: "Awraq Shakhsiyah"* (Expeditionary raid: "Private papers") (Cairo: Dar al-Hilal, 1992).

69. Interview with Latifah al-Zayyat, May 3, 1990. See also Badran, "Gender Activists: Feminists and Islamists in Egypt," in *Identity Politics and Women: Cultural Reassertions and Feminisms in International Perspective*, ed. Valentine Moghadam (Boulder: Westview Press, 1994).

70. Interview with Mustafa Thabit, the brother of Munirah Thabit, Feb. 6, 1972, Cairo.

71. "La femme orientale et les hautes études," *E*, Sept. 1925, p. 256. *E* had just hailed Sara Levy as the "first Eastern woman" to take a diploma in an "Eastern university." She was a Jewish woman from Jerusalem, who had specialized in chemisty and pharmaceutics at the American University in Beirut.

72. "Hors-texte," *E*, Sept. 1930.

73. Ibid. In 1934 only two of the twenty-eight women at the university were Muslims. See Woodsmall, *Moslem Women Enter a New World*, p. 214.

74. Al-Masri, *Memoirs of an Egyptian American*, pp. 6–7. On the admittance of women to the American University in Cairo see also Lawrence R. Murphy, *The American University in Cairo: 1919–1987* (Cairo: The American University in Cairo Press, 1987), p. 42. By 1934 there were fifteen women students, constituting nearly ten percent of the total enrollment, most of whom were Christian graduates of the American College for Girls.

75. Al-Masri, *Memoirs*, p. 18.

76. The biographical information is gleaned from my two interviews with Duriyah Shafiq, Jan. 23, 1968, and Apr. 10, 1974, Cairo, and from Cynthia Nelson in "The Voices of Doria Shafiq: Feminist Consciousness in Egypt, 1940–1960," *Feminist Issues* 6, no. 2 (1986): 15–31.

77. Her articles include "Une femme a-t-elle le droit de philosopher?" Dec. 1930; "Reverie d'une femme d'aujourd'hui," Aug. 1932; "Voyage gratis," Feb. 1936; and "L'art pour l'art dans l'Egypte," Apr. 1940.

78. Interviews with Duriyah Shafiq, Jan. 23, 1968, and Apr. 10, 1974, Cairo.

79. The association was headed by Najib al-Hilali, a former minister of education.

80. "Ouverture d'une école nouvelle de service social," *E*, Sept. 1937, p. 36, and "Al-Mar'a a-Misriyya wa Khidma al-Ijtimaʿi," *M*, Oct. 16, 1937, pp. 10–12.

81. Interview with Ihsan al-Qusi, Feb. 22, 1972.

82. "Pour la culture intellectuelle et morale de la femme égyptienne," *E*, Nov. 1930, p. 40, and "Echos d'Orient," *E*, Dec. 1930, pp. 35–37. Al-Qusi and Saiza Nabarawi were members of the joint EFU–Ministry of Education committee.

83. See Mahmud Kamil, *Tadhawwuq al-Musiqa al-ʿArabiyah* (Cairo, 1975), pp. 26–27.

84. See Virginia Danielson, "Artists and Entrepreneurs: Female Singers in Cairo during the 1920s," in Keddie and Baron, *Women in Middle Eastern History*, pp. 292–309.

85. See Poole, *The Englishwoman in Egypt*, 2:61–67.

86. See Tugay, *Three Centuries*, pp. 170–77.

87. HS and SN's (then future) stepmother attended performances in the 1890s. See HS, *Harem Years*, p. 62.

88. Ibid.

89. Wassif, unpublished memoirs.

90. "Hors-texte," *E*, Mar. 1927.

91. Communication from Virginia Danielson.

92. See Danielson, "Artists and Entrepreneurs."

93. On the life of Umm Kalthum see her memoirs, published in serial form in the journal *Akhir Saʿah* from Nov. 1937 to Jan. 1938 "with the pen of" Muhammad Hammad; they were republished as *Umm Kulthum allati la Yaʿrifuha Ahad* (The Umm Kulthum nobody knows) (Cairo: Mu'assasat Akhbar al-Yawm, 1971) by Mahmud Awad, who added new material. For an English translation of part of the memoirs see "Excerpts from *The Umm Kulthum Nobody Knows*," trans. Elizabeth Fernea, in *Middle Eastern Muslim Women Speak*, ed. Elizabeth Fernea and Basima Qattan Bezirgan (Austin: University of Texas Press, 1977), pp. 135–67. See also Mahmoud Kamil's introduction to *al-Nusus al-Kamilah li-Aghani Umm Kalthum* (Complete editions of the songs of Umm Kalthum) (Cairo, 1975); Muhammad al-Sayyid Shushah, *Umm Kulthum: Hayat Nagham* (Cairo: Ruz al-Yusif, 1976); Niʿmat Ahmad Fu'ad, *Umm Kulthum wa ʿAsr min al-Fann* (Cairo: al-Hay'ah al-Misriyah al-ʿAmah lil-Kitab, 1976); and Virginia Danielson, "Shaping Tradition in Arabic Song: The Career and Repertory of Umm Kulthum" (Ph.D. diss., University of Illinois, Champaign-Urbana, 1991).

94. See SN, "Le Conservatoire de musique orientale," *E*, Dec. 1930, pp. 6–10, and ibid., "Hors-texte," featuring ʿAziza Musa, p. 1.

95. See SN, "Une nouvelle étoile au firmament égyptien," *E*, Sept. 1928, pp. 5–9. Around that time a group of upper-class women were forming a Committee for Friends of Music to promote music and nurture artists, but it is not clear whether women themselves benefited.

96. Celebrated European musicians and musicologists from abroad attended, including Béla Bartók from Hungary and Paul Hindemith from Germany.

97. On artists from the 1920s to the early 1970s see the exhibition catalog *Egyptian Women Painters over Half a Century* (Cairo, 1975).

98. SN, "Vers la solution de grands problèmes sociaux: quelques minutes avec le Ministre de l'Instruction Publique," *E*, July–Aug. 1938, pp. 5–11; see p. 9.

99. Ibid., p. 9.

100. SN, "La femme et le mouvement artistique," *E*, Mar. 1938; pp. 2–4, see p. 3.

101. Ibid., p. 4.

102. See "Hors-texte: Moukhtar," *E*, Mar. 1934, p. 2; "Hors-texte: le monument

à Saad Zaghloul par Moukhtar" and Isma'il Kamel, "Moukhtar: symbole d'une époque," *E*, Apr. 1934, pp. 2 and 6, respectively; "Hors-texte: la fiancée du Nil de Moukhtar," *E*, Mar. 1938; SN, "Pour que l'oeuvre de Moukhtar revienne à l'Egypte," *E*, June 1934, pp. 2–7, declaring that helping artists of the present was as much a national duty as cherishing the treasures of the past (p. 3); and SN, "Le concours Moukhtar 1940," *E*, Mar. 1940, pp. 2–5.

103. See SN, "Décembre de gloire!" *E*, Dec. 1933, pp. 2–6, and SN, "A l'Union féministe égyptienne," *E*, Dec. 1933, pp. 7–9. The EFU published her picture on the frontispiece of *E* in January and in May of 1934.

104. Markham's autobiography, *West with the Night* (Boston: Houghton, 1942), mentions her stop in Cairo, but there is no reference to Lutfi.

105. A photograph of a class of women pilots was published in *M*, Aug. 1, 1940, p. 11.

106. *M*, Apr. 15, 1939.

107. *E*, Dec. 1933, p. 7.

108. See Tawfiq al-Hakim, *al-Jins al-Latif*, in *al-Masrah al-Munawwa'* (Cairo: Maktabat al-Adab wa-Matbaatuha, 1956), pp. 687–703. It was produced for the first time on the stage at the EFU with members and friends playing the parts.

109. SN, "Réponse aux réactionnaires," *E*, Sept. 1932, p. 2.

110. Ibid., pp. 2–8.

111. "Parliamentary Affairs," *M*, May 15, 1937, p. 37.

112. Interview with Aminah al-Sa'id, Oct. 1989, Cairo. Reid interview with Zaynab Hassan, Apr. 26, 1988, cited in his book, *Cairo University*; see pp. 108 and 254n.32. A woman in Cairo told Ruth Woodsmall that "before the nationalist movement [presumably 1919–1922] we kept it a secret if we played tennis." Woodsmall wrote (1936), "Now people are quite proud of the fact." See Woodsmall, *Moslem Women Enter a New World*, p. 81.

113. SN, "Alexandrie, reine des cités méditerranéennes," *E*, Aug. 1932, p. 7.

114. On this press censorship, and general loss of liberties see SN, "La liberté sous la nouvelle constitution," *E*, June 1931, pp. 6–8. On the student movement and protests during this period see Abdalla, *The Student Movement and Nationalist Politics in Egypt*, pp. 39–57.

115. The mixing of the sexes at the university came up again in 1937 in struggles between Wafdists and non-Wafdist students when religion was also an issue; see Abdalla, *The Student Movement and Nationalist Politics in Egypt*, p. 44.

116. Extracts from the Hilmi 'Isa interview with *al-Ahram* derive from the French translation done by *La réforme*, which was reproduced in *E*; SN, "Pudeur ministérielle!" *E*, Sept. 1931, pp. 6–11; see p. 7.

117. SN, "A la dérive," *E*, Jul–Aug. 1933, p. 9.

118. Ibid., p. 7.

119. Ibid., pp. 8–9.

120. Ibid., pp. 2–9.

121. "A Quiet Talk: Boys and Girls in the Halls of Learning," *M*, Mar. 15, 1937, p. 30, cont. p. 40.

122. "The Question of the Mixing of the Two Sexes," *M*, Apr. 1, 1937, p. 8.

123. Ibid.

124. "A Quiet Talk: Boys and Girls in the Halls of Learning," *M*, Mar. 15, 1937, p. 30, cont. p. 40.

125. Tawfiq al-Hakim, "About the Mixing of the Sexes,"*M*, Apr. 1, 1937, p. 1.

Chapter Nine
Women Have Always Worked

1. *Al-Mar'ah al-Misriyah*, no. 10 (Dec. 1920): 350.

2. See Tucker, *Women in Nineteenth Century Egypt*, and Hammam, "Women and Industrial Work in Egypt," pp. 50–60, see pp. 51–54.

3. For various interpretations see Cole, "Feminism, Class, and Islam in Turn-of-the-Century Egypt,"and Thomas Philipp, "Feminism and National Politics in Egypt," in Beck and Keddie, *Women in the Muslim World*, pp. 295–308.

4. See Judith Tucker, "Decline of the Family Economy," *Arab Studies Quarterly* 1, no. 3 (1979): 245–71.

5. Bahithat al-Badiyah, "A Lecture in the Club of the Ummah Party," in *al-Nisa'iyat.*

6. NM, *The Woman and Work*, pp. 3–5.

7. "Egypt's Need for Women Doctors, Teachers, Dressmakers, and Other Professions," in ibid., pp. 65–77.

8. Bahithat al-Badiyah, "A Lecture in the Club of the Ummah Party," in *al-Nisa'iyat.*

9. NM, "The Differences between the Man and the Woman and Their Capacities for Work," in *The Woman and Work*, pp. 21–36.

10. Ibid., and NM, "Introduction," in *The Woman and Work*, pp. 3–5.

11. Bahithat al-Badiyah, "A Lecture in the Club of the Ummah Party,"in *al-Nisa'iyat.*

12. NM, "The Differences between the Man and the Woman and Their Capacities for Work," in *The Woman and Work*, pp. 21–36.

13. Ibid.

14. SN, "Des inaugurations . . . des horizons nouveaux," *E*, Oct. 1930, p. 2.

15. HS, "Lettre ouverte de Mme Charaoui Pacha à S.A. le Prince Omar Tousson," *E*, Mar. 1935, pp. 6–7.

16. Ihsan al-Qusi recited examples of women in Islamic history at a lecture at the American University in Beirut in Feb. 1925. Majd al-Din Hifni Nasif had done likewise in a lecture in Paris sponsored by Maria Verone the same month. See "Nos féministes à l'étranger," *E*, Apr. 1925, pp. 81–85.

17. SN, "La jeune fille et le travail," *E*, Nov. 1930, pp. 3–4.

18. Jeanne Marques, "Le prééminence du point de vue social dans les divers problèmes traités par les associations féministes," *E*, Apr. 1934, pp. 17–20.

19. SN, "La jeune fille et le travail," *E*, Nov. 1930, pp. 2–8; see p. 3.

20. Ibid.

21. *Report of the Eleventh Congress of the International Alliance of Women for Suffrage and Equal Citizenship Held in Berlin June 17–22, 1929* (London, 1929), p. 195. *Report of the Twelfth Congress of the International Alliance of Women for Suffrage and Equal Citizenship Held in Istanbul April 16–25, 1935* (London, 1935) p. 134.

22. Marques, "Le prééminence du point de vue social dans les divers problèmes traités par les associations féministes," *E*, Apr. 1934, p. 19.

23. On women's work in Europe see Renate Bridenthal, "Something Old, Something New: Women between the Two World Wars," in *Becoming Visible: Women in European History*, ed. Renate Bridenthal, Claudia Koonz, and Susan Stuard, 2d ed. (Boston: Houghton Mifflin, 1987), pp. 473–98; on the IAW positions, especially regarding the United States and Europe, see Susan Becker, "International Feminism

between the Wars: The National Woman's Party versus the League of Women Voters," in *Decades of Discontent*, ed. L. Scharf and J. Jensen (Westport, Conn.: Greenwood, 1983), pp. 223–42; and on women and work in France see Karen Offen, "Body Politics: Women, Work, and the Politics of Motherhood in France, 1920–1950," in *Maternity and Gender Policies: Women and the Rise of the European Welfare States, 1880s-1950s*, ed. Gisela Bock and Pat Thane (London and New York: Routledge, 1991).

24. Fatma Nimet Rached, "Notre enquête," *E*, Apr. 1934, pp. 30–31.

25. Ibid., pp. 28–29.

26. Ibid., pp. 32–33.

27. "Un intéressant débat à la faculté de droit," *E*, Nov. 1931, p. 32.

28. See Tucker, *Women in Nineteenth Century Egypt*, pp. 84–91.

29. See Ester Boserup, *Women's Role in Economic Development* (London: Allen and Unwin, 1970).

30. See J. Vallet, *Contribution à l'étude de la condition ouvrière dans la grande industrie au Caire* (Valence, 1911).

31. SN, "Des inaugurations des horizons nouveaux," *E*, Oct. 1930, p. 14. The al-Luzi family were wealthy merchants who imported silk from Lebanon and were among the backers of Bank Misr. On employment and exploitation of women workers because of both assumed and observed "gender traits" in Egypt see James Toth, "Pride, Purdah, or Paychecks: Gender Division of Labor in Rural Egypt," *International Journal of Middle Eastern Studies* 23, no. 2 (1991): 213–36. See Tucker, *Women in Nineteenth Century Egypt*, on women's work and lower pay. Also see Boserup, *Women's Role in Economic Development*.

32. "Une industrielle égyptienne: Helama Abdel Malek," *E*, Aug. 1925, pp. 209–10.

33. SN, "L'enseignement d'une exposition," *E*, Mar. 1931, p. 4.

34. The director was James-Alfred Coulon, who had studied at l'Ecole des Arts Décoratifs in Paris. See Jeanne Marquès, "La renaissance de la céramique arabe," *E*, Jan. 1926, pp. 15–16; and Louis Marcerou, "Une renaissance de la céramique arabe en Egypte," *E*, Oct.–Nov. 1926, pp. 48–50. Hasan al-Hawari, *al-Marʿah wa al-Fann* (Cairo, n.d.), p. 427. There is some evidence that women engaged in ceramic production in Cairo in earlier centuries. A faience shard of Mamluk fabrication, for example, found at Fustat was signed "the work of Khadijah." There is a living tradition of women potters in certain villages in both the Delta and Upper Egypt.

35. Woodsmall, *Moslem Women Enter a New World*, p. 184, remarked with favor on this enterprise after her 1929 trip to Egypt.

36. HS recalls women peddlers who came to her family house in Cairo when she was a young girl, and her description of first going to a new department store in Alexandria indicates that there were saleswomen. See *Harem Years*, pp. 48 and 68–69.

37. See Becker, "International Feminism between the Wars."

38. "Règlementation du travail des femmes en Egypte," *E*, June 1932, pp. 36–38; see p. 36. See also "Notre législation ouvrière," *E*, Nov. 1932, pp. 32–33.

39. "Règlementation du travail des femmes en Egypte," *E*, June 1932, pp. 36–38.

40. "Règlementation de l'emploi des femmes dans le commerce et l'industrie [Law 80]," *E*, Sept. 1933, pp. 17–21.

41. See Boserup, *Women's Role in Economic Development*.

42. Agricultural work for women, harvesting onions from March through June, harvesting fruits and vegetables from October through March, and sorting and crat-

ing eggs from November through March; *Arrêté*, Dec. 31, 1933. Night work for women was further regulated by Convention no. 41 of June 19, 1934 (ratified July 11, 1947). Work between 10 P.M. and 5 A.M. was prohibited to women.

43. Joan Scott, "The Woman Worker," in Fraisse and Perrot, *A History of Women in the West*, pp. 398–426; see pp. 420–22.

44. "Les droits de nos ouvrières," *E*, May 1934, p. 28.

45. See "Lutte effective contre le chômage," *E*, Apr. 1934, pp. 34–35; see p. 34.

46. "Les femmes et le travail en Egypte," *E*, Feb. 1935, pp. 17–18.

47. Ibid., p. 16.

48. SN, "Honneur au Ministre de l'Instruction Publique," *E*, Oct. 1935, p. 7. Interview with Naʿimah al-Ayyubi, Feb. 8, 1975, Cairo.

49. SN, *L'évolution féministe et les profits que peut en retirer le bien public* (Cairo, 1936); also published in *E*, Mar. 1936, pp. 11–18. SN also used this essay to argue for women's political rights, as we shall see in chapter 11.

50. J. C., "L'action social des femmes dans l'enseignement officiel en Egypte," *E*, Feb. 1925, pp. 27–28.

51. See SN, "Dans les domaines de notre action," *E*, May 1925, pp. 108–9.

52. ʿAsmah Fahmi wrote memoirs of her teaching experience, *Dhikrayat ʿan Madrasat al-Hilmiyah al-Thanawiyah lil-Banat*. Nazirah Niqula later published a widely used cookbook.

53. See Woodsmall, *Moslem Women Enter a New World*, p. 183. She reported that there had been 110 applications submitted by women for eight scholarships in 1930.

54. SN, "Le Gouvernement Egyptien et l'enseignement des jeunes filles," *E*, Sept. 1930, pp. 2–7.

55. SN, "La jeune fille et le travail," *E*, Nov. 1930, p. 3.

56. SN, "A la dérive," *E*, July–Aug. 1933, pp. 2–9.

57. Woodsmall, *Moslem Women Enter a New World*, p. 183.

58. "Infitah Nisaʾi Jadid: al-Muʿallimat Yatakhassasna bi-al-Lughah al-ʿArabiyah," *M*, Aug. 15, 1938, p. 27.

59. See J. C., "L'action sociale des femmes dans l'enseignement officiel en Egypte," *E*, Feb. 1925, p. 28, and SN, "La jeune fille et le travail," *E*, Nov. 1930, p. 3.

60. *D*, "They Wanted to Destroy Me and Their Wish Ended in My Promotion," 1st ser., no. 12.

61. For a comparative example of a school principal who displayed a stern authoritarian manner associated with male traits see Elizabeth Edwards, "Alice Havergal Skillicorn, Principal of Homerton College, Cambridge, 1935–60: A Study of Gender and Power," *Women's History Review* 1, no. 1 (1992): 89–108.

62. In her memoirs she tells how trumped-up charges were leveled against her. She also speaks of the difficulties of finding adequate legal defense and how she finally took up her own defense in court and won compensation. See *D*, "The Story of the Wolf and the Lamb," 1st ser., no. 37, and "The Day in Court," 1st ser., no. 38. For a discussion of her representation of these events see my "Expressing Feminism and Nationalism." NM's dismissal, the allegations, and the court case require thorough investigation before the full story can be unraveled. Later, she also fought successfully to obtain her pension from the state.

63. Interview with Ihsan al-Qusi, Feb. 22, 1972, Cairo. Al-Qusi wrote two books: *Fi Maydan al-Khidmah al-Ijtimaʿiyah* (In the field of social work) (Cairo, 1949) and *al-Khidmah al-Ijtimaʿiyah fi al-Qarn al-ʿIshrin* (Social work in the twenti-

eth century) (Cairo, 1956). She also translated into Arabic *Democracy and Education* by Thomas Dewey and *Men Who Make the Future* by Bruce Bliven.

64. Interviews with Karimah al-Saʿid, Jan. 21, 1968, and Apr. 4, 1972, Cairo.

65. *E* applauded her appointment in "Hors-texte," Oct. 1930, p. 1. According to Reid, *Cairo University*, p. 108, who interviewed Zaynab Hasan, "Rector Lutfi Sayyid tried to divert her back to secondary school teaching but Dean Bangham and Ali Mosharrafa backed up her university ambitions."

66. The EFU widely publicized the launching of her career. In 1956 she became chair of the department. Interview with Suhayr al-Qalamawi, Apr. 9, 1968, Cairo.

67. Interview with ʿA'ishah ʿAbd al-Rahman (Bint al-Shatiʾ), July 8, 1968.

68. Woodsmall, *Moslem Women Enter a New World*, p. 245. Married women could also teach in India and Iran at the time.

69. SN, "Honneur au Ministre de l'Instruction Publique," *E*, Oct. 1935, pp. 5–7, and "Le droit de travail est reconnu aux institutrices mariées," *E*, Dec. 1937, p. 38.

70. Letter to HS from a group of graduates from al-Saniyah School, Cairo, n.d., in Private Papers of HI. See HS, "Qasim Amin: Khitab Huda Hanim Shaʿrawi," *M*, May 1, 1940, pp. 7–9; SN, "A propos de droit au mariage des institutrices," *E*, Jan. 1940, pp. 2–3; and idem, "Muʿallimat Mutazawwijat," *M*, Oct. 1, 1939, p. 10.

71. SN, "A propos de droit au mariage des institutrices," *E*, Jan. 1940, pp. 2–3.

72. Blackman, *The Fellahin of Upper Egypt*, pp. 201–17. She gives many examples of different cures achieved by both sexes. Her evidence does not indicate any correlation between the sex of the practitioner and the kinds of cures performed.

73. See Mahfouz, *The History of Medical Education in Egypt*. The author was a gynecologist at the Qasr al-ʿAyni Hospital.

74. Sonbol, *The Creation of a Medical Profession*, p. 110. Some of the foreign doctors were women, including the British Dr. Elgood, a government doctor (her husband was an officer in the British army), and Dr. A. Panayotatou, a graduate of the School of Tropical Medicine in Paris, who worked in Alexandria.

75. Kathleen Howard-Merriam, "Women, Education, and the Professions in Egypt," *Comparative Education Review*, June 1979, pp. 256–70, notes the persistence of this pattern from the 1950s to the end of the 1970s (pp. 263 and 265).

76. The text is from *al-Mazini's Egypt: Midu and His Accomplices; Return to a Beginning; The Fugitive. A Short Story and Two Novels of Ibrahim Abd al-Qadir al-Mazini*, trans. and introd. William M. Hutchins (Washington, D.C.: Three Continents Press, 1983), p. 33.

77. Interview with Hilanah Sidarus, Dec. 5, 1975, Cairo. ʿAli Ibrahim told Fatma Niʿmat Rashid in an interview for *E* that women were especially fitted to be nurses, midwives, and doctors. See Fatma Niʿmat Rashid, "Notre enquête," *E*, Mar. 1935, pp. 27–30.

78. Her work with women patients provided her with a detailed awareness of the practice of female circumcision, which was taken up as a public feminist issue in the 1970s. She said that all her Muslim women patients and Copts coming from Upper Egypt were circumcised, but this practice declined in the 1950s. Interview with Hilanah Sidarus, Dec. 5, 1975, Cairo.

79. On the importance attached to virginity in Egypt and related social and psychological problems see al-Saʿdawi, *al-Mar'ah wa-al-Jins* (The woman and sex); and for a comparative look at Morocco see Fatima Mernissi, "Virginity and Patriarchy," in Azizah al-Hibri, *Women and Islam*, pp. 183–92.

80. For views on this subject earlier this century see Aletta Jacobs, "De Staats-

opleiding van verpleegsters in Egypte" (State training of nurses in Egypt), *Nosokomos*, no. 12 (Apr. 10, 1912): 247–50, cited in Feinberg, "A Pioneering Dutch Feminist Views Egypt," pp. 70–71.

81. Interview with Hilanah Sidarus, Dec. 5, 1975, Cairo, and interview with Gertrude Butrus Ghali, Sept. 12, 1975, Cairo.

82. See *Taqrir ʿan Aʿmal al-Ittihad al-Nisaʾi al-Misri min Sanat 1923 ila 1955* (Cairo, 1955), a publication of the EFU, p. 35.

83. HS, "Le Cabinet Ali Maher Pacha et son vaste programme de réformes sociales," *E*, Mar.–Apr. 1936, pp. 6–7.

84. "Al-Akhbar," *M*, Mar. 1, 1938, pp. 14–15.

85. Interview with Gertrude Butrus Ghali, Sept. 12, 1975, Cairo. She produced a training manual for nurses, *Adab al-Tamrid* (The etiquette of nursing), which was an adaptation of Charlotte A. Aikens, *Ethics for Nurses*. Butrus Ghali also wrote a number of papers including "Programme pour des cours d'infirmières auxiliaires et volontaires," n.d.; "Ecole de perfectionnement pour infirmières, formation d'infirmières-chefs," n.d.; and "Nursing," n.d.

86. Before the 1890s it had not been a respectable profession.

87. On law as a career for men in Egypt see Donald M. Reid, *Lawyers and Politics in the Arab World: 1880–1960* (Chicago: Biblioteca Islamica, 1981); idem, "Educational and Career Choices of Egyptian Students, 1882–1922," *International Journal of Middle East Studies* 8 (1977): 349–78; and Ziadeh, *Lawyers, the Rule of Law and Liberalism*. Reid notes that six future ministers including prime ministers studied law before 1900 (p. 17), that ten out of fourteen prime ministers between 1919 and 1952 were lawyers, and that most of the governments in the period included a majority of lawyers (p. 118).

88. "Nos avocates," *E*, Aug. 1926, pp. 217–18, an interview with Mrs. Bernard Michel. SN, "Une heure avec Maître Garzouzi," *E*, May 1930, pp. 12–16, an interview with Eva Garzouzi upon her return from a trip to the United States. She had given several talks, among which were "La profession d'avocat pour la femme orientale" and "La femme nouvelle dans l'ancien orient" both delivered in New York.

89. See Reid, "Educational and Career Choices of Egyptian Students."

90. Makram ʿUbayd, a Wafdist, was head of the bar at the time. The committee postponed taking a decision until October. See SN, "A la dérive," *E*, July–Aug. 1933, p. 8. Interview with Naʿimah al-Ayyubi, Feb. 8, 1975. Munirah Thabit had qualified as a lawyer at the French School of Law in Cairo in 1928 but never practiced law.

91. SN, "A la dérive," *E*, July–Aug. 1933, p. 5.

92. Woodsmall, *Moslem Women Enter a New World*, p. 122.

93. SN, "A la dérive," *E*, July–Aug. 1933, p. 6.

94. Ibid., p. 7.

95. Ibid.

96. "A l'Union féministe égyptienne," *E*, Dec. 1933, pp. 7–10; see p. 7. Muhammad ʿAli ʿAllubah repeated al-Ayyubi's words to him at their first meeting when he addressed the group assembled at the EFU ceremony honoring the first women university graduates.

97. "Kalimat Kharijat al-Jamiʿah," in *Dhikra Faqidat al-ʿUrubah Huda Hanim Shaʿrawi*, p. 69.

98. "Muhamiyatan Misriyatan Tatarafaʿan al-Awwal Marʾah," *M*, Dec. 1, 1939, pp. 12–13. It was reported that a great crowd came to witness the unfamiliar scene.

99. Interview with Mufidah ʿAbd al-Rahman, Apr. 28, 1968, Cairo.

100. Interview with Naʿimah al-Ayyubi, Feb. 8, 1975, Cairo.

101. Hind Nawfal's *al-Fatah* was founded in 1892, only eight years after Yaʿqub Sarruf moved *al-Muqtataf* to Cairo and two years before Jurji Zaydan started *al-Hilal.*

102. For a study of four women's journals during this period see Fenoglio-Abd El Aal, *Défense et illustration.*

103. Hashim published *Kitab fi al-Tarbiyah* and Saʿd published *Rabbat al-Dar.*

104. See Ijlal Hanim Mahmoud Khalifah, "al-Sihafah al-Nisa'i fi Misr min 1919 ila 1939" (M.A. thesis, Cairo University, 1966), p. 478.

105. Interview with Mustafa Thabit, Feb. 6, 1972, Cairo. See her *Thawrah fi al-Burj al-ʿAji: Mudhakkirat fi ʿAshrin ʿAm* (Revolution in the ivory tower: Memoirs of twenty years).

106. Interview with Ihsan ʿAbd al-Qaddus, Sept. 3, 1971, Cairo. On Ruz al-Yusif see *Dhikrayat Ruz al-Yusif* (The memoirs of Ruz al-Yusif); this was written by the then young journalist Ahmad Baha al-Din. See also Ibrahim ʿAbduh, *Ruz al-Yusif* (Cairo, 1961), and Sonia Dabbous, "Studying an Egyptian Journalist: Rose al-Youssef, a Woman and a Journal," *Islamic and Mediterranean Women's History Network Newsletter* 1, nos. 2–3 (1988): 11–12.

107. SN, "A propos de journalisme," *E*, Feb. 1926, p. 10; this article contains the most complete statement by SN on how she viewed her role as a journalist. See "Discours de Mlle Céza Nabaraoui au banquet offert à la presse berlinoise par l'Alliance Internationale des Femmes," *E*, Oct. 1929, p. 31, and SN, "Le congrès de la presse latine," *E*, Jan. 1932, pp. 2–4.

108. See "Le IV banquet de la presse," *E*, June 1928, pp. 2–5.

109. "Discours de Mademoiselle May au Xème banquet de la presse," *E*, Nov. 1928, pp. 38–41.

110. See my "Expressing Feminism and Nationalism."

111. *La femme nouvelle*, no. 2.

112. Interviews with Duriyah Shafiq, Jan. 23, 1968, and Apr. 10, 1974, Cairo.

113. Interviews with Aminah al-Saʿid, Jan. 21, 1968, and Mar. 29, 1972, Cairo.

114. These women could not be allowed space because SN was considered to be too far to the left and Shafiq had been too outspokenly critical of the president.

115. See, for example, Foulad Yeghen, "La femme," *E*, Feb. 1927, pp. 49–51.

116. "Discours de Mme Charaoui Pacha," *E*, Dec. 1933, pp. 10–13. See also SN, "A la dérive," *E*, July–Aug. 1933, pp. 2–9.

117. See "Barlamaniyat," *M*, Aug. 1938, pp. 3–4.

118. Interview with SN, Jan. 18, 1972, Cairo. She noted the cooperation between the EFU and the Ministry of Social Affairs that began as soon as the new ministry was established.

119. Interview with Naʿimah al-Ayyubi, Feb. 8, 1974, Cairo. Ruth Frances Woodsmall Papers, Box 62, File 3, interview with Suhayr al-Qalamawi, Jan. 12, 1955; al-Qalamawi said that the first women's student hostel was created in 1938 with fourteen girls.

120. Interview with Hikmat Abu Zayd, June 27, 1968.

121. "L'entrée de l'Egypte à la Société des Nations," *E*, June 1937, pp. 2–3.

122. Interview with SN, Feb. 21, 1972, Cairo.

123. See Howard-Merriam, "Women, Education, and the Professions in Egypt."

124. Interviews with Karimah al-Saʿid, Jan. 21, 1968, and Apr. 4, 1972.

125. Danielson, "Artists and Entrepreneurs," pp. 293–95, on women singers in the nineteenth century. On women entertainers in earlier periods, see Lane, *Manners and Customs*, 1:28–30, and ʿAbd al-Raziq, *La femme au temps des mamlouks en Egypte*, pp. 66–70. HS recalled performances of Salama Hijazi in Helwan (*Harem Years*, p. 53).

126. Interview with Buthaynah Farid, Nov. 20, 1975, Cairo (a dean at the Maʿhad li-Dirasat al-Musiqa al-ʿArabiyah, Institute for the Study of Arab Music), for information on early-twentieth-century women in entertainment.

127. See Danielson, "Artists and Entrepreneurs," p. 296, and Mahmud Kamil, *Tadhawwuq al-Musiqa al-ʿArabiyah* (Cairo: Muhammad al-Amin, 1975), pp. 166–67. Other entertainers included Fathiyah Ahmad, who first appeared on stage as a singer in the 1910s and later went on to concert singing.

128. Interview with her son, Ihsan ʿAbd al-Qaddus, Sept. 3, 1971, Cairo.

129. On her life and work see Badʿiyah al-Masabni, *Mudhakirrat Badʿiyah Masabni* (The memoirs of Badʿiyah Masabni), "with the pen of" Nazik Basilah (Beirut: Dar Maktabat al-Hayat, n.d.). For information about this memoir and those of other entertainers I am indebted to Virginia Danielson, who completed a dissertation on the Egyptian singer Umm Kalthum and the evolution of entertainment in Egypt from the late nineteenth century. See also Graham-Brown, *Images of Women*, p. 184.

130. See Wendy Buonaventura, *Serpent of the Nile: Women and Dance in the Arab World* (London: Saqi Books, 1989), pp. 149–51. On the export of "oriental" dance to the West, see chap. 5. Fahreda Mahzar from Syria danced at the Great Columbia Exposition in Chicago in 1893 where she became known as "Little Egypt." "Oriental dance" made its way into late-nineteenth-century American vaudeville. Another dancer from the East was Armen Ohanian, an Armenian from Iran, who performed in Egypt before going on to Europe. Her memoirs are narrated in two books published under her name: *The Dancer of Shamanhka* (London: Jonathan Cape, 1922) and *Rires d'une charmeuse* (Paris: Les Revues, 1931). In *The Dancer of Shamanhka* she writes of the vulgarization of a traditional folk dance celebrating "the mystery and pain of motherhood" in "olden Asia" in a stage performance in Cairo (p. 246).

131. Her life and singing career are recalled in *ʿAsmahan Tirwi Qissataha* (ʿAsmahan tells her story) "with the pen of" Muhammad al-Tabaʿi (Beirut: Dar al-Kutub, 1961). See also Graham-Brown, *Images of Women*, pp. 182–83.

132. "Hors-texte," *E*, Oct. 1929. Her grandfather was al-Qasim ibn Sidarah.

133. SN, "Une nouvelle étoile du firmament égyptien," *E*, Sept. 1928, pp. 5–9; "Hors-texte," *E*, Jan. 1930; and Bahigah Hafiz, "Athar ʿal-Misriyah fi al-Sinima wa-Nashahati la-ha," *M*, June 1, 1937, pp. 33–34.

134. SN, "Une nouvelle étoile du firmament égyptien," *E*, Sept. 1928, p. 7.

135. Fatma Rushdi was another pioneering actress. She has told the story of her work in the first half of the century in *Kifahi fi Masrah wa-Sinima* (My struggle in theater and cinema) (Cairo: Dar al-Maʿarif, 1971); she also wrote *Fatma Rushdi bayna al-Hubb wa-al-Fann* (Fatma Rushdi between love and art) (Cairo: Matbaʿat Saʿdi wa-Shandi, 1981).

136. Etel Adnan, "In the Heart of the Heart of Another Country," *Mundus Artium* 10, no. 1 (1977): 20–34; see 28–29.

Chapter Ten
Traffic in Women

1. Josephine Butler, *Personal Reminiscences of a Great Crusade* (London: H. Marshall and Son, 1896; new ed., 1911), p. 13.

2. See Edward Bristow, *Vice and Vigilance* (Dublin: Gill and Macmillan; Totowa, N.J.: Rowman and Littlefield, 1977), p. 86.

3. Marion Kaplan believes that a minority of "white slaves" were abducted; she writes: "Most were semiwilling victims who answered what appeared to be job announcements. Employment ads for waitresses, cooks, maids, and governesses were commonly used as ploys. The ads demanded a picture of the girl. If she was accepted by the alleged employer, she received money for her voyage and was met by the trafficker at the train or boat" (*The Jewish Feminist Movement in Germany*, p. 106). Judith Walkowitz, *Prostitution and Victorian Society: Women, Class, and the State* (Cambridge: Cambridge University Press, 1980), p. 247, says of late-nineteenth-century Britain, "The evidence for widespread involuntary prostitution of British girls at home or abroad is slim." Mary Gibson, *Prostitution and the State in Italy, 1860–1915* (New Brunswick: Rutgers University Press, 1986), p. 83, asserts in regard to Italy that "proof of widespread trafficking in women against their will is lacking."

4. Quoted in Edward Bristow, *Prostitution and Prejudice: The Jewish Fight against White Slavery 1870–1939* (New York: Schocken Books, 1983), p. 194; S. M. Edwardes, commissioner of police in Bombay, addressed this to the secretary to government, Judicial Department in Bombay, on Jan. 2, 1913 (p. 194n.33).

5. *D*, "How the English Maintain Their Reputation among Nations," 1st ser., no. 19.

6. On the Capitulations see Ziadeh, *Lawyers, the Rule of Law and Liberalism*; Hill, *Mahkama!*; and M. Sabry, "Note sur les Capitulations," *E*, Apr. 1937, pp. 7–9. On the impact of the Capitulations on Egyptians see Marsot, *Egypt and Cromer*, p. 161.

7. See Tucker, *Women in Nineteenth Century Egypt*, pp. 151–53.

8. See ibid., and idem, "Decline of the Family Economy," *Arab Studies Quarterly* 1, no. 3 (1979): 245–71.

9. Between 1877 and 1905 some twenty-five thousand slaves, the majority of whom were women, were freed; see Tucker, *Women in Nineteenth Century Egypt*, pp. 164–93, and Baer, "Slavery and Its Abolition," in *Studies in the Social History of Modern Egypt*, pp. 161–89.

10. Baron Jacques de Menasce, a prostitution abolitionist in Alexandria, reported that the common path for traffic from Europe was through "Alexandria, Cairo, or Port Said, Bombay, Columbo, Singapore, Saigon, Hong Kong, and Shanghai." From *Rapport du Comité Exécutif, Société Internationale Pour la Repression de la Traite des Blanches à Alexandrie* (1907), Alexandria IC, 13, AIU, p. 4, cited in Bristow, *Prostitution and Prejudice*, p. 182.

11. For a mapping of foreign prostitution in Egypt and problems combating it see Bristow, *Prostitution and Prejudice*, chap. 6, "Roads to Asia and Africa," pp. 181–214.

12. M. H. Haekal [Haykal], "Les causes de l'incompréhension entre l'Europe et les Musulmans, et les moyens d'y remédier," *E*, Apr. 1935, p. 27.

13. In *Bayna al-Qasrayn* (Palace walk) Mahfuz speaks of prostitution and the

merchant elite early in the twentieth century. In *Midaq Alley* Mahfuz takes readers into the world of the Egyptian prostitute and British soldiers during the Second World War.

14. See, for example, *Flaubert in Egypt: A Sensibility on Tour*, trans. and ed. Francis Steegmuller (Chicago: Academy Chicago Limited, 1979), pp. 112–20, where he describes his experience in Upper Egypt with Kuchuk Hanem, well-known to European travelers.

15. See Walkowitz, *Prostitution and Victorian Society*, and Gibson, *Prostitution and the State in Italy*.

16. In 1875, Butler and European activists, fighting similar laws in their countries, formed the British, Continental and General Federation to extend and strengthen their campaign.

17. See Ronald Hyam, *Empire and Sexuality: The British Experience* (Manchester and New York: Manchester University Press, 1990), p. 66 and passim. After 1886, a group called the British Committee for the Abolition of the State Regulation of Vice in India and the Dominions concentrated efforts against state regulation in some parts of the empire, but not in Egypt. Burton deals with this in her book *Burdens of History*, in chap. 5, "The White Woman's Burden: Josephine Butler and the Indian Campaign, 1886–1915." Philippa Levine, "Venereal Disease, Prostitution, and the Politics of Empire: The Case of British India," *Journal of the History of Sexuality* 4, no. 4 (1994): 579–602.

18. On the antiregulationists and anti–white slavery forces, and contemporary debates on sexuality in England, see Jeffreys, "'Free from All Uninvited Touch of Man.'"

19. For example, in Italy, an important country of supply of women destined for prostitution in Egypt, a National Committee for the Suppression of the Traffic in Women was created in 1901, with branches in four major cities; the Milan branch, which remained the most active, stressed prevention over rehabilitation. See Gibson, *Prostitution and the State in Italy*, p. 77. A German National Committee was established in 1899. On private associations created in France to protect girls from traffickers, and on the alliance of European anti–white slavery forces with regulationists, see Alain, Corbin, *Women for Hire: Prostitution and Sexuality in France after 1850*, trans. Alan Sheridan (Cambridge: Harvard University Press, 1990), pp. 278–80.

20. See Russell, *Egyptian Service*.

21. Interview with Alexandra Farag, Sept. 17, 1975, Alexandria.

22. On the life and work of Pappenheim see Kaplan, *The Jewish Feminist Movement in Germany*.

23. The full title of the work is *Sisyphus Arbeit: Reisebriefe aus den Jaren 1911 und 1912* (Leipzig: Verlag Paul E. Linder, 1924). On her trip see Kaplan, *The Jewish Feminist Movement in Germany*, pp. 111–12, and idem, "Prostitution, Morality Crusades and Feminism: German-Jewish Feminists and the Campaign against White Slavery," *Women's Studies International Forum* 5, no. 6 (1982): 619–27. Pappenheim also visited Constantinople where, she reported, around 90 percent of the prostitutes, and all the traffickers, were Jews.

24. The information in this section on Pappenheim's Alexandria visit is taken from her journal entries for May 19–24, 1911, published in *Sisyphus Arbeit*, pp. 129–35. I wish to thank Silvia Schmitz-Burgard for her help with translation.

25. Ibid.

26. Copy of police report, the assistant commandant, Cairo City Police, May 5, 1929, in the Private Papers of Mary Kahil.

27. Police Report, the assistant commandant, Cairo City Police, Apr. 21, 1929, copy in the Private Papers of Mary Kahil.

28. SN, "Pour la suppression du traffic des femmes et des enfants," *E*, Mar. 1930, p. 3.

29. Report to the 1926 conference, in the Private Papers of Mary Kahil.

30. HS, *Mudhakkirat Raʿidat al-ʿArabiyah al-Haditha*, p. 270.

31. Ibid.

32. See SN, "En marge de la Conférence de Montreux," *E*, Apr. 1937, pp. 2–4; see p. 2.

33. HSM, pp. 306–9, and "Propositions présentées par Mme Hoda Charaoui au IVe Congrès international tenu à Graz le 18, 19, 20 septembre 1924 pour la suppression de la traite des femmes et des enfants," from the Private Papers of SN.

34. See SN, "Discours de Mlle Céza Nabaraoui, Secrétaire de l'Union féministe égyptienne à la Grande Réunion publique du Xe Congrès de l'Alliance internationale pour le Suffrage des femmes (le 31 mai à la Sorbonne)," *E*, July 1926, p. 191. For more on the EFU position see SN, "Le congrès de Paris," *E*, July 1926, pp. 190–91.

35. HS, "Conférence d'Amsterdam pour la paix," *E*, Dec. 1927, pp. 2–13.

36. "Pour la suppression de la traite des femmes et des enfants: copie de la lettre adressée par l'Alliance Internationale des Femmes pour le Suffrage au Président du Conseil des Ministres du Royaume d'Egypte," *E*, Feb. 1928, pp. 17–18. The letter was dated Dec. 19, 1927.

37. Mary Kahil proposed the resolution, which was seconded by Marcelle Kraemer-Bach, of the French delegation; see SN, "Le Congrès de Berlin," *E*, Oct. 1929, pp. 21–22.

38. SN, "Impressions de Congrès," *E*, Oct. 1929, p. 21 and HS, *Mudhakkirat Raʿidat al-ʿArabiyah al-Haditha*, p. 242.

39. SN, "Les femmes dans la police," *E*, Nov. 1929, pp. 21–27. See also "L'arrivée au Caire de Commandant Mary Allen," *E*, Feb. 1930, p. 36.

40. "Un manifeste de Miss Higson," *E*, Mar. 1930, p. 4; see also SN, "Pour la suppression du traffic des femmes et des enfants," *E*, Mar. 1930, pp. 2–4.

41. *E*, Mar. 1930, p. 4, and SN, "Pour la suppression du traffic des femmes et des enfants," *E*, Mar. 1930, pp. 2–4.

42. Information on the Jamʿiyat Misr li-Himayat al-Mar'ah wa-al-Tifl comes from interviews with Bahigah Rashid, Oct. 7, 1975, Cairo (president from 1954 to 1964) and Alexandra Farag, Sept. 17, 1975, Cairo (president from 1964 to 1974); and from *Jamʿiyat Misr li-Himayat al-Mar'ah wa-al-Atfal* (Cairo, 1969), and Alexandra Farag, "Situation de l'Association pour la protection de la femme et de l'enfant en Egypt" (Speech at the Geneva conference of the International Abolitionist Federation, June 16, 1973), which includes historical notes. The new Egyptian members included Bahigah Rashid, Alexandra Farag, Basimah Fu'ad, and Diana al-Bakri.

43. Dr. Samy Kamal, Dr. Abdel Hamid Waffa, Dr. Hussein Gamaly, Dr. Mohammed Tewfiq Naggar, "Rapports des médecins du dispensaire de l'Union féministe égyptienne," *E*, Apr. 1926, pp. 75–82. The doctors' reports revealed a high incidence of venereal disease among the women examined, which the doctors related to widespread prostitution in the poor quarters of Cairo. See also "Discours de S.E. Chahine Pacha à l'Assemblée Générale de l'Union internationale contre le péril vénérien mai

1932," *E*, July 1932, pp. 6–11, and SN, "Vers l'abolitionnisme," *E*, July 1932, pp. 2–5.

44. The questionnaire was reprinted in *E*, July 1932, p. 5.

45. "La Commission de l'Hygiene Publique a decidé la suppression de la prostitution officielle," *E*, Mar. 1934, p. 30. Turkish laws concerning prostitution and venereal diseases were being studied by the commission. On the history of prostitution in Marseilles see Corbin, *Women for Hire*, passim.

46. Verone, who was highly regarded by Egyptian feminists, was featured in "Hors-texte," in *E*, April 1933. Notice was also given when she died, in "Mme Maria Verone est Morte," *E*, May 1938, p. 42.

47. "Traite des femmes en Orient," in IAW *Report of 1935 Congress*, pp. 75–76.

48. "Echos d'Orient," *E*, Oct. 1932.

49. SN, "Les journées féministes de Marseille et du midi de la France," *E*, Apr. 1933, pp. 10–11, for the text of the IAW resolution.

50. SN, "Discours de Mademoiselle C. Nabaraouy à la réception de la presse donnée par le Bureau de l'A.I.S.F. au Splendid Hôtel à Marseille le 18 mars 1933," *E*, May 1933, p. 8.

51. See *Report of the Twelfth Congress of the International Alliance of Women for Suffrage and Equal Citizenship Held at Istanbul from 15 through 25 April 1935*, reprinted in SN, "En marge de la Conférence de Montreux," *E*, Apr. 1937, p. 4.

52. "La suppression de la prostitution officielle en Egypte," *E*, Aug–Sept. 1935, pp. 31–32.

53. HS, "ʿAla Wataniyat al-Wafd al-Rasmi wa-Hirsuhu Yatawaqqafa Nijahuhu fi Mu'tamar Muntru," *M*, Apr. 15, 1937, pp. 2–3.

54. "L'U.F.E. et la Conférence des Capitulations," *E*, Apr. 1937, p. 6.

55. See al-Shafiʿi al-Labban, "Fi Suq al-Raqiq al-Abyad," *M*, Nov. 1, 1937, pp. 21–22; "al-Bigha' fi Misr," *M*, Dec. 1, 1937, pp. 13–15; and "al-Tashriʿ wa-al-Qada' al-Misri wa-ma Arju la-huma fi ʿAhd al-Faruq," *M*, Jan. 20, 1938, pp. 40–41.

56. Muhammad Ahmad Jad al-Mawla, "Fi Sabil al-Islah al-Ijtimaʿi," *M*, Nov. 1, 1937, pp. 21–22.

57. "Vers l'abolition de la prostitution en Egypt," *E*, June 1933, pp. 37–38.

58. "Report of the Committee on an Equal Moral Standard," in *Proceedings of the IAW Congress*, Istanbul, 1935, p. 128.

59. "Vers l'abolition de la prostitution," *E*, Feb. 1940, p. 37.

60. See SN, "Wajib al-Mar'ah fi al-ʿAhd al-Jadid," *M*, Mar. 1, 1937, p. 11. Also interview with Bahigah Rashid, Oct. 7, 1975, Cairo.

61. "Barlamaniyat," *M*, July 15, 1937, p. 36.

62. The criticism was leveled in the context of the review of the ministry's financial committee report. See "Barlamaniyat," *M*, June 1, 1940, pp. 34–36.

63. HS, "Kalimat Huda Hanim Shaʿrawi fi Haflat Dhikra al-Marhum Qasim Amin," *M*, May 1, 1940, pp. 8–9.

64. Bahigah Rashid, speech, *MAQF*, pp. 197–200.

65. "The Proposals of the Society for the Protection of the Woman and Child," *MAQF*, pp. 146–47.

66. *MAQF*, pp. 328–36.

67. Al-Markaz al-Qawmi lil-Buhuth al-Ijtimaʿi wa-al-Jina'iyah, *al-Bigha' fi al-Qahirah* (Cairo, 1961); see Introduction and pp. 4–5 for ending of legalized prostitution. On a comparative note, state regulation was ended in France in 1946 and in Italy in 1958.

Chapter Eleven
Suffrage and Citizenship

1. Outside the IAW there were some women from colonizing countries who supported both national independence movements and female suffrage, such as Irishwomen Annie Besant and Margaret Cousins in 1917 in India. See Strobel, *European Women and the Second British Empire*, pp. 64–65.

2. On this party see Afaf Lutfy al-Sayyid Marsot, *Egypt's Liberal Experiment, 1922–36* (Berkeley and Los Angeles: University of California Press, 1977).

3. "Nous avions le droit de vote," *E*, Feb. 1925, pp. 29–30, with the list of "elected" members of parliament in attached supplement; "Nos enquêtes," *E*, Feb. 1925, pp. 17–18; and "Nos enquêtes," *E*, Mar. 1925, pp. 52–56.

4. The EFU congratulated Thabit and the new review in "Echos d'Orient," *E*, Dec. 1925, p. 358.

5. Interview with Mustafa Thabit (brother of Munirah Thabit), Feb. 6, 1972, Cairo. See Munirah Thabit, *Thawrah fi al-Burj al-ʿAji*, pp. 31–44.

6. "Les revendications des dames égyptiennes," *E*, Feb. 1, 1925, pp. 8–11, Partie Féminine, no. 5. Girls from the workshop of the New Woman Society carried placards in Arabic and French with this and other demands outside the gates of the parliament building.

7. Egyptian scholar Ahmed Abdalla has noted that illiterate male citizens had been "tutored" in voting by pro-Wafdist students. See Abdalla, *The Student Movement and National Politics in Egypt*, pp. 43–44.

8. SN, "L'évolution du féminisme en Egypt," *E*, Mar. 1925, pp. 46–47.

9. SN, "Impressions du congrès," *E*, Oct. 1929, p. 11, and SN, "Entre deux conférences," *E*, Mar. 1933, pp. 13–14.

10. SN, "Discours de Mademoiselle C. Nabaraouy au banquet d'Hyères le 24 mars 1933," *E*, May 1933, pp. 14, 17.

11. HS, "Discours de Madame Hoda Charaoui Pacha à l'Hôtel de Ville de Marseilles 18 mars 1933," *E*, Apr. 1933, p. 4.

12. SN, "Les femmes dans le mouvement national," *E*, May 1931, p. 28.

13. See *D*, "Forced Demonstration," 1st ser., no. 88. The demonstrators she mentions by name include Mrs. Khashabah Pasha, Sharifah Riyad, and Mrs. ʿAli Pasha Shawqi; the first, she notes, was among the women arrested.

14. SN, "Les femmes dans le mouvement national," *E*, May 1931, p. 29.

15. See "Résolutions du congrès national égyptien," *E*, May 1931, pp. 5–14. There were 145 women's signatures.

16. "Un manifeste des dames égyptiennes: toutes les associations féminines adhèrent aux résolutions du congrès national et protestent contre la politique du Cabinet Sedky," *E*, May 1931, pp. 20–31.

17. See "Une grande manifestation des dames égyptiennes," *Le Journal du Caire*, May 6, 1931, for an account of the demonstration, a list of women arrested, and the text of their manifesto. See also SN, "Les femmes dans le mouvement national," *E*, May 1931, pp. 28–29, and idem, "Protestation de l'Union féministe égyptienne," *E*, May 1931, p. 30. Interview with SN, Cairo.

18. Interview with Aminah al-Saʿid, Mar. 29, 1972, Cairo, and *D*, "Forced Demonstration," 1st ser., no. 88; "Another Demonstration Fate Had Hidden from Me," 1st ser., no. 90; "Demonstrations and the Morals of Girl Students," 2d ser., no. 68.

19. See "La plainte de Nahas Pacha au Procureur General," *E*, May 1931, p. 22, for a copy of this complaint.

20. *D*, "Another Demonstration Fate Had Hidden from Me," 1st ser., no. 90. Among the women cited were Mrs. Amin Bey Lutfi, Mrs. Raghib Pasha, and Mrs. Mahmud Bey al-Namrusi.

21. See "Message des dames égyptiennes aux familles des victimes tombées à la Journée Electorale du 14 Mai," *E*, May 1931, p. 31. The WWCC held a benefit at NM's school in Alexandria for workers shot by police during the Sidqi period. *D*, "The Wafdist Women's Central Committee at Banat al-Ashraf School in Alexandria," 1st ser., no. 71.

22. "Protestation de l'Union féministe égyptienne," *E*, May 1931, p. 30.

23. "Un parlement non représentatif," *E*, May 1931, p. 3.

24. SN, "Les femmes dans le mouvement national," *E*, May 1931, p. 28.

25. SN, *Majallat al-Usbuᶜ*, no. 29 (June 13, 1934): 9.

26. See SN, "La semaine de la femme," *E*, Feb. 1935, pp. 3–12.

27. "Revue de la presse," *E*, Feb. 1935, p. 13, from *al-Siyasah*.

28. Interview with Margery Corbett Ashby, Nov. 16, 1971, London.

29. See Afet Inan, *The Emancipation of the Turkish Woman* (Paris: UNESCO, 1962).

30. See Deniz Kandiyoti, "End of Empire: Islam, Nationalism, and Women in Turkey," in Kandiyoti, *Women, Islam and the State*, pp. 22–47; see pp. 41–42.

31. "Discours prononcé par Mme Esther Fahmi Wissa à la séance du 23 avril," *E*, May 1935, p. 38. "Discours de Mlle Céza Nabaraoui au thé offert à la presse à l'hôtel Pera Palace, le 15 avril," *E*, May 1935, p. 37.

32. HS, *Mudhakkirat al-Raᶜidat al-ᶜArabiyah al-Haditha*, p. 453.

33. See "Echos d'Orient," *E*, Apr. 1937, p. 34.

34. HS, "Après le Congrès d'Istanboul," *E*, Aug.–Sept. 1935, pp. 7–9; see p. 8.

35. HS, "Le Cabinet Ali Maher Pacha et son vaste programme de réformes sociales," *E*, Mar.–Apr. 1936, pp. 4–7; see p. 7 for resolution on political rights. HS, "Lettre adressée à S.E. Nahas Pacha par la Présidente de l'U.F.E.," *E*, May 1936, pp. 4–5.

36. SN, *l'évolution féministe et les profits que peut en retirer le bien général*, p. 7. The essay was also published in *E*, Mar.–Apr. 1936, pp. 11–18.

37. Ibid.

38. The leaflet was published in *E*, "Debout les femmes, debout les morts!" Oct. 1936, pp. 2–3; quotation from p. 3.

39. Private Papers of HI; see also Mustafa Hifnawi, ed., *al-Sifr al-Khalid: Majmuᶜat Khutab wa kitabat al-Zuᶜama*, vol. 1 (Cairo, 1937), pp. 143–44.

40. *Al-Musawwar*, Sept. 18, 1936.

41. *Ruz al-Yusuf*, Nov. 18, 1936.

42. See SN, "La mission de la femme dans l'ère nouvelle," *E*, Jan. 1937, pp. 2–7. For feminist criticism of the Anglo-Egyptian treaty, see "Discours de S.E. Allouba Pacha," *E*, Oct. 1936, pp. 4–15, and SN, "Après la ratification du traité," *E*, Nov. 1936, pp. 14–16.

43. Munirah Thabit, "Naqd fi Diᶜaba min Wahi al-Misriyya," *M*, Mar. 1, 1937, pp. 9–11.

44. See *al-Ahram*, Feb. 6, 1937.

45. ᶜAliyah Fahmi, *M*, Feb. 15, 1939.

46. *M*, Feb. 15, 1937, pp. 8–9.

47. *Al-Misri*, Sept. 1936.

48. HS, "Hawla Tasriʿ Muhammad Mahmud Pasha," *M*, Apr. 1, 1938, p. 3. See also Thabit, *Thawrah fi al-Burj al-ʿAji*, pp. 56–58.

49. HS, *M*, July 1, 1938, p. 2.

50. Fatma Niʿmat Rashid, *E*, Apr. 1934, pp. 31–32; May 1934, pp. 24–26; and Sept. 1936, pp. 30–32, respectively.

51. Majd al-Din Saʿfan, "Maʿna al-Dimuqratiyah al-Harakah al-Nisaʾiyah," *M*, Apr. 1, 1937, p. 4.

52. Mounira Sabet, "La jeunesse et le féminisme," *E*, July–Aug., 1939, p. 19.

53. *MNA*, pp. 77–84, for text of entire speech.

54. Ibid., pp. 272–75.

55. Ibid., pp. 244–60.

56. Ibid., p. 328.

57. Interview with Bahigah Rashid, Apr. 10, 1974, Cairo.

58. Interviews with Duriyah Shafiq, Jan. 23, 1968 and Apr. 10, 1974, Cairo. On Shafiq's feminism and her fight for political rights see Cynthia Nelson, "Biography and Women's History: On Interpreting Doria Shafik," in Keddie and Baron, *Women in Middle Eastern History*, pp. 310–33, and idem, "The Voices of Doria Shafik."

Chapter Twelve
Arab Feminism

1. See Matiel Mogannam, *The Arab Woman and the Palestine Problem* (London: H. Joseph, 1937), pp. 69–77; Julie Peteet, *Gender in Crisis* (New York: Columbia University Press, 1991), pp. 45–49; and "En Palestine, musulmanes et chrétiennes ont manifeste, sans voile," *E*, Nov. 1929, p. 40. When *E* reported the demonstration, it underscored the feminist dimension of this nationalist act: "During the recent regrettable events, our Muslim and Christian sisters formed a block—without veil—proving to public opinion that they were conscious of their social duty . . . by their free act they showed that no one—including a woman—would hide herself to demand that which all men, all of the accused population, had not only the right but the duty to demand impartiality and justice."

2. Mogannam, *The Arab Woman*, p. 77.

3. See Ann Lesch, "Part I: The Palestine Arab Nationalist Movement under the Mandate," in William B. Quandt, Fuad Jabber, and Ann Mosely Lesch, *The Politics of Palestinian Nationalism* (Berkeley and Los Angeles: University of California Press, 1973), pp. 21–22.

4. "L'activité des femmes arabes palestiniennes," *E*, Mar. 1935, pp. 38–39. The Haifa meeting also resolved to work toward uniting Palestinians who were plagued by internal divisions, asked for pardon for political prisoners, and resolved to encourage women to support national industries and to boycott foreign goods.

5. On the Arab revolt see Tom Bowden, "The Politics of the Arab Rebellion in Palestine 1936–1939," *Middle East Studies* 11 (1975): 147–74; James P. Jankowski, "The Palestinian Arab Revolt of 1936–1939," *The Muslim World* 63 (1973): 220–33; Ghassan Kanafani, *The 1936–39 Rebellion in Palestine* (Committee for Democratic Palestine, n.d.); Yehoshua Porath, *The Palestinian Arab National Movement 1929–1939*, vol. 2 (London: F. Cass, 1977); and Ylana Miller, *Government and Society in Rural Palestine 1920–1948* (Austin: University of Texas Press, 1985).

6. On the roles of women in the Arab revolt see Peteet, *Gender in Crisis*, pp. 52–57; Soraya Antonius, "Fighting on Two Fronts: Conversations with Palestinian Women," *Journal of Palestine Studies* 8, no. 3 (1979): 26–45; and Mogannam, *The Arab Woman*, p. 305.

7. *MAQF*, pp. 14–15. On the two appeals see Mogannam, *The Arab Woman*, p. 81n. For a general treatment of the involvement of Egyptian women in the Palestine question, see Ijlal Khalifah, *al-Mar'ah wa-Qadiyat Filastin* (Cairo, 1974).

8. *MAQF*, pp. 12–13. See "L'Union féministe égyptienne et les victimes de Palestine," *E*, July–Aug. 1936, p. 33.

9. "Section Egyptienne de la Lique internationale des mères et des educatrices pour la paix," *E*, Mar. 1935, pp. 12–15.

10. On the WILPF, see Gertrude Bussey and Margaret Tims, *Women's International League for Peace and Freedom: 1915–1965* (London: Allen & Unwin, 1965).

11. On a comparative note, Bohachevsky-Chomiak in *Feminists despite Themselves*, p. 271, says that Western Ukrainians, believing that Ukrainians had lost their independence because of their inability to defend themselves, held a position similar to that of the Egyptians.

12. See "Activités depuis le Congrès de Luhacovice (July 1937)," in *Rapport de la Section Egyptienne de la Ligue internationale des femmes pour la paix et la liberté*; G. Lankester, "India and Egypt," WILPF, *British Section Newssheet* 30, no. 4 (1937): 2–3; and "Our Section in Egypt," *Pax* (WILPF organ), 14, no. 2 (1938): 4. A WILPF meeting was held on Nov. 11, 1937, at the EFU where Zaynab al-Hakim, a schoolteacher, denounced fascism. Peace meetings were not without some risks; at the Dec. 10, 1937, meeting, where Ester Fahmi Wissa and others were speaking, some Italian fascists threw stink bombs and yelled insults. In Jan. 1938, the director of the Jewish Schools (Ecoles Israelites) in Egypt spoke at a WILPF meeting on "Peace through Education." The same year, the Egyptian Section received Rosa Gutman, a Russian Jew recently settled in Tel Aviv, visiting from Palestine. On Jews in peace work in Egypt see Gudrun Kramer, "Political Participation of the Jews in Egypt between World War I and the 1952 Revolution," in *The Jews of Egypt: A Modern Mediterranean Society in Modern Times*, ed. Shimon Shamir (Boulder and London: Westview Press, 1987), pp. 68–84; see p. 76. On Zionism in Egypt during the period between the two world wars see Michael M. Laskier, *The Jews of Egypt, 1920–1970: In the Midst of Zionism, Anti-Semitism, and the Middle East Conflict* (New York: New York University Press, 1992), chap. 1, "The Jews of Egypt and the Yishuv: Aspects of Jewish Solidarity, 1920–1939," pp. 17–54.

13. When the EFU sent assistance to the Association of Ethiopian Women, Eugenie Taf Bellow wrote saying that when Ethiopian women had decided to take part in the defense of the nation, they realized that "new times required a new woman." See "La femme abyssine," *E*, Nov. 1935, pp. 15–19.

14. SN, "Rassemblement pour la paix et la S.D.N. à Alexandrie le 4 juin," *E*, June 1936.

15. "Rassemblement pour la paix et la S.D.N. au Caire le 26 juin 1936," *E*, July–Aug. 1936. Ester Fahmi Wissa and Surayya Shafiq also attended the meeting. *E* said the views of the masses on an independent Egypt in a peaceful world must be taken into account.

16. SN, "Rassemblement pour la paix et la S.D.N. à Alexandrie le 4 juin," *E*, June 1936, pp. 2–4; "Rassemblement pour la paix et la S.D.N. au Caire le 26 juin 1936," *E*, July–Aug. 1936, pp. 26–28; and *MAQF*, pp. 12–14.

17. "Suggestions presentées par l'U.F.E. au rassemblement universel pour la paix à Bruxelles," *E*, Sept. 1936, pp. 21–23. Also see "Rassemblement universel pour la paix: Congrès de Bruxelles, 3–6 septembre 1936," *E*, July–Aug. 1936, pp. 21–23.

18. Egypt and Britain were locked into a mutual defense pact.

19. *MAQF*, pp. 14–17.

20. The British ambassador forwarded to London a copy of the telegram from the Women's Committee of ʿAkka to HS and her reply, noting, "We may expect an increasing number of these protests and petitions." FO 371 (20809) E4206, from Lampson, Cairo, July 17, 1937, no. 52.

21. FO 371 (21875) 4917, Communication from Arab women (about two hundred signatures) to high commissioner, Jerusalem, Feb. 5, 1938.

22. FO 371 E2117 (21875), Jan. 27, 1938.

23. On plans for a women's congress in Syria, see HS, "Rendez justice à la Palestine et secourez l'humanité martyrisée," *E*, May 1938, pp. 6–7. MacKereth, Damascus, to Halifax, June 17, 1938, tel. no. 31, FO 371 E3591 (21877), relates details of proposed plans for a women's congress in Syria. See also Muhammad ʿAli ʿAllubah, *Filastin wa-al-Damir al-Insani* (Cairo: Dar al-Hilal, 1964). In an interview with ʿAli ʿAllubah and Na'ilah ʿAllubah (the son and niece of Muhammad ʿAli ʿAllubah) on Jan. 24, 1968, Cairo, it was related that Muhammad ʿAli ʿAllubah had encouraged HS to organize a women's congress.

24. See Philip S. Khoury, *Syria and the French Mandate: The Politics of Arab Nationalism, 1920–1945* (Princeton: Princeton University Press, 1987), pp. 554–59. One hundred and thirty-eight participants from Palestine, Syria, Trans-Jordan, Lebanon, Iraq, and Egypt attended the congress. Egyptians Muhammad ʿAli ʿAllubah and ʿAbd al-Hamid Saʿid chaired the conference.

25. The British consul in Damascus said in a dispatch on July 2, 1938, "The Syrian Prime Minister has forbidden the holding of a Women's Congress in Syria to discuss Palestine and has taken steps to ensure that negotiations for it cease." MacKereth, Damascus, to Halifax, July 2, 1938, tel. no. 34, FO 371 E4049 (21878). On the general political climate following Bludan see Khoury, *Syria and the French Mandate*, pp. 554–59. On the women's correspondence see FO 371 E4049 (21877), from Consul MacKereth, Damascus, no. 31, June 17, 1938, to Halifax.

26. *MAQF*, p. 18.

27. FO 371, Egypt, Palestine, and Trans-Jordan, from Mr. Bateman, Cairo, Sept. 26, 1938, no. 10077 (8/259/38).

28. Ibid.

29. See Lampson to Halifax, Oct. 4, 1938, tel. no. 513, FO 371 E 5816 (21882).

30. *MAQF*, p. 4.

31. *M* reported on the congress extensively on Oct. 15, 1938, and Nov. 1, 1938. *E* carried the following articles: in July–Aug., 1938, "Un grand événement historique en perspective: Premier Congrès au Caire des Femmes d'Orient en faveur de la Palestine," p. 2; and in Oct. 1938, SN, "Le Congrès des Femmes d'Orient pour le Défense de la Palestine," pp. 2–14; HS, "Résolutions du Congrès des Femmes d'Orient pour la Défense de la Palestine tenu au Caire du 15 au 18 octobre 1938," pp. 15–17; and "Lettres échangées entre la Presidente du Congrès et les Souverains des pays Arabes," pp. 18–19.

32. As the congress was convening, the second phase of the Arab Revolt in Palestine was at its height. By October, British administration in the old city of Jerusalem and in several cities of the interior had virtually collapsed. In an interview on Apr. 25,

1972, Cairo, Katy Antonius recalled how difficult it was for a Palestinian delegation to be able to come to the congress.

33. Women's political life was not a mirror of men's political life. Women did not automatically associate themselves with the political groups of their fathers or husbands. Laila Mogannam (daughter of Matiel Mogannam) explained the broad coalescing of Palestinian women in the 1920s and 1930s to Julie Peteet. Men applauded the women's cohesiveness, which signaled the broad unity that men's political differences might appear to diminish. There were also practical advantages ensuing to men from the broader and more cohesive women's networks, including helping to keep up good relations among men. Laila Mogannam also acknowledged a hierarchy among the women: "It was almost like a monarchy. There were two or three women up there, they were acknowledged" (Peteet, *Gender in Crisis*, p. 49). Matiel Mogannam, looking back, said: "During this period most of the women didn't compete with each other. This was the only intellectual activity they really had. So they felt they had just better do a good job together." There was a broad gender cohesiveness, but not altogether without disagreements. In the Arab Women's Union in Haifa there was some conflict over the issue of dress between women who upheld veiling and those who unveiled. See Rosemary Sayigh, "Femmes palestiniennes: une histoire en quête d'historiens," *Revue d'études palestiniennes*, no. 23 (Spring 1987): 29.

34. *MAQF*, pp. 46–47.

35. Ibid., pp. 142–43. This exhortation came from a conservative woman who in "normal" times extolled women's "primary role" in the home and stressed the separation of the sexes.

36. SN, "Le Congrès des Femmes d'Orient pour la Défense de la Palestine," *E*, Oct. 1938, pp. 5–6.

37. *MAQF*, pp. 204–6.

38. Ibid., pp. 128–30.

39. Ibid., pp. 46–47.

40. Ibid., pp. 71–75.

41. See "Sadhij Nassar, the Enemy of the British Mandate Authority in Palestine," signed "An Arab," *M*, Sept. 1, 1939, p. 28.

42. *MAQF*, pp. 58–62.

43. Ibid., pp. 174–78. See also Mogannam, *The Arab Woman*.

44. *MAQF*, pp. 79–92.

45. HS led a deputation that delivered the conference resolutions to ʿAbdin Palace in Cairo and to foreign ambassadors and heads of legations. Telegrams were sent to world political and religious leaders, including British prime minister Chamberlain, French premier Daladier, President Theodore Roosevelt, Hitler, Mussolini, the pope, and the archbishop of Canterbury. See ibid., pp. 170–73.

46. Ibid., p. 218.

47. Ibid., p. 215.

48. Ibid., p. 222.

49. FO 371 E5990 (21881), minute by Colville (Oct. 17, 1938).

50. FO 371 E6209 (21881), dispatch no. 1131, from Lampson, Cairo, Oct. 20, 1938, minute by Colville (Oct. 20, 1938).

51. FO 371 E6432 (21883), from Lampson, Cairo, Oct. 24, 1938. The Diaries of Lord Killearn (Lampson), Oct. 21, 1938, related the visit of a delegation from the Women's Congress headed by HS, "a considerably intense and at moments rather

fierce, but on the whole, I should say, an intelligent and not unattractive lady. It was clear that they all felt very strongly about Palestine."

52. FO 371 E6302 21881, from Lampson, no. 1133, Oct. 21, 1938.

53. Two charity benefits were held by the permanent central committee on Oct. 24, 1938, at the EFU, netting £E103.720, and on Dec. 1, 1938, at the Royal Opera House, netting £E322.700. The rest of the money was obtained through private subscription. See *MAQF*, pp. 239, 248. The British were concerned about the spending of the funds; see FO 371 E5914 (21881), from Harold MacMichael, high commissioner of Palestine, Sept. 28, 1938, secret communication, and FO 317 E6733 (21884), dispatch no. 63, secret, from acting consul, Gen. Furlonge, Beirut, Oct. 11, 1938.

54. HS immediately sent a telegram to the British ambassador in Cairo. See FO 371 E7438 (21868) 1287, from Lampson, Cairo, to FO, Dec. 6, 1938, and no. 52, Dec. 6, 1938, to the high commissioner, Palestine.

55. *MAQF*, pp. 252–53. HS sent a telegram to Corbett Ashby on Mar. 1, 1939.

56. *M*, May 15, 1939, p. 5.

57. *MAQF*, pp. 252–53.

58. Ibid., pp. 188–93. Nassar later wrote pamphlets for the Arab League. In the 1950s the office of the Arab Women's Union that Nassar had opened in Damascus was closed down by the government. In the early 1970s in Damascus she died "forgotten." See Sayigh, "Femmes palestiniennes," pp. 16–17.

59. Text reproduced in Margaret Mathieson and Adele Schreiber, *Journey towards Freedom: Written for the Golden Jubilee of the International Alliance of Women* (Copenhagen: International Alliance of Women, 1955), p. 51. SN, "La délégation égyptienne au Congrès de Copenhague," *E*, July–Aug. 1939, p. 5, speaks of intense debate over this declaration. Rosa Manus refers to the debate in her letter to Carrie Chapman Catt, July 31, 1939, Amsterdam, in which she also says that the declaration passed with only a slight majority. Schreiber and Mathieson claimed that the vote was unanimous (p. 52).

60. *The Congress Report, Istanbul 1935, Constitution and By-Laws*, p. 182: "to respect the independence of each affiliated association, and to leave it entirely free to act on all matters within its own country."

61. SN, "La délégation égyptienne au Congrès de Copenhague," *E*, July–Aug. 1939, pp. 2–9; see p. 3.

62. Ibid., pp. 5–6.

63. For accounts by participants of the meetings at Copenhagen, see ibid., pp. 2–9; Munirah Thabit, *Thawrah fi al-Burj al-ʿAji*, pp. 106–10; and Dr. Brachayahu (Palestine Jewish Women's Rights Association), "The Thirteenth International Alliance of Women Congress in Copenhagen: Bulletin on the Women's Union for Equal Rights," *Davar Hapoelet*, no. 8 (Nov. 21, 1939), translated for the author by Schlomo Ben Ami. The accounts all basically agree upon what happened at the congress. Both the EFU and the Palestinian organization thought that hostility had been directed specifically at them; in the first case on the part of the congress collectively and in the second case on the part of the EFU.

64. SN, "La délégation égyptienne au Congrès de Copenhague," *E*, July–Aug. 1939, p. 5.

65. Letter from Rosa Manus to Carrie Chapman Catt, Amsterdam, July 31, 1939, reprinted in Bosch and Kloosterman, *Politics and Friendship*, pp. 246–52;

quotation from p. 247. Also see chap. 7, pp. 221–23, for a brief discussion of the subject entitled "Crisis within the IWSA."

66. A resolution was put forward by the Swiss delegation calling upon IAW affiliates to demand that their governments sign and ratify the League of Nations convention (of Feb. 10, 1938) concerning the legal and civil status of refugees; it was adopted. The EFU delegation abstained from voting. See SN, "La délégation égyptienne au Congrès de Copenhague," *E*, July–Aug. 1939, pp. 6–7.

67. Ibid., p. 7.

68. Ibid., pp. 7–8.

69. Ibid., p. 8.

70. Dr. Brachayahu, in "The Thirteenth International Alliance of Women Congress in Copenhagen," *Davar Hapoelet*, no. 8 (Nov. 21, 1939), also reported that the Jewish delegation introduced a resolution, which passed, asking for removal from the agenda of resolutions dealing with immigration. She said that the Jewish delegation had many allies (the Egyptians concurred in this).

71. "The Withdrawal of the EFU Delegation to the Thirteenth Congress of the International Alliance of Women in Copenhagen: Telegram from Huda Shaʿrawi," *M*, Aug. 1, 1939, p. 11. SN, "La délégation égyptienne au Congrès de Copenhague," *E*, July–Aug. 1939, p. 9. Interview with Luli Abu al-Huda, Nov. 4, 1972, Oxford. Corbett Ashby in a letter to her husband said, "Charaoui has resigned and withdrawn her delegation because we refused to send a letter saying we stood for the immediate cessation of all Jewish immigration into Palestine." In Whittick, *Woman into Citizen*, p. 144.

72. SN, "La délégation égyptienne au Congrès de Copenhague," *E*, July–Aug. 1939, pp. 3–4.

73. "The Success of the Delegation from Egypt at the Congress of the International Alliance of Women: The Ignorance of the Women of Northern Europe on the Palestine Question," *M*, Sept. 1, 1939, p. 6, includes a translation of the letter from Margery Corbett Ashby to HS, from Stavangar, Norway, Aug. 14, 1939. This letter was reproduced in HI, "Ana wa-al-Sharq," pt. 2, pp. 439–41, with first and last paragraphs that were not reprinted in *M*.

74. Letter from HS to Margery Corbett Ashby, Cairo, n.d. (Aug. 1939), in HI, "Ana wa-al-Sharq," pt. 2, pp. 433–35.

75. Letter from Margery Corbett Ashby, Horsted Keynes, Sussex, June 18, 1973, to Margot Badran, Oxford. Interviews with Margery Corbett Ashby, June 12, 1972, Horsted Keynes, and Nov. 9, 1972, London.

76. Authors Adele Schreiber and Margaret Mathieson became IAW board members in 1923 and 1952, respectively. Whittick's history of the IAW, *Woman into Citizen*, is equally silent.

77. "Sadhij Nassar, the Enemy of the British Mandate Authorities in Palestine," signed "An Arab," *M*, Sept. 1, 1939, pp. 27–28. In this interview Nassar, in saying that unveiling was widespread in Egypt, felt it necessary to stress that at the same time women retained their moral and religious values.

78. "Interview with Najlah Kafuri [a member of the Jamʿiyat al-Nahdah al-Nisaʿiyah in Beirut]," *M*, Oct. 15, 1938, pp. 28–29.

79. On changing styles of dress in the Middle East in the nineteenth and early twentieth centuries see Graham-Brown, *Images of Women*, chap. 4, pp. 118–43.

80. Interview with Sara Shahbandar, Apr. 13, 1974, Cairo.

81. Graham-Brown, *Images of Women*, p. 141, citing an obituary by Tarif al-

Khalidi in the *Times* (London), June 18, 1986. See ʿAnbarah Salam al-Khalidi, *Jawlah fi Dhikrayat bayna Lubnan wa-Filastin* (Beirut: Dar al-Nahar lil-Nashr, 1978).

82. Interview with Tarab ʿAbd al-Hadi, Apr. 20, 1974, Cairo.

83. Tuqan, *A Mountainous Journey*, pp. 93 and 105.

84. Woodsmall, *Moslem Women Enter a New World*, chaps. 1, 2, and 4.

85. Her rebuttal was entitled *al-Fatat wa-al-Shuyukh: Nazarat wa-Munazarat fi al-Sufur wa-al-Hijab* (Beirut, 1929). For a short biographical reference see Badran and Cooke, *Opening the Gates*, pp. 270–71, and, for a translated extract from *Unveiling and Veiling* entitled "Unveiling and Veiling: The Liberation of the Woman and Social Renewal in the Islamic World," pp. 272–76. For another extract translated into English see "Removing the Veil and Veiling," trans. Salah-Dine Hammoud, in al-Hibri, *Women and Islam*, pp. 221–26.

86. Zaynab Fawwaz in *al-Durr al-Mandhur*, pp. 497–510, relates that Makarius had proposed that girls take the names of both their mother and father, following Spanish practice.

87. *MNA*, the conference proceedings and related materials, p. 19.

88. Ibid., p. 27.

89. SN, "Le reveil des femmes de l'Asie," *E*, Apr. 1930, p. 4.

90. See Ahmad Mahmoud Gomaa, *The Foundation of the League of Arab States* (London: Longmans, 1977).

91. Later, HS was decorated "in recognition of her efforts on the woman question" by the governments of Syria, Lebanon, and Trans-Jordan.

92. On the trip see *MNA*, pp. 27–28; HI, "Ana wa-al-Sharq," pt. 1, pp. 84–85; in an interview on Mar. 29, 1972, in Cairo, Aminah al-Saʿid mentioned that they helped to form local feminist societies.

93. The EFU women from Minya included Mrs. ʿAbd al-Hamid Jawish Bey, Mrs. Mustafa al-Tawil Bey, and Berlant al-Sayyid.

94. *MNA*, pp. 77–84, for entire speech.

95. Ibid., pp. 72–76.

96. Ibid., pp. 272. On the difficulty for Palestinian women to struggle for women's liberation along with national liberation during the fight for the survival of their country see Sheila Rowbotham, *Women, Resistance, and Revolution* (London: Allen Lane, 1972), p. 204. More recently Palestinian women have been able to struggle for national liberation and women's liberation at the same time, and they have been more fully involved in all aspects of the national liberation struggle. See Rosemary Sayigh, *Palestinians: From Peasants to Revolutionaries* (London: Zed Press, 1979); Nahla Abdo, "Nationalism and Feminism—Palestinian Women and the Intifada: No Going Back?" in *Gender and National Identity: Women and Politics in Mulsim Societies*, ed. Valentine Moghadam (London: Zed Press, 1994); Julie Peteet, Rita Giacaman, and Muna Odeh, "The Palestinian Women's Movement in the Israeli-Occupied West-Bank and Gaza Strip," in *Women in the Arab World*, ed. Nahid Toubia (London: Zed Press, 1988), pp. 57–65; Rema Hammami, "Women, the Hijab and the Intifada," *Middle East Report*, nos. 164–65 (May–Aug. 1990); Joost Hiltermann, "The Women's Movement during the Uprising," *Journal of Palestine Studies* 20, no. 3 (1991); and Rita Giacaman and Penny Johnson, "Building Barricades and Breaking Barriers," in *Intifada: The Palestinian Uprising against Israeli Occupation*, ed. Zachary Lockman and Joel Benin (Boston: South End Press with MERIP, 1989).

97. *MNA*, pp. 319–21.

98. Ibid., p. 339.

99. Sabri, who began law practice in 1921, worked in the office of the public prosecutor in 1922. He was first elected to parliament in 1929 and ran several more times. For his speech see ibid., pp. 251–60.

100. See Malifah Rifᶜat al-Habib from Palestine, who stressed Islamic modernist arguments in her speech and pointed in particular to curbing polygamy. Ibid., pp. 214–15.

101. The effects of Western-modeled education are vividly portrayed by Lebanese Etel Adnan in "Growing Up to Be a Woman Writer in Lebanon," in Badran and Cooke, *Opening the Gates*, pp. 5–20. Egyptian Wadidah Wassif also conveys this in her unpublished memoirs.

102. For her speech see ibid., pp. 120–29.

103. For Zahiyah Dughan's speech see ibid., pp. 153–60. An edited extract translated into English was published in Badran and Cooke, *Opening the Gates*, p. 342.

104. *MNA*, pp. 268–71.

105. Ibid., pp. 184–88. Harfush received her degree in pediatrics at the American University in Beirut in 1941 and subsequently taught at the university's school of medicine. In 1959 she took a degree in social health and hygiene and in 1965 a doctorate in public health at Harvard University. She has written a book on her life: *Fi Tariqat Hayah* (Beirut: Maᶜhad al-Dirasat al-Nisaʾiyah fi al-ᶜAlam al-ᶜArabi Kulliyat al Bayrut al-Jamᶜiyah al-Tawziᶜ Muʾassasat Nawfal, 1987).

106. *MNA*, pp. 89–96.

107. *Al-Muqattam*, Dec. 13, 1944, and *al-Balagh*, Dec. 26, 1944.

108. FO 371 (41335) J4576, no. 353, Killearn from Cairo, Dec. 13, 1944.

109. FO 371 J 90 (45916), A. Eden to J. Nall.

110. See Gomaa, *The Foundation of the League of Arab States.*

111. *MNA*, p. 342–43.

112. Ibid., p. 343.

113. Ibid., p. 343–44.

114. IAW *Report of the Congress at Interlaken, 1946*, "Egypte," pp. 51–53.

115. Ibid., "Lebanon," pp. 62–64.

116. See *MNA*, p. 35, for the letter from Kamala Devi Chattopadhyay to HS and the telegram from HS to Kamala Devi Chattopadhyay, and pp. 319–21 for HS's closing speech.

117. Interview with SN, Sept. 11, 1971, Cairo.

118. Interview with Aminah al-Saᶜid and Karimah al-Saᶜid, Jan. 21, 1968, Cairo.

• BIBLIOGRAPHY •

Interviews

ʿAbd al-Hadi, Tarab	Apr. 20, 1974, Cairo
ʿAbd al-Malak Saʿd, Munirah	Sept. 17, 1975, Cairo
ʿAbd al-Qaddus, Ihsan	Sept. 3, 1971, Cairo
ʿAbd al-Rahman, ʿAʾishah (Bint al-Shatiʾ)	July 8, 1968, Cairo
ʿAbd al-Rahman, Mufidah	Apr. 18, 1968, Cairo
Abu al-Huda, Luli	Nov. 4, 1972, Oxford
Abu Zayd, Hikmat	June 27, 1968, Cairo
Aflatun, Inji	Sept. 17, 1975, Cairo
	Mar. 1988, Cairo
al-ʿAlam, Mahmud Amin	June 1974, Oxford
ʿAllubah, Naʿilah	Jan. 24, 1968, Cairo
Antonius, Katy	Mar. 25, 1972, Cairo
al-Ayyubi, Naʿimah	Feb. 8, 1975, Cairo
ʿAzzam, Marguerite	Nov. 18, 1975, Cairo
Bakhit, Salah al-Din ʿAbd al-Halim	Dec. 2, 1975, Minya
Barakat, Layla	Apr. 9, 1974, Cairo
de Bono, Jeannette Ayrut	Nov. 10, 1975, Cairo
Bulus Hanna, Jeannette M.	Sept. 26, 1975, Cairo
Corbett Ashby, Margery	Nov. 16, 1971, London
	June 12, 1972, Horsted Keynes
	Nov. 9, 1972, London
Daʾud, Princess Fatma	Dec. 4, 1975, Cairo
Doss, Layla	Feb. 13, 1968, Cairo
	Oct. 5, 1975, Cairo
	Jan. 1985, Cairo
	May 19, 1990, Cairo
Fahmi, Andrée	Aug. 20, 1968, Cairo
	From 1973 to 1990, Cairo
Fahmi, Fatma	June 27, 1968, Cairo
Fahmi, Virginie Rousseau	June 12, 1968, Cairo
Farag, Alexandra	Sept. 17, 1975, Cairo
Farid, Buthaynah	Nov. 20, 1975, Cairo
Farr, ʿAliyah	July 20, 1968, Cairo
Fuʾad ʿIzzat, Princess Khadijah	Feb. 15, 1972, Cairo
Ghali, Anna Nagib	Sept. 10, 1975, Cairo

Ghali, Gertrude Butrus	Sept. 12, 1975, Cairo
Ghali, Ibrahim	Mar. 31, 1974, Cairo
al-Ghazali, Zaynab	Feb. 1988, Cairo
Greis, Matilda	July 15, 1968, Cairo
Habib al-Masri, Eva	Dec. 2, 1974, London
al-Hakim Tawfiq	Feb. 12, 1968, Cairo
Hasan, Prince Hasan	Feb. 12, 1975, Cairo Aug. 1988, Cairo
Haykal, Ahmad	Feb. 15, 1972, Cairo
Haykal, ʿAzizah	Feb. 12, 1972, Cairo
Idris, Hawwaʾ	From 1967 to 1989, Cairo
Kahil, Mary	Mar. 3, 1972, Cairo
Kahil, Ra’uf	Feb. 10, 1973, Oxford
Kazim, Safinaz	From 1988 to 1990, Cairo
Kher, Amy	Oct. 19, 1975, Oxford
Khayyat, Edna	Mar. 9, 1972, Cairo
Madhkur, Ibrahim	Mar. 6, 1968, Cairo
Nabarawi, Saiza	From 1967 to 1984, Cairo
Nasr Allah, ʿA’idah	From 1988 to 1990, Cairo
Qalamawi, Suhayr	Apr. 9, 1968, Cairo
al-Qalini, Rawhiyah	Apr. 11, 1974, Cairo
Qasim, Munirah	Sept. 16, 1967, Cairo
al-Qusi, Ihsan Ahmad	Feb. 22, 1972, Cairo
Raghib, Aminah Idris	Apr. 18, 1974, Cairo
Rashid, Bahigah	Apr. 10, 1974, Cairo Oct. 7, 1975, Cairo
al-Saʿdawi, Nawal	From 1985 to 1990, Cairo
al-Saʿid, Aminah	Jan. 21, 1968, Cairo Mar. 29, 1972, Cairo Oct. 1989, Cairo
al-Saʿid, Karimah	Jan. 21, 1968, Cairo Apr. 4, 1972, Cairo
Saqqaf, Abqar	Nov. 28, 1975, Cairo
Sarruf, Ellen	Mar. 31, 1974, Cairo
Shafiq, Duriyah	Jan. 23, 1968, Cairo Apr. 10, 1974, Cairo
Shahbandar, Sarah	Apr. 13, 1974, Cairo
Sidarus, Hilanah	Dec. 5, 1975, Cairo Sept. 10, 1990, Cairo
Sidqi, ʿAbd al-Rahman	June 28, 1968, Cairo
Thabit, Mustafa	Feb. 6, 1972, Cairo
Wakid, Fu’ad	Feb. 5, 1968, Cairo

Wissa, Ester Fahmi	Aug. 15, 1968, Alexandria
al-Zayyat, Latifah	May 3, 1990, Cairo

Women's Memoirs (Published and Unpublished)

Aflatun, Inji. *Mudhakkirat Inji Aflatun*. Edited and introduced by Sa'id al-Khayy. Kuwait: Dar Su'ad al-Sabah, 1994.

'Asmahan (Amal al-Atrash). *'Asmahan Tirwi Qissataha*. Beirut: Dar al-Kutub, 1961.

Bint al-Shati' ('A'ishah 'Abd al-Rahman). *'Ala Jisr: Usturat al-Zaman*. Cairo: Dar al-Hilal, 1967.

———. *Sirr al-Shati'*. Cairo: Ruz al-Yusif, 1952.

Djavidan Hanum. *Harem Life*. New York: Dial Press, 1931.

Fahmi 'Asmah. *Dhikrayat 'an Madrasat al-Hilmiyah al-Thanawiyah lil-Banat*. Cairo, 1955.

Harfush, Jamal Karam. *Fi Tariqat al-Hayah*. Beirut: Ma'had al-Dirasat al-Nisa'iyah fi al-'Alam al-'Arabi Kulliyat al-Bayrut al-Jam'iyah al-Tawzi' Mu'assasat Nawfal, 1987.

Husni, Munirah. *Ayyam fi al-Hay'ah al-Nisa'iyah*. Cairo, n.d.

Idris, Hawwa'. "Ana wa-al-Sharq." Unpublished memoirs. Cairo, 1975.

Jacobs, Aletta. *Herinneringen van Aletta Jacobs*. Amsterdam: Socialistische Uti-geuerij Nijmegen, 1924.

al-Khalidi,' Anbarah Salam. *Jawlah fi Dhikrayat bayna Lubnan wa-Filastin*. Beirut: Dar al-Nahar lil-Nashr, 1978.

al-Masabni, Bad'iyah. *Mudhakirrat Bad'iyah Masabni*. Beirut: Dar Maktabat al-Hayah, n.d.

al-Masri, Eva Habib. *Memoirs of an Egyptian American or the Life Story of the First Co-Ed at the American University in Cairo*. Jasper, Ark., n.d.

Musa, Nabawiyah. "Dhikrayati." *Majallat al-Fatah*, May 1938–Aug. 1943.

Rushdi, Fatma. *Kifahi fi Masrah wa-Sinima*. Cairo: Dar al-Ma'arif, 1971.

Sha'rawi, Huda. *Harem Years: The Memoirs of an Egyptian Feminist*. Translated, edited, and introduced by Margot Badran. London: Virago Press, 1986; New York: The Feminist Press, 1987.

———. *Mudhakkirat Ra'idat al-'Arabiyah al-Hadithah Huda Sha'rawi*. Introduced by Aminah al-Sa'id. Cairo: Dar al-Hilal, 1981.

Thabit, Munirah. *Thawrah fi al-Burj al-'Aji: Mudhakkirat fi 'Ashrin 'Am*. Cairo: Dar al-Ma'arif bi-al-Tiba'ah wa-al-Nashr, 1945.

Tugay, Emine Foat. *Three Centuries: Family Chronicles of Turkey and Egypt*. London: Oxford University Press, 1963.

Tuqan, Fadwa. *A Mountainous Journey: An Autobiography*. Translated by Olive Kenny. London: The Women's Press, 1990.

Umm Kulthum. *Umm Kulthum allati la Ya'rifuha Ahad*. With Mahmud Awad. Cairo: Mu'assasat Akhbar al-Yawm, 1971.

Wassif, Wadidah. Unpublished memoirs. Alexandria.

al-Yusif, Fatma. *Dhikrayat Ruz al-Yusif*. Cairo: Mu'assasat Ruz al-Yusif, 1953 and 1959.

al-Zayyat, Latifah. *Shaykhukhah*. Cairo: Dar al-Mustaqbal al-'Arabi, 1986.

———. *Hamlat Taftish*. "*Awraq Shakhsiyah*." Cairo: Dar al-Hilal, 1992.

Unpublished sources

Private Collections

Corbett Ashby, Margery. "Memories of Madame Charaoui Pacha." Horsted Keynes, Sussex, 1971.

Ghali, Anna Nagib Butrus. "Mariage." Eyewitness account of the wedding reception for ʿAtiyah, the daughter of Khedive ʿAbbas Hilmi II, to Celaleddin Vlora Pasha. Cairo, 1909.

Ghali, Gertrude Butrus. Diary kept in Upper Egypt during cholera epidemic, 1944. "Programme pour des cours d'infirmières auxiliaires et volontaires," Cairo, n.d.; "Ecole de perfectionnement pour infirmières, formation d'infirmières-chefs," Cairo, n.d.; "Nursing," Cairo, n.d. Newspaper clippings.

Ghali, Louise Majorelle. In the Ghali Family Private Papers.

Hasan, Prince Hasan. Photograph collection.

Husni, Fikriyah. Letters to Huda Shaʿrawi.

Idris, Hawwa'. Misc. papers, newspaper clippings, and photograph collection; seen at her residence, the collection is now housed at the American University in Cairo.

Kahil, Mary. Misc. papers including materials from IAW conference in Berlin, 1929, and materials on prostitution in Egypt.

Nabarawi, Saiza. Vast private papers collection including newspaper clippings and photograph collection.

Richard, Mme. Letters from Huda Shaʿrawi.

Saqqaf, Abqar. Photograph collection.

Shaʿrawi, Huda. Private letters.

Thabit, Aminah. Letters to Huda Shaʿrawi.

Archival Collections

Catt, Carrie Chapman. Correspondence. New York Public Library. Diaries. Library of Congress, Washington, D.C.

Crane, Charles. Private Papers, Memoirs. Institute of Current World Affairs, New York.

International Alliance of Women. London Office. Minutes of Executive Board Meetings.

Milner Papers. New College, Oxford.

(British) Public Records Office, London. Consular and Embassy Archives, File 14086, FO 141, and Foreign Office, Political, FO 371.

Russell Papers. St. Antony's College, Oxford.

Women's International League for Peace and Freedom. Branch Reports, Correspondence, and Memoranda. London.

Woodsmall, Ruth Frances. Private Papers. Sophia Smith Collection. Smith College, Northampton, Mass.

Published Sources

Egyptian Feminist Union

Dhikra Faqidat al-Adibah al-Nabighah Mayy. 1941.

Dhikra Faqidat al-ʿUrubah Huda Hanim Shaʿrawi. Cairo, 1947.

L'Egyptienne. 1925–1940.
al-Mar'ah al-ʿArabiyah wa-Qadiyat Filastin: al-Mu'tamar al-Nisa'i al-Sharqi. 1938.
al-Misriyah. 1937–1940.
al-Mu'tamar al-Nisa'i al-ʿArabi. 1944.
Nabaraouy, Céza. *Vingt-six ans d'activité de L'Union féministe égyptienne 1923–49*. 1950.
Nizam Jamʿiyat Huda Shaʿrawi lil-Nahdah al-Nisa'iyah. 1964.
Nizam Jamʿiyat al-Ittihad al-Nisa'i al-Misri. 1957.
Qanun Jamʿiyat al-Ittihad al-Nisa'i al-Misri. 1947.
Rashid, Bahigah, Tahiyah Isfahani, and Samiyah Sidqi Murad. *al-Yubili al-Dhahabi: 1923–1973*. 1973.
Les revendications des dames égyptiennes. 1925.
Taqrir ʿan ʿAmal al-Ittihad al-Nisa'i al-Misri min Sanat 1923 ila Sanat 1955. Cairo, 1955.
L'Union féministe égyptienne: rapport 1928–33. Cairo, 1933.

Women's Societies, Egypt

Association Intellectuelle des Dames égyptiennes. Cairo, 1914.
al-Jamʿiyah al-Nisa'iyah li-Tahsin al-Sihhah: Qissat Khamsah wa-ʿIshrin Sanah, 1936–1961. Cairo, 1961.
Jamʿiyat al-Mar'ah al-Jadidah: The Welfare Modern Woman Society. Cairo, ca. 1974.
Jamʿiyat Misr Himayat al-Mar'ah wa-al-Atfal. Cairo, 1969.
Nidaʿ Jamʿiyat al-Mar'ah al-Jadidah. Cairo, n.d.
Oeuvre Mohamed Aly el Kebir. Cairo, 1950.
Statute de Club union féminine. Cairo, 1925.

Women's Organizations, International

International Woman Suffrage Alliance (from 1926: International Alliance of Women for Suffrage and Equal Citizenship), London. Congress Reports: Budapest 1913, Rome 1923, Paris 1926, Berlin 1929, Istanbul 1935, Copenhagen 1939, Interlaken 1946. *Jus Suffragi* (official journal).
al-Ittihad al-Nisa'i al-ʿArabi. *al-Mar'ah al-ʿArabiyah* (official journal), 1946.
Women's International League for Peace and Freedom, London. *Pax* (official journal). *British Section Newssheet*. Correspondence.

Women's Lectures, Speeches, Essays, Letters, and Manuals

Association Intellectuelle des Dames Egyptiennes. *Conférences données au Caire chez Madame Ali Pacha Charaoui et à l'Université égyptienne par Mlle Clément*. Cairo, 1914.
Bahithat al-Badiyah (Malak Hifni Nasif). *al-Nisa'iyat*. Cairo: Matbaʿat al-Jaridah Press, 1909.
Couvreur, A. *Conférences faites aux dames égyptiennes*. Paris: Peyriller, 1910.
Dhikra Bahithat al-Badiyah. Cairo, 1920.
Fawwaz, Zaynab. *al-Durr al-Manthur fi al-Tabaqat Rabbat al-Khudur*. Cairo: Matbaʿat al-Kubra al-Amiriyah, 1312 H.
———. *al-Rasa'il al-Zaynabiyah*. Cairo, 1897.
Ghali, Gertrude Butrus. *Adab al-Tamrid*. Cairo, n.d.
Hashim, Labibah. *Kitab fi al-Tarbiyah*. Cairo: Matbaʿat al-Maʿarif, 1911.

Hifnawi, Mustafa, ed. *al-Sifr al-Khalid: Majmuʿat Khutab wa-Kitabat al-Zuʿamaʾ*. Vol. 1. Cairo, 1937.

Husayn, Qadriyah. *Shahirat al-Nisaʾ fi al-ʿAlam al-Islami*. Cairo: Maktabat al-Misriyah, 1924.

"Khitab al-Sayidah Huda Hanim Shaʿrawi fi al-Ijtimaʿ al-Nisaʾi al-Watani al-Kabiri." In *al-Marʾah al-Jadidah* 2, no. 9 (1924): 84.

Majmuʿat al-Khutab allati Ulqiyat fi Ijtimaʿ al-Sayyidat al-Misriyat bi Dar al-Marhum Husayn Basha Abu ʿUsbaʿ yawm al-Jumʿah 5 Mayu 1922 wa Yawm al-Jumʿah 27 Disimbir 1922.

Mursi, Zaynab. *al-Ayat al-Bayyinat fi Tarbiyat al-Banat*. Cairo: Matbaʿat Kararah, 1912.

Musa, Nabawiyah. *Diwan al-Fatah*. Cairo, 1938.

———. *al-Marʾah wa-al-ʿAmal*. Alexandria: al-Matbaʿah al-Qawmi, 1920.

———. "al-Muhadarat al-Nisaʾiyah al-Misriyah fi Jamiʿat al-Misriyah." In *al-Ahram, Shuhud al-ʿAsr 1876–1986*. Cairo, 1986.

———. *Riwayat Nabhutub*. Cairo, n.d. [pub. by 1938].

Nabaraouy, Céza. *L'évolution féministe et les profits que peut en retirer le bien publique*. Premier Prix de Concours du Gouvernement. Cairo, 1936.

Nasif, Majd al-Din Hifni. *Athar Bahithat al-Badiyah Malak Hifni Nasif: 1886–1918*. Cairo: Wizarat al-Thaqafah wa-al-Irshad al-Qawmi, 1962.

Nidaʾ min al-Sayidah al-Jalilah Huda Hanim Shaʿrawi Zaʿimat al-Nahdah al-Nisaʾiyah. Cairo, 1936.

al-Qusi, Ihsan. *Fi Maydan al-Khidmah al-Ijtimaʿiyah*. Cairo, 1949.

———. *al-Khidmah al-Ijtimaʿiyah fi al-Qarn al ʿIshrin*. Cairo, 1956.

Saʿd, Malikah. *Rabbat al-Dar*. Cairo: Matbaʿat al-Tawfiq, 1915.

Shaʿrawi, Huda. *Muhadarah: Dawr al-Marʾah fi al-Nahdah al-Sharqiyah*. Cairo, 1935.

Works in Arabic

BOOKS AND THESES

ʿAbd al-Halim, Ahmad Zaki. *Nisaʾ fawq al-Qima*. Cairo: Dar al-Faisal, n.d.

ʿAbd al-Karim, Ahmad ʿIzzat. *Tarikh al-Taʿlim fi Misr*. Cairo: Dar al-Kutub al-Misriyah, 1945.

ʿAbduh, Ibrahim. *Ruz al-Yusif*. Cairo, 1961.

ʿAbduh, Ibrahim, and Duriyah Shafiq. *al-Marʾah al-Misriyah min al-Faraʾina ila al-Yawm*. Cairo: Matbaʿat al-Misr, 1955.

———. *Tatawwur al-Nahdah al-Nisaʾiyah fi Misr*. Cairo: Maktabat al-Tawwakul, 1954.

ʿAbduh, Muhammad. *al-ʿAmal al-Kamilah li-Muhammad ʿAbduh*. Edited by Muhammad ʿImarah. 6 vols. Cairo, 1972. Beirut: al-Muʾassasah al-Arabiyah lil-Dirasat wa al Nashr, 1974.

Abu Zayd, Hikmah. *al-Takyif al-Ijtimaʿi fi al-Rif al-Misri al-Jadid*. Cairo, n.d.

Aflatun, Inji. *Imraʾ Maʿna*. Cairo, 1947.

———. *Nahdat al-Nisaʾ al-Misriyat*. Cairo, 1950.

———. *al-Salam wa-al-Jalaʾ*. Cairo, 1950.

———. *Thamani Milyun Imraʾ*. Cairo, n.d.

Ahmad, Ahmad Taha. *al-Marʾah Kifahuha wa-ʿAmaluha*. Cairo, 1964.

ʿAlluba, Muhammad ʿAli. *Filastin wa al-Damir al-Insani*. Cairo: Dar al-Hilal, 1964.

Amin, Qasim. *al-ʿAmal al-Kamilah li-Qasim Amin*. Edited by Muhammad ʿImarah. 2 vols. Beirut: al-Mu'assasah al-ʿArabiyah lil-Dirasat wa-al-Nashr, 1976.

———. *al-Mar'ah al-Jadidah*. Cairo, 1900.

———. *Tahrir al-Mar'ah*. Cairo, 1899.

Anis, Muhammad. *Dirasat fi Watha'iq Thawrat Sanat 1919*. Cairo, 1963.

Barakat, Hidayah. *Nubdhah ʿan al-ʿAmal al-Siyasi wa-al-Ijtimaʿi al-Nisa'i fi Misr*. Cairo, n.d.

Fahmi, Murqus. *al-Mar'ah fi al-Sharq*. Cairo, 1894.

Fahmi, Qalini. *Mudhakkirat*. Cairo: al-Shinnawi, 1943.

Farid, Zaynab Muhammad, "Tatawwur Taʿlim al-Banat fi Misr min al-Ihtilal al-Baritani, 1882 hatta al-An." 2 vols. Ph.D. diss., Kulliyat al-Banat, ʿAyn Shams University, Cairo, 1966.

Fu'ad, Niʿmat Ahmad. *Umm Kulthum wa ʿAsr min al-Fann*. Cairo: al-Hay'ah al-Misriyah al-ʿAmah lil-Kitab, 1976.

Halim, ʿAsmah. *Sittat Ayyam fi Saʿid*. Cairo: The New Dawn Publisher, 1944.

Hamadah, Husayn ʿUmar. *Ahadith ʿAn Mayy Ziyadah*. Damascus: Dar Qutaybah lil-Nashr, 1983.

Harb, Talʿat. *Tarbiyat al-Mar'ah wa al-Hijab*. Cairo, 1899. 2d ed. 1905.

———. *Fasl al-Khitab fi al-Mar'ah wa-al-Hijab*. Cairo, 1901.

al-Ittihad al-ʿAmm al-Nisa'i. *al-Mar'ah al-ʿArabiyah fi Qutr al-ʿArabi al-Suri*. Damascus, ca. 1974.

al-Jaziri, Ibrahim. *Saʿd Zaghlul: Tarqiyat Tarifah*. Cairo, 1887

Junaydi, Muhammad Farid. *ʿAzmat al-Zawaj fi Misr*. Cairo, 1933.

Khalifah, Ijlal Hanim Mahmud. *al-Harakah al-Nisa'iyah al-Hadithah*. Cairo: al-Matbaʿah al-ʿArabiyah al-Hadithah, 1974.

———. *al-Mar'ah wa-Qadiyat Filastin*. Cairo, 1974.

———. "al-Sihafah al-Nisa'iyah fi Misr min 1919 ila 1939." M.A. thesis, Cairo University, 1966.

al-Kuzbari, Salma H. *Mayy Ziyada: Maʿsat al-Nubuʿ*. Beirut: Mu'assasat Nawfal, 1978.

al-Markaz al-Qawmi lil-Buhuth al-Ijtimaʿi wa-al-Jina'iyah. *al-Bighah fi al-Qahirah*. Cairo, 1961.

Musa, Salamah. *al-Mar'ah Laysat Luʿbat al-Rajul*. Cairo, 1956.

al-Nahhas, Maryam. *Maʿrid al-Hasna' fi Tarajim Mashahir al-Nisa'i*. Alexandria, 1879.

al-Qalamawi, Suhayr. *Ahadith Jaddati*. Cairo: Dar al-Qawmiyya, , 1935.

al-Rafiʿi, ʿAbd al-Rahman. *Thawrat Sanat 1919*. Cairo, 1946.

Ragib, Nabil. *Huda Shaʿrawi wa ʿAsr al-Tanwir*. Cairo, 1988.

Rida, Rashid. *Nida' lil-Jins al-Latif*. Cairo, 1351 A.H.

al-Saʿdawi, Nawal. *al-Mar'ah wa-al-Jins*. Beirut, 1972.

Safwat, Ahmad. *Qa'idat Islah Qanun al-Ahwal al-Shakhsiyah*. Alexandria, 1917.

Salim, Latifah. *al-Mar'at al-Misriyat wa-al-Taghyir al-Ijtimaʿi*. Cairo: al-Hay'ah al-Misriyah al-ʿAmmah lil-Kitab, 1984.

al-Sayyid, Ahmad Lutfi. *al-Muntakhabat*. Cairo, 1938.

Shafiq, Ahmad. *Hawliyat Misr al-Siyasiyah*. 6 vols. Cairo: Matbaʿat Shafiq Basha, 1926–1931.

Shafiq, Duriyah. *al-Kitab al-Abyad li-Huquq al-Mar'ah al-Siyasiyah*. Cairo: Matba'at al-Sharqiyah, 1953.

Shushah. *Umm Kalthum: Hayat Nagham*. Cairo: Ruz al-Yusif, 1976.

al-Subki, Amal. *al-Harakat al-Nisa'iyah fi Misr bayna al-Thawrayn 1919 wa 1952*. Cairo: al-Hay'ah al-Misriyah al-ʿAmmah lil-Kitab, 1986.

al-Tahtawi, Rifaʿi. *al-Murshid al-Amin lil-Banat wa-al-Banin*. Cairo, 1875.

al-Taymuriyah, ʿA'ishah. *Hilyat al-Tiraz*. Cairo: al-Matbaʿat al-Amirah al-Sharafiyah, 1909.

———. *Mir'at al-Taʿammul fi al-ʿUmur*. Cairo, ca. 1890s.

———. *Nata'ij al-Ahwal fi al-Aqwal wa-al-Faʿal*. Cairo, 1887.

Wajdi, Muhammad Farid. *al-Mar'ah al-Muslimah*. Cairo, 1912.

Yahya, Muhammad Kamal. *al-Juzur al-Tarikhiyah li-Tahrir al-Mar'ah al-Misriyah*. Cairo: al-Hay'ah al-Misriyah al-ʿAmmah lil-Kitab, 1983.

Zayn al-Din, Nazirah. *al-Fatat wa-al-Shuyukh: Nazarat wa-Munazarat fi al-Sufur wa-al-Hijab*. Beirut, 1929.

———. *al-Sufur wa-al-Hijab*. Beirut, 1928.

al-Zirkili, Khayr al-Din. *al-Aʿlam Tarajim li-Ashar al-Rijal wa al-Nisa' min al-ʿArab wa Mustaʿrabin wa Mustashriqin*. Cairo, 1954–1959.

Ziyadah, Mayy. *ʿA'ishah Taymur: Shaʿirat al-Taliʿah*. Cairo: Matbaʿat al-Muqtataf, 1926.

———. *Bahithat al-Badiyah: Bahth Intiqadi*. Cairo, 1920.

———. *Sawanih Fatah*. Cairo, n.d.

ARTICLES

This selective list does not include articles from *L'Egyptienne* and *al-Misriyah* and other women's journals of the period.

ʿAllubah, Naʿilah, Muhammad Rifʿat, et al. "Thawrat 1919 Rafʿat al-Hijab wa-al-Yashmak ʿan Wajh al-Mar'ah al-Misriyah." *al-Musawwar*, Mar. 7, 1969.

Amin, Wadiʿ. "al-Judhur al-Tarikhiyah li-Kifah al-Mar'ah." *al-Taliʿah*, Nov. 1969, 66–73.

al-ʿAyyubi, Naʿimah. "Kayfa wa-li-madha Ikhtartu ʿan akuna Muhamiyah." *Majallat al-Usbuʿ*, no. 29 (June 13, 1934): 15.

Badran, Margot. "al-Harakah al-Nisa'iyah wa-al-Wataniyah fi Misr min 1870 ila 1925." *Nun* (Cairo), 1989, and *Nun* (Algiers), 1990.

———. "Ma hiya al-Nisa'iyah?" *Nisf al-Dunya* (Cairo), Sept. 21, 1990.

———. "al-Nisa'iyah ka-Quwah fi al-Alam al-ʿArabi." *Fikrah al-ʿArabi al-Hadith fi al-Alam al-ʿArabi*. Cairo: Matbaʿat al-Tadammun al-ʿArabi, 1989.

al-Hakim, Tawfiq. "Ta'thir al-Mar'ah ʿala Kuttabina al-Muʿasirin." *al-Thaqafah*, Apr. 11, 1939, pp. 6–8.

Kazim, Safinaz. "al-Ra'idah Nabawiyah Musa wa-Inʿash Dhakirat al-Ummah." *Majallat al-Hilal*, Jan. 1984.

Majalla al-Usbuʿ, no. 29 (June 13, 1934). Special issue on women.

Nabarawi, Saiza. "Baʿda Khamsat ʿAshar ʿam, hana al-Waqt li-Husul al-Mar'ah ʿala Haqq al-Intikhab wa-al-Tarshih lil-Barlaman. *Majallat al-Usbuʿ*, no. 29 (June 13, 1934): 9.

al-Saʿid, Aminah. "Fi Dhikra Huda Shaʿrawi—Imra'ah Jadirah bi-al-Khulud." *Hawwa'*, Dec. 16, 1967, 4–5.

———. "Kalimah Sarihah ʿan Tarikh al-Nahdah al-Nisa'iyah." *Hawwa'*, Dec. 2, 1967, 4–5.

Shaʿrawi, Huda. "Assasa al-Nahdah al-Nisa'iyah wa-Tatawwuratuha fi Misr." *Majallat al-Shu'un al-Ijtimaʿiyah*, Aug. 1941, 16–24.

———. "Kayfa ussisa al-Ittihad al-Nisa'i." *al-Hilal*, May 1949, 85–87.
———. "al-Mar'ah al-Muta'allimah fi Maydan al-Hay'ah al-Misriyah." *Majallat al-Shu'un al-Ijtima'iyah*, Feb. 1941, 42–50.

Works in Western Languages

BOOKS AND THESES

'Abd al-Raziq, Ahmad. *La femme au temps des mamlouks en Egypte*. Cairo: Institut français d'archéologie oriental du Caire, 1973.
Abdalla, Ahmed. *The Student Movement and National Politics in Egypt*. London: al-Saqi Books, 1985.
Abu-Lughod, Janet. *Cairo: 1001 Years of the City Victorious*. Princeton: Princeton University Press, 1971.
Abu-Lughod, Lila. *Veiled Sentiments: Honor and Poetry in a Bedouin Society*. Berkeley and Los Angeles: University of California Press, 1986.
———. *Writing Women's Worlds: Bedouin Stories*. Berkeley and Los Angeles: University of California Press, 1993.
Adams, Charles C. *Islam and Modernism in Egypt*. New York: Russell and Russell, 1933.
Ahmed, J. M. *The Intellectual Origins of Egyptian Nationalism*. London: Oxford University Press, 1960.
Ahmed, Leila. *Women and Gender in Islam*. New Haven: Yale University Press, 1992.
Allen, Roger, *A Period of Time*. Reading, England: Garnet Press, 1992.
Ammar, Hamed. *Growing Up in an Egyptian Village*. London, 1954.
Anderson, Benedict. *Imagined Communities: Reflections on the Origin and Spread of Nationalism*. London: Verso, 1983.
Anderson, J.N.D. *Islamic Law in the Modern World*. New York: New York University Press, 1959.
Arat, Yesim. *The Patriarchal Paradox: Women Politicians in Turkey*. Rutherford, N.J.: Fairleigh Dickinson University Press, 1989.
Arnett, Mary Flounders. "Qasim Amin and the Beginnings of the Feminist Movement in Egypt." Ph.D. diss., Dropsie College, Philadelphia, 1965.
Babazogli, Sophie. *L'éducation de la jeune fille musulmane en Egypt*. Cairo, 1928.
Badran, Margot, and Miriam Cooke, eds. *Opening the Gates: A Century of Arab Feminist Writing*. London: Virago; Bloomington: Indiana University Press, 1990.
Baer, Gabriel. *Studies in the Social History of Modern Egypt*. Chicago: University of Chicago Press, 1969.
Baron, Beth Ann. "The Rise of a New Literary Culture: The Women's Press of Egypt, 1892–1919." Ph.D. diss., University of California, Los Angeles, 1988.
Beck, Lois, and Nikki Keddie, eds. *Women in the Muslim World*. Cambridge: Harvard University Press, 1978.
Beinin, Joel, and Zachary Lockman. *Workers on the Nile: Nationalism, Communism, Islam, and the Egyptian Working Class, 1882–1954*. Princeton: Princeton University Press, 1987.
Berque, Jacques. *Egypt: Imperialism and Revolution*. Translated by Jean Stewart. London: Faber and Faber, 1972.
———. *Histoire sociale d'un village égyptien au XXème siècle*. Paris, 1957.
Blackman, Winifred S. *The Fellahin of Upper Egypt*. London: G. G. Harrap, 1927.
Bohachevsky-Chomiak, Martha. *Feminists despite Themselves: Women in Ukrain-*

ian Community Life, 1884–1939. Edmonton: Canadian Institute of Ukrainian Studies, University of Alberta, 1988.

Boktor, Amir. *School and Society in the Valley of the Nile*. Cairo: Elias' Modern Press, 1936.

Bosch, Mineke, and Annemarie Kloosterman, eds. *Politics and Friendship: Letters from the International Woman Suffrage Alliance, 1902–1942*. Columbus: Ohio State University Press, 1990.

Boserup, Ester. *Women's Role in Economic Development*. London: Allen and Unwin, 1970.

Bridenthal, Renate, Claudia Koonz, and Susan Stuard. *Becoming Visible: Women in European History*. 2d ed. Boston: Houghton Mifflin, 1987.

Bristow, Edward. *Prostitution and Prejudice: The Jewish Fight against White Slavery 1870–1939*. New York: Schocken Books, 1983.

———. *Vice and Vigilance*. Dublin: Gill and Macmillan; Totowa, N.J.: Rowman and Littlefield, 1977.

Buonaventura, Wendy. *Serpent of the Nile: Women and Dance in the Arab World*. London: Saqi Books, 1989.

Burton, Antoinette. *Burdens of History: British Feminists, Indian Women, and Imperial Culture, 1865–1915*. Chapel Hill: University of North Carolina Press, 1994.

Bussey, Gertrude, and Margaret Tims. *Women's International League for Peace and Freedom: 1915–1965*. London: Allen & Unwin, 1965.

Butcher, E. L. *Things Seen in Egypt*. Paris: Librarie Vuibert, 1913.

Butler, Judith, and Joan W. Scott, eds. *Feminists Theorize the Political*. New York and London: Routledge, 1992.

Callaway, Helen. *Gender, Culture and Empire*. Houndmills, Basingstoke, Hampshire: Macmillan Press in association with St. Antony's College, Oxford, 1987.

Cannon, Bryon. *Politics of Law and the Courts in Nineteenth-Century Egypt*. Salt Lake City: University of Utah Press, 1988.

Chatterjee, Partha. *The Nation and Its Fragments: Colonial and Postcolonial Histories*. Princeton: Princeton University Press, 1993.

Chaudhuri, Nupur, and Margaret Strobel, eds. *Western Women and Imperialism*. Bloomington: Indiana University Press, 1992.

Chedid, Andrée. *Le sixième jour*. Translated into English by Isobel Strachey as *The Sixth Day*. London: The Serpent's Tail, 1978.

———. *Le sommeil délivré*. Translated into English by Sharon Spenser as *From Sleep Unbound*. Athens, Ohio: Swallow Press, 1983.

Chennells, Ellen. *Recollections of an Egyptian Princess by Her English Governess*. 2 vols. Edinburgh and London: W. Blackwood & Sons, 1893.

Chirol, Valentine. *The Egyptian Problem*. London: Macmillan and Co., 1920.

Clerget, Marcel. *Le Caire: étude de géographie urbaine et d'histoire économique*. 2 vols. Cairo: Imprimerie E. & R. Schindler, 1934.

Cole, Juan Ricardo. *Colonialism and Revolution in the Middle East: Social and Cultural Origins of Egypt's ʿUrabi Movement*. Princeton: Princeton University Press, 1993.

———. *Comparing Muslim Societies*. Ann Arbor: University of Michigan Press, 1992.

Cooper, Elizabeth. *The Harim and the Purdah: Studies of Oriental Women*. London, 1915.

———. *The Women of Egypt*. London: F. A. Stokes, 1914.

Corbin, Alain. *Women for Hire: Prostitution and Sexuality in France after 1850*. Cambridge: Harvard University Press, 1990.

Cott, Nancy. *The Grounding of Modern Feminism*. New Haven: Yale University Press, 1987.

Coulson, Noel J. *Conflicts and Tensions in Islamic Jurisprudence*. Chicago: University of Chicago Press, 1969.

———. *Succession in the Muslim Family*. Cambridge: Cambridge University Press, 1971.

Cromer, earl of. *Modern Egypt*. 2 vols. New York: Macmillan, 1908.

Davis, Eric. *Challenging Colonialism*. Princeton: Princeton University Press, 1983.

Davis, Fanny. *The Ottoman Lady, A Social History: 1718 to 1918*. Westport, Conn.: Greenwood Press, 1986.

Deeb, Marius. *Party Politics in Egypt: The Wafd and Its Rivals, 1919–1939*. London: Ithaca Press, 1979.

Dirks, Nicholas B., ed. *Colonialism and Culture*. Ann Arbor: University of Michigan Press, 1992.

Dirks, Nicholas B., Geoff Eley, and Sherry B. Ortner, eds. *Culture/Power/History*. Princeton: Princeton University Press, 1994.

Duff Gordon, Lucy. *Letters from Egypt, 1863–65*. London: Macmillan, 1865.

Eccel, A. Chris. *Egypt, Islam, and Social Change: Al-Azhar in Conflict and Accommodation*. Berlin: Klaus Schwarz, 1984.

Egyptian Women Painters over Half a Century. Exhibition catalog. Cairo, 1975.

Esposito, John. *Women in Muslim Family Law*. Syracuse: Syracuse University Press, 1982.

Evans, Richard. *The Feminists: Women's Emancipation Movements in Europe, America and Australasia 1840–1920*. London: Croom Helm, 1977.

Fahmi, Qallini. *Souvenirs du Khedive Ismail au Khedive Abbas II*. Cairo: Editions de la Patrie, n.d.

Fahmy, Mansur. *La condition de la femme dans la tradition et l'islamisme*. Paris, 1913.

Fanon, Frantz. *A Dying Colonialism*. New York: Monthly Review Press, 1965.

Farag, Nadia. "*Al-Muqtataf*, 1876–1900: A Study of the Influence of Victorian Thought on Modern Arabic Thought." D.Phil. thesis, Oxford University, 1969.

Fenoglio-Abd El Aal, Irene. *Défense et illustration de l'Egyptienne: aux débuts d'une expression féminine*. Cairo: Centre d'Etudes et de Documentation Economique, Juridique et Social (CEDEJ), 1988.

Fernea, Elizabeth, ed. *Women and the Family in the Middle East*. Austin: University of Texas Press, 1985.

Fernea, Elizabeth, and Basima Qattan Bezirgan, eds. *Middle Eastern Women Speak*. Austin: University of Texas Press, 1977.

Fowler, Robert Booth. *Carrie Catt, Feminist Politician*. Boston: Northeastern University Press, 1986.

Fraisse, Geneviève, and Michelle Perrot, eds. *A History of Women in the West: Emerging Feminism from Revolution to World War*. Cambridge: Harvard University Press, Belknap Press, 1993.

Gallagher, Nancy. *Egypt's Other Wars: Epidemics and the Politics of Public Health*. Syracuse: Syracuse University Press, 1990.

Gershoni, Israel, and James P. Jankowski. *Egypt, Islam, and the Arabs: The Search for Egyptian Nationhood, 1900–1930*. New York: Oxford University Press, 1986.

Gibson, Mary. *Prostitution and the State in Italy, 1860–1915*. New Brunswick: Rutgers University Press, 1986.

Gomaa, Ahmad Mahmoud. *The Foundation of the League of Arab States*. London: Longmans, 1977.

Graham-Brown, Sarah. *Images of Women*. New York: Columbia University Press, 1992.

Harry, Myriam. *Les derniers harems*. Paris: E. Flammarion, 1933.

Heyworth-Dunne, J. *An Introduction to the History of Education in Modern Egypt*. London: Luzac & Co., 1939.

Hijab, Nadia. *Womanpower: The Arab Debate on Women and Work*. Cambridge: Cambridge University Press, 1988.

al-Hibri, Azizah, ed. *Women and Islam*. New York: Pergamon Press, 1982.

Hill, Enid. *Mahkama! Studies in the Egyptian Legal System, Courts and Crimes, Law and Society*. London: Ithaca Press, 1979.

———. *Al-Sanhuri and Islamic Law*. Cairo Papers in Social Science, vol. 10, monograph 1. Cairo: American University in Cairo Press, 1987.

Hobsbawm, E. J. *Nations and Nationalism since 1780*. Cambridge: Cambridge University Press, 1990.

Holt, P. M., ed. *Political and Social Change in Modern Egypt: 1850–1950*. London: Oxford University Press, 1968.

Hourani, Albert. *Arabic Thought in the Liberal Age*. Cambridge: Cambridge University Press, 1983.

———. *A History of the Arab Peoples*. Cambridge: Harvard University Press, 1991.

Hunter, Robert. *Egypt under the Khedives, 1805–1879: From Household Government to Modern Bureaucracy*. Pittsburgh: University of Pittsburgh Press, 1984.

Hyam, Ronald. *Empire and Sexuality: The British Experience*. Manchester and New York: Manchester University Press, 1990.

Inan, Afat. *The Emancipation of the Turkish Woman*. Paris: UNESCO, 1962.

Issawi, Charles. *Egypt: An Economic and Social Analysis*. London: Oxford University Press, 1947.

———. *Egypt at Mid-Century*. London, 1954.

Jacobs, Aletta. *Reisbrieven unit Afrika en Azie*. Almelo: W. Hilarius Wzn., 1913.

Jayawardena, Kumari. *Feminism and Nationalism in the Third World*. London: Zed, 1986.

Kanafani, Ghassan. *The 1936–39 Rebellion in Palestine*. Committee for Democratic Palestine, n.d.

Kandiyoti, Deniz, ed. *Women, Islam and the State*. London: Macmillan; Philadelphia: Temple University Press, 1991.

Kaplan, Marion. *The Jewish Feminist Movement in Germany: The Campaigns of the Jüdischer Frauenbund, 1904–1938*. Westport, Conn.: Greenwood Press, 1979.

———. *Making of the Jewish Middle Class: Women, Family, and Identity in Imperial Germany*. New York: Oxford University Press, 1991.

Keddie, Nikki, and Beth Baron, eds. *Women in Middle Eastern History*. New Haven: Yale University Press, 1992.

Kher, Amy. *Mes soeurs*. Cairo: R. Schindler, 1942.

———. *Visages d'Egypte*. Cairo: Atlas, 1972.

———. *Visages de Liban, visages de Syrie*. Cairo: Mondiale, 1972.

Khoury, Philip S. *Syria and the French Mandate: The Politics of Arab Nationalism, 1920–1945*. Princeton: Princeton University Press, 1987.

Knauss, Peter R. *The Persistence of Patriarchy: Class, Gender, and Ideology in Twentieth Century Algeria*. New York: Praeger, 1987.

Kramer, Gudrun. *The Jews in Modern Egypt, 1914–1952*. London: I. B. Tauris, 1989.

Kuhnke, Laverne. *Lives at Risk: Public Health in Nineteenth Century Egypt*. Berkeley and Los Angeles: University of California Press, 1990.

Lane, Edward W. *Cairo Fifty Years Ago*. Edited by S. Lane-Poole. London: J. Murray, 1896.

———. *The Manners and Customs of the Modern Egyptians*. 1871. 2 vols. London: J. M. Dent & Co., 1908.

Mabro, Judy. *Veiled Half-Truths: Western Travellers' Perceptions of Middle Eastern Women*. London and New York: I. B. Tauris, 1991.

Mahfuz, Najib. *Cairo Trilogy*. I. *Palace Walk* (*Bayn al-Qasrayn*). Translated by William Maynard Hutchins and Olive E. Kenny. New York: Doubleday, 1990. II. *Palace of Desire* (*Qasr al-Shawq*). Translated by William Maynard Hutchins, Lorne M. Kenny, and Olive E. Kenny. New York: Doubleday, 1991. III. *Sugar Street* (*al-Sukkariyah*). Translated by William Maynard Hutchins and Angèle Botros Samaan. New York: Doubleday, 1992.

———. *Mirrors*. Translated by Roger Allen. Minneapolis: Biblioteca Islamica, 1977.

Mahfouz, [Dr.] Naguib, *The History of Medical Education in Egypt*. Cairo: Government Press, 1935. London, 1935.

———. *The Life of an Egyptian Doctor*. London, 1966.

Marsot, Afaf Lutfi al-Sayyid. *Egypt and Cromer: A Study in Anglo-Egyptian Relations*. London: John Murray, 1968.

———. *Egypt in the Reign of Muhammad Ali*. Cambridge: Cambridge University Press, 1984.

———. *Egypt's Liberal Experiment, 1922–36*. Berkeley and Los Angeles: University of California Press, 1977.

Martineau, Harriet. *Eastern Life: Present and Past*. New ed. London: E. Moxon, 1875.

Mathieson, Margaret, and Adele Schreiber. *Journey Towards Freedom: Written for the Golden Jubilee of the International Alliance of Women*. Copenhagen: International Alliance of Women, 1955.

Melman, Billie. *Women's Orients: English Women and the Middle East, 1718–1918, Sexuality, Religion and Work*. Ann Arbor: University of Michigan Press, 1992.

Mernissi, Fatima. *Beyond the Veil: Male-Female Dynamics in a Modern Muslim Society*. Rev. ed. Bloomington: Indiana University Press, 1987.

———. *Islam and Democracy: Fear of the Modern World*. Translated by Mary Jo Lakeland. New York: Addison-Wesley, 1992.

———. *The Veil and the Male Elite: A Feminist Interpretation of Women's Rights in Islam*. Translated by Mary Jo Lakeland. Reading, Mass.: Addison-Wesley, 1991.

Miller, Ylana. *Government and Society in Rural Palestine 1920–1948*. Austin: University of Texas Press, 1985.

Mitchell, Timothy. *Colonising Egypt*. Cambridge: Cambridge University Press, 1989.

Mogannam, Matiel. *The Arab Woman and the Palestine Problem*. London: H. Joseph, 1937.

Moghadam, Valentine, ed. *Gender and National Identity: Women and Politics in Muslim Societies*. London: Zed Press, 1994.

———, ed. *Identity Politics and Women: Cultural Reassertions in Feminisms in International Perspective*. Boulder: Westview Press, 1994.

Musa, Salama. *The Education of Salama Musa*. Translated by L. O. Schuman. Leiden: E. J. Brill, 1961.

Musallam, Basim F. *Sex and Society in Islam*. Cambridge: Cambridge University Press, 1983.

Niyya Salima (Eugénie Le Brun, Mme Rushdi Pasha). *Harem et les musulmanes*. 2d ed. Paris: Librairie Félix Juven, 1902.

———. *Les répudiées*. Paris: Librairie Félix Juven, 1908.

Out El Kouloub. *Harem*. Paris: Gallimard, 1937.

———. *Ramza*. Paris: Gallimard, 1958. Also translated and introduced by Nayra Atiya. Syracuse: Syracuse University Press, 1994.

Owen, E.R.J. *Cotton and the Egyptian Economy, 1820–1914*. Oxford: Oxford University Press, 1969.

Pappenheim, Bertha. *Sisyphus Arbeit: Reisebriefe aus den Jaren 1911 und 1912*. Leipzig: Verlag Paul E. Linder, 1924.

Peck, Mary Gray. *Carrie Chapman Catt: A Biography*. New York: H. W. Wilson Company, 1944.

Penzer, N. M. *The Harem*. London: G. Harrop, 1936.

Peteet, Julie. *Gender in Crisis*. New York: Columbia University Press, 1991.

Philipp, Thomas. *The Syrians in Egypt, 1725–1975*. Stuttgart: Franz Steiner Verlag Wiesbaden GMBH, 1985.

Pierce, Leslie. *The Imperial Harim: Women and Sovereignty in the Ottoman Empire*. New York: Oxford University Press, 1993.

Poole, Sophia Lane. *The Englishwoman in Egypt: Letters from Cairo Written during a Residence There in 1842, 3, 4*. 2 vols. London: C. Knight & Co., 1844. 2d ed., 1846.

Porath, Yehoshua. *The Palestinian Arab National Movement 1929–1939*. London: F. Cass, 1977.

Quandt, William B., Fuad Jabber, and Ann Mosely Lesch. *The Politics of Palestinian Nationalism*. Berkeley and Los Angeles: University of California Press, 1973.

Radwan, Abu al-Futouh Ahmad. *Old and New Forces in Egyptian Society*. New York: Bureau of Publication, Teachers College, Columbia University, 1951.

Raymond, André. *Le Caire*. Paris: Fayard, 1993.

Reid, Donald. *Cairo University and the Making of Modern Egypt*. Cambridge: Cambridge University Press, 1990.

———. *Lawyers and Politics in the Arab World, 1880–1960*. Chicago: Biblioteca Islamica, 1981.

Rowbotham, Sheila. *Women, Resistance, and Revolution*. London: Allen Lane, 1972.

Russell, Thomas. *Egyptian Service*. London, Murray, 1949.

El Saadawi, Nawal. *The Hidden Face of Eve*. Translated by Sherif Hetata. London: Zed Books, 1979.

———. *The Memoirs of an Egyptian Doctor*. Translated by Sherif Hetata. London: Zed Books, 1983.

———. *Woman at Point Zero*. Translated by Sherif Hetata. London: Zed Books, 1983.

Sabah, Fatna A. *Women in the Muslim Unconscious*. Translated by Mary Jo Lakeland. New York: Pergamon Press, 1984.

Sayigh, Rosemary. *Palestinians: From Peasants to Revolutionaries*. London: Zed Press, 1979.

Schölch, Alexander. *Egypt for the Egyptians!: The Socio-Political Crisis in Egypt, 1878–1882*. London: Ithaca Press for the Middle East Centre, St. Antony's College, Oxford, 1981.

Shafiq, Duriyya. *La femme et le droit religieux de l'Egypte contemporaine*. Paris: Geuthner, 1940.

———. *La femme nouvelle en Egypte*. Cairo: Schindler, 1944.

Shamir, Shimon, ed. *The Jews of Egypt: A Modern Mediterranean Society in Modern Times*. Boulder and London: Westview Press, 1987.

Smith, Charles. *Islam and the Search for Social Order in Modern Egypt: A Biography of Muhammad Husayn Haykal*. Albany: State University of New York Press, 1983.

Smith, Sidonie, and Julia Watson. *De/Colonizing the Subject: The Politics of Gender in Women's Autobiography*. Minneapolis: University of Minnesota Press, 1992.

Sonbol, Amira. *The Creation of a Medical Profession*. Syracuse, N.Y.: Syracuse University Press, 1991.

Sproul, Christine. "The American College for Girls, Cairo, Egypt: Its History and Influence on Egyptian Women, a Study of Selected Graduates." Ph.D. diss., University of Utah, 1982.

Storrs, Ronald. *Orientations*. London: I. Nicholson and Watson, 1945.

Strobel, Margaret. *European Women and the Second British Empire*. Bloomington: Indiana University Press, 1991.

Sullivan, Earl. *Women in Egyptian Public Life*. Syracuse: Syracuse University Press, 1986.

Tignor, Robert. *Modernization and British Colonial Rule in Egypt, 1882–1914*. Princeton: Princeton University Press, 1966.

Tillion, Germaine. *Le harem et les cousines*. Paris: Editions du Seuil, 1966.

Toubia, Nahid, ed. *Women in the Arab World*. London: Zed Press, 1988.

Tucker, Judith. *Arab Women: Old Boundaries, New Frontiers*. Bloomington: Indiana University Press, 1993.

———. *Women in Nineteenth Century Egypt*. Cambridge: Cambridge University Press, 1985.

Vallet, J. *Contribution à l'étude de la condition ouvrière dans la grande industrie au Caire*. Valence, 1911.

Van Voris, Jacqueline. *Carrie Chapman Catt: A Public Life*. New York: Feminist Press, 1987.

Vidal, Fina Gued. *Safia Zaghlul*. Cairo, n.d.

Walkowitz, Judith. *Prostitution and Victorian Society: Women, Class, and the State*. Cambridge: Cambridge University Press, 1980.

Whittick, Arnold. *Woman into Citizen*. Santa Barbara, Calif.: ABC-Clio, 1979.

Woodsmall, Ruth Frances. *Moslem Women Enter a New World*. New York: Round Table Press, 1936.

———. *Women and the New East*. Washington, D.C.: The Middle East Institute, 1960.

Wright, Arnold, ed. *Twentieth Century Impressions of Egypt*. London, 1909.

Zaalouk, Malak. "The Social Structure of Divorce Adjudication in Egypt." M.A. these, The American University in Cairo, 1975.

Ziadeh, Farhat. *Lawyers, the Rule of Law and Liberalism in Modern Egypt*. Stanford: Hoover Institution on War, Revolution, and Peace, 1968.

ARTICLES

Abdo, Nahla. "Nationalism and Feminism—Palestinian Women and the Intifada: No Going Back?" In Moghadam, *Gender and National Identity*.

Abu-Lughod, Lila. "The Romance of Resistance: Tracing Transformations of Power through Bedouin Women." *American Ethnologist* 17, no. 1 (1990): 41–55.

———. "Zones of Theory in the Anthropology of the Arab World." *Annual Review: Anthropology* 18 (1989): 267–308.

Adnan, Etel. "In the Heart of the Heart of Another Country." *Mundus Artium* 10, no. 1 (1977): 20–34.

Alcoff, Linda. "Cultural Feminism versus Post-Structuralism: The Identity Crisis in Feminist Theory." *Signs* 13 (1988): 405–36.

Allen, Roger. "Drama and Audience: The Case of Arabic Theatre," *Theater Three*, Spring 1989, pp. 7–20.

———. "Writings of Members of the Nazli Circle." *Journal of the American Research Center in Egypt* 8 (1969–1970): 79–84.

Anderson, J.N.D. "Law Reform in Egypt." In Holt, *Political and Social Change in Modern Egypt*.

———. "Recent Developments in Shariʿa Law III." *The Muslim World* 41, no. 3 (1951): 113–21.

———. "The Role of Personal Status in Social Development in Islamic Countries." *Comparative Studies in Society and History* 13, no. 1 (1971): 16–31.

Antonius, Soraya. "Fighting on Two Fronts: Conversations with Palestinian Women." *Journal of Palestine Studies* 8, no. 3 (1979): 26–45.

Arnett, Mary Flounders. "Marie Ziyada." *Middle Eastern Affairs*, Aug.–Sept. 1957, pp. 288–94.

Badran, Margot. "Competing Agenda: Feminists, Islam, and the State in Nineteenth and Twentieth Century Egypt." In Kanidyoti, *Women, Islam, and the State*.

———. "Dual Liberation: Feminism and Nationalism in Egypt, 1870s–1925." *Feminist Issues* 8, no. 1 (1988): 15–34.

———. "Expressing Feminism and Nationalism in Autobiography: The Memoirs of an Egyptian Educator" In Smith and Watson, *De/Colonizing the Subject*.

———. "Feminism as a Force in the Arab World." In *Contemporary Arab Thought and Women*. Arab Women's Solidarity Press: Cairo, 1989.

———. "From Consciousness to Activism: Feminist Politics in Early Twentieth Century Egypt." In *Problems of the Middle East in Historical Perspective*, edited by John Spagnolo. St. Antony's College, Oxford, monograph series. London: Ithaca Press, 1992.

———. "Independent Women: More Than a Century of Feminism in Egypt." In Tucker, *Arab Women*.

———. "Islam, Patriarchy, and Feminism in the Middle East." *Trends in History* 4, no. 1 (1985): 48–71.

———. "The Origins of Feminism in Egypt." In *Current Issues in Women's History*, edited by Arina Angerman et al. London: Routledge, 1989.

———. "Women and Production in the Middle East and North Africa." *Trends in History* 2, no. 3 (1982): 59–88.

Baron, Beth. "The Making and Breaking of Marital Bonds in Modern Egypt." In Keddie and Baron, *Women in Middle Eastern History.*

———. "Mothers, Morality, and Nationalism in Pre-1919 Egypt." In *The Origins of Arab Nationalism*, edited by Rashid Khalidi, et al. New York: Columbia University Press, 1991.

———. "Unveiling in Early Twentieth Century Egypt: Practical and Symbolic Considerations." *Middle Eastern Studies* 24, no. 3 (1989): 370–86.

Becker, Susan. "International Feminism between the Wars: The National Woman's Party versus the League of Women Voters." In *Decades of Discontent*, edited by L. Scharf and J. Jensen. Westport, Conn.: Greenwood, 1983.

Bohdanowicz, Arslan. "The Feminist Movement in Egypt." *Islamic Review* 8 (Aug. 1951): 24–33.

Booth, Marilyn. "Biography and Feminist Rhetoric in Early Twentieth Century Egypt: Mayy Ziyada's Studies of Three Women's Lives." *Journal of Women's History* 3, no. 2 (1991): 38–64.

———. "Imprinting Lives: Biography, Subjectivity, and Feminism in the Egyptian Women's Press, 1892–1935." Unpublished paper.

Botman, Selma. "The Experience of Women in the Egyptian Communist Movement, 1939–1954." *Women's Studies International Forum* 2, no. 5 (1988): 117–26.

———. "Women's Participation in Radical Egyptian Politics, 1939–1952." *Khamsin*, no. 6 (1987): 12–25.

Bowden, Tom. "The Politics of the Arab Rebellion in Palestine 1936–1939." *Middle East Studies* 11 (1975): 147–74.

Bridenthal, Renate. "Something Old, Something New: Women between the Two World Wars." In Bridenthal, Koonz, and Stuard, *Becoming Visible.*

Burton, Antoinette. "The Feminist Quest for Identity: British Imperial Suffragism and 'Global Sisterhood,' 1900–1915." *Journal of Women's History* 3, no. 2 (1991): 46–81.

Butler, Josephine. *Personal Reminiscences of a Great Crusade*. London: H. Marshall and Son, 1896. New ed., 1911.

Cale, Patricia. "A British Missionary in Egypt: Mary Louisa Whately." *Vitae Scholasticae* 3, no. 1 (1984): 131–43.

Cannon, Byron D. "Nineteenth-Century Writing on Women and Society: The Interim Role of the Masonic Press in Cairo—*Al-Lataif*, 1885–1895." *International Journal of Middle East Studies* 17, no. 4 (1985): 463–84.

Castagné, J. "Le mouvement d'émancipation de la femme musulmane en orient." *Revue des Etudes Islamiques* 2 (1929): 162–226.

Cole, Juan Ricardo. "Feminism, Class, and Islam in Turn-of-the-Century Egypt." *International Journal of Middle East Studies* 13 (1981): 397–407.

Contu, Giuseppe. "Le donne comuniste e il movimento democratico femminile in Egitto fino al 1965." *Oriente Moderno*, May–June 1975, pp. 237–47.

Cooke, Miriam. "Telling Their Lives: A Hundred Years of Arab Women's Writings." *World Literature Today* 60 (Spring 1986): 212–16.

Coulson, Noel J., and Doreen Hinchcliffe. "Women and Law Reform in Contemporary Islam." In Beck and Keddie, *Women in the Muslim World.*

Crabitès, Pierre. "Woman and the Crisis in Egypt: How the Social Estrangement of

Egyptian and European Women Breeds Political Ill." *Asia* 25 (1925): 568–72, 615–18.

Crecelius, Daniel. "The Course of Secularization in Modern Egypt." In *Religion and Political Modernization*, edited by Donald E. Smith. New Haven: Yale University Press, 1974.

Dabbous, Sonia. "Studying an Egyptian Journalist: Rose al-Youssef, a Woman and a Journal." *Islamic and Mediterranean Women's History Network Newsletter* 1, nos. 2–3 (1988): 11–12.

Danielson, Virginia. "Artists and Entrepreneurs: Female Singers in Cairo during the 1920s." In Keddie and Baron, *Women in Middle Eastern History*.

Deeb, Marius. "The 1919 Popular Uprising: A Genesis of Nationalism." *Canadian Review of Studies in Nationalism*, Fall 1973, pp. 105–19.

Edwards, Elizabeth. "Alice Havergal Skillicorn, Principal of Homerton College, Cambridge, 1935–60: A Study in Gender and Power." *Women's History Review* 1, no. 1 (1992): 89–108.

Eliraz, Giora. "Egyptian Intellectuals and Women's Emancipation, 1919–1939." *Asian and African Studies* 16 (1986): 95–120.

Feinberg, Harriet. "A Pioneering Dutch Feminist Views Egypt: Aletta Jacobs' Travel Letters." *Feminist Issues* 10, no. 3 (1990): 65–78.

Fenoglio-Abd El Aal, Irene. "L'activité culturelle francophone au Caire durant l'entre-deux-guerres." In *D'un Orient l'autre: les metamorphoses des perceptions et connaissances*. Cairo: CEDEJ, 1989.

Gran, Judith. "Impact of the World Market on Egyptian Women." *Merip Reports*, no. 58 (June 1977): 3–7.

Haddad, Yvonne. "The Case of the Feminist Movement." In *Contemporary Islam and the Challenge of History*. Albany: State University of New York Press, 1982.

———. "Islam, Women and Revolution in Twentieth Century Arab Thought." *The Muslim World* 124, nos. 3–4 (1984): 137–60.

Hammam, Mona. "Women and Industrial Work in Egypt: The Chubra al-Kheima Case." *Arab Studies Quarterly* 2 (1980): 50–59.

Hatem, Mervat. "Egyptian Upper-and Middle-Class Women's Early Nationalist Discourses on National Liberation and Peace in Palestine (1922–1944)." *Women and Politics* 9, no. 3 (1989): 49–70.

———. "The Enduring Alliance of Nationalism and Patriarchy in Muslim Personal Status Laws: The Case of Modern Egypt." *Feminist Issues* 6, no. 1 (1986): 19–43.

———. "The Politics of Sexuality and Gender in Segregated Patriarchal Systems: The Case of Eighteenth and Nineteenth Century Egypt." *Feminist Studies* 12, no. 2 (1986).

———. "Through Each Other's Eyes: Egyptian, Levantine-Egyptian, and European Women's Images of Themselves and of Each Other (1862–1920)." *Women's Studies International Forum* 12, no. 2 (1898):183–98.

al-Hibri, Azizah. "Marriage Laws in Muslim Countries: A Comparative Study of Certain Egyptian, Syrian, Moroccan, and Tunisian Laws." *International Review of Comparative Public Policy* 4 (1992): 227–44.

Howard-Merriam, Kathleen. "Women, Education, and the Professions in Egypt." *Comparative Education Review*, June 1979, pp. 256–70.

Hunter, Robert. "The Making of a Notable Politician: Muhammad Sultan Pasha (1825–1884)." *International Journal of Middle East Studies*, no. 15 (1983): 537–44.

d'Ivray, Mme Jehan. "L'Orient et le féminisme." *Le lotus* 1, no. 1 (1901): 46–50.

Jankowski, James P. "The Palestinian Arab Revolt of 1936–1939." *The Muslim World* 63 (1973): 220–33.

Jeffreys, Sheila. "'Free from All Uninvited Touch of Man': Women's Campaigns around Sexuality, 1880–1914." *Women's Studies International Forum* 5, no. 6 (1982): 629–45.

Kaplan, Marion. "From Chevra to Feminism: Jewish Women's Social Work in Imperial Germany." Paper presented to the Colloquium on Women in Religion and Society at the Annenberg Institute, May 1991.

———. "Prostitution, Morality Crusades and Feminism: German-Jewish Feminists and the Campaign against White Slavery." *Women's Studies International Forum* 5, no. 6 (1982): 619–27.

Käppeli, Anne-Marie. "Feminist Scenes." In Fraisse and Perrot, *A History of Women in the West.*

Khater, Adram, and Cynthia Nelson. "al-Harakah al-Nissa'iyya: The Women's Movement and Political Participation in Modern Egypt." *Women's Studies International Forum* 2, no. 5 (1988): 465–83.

Kooij, C. "Bint al-Shat': A Suitable Case for Biography?" Paper published by the Institute for Modern Near Eastern Studies, University of Amsterdam, 1982.

Kuhnke, Laverne. "The 'Doctoress' on a Donkey: Women Health Officers in Nineteenth Century Egypt." *Clio Medica* 9, no. 3 (1974): 193–205.

Lazreg, Marnia. "Feminism and Difference: The Perils of Writing as a Woman on Women in Algeria." In *Conflicts in Feminism*, edited by Marianne Hirsch and Evelyn Fox Keller. New York and London: Routledge, 1990.

———. "Gender and Politics in Algeria: Unraveling the Religious Paradigm." *Signs* 15, no. 4 (1990): 755–80.

Le Balle, R. "La condition de la femme musulmane égyptienne." *Egypte Contemporaine* 24 (1933): 415–34.

Levine, Philippa. "Venereal Disease, Prostitution, and the Politics of Empire: The Case of British India." *Journal of the History of Sexuality* 4, no. 4 (1994): 579–602.

McBarnet, A. C. "The New Penal Code: Offenses against Morality and the Marriage Tie and Children." *L'Egypte Contemporaine* 10, no. 46 (1919): 382–86.

"Madame Hoda Charaoui—a Modern Woman of Egypt." *The Woman Citizen*, Sept. 1927.

Maher, Vanessa. "Divorce and Property in the Middle Atlas of Morocco." *Man: Journal of the Royal Anthropological Institute*, n.s., 9 (1974): 103–22.

Marsot, Afaf Lutfi al-Sayyid. "The Revolutionary Gentlewomen in Egypt." In Beck and Keddie, *Women in the Muslim World.*

Melman, Billie. "Desexualizing the Orient: The Harem in English Travel Writing by Women 1763–1914." *Mediterranean Historical Review* 4 (1984): 301–39.

Fatima Mernissi. "Democracy as Moral Disintegration: The Contradiction between Religious Belief and Citizenship as a Manifestation of the Ahistoricity of the Arab Identity." In Toubia, *Women of the Arab World.*

———. "Virginity and Patriarchy." In Azizah al-Hibri, *Women and Islam.*

Mosseri, Victor M., and Charles Audebeau. "Quelques mots sur l'histoire de l'ezbeh égyptienne." *Institut d'Egypte Bulletin* 3 (1921): 27–48.

Muir, W. "The Emancipation and Elevation of Egyptian Woman." *Asiatic Quarterly Review* 12 (1901): 194ff.

Mundy, Martha. "Women's Inheritance of Land in Highland Yemen." *Arabian Studies* 5 (1979): 161–87.

Nelson, Cynthia. "Biography and Women's History: On Interpreting Doria Shafiq." In Keddie and Baron, *Women in Middle Eastern History.*

———. "The Voices of Doria Shafiq: Feminist Consciousness in Egypt, 1940–1960." *Feminist Issues* 6, no. 2 (1986): 15–31.

al-Nowaihi, Magda. "Gender as Seen through Children's Eyes." Paper presented to the Colloquium on Women in Religion and Society at the Annenberg Institute, May 1991.

Offen, Karen. "Body Politics: Women, Work, and the Politics of Motherhood in France, 1920–1950." In *Maternity and Gender Policies: Women and the Rise of the European Welfare States, 1880s-1950s*, edited by Gisela Bock and Pat Thane. London and New York: Routledge, 1991.

———. "Defining Feminism: A Comparative Historical Approach." *Signs* 14, no. 1 (1988): 119–57.

———. "Ernest Legouvé and the Doctrine of 'Equality in Difference' for Women." *Journal of Modern History* 58 (June 1986): 452–84.

———. "Exploring the Sexual Politics of Republican Nationalism." In *Nationhood and Nationalism in France from Boulangism to the Great War, 1889–1918*, edited by Robert Tombs. New York: Harper Collins, 1991.

———. "Feminism and Sexual Difference in Historical Perspective." In *Theoretical Perspectives on Sexual Difference*, edited by Deborah L. Rhode. New Haven: Yale University Press, 1990.

———. "On the French Origin of the Words *Feminism* and *Feminist*." *Feminist Issues* 8, no. 2 (1988): 45–51.

———. "The Second Sex and the Baccalaureate in Republican France, 1880–1924." *French Historical Studies* 13, no. 2 (1983): 252–86.

Papanek, Hanna. "Purda: Separate Worlds and Symbolic Shelter." *Comparative Studies in Society and History* 10 (1973): 289–323.

Philipp, Thomas. "Feminism and Nationalist Politics in Egypt." In Beck and Keddie, *Women in the Muslim World.*

Philips, Daisy Griggs. "The Awakening of Egypt's Womanhood." *Moslem World* 8, no. 18 (1928): 402–8.

———. "The Growth of the Feminist Movement in Egypt." *Moslem World* 8, no. 16 (1926): 277–85.

Ramusack, Barbara. "Catalysts or Helper? British Feminists, Indian Women's Rights, and Indian Independence." In *The Extended Family: Women and Political Participation in India and Pakistan.* Columbia, Mo.: South Asia Books, 1981.

Rao, Juliette. "The Arab Woman." *Pax* 5, no. 3 (Jan. 1930).

Reid, Donald. "Educational and Career Choices of Egyptian Students, 1882–1922." *International Journal of Middle East Studies* 8 (1977): 349–78.

———. "Indigenous Egyptology: The Decolonization of a Profession?" *Journal of the American Oriental Society* 105, no. 2 (1985): 233–46.

———. "The 'Sleeping Philosopher' of Nagib Mahfuz's *Mirrors*." *The Muslim World* 74, no. 1 (1984): 1–11.

Rupp, Leila J. "Conflict in the International Women's Movement, 1888–1950." Paper presented at the Berkshire Conference of Women Historians, Rutgers University, 1990.

El Saadawi, Nawal. "The Political Challenges Facing Arab Women at the End of the Twentieth Century." In Toubia, *Women of the Arab World.*

Sayigh, Rosemary. "Femmes palestiniennes: une histoire en quête d'historiens." *Revue d'études Palestiniennes*, no. 23 (Spring 1987): 13–33.

Scott, Joan. "The Woman Worker." In Fraisse and Perrot, *A History of Women in the West*.

Shepherd, William. "The Myth of Progress and Gender Relations in the Thought of Sayyid Qutb." Unpublished paper.

Sherrick, Rebecca L. "Towards Universal Sisterhood." *Women's Studies International Forum* 5–6 (1982): 655–62.

Sievers, Sharon. "Six (or More) Feminists in Search of an Historian." *Journal of Women's History* 2 (1989): 134–46.

Stewart, Frank H. "The Woman, Her Guardian and Her Husband in the Law of the Sinai Bedouin." *Arabica* 38 (1991):102–29.

"The Thirteenth International Alliance of Women Congress in Copenhagen: Bulletin of the Women's Union for Equal Rights." *Davar Hapoelet*, no. 8 (Nov. 21, 1939).

Thompson, Anna Y. "The Woman Question in Egypt." *Moslem World* 4, no. 3 (1914): 266–72.

Tomiche, Nada. "La femme dans l'Egypte moderne." *Etudes méditerranéennes*, Summer 1957, pp. 99–111.

Toth, James. "Pride, Purdah, or Paychecks: Gender and the Division of Labor in Rural Egypt." *International Journal of Middle East Studies* 23, no. 2 (1991): 213–36.

Tucker, Judith. "Decline of the Family Economy." *Arab Studies Quarterly* 1, no. 3 (1979): 245–71.

———. "Egyptian Women in the Work Force: An Historical Survey." *Merip*, no. 50 (1976): 3–9.

———. "Problems in the Historiography of Women in the Middle East: The Case of Nineteenth Century Egypt." *International Journal of Middle East Studies* 15, no. 3 (1983): 321–36.

Vreeda de Stuers, Cora. "Parda." *Revue des études islamiques* 30, pt. 1 (1962): 151–212.

"The Women's Movement in the Near and Middle East." *Asiatic Review*, April 1928, p. 188.

"World News about Women." *The Woman Citizen* 10, no. 7 (1925): 33.

Zaghloul, Safia. "La femme égyptienne pendant l'autre guerre." In *Livre d'or du Journal la réforme: 1895–1945*.

Ziade, May. "Il risveglio della donna in egitto negli ultimi centi anni." *Oriente Moderno* 9, no. 5 (1929): 237–48.

• INDEX •

Abazah, Fikri, 107, 136
ʿAbazah, Dr. Mahmud, 115
ʿAbbas, Hilmi II, Khedive, 51, 103, 134
ʿAbbas Primary School, Girls' Section, 9, 38, 39, 43, 54, 57, 58, 99
ʿAbd Allah, Muhammad Jamil, 159
ʿAbd al-ʿAziz, Zahirah, 148
ʿAbd al-Hadi, Tarab, 237
ʿAbd al-Haqq, ʿAbd al-Hamid, 215
ʿAbd al-Malak, Balsam, 102, 184
ʿAbd al-Malak, Halima, 172
ʿAbd al-Masih, Matilde, 156
ʿAbd al-Masih, Sophie, 155–56
ʿAbd al-Nasir, Jamal, 249
ʿAbd al-Qadir, Amir, 104
ʿAbd al-Qadir, ʿAdilah Bayham, 239, 244
ʿAbd al-Rahman, ʿA'ishah (Bint al-Shati'), 106, 119, 150–51, 154, 178
ʿAbd al-Rahman, Mufidah, 183, 216–17, 242
ʿAbd al-Rahman, Tawhida, 147, 148
ʿAbd al-Razik, Shaykh Mustafa, 101
ʿAbd al-Razzaq, ʿArif, 230
ʿAbd al-Salam, Dr., 116
ʿAbd al-Salam, Khadijah, 81, 96
ʿAbd al-Wahid Wafi, ʿAli, 104
ʿAbdin, Fatma Hafiz, 150
ʿAbduh, Muhammad, 11, 18, 49, 125, 129, 130, 134
ʿAbdulla, Amin Pasha, 98
Abu al-Huda, Luli, 232, 235, 239
Abu al-Saʿud, 129–30
Abu Shadi, Ahmad Zaki, 107
Abu ʿUsba, ʿAtiyah, 77
Abu ʿUsbah, Mrs. Ahmad, 75, 80
Abu Zayd, Hikmat, 188
Abyad, Dawlat, 190
Academy of Arabic Language in Cairo, 243
actresses, 76, 189–91
Adli, Suzanne, 157
Adnan, Etel, 191
Afghanistan, 93, 129
ʿAfifi, Ahmad, 114
ʿAfifi, Firdus, 96
ʿAfifi, Hafiz, 107, 215–16
Aflatun, Inji, 104, 152, 157, 248
Aflatun, Muhammad, 104
Aflatun, Sulha, 117
Agricultural and Industrial Exposition, 172
Ahmad, Labibah, 61, 93, 184
ʿA'ishah, 105, 145, 170
Akad, Teo, 104
al-ʿAla'ili, Jamilah, 106, 119, 138
ʿAlam, Tafida, 184
Alexandria, 6, 58, 78, 81, 85, 87, 92, 98, 117, 144, 151, 153, 155, 157, 158, 159, 161, 177, 178, 189, 190, 193, 194–98, 202, 226, 236
al-Alfi, Hafizah, 244
Algeria, 23, 48, 72, 104, 190; veil and traditional woman as cultural defense of, 23, 48
ʿAli, Surayya, 101
ʿAli, Zaki, 102
alimony. See *nafaqah*
All-India Women's Conference, 186, 232, 247
Allen, Mary, 201
Allenby, 85
ʿAllubah, Amina, 121
ʿAllubah, Duriyah, 114
ʿAllubah, Ida, 114
ʿAllubah, Nafisa Muhammad ʿAli, 229
ʿAllubah, Muhammad ʿAli, 107, 150, 171, 183
ʿAlwai Pasha, 53
American College for Girls in Cairo, 10, 97, 101, 153
American Presbyterian Mission, 97
American University in Beirut, 93, 132, 145, 153
American University in Cairo, 102, 151, 153
American Woman Suffrage Association, 65
Amie de la Jeune Fille, L'(Alexandria), 197
Amin, Ahmad, 138
Amin, Qasim, 18–19, 38, 47, 52, 62, 179
Amina Hanim Afandi, 50, 99, 103, 134
Amina Hanim (al-Silahdar), 49
Amira Fayzah School (Alexandria), 147, 151
Amirah, ʿAzizah, 190
Amirah Fawziyah School, 147, 177, 178
al-Amrusi, Muhammad Fahmi, 101
Amsterdam, 200
Anglo-Egyptian Treaty (1936), 109, 214–15, 223
al-ʿAqqad, ʿAbbas, 38, 107
Arab Feminist Conference, 116, 120, 180, 205, 216–17, 237, 238–47

Arab Feminist Union (al-Ittihad al-Nisa'i al-ʿArabi al-ʿAmm), 110, 186, 244–45, 250
Arab League, 245–45, 247
Arab revolt, 225, 230
Arab Women's Committee in Jerusalem, 228–29, 230
Arab Women's Congress in Jerusalem, 224, 228
Arab Women's Executive Committee (later Arab Women's Committee), 224–25
Arabia, 37, 104, 129, 139
Arabian Peninsula, 24, 238
Arabic Academy (Cairo), 107
Arabic language: articulation of feminism in, 91, 96, 105–8, 143, 244, 277n.56; and class, 22; teaching of by Egyptian women, 58, 176, (and literature) 178; used by Egyptian women, 33–34, 38–40; and women's demand to drop feminine word endings in, 180, 243; and women's demands for translating books into, 94
Arabic language and literature; Egyptian women at university and, 119, 147, 148, 149, 150–51, 178, 243, 249
archaeology, 150
ʿArif, Fadilah, 150
Armenians, 48, 50, 121
Ashmawi, Shafiqah bint Muhammad, 77
ʿAsim, Fatimah, 55
al-ʿAskari, Nadhimah, 239, 244
ʿAsmahan (Amal al-Atrash), 190
ʿAsmat, Asim, 247
al-Asqalani, Haghir, 104
Association for Social Studies, 154
Association of Women Journalists (Hay'at al-Sihafiyat), 185
Association of Writers in the French Language in Egypt, 104
Asyut, 69, 77, 96, 97, 114, 120, 143, 205; secondary school for girls in, 147
ʿAtiyah, Jamila, 77, 96
al-Atrash, Farid, 190
Auclert, Hubertine, 72
Awad, Matilda, 147
ʿawrah, 16
ʿAyn, al-Hayat, Princess, 53
ʿAyn Shams University. *See* Ibrahim Pasha University
Ayrut, Henry Habib, 121
Ayrut, Jeannette, 121
Ayrut, Yvette, 121
al-Ayyubi, Naʿimah, 106, 137, 140, 143, 146–48, 154, 171, 175, 182, 183, 187, 242, 289n.6
al-Azhar, 10, 40, 49, 54, 93, 125, 150, 163–64, 198–99, 228; College for Girls of, 151
al-ʿAzim, Fayzah al-Muʿayyad, 244
ʿAziz, Zakiyah, 114
al-ʿAzmah, Bahirah, 227–28, 230
al-ʿAzmah, Nabi, 227
ʿAzmi, Mahmud, 134
ʿAzmi, Sulayman, 217
Azzam, Marguerite, 121

Baghdad, 236
Bahithat al-Badiyah (Malak Hifni Nasif); articulation of feminism by, 54, 66, 148, 167–68, 179; articulation of nationalism by, 166, 179; biography of, 54, 57; and Elizabeth Cooper, 70; eulogy of, 73; hails al-Taymuriyah as feminist, 14; and intellectual societies, 55; languages of, 22; as lecturer, 54; on marriage, polygamy, and divorce, 124, 129, 131; on national identity, 54–55; and *Nisa'iyat*, 54, 65; philanthropy of, 50; presentation of feminist demands by at Egyptian Congress, 69; and recreation, 146; and social construction of gender, 66; and veiling, 23, 54, 67, 146
al-Bahrawi, Jalilah, 96
Bakir, Latife, 213
Bakurat Suriyah (Beirut), 237
Banat al-Ashraf School: aborted nineteenth-century school, 9; twentieth-century school, 144
Bank Misr, 165, 172, 190; women sell shares in, 81, 83–84
Barakat, Bahi al-Din, 107, 114, 149
Barakat, Hidiyah, 77, 114, 187; decorated by state, 114
al-Bassal, ʿAbd al-Sattar, 54
al-Bayadi, Munirah, 121
bayt al-taʿah, 126–27, 131–32, 153, 158
Bayt al-Ummah (House of the Nation), 76, 81
Beirut, 236, 237; and meeting of Arab women, 228
Berlin, 69, 171, 200–201, 209
Bint al-Shati'. *See* ʿAbd al-Rahman, ʿA'ishah
Birzeit College (later Birzeit University), 231
Birzi, Niʿmat, 114
Bisharat, Emily, 244
Booth, Marilyn, 65
Bosch, Mineke, 109–10
boycotts, women's, 81, 83–84, 87
Brachayahu, Dr., 235
Britain: sending of Egyptian women for education in, 148–50, 152–53, 176–77

British colonial state in Egypt: and British women teachers and administrators in state schools, 42–44, 56–57, 59–60, 64, 176–77; and lack of state secondary schools for girls, 10, 41–44, 142; and military presence, 84, 109, 152, 195, 214, 223, 226, 248
British mandate in Palestine, 233–36 passim, 238–48, passim
Brun, Eugénie Le (Mrs. Husayn Rushdi), 15, 37, 38, 131
Brussels, 74
Budapest, 71
Bulaq Women Teachers' Training School, 57
Bulus Hanna, Jeannette Makar Kamal, 121
Buonaventura, Wendy, 190
burqa, 22
Burton, Antoinette, 71
Bustrus, Evelyn Jibran, 229
Butler, Josephine, 192, 195

Cairo University. *See* Fu'ad I University
Cairo Women's Club, 157, 239
Cama, Bhikaji, 74
Canal Zone, 152, 214, 248
Capitulations, 13, 94, 193, 195–96, 199–204, 210, 223, 238
Capy, Marcelle, 105
Carioca, Tahiyah, 190
Catt, Carrie Chapman, 69–73, 109, 234
Cattawi, 197
Cattawi, Celine, 122
Caucasus, 6, 32, 155, 189, 194
Cemile, 7
Central Committee for the Defense of Palestine in Damascus, 227
Chattopadhyay, Kamala Devi, 247
child custody (*hadana*), 126, 132, (Arab) 242
cholera, 119, 122
Christian Public Charity Society for Ladies (Haifa), 237
Christians, 49–50, 55, 95–96, 98, 106, 113–14, 121, 124–25, 173
Churchill, Winston, 242
Circassian, 9, 14, 22, 101
citizenship, 51, 128, 132, 133, 145, 162, 192, 203, 207, 208, 211, 219, (Arab) 232, 239, 240, 247; and the IAW, 92
Clément, Marguerite, 52, 55–56
coeducation, 148–50, 159–64, 212
College Qasr al-Dubara, 143
colonialism: and Egyptians demanding an end to, 74–85; ignoring of by imperial feminists, 108–10, 208. *See also* British colonial state in Egypt; British mandate in Palestine
Committee of Sa'dist Women (Lajnah al-Sa'diyah lil-Sayyidat), 87
Committees for the Defense of Palestine, 227
concubines, 6, 32, 155
Conservatory of Oriental Music, 155, 156
constitution of Egypt, 13, 86, 160, 207, 210, 211
Cooper, Elizabeth, 70
Coote, William, 195–96
Copenhagen, 236, 245
Coptic Ladies' Society for the Education of Children (Jam'iyat al-Sayyidat al-Qibtiyah li-Tarbiyat al-Tufulah), 121
Coptic Philanthropic Society, 239
Coptic Primary School (Tanta), 180
Copts, 19, 96–97, 133, 176; as church officials, 5, 9; and nationalist congress (1911), 69; and nationalist unity with Muslims, 75; and welfare societies, 49–50, 121; women 6, 47, 62, 69, 106, 189
Corbett Ashby, Margery, 109, 204, 212–13, 233–36, 247–48
Council of State, 188
Couvreur, Mlle A., 54
crafts workshops for girls, 51, 99, 112, 113, 173
Cromer, Lord (Evelyn Baring), 12
cult of domesticity, 52, 62–65, 166
Curzon Plan, 81, 84
Cyril IV, 9

Daccache, Laure, 190
Damietta, 96, 150, 172
Dar al-Hadanah, EFU, 100–101, 116
Dar al-'Ulum, 54, 59–60, 107, 205
Daughter of the Nile Union (al-Ittihad Bint al-Nil), 151, 186, 217, 249
Davson, Florence, 42
Dayr al-Bahri, 145
democracy, 203, 207, 209, 215, 217, (Arab) 232–33, 240, 242, 247
demonstrations, Egyptian, 74, 75; by women, 75–78, 99, 211, 248; by women and men together, 76–77
demonstrations, Palestinian women's, 224, 309n.1
demonstrations, Syrian women's, 237
Department of Public Health: Section for the Protection of Childhood, 113
Detroit, 113
Dib, Akilah Shukri, 230

al-Din, Nazirah Zayn, 93, 237, 315n.85
dispensaries run by women, 50, 98, 99, 111–12, 113, 150, 202
divorce, 19, 95, 127, 129, 132, 133, 135, 141, 168, (Arab) 242; *talaq* (repudiation), 11, 19, 124, 125–26, 130–31; *tatliq* (judicial divorce), 130–31, 132
Diyab, Falak, 244
Djavidan Hanim, 51, 117
doctors, women, 137, 167, 169, 179–81
Doss, Layla, 114–16, 121, 144
dower. See *mahr*
Dughan, Zahiyah, 243
Dunlop, Douglas, 43, 177
durra (co-wife), 6, 32
Duzdar, Shahindah, 228

Eastern Women's Conference for the Defense of Palestine, 228–32
Ecole de Louvre, L', 150
Edib, Halide, 65
Education, Ministry of; jobs for women in, 58, 146–47, 177–78, 187–88
education of women: and Arab women's call for Arab-centered curriculum, 242–43; and debates on gender-specific curricula, 63–64, 147–48; demands for, 66, 69, 95, 142–45; early gains in, 63, 70; at home, 14, 98; opening state schools for, 143–44; and sports, 146. *See also* coeducation; individual names of schools and universities; university
Egypt Society for the Protection of the Woman and Child, 202
Egyptian Anti-Smoking Society, 239
Egyptian Feminist Union (al-Ittihad al-Nisa'i al-Misri), 112, 173; and Arab feminism, 223–50; and Arab Feminist Union, 244; bylaws of, 91; creation of, 3, 33, 86; daycare by, 100–101, 116; dispensary of, 99, 100, 111–12, 202; fight against prostitution and Capitulations by, 192, 198–206; and support for first women at university in Egypt, 149–50; founders and early members of, 96–99; House of Cooperative Reform (Dar al-Taʿawun al-Islahi) of, 99; IAW conferences attended by, 91–92, 198, 200–204, 213, 216, 232–38, 245, 247–49; joint demands with WWCC by, 87, 94–96, 199, 209; journals of, 102–8, 184–85; male advisers to, 101–2; Minya branch of, 239; new headquarters of, 100–101, 212; and reform of personal status code, 126, 127, 133, 134; Professional and Domestic School of, 100, 112–13; and reinstituting as Huda Shaʿrawi Association, 219, 249; and rural needs, 111, 113, 116, 118–20; rural outreach of, 101, 120; Shaqiqat of, 101, 120, 140, 143, 151, 213, 249; and victims of antigovernment protest, 211–12; Youth Committee (Lajnat al-Shabbat) of, 248, 152
Egyptian Geographical Society, 155
Egyptian National Congress (Heliopolis), 69
Egyptian Section of the International League of Mothers and Educators for Peace, 225
Egyptian Section of the Women's International League of Peace and Freedom, 226
Egyptian Society for the Protection of the Mother and Child, 244
Egyptian University, 39, 49, 53, 72, 148; Women's Section of, 39, 53–55
Egyptian Women Lawyers' Union (Ittihad al-Muhamiyat al-Misriyat), 183
Egyptian Young Women's Christian Association, 97
Egyptienne, L', 102–8
Egyptology, 150
election of women to parliament, 11, 212, (Arab) 242
electoral law, 86, 207
Elgood, Dr., 70
English National Vigilance Association, 195
Ethiopia, 194
eunuch, 5

factory work for women, 165, 172–75
al-Fadl, Muhammad Abu (shaykh al-Azhar), 198
Fadli, Mrs. Ahmad, 113
al-Faggalah, 49
Fahmi,ʿAbd al-ʿAziz, 75, 118
Fahmi,ʿAbd al-Rahman, 80
Fahmi, ʿAli Pasha, 35
Fahmi, ʿAliyah, 215
Fahmi, ʿAsma, 176
Fahmi, Bertha Kamal, 154
Fahmi, Duriyah, 104, 137
Fahmi, Fatma, 148
Fahmi, Mansur, 101
Fahmi, Murqus, 17, 18–19, 39, 129
Fahmi, Mustafa Pasha, 80
Fahmi, Sumayya, 106, 141
family law. *See* personal status code
family life, 17–19, 132, 147, 169, 178
Farazli, Mimi, 121
Faridah, Queen, 117, 239
Faruk, King, 122

Faruk University (Alexandria), 151, 178
Faryal, Princess, 117
father, role of, 133, 141, 168. *See also* family life
Fathi, Hasan, 117
Fatma Hanim (birth mother of Saiza Nabarawi), 98
fatwa, 10
Fatwa Committee of al-Azhar, 93–94, 218
Fawwaz, Zaynab, 14, 15, 20, 64, 65, 66, 168
Fawzi, ʿAzizah, 85, 96
Fayyum, 23, 48, 54, 57, 58, 59, 129
Fayyum Primary School for Girls, 9, 39
Fazil, Prince Haydar, 104
Fazil, Prince Mustafa, 7
Fazil, Princess Nazli, 7, 18, 56, 81, 106, 150
Feinberg, Harriet, 72
feminism, Arab, 223, 232–48, 250
feminism, Egyptian men's, 16–19, 47, 129; and nationalism, 13, 92
feminism, Egyptian women's: definitions of, 19–20, 91; demands of, 69, 87; and first public claim of identity, 19; emergent discourse of, 14–16, 65–69. *See also* Eastern Women's Conference for the Defense of Palestine; Egyptian Feminist Union; Islam: and feminist women's discourse; nationalism, Egyptian: of feminist women
feminism, imperial, 13, 21, 69–73, 274n.9. *See also* International Alliance of Women
feminist consciousness, 3, 4, 20, 31–46 passim, 125
Feodorova, Tatiana, 246
Fikri, Ahmad, 104
fitna (chaos), 67, 218
flying, sport of, 158
France: and colonialism in Algeria, 23, 72; and education and cultural influences in Egypt, 22–24, 54, 96–98, 114, 142, 152–53, 189, 277n.52, 278n.67; imperial feminism of, 21, 72; national feminism of, 19; and prostitution in Egypt, 197–98; women admitted to bar in, 182; women of, supporting Egyptian feminism and nationalism, 37–38, 52, 54–56, 201, 210, 212
French contributors to *L'Egyptienne*, 104–5
French Institute of Archaeology in Cairo, 103
French language: and coining of *féminisme*, 19, 258n.79; as used by Egyptians, 7, 9, 21–22, 24, 33, 34, 75, 87, 102–5, 149
French mandate in Syria, 223
Fu'ad, King, 97, 176
Fu'ad, ʿAtiyah, 96
Fuʿad I University (later Cairo University), 107, 142, 148–51, 158, 176, 182, 188, 249; political protests at, 152
Fumaroli, Arlette, 121

Gamal, Samiyah, 190
Garzouzi, Eva, 182
gender: and IAW stress of similarity among women, 92; and mixing of the sexes, 58, 116, 159, 160–64, 170; and seclusion of women, 4–6, 11, 14–15, 17, 19, 22, 47–48, 55–56, 61, 64–67, 91, 93, 162, 252n.4; and sex segregation, 4, 35, 48, 56, 58, 59, 79, 143, 149, 160–64, 170; social construction of, 66–67; suspension of social rules of, 74; women's consciousness of, 12, 22, 32, 34, 154. *See also* sexuality; veiling
Geneva, 86, 188
Ghali, Anna Dadian Nagib, 121
Ghali, Butrus Butrus, 122
Ghali, Gertrude, 117, 122, 181, 300n.85
Ghali, Louise Majorelle Wasif, 80, 85
Ghali, Mirrit, 117
Ghali, Sophie Butrus, 122
Ghali, Wasif, 80, 84, 85
Ghamrawi, Nafisah, 106, 147, 158
al-Ghazali, Zaynab, 163, 229, 248
Girgus, Sidarus, 180
Girl Guides, 146, 161
Girls' College (Kulliyat al-Banat), ʿAyn Shams, 151
Girls' College (Kulliyat al-Banat) (Gizah), 177
Girls' College (Kulliyat al-Banat) (Zamalek), 101, 114, 144, 178
girls' gymnastic exhibition at Gazirah sporting grounds, 146
Gourd, Emilie, 188
Greeks, 50, 195, 197; women, 48
Green, Suzy, 157
Guibon Poulleau, Alice, 105

Habib, Mrs. Muhammad Ahmad, 147
Haddad, Marie Nikula, 180
hadith (Prophet Muhammad's sayings), 64, 145, 170
Hafiz, Bahija, 102–3, 156, 190–91
Hakim, Nazla, 176
al-Hakim, Tawfiq, 107, 138, 158, 164
hakimah (woman health professional), 179

Halbawi, Ibrahim, 102
Hamid, Fathiyah, 148
Hamzah, ʿAbd al-Qadir, 130, 209
Hamzah, Amina, 101
Hanafi school, 93, 133
al-Harawi, Muhammad, 107
Harb, Munirah, 247
Harb, Talʿat, 62, 66
Harcourt, duc d', 18
harem, 4, 5, 6, 14, 22, 32, 47, 67, 69, 96, 128, 143, 149, 154–56, 162, 251n.3, 252n.12
Harfush, Jamal Karam, 244, 316n.105
Harry, Myriam, 105
Hasan, Hasan Ibrahim, 107
Hasan, Saʿidah, 77
Hasan, Salim, 104
Hasan, Zaynab, 159, 178
Hashim, Labibah, 54, 184
Hashimi, Sabihah, 229
Hasibah (*Umm Kabirah*), 32, 34
Hatshepsut, 145
Haykal, ʿAziza, 93, 97, 138
Haykal, Ihsan, 95
Haykal, Muhammad Husayn, 97, 101–2, 107, 138, 157, 171, 191, 195, 216, 239, 240–41
health: of mothers and children, 50, 113, 119–20, (Arab) 243–44
Health, Public: Ministry of, 122, 115, 187; Department of, 113, 202; jobs for women in Ministry of, 179, 180, 187
health and hygiene, 175; basic instruction in for women and girls, 51, 98, 112, 113, 120, (Arab) 242–43; in rural areas, 98, 101, 111, 119–23, (Arab) 242–43
Helwan: as resort, 8, 143, 189
Helwan Secondary School for Girls, 143, 147, 177
Helwan Women Teachers' Training School, 99
Hifni Nasif, Kawkab, 106, 148, 179
Hifni Nasif, Majd al-Din, 107
Hifni Nasif, Malak. *See* Bahithat al-Badiyah
Higher Institute of Social Work for Women, 154
Higher Institute of Teacher Training, 162
Higher Institute of Women Music Teachers, 156
Higson, Miss, 201
Hijazi, Salamah, 189
al-Hilali, Ahmad Najib, 178
Hill, Enid, 127
Hilmiyah School: becomes full secondary school for girls, 143; Girls' Section of, 9
Husayn, Princess Qadriyah, 104
Husayn, Samihah, 157
Husayn, Taha, 101, 138, 148–50, 151–52, 160–61, 163–64, 171, 178
al-Husayni, Hajj Amin, 230
husband, role of, 138, 141, 168. *See also* family life; *nafaqah*
Husni, Fikriyah, 80, 81, 96, 99

Ibrahim, ʿAli, 180
Ibrahim, Hafiz, 107
Ibrahim, Mary, 76, 190
Ibrahim Pasha University (later ʿAyn Shams University), 151, 178
ʿiddah, 133
Idris, Ahmad, 101
Idris, Hafsah, 101
Idris, Hawwa', 49, 101, 112, 116, 122, 144, 238, 249
Idris, Hurriyah, 101, 140, 144
ʿIffat, Muhammad, 139
ijtihad, 11
imperialism: and international feminists, 13, 92, 171
independence of Egypt: Egyptians fight for, 74–85; feminists' condemnation of British unilateral declaration of, 84–85
India, 104, 122, 139, 172–73, 193, 215, 247
Indian women, 71, 74, 228
inheritance, 100, 124, 125, 133–34
al-Injlizi, ʿAbd Allah Pasha, 98
Inshas, 117
Institute for the Education of Girls (Ma'had al-Tarbiyat lil-Banat), 106, 141
Institute of Archaeology of Fu'ad I University, 150
Institute of Education, 176
Institute of Physical Education, 147
intellectual programs and societies: of women in Arab East, 237; of women in Egypt, 52–56
Inter-Parliamentary Congress of Arab and Islamic Countries for the Defense of Palestine, 228
Interior, Ministry of: woman censor in, 187
Interlaken, 246
International Alliance of Women: changing of name by, 108; imperial feminism of, 108–10, 208, 232–38; and joining of by Arab feminist unions, 225; and joining of

by EFU, 86, 108; and Palestine case, 228, 232–36; stress of similarity among women by, 92; visit to Egypt by leaders of, (1911) 69–73, (1935) 212; Women's Charter of, 108–9; and work for women, 171, 173. *See also* Capitulations; Egyptian Feminist Union: IAW conferences attended by; peace; prostitution
International Congress for the Suppression of the White Slave Traffic, 195, 200
International Labor Office, 173
International League for the Suppression of Traffic in Women and Children: Graz conference, 199
International Woman Suffrage Alliance. *See* International Alliance of Women
Iqbal Hanim, 32, 37, 38, 50
Iran, 129, 229
Iraq, 199, 228–29, 241
ʿIsa, Muhammad Hilmi, 159, 160–63
Isfahani, Tahiyah Muhammad, 77
Iskandar, ʿAfifah, 150
Islam: and refutation of seclusion and veiling of women in name of, 11, 19, 47; and women in early Islamic history, 55, 91, 144, 145, 170, 240; and women's conservative discourse, 52, 61, 62, 65; and feminist women's discourse, 64–65, 66–67, 95–96, 125–26, 134–35, 146, 152, 168, 176, 179, 192, 198, 216, 223, 237; and conflicting interpretations of women's suffrage by Egyptian religious authorities, 218
Islamic Benevolent Society (al-Jamʿiyah al-Khayriyah al-Islamiyah), 49
Islamism (late twentieth century), 25, 159, 160
ʿisma, 36, 130
Ismaʿil, Khedive, 6, 7, 98
Ismaʿil, Princess Fatma, 49, 53
Ismaʿil, Najiyah Saʿid, 77
Israel, 250
Istanbul, 10, 102, 109, 121, 151, 171, 203, 213, 225
Iwis, Habibah, 148
ʿIzbat al-Basri, 117
ʿIzzat, Khadijah Fu'ad, 150

Jabra, Sami, 104
Jacobs, Aletta, 50, 69–73
Jamali, Husayn, 111
Jamʿiyat Nur al-Fiyah (Beirut), 237
Jawdat, Naziq, 228
Jazaʿiri, ʿAdilah Bayham Mukhtar, 229
Jerusalem, 225, 227, 236
Jewish immigration to Palestine, 216, 225–26, 228, 230, 233, 241, 247
Jewish Women's Rights Association (Palestine), 108, 232, 233–35
Jewish Women's Union, 196
Jews in Egypt, 50, 104, 125, 173, 195–97, 226; women, 16, 47, 48, 55, 61, 195
Jews in Palestine: acquisition of land by, 230, 241
jins (sex, or race), 161
journalism: women in, 15–16, 61–65, 70, 183–87
journals, women's (excluding *L'Egyptienne* and *al-Misriyah*), 15, 16, 39, 61–65, 140
Jubran, Mary (Mary Jamilah), 190
Jumayyil, Antun, 102
Junaydi, Muhammad Farid, 136
Justice, Ministry of: and employment for women, 188

al-Kaddurah, Ibtihaj, 228
Kafuri, Najla, 236
Kahil, Mary, 96, 100, 113–14, 118, 122, 187, 200–201; decorated by state, 114
Kamal, Zaynab, 176
Kami Hanim, 98
Kamil, Mustafa (Ataturk), 92, 213
Kamil, Mustafa (Egyptian nationalist leader), 38, 99
Kamil, Sami, 111, 150
Kamil, Zaynab, 187
Kawrani, Hanna', 15
Keatinge, Dr., 50
Khadduri, Rose, 243
Khadijah, 64, 170
al-Khadra, Anisah, 227
al-Khalidi, ʿAmbarah Salam, 237
al-Khalidi, Wahida, 229–30
Khalil, Hamidah, 75, 76
Khartabil, Wadiʿah, 241
Khayyat, Edna, 114
Khayyat, Habib, 97
Khayyat, Regina Habib, 80, 81, 96, 114
Kher, Amy, 104, 278n.66
al-Khujah, Sirriyah, 244
al-Khuli, Amin, 151, 178
Khulusi, Wajidah, 96
Khunum Khtub, 145
al-Khuri, Faris, 246
Khurshid, Muhammad, 107, 136
Kilani, Kamil, 107, 140

Kitchener Memorial Hospital, 179
Kraemer-Bach, Marcelle, 201
kuttab: attendance of by girls, 10

La Mazière, Marcelle, 105
Labban, Shaykh Shafaʿi, 107, 206
labor law: call for in Arab countries, 243
Labor Law, Egyptian, 173–74, 187
Labor Office of Ministry of Interior in Egypt: woman inspector in, 175, 187
Ladies Literary Improvement Society (Jamʿiyat al-Raqy al-Adabiyah li-al-Sayyidat al-Misriyat), 55, 56
Ladies National Association (Britain), 195
Lady Cromer Society, 50
Lampson, Miles, 227
lawyers, women, 158, 171, 181–83, 188
al-Laythi, ʿAli, Shaykh, 98
al-Laythi, Fatma ʿAli, 98
League for the Suppression of the Traffic in Women, 202; Alexandria committee of, 196; Cairo committee of, 196
League of Nations, 173, 188, 200, 223, 225–26, 228
League of University and Institutes' Young Women (Rabitat Fatayat al-Jamʿiat wa-al-Maʿahid), 152, 248
Lebanese Arab Women's Union, 228, 237, 247
Lebanon, 14, 182, 190, 199, 223, 228–29, 238, 241
lectures for women, 33, 55, 70, 96, 142
Leider, Mrs., 9
Liberal Constitutionalist Party, 97, 208–9, 211, 214
Ligue française pour le droit des femmes, 202, 210
literacy, female, 63, 137, 292n.60; and morality, 255n.35, 289n.89; and the vote, 215
literacy instruction for females, 51, 121, 217
London, 81, 83, 85, 158, 178, 202
London University, 148, 149
Lutfi, Sharifah, 101
al-Luzi, ʿAbd al-Fattah, 172
Lycée Français (Cairo), 152
Lycée de Versailles, 98

Mabarrat Amirah Faryal, 116, 239
Mabarrat Muhammad ʿAli, 50, 51, 96, 113, 114, 116, 121, 122, 239
maʿdhun (marriage registrar), 128, 140
al-Mahalla al-Kubra, 87, 172
al-Mahdiyah, Munirah, 156, 189
Mahfuz, Najib, 149
Mahir, ʿAli, 116, 127, 143, 176, 181, 214
Mahmud, Ivy Najib, 114
Mahmud, Muhammad, 59, 215
mahr (dower), 134, 139–40
Makhluf, Shaykh Hasanayn, 218
malaria, 121–22
Malaterre-Sellier, Germaine, 212
Maliki school, 93, 132–33
Manshari, Habibah, 93
Mansurah, 117, 143
Mansurah Women Teachers' Training School, 9, 57, 59
Manus, Rosa, 212, 234
al-Maraghi, Mustafa, 163, 230
Marʿai, Nur, 120
Markham, Beryl, 158
Marques, Jeanne, 103, 225, 277n.60
marriage: Coptic church set minimum age of, 5; Egyptian feminists' views of, 15, 35–36, 44–45, 54, 125, 135, 138–39, 288n.71; and law setting minimum age, 126–28, (Arab) 242; legal reform of, 127, (Arab), 242;
Marseilles, 198, 202–3, 210
Masabni, Bad'iyah, 190
al-Masri, Eva Habib, 106, 114, 115, 121, 136, 140, 153, 184–85, 280n.19
al-Masri, Habib, 136, 246
al-Masri, Iris Habib, 121
al-Mawla, Shaykh Jad, 205
al-Mazini, ʿAbd al-Qadir, 180
al-Mazini, Ibrahim, 107
Mead, Miss, 57
Melman, Billie, 72
Menasce, Baron Jacques de, 196–97
Mernissi, Fatima, 67
Michel, Mme Bernard, 182
midwifery, 50, 113, 179
Mihriz, Sharifah, 114
Milner Mission, 77
Minya, 6, 32, 33, 81, 99, 120, 121, 239
Misr Spinning and Weaving Company, 172
al-Misriyah, 184–85
Mixed Courts, 182
modesty (*hismah*), female, 48, 67–68, 159, 161, 169
Mogannam, Matiel, 230
Montreux conference, 204
morality, 16–18, 41, 58–60, 68, 79, 145–46, 149, 160–63, 168, 170, 171, 187, 192, 198, 200, 205, 255n.35
Mosseri, Emil, 104

mother, role of, 63, 135, 136, 137, 140–41, 145, 147–48, 161, 166, 168, (Arab) 242
mothers and children: call for creation of Arab agencies for protection of, 244
Movement of the Friends of Peace (Harakat Ansar al-Salam), 152, 248
Mubarak, ʿAli Pasha, 9
Muddaris, Faykah, 229
mufti, 10, 11
Muhammad, Shaykh Abu al-ʿIla, 156
Muhammad, Aminah, 190
Muhammad, Musa, 12, 20, 21, 38
Muhammad, Niʿmat Hamid, 138
Muhammad, Nur, 147
Muhammad ʿAli, 6, 9, 10
Muharram Bey Primary School for Girls (Alexandria), 177
Mukhtar, Muhammad, 158
al-Mulla, Muhammad Jad, 107
Munirah, 50, 51
Murad, Muhammad, 98
Mursi, ʿAbd al-Hamid Fahmi, 33
Murtagi, Layla Barakat, 114
Musa, ʿAziza, 156
Musa, Nabawiyah: and antigovernment protest, 211; and articulation of feminism, 49, 65–69, 142, 145–46, 168–69, 172, 177, 179, 192; and articulation of feminist nationalism, 60, 69, 78–80, 142, 145–46, 166–67, 177, 179, 193; and attempt to enroll at the Egyptian University, 53–54, 49; and attempt to study law, 182, 264n.27; claimed as foremother by feminist and Islamist women, 25; and EFU, 20, 91–92, 96; formative years of, 38–45; and imperial feminism, 232–33; and intellectual societies, 55; and international links, 70, 91–92; journalism of, 39; lectures for women by, 53–54; and *The Magazine of the Young Woman*, 39, 103; as nationalist, 60, 78–80, 145–46; obtaining secondary school diploma, 42–44, 53, 143; personal views on marriage by, 44–45, 124, 136; and social construction of gender, 66; as teacher and educational official, 56–60, 149, 165, 176–80, 187; and veiling and unveiling, 23, 48, 58, 67–78; and *The Woman and Work*, 39, 64–65, 68, 78, 167, 192; and women's education, 63–64, 138, 142, 144–46, 148, 177
Musa, Salamah, 14, 134, 261n.41
Muslim Brothers, 163
Muslim Women's Association (Beirut), 237
Muslim Women's Society, 163, 229, 239
Mutran, Khalil, 107
al-Muwaylihi, Muhammad, 7

Nabarawi, ʿAdilah, 37, 67, 98
Nabarawi, Ibrahim, 98
Nabarawi, Saiza: accuses government of sexism, 161; and anticolonialism, 226; and antigovernment protest, 211–12; and anti-imperial feminism, 232; articulation of feminism by, 113, 145, 156–57, 159; becomes EFU vice president, 248–49; biography of, 98–99; creation of EFU Youth Committee by, 152, 248; as editor of *L'Egyptienne*, 95, 99, 102; and education of women, 143, 145; and EFU, 100, 113, 115, 118, 152; and journalism, 184–85, 187; marriage of, 139; and nationalism, 169; and Palestine case at the IAW Copenhagen conference, 233–35; and personal status reform, 128, 129, 130, 131–32, 134; veiling and unveiling of, 67, 92–93, 98; and women's political rights, 213
Nadi, Lutfiyah, 158
Nadirah, 190
nafaqah (family maintenance; also alimony), 131, 168
Nafisah, 64, 170
al-Nahhas, Maryam, 14, 15, 64
Nahhas, Mustafa, 214, 227
Najdi, Ibrahim, 107
Naji, Anisah, 148
Najib, General Muhammad Najib, 121, 218
Najib, Mustafa, 139–40
Najjar, Cecile, 9
Najjar, Rose, 9
Najjar, Tawfiq, 111
Nakhlah, Marguerite, 157
Naples, 249
nashizah (disobedient wife, legal term), 131
Nasif, Hifni, 54
Nasim, Tawfiq, 138, 214
Nasir, Nabihah, 231
Nassar, Shaykh Allam, 218
Nassar, Sadhij, 225, 230, 232–34, 236, 244, 313n.58
National American Woman Suffrage Association, 70
National Council of Frenchwomen, 105
National Courts, 97, 182
National Feminist Party (al-Hizb al-Nisaʾi al-Watani), 217
National Party (Hizb al-Watani), 99, 208; congress in Brussels of, 74

nationalism, Arab, 13, 105–6, 110, 223, 230–32, 238–39, 242. *See also* Arab Feminist Conference
nationalism, Egyptian: of conservative men, 13, 24, 166; of conservative women, 13, 63; of feminist women, 4, 13, 21, 24, 48, 53, 57, 60, 74, 84–85, 87, 94, 154, 166, 169, 173, 214–15, 239–40; of men in general, 57, 74–78 passim; of progressive men, 4, 12–13, 16–19, 24, 53–54, 57, 74, 166; of women in general, 53, 70–88
nationalism, Egyptian men's: conservative, 12, 24, 166; progressive, 12, 13, 53, 74, 166
nationalism, Palestinian: of women, 223–25, 227–32, 238, 241–42, 247–48. *See also* Arab Feminist Conference; Eastern Women's Conference for the Defense of Palestine
nationality, 203–4
Nawfal, Hind, 15
Netherlands Woman Suffrage Association, 70
new woman: construct of, 48, 74
New Woman Society (Jamᶜiyat al-Mar'ah al-Jadidah), 51, 81, 83, 113, 114, 173, 239
Nimr, Amy, 157
niqab, 23
Niqula, Nazira, 176
nisa'i/yah (adj.: feminist), 19, 91
Notre Dame de la Mère de Dieu School (Cairo), 96, 114
Notre Dame de Sion School (Alexandria), 97, 98
al-Nuqrashi, Mahmud, 39, 246
nurses, 113, 169, 179, 181

Oeuvre des Ecoles Gratuites des Villages de Haute-Egypte, 121

Palestine: and British rule, 215; and end of Capitulations, 199; and nonmembership in Arab League, 245
Palestinian Arab Women's Unions (Jerusalem, Jaffa, Nablus, Haifa), 224–25, 233–34, 237
Pan-Arab Conference for the Defense of Palestine (Bludan), 227
Pappenheim, Bertha, 196–97
Paris, 37, 54, 82, 93, 98, 99, 156, 200–201
parliament, 128, 160, 205, 210, 215; sit-in of, 218; women barred from opening of, 86, 185, 208; women's picketing of, 87
patriarchy, colonial, 33, 42, 56, 60, 177
patriarchy, imperial, 109
peace, 200, 203, 216, 225–42 passim, 248–49
peasants, 4, 5, 54–55, 68, 92, 94, 98, 105, 118, 150, 166, 169, 171, 172, 194, 225
Persian language and literature, 14, 141
personal status code (*ahwal shakhsiyah*), 39, 95, 124–27, 133, 183, 186, 207, 217, (Arab) 241–42, 249; and the 1927 draft proposal, 127, 131; and the 1929 revised law, 127, 130, 131, 132, 133
pharaonic era, 91, 155
philanthropy: of Arab women, 237; of Egyptian women, 33, 48, 48–52, 56, 70, 72, 96, 113, 114, 115, 120–22, 154, 187, 192, 241, 263n.8, 280n.19; men's, 49–50
Philipp, Thomas, 62
physical education, girls', 106, 161
Pioneers (al-Ruwwad), 115–16
Plaminkova, Frantiska, 233
policewomen, 201, 203
political rights for women, 98
polygamy (*taᶜaddud al-zawjat*), 6, 11, 19, 95, 124–30, 132, 133, 135, 209, (Arab) 242
Port Said, 193, 195, 197
Pressly Memorial Institute for Girls (Asyut), 96, 98
primary school education for girls: and first class to take diplomas, 54; and first provision for by state, 9
Professional and Domestic School, EFU, 100, 112–13, 173
prostitution, 98, 112, 159, 169, 192–206, (Arab) 238, 288n.84

al-Qalamawi, Suhayr, 101, 148, 151, 171, 178, 225, 249
al-Qalini, Rawhiyah, 150–51, 292n.58
Qazun, Qamar, 243
Qirabiyah School, 9
Qur'an, 34, 40, 48, 129, 132, 145, 149, 156, 191, 251n.4
al-Qusi, Shaykh Ahmad ᶜAli
al-Qusi, Ihsan, 51, 80, 84, 93, 96, 98, 132, 145, 154, 155, 177, 298- 99n.63
Qutb, Sayyid, 107

Rabbat, Nadia, 121
race, 193
Raghib, Idris, 56
Rami, Ahmad, 107
Rashid, Bahigah, 97–98, 147–48, 205, 218
Rashid, Fatma, 52, 62

Rashid, Fatma Ni'mat, 104, 171, 184–85, 216
Rashid, Hasan Ahmad, 97
Rashid, Nadiyah, 96
Ratib, 'Aishah, 188
Ratib, 'Ulfat, 80
Ra'uf, 'Afifah, 243
Red Crescent Society (Jam'iyat al-Hilal al-Ahmar), 51, 116, 117; Women's Committee, 51, 117, 122, 181, 239; Young Women's Committee, 117
revolution (of 1919), 73, 74, 97
revolution (of 1952), 142, 151, 164, 183, 206, 249
Richard, Mme, 36
Rida, 'Abd al-Rahman, 97
Rida, Rashid, 134
al-Rihani, Najib, 189
Riyad, 'Abd al-Mu'min, 205
Riyad, Sharifah, 80, 82
Riyad, Su'ad, 116
Rome, 70, 86
Roosevelt, Eleanor, 241
Roosevelt, Franklin Delano, 241
Royal Academy of Music (London), 156
rural population: in Arab countries, 243; in Egypt, 101, 111, 113, 118–22, 126, 127
Rushdi, Sabihah, 157
Russell, Thomas, 76, 196, 200–201
Rustam, Rashad, 119

Sabri, Salim, 111
Sabri, Sayyid, 218
Sabri, 'Uthman, 104
Sabri, Zuhayr, 217, 252
Sa'd, Malikah, 184
Sa'd al-Din Bey, 35
Sadat, Anwar, 135
Sadat, Jehan, 135
Sadiq, Munirah, 176
Sa'fan, Majd al-Din, 216
Safwat, Ahmad, 129
al-Sa'id, Aminah, 101, 143, 152, 159, 186, 225, 238, 244, 249–50, 289n.6
al-Sa'id, 'Azimah, 101, 177
al-Sa'id, Karimah, 106, 177; as deputy minister of education, 178, 188, 250
Said Agha (also Sayyid Agha), 34, 35, 82
Saifi, Angelina, 96
Saint Mark's Coptic Cathedral, 77, 99
Saint Vincent de Paul School (Alexandria), 153
Sainte-Croix, Avril de, 104
Sakina, 145
Salim, 'Abd al-Wahhab Muhammad, 187
Salim, Fatma, 148, 178
Samahah, Nafisah, 150
Samalut (in Minya), 101, 120
Samat, Mary, 190
Sanhuri, 'Abd al-Razzaq, 107
Saniyah School, 9, 39, 41–44, 57, 77, 78, 143, 177, 178, 180
Saqqaf, 'Atiyah, 37, 156
Sarruf, Ellen, 113
Sarruf, Rahmah, 54
Saudi Arabia, 246
al-Sawi, Ahmad, 140
al-Sayyid, Ahmad Lutfi, 18, 101, 148, 160, 216
Sayyidah Khadijah, 34–35
Sayyidah Zaynab, 99, 111, 173
School for Hakimahs (Abu Zabal), 8, 9, 179
School of Fine Arts (Ecole des Beaux Arts) (Cairo), 156–57
School of Fine Arts (Istanbul), 157
School of Social Work (Cairo), 154
School of Social Work (University of Liège), 106, 154
schools of feminine culture, 147
Scott, Joan, 174
seclusion of women. *See* gender
secondary schools for girls: feminist demands to state for, 95, 141–43; and first Egyptian woman to take secondary school diploma, 42–44; first opening of by state, 143
seductiveness (*tabarruj*), 68–69
segregation of sexes. *See* gender
Sennemut, 145
sex education for children, 141
sexism, 161
sexuality: and double standard, 187; and honor, 5; and sexual purity of women, 5, 16, 18, 169; and single standard, 59–60, 192, 198–99; social construction of, 66–67; and social construction of the woman, 17, 67. *See also* gender; prostitution; veiling; white slavery
Seychelles, 83
al-Shafi'i, Immam, 170
al-Shafi'i, 'Atiyah Husayn, 183
Shafi'i School, 132
Shafiq, Ahmad, 104
Shafiq, Duriyah, 104, 140, 153–54, 184, 186–87, 218, 249
Shahbandar, Sara, 237
Shahfa, Rose, 244
Shahin, Dr., 102, 202

Shaᶜiah Courts, 183
Shaᶜrawi, ᶜAli, 32–33, 35, 36, 75, 82, 84
Shaᶜrawi, Bathna, 38, 248
Shaᶜrawi, Huda: advocacy of the Palestinian cause in international forums by, 225–27, 234–36; and Anglo-Egyptian Treaty (1936), 214–16; and Arab League, 245–46; and Arab Feminist Conference, 238, 240–42; and Arab Feminist Union, 244; articulation of feminist demands by, 170, 179, 187, 188, 192; and attempts to form federation of women's societies, 118, 217, 239; and charity and philanthropy, 49–51, 192; and creation of EFU structure, 86, 96, 100, 102, 105; defense of women workers by, 175; and education of women, 143, 144, 150, 151; and EFU's social service, 112, 187; eulogy for Bahithat al-Badiyah by, 73; fight against prostitution and Capitulations by, 198–99, 200–202, 204–5; formative years of, 15, 32–38, 45–50, 124, 155; and IAW, 91–92, 109, 234–36; and intellectual societies, 55; and Islamic religious authorities, 163, 198; and lectures for women, 52, 55–56; nationalist activism of, 50, 75–78, 173, 214–16; opening of ceramic factory by, 173; and Palestine conference, 228–31; and personal status code reform, 127, 128; and political rights for women, 213, 215–16; and rural needs, 101, 120, 122; and veiling and unveiling, 23, 25, 67, 92–93, 98; as WWCC president, 80–88
Shaᶜrawi, Muhammad, 38
sharᶜiah (Islamic law), 83, 126, 130, 135, 216, 240
sharᶜiah courts, 107
Sharjarat al-Durr, 170
Sharq (in Minya), 101, 120
al-Shawarbi, Layla, 117, 122
Shawqi, Ahmad, 104, 107
Shawqi, Inshirah, 74
al-Shihabi, Zulaykhah, 228–29, 244
Shita, Firdus, 96, 122
shopsellers, women, 173, 175
Shubra Secondary School for Girls, 101, 143, 148
Shurbagi, Dr., 102
Sid Ahmad, Murad, 101, 145, 157, 176
Sidara, Laila Bin, 190
Sidarus, Hilanah, 77, 179, 180
Sidqi, Amina, 122
Sidqi, Ismaᶜil, 100, 122, 150, 152, 159, 162, 210, 212
Sidqi, Mahmud, 97
al-Silahdar, Salim Pasha, 49
Simmons College (Boston), 154
singers, women, 189–91
single mothers, 168
al-Sirafi, Hasan Kamil, 107
Sirri, Husayn, 144
Sirri, Insaf, 143, 289n.4
Sirri, Nahid, 51, 117, 122
Siyufiyah School, 9
slaves, 6, 9, 67, 104, 129, 135, 155, 189, 194, 203
Smith College, 106, 114
Social Affairs, Ministry of, 121, 122, 127, 140, 154, 187–88, 205, 250
Social Reform League (Rabitat al-Islah al-Ijtimaᶜi), 97
social service, voluntary, 48–52, 120, 121, 154; men's, 51; women's, 48, 56, 95, 101, 111, 113–14, 116, 117, (Arab) 237
social services, state: feminist demands for, 94, 120, (Arab) 243–44
social work, 112, 147, 177, 187
socialism, 151, 164, 188–89, 219, 249
Society for the Advancement of Women (Jamᶜiyat al-Tarqiyat al-Fatah): founded by Fatma Rashid, 52; founded by Nabawiyah Musa, 144
Society for the Training of Orthodox Girls in Jerusalem, 230
Society of Mothers of the Future (Jamᶜiyat Ummuhat al-Mustaqbal), 81
Society of Muslim Brothers, 107
Society of the Friends of Art, 157
Society of the Renaissance of the Egyptian Woman (Jamᶜiyat Nahdat al-Sayyidat al-Misriyat), 81, 184
Society of Union and Progress (Jamᶜiyat al-Ittihad wa-al-Tarqiyah), 81
Sorbonne, 104, 154
Soviet Women's Anti-Fascist Committee, 246
sports for women, 146
Stack, Lee (Sirdar), 87
state bureaucracy: and employment for women, 187–89, (Arab), 243. *See also* under various ministries
Stone, Lucy, 65
Sudan, 38, 87, 94, 183, 194
Suez, 159
Suez Canal, 6, 7, 11, 94, 194, 195
suffrage, 11, 71, 92, 95, 108–9, 207–19 passim, (Arab) 240–42, 268–69n.48; Egyptian women's support of Frenchwomen in

struggle for, 210; French women's support for Egyptian women in struggle for, 212; in international arena, 69–73, 92, 208. *See also* election of women to parliament; electoral law; International Alliance of Women
Sukaynah, Sayyidah, 170
Sultan, Aminah Fu'ad, 229
Sultan, ʿUmar, 34, 37, 38
Sultan Pasha, 11, 32
Surayya (queen of Afghanistan), 93
Syria, 178, 182, 189, 199, 223, 227, 228–29, 237, 242
Syrian Arab Women's Union, 225, 237
Syrians, women: articulating of cult of domesticity by, 62; creating of women's press by, 16, 61, 184; early feminist voice of, 66; and educational, social, and nationalist activities in Syria, 236–37; as educators, 9; as entertainers, 189–90; and founding of philanthropies, 49–50; and intellectual activities, 54, 55; as minority freer to innovate, 47–48; as peddlars, 173. *See also* Arab Feminist Conference; Eastern Women's Conference for the Defense of Palestine

Tagart, Helene, 201
Tahir, Muhammad, 158
Tahsin al-Sihha (Women's Society for the Improvement of Health), 114–16, 121
Tahtawi-al, Rifaʿi, 9
Talat, Zaynab, 77
Tanta, 81, 121, 143, 151, 153, 172, 211
Tanta Secondary School for Girls, 143, 147
Tarqiyat al-Fatah School (Alexandria), 144
Tawfiq, Khedive, 32, 102, 134
Tawfiq Coptic Society, 49
Taymur, Ismaʿil Pasha, 14
Taymur, Mahmud, 107
al-Taymuriyah, ʿA'isha, 14, 15, 23, 40, 65, 124, 180
Tcheshme Hanim, 9
teachers and school administrators, 9, 39, 42, 44, 54, 56–60, 64, 95, 143–44, 165, 167, 174–79
teaching, 56, 64, 95, 164, 175–79
technical education for Arab women: call for state to provide, 243
Thabit, Anisah, 153
Thabit, Hasan, 153
Thabit, Hayat, 81
Thabit, ʿIffat, 141
Thabit, Munirah, 106, 130, 153, 184, 215
Tharwat, ʿAbd al-Khaliq, 83–84, 200
al-Tilmisani, Kamil, 107
al-Tinai, Mustafa
Tinayre, Marcelle, 105
Tirsa, 120
Trans-Jordan, 199, 215, 223, 241
Tulaymat, Zaki, 107
Tunis, 93
al-Tunisi, Sarwat, 150
Tunisia, 105
Tuqan, Fadwa, 237
Turco-Circassians, 6, 11, 32, 33, 38, 86
Turkey, 7, 24, 32, 38, 104, 105, 117, 140, 153, 157, 182, 188, 199, 203, 213, 215, 237; Civil Code of, 126; veiling in, 23, 93
Turkish language, 14, 22, 34, 213
Turkish Women's Federation, 213
Tusun, Prince ʿUmar, 169
Tutankhamen, 145

ʿUmar, ʿA'ishah bint, 77
Umm Kalthum, 100, 107, 156, 191
Umma Party, 53
Union français pour le suffrage des femmes, 201
Union of Muslim Associations, 218
United Nations, 122, 135, 247
United Nations Forum, 135
United States, 69, 76, 103, 140; and education in Egypt, 9, 142
Universal Peace Congress in Brussels, 226
university: and attendance of women abroad, 153–54; and attendance of women in Egypt, 148–53; coeducation at, 149, 160–64, 212; demand for chairs in women's literature at, 243; demands of Arab women to teach women's heritage at, 243; Nabawiyah Musa forbidden to attend, 43–54; Women's Section of Egyptian University, 54–55
University Women's Club (Cairo), 134
ʿUrabi revolution, 11, 32, 38
ʿUthman, Zaynab bint Muhammad ibn, 170

Vacaresco, Hélène, 150
veiling (*hijab*) and unveiling (*sufur*), 4, 8, 11, 19, 22–23, 42, 47, 48, 52, 55, 58, 62, 67–69, 75, 85–86, 91–94, 98, 104, 146, 153, 159, 169, 205, (Arab) 236–37, 251n.4, 261n.41, 314n.77. *See also* gender; sexuality
venereal disease, 112
Verone, Maria, 104, 202, 210, 279n.78
Versailles, 13

Villon, Margo, 157
votes for women. *See* suffrage

Wafd (al-Wafd al-Misri), 75, 80–88, 153, 185, 208, 211, 212, 214, 215–16, 228
Wafdist Women's Central Committee (Lajnat al-Wafd al-Markaziyah lil-Sayyidat), 80–88, 99, 199, 208, 209, 210
Waffa, ʿAbd al-Halim, 111
Wahbi, Yusuf, 189
Wajdi, Muhammad Farid, 62, 66
Wakil, Mukhtar, 107
waqf (pl. *awqaf*, religious endowment), 32, 78
Wardiyan Women Teachers' Training School, 9, 58, 177
Wassif, Wadidah, 149, 155
Wazir, Mary, 229
white slavery, 192, 195–96
wife, role of, 63, 136, 139, 147, 161, 166, (Arab) 242
Wilson, Woodrow, 76
Wingate, Reginald, 75
Wissa, Boctor Wissa, 96
Wissa, Ester Fahmi, 80, 81, 85, 213
Wissa Wasif, Mrs. 80
Women Teachers' Training College (Heliopolis) (later Girls' College of ʿAyn Shams), 151
Women's Awakening Society (Jamʿiyat al-Nahda al-Nisa'iyah), 55
Women's Committee for the Defense of Palestine in Syria, 227–28, 230
Women's Committee of ʿAkka, 227
Women's Indian Association, 108
Women's International Democratic Federation, 246–47, 249
Women's Political Party (Turkey), 213
Women's Popular Resistance Committee (Lajnat al-Nisa'iyah lil-Muqawamah al-Shaʿbiyah), 248
Women's Refinement Union (al-Ittihad al-Nisa'i al-Tahdhibi), 55
Women's Renaissance Society (Beirut), 237
Women's Society for the Improvement of Health. *See* Tahsin al-Sihha
Women's Union of Minya (Ittihad al-Sayyidat bil-Minya), 81
Woodsmall, Ruth, 176, 237
World War I, 13, 57, 75–77, 79, 92, 117, 120, 202, 208, 223
World War II, 51, 108, 109, 117, 200, 202, 206, 216, 237, 244, 246

Yakan, ʿAdli, 83
yashmak, 22
al-Yaziji, Warda, 14, 65
Yeghen, Foulad, 104
Younan, Nelly, 121
Young Women's Society (Jamʿiyat al-Shabbat al-Misriyat), 184
Yunis, ʿAbd al-Hamid, 107
Yusif, Rifqah ʿAtiyah, 138
al-Yusif, Ruz (Fatma), 76, 184–85, 190
Yusri, Lutfiyah, 122
YWCA, 114

Zafir, ʿAsmah, 104
Zaghlul, Saʿd, 59, 75, 81, 81–88, 189, 208; deportation of, 75
Zaghlul, Safiyah, 80–81, 85–86, 210
Zaki, Ahmad, 104
Zananiri, Nelly, 104
Zawiyat al-Amwat (in Minya), 101, 120
Zaynab, 145
al-Zayyat, Latifa, 152
Zionism, 109, 223, 224, 227, 230, 232–34, 241
Ziyadah, Mayy, 14, 54, 55, 56, 104, 158, 185
Zulfiqar, Muhammad, 104